M000289211

THE
HOUSE
OF THE
LORD

THE
HOUSE
OF THE
LORD

A Catholic Biblical Theology
of God's Temple Presence in the
Old and New Testaments

STEVEN C. SMITH

FRANCISCAN UNIVERSITY PRESS

Copyright © 2017 by Franciscan University Press
All rights reserved.
No part of this publication may be reproduced or transmitted in any
form or means, electronic or mechanical, including photography,
recording, or any other information storage or retrieval system, without
permission in writing from the publisher. Requests for permission to
make copies of any part of the work should be directed to:

Franciscan University Press
1235 University Boulevard
Steubenville, OH 43952
740-283-3771
Distributed by:
The Catholic University of America Press
c/o HFS
P.O. Box 50370
Baltimore, MD 21211
800-537-5487

Library of Congress Cataloging-in-Publication Data
Names: Smith, Steven C. (Ph.D.), author.
Title: The house of the Lord : a Catholic biblical theology of God's
temple presence in the Old and New Testaments / Steven C. Smith.
Description: Steubenville : Franciscan University Press, 2017. |
Includes bibliographical references and index.
Identifiers: LCCN 2016049214 | ISBN 9780996930543
Subjects: LCSH: Presence of God—Biblical teaching. |
Worship in the Bible. | Temple of God—Biblical teaching. |
Tabernacle—Biblical teaching. | Catholic Church—Doctrines.
Classification: LCC BT180.P6 S65 2017 | DDC 296.4/91—dc23
LC record available at hlps://lccn.loc.gov/2016049214
Cover Design: Kachergis Book Design
Cover Image: *The Finding of the Saviour in the Temple*, William Holman
Hunt, 1860. Courtesy of Birmingham Museum and Art Gallery
Printed in the United States of America.
ISBN: 978-0-9969305-4-3

This book is lovingly dedicated to four special women in my life. To my mother, Betty, who did everything possible to make our home a place where God's warm presence was felt. To my dear wife, Elizabeth, who never ceases to remind me that, in the end, how we love is all that matters. Elizabeth embodies God's compassionate presence in our marriage and family. And to my two darling daughters, Isabelle and Olivia, who patiently forgave me whenever the writing of this book interfered with *truly important stuff*, like making impromptu doughnut runs and bringing them home to eat while watching cartoons together. I am grateful most of all to God the Father, who makes his presence known to me each day through these lovely women, and in so many other ways.

CONTENTS

ACKNOWLEDGMENTS

This origins of this book may be traced back a number of years, at least to the time when I was researching and writing my first book, *The Word of the Lord: 7 Essential Principles for Catholic Scripture Study*. After that book was written, I was fortunate enough to use it as a Seminary textbook and additionally gave many lectures and presentations across the United States and Canada concerning its subject matter, that is, the principles underpinning a sound Catholic approach to biblical interpretation.

Soon, however, I realized that *The Word of the Lord*, while it offered a number of biblical examples, was not, strictly speaking, a work of "biblical theology." Rather, it was an iteration of the ingredients that comprise sound Catholic biblical theology.

The present book picks up, so to speak, just where *The Word of the Lord* finished off. *The House of the Lord* builds upon and applies the various principles, for example, of biblical inspiration, the "dynamic unity" of the Old and New Testaments, apprehending the Word of God according to the Four Senses, and so on. In other words, this book is an articulation of a Catholic biblical theology that is informed and guided by principles of Catholic biblical interpretation. As a Catholic biblical scholar, I have been interested in making some contribution to the need for a reintegration of "exegesis and theology" (Pope Benedict XVI, *Verbum Domini* §31). It is hoped that the present work is a helpful example of such reintegration that is greatly needed today.

There are many people who deserve my sincere thanks. At furthest reach, I suppose that I could begin by expressing gratitude to my master teachers, whose works taught me the meaning and value of biblical theology. Among others, this list includes the likes of Joseph Ratzinger, Yves Congar, Jean Daniélou, and Louis Bouyer. They and other Catholic theologians like them not only had profound expertise in biblical exegesis, but also capably demonstrated what it looks like when exegesis and theology are properly integrated. Any success achieved in this book, in articulating a Catholic biblical theology today, owes much to their wisdom from such works, many of which are mentioned in the present volume.

Closer to home, I wish to thank the administration, seminarians, faculty, and staff at Mount St. Mary's Seminary in Emmitsburg, Maryland, where I have been blessed to form, mentor, and train tomorrow's priests. In particular, I thank our rector, Monsignor Andrew Baker, as well as Fr. Dan Mindling, OFM, Cap., academic dean, for their continued leadership, support, and friendship. Additionally, I wish to acknowledge all of my peers on the Seminary faculty, especially Fr. Tommy Lane and Dr. William Bales, my colleagues in Sacred Scripture at the Seminary. All of my research and writing are intimately connected with my classroom teaching, and so I remain deeply grateful to all of the seminarians (past, present, and future) at "The Mount."

I am equally grateful that *The House of the Lord* has a "home," and that home is Franciscan University Press. From beginning to end, *everyone* at FUS Press has not only been professional, smart, and engaging, but warmly so. Special thanks go to Stephen Hildebrand, Sarah Wear, and Ashleigh McKown for the countless hours involved in bringing *The House of the Lord* to fruition. Likewise, Joyce and Anne at Kachergis Book Design did a remarkable job with the cover design and art for the book jacket.

Finally, I again wish to express special thanks to my family, especially my dear wife, Elizabeth. She is not only my spouse but my best friend. In many ways, Elizabeth was a "silent partner" and co-laborer with me, as I could not have written this book without her love and support. I thank my children, Isabelle and Olivia, and additionally my spiritual director, pastor, and friend, Monsignor Bill King, who allows me to darken his door with riddles of every kind.

Thank you all—and to all I have failed to mention by name. My heart is filled with gratitude for all of your support.

FOREWORD

It is well over ten years ago since I read my first full-length study of the Temple: G. K. Beale's thought-provoking book *The Temple and the Church's Mission: A Biblical Theology of the Dwelling Place of God*.[1] I can still remember the sense of wonder I felt as I read it in the airport terminal on my way home from the 2004 Annual Meeting of the Society of Biblical Literature. With every turn of the page and every new insight into the Temple, I felt like pieces of the biblical puzzle that I had not even known were missing began suddenly appearing, and then falling into place. To take but one example: Beale shows that the story of the sanctuary does not begin (as I always assumed) with the Temple of Solomon, or even with the Tabernacle of Moses. Instead, the Book of Genesis describes *the Garden of Eden itself* as a primordial temple sanctuary, with Adam as its priest and guardian. And ancient Jewish readers of Scripture knew it. In other words, the story of Scripture and the story of the sanctuary of God are *one story*. I was completely blown away by this and other insights in its pages. After finishing Beale's book, I began devouring a steady stream of books and articles on the Jewish Temple, most notably of all that of the great Catholic scholar Yves Congar, OP, and his still-classic work *The Mystery of the Temple*.[2] Taken together, these works showed me the truth of what E. P. Sanders once wrote: "it is almost impossible to make too much of the Temple in first-century Jewish Palestine."[3] For ancient Jews, the Temple was nothing less than the dwelling place of God on earth, the sole place of sacrificial worship, and a literal "microcosm"—a "little universe"—in stone and mortar.

And yet I also felt like something important was missing from these otherwise excellent books. Some of them, like that of Yves Congar, do a fine job of theological synthesis, but do not have the space to go into exegetical

---

1. G. K. Beale, *The Temple and the Church's Mission: A Biblical Theology of the Dwelling Place of God* (Downers Grove, IL: InterVarsity Press, 2004).

2. Yves Congar, *The Mystery of the Temple* (New York: Newman Press, 1962).

3. E. P. Sanders, *The Historical Figure of Jesus* (London: Penguin, 1994), 262.

depth, and do not reflect the important research that has taken place in the last twenty years or so. Others, like that of E. P. Sanders, give a precise and impeccable historical description of the day-to-day cultic activities within the Temple, but say almost nothing about the theological symbolism of the sanctuary. Other books offer in-depth studies of the Temple or the Tabernacle in a particular section of Scripture, but they don't give the full canonical story of the Temple, from Genesis to Revelation. Finally, still others, like G. K. Beale's excellent study, do so from a distinctly Protestant point of view. As such, they tend to pay little attention to patristic and medieval interpretations of the biblical text, to say nothing of later Catholic theology and the liturgy of the Church. In other words, I found myself wishing there were a robustly *Catholic* and up-to-date study of the Temple in Sacred Scripture. I even considered writing one myself.

That is, until now. In *The House of the Lord*, Steven Smith has given us something truly remarkable: a thoroughly exegetical and robustly theological study of the Temple of God in Scripture, starting with Genesis and ending with the Book of Revelation. In other words, he has given us a truly "biblical theology" of the Temple. In it, Smith unlocks the meaning of the Temple in both the Old *and* New Testaments using both historical exegesis *and* theological synthesis. Moreover, unlike virtually every other contemporary study of the Temple, Smith does not confine himself to the results of modern exegetes and theologians. Instead, he draws on the wellspring of ancient and medieval interpreters, both Eastern and Western: interpreters such as Justin Martyr, Origen of Alexandria, Augustine, Ephrem the Syrian, and Thomas Aquinas, to name just a few. Perhaps most significant of all, Smith brings all of these insights together in what he refers to as a "typological-sacramental" reading of the Scriptures. Drawing on the work of great patristic scholars such as Cardinal Jean Daniélou, Smith thereby models for us a typological approach to the Temple in Scripture that is not merely salvation-historical but also sacramental and liturgical.

The result is an exegetical feast of insights into what is arguably one of the most central topics in the Bible—the Temple—the house of God, the gate of heaven, the concrete embodiment of the creator's plan to not only save humanity from sin and death, but also *dwell with them* forever in a covenant relationship of communion and life-giving love. As the Gospel of John puts it in its famous Prologue, "And the Word became flesh, and *tabernacled*

[Greek: *eskēnōsen*] among us" (John 1:14). It gives me great pleasure to recommend *The House of the Lord* to all readers who want to understand the mystery of the Temple, and through it the mystery of salvation, in a fresh and exciting new light.

Brant Pitre

THE
HOUSE
OF THE
LORD

INTRODUCTION

An Invitation to Temple Theology

One thing I ask of the Lord, this I seek: To dwell in *the House
of the Lord* all the days of my life, that I may gaze on the loveliness of the Lord and contemplate *his Temple.*

Psalm 27:4

It was the duty of the trumpeters and singers to make themselves heard in unison in praise and thanksgiving to the Lord,
and when the song was raised, with trumpets and cymbals
and other musical instruments, in praise to the Lord, "For he
is good, for his steadfast love endures forever," *the House, the
House of the Lord,* was filled with a cloud, so that the priests
could not stand to minister because of the cloud, *for the glory
of the Lord filled the house of God.*

1 Chronicles 5:13–14

The Thread of the Temple

This book invites the reader to participate in a unique journey: into a
deep exploration of the Old and New Testaments, searching out and contemplating the reality of God's "temple presence" with his people. God has
indeed revealed himself "in many and various ways" in Sacred Scripture
(Heb. 1:1). The raison d'être of this particular book is to investigate God's
self-revelation to his people in and through his temple presence—in and
through the various stages of the biblical Temple.

At times the Bible unveils this mystery of God's temple presence in clear
and unmistakable ways. Other times, this mystery unfolds more gradually
and subtly. A search of both the obvious and more inconspicuous dimen-

sions of God's temple presence in Scripture is required. Consequently, this journey cannot and will not engage in "shortcuts."

The reader is invited to partake in a rather *expansive journey* that will involve a careful and thorough treatment of the entire biblical canon. And beyond it as well. The patient reader will be richly rewarded! By journey's end, a rich theological pattern will be evident, a pattern discernible across the canon—a pattern of God's temple presence with his people. *The goal of this book is to help the reader to recognize, make sense of, and appreciate God's temple presence in Sacred Scripture.*

What exactly is meant by God's "temple presence"? Several synonymous phrases may help to clarify, such as a "theology of the temple" or, better, "temple theology." The latter will be the one used throughout the book. Again, it may be asked, what is "temple theology," and what role does it play in the overall drama of Sacred Scripture?

For the purpose of this book, temple theology may be defined as the study of the Jerusalem Temple—its history and theology, signs and symbols, sacrifices and priesthood, and its purpose and meaning within the canon of Scripture. This book deals with temple theology on both a micro and a macro level. As to the former, the reader will become attuned to many fascinating elements that comprise daily life within the Temple. As to the latter, the reader will come to think about the Temple in fresh ways, and grasp its significance in the overall story of the biblical narrative.

This book examines the intricacies and practices of the Temple at every stage of its development over time.[1] By necessity, this investigation will explore crucial topics such as the following: (1) the promise and purpose of the Temple; (2) the "physicality" of the Tabernacle/Temple (structure and design); (3) Temple sacrifices, festivals, and feasts; and (4) various social groups associated with the Temple.

In terms of significance, chief among these topics is that of Temple priest-

---

1. Discussions of the Temple are by no means limited to the structure constructed in the reign of King Solomon. Rather, this book will investigate the Temple *at every stage in the biblical epic*, from the earliest hints of its conception to various physical manifestations of it. There are important developments to consider, leading up to the Jerusalem Temple, such as the theme of the "Temple of Creation" in ancient Jewish writings and the Tabernacle of the wilderness. Similarly, there are numerous related developments following the destruction of Solomon's Temple, such as the erection of the Second Temple and, later, a massive expansion of the Jerusalem Temple during the reign of Herod the Great.

hood. As will be made clear over the course of the book, the meaning of the Temple is intricately tied to its priests and their sacrifices. In fact, priesthood plays such a significant role in the study of the Temple that this book would not dare study the one without the other. To diminish the relationship of the two (as some have done) would be not only unhelpful, it would also jeopardize the entire study. This point needs to be underscored: this study of temple theology has a priest *in the center of it—and unapologetically so*—in keeping with the biblical narrative.

At the outset, it is asserted that the Temple looms over the entirety of the Old and New Testaments in such a remarkable way that it is hard to not stand under (or near) the shadow that is casts across the pages of the canon. The "thread" of temple theology is woven throughout the Scriptures in an unmistakable and intentional way.

The first and immediate goal will be, broadly speaking, to persuade the reader of the reasonability of the above claims. (Are these claims valid—and do they warrant a book-length study?) The sooner this initial goal is met, the better, as a second and more far-reaching objective follows upon its heels and requires the reader's attention throughout the entire book. Namely, *to discover the majestic and mysterious thread of temple theology in Scripture and to inquire why the human authors of Scripture—indeed, why the Divine author—has woven it through the biblical canon.* Part and parcel with this second objective is to appropriately ascertain the "meaning" of the Temple: first, within each particular context in which it is found and second, its significance within the larger framework of the biblical canon.

An exploration of Sacred Scripture—one that is properly attentive to the centrality of the Temple within the horizon of biblical theology—is vitally needed today. Of pressing concern is that far too many readers of the Bible (even fairly proficient ones) are not always able, on their own, to grasp the extraordinary influence of the Temple upon the biblical story. Likewise, far too many readers do not appreciate the theological "grip" that the Temple had upon the biblical authors of both the Old and New Testaments. This is not to criticize readers of good will; rather, it is to call attention to a kind of temple illiteracy that is quite common today. This illiteracy is present in the pulpit and pew as well as in the classroom and faculty lounge.

To be fair, it is not as though the thoughtful reader of Scripture cannot grasp "the big idea" without a deeper appreciation of the Temple's centrality to the biblical narrative. Indeed, one can. Rather, it is that when the Temple is in its proper place at center stage, the entire canonical drama becomes more coherent. The big idea becomes even bigger, and clearer.

But this book is not somehow advocating a "placing" of the Temple at the center of the biblical story in some arbitrary fashion. Rather, this book asserts that the Temple *was always there*, placed at the epicenter of the Scriptural drama by the biblical authors and the Divine author himself.

Returning to the illiteracy of the Temple, what provoked it, and what are some of the causes of the Temple not being properly appreciated or not being given its due? Among various causes, one may look to modern and contemporary biblical criticism. Far too often, the Temple has, for one or another reason, been eclipsed or diminished of its significance by biblical scholars. In particular, the past several centuries of historical-critical scholarship of the Hebrew Scriptures has frequently yielded rather negative views of the Temple and those closest to it, specifically the priestly cult. Among the reasons for a widespread illiteracy about the Temple today is the *drip, drip, drip* effect that such academic scholarship has had upon the classroom, pew, pulpit, and so on.

Here, an example of this type of biblical criticism may prove helpful; specifically, consider the question of the authorship of the Five Books of Moses (Genesis–Deuteronomy). Beginning in Europe, in the late seventeenth century, the traditional view of Mosaic authorship began to collapse. Over the course of the next century, the idea of a single Mosaic author was gradually displaced in favor of approaches that involved the grafting together of multiple, independent written sources into a single document over time. Julius Wellhausen (1844-1918), often referred to as the father of source criticism of the Hebrew Bible, emerged as the leading voice of such critical approaches.

When the dust settled, it was Wellhausen's "Documentary Hypothesis" (DH) that gained the majority of adherents over other proposals.[2] The many

---

2. Julius Wellhausen, *Prolegomena to the History of Israel* (Atlanta: Scholars Press, 1994 [1885]). On the "legacy" the Documentary Hypothesis, see also M. Noth, *A History of Pentateuchal Traditions* (Englewood Cliffs, NJ: Prentice-Hall, 1972); idem, *The Deuteronomistic History,* JSOT Supplement Series 15 (Sheffield, UK: JSOT, 1981); R. Rendtorff, *The Problem of the Process of Transmission in the Pentateuch*, JSOT Supplement Series 89 (Sheffield, UK: Sheffield Academic Press, 1990); E. W. Nicholson, *The Pentateuch in the Twentieth Century: The Legacy of Julius Wellhausen* (Oxford: Clarendon, 1998); G. von Rad, *The Problem of the Hexateuch and Other Essays* (New York: McGraw-Hill, 1966); R. N. Whybray, *Introduction to the Pentateuch* (Grand Rapids, MI: Eerdmans, 1995).

complexities of Wellhausen's influential hypothesis need not be rehashed here. For the sake of discussion, five key facts about the DH may be summarized here:

1. The Pentateuch did not originate in the time of Moses (1400s BC) but over approximately five centuries (950–500 BC).

2. The Pentateuch was not the product of a single author who composed in as a kind of unity, but it rather developed out of a long, complex process from four separate editors (or "schools").

3. The four schools were the *Yahwist* (J), the *Elohist* (E), the *Deuteronomist* (D), and the *Priestly* (P) source. The schools—J, E, D, and P—composed independent written sources, the oldest being J (and E), and the most recent being P. Over time, the sources were integrated and melded into an evolving document, shaped by each subsequent school.

4. Importantly, the editors of J, E, D, and P each had their own understanding of what Israel was, as well as particular interests, theological approaches, and so on.

5. By approximately 500 BC, in the postexilic period, the editing of the document was more or less brought to a conclusion. Given their belief that the Priestly school had the final editorial role in forming the Pentateuch, Wellhausen and other source critics asserted that it was this group of Temple loyalists that decisively shaped the text as we now have it.

Wellhausen and subsequent generations of source critics assigned the final editing of the Pentateuch to the so-called Priestly school.[3] This is precisely where the present example proves helpful. Why? Because of the rather

---

3. Over the past fifty years or so, the tide has begun to turn in Old Testament studies, away from the conclusions of Wellhausen and other source critics: "The second half of the twentieth century witnessed the collapse of the older consensus on the Documentary Hypothesis and its various applications in form and tradition criticism." B. T. Arnold, *Dictionary of the Old Testament: Pentateuch*, s.v. "Pentateuchal Criticism, History of." For recent critiques of the Documentary Hypothesis, see Gordon Wenham, "Pondering the Pentateuch: The Search for a New Paradigm," in *The Face of Old Testament Studies: A Survey of Contemporary Approaches*, ed. D. W. Baker and B. T. Arnold (Grand Rapids, MI: Baker, 1999), 116–44; Umberto Cassuto, *The Documentary Hypothesis and the Composition of the Pentateuch: Eight Lectures* (Jerusalem: Magnes, 1961); Desmond Alexander, *From Paradise to the Promised Land: An Introduction to the Pentateuch*, 2nd ed. (Grand Rapids, MI: Baker, 2002); Konrad Schmid, "Has European Scholarship Abandoned the Documentary Hypothesis? Some Reminders on Its History and Remarks on Its Current Status," in *The Pentateuch: International Perspectives on Current Research*, Forschungen zum Alten Testament 78, ed. Thomas Dozeman et al. (Tübingen: Mohr Siebeck, 2011).

dim view of the Priestly school, it might be asked whether Wellhausen and other biblical critics saw *anything virtuous or true* in the work of the Priestly editors.

A close reading of Wellhausen yields the following assessment: that the Priestly school had usurped the intent of the earlier schools that were developing the Torah as a kind of legislation of moral and civil law. The Priestly school, Wellhausen believed, co-opted the purer intentions of earlier sources. The Priestly redaction shifted the balance of Judaism, away from a "folk religion" of justice into something much more partisan and bloodthirsty, in keeping with the will of a small but powerful class of priests in Jerusalem in the fifth century BC. And so Wellhausen (and really a generation of source critics after him) asserted that the entire sacrificial apparatus of the Temple cult was a late development, and a kind of unfortunate development. For Wellhausen, the Priestly source was a theological blemish upon the older, more ethically minded religion known as ancient Judaism.

For Wellhausen, the earlier editors of the Pentateuch had promoted a "purer form" of Israelite religion that shared numerous attributes of other ancient near eastern religions. He looked especially to the values of the *Deuteronomist* and its many social concerns, for example, the building of a just and moral society, proper care for the impoverished, and so on. In sharp contrast, he conjectured that the Priestly editors had far different and parochial designs upon the evolving religion of Judaism. The Priestly elite were preoccupied with the Temple and their powerful place within it.

In sum, the Priestly school was for Wellhausen a kind of regrettable development. Moreover, a close reading of Wellhausen's own words suggests that the theological realities propagated by the Priestly school were largely *mythical in nature*, the output of a small but powerful minority of priestly scribes sympathetic to the Temple. As such, Leviticus and other priestly texts in the Books of Moses represented a kind of *devolution* away from the purer moral law of Deuteronomy that preceded it. Wellhausen asserted that the burnt offerings and other Temple offerings were a theological imposition upon the earlier Jewish tradition, forged by an elitist priestly class that foisted their influence upon earlier Israelite customs and beliefs. As a result of Wellhausen's influential, pioneering work, many biblical scholars of subsequent generations wrote about the Temple and the Old Testament priesthood with a notable amount of *skepticism,* if not *outright disdain.*

Regarding such skeptical criticism, the French have several helpful proverbs that come to mind. The first is: *L'habit ne fait pas le moine.* The second is just as priceless: *La barbe ne fait pas le philosophe.* Indeed, "the vestments do not make the monk" any more than "a beard makes one a philosopher."[4]

Comprends? Things are not always as they are reported to be, and one need not be distraught by the cynical conclusions of erudite scholars. In fact, one may rightly *critique de la critique.* Turnabout is certainly fair play in biblical interpretation. Certainly the underlying *suppositions* of source critics as Wellhausen and others are to be objectively examined, challenged, and critiqued. Not only this, but also the *implications* of such historical-critical interpretations of Scripture should be carefully thought through before they are embraced.

To be sure, not all roads of today's temple illiteracy can be traced back to Wellhausen or similarly minded skeptics. Nor are such negative perceptions of Temple and priesthood limited to Old Testament studies. By the late nineteenth and early twentieth centuries, similar trends can be seen within New Testament scholarship.

In fact, far too many modern New Testament studies (and, in particular, those dealing with Jesus and the Gospels) have likewise ignored or greatly diminished the role of the Temple and the priesthood. In particular, the characterization of Jesus as a priestly Messiah or of the priestly identity of Jesus's Apostles are all but absent in many studies of the Gospels today.[5]

There are other developments, too, that contributed to a diminishment of the Temple and priesthood in biblical criticism. Collectively, such skepticism

---

4. "Yet historical criticism does not tell the whole story of twentieth-century exegesis. At mid-century, in Europe, came a revival of spiritual exegesis. The *nouvelle theologie* (new theology) encouraged a return to patristic sources. This new theology found expression in the work of Henri de Lubac, Hans Urs von Balthasar, Yves Congar, Jean Daniélou, and Louis Bouyer. These men practiced spiritual exegesis as a truly critical science and spiritual art. Their movement of *ressourcement*—a return to the sources—was canonized to a certain extent by the documents of Vatican II, which repeatedly quote the Fathers as authorities." S. W. Hahn, *Scripture Matters: Essays on Reading the Bible from the Heart of the Church* (Steubenville, OH: Emmaus Road, 2003), 17.

5. See Brant Pitre, "Jesus, the New Temple and the New Priesthood," *Letter & Spirit* 4 (2008): 47–83. Pitre cites a good example of such oversight: "In the first century ... the Temple was not the center of piety in the way that synagogue and home were." Luke Timothy Johnson, *The Writings of the New Testament: An Interpretation* (Minneapolis: Fortress, 1999), 59. In response, Pitre writes that Johnson's comment "totally ignores the centrality of sacrifice in worship (which ... could only be carried out in Jerusalem), and that Jewish synagogues themselves reflected their subordination to the Temple by the fact that they were oriented toward the Temple, so that 'the people prayed standing with their faces turned toward the Holy of Holies, towards Jerusalem.'"

has had a pronounced effect upon the reception of the Bible, across a broad spectrum, clear through from academic hallways to the pulpit, pew, and family room.

What is a healthy response to all of this?

From the viewpoint of Catholic biblical theology, developments such as those discussed above are highly problematic. The sort of historical-critical theorizing and diminishing of the Temple and its priesthood, as exemplified by Wellhausen and others, is in need of legitimate critique. As renowned Jesus scholar E. P. Sanders wrote:

> I think that it is almost impossible to make too much of the Temple in first-century Jewish Palestine. Modern people so readily think of religion without sacrifice that they fail to see how novel that idea is.[6]

All of this leads to the "why" question. Why has so much modern biblical scholarship, right up to the present day, insufficiently appreciated the role of one of the primary institutions in the larger biblical drama? Surely not all of the responsibility may be laid at the feet of Wellhausen. Nor is affixing blame to any particular scholar of interest here.

The point is clear: there has been a woeful neglect of the Temple and its priesthood over the past several hundred years. And such neglect created a theological vacuum that was often filled by other, often less helpful, ideas. Meanwhile, this grand institution (and, theologically speaking, gift of God) remains insufficiently appreciated writ large. *For this reason alone, this book is undoubtedly warranted.*

For the time being, the reader is only asked to be aware of these trends in biblical theology and the need for studies such as this, which challenge questionable conclusions. There is a gap between the true significance of the Temple (and its priesthood) in the biblical narrative on one hand, and its recognition among biblical critics on the other hand. The present volume attends to this gap and in place of such deficiencies in biblical criticism offers to the reader not only a positive assessment of the Temple but also an explanation of the true importance, and indeed the true grandeur, of temple theology in the biblical canon.[7]

Yet moving beyond academic and critical treatments of the Temple, a

---

6. E. P. Sanders, *The Historical Figure of Jesus* (London: Penguin, 1994), 262.

7. While the present study does not claim to be "the" solution to the sort of mishandling of the

separate but related question may be asked: To what degree, on a cultural level does today's general reader or student of Scripture grasp the true significance and centrality of the Temple as it pertains to the Bible as a whole?

An educated guess may be offered: many modern readers of Scripture possess minimal or no understanding of the Temple or its greater significance in the biblical story. First, cultural evidence suggests that there is generally far less biblical literacy today than perhaps ever before. This point need not be debated here. Second, there is likely a "trickle-down" effect from such critical scholarship described above. It is plausible that such dismissive conclusions about the Temple eventually influence the general population.

Third, even if one dutifully attempts to make his or her way through the Old Testament, temple theology may not always jump off the page. At times, temple theology is a subtle and silent presence in the text. Meanwhile, an array of colorful characters capture the reader's attention: Lot's wife turning into a pillar of salt, Jonah being swallowed by the whale, and so on. In some places within the biblical narrative the centrality of the Temple is hard to miss, for example, in Leviticus and in a good number of texts in the Book of Psalms. In other words, the "thread" of the temple is woven from page to page. At times in the foreground, though often enough in the background.

Given this, it is perfectly understandable if readers are somewhat skeptical as to the claims stated in this introduction. Some may feel that the metaphor of the temple thread "weaving its way through Scripture" is excessive. Such readers are asked to press on, as they may benefit as much as (if not more) than the less skeptical over the course of the book. This book will vigorously engage such readers in this respect, arguing that the Temple was indeed one of the most—if not *the most*—enduring of institutions in the entire canon of Scripture. The Temple and its keepers, its high priests, priests, and sacrifices all lie just under the surface of many of the narratives of Sacred Scripture. As will become evident, the Temple was a central preoccupation of the writers of the Old and New Testaments. Other than God himself and perhaps the Torah, nothing else approaches the Temple as a central shaping force in the biblical narrative.

The status of the Temple—it meaning and its priesthood—has been re-

---

Temple/priesthood as seen in some historical-critical approaches, it is hoped that this book, in putting forth a study of temple theology (and priesthood), will make a positive contribution to biblical theology in the twenty-first century.

grettably placed in doubt by far too many biblical critics. And so the need for a fresh study of the Temple is called for in biblical theology today.[8] It is true that in recent years there have been some encouraging temple trends among scholars. Once again, positive light is again being cast upon the Temple. There is nevertheless a surprising paucity of book-length treatments of the Temple as it pertains to biblical and theological study. There are a fair number of monographs that deal with Second Temple Judaism *as a matter of history*. Yet such studies are often technical and limited in nature. Additionally, various introductions to Second Temple Judaism exist, many of which are accessible to the general reader. From such books, a sense of the Temple's significance may be gleaned. Yet while such studies will often enough *mention* or *describe* the Temple, they often fail, ironically, to *assess* or *explain the meaning of the Temple* in any sustained way. Such books often take the reader *to the vicinity of the Temple*, yet quickly move on before one can breathe in the incense rising above its altar, or ask what it all means.

In sharp contrast, *The House of the Lord* invites the reader to inhale deep-

---

8. It is not asserted that there are no positive trends in biblical scholarship today as it pertains to temple theology. In fact, over the past few decades, there have been a number of welcome investigations into the topic. Some of the significant works on the Temple/temple theology in Sacred Scripture that will be engaged in the present study include: Gregory K. Beale, *The Temple and the Church's Mission: A Biblical Theology of the Dwelling Place of God* (Downers Grove, IL: InterVarsity Press, 2004); Matthew Levering, *Christ's Fulfillment of Temple and Torah: Salvation According to Thomas Aquinas* (Notre Dame, IN: University of Notre Dame Press, 2002); Nicholas Perrin, *Jesus the Temple* (Grand Rapids, MI: Baker Academic, 2012); Craig R. Koester, *The Dwelling of God: The Tabernacle in the Old Testament, Intertestamental Jewish Literature, and the New Testament*, Catholic Biblical Quarterly Monograph Series 22 (Washington, DC: Catholic Biblical Association of America, 1989); Crispin Fletcher-Louis, *All the Glory of Adam: Liturgical Anthropology in the Dead Sea Scrolls* (Leiden: Brill Academic, 2001); "God's Image, His Cosmic Temple and the High Priest," in *Heaven on Earth*, ed. T. Desmond Alexander and Simon Gathercole (Carlisle, UK: Paternoster Press, 2004); Yves Congar, *The Mystery of the Temple* (New York: Newman Press, 1962); M. Barber, "Jesus as the Davidic Temple Builder and Peter's Priestly Role in *Matthew* 16:16-19," *Journal of Biblical Literature* 132, no. 4 (2013): 933–51; Margaret Barker, *The Gate of Heaven: The History and Symbolism of the Temple in Jerusalem* (London: SPCK, 1991); idem, *Temple Themes in Christian Worship*, 3rd ed. (London: Bloomsbury, 2013); idem, *Temple Theology in John's Gospel* (London: SPCK, 2014); Pitre, "Jesus, the New Temple, and the New Priesthood," 60–71; Oskar Skarsuane, *In the Shadow of the Temple: Jewish Influences on Early Christianity* (Downers Grove, IL: InterVarsity Press, 2002); Michael L. Morales, *The Tabernacle Pre-Figured: Cosmic Mountain Ideology in Genesis and Exodus* (Leuven: Peeters, 2012); Alan Kerr, *The Temple of Jesus' Body: The Temple Theme in the Gospel of John*, Journal for the Study of the New Testament Supplement Series 220 (Sheffield, UK: Sheffield Academic, 2002).

ly, and breathe in the Temple in all of its stages. This book will lead the reader through every court and corner of the Temple, in an immersive and complete way.

Among the earliest readers of the Scriptures, a mere whisper of the Jerusalem Temple immediately called to mind words and concepts such as: *worship, creation, holiness, prayer, fellowship, unity, sacrifice, priesthood, atonement, covenant, forgiveness of sin*, and, above all, *the presence of God*. Almost paradoxically, over the course of time, its mention could equally call to mind words and concepts such as: *idolatry, sin, estrangement, destruction, judgment, exile* and *the silence of God*.

A study of the Temple in Scripture leads to an examination of the relationships between the Temple and concepts such as the ones mentioned above. There is no full resolution of the paradox. But a broad consideration of the Temple and its meaning should strengthen the reader's understanding of the nature of this paradox. The remainder of this introduction leads the reader through a few initial steps in a positive direction.

Temple Theology in the Old Testament: The Dwelling Place of God

How did ancient Jews perceive the Temple? For the ancient Jewish believer, nothing was greater than the Jewish Temple than the Law or God himself. Ample evidence supports this claim. As N. T. Wright summarizes, it is impossible to overstate the Temple's centrality in ancient Judaism: "The Temple was the focal point of every aspect of Jewish national life. Local synagogues and schools of Torah in other parts of Palestine, and in the Diaspora, in no way replaced it, but gained their significance from their implicit relation to it. Its importance at every level can hardly be overestimated."[9]

The primary reason why the Temple was so central is this: for the ancient Israelites, it wasn't merely a place to worship a far-off, distant God. It was the very dwelling place of the living God: "Attitudes toward the Temple at Jerusalem varied considerably from time to time and from group to group within Judaism ... the Temple was considered to be the very dwelling place of God, in a way shared by no other place on earth.[10] Even the prophets who had

---

9. N. T. Wright, *The New Testament and the People of God* (Minneapolis: Fortress, 1992), 224.

10. See, e.g., Psa. 27:4: "One thing I ask of the Lord, this I seek: *To dwell in the house of the Lord* all the days of my life that I may gaze on the loveliness of the Lord and contemplate his Temple." See also

grave reservations about the cultic practices going on in their own time believed that the Temple was nevertheless God's dwelling among humankind. Ezekiel, for example, who says that he saw the glory of God depart the Temple because of defiling practices (Ezek. 8–10), also says that God will return to live forever in a new Temple (Ezek. 43:1–12)."[11]

The above sketch ought to be enough to warrant this study. Yet there are other significant reasons that could be added:[12]

1. The Jerusalem Temple was a sign of Israel's election from among the peoples of the earth.

2. It stood on a site chosen by theophany long before its construction.

3. Zion was "the mountain of God" (Psa. 68:17).[13]

4. The Temple was "even identified with the original location of the Garden of Eden."[14]

5. "Even the destruction of [the Temple in] 587 B.C. did not disprove Israel's election; rather, God would return and once more make Jerusalem His choice (Zech. 1:17)."[15]

6. All of humanity would one day *stream to Jerusalem* to worship Israel's God, and Israel would stand at the head of the nations (see Isa. 2:1–4).[16]

But where would a proper study of the Temple in Scripture logically begin? It may surprise some readers that the origins of temple theology are not in the Book of Exodus, for example, with Moses and Aaron receiving the divine "blueprint" for constructing the Tabernacle (Exod. 25-40). Temple theology can be traced back far earlier in the Old Testament, to the very "beginning," within the opening pages of the Book of Genesis. There, the first hint of the Temple in Scripture appears, in the Creation narratives of Genesis 1-2 and the Fall of Man in chapter 3.

Exod. 23:19; 2 Sam. 24:20; 1 Ki. 3:1, 6:1, 6:37, 7:9, 7:12, 7:40; 2 Ki. 25:40; Zech. 14:20, 14:21; Matt. 12:4; Mark 2:26; Luke 6:4; Heb. 10:21.

11. Bruce Chilton, P. W. Comfort, and M. O. Wise, *Dictionary of New Testament Background: A Compendium of Contemporary Biblical Scholarship* "Temple, Jewish" (emphasis added).

12. On these points listed here, see ibid.

13. See Psa. 68:17: "Sinai is now in the sanctuary."

14. See Ezek. 28:13-14, 34:1ff.

15. See Zech. 1:17.

16. See Isa. 2:2-3: "Many peoples shall come, and say: 'Come, let us go up to the mountain of the Lord, to the house of the God of Jacob; that he may teach us his ways and that we may walk in his paths.'"

Much more than a horticultural paradise, the Garden of Eden was the Holy Place of God's Temple of Creation. Adam was created as the first man and first husband, yes, but also as the high priest of the sanctuary of Eden. As will become clear, Adam was tasked to "fill the earth" with God's holy presence, his glorious temple presence. In this mystical beginning, the concept of the Temple lies just underneath numerous episodes in Genesis alone: in the flood story, the building of the Tower of Babel, the call of Abraham, and Jacob's ladder, to name just a few.

The ancients contemplated the Temple in Genesis as much as in the Psalms and 1 Kings. Indeed, Genesis 1-3 is merely the beginning of temple theology. As roots are to a great tree, these three chapters of Genesis are the first stages of the temple story, and of temple patterns that repeat over and over, even as they grow this way and that. The motif of the temple resonates throughout the Five Books of Moses: in the divine instructions for the building of the Tabernacle in Exodus; in the entirety of Leviticus with its many temple sacrifices (most especially, the Day of Atonement); and in the Shekinah, the glory cloud of the wilderness in the Book of Numbers.

The more one looks into the Old Testament, the clearer it becomes that long before the first stones of the sanctuary were laid, there was an expectation of the Temple's eventuality:

But you shall seek the place that the Lord your God will choose out of all your tribes to put his name *and make his habitation* there. There you shall go, and there you shall bring your burnt offerings and your sacrifices, your tithes and the contribution that you present, your vow offerings, your freewill offerings, and the firstborn of your herd and of your flock." (Deut. 12:5-7, ESV)[17]

Likewise, temple theology lies under books like Joshua and Judges, as God's people edge closer to Jerusalem and the holy hill of Zion. Without any doubt, temple theology dominates the narrative of David's story and God's holy covenant with him. The theology of the Psalter becomes senseless apart from the reality of the Temple and God's presence within it. And just as the deeper meaning of a psalm diminishes the further one moves away from the shadow of

---

17. Unless otherwise indicated, all Scripture references are taken from the *Holy Bible: Revised Standard Version*, Catholic ed. (New York: National Council of Churches of Christ in the USA, 1994), i.e., RSV-CE. In certain instances, the *English Standard Version* (ESV) or other translations will be used. Where helpful, transliterations of passages in biblical Hebrew and Greek will be provided for the reader.

the Temple, one cannot consider the message of the Old Testament Wisdom books apart from the figure of Solomon who oversaw its construction.

The voice of the biblical prophets would be squelched if a reader attempted to interpret their writings apart from the reality of the Temple. This is not only the case in the major biblical prophets, such as Isaiah, Ezekiel, and Daniel, but also in the minor prophets, such as Haggai and Zechariah. Their visions would be emptied of their vivid eschatological hope apart from the once glimmering but now diminished Temple of their age. Students of the prophetic genre may be aware of how much ink has been spilt upon subjects such as idolatry and high places in early Israelite society. Yet these subjects, from the vantage point of the biblical story, are but reflections of the true worship of the Temple. One need only recall that the exhortations of the prophets rest upon a return to God, and to a right understanding of worship in God's holy Temple.

This is clear from a text at the beginning of Isaiah. In reading the following text, pay attention to the pairing of the phrases "the *mountain* of the Lord" and "the *House* of the Lord." Although this is not the place to elaborate on the significance of these terms, they will surface as an idea critical to the entire book:

It shall come to pass in the latter days that *the mountain* of the *House of the Lord* shall be established as *the highest of the mountains* and shall be raised above the hills; and all the nations shall flow to it, and many peoples shall come, and say: 'Come, let us go up to *the mountain of the Lord*, to the *House of the God of Jacob*; that he may teach us his ways and that we may walk in his paths. (Isa. 2:2-3)

Stepping back from the Old Testament canon, the significance of the Temple to ancient Judaism may be seen from the history of Israel itself. Unquestionably, the defining moment in the whole history of ancient Judaism was the destruction of Solomon's Temple in 587 BC. A remnant of Judeans that returned to Jerusalem constructed Zerubbabel's Temple, or, as it is commonly known today, the Second Temple. With its reconstruction, sacrificial worship was restored. Yet deep questions abounded as to God's presence with his people in light of its earlier destruction.

In this Second Temple period, new realities emerge, giving expression in various forms of Judaism, particularly a growing strand of messianism that, among other convictions, yearned for a future judgment and restoration of the Temple. Much later, the Second Temple was greatly expanded to include opulent palaces, spacious courts, and a great portico. Here, one thinks of the

Herodian Temple, in which Joseph and Mary "presented" Jesus and where he often taught.

In short, nearly every biblical book of the Old Testament was composed "in the shadow of the Temple." This is true not only for biblical texts that originate in or focus on Jerusalem (e.g., Ezekiel), but also even for deuterocanonical outliers such as Sirach and Wisdom of Solomon, which were popularized among the Hellenistic Jewry of Alexandria. These Wisdom books of the latter Old Testament period lead directly to the pages of the New Testament as a bridge across a vast river.

Temple Theology in the New Testament

Nearly every page of the New Testament bears witness to the profound importance of the Jerusalem Temple. The New Testament is deeply indebted to the temple theology of the Old Testament. The New builds upon the Old, yet clearly develops its own rich temple theology around the proclamation of Jesus Christ and his Gospel. Put simply, it is difficult if not impossible to fully grasp the life, death, and Resurrection of Jesus Christ or the proclamation of the Gospel message apart from the reality of the Temple. Likewise, any serious study of St. Paul's epistles, or books such as Hebrews and Revelation, is unadvisable without a sufficient understanding of the Temple with regard to their respective content. In the Gospel of Luke, the Jerusalem Temple becomes a kind of literary frame, as Luke both begins and ends his Gospel in the Temple.[18]

As one reads through the Four Gospels, it becomes clear that, for the Evangelists, the Jerusalem Temple was more than a framing device or some sort of literary backdrop from which to tell their story. No, the Temple was instrumental to the narrative of each respective Evangelist. The Temple was for each of the Gospel authors the theological engine that propelled the Jesus story forward from beginning to end, from the Infancy Narratives to his death and Resurrection and glorious Ascension.

Many of Jesus's teachings are given in or near the vicinity of the Temple. Regardless of their geographical context, whether in Jerusalem or in Galilee, many of Jesus's sayings, parables, and even exorcisms reveal his attitudes and beliefs about the Temple. Certainly, in a number of Gospel texts, references

18. See Luke 1:5-2:50 and 24:52-53.

to the Temple are straightforward, that is, pertaining to settings in Jerusalem. Yet looks can deceive. A close reading of the Gospel texts supports the claim that there is often more to it than that. The House of the Lord was not just a spectacular backdrop; it held and signified unspeakable mysteries, such as forgiveness and reconciliation, God's presence with his people, and the renewal of Israel and in fact all of Creation.

On at least one occasion in the Gospels, the Temple becomes a synonym for Jesus's own body (Matt. 12:6; John 2:21). *How is this possible?* As will be discussed, each of the Evangelists developed a unique Christological portrait of Jesus, and the Temple was integral in their development. Collectively, the Gospels present Jesus as the "something greater than" the Temple.

Collectively, the authors of the Gospels present Jesus as the Temple's true worshipper and true destiny, revealing God's people to his glorious presence. In particular, in the Synoptic Gospels, Jesus is depicted as the true Prophet, leading a New Exodus, and he is the new Moses who will bring it about, leading God's people to a restored Temple. In the Gospel of John and in the other Johannine writings of the New Testament, temple theology ascends higher still. John presents Jesus as *the new Temple*, the fleshly manifestation of Temple holiness, raised by God in the Resurrection.

There are a number of strong links between the Four Gospels and texts from the Old Testament, connected in some way because of a particular temple motif present in both. And yet, when not knowing what to look for, one may miss such links. As the reader of this book becomes more acquainted with its temple theology, identifying such connections in Scripture will become easier. Not only this, but the reader will also be better able to comprehend the logical relationship between passages.

For instance, the announcement of the Kingdom of God by Jesus (e.g., Mark 1:15; Luke 4:43), along with his words spoken to the Apostles in the Great Commission—"*Go* and make disciples" (Matt. 28:19-20)—may not initially strike the reader as particularly linked to Genesis 1:28, but in fact they are connected on a theological level.

The first commandment given to Man in Genesis was to "be fruitful and multiply." This point may not seem to suggest a connection in any way. Yet there is sufficient evidence throughout Genesis 1-3 to support the claim that Adam is portrayed as the high priest of Eden, and that as high priest he was given two interrelated duties. Specifically, God called Adam: (1) to serve God in the "Holy Place" of the Garden and (2) to multiply the holiness of the Garden sanctuary *beyond Eden*. There is more within the command to "be fruitful" than, strictly speaking, human fertility. Adam was called to *multiply* the holiness of the Temple over the face of the earth, and to "subdue" it, that is, to continue with the ordering and perfecting of everything toward its end, which is the worship of God in his holy Temple.

Armed with this explanation of Adam's high priesthood and the "temple-building" vocation given him by God, one's interpretation of Jesus's announcement of the Kingdom, as well as of his words of the Great Commission, takes on deeper levels of meaning. Over the course of this study, the reader will come to see that the first command given in Genesis (1:28) was the "First Great Commission," later to be recapitulated and brought to its fullness in Jesus Christ, the New Adam.

In this light, God's inaugural command to Adam was not merely a divine directive about procreation. It was a glorious invitation to extend the holy radiance God's temple presence from Eden to ends of the earth. Echoes of God's command are heard throughout the entire canon, at Sinai, at Zion, and, ultimately, in Jesus. Canonically, God's words to Man in Genesis have their *telos*, their end, in Jesus. And so this richer portrait of the Garden, of Eden as the Holy Place of God's cosmic temple, will lead to a thorough rethinking of many of Jesus's actions and words in the Four Gospels. Jesus's proclamation of the Kingdom of God, so central to his identity and message in the Gospels, as well as his final words to the Apostles in Matthew, to "go and to make disciples" (Matt. 28:18-20), will be seen in a fresh light. Specifically, these Gospel texts will be seen as the full flowering of the first command to "be fruitful and multiply" in Genesis.[19]

The above is but one of many examples of textual analysis that will be involved over the course of the book. Numerous others will be brought forward in similar investigations. Many other mysteries of Christ's life as pre-

---

19. As will be explained, the growth of the Kingdom of God—a central theme of Jesus's ministry and teaching—is undergirded by the *biblical* idea that the Temple was always intended, from the outset in Genesis, to be *an expansive entity that covered the earth*, and not merely Mt. Zion in Jerusalem. See Mark 4:31-32: "[The Kingdom of God] is like a grain of mustard seed, which, when sown upon the ground, is the smallest of all the seeds on earth; yet when it is sown *it grows up and becomes the greatest of all shrubs,* and puts forth large branches, so that the birds of the air can make nests in its shade." See also Dan. 2:1-49. Beale's study is particularly important in this regard: "My thesis is that the Old Testament tabernacle and Temples were symbolically designed to point to the cosmic eschatological reality that God's tabernacling presence, *formerly limited to the holy of holies, was to be extended throughout the whole earth.*" *The Temple and the Church's Mission*, 25 (emphasis added).

sented in the Four Gospels beckon to be read anew, in light of insights drawn
from temple theology. The reader will come to see all of Jesus's life and ministry in the Gospels as one continual "coming and going" to and from the
Temple:

- Jesus's presentation in the Temple[20]
- The finding of the boy Jesus in the Temple[21]
- Jesus's many pilgrimages to the Temple[22] and his critique of Temple, in-
  cluding the driving out of the merchants from its courts[23]
- Jesus's prophecies of the Temple's destruction[24]
- Jesus's frequent teaching in the Temple[25]
- The mystery of the Last Supper, occurring within a stone's throw of the
  gates of the Temple
- Finally, and above all, Jesus's crucifixion, which can only be fully grasped
  within the shadow of the Temple[26]

Similarly, one can think about the various people groups active within
the Gospels. Most all of the significant Jewish groups of Jesus's day were, in
one way or another, decisively shaped by the reality of the Temple:

- The Sanhedrin and High Priest, who together were *the singular authority of the Temple*
- The Pharisees, who urged all of Israel to adopt a lifestyle of radical purity, *so that God would once again bless his Temple people and return to it
  in glory*
- The Sadducees, who were *the elite class of Temple privilege*
- The Essenes, the mysterious Jewish sect *that rejected a "corrupted Temple," and fervently awaited the Messiah's purification of it*

This study of temple theology will open up fresh, energizing possibilities for interpretation of the Four Gospels. And such temple patterns do not
end with the Gospel of John. They continue throughout the remainder of
the New Testament right through to St. John's *Apocalypse*—especially there.
Early in the narrative of Acts of the Apostles, the Temple takes center stage

---

20. Luke 2:22-39.   21. Luke 2:46-49.
22. See John 2:13–14, 5:1, 5:14, 7:1, 7:10, 7:14, 8:2, 10:22–23.
23. Matt. 21:23; see John 2:13-22.   24. Matt. 24:1-12; Mark 13:1-23.
25. Matt. 26:55; Luke 19:47; John 5:14, 7:28, 8:28, 18:20.
26. Mark 15:37-38.

to Peter's first post-Resurrection sermon (Acts 2:14*ff.*). There, Peter sets the stage for a sustained engagement/critique of Jewish beliefs concerning the Temple, which carry through over and again throughout Acts.[27] As numerous fathers of the Church saw, Pentecost itself (Acts 2:1-13) was a reversal and righting of the sinful, primordial temple of Babel.[28] Stephen's speech and James's testimony were likewise steeped in Temple critiques.[29] In Acts, the Temple provided the context and contrast for the worship and beliefs of the emerging Church. Again and again, the Temple and its meaning shaped the story of the early Church in Acts, such that it was never far from the shadow of its mighty walls.

Following Acts, the temple theology of the New Testament reaches a new height in the letters of St. Paul. The entire Church was, for St. Paul, a participation in the new Temple. He perceived that the Church was sacramentally joined to Christ, the Head and Cornerstone of the Temple. St. Paul would go even further, with moral teachings that are sensible only in light of his "Christ as cornerstone" theology: those who are "in Christ" are indeed a New Creation and the very dwelling place of God. "Do you not know that you are God's Temple and that God's Spirit dwells in you? If anyone destroys God's Temple, God will destroy him. For God's Temple is holy, and that Temple you are" (1 Cor. 3:16-17).

Many all of St. Paul's letters are saturated with temple motifs, from his opening critique of idolatry in Romans[30] to his images of the Church as the "temple of the Holy Spirit" in Corinthians and Ephesians[31] to his admonition for believers to conduct their lives and bodies as a "temple of the Holy Spirit."[32]

As one gazes into the mysteries presented in Book of Hebrews, a new height of temple theology in the New Testament is realized. Perhaps more

---

27. Acts 2:5-47.

28. "The church's humility recovers the unity of languages that the pride of Babylon had shattered." Venerable Bede, *Commentary on the Acts of the Apostles 2.4*, Cistercian Studies (Kalamazoo, MI: Cistercian, 1973), 117:29. "The multitude of those listening was confounded; it was a second confusion, in contrast to the first evil confusion at Babylon. In that former confusion of tongues there was a division of purpose, for the intention was impious. Here there was a restoration and union of minds, since the object of their zeal was righteous. Through what occasioned the fall came the recovery." St. Cyril of Jerusalem, *Catechetical Lectures* 17.16–17. P. Schaff et al., eds., *A Select Library of the Nicene and Post Nicene Fathers of the Christian Church* (Buffalo: Christian Literature, 1887, 1894; reprint, Peabody: Hendrickson, 1994), 7:128.

29. See Acts 6:13-14, 7:48-50, 15:16-17.

30. See Rom. 1:18-25.

31. See 1 Cor. 3:16-17; 2 Cor. 6:16; Eph. 2:21.

32. 1 Cor. 6:19.

than any book, Hebrews fashions a Christology of Jesus's eternal high priesthood. This complex presentation of the risen Christ rests firmly upon a sustained critique of the high priesthood of the Jerusalem Temple.[33]

Finally, in his glorious and mystical vision in the Book of Revelation, St. John envisions a garden-like city in the shape of a Temple, a new heavens and new earth.[34] All of Revelation hinges upon the figure of a lamb, "standing as though slain" (Rev. 5:6), a reference to the offerings of the Jerusalem Temple and the once for all offering of Jesus, the Lamb of God (John 1:29, 1:36). This final book of the Bible depicts this lamb as *standing as though slain*, a direct allusion to the sacrificial death and Resurrection of Jesus, who has himself become both priest and offering of the new Temple.[35] From this basis, St. John develops a theology of "worship of the lamb," a singular image of Temple sacrifice that he develops again and again in the Apocalypse.[36]

Stepping back from this brief overview of the Old and New Testaments, it should now be clear that this book is concerned with something more than a number of loosely connected texts. Rather, this book will bring into focus a prevalent theme, a "glorious temple pattern," that may have gone previously unnoticed by the reader. As the investigation unfolds, and as texts are identified and evaluated, an unmistakable biblical theology emerges, one that is woven through both biblical canons with the Temple near the very center of things.

One may ask, "Which of the biblical authors is chiefly responsible for perpetrating such an orchestration of temple theology in the Scriptures?" On a purely human level, there are a number of good candidates: the author of Genesis, various psalmists, St. John. Yet, on a deeper level that fully embraces biblical inspiration as a reality, the subtle hand of a Conductor is evident. This book will consider temple theology from the level of both the human authors and that of the Divine authorship of Sacred Scripture.

Temple theology, in other words, ought not to be engaged as a mere intellectual activity. Spiritually speaking, this book is a deep invitation to the

---

33. See Heb. 8:1-10:39.   34. See Rev. 21:1-22:5.

35. Rev. 22:3-5: "There shall no more be anything accursed, but the throne of God and of the Lamb shall be in it, and his servants shall worship him; they shall see his face, and his name shall be on their foreheads. And night shall be no more; *they need no light of lamp or sun, for the Lord God will be their light, and they shall reign for ever and ever.*"

36. See Rev. 5:6, 5:8, 5:12, 5:13, 6:1, 6:16, 7:9, 7:10, 7:14, 7:17, 8:1, 12:11, 13:8, 13:11, 14:1, 14:4, 14:10, 15:3, 17:14, 19:7, 19:9; 21:9, 21:14, 21:22, 21:23, 22:1, 22:3.

contemplative reader: to listen carefully to "the God who speaks" and to un-cover within the rich temple theology of Sacred Scripture God's intentions for the human soul: *that God belongs to man and man to God*. The widely respected Catholic theologian Thomas Dubay aptly describes the sort of in-terior, mystical contemplation that lies deep below a purely academic exami-nation of the topic:

The Temple that we are is to be transfigured in body as well as in soul, that it might become at last a worthy habitation for the divine fire within ... God has purchased this temple-soul by his own blood; it belongs to Him alone as his own delightful dwelling. His love for this soul must be inconceivable for he has paid an almost in-credible price for it. It is his. Yet at the same time, and even more inconceivably, He is its possession. God belongs to man.[37]

Electrifying Holiness

It is hoped that the skeptical reader has been provided with enough ini-tial cause to warrant further inquiry. Yet it is readily acknowledged that the above sketch raised other key questions that might not have been addressed, such as these:

- What drove such preoccupation with the Temple by the biblical writers?
- Did they share common beliefs about the Temple, or can they be distin-guished from one another in their vision and meaning of the Temple?
- Can all of these strands and possibilities of temple theology be brought together, and if so, what conclusions may follow in terms of how one reads and experiences the biblical texts today?

Such questions hint at complexities and tensions within temple theol-ogy. Such complexities and tensions are real, and in some sense nailing down temple theology can be like hitting a moving target: its shape and size and meaning all take shape in different ways throughout the biblical narrative.

Such complexities could make this study taxing for the reader. Despite this, every effort will be taken to help the reader *make sense* of the big picture of temple theology, without unduly simplifying that which is rightly com-plex. Over the course of the book, the diligent reader will come to see what invigorates its author: that within the Old and New Testaments, there is an

---

37. Thomas Dubay, "The Indwelling of Divine Love," *Letter & Spirit* 4 (2008) (emphasis added).

unbreakable thread, a divine fiber that weaves these distinct theological fabrics together: the steadfast proclamation that God dwells in the midst of his people in all of his glory. The visible sign of this is the glorious Temple of God, *the House of the Lord.*

This conviction is not only found within the pages of the Bible. It is also the lively and firmly held dogma that is the essence of Jewish and Christian belief. For these interrelated religions, the Temple is not merely a destination to which one traveled to worship God. For those of biblical faith, the Temple is where one goes *to be with God.*

And so all of Israel's hopes in Sacred Scripture anticipate the arrival of the House of the Lord, the holy Temple. From the sanctuary of Eden on the opening pages of Genesis to the consummation of salvation history at the end of Revelation, where the new Temple that descends from heaven, all of the Bible and its interpretation are shaped by the reality of the Temple and God's presence within it. At the epicenter of this temple story is Jesus Christ, the Living Temple of the New Covenant.

In closing, it is fitting to describe this project not only as a pursuit of temple theology but also as *a full-fledged biblical theology of the Old and New Testaments through the lens of the Temple.* Esteemed theologian Yves Congar writes, "The essential point of God's plan ... could be well formulated in terms of a Temple built of living stones; for God's whole purpose is to make the human race, created in his image, a living, spiritual Temple in which he not only dwells, but to which he communicates himself and in turn receives from it the worship of a wholly filial obedience."[38] Importantly, Congar adds that the entire story of salvation history may be grasped as that of God's "ever more generous, ever deeper presence among his creatures."[39]

This book is a study of the deeper presence of God with his people in Sacred Scripture. Jon Levenson does not overstate things when he describes the Jerusalem Temple as a place of "electrifying holiness."[40] This singular conviction will undergird the book, as biblical texts are explicated in their ancient contexts, and as their implications for people of faith today are made clear. This study is written from the vantage point of Catholic biblical theology,

---

38. Congar, *Mystery of the Temple,* ix. Emphases added.

39. Ibid.

40. Jon Levenson, *Sinai and Zion: An Entry into the Jewish Bible* (San Francisco: Harper & Row, 1985), 77.

and aims to assist all those with such interests. Accordingly, *The House of the Lord* can and should be described as a work of Catholic biblical theology. Nevertheless, it is hoped that numerous other readers will benefit from such a study of Sacred Scripture, a study that can be more precisely described as a *theology of presence—God's presence with his people.* This book is an invitation to investigate God's presence with his people in Sacred Scripture.

The Methodology of Biblical Interpretation in This Book

The brief sketch of temple theology offered above suggests that the "fiber optics" of temple theology is woven through the sacred texts of the Old and New Testaments. Yet this "thread" has too often been missed or mishandled in the past. It was suggested that faulty suppositions, a lack of evidence, or ideological biases about evidence likely played a role in such conclusions. That discussion need not be taken up again here. It need only be added that the true culprit that led to such conclusions was *poor methodology.* The present study seeks to avoid such errors.

In moving forward, this study will not rely upon hastily drawn deductions or personal biases. Rather, a clear and consistent method of inquiry was carefully developed and adhered to throughout the study. The methodology that governs this entire study may be summarized as follows.

1. The method of approach may be considered *textual* in that the claims asserted in the book will be supported with solid literary evidence. Every effort will be made to stay close to the Scriptural texts and other primary sources relevant to the inquiry. Wherever necessary, appropriate contexts will be explained for the clarity of the reader, with an eye to their import upon temple theology. While a plethora of secondary sources will be engaged throughout the book, textual data from primary sources will be preferenced over secondary ones, and proven arguments over presumption or mere hypothesis.

2. The method of approach may be described as *canonical* inasmuch as the book generally follows the narrative of the Old and New Testaments, respectively. While studying Scripture in an "Old to New Testament" manner is something that many will have some experience with, the reader may discover more than a few surprises along the way. The reader will be spared the tedium of undisputed matters wherever possible, and introduced to fresh

voices and lively discussions pertinent to the topic. In the process, the reader will gain clearer understanding not only of the Temple itself, but also of the biblical context in which they are located.

3. The method of approach may be described as *historical* inasmuch as the Temple cannot and should not be studied in isolation from the historical persons, places, and things, whose stories intersect with the Temple. Credible analysis will be distinguished from fanciful or subjective opinion. Objective, authoritative voices will be sought. In seeking to avoid the pitfalls of the source critics described above, a sound and balanced hermeneutic is demanded.[41] Ratzinger's critique of modern biblical skepticism sheds important light on this:

The initiate, however, no longer reads the Bible, but dissects it into the elements from which it is supposed to have grown. The method itself seems to require this radicalizing process: it cannot stand still anywhere in the process of getting to the bottom of the human activity in sacred history. It must try to remove the irrational remnant and explain everything. Faith is not a component of this method, and God is not a factor in the historical events with which it deals.[42]

Ratzinger adds that such historical-critical approaches seek to go "behind the surviving sources—the books of the Bible—[so that] more original sources must be found, which then become the criteria for interpretation." He rightly assesses, "No one can be surprised that in the course of this, hypotheses increasingly branch out and subdivide and finally turn into a jungle full of contradictions. In the end, we find out, no longer what the text says, but what it ought to say and to what components it can be traced back."[43]

This study will not shirk any historical topic of merit as it pertains to the Temple or its priesthood. *Whenever history is engaged in the book, it will be done with responsible and careful handling of data.*

4. The method of approach may be described as *theological* and even "spiritual" in that the primary interest of the book is not with enumerating a plethora of trivial matters, for example, the number of stones used in the

---

41. Steven C. Smith, *The Word of the Lord: 7 Essential Principles for Catholic Scripture Study* (Huntington, IN: OSV Press, 2012), 199-213. The sort of healthy approach that is employed in the present study is described in the previous book, in the discussion of the sixth of seven key principles of Catholic biblical interpretation.

42. Joseph Ratzinger (Benedict XVI), "Biblical Interpretation in Conflict: The Question of the Basic Principles and Path of Exegesis Today," in *God's Word: Scripture—Tradition—Office*, ed. Peter Hünermann and Thomas Söding, trans. Henry Taylor (San Francisco: Ignatius Press, 2008), 92.

43. Ibid., 92–93.

construction of Solomon's Temple. No—this is a study of temple theology, not *temple minutiae*. The deepest interest is in providing the reader with a sound theological assessment of this grand theme in Sacred Scripture.

In fact, the theological approach adhered to may be described with even greater precision. In sum, the methodology of this book is rooted in and informed by *Catholic biblical theology*.[44] This is not simply because the book was written by a practicing Roman Catholic. Rather, the book is sustained from beginning to end by a number of principles of biblical interpretation and biblical theology that are founded upon and flow from the teachings of the Catholic Church.

Principles of Catholic Biblical Theology and Their Import in This Study

Among the various principles of Catholic biblical theology that inform the discussions in this book, there is one particular concept that plays a considerable role: *biblical typology*. Strictly speaking, typology involves "specific persons, institutions, and the like that prefigure or foreshadow a reality made known by God in a later biblical text."[45] The contributions of such readings of Scripture will become evident over the course of the present study. The *Catechism* explains that typological readings of Scripture engage the reader in the ancient Jewish and Christian art of intertextuality, such that an earlier biblical text foreshadows a later one, often in cryptic ways: "It is on this harmony of the two Testaments that the Paschal catechesis of the Lord is built, and then, that of the Apostles and the Fathers of the Church. Typological reading concerns attentive reading to 'what lay hidden under the letter of the

---

44. This is a work of Catholic *biblical* theology, not dogmatic or systematic theologies. As such, it is not the aim of this book to develop or articulate various Catholic dogmas (e.g., the Real Presence of Christ in the Eucharist, the Immaculate Conception of Mary). Nevertheless, to the extent that such teachings become particularly relevant to the study, the book will not hesitate to discuss them.

45. "The basis of such study is the belief that God, who providentially shapes and determines the course of human events, infuses those events with a prophetic and theological significance. Typology thus reveals the unity of salvation history as a carefully orchestrated plan that God unfolds in stages of ever-increasing fulfillment." Scott Hahn, ed., *Catholic Bible Dictionary* (New York: Doubleday, 2009), 929. See also L. Goppelt, *Typos: The Typological Interpretation of the Old Testament in the New* (Grand Rapids, MI: Eerdmans, 1982); Richard Longenecker, *The Christology of Early Jewish Christianity*, Studies in Biblical Theology 17 (London: SCM, 1970); C. A. Evans and L. Novakovic, *Dictionary of Jesus and the Gospels*, 2nd ed., "Typology."

Old Testament: the mystery of Christ.'"[46] Reading Scripture in this manner is typological "because it reveals the newness of Christ on the basis of the *figures* (types) which announce him in the deeds, words, and symbols of the first covenant. By this re-reading in the Spirit of Truth, starting from Christ, the figures are unveiled."[47]

One of the leading practitioners of this ancient way of reading Scripture in the modern age was Jean Cardinal Daniélou. In *The Bible and the Liturgy*, Daniélou explains that typological readings of Scripture did not, strictly speaking, originate with the authors of the New Testament, but rather from ancient Judaism: "The New Testament, therefore, did not invent typology, but simply showed that it was fulfilled in the person of Jesus of Nazareth."[48] Yet, whereas many theologians who engage in typological readings are content in identifying the correspondence between an Old Testament "type" and its corresponding New Testament "antitype," Daniélou goes further.

In *The Bible and the Liturgy*, the reader is immersed in the world of patristic exegesis, and in what may be described as a typological-sacramental study of both Sacred Scripture and the liturgical practices of the early Church. For Daniélou, the "end" of typology is not the New Testament passage to which the Old Testament text was "pointing," but rather the liturgical and sacramental reception of biblical truths: "This biblical symbolism, therefore, *constitutes the primitive foundation which gives us the true significance of the sacraments in their original institution.*"[49] From this basis, Daniélou examines numerous biblical types and, drawing upon the rich treasury of early patristic thinkers, not only explains Scriptural correspondences between the Old and New Testaments but also points to their *typological reality* in the lived experi-

46. Catholic Church, *Catechism of the Catholic Church*, 2nd ed. (Washington, DC: US Catholic Conference, 2000), §1094. (Note: In this study, all citations from the *Catechism* will be referenced by the paragraph number from which it is taken, not the page number.)

47. *Catechism of the Catholic Church*, §1094. In this description, several classic examples of biblical typology: "Thus the flood and Noah's ark prefigured salvation by Baptism, as did the cloud and the crossing of the Red Sea. Water from the rock was the figure of the spiritual gifts of Christ, and manna in the desert prefigured the Eucharist, "the true bread from heaven."

48. Jean Daniélou, *The Bible and the Liturgy* (Notre Dame, IN: Notre Dame Press, 1951, 1961, 1964, 1987), 5. See also Jean Daniélou, *From Shadows to Reality: Studies in the Biblical Typology of the Fathers* (London: Burns & Oates), 1960; Henri De Lubac, *Medieval Exegesis: The Four Senses of Scripture*, vol. 1, *Ressourcement: Retrieval & Renewal in Catholic Thought* (Grand Rapids, MI: Eerdmans, 1998). For an extensive study of Jewish typology, see Goppelt, *Typos*, esp. chaps. 2-3.

49. Daniélou, *The Bible and the Liturgy*, 7.

ence of the early Christian Church, especially in the life of the sacraments.

With great clarity and magnificent depth, Daniélou leads the reader on a typological tour de force in considering early baptismal liturgies as well as the sacraments of Confirmation and the Holy Eucharist. Virtually no liturgical stone is left unturned, as Daniélou explores other ecclesial customs and beliefs in discussing the mystery of the Sabbath, the "Eighth Day of Creation," the celebration of Easter, and more.

Unfortunately, many Catholic readers today are unfamiliar with Daniélou's contributions to Catholic biblical theology. Such students of the Bible may well understand and appreciate biblical typology yet suffer from a more "linear" and limited understanding of it. *This book threatens to change that*, as the present study looks to Daniélou as well as Yves Congar, Henri De Lubac, Ratzinger, and other biblical masters of typology with a kindred sense of affinity. Recognizing that some contemporary readers may be unfamiliar with this sort of *typological-sacramental* way of engaging this topic, explanations will be provided wherever necessary for the clarification of the reader.

In addition to biblical typology, there are other principles at play in this book, which are informed by both classical and contemporary currents in Catholic biblical theology. For the sake of completeness, there are four additional points regarding the methodology of this book as being informed by Catholic biblical theology:

1. *The God Who Speaks.* First and foremost, all truly Catholic approaches to biblical theology are rooted upon the solemn belief that all Scripture is "God-breathed" (2 Tim. 3:16). As Pope Benedict XVI expressed, "The God who speaks to us in His word."[50] This book wholly affirms this conviction as the starting point of all biblical exegesis and theological reflection.

---

50. Benedict XVI, *Verbum Domini* (Vatican City: Libreria Editrice Vaticana, 1998), 24. Unpacking this concept of the God who speaks, the pope looks to the example of Mary in Scripture, particularly in her *Magnificat*: "Here I would like to mention Mary's familiarity with the word of God. This is clearly evident in the *Magnificat*. There we see in some sense how she identifies with the word, enters into it; in this marvelous canticle of faith, the Virgin sings the praises of the Lord in his own words: The *Magnificat*—a portrait, so to speak, of her soul—is entirely woven from threads of Holy Scripture, threads drawn from the word of God. Here we see how completely at home Mary is with the word of God, with ease she moves in and out of it. She speaks and thinks with the word of God; the word of God becomes her word, and her word issues from the word of God. Here we see how her thoughts are attuned to the thoughts of God, how her will is one with the will of God. Since Mary is completely imbued with the word of God, she is able to become the Mother of the Word Incarnate" (28).

That "God speaks to us in His word" is not merely the opinion of this or that Catholic scholar but is dogmatic faith, and at the bedrock of all Catholic teachings about Sacred Scripture, as articulated by the Second Vatican Council (*Dei Verbum §11*). In describing the principle of biblical inspiration, one rightly looks to *Dei Verbum*. Yet the roots of the principle, that "God speaks" through Scripture, are of course ancient, and the deepest roots are not merely Christian but Jewish.[51] Louis Bouyer explains, "For the pious Jew ... the divine Word signified an intensely living reality. From the outset, it is not merely basic ideas that are to be shaped, but a fact, an event, *a personal intervention in their existence*. For them the temptation to identify the religion of the Word with an intellectual religion was nonexistent. *The mere mention of such an identification would have seemed absurd to them, and even bereft of meaning.*"[52] In sum, this study recognizes biblical inspiration not only as a logical and intelligent supposition, but also as the harbor from which all sound biblical exegesis sets sail. The conviction underlying this book is that the Word of God is living, breathing, and inspired by the Holy Spirit—and not merely a human word, a thing of the past.[53]

2. *Dei Verbum.* Second and closely related to this above conviction, this study looks to *Dei Verbum* as the lodestar in Catholic biblical interpretation in the present age.[54] Certainly, a number of concepts crucial to Catholic biblical exegesis emerged over many ages of the Church. And yet they are

---

51. "These hermeneutical assumptions bring Irenaeus quite close to the rabbis of the intertestamental period who, as James Kugel argues, operated out of four fundamental convictions—namely, that God in a very real sense is the author of the whole Scripture, that the Bible is consistent with itself, that its meaning is often cryptic, and that it has relevance for us today." Robert Barron, "Biblical Interpretation and Theology: Irenaeus, Modernity, and Vatican II," *Letter & Spirit* 5 (2009): 178. See also James Kugel, *How to Read the Bible: A Guide to Scripture, Then and Now* (New York: Simon and Schuster, 2007), 14–17.

52. Louis Bouyer, *Eucharist: Theology and Spirituality of the Eucharistic Prayer*, trans. Charles Underhill Quinn (Notre Dame, IN: University of Notre Dame, 1968), 31–32.

53. *Dei Verbum §21*: "The Church has always venerated the divine Scriptures just as she venerates the body of the Lord, since, especially in the sacred liturgy, she unceasingly receives and offers to the faithful the bread of life from the table both of God's word and of Christ's body. She has always maintained them, and continues to do so, together with sacred tradition, as the supreme rule of faith, since, as inspired by God and committed once and for all to writing, *they impart the word of God Himself without change, and make the voice of the Holy Spirit resound in the words of the prophets and Apostles.*"

54. Second Vatican Council, *Dei Verbum* [The Word of God], Dogmatic Constitution on Divine Revelation, November 18, 1965, in *The Scripture Documents: An Anthology of Official Catholic Teachings*, ed. Dean P. Béchard (Collegeville, MN: Liturgical Press, 2002).

brought together, synthesized, and given doctrinal teeth in Vatican II's Dogmatic Constitution on Divine Revelation (i.e., *Dei Verbum*). While the present study naturally embraces and looks to the authoritative wisdom of *Dei Verbum* as a whole for guidance, certain of its concepts are particularly important here, among them: biblical inspiration, the historicity and believability of the Four Gospels, the unity of the Old and New Testaments,[55] and the integration of Sacred Scripture and Sacred Tradition as originating from the "same Divine Wellspring" (*Dei Verbum* §9).[56] The Gospel writers themselves engaged in typological readings of the Old Testament, and biblical typology subsequently became a chief means in the patristic age for explaining Christ in light of the Old Testament. Though overlooked by many biblical scholars today, typology has always been revered by the Catholic Church, and it, too, is included in the teachings of *Dei Verbum*.[57] Additionally, this book looks to a rich concept that goes back to St. Irenaeus, known as "recapitulation," or

55. *Dei Verbum* §16: "God, the inspirer and author of both Testaments, wisely arranged that the New Testament be hidden in the Old and the Old be made manifest in the New." See also *Catechism of the Catholic Church*, §129).

56. *Dei Verbum* §9: "Hence there exists a close connection and communication between sacred Tradition and Sacred Scripture. For both of them, flowing from *the same divine wellspring*, in a certain way merge into a unity and tend toward the same end. For Sacred Scripture is the word of God inasmuch as it is consigned to writing under the inspiration of the divine Spirit, while sacred tradition takes the word of God entrusted by Christ the Lord and the Holy Spirit to the Apostles, and hands it on to their successors in its full purity, so that led by the light of the Spirit of truth, they may in proclaiming it preserve this word of God faithfully, explain it, and make it more widely known. Consequently, it is *not from Sacred Scripture alone* that the Church draws her certainty about everything which has been revealed." Pope Benedict XVI offered the following lively description of the "handing on" of Sacred Tradition and its importance up to today: "Tradition is the living Gospel ... Thanks to tradition ... the water of life that flowed from Christ's side and his saving blood reach the women and men of all times.... Tradition is the living river that links us to the origins, the living river in which the origins are ever present, the great river that leads us to the gates of eternity." From Pope Benedict XVI, General Audience, April 26, 2006, in *L'Osservatore Romano*, May 3, 2006, 11.

57. See *Dei Verbum* §15. The *Catechism of the Catholic Church* adds this about how various mysteries of the Old Testament are "unveiled" in Christ: "It is on this harmony of the two Testaments that the Paschal catechesis of the Lord is built, and then, that of the Apostles and the Fathers of the Church. This catechesis unveils what lay hidden under the letter of the Old Testament: the mystery of Christ. It is called '*typological*' because it reveals the newness of Christ on the basis of the 'figures' (types) which announce him in the deeds, words, and symbols of the first covenant. By this re-reading in the Spirit of Truth, starting from Christ, the figures are unveiled. Thus the flood and Noah's ark prefigured salvation by Baptism, as did the cloud and the crossing of the Red Sea. Water from the rock was the figure of the spiritual gifts of Christ, and manna in the desert prefigured the Eucharist, 'the true bread from heaven'" (§1094; see also §128-29).

the idea that Christ the New Adam renews, restores, and transforms fallen humanity, and the whole Creation.[58]

3. *Word and Sacrament.* Third, the present study rests upon the Catholic principle that the liturgy is the home of Sacred Scripture and is crucial to its proper interpretation in the Church. As such, the book affirms the profound unity that exists between "Word and Eucharist,"[59] and that one's understanding of Sacred Scripture is imperfect and lacks something of its fullness without the unity of Word and Sacrament: Word and Eucharist are so deeply bound together that we cannot understand one without the other: the word of God sacramentally takes flesh in the event of the Eucharist. The Eucharist opens us to an understanding of Scripture, just as Scripture for its part illumines and explains the mystery of the Eucharist. Unless we acknowledge the Lord's real presence in the Eucharist, our understanding of Scripture remains imperfect.[60]

4. *Ancient and Modern.* Fourth, while it is *Dei Verbum* that specifically undergirds the conclusions derived here, the book readily draws from the wellspring of two millennia of the Catholic biblical and intellectual tradition. Ancient and medieval voices—such as St. Justin Martyr, Origen, St. Augustine, St. Ephrem the Syrian, and St. Thomas Aquinas—will be heard from time and again, as will modern and Catholic biblical thinkers such as Joseph Ratzinger, Jean Daniélou, Yves Congar, Louis Bouyer, and Matthew Levering. While the study will always seek to "begin with the literal," neither the spiritual senses of Scripture nor various spiritual exegetes will be neglected here.

Having clarified the methodology that underlies the book, and more par-

---

58. *Catechism of the Catholic Church:* "When Christ became incarnate and was made man, he *recapitulated* in himself the long history of mankind and procured for us a 'short cut' to salvation, *so that what we had lost in Adam, that is, being in the image and likeness of God, we might recover in Christ Jesus.* For this reason Christ experienced all the stages of life, thereby giving communion with God to all men" (§118). See also St. Irenaeus, *Against Heresies,* III.18.

59. Pope Benedict XVI, *Verbum Domini.* Benedict adds that this unity "is grounded in the witness of Scripture (cf. Jn 6; Lk 24), attested to by the Fathers of the Church, and reaffirmed by the Second Vatican Council."

60. Ibid., 55. Similarly, St. Pope John Paul II explained in *Fides et Ratio* that there is a "sacramental character" to Sacred Scripture, "and especially to the sign of the Eucharist, in which the indissoluble unity between the signifier and signified makes it possible to grasp the depths of the mystery." *Fides et Ratio* (Vatican City: Libreria Editrice Vaticana, 1998), §13.

ticularly the Catholic hermeneutic that deeply informs this study, one final question remains: *How will this approach affect the reader's experience of the book?* The answer depends upon one's expectations (and experiences) in reading a work of Catholic biblical theology. In no way will non-Catholic readers be left out or diminished. Numerous present-day biblical theologians will be sought for their expertise, such as Matthew Levering, Michael Barber, and Brant Pitre. Alongside Catholic biblical theologians as these, the insights of Jewish and Protestant (and other non-Catholic theologians) will also be included. In fact, certain concepts developed by non-Catholic theologians such as Gregory Beale, N. T. Wright, Margaret Barker, and Nicholas Perrin are particularly crucial to the study. Their input will be thoughtfully incorporated into the book in light of the strengths they bring to this discussion.

Concluding Remarks

The above discussion points are intended to give the reader the clearest possible understanding of the Catholic biblical of methodology that undergirds this book. It is hoped that the approach employed here in no way imposes a hermeneutic upon other readers, nor diminishes such readers' engagement of this topic. To the contrary, the approach embraced in this book is put forth as a sound and reliable manner of engaging not only *temple* theology, but also other avenues of theological and biblical inquiry.[61]

For Catholic readers in particular, it is especially hoped that this discussion serves as a reminder that all biblical theology is in dialogue with and out of loyalty to the doctrines of the Church and can provide guideposts, even for developing personal study habits of Sacred Scripture. Overall, the book will have much to offer various types of Catholic readers, from the serious academic reader to the nonspecialist and even those with primarily personal, even devotional, interests in the topic. And yet in no way is the non-Catholic reader discouraged from engaging this study. To the contrary, such readers will quickly see that there is a lively spirit of collaboration in play, as alluded to by the welcoming of non-Catholic experts into the study of the Temple in Scripture.

Nothing more needs to be added about methodology. The merits of

---

61. Regarding the approach adopted here, if in the course of the book the reader feels confused or misled for any reason, it is hoped that charity will prevail.

methods employed in the book will speak for themselves, and the reader will ascertain their profitability. Those interested in a more extensive study of the main principles of Catholic biblical interpretation are directed to the previous book, *The Word of the Lord: 7 Essential Principles for Catholic Scripture Study*.[62]

62. Smith, *The Word of the Lord*. Additionally, the following studies may be helpful regarding Catholic biblical interpretation: Ratzinger, "Biblical Interpretation in Conflict"; Aidan Nichols, *The Shape of Catholic Theology: An Introduction to its Sources, Principles and History* (San Francisco: Ignatius Press, 1991); Daniélou, *From Shadows to Reality*; Matthew L. Lamb and Matthew Levering, *Vatican II: Renewal within Tradition* (New York: Oxford University Press, 2008); Pope Benedict XVI, General Audience, April 26, 2006; Richard N. Longenecker, *Biblical Exegesis in the Apostolic Period*, 2nd ed. (Grand Rapids, MI: Eerdmans, 1999); Peter Williamson, *Catholic Principles for Interpreting Scripture: A Study of the Pontifical Biblical Commission's The Interpretation of the Bible in the Church*, Pontificia Universita Gregoriana 2000, Subsidia Biblica 22 (Rome: Pontificio Instituto Biblico, 2001); Matthew Levering, *Participatory Exegesis: A Theology of Biblical Interpretation* (Notre Dame, IN: University of Notre Dame Press, 2008).

I

TEMPLE THEOLOGY IN THE OLD TESTAMENT

EDEN, THE
COSMOLOGICAL TEMPLE

The Temple of Creation (I/III)

He built his sanctuary like the high heavens,
like the earth, which he has founded forever.

Psalm 78:69

The Story Begins: Seeing Eden
in Three Dimensions

Where exactly does the temple thread begin to weave its way into the story of the Old Testament? With the opening words of the Bible, *"In the beginning God created the heavens and the earth"* (Gen. 1:1). This is where the epic story of God's presence with his people begins.

All readers of Scripture (in fact, most everyone else, too) have some image quickly spring to mind at the mention of "the Garden of Eden." Beyond its biblical roots, the concept of Eden enjoys wide cultural and social recognition today. Yet the two worlds do not always converge well. For many casual observers, Eden is simply a two-dimensional fantasy, a fairy tale. More often than not, in an age of disproportionate biblical illiteracy and "none's" (people with no discernible religious background), Eden is imagined from *cultural misconceptions* rather than from biblical or theological conceptions of one sort or another.

Too often, a rather whimsical and overly simplistic portrait is foisted upon the biblical text, with two naked, rather bored individuals prancing around a make-believe tree. Such is a two-dimensional conception, the sort of picture a child might draw and not the reality of God's inspired Word and not the biblical Eden.

This book pushes back strenuously against such popular misconceptions and asserts that the true biblical Eden is vastly more complex and interesting than the commonly flat cultural impressions. There is more "there" there, more than meets the eye from only a cursory glance at the biblical text. Eden springs forth from Genesis as a robustly alive landscape, with rays of morning sunlight streaming down upon majestic, three-dimensional, living beings. Birdsong fills the crisp air, and one's attention is drawn to the beauty and splendor of the man and the woman, united in a living and human embrace. No human words can fully describe or comprehend the splendor of Eden. Still, the following depiction offered in St. Ephrem's *Hymn of Paradise* invites the reader to peer deeply into the remarkable biblical vision of Eden:

Joyfully did I embark on the tale of Paradise—a tale that is short to read but rich to explore. My tongue read the story's outward narrative, while my intellect took wing and soared upward in awe as it perceived the splendor of Paradise—*not indeed as it really is but insofar as humanity is granted to comprehend it.*

With the eye of my mind I gazed upon paradise; the summit of every mountain is lower than its summit, the crest of the Flood reached only its foothills; these it kissed with reverence before turning back to rise above and subdue the peak of every hill and mountain. The foothills of Paradise it kisses while every summit it buffets.

Not that the ascent to Paradise is arduous because of its height, for those who inherit it experience no toil there. With its beauty it joyfully urges on those who ascend. Amidst glorious rays it lies resplendent, all fragrant with its scents; magnificent clouds fashion the abodes of those who are worthy of it.[1]

As St. Ephrem's liturgical poetry rightly depicts, Eden is a vast, mysterious mountain that the reader reverently ascends, and its glorious heights cannot be ascended by human reason alone. One's image of Eden must go beyond the surface of the text, beyond literalistic first impressions, beyond cultural misconceptions, and beyond the untrained imagination.

Yet with the interpretative counsel of the likes of St. Ephrem, the intellectually—and spiritually—inquisitive reader may begin to see much more within the biblical text than one might imagine possible. But Eden's glorious heights cannot be easily ascended if, in the reader's mind, it is restricted to

---

1. St. Ephrem, *Hymns on Paradise*, 78–79 [Hymn I, §§3–5].

two dimensions—or if its exalted meaning is grasped from a hastily drawn sketch.

The true, biblical vision of Eden invites the reader into a richly symbolic and evocative "living environment," composed of at least three distinct regions. Such a vision of Eden will be developed in this book, and it matters, as Eden is at the epicenter of temple theology in Sacred Scripture.

The Fiber Optics of Temple Theology

There are numerous valid ways of interpreting Genesis 1-3, some of which may not necessarily lead the reader to "see" a temple in the text. This does not make them any less valid. Yet when one does read the text *as a whole*—and, importantly, when one interprets Genesis 1–3 *in the light of the entire biblical canon*—a far deeper connection between Genesis 1–3 and the rest of the biblical canon begins to emerge.

How deep?

In a manner of speaking, as deep as the ocean. Beginning in the 2000s, global telecommunications firms raced to bridge the oceanic gap on the Internet superhighway. Hi-tech submarines were used to embed fiber optical cables within the dark depths of the ocean floor. The most advanced of the fiber optical cables have a diameter slightly larger than a human hair. Among such governmental, commercial, scientific clients, Wall Street is able to conduct global business at the speed of light. Though not one of the millions of people depending upon global communications can "see" these hair-like fibers, there would be no connection without them.

This is an analogy worth holding on to as the book unfolds because, *theologically speaking, deep in the ocean floor of the biblical canon runs a nearly transparent cable called temple theology.* Like a divine, hair-like fiber, temple theology connects the Old and New Testaments in profound ways. One may not always see it, but in its absence, the deeper meaning of Sacred Scripture would go offline. This divine fiber runs clear from Genesis onward, branching off at numerous places in between, winding its way slowly but steadily to the Book of Revelation.

Within this analogy, the "hub" of the fiber optical highway is Genesis. There, chapters 1–3 depict the whole of Creation as God's holy Temple. The starting point of this thread is embedded within the opening verses of Genesis, running clear through chapters 1–2 and culminating in the dark moment of the expulsion of the Man and Woman from Eden at the conclusion of chapter 3.

Numerous clues from Scripture support this claim as wholly accurate.[2] A close examination of the foundational biblical texts of Genesis reveals that the whole of Creation—and specifically the Garden of Eden—is depicted as a *cosmological sanctuary*. Such a depiction is not without precedent. Numerous texts both within and beyond ancient Judaism bear this out and follow along similar lines as the biblical narrative of Genesis 1–3.[3]

Certainly, Eden is the centerpiece of Creation of Genesis 1–2. That much is undisputed and clear to anyone who reads the text with care. What may be less evident to some readers, though no less important, is the reality that Eden is not merely a garden, but a holy mountain. *This book will show that Genesis 1–2 presents Eden as a sacred mountain, an archetypal Temple.*

Though it may come as a surprise to some biblical readers, this book will nevertheless demonstrate that the author of Genesis conceived of Eden as much more than a perfectly cultivated garden. No—Eden was God's mountain, with a Divine garden at the base of the mountain of God. Specifically, Genesis depicts the home of Adam and Eve as a garden sanctuary named Eden, with its holy, inner sanctum at the center called the "Tree of Life."[4] This temple of Creation belongs wholly to its Creator, *Yahweh Elohim*. It is

2. That the author of Gen. 1–2 clearly intends a cosmological temple reading will be discussed below. Corroborating evidence will be provided in the form of parallel biblical texts, early primary sources, as well as insights from contemporary Jewish and Christian scholars.

3. See esp. G. K. Beale, *The Temple and the Church's Mission: A Biblical Theology of the Dwelling Place of God* (Downers Grove, IL: InterVarsity Press, 2004), 44–66; T. Desmond Alexander, "God's Temple City," in *From Paradise to the Promised Land: An Introduction to the Pentateuch*, 2nd ed. (Grand Rapids, MI: Baker Academic, 2012), 119–33; idem, *From Eden to the New Jerusalem* (Grand Rapids, MI: Kregel, 2008), 13–73; E. P. Sanders, *Judaism: Practice and Belief, 63BCE–66 CE* (Philadelphia: Trinity Press International, 1992), 47–145; Emil Schürer, *The History of the Jewish People in the Age of Jesus Christ (175 B.C.—A.D. 135)*, 3 vols., rev. and ed. Geza Vermes et al. (Edinburgh: T & T Clark, 1973, 1979, 1986, 1987), 2:237–313; Menahem Haran, *Temples and Temple Service in Ancient Israel* (Oxford: Clarendon, 1978); Joachim Jeremias, *Jerusalem in the Time of Jesus*, trans. F. H. Cave and C. H. Cave (Philadelphia: Fortress, 1969), 21–27, 84–86, 147–221; H. H. Rowley, *Worship in Ancient Israel* (London: SPCK, 1967), 71–110; Yves Congar, *The Mystery of the Temple* (New York: Newman Press, 1962); L. Michael Morales, *The Tabernacle Pre-Figured: Cosmic Mountain Ideology in Genesis and Exodus* (Leuven: Peeters, 2012); Jacob Chanikuzhy, *Jesus the Eschatological Temple* (Leuven: Peeters, 2012); Margaret Barker, *Temple Themes in Christian Worship*, 3rd ed. (London: Bloomsbury, 2013); Nicholas Perrin, *Jesus the Temple* (Grand Rapids, MI: Baker Academic, 2012).

4. Gen. 2:9; see 3:22, 3:24.

he who nourishes it with "living waters" that flow down Mt. Eden to fill the earth and fructify the entire Creation with his life and goodness.[5] In the figurative language of Genesis, a *threefold cosmological Temple* comes into view:

1. Above the mountain of Eden was the "inner and uppermost" sanctum of the Temple. In a sense it was part of the cosmological temple; in another sense, it was wholly other, for above the mountain was simply "the heavens," the dwelling place of God and God alone. This "Holy of Holies" is where *Yahweh Elohim* dwells in all of his transcendent holiness and resplendent glory.

2. Below the Holy Place, down upon the mountain itself, was the "Holy Place" of this cosmological temple. This was the sacred space of the Garden itself, which the Man and Woman inhabited in perfect communion to God above and each other. In the center of this Garden was the Tree of Life, an icon and constant reminder to the Man and Woman of God's nearness, of his holiness. From it they drew on his own divine life as their own, as they free "ate" from it. The Tree of Life was the center of their reality and communion with one another. It conveyed that all of their life is from God and a gift to be given back to God, in every thought, every word, every action, every choice. They were to "be holy" just as he "is holy." Thus the Tree of Life was for the Man and Woman a tangible sign, a *typological-sacramental* icon of God's own life, shared with man. Its holy presence was a sign of God's holy presence "above and beyond" them, above Mt. Eden.[6] This Holy Place was created by God as an icon of heaven, and importantly Eden is the primary place where those who dwelt there were able to encounter the Divine Presence, provided that they continually "remembered God." Adam, God's first and filial High Priest of Eden, failed at his priestly duties. Later, Adam's choice of disobedience is contrasted by another priest in early Creation, Noah. Yet, unlike Adam, Noah obeyed, remembered God (Gen. 8:1), and in return was remembered *by God*. Those who lived by faith had access to God's divine life, and a divine mission to sanctify the world beyond Eden with God's temple presence.

---

5. See Gen. 2:10–14.

6. The Tree of Life plays a symbolic role *beyond* the text of Genesis itself. In the larger schema of the canon of Scripture, it came to prefigure the Holy Place of the Jerusalem Temple, in which a *menorah* was set, a "tree of light and life" that illuminated the sacred space of the Holy Place for the work of priests.

3. Beyond the Garden were the Outer Courts of the cosmological temple. It was "the world beyond." Though created good, it was in need of taming by the Man and Woman, as they were called to "be fruitful and multiply" and to "fill the earth." In one sense, the Outer Courts posed dangers, limits, in that the Outer Courts were not near to God as they were. There was *potential* for life and goodness to be brought to it, but make no mistake: *it had to be brought* from within the Garden. Here is the pattern: from God above, to the Man and Woman, and out to the "world beyond." There was a clear "boundary" between that which was in the Holy Place of the Garden (i.e., that which was holy, sanctified) and that which was beyond the Garden (i.e., that which was unholy, not yet sanctified). As will be shown, Adam (and Eve with him) was called to preserve and protect the holiness of the Holy Place. This, first and foremost, was his duty: to keep the unholy out and to assure that all Creation within the Garden was indeed holy and set apart for God. But secondarily, and of no small significance, was a future command, in fact, a "divine commission" from God to Adam: to *expand the holiness of the Temple to the world beyond.* Adam was called to "spread" the holiness of the Holy Place to that which yet needed to be sanctified in the world beyond.

This is, in sum, the threefold temple reality and cosmology of Genesis. The Jewish apocryphal Book of Jubilees, written approximately 200 BC, was itself a retelling of the Creation narratives of Genesis. It reflects this ancient way of interpreting Genesis 1–2, when it boldly declares that "[Noah] knew that the Garden of Eden was the *Holy of Holies* of the Lord."[7] For the authors of Jubilees, such a connection between Noah and Eden was anything but obscure. The reasoning is this: Adam was created by God to be the priestly caretaker of the Garden Temple. Yet Adam failed to keep the Holy Place holy, and was himself expelled from it.

Later in Genesis, Noah emerges as the righteous man, the man whom God "remembered" (Gen. 8:1), redeeming him and his family. As the waters of the flood recede, Noah builds a *mizbeah*, the first altar in Scripture. He offers burnt offerings in thanksgiving to God, an archetype of the Levitical priests yet to come. In other words, Noah typifies priestly sanctity. God remembered Noah the priest, because unlike the failed priesthood of Adam,

---

7. Jubilees 8:19. See James Charlesworth, ed., *The Old Testament Pseudepigrapha*, vol. 2 (New York: Doubleday, 1998), 73.

Noah's priesthood got worship right: Noah remembered God and "called upon the name of the Lord" (see Gen. 4:26). So, for Jubilees, the Garden was the Holy Place and Noah "knew it."

Here is something of great importance: temples are not without priests. As such, Adam, the first man, was given the investiture of a priest in his innermost being. To be clear: Adam was *the archetypal high priest of Creation*. He was created and called by God, and as God's son, was given stewardship over the sanctuary of Eden, the Holy Place of this temple.

As guardian-priest of the Holy Place of Eden, he was charged by his Father to preserve the holiness of the temple, for all who dwell within its sacred space. Again, Adam's vocation required keeping out anything that maliciously threatened the holiness of the temple. In some sense, Eve, "mother of the living,"[8] shares in Adam's priestly dignity and duties. (Eve's feminine dignity holds equally profound and mysterious implications, yet these will not be touched upon in the book.) In Genesis, it is specifically Adam, and Adam alone, who is given priestly responsibilities by God.

This identity of Creation as God's holy Temple, with Eden as the Holy Place and Adam as its high priest, is at the foundation of temple theology, upon which the larger study rests.[9] More specifically, the depiction of Eden as the archetypal temple and Adam as its high priest invites the biblical reader into the mysteries of temple theology that unfold across the pages of both the Old and New Testaments.[10]

Now, in what follows, four major lines of evidence will be brought forth that support the above claims. Scriptural data and supporting textual evidence will be examined that collectively and powerfully suggest that the opening chapters of Genesis present the whole of Creation as God's cosmological Temple, with Eden as its Holy Place, Adam as its high priest, and the Tree of Life as the icon of God's presence with humanity in the Temple.

8. Gen. 3:20.

9. As discussed previously, the evidence for a temple theology reading of Sacred Scripture advances far beyond the text of Gen. 1–2.

10. The present topic focuses primarily on Old Testament texts (and Genesis in particular). A few ideas will be sketched out that point the reader toward apprehending creation theology in the New Testament as well.

Eden, the Holy Mountain

The idea that Eden is a *mountain*—and not merely a garden—may come as a surprise to some. Yet a close reading of Genesis 2 reveals clues that the paradise of Eden is actually atop a mountain, from which four rivers flow outward and fructify the earth: "*A river flowed out of Eden* to water the garden, and there it divided and became four rivers" (Gen. 2:10–14). This may not seem like a smoking gun in terms of the claim that Eden was a high place, a mountain.

But a key piece of supporting evidence is found elsewhere in Scripture. Specifically, the following passage from Ezekiel describes the king of Sidon, arrayed with the splendor of Adam. For the purposes of this study, what is crucial is that the biblical prophet identifies Eden with the holy mountain of God: "You were in Eden, the garden of God; every precious stone was your covering, carnelian, topaz, [etc.] … With an anointed guardian cherub I placed you; *you were on the holy mountain of God;* in the midst of the stones of fire you walked" (Ezek. 28:13–14).

Eden is the mountain above which God himself dwells as the source of both physical and spiritual life. It is the mountain abode of God himself.[11] Beale's description is helpful: "The Garden itself is a sacred space separate from the outer world, where God's priestly servant worships God by obeying him, by cultivating and guarding."[12]

If Mt. Eden is the Holy of Holies, the dwelling of God, then below the Garden is the Holy Place, the special abode created for Adam and Eve. It is sustained by the love of God and nourished by his immortal life, the Tree of Life. Finally, beyond the mountain of Eden and its adjacent Garden paradise is "the world beyond." In temple language, the world beyond Eden is the Outer Courts.

The world of Genesis depicts all of reality as concentric spaces as nearness or distance from the holy God of the mountain. Another biblical theologian agrees, stating that "At the heart of the theology of the Bible is … its principle theme: the dwelling of the Divine Presence…. This theme is given historical movement and literary expression through a particular pattern of approaching God: through the waters to the mountain of God for worship,

---

11. "Eden is the source of the waters and [is the palatial] residence of God; and the garden adjoins God's residence." John Walton, *Genesis* (Grand Rapids, MI: Zondervan), 167.

12. Beale, *The Temple and the Church's Mission*, 75.

that is, for the abundant life of the Divine Presence."[13] In fact, one of God's names in Scripture supports this idea. Specifically, the oldest name for God in Israel is *El Shaddai*, often translated "mighty God" or "God Almighty," but more precisely "*El*, the one of the mountain."[14]

A contemporary theologian uses the language of archetype with respect to Eden. This is correct, and prepares the reader to see Eden long after our reading of Scripture has moved on from Genesis: "Eden ... may be considered an archetype for the cosmic mountain [and] the foremost world mountain for Israel. Further, the Israelite cultus of the Tabernacle/Temple—and specifically the Sabbath ... opened the way to that Edenic reality."[15] This is evident in the deuterocanonical Wisdom of Solomon: "Thou hast given command to build a temple on thy holy mountain, and an altar in the city of thy habitation, a copy of the holy tent which thou didst prepare from the beginning" (Wisd. 9:8).

Clearly, these lines of evidence support what was said by Ezekiel concerning Eden. It can be fairly asserted that, according to some ancient Jewish conceptions, the Eden was not merely a sacred space upon God's holy mountain, Mt. Eden. Gordon Wenham discusses the connection between the Garden of Eden and Ezekiel's more precise interpretation of it as part of the "holy mountain of God." As he explains, "The Garden of Eden is not viewed by the author of Genesis simply as a piece of Mediterranean farmland, *but as an archetypal sanctuary, that is a place where God dwells and where man should worship him.* Many of the features of the Garden may also be found in later sanctuaries, particularly the Tabernacle or Jerusalem Temple. These parallels suggest that the Garden itself is understood as a sort of sanctuary."[16]

13. Morales, *The Tabernacle Pre-Figured*, 1.

14. See 1 Ki. 20:28–29: "And a man of God came near and said to the king of Israel, 'Thus says the Lord, "Because the Syrians have said, '*The Lord is a god of the hills but he is not a god of the valleys*,' therefore I will give all this great multitude into your hand, and you shall know that I am the Lord."'" And they encamped opposite one another *seven days*. Then *on the seventh day* the battle was joined; and the people of Israel smote of the Syrians a hundred thousand foot soldiers in one day." Note the occurrence of "seven" following *El Shaddai*. Much more will be explained about the significance of "seven" in a subsequent discussion.

15. Morales, *The Tabernacle Pre-Figured*, 16. The connection between temple/mountain, Sabbath, and covenant is seen clearly in Isa. 56:6–7: "*Everyone who keeps the Sabbath*, and does not profane it, and *holds fast my covenant—these I will bring to my holy mountain*, and make them joyful in my *house of prayer*; their burnt offerings and their sacrifices will be accepted on my altar; *for my house shall be called a house of prayer for all peoples*."

16. Gordon Wenham, "Sanctuary Symbolism in the Garden of Eden Story," *Proceedings of the*

It will suffice to say that all such two-dimensional concepts of a man and woman next to a fruit tree need to now be set aside once and for all, and replaced with the rich and multidimensional vision with which the Bible itself presents Eden. Along these lines, the idea of "Eden as mountain of God" may now be brought into sharper focus.

First, the mountain image stays closer to the biblical depiction of Eden compared with flat (pun intended) cultural conceptions. Yet there is a second reason to prefer the mountain imagery; in Sacred Scripture, mountains often have an intrinsic spiritual value. Time and again in the canon of both the Old and New Testaments, it is upon holy mountains that God reveals himself. More precisely, it is on the mountaintop *that God meets and covenants with his people.* This is a recurrent pattern throughout the major covenants described in the Old Testament:

God covenants with Adam (and Eve) in the garden of Mt. Eden (Gen. 1–2).[17]

God covenants with Noah (and his family) on Mt. Ararat (Gen. 8:4, 9:1–8, 9:17).

God covenants with Abraham (and his descendants) on Mt. Moriah, after the binding of Isaac (Gen. 22, 12:1–3, 17:1–21).

God covenants with Moses (and the Israelites) on Mt. Sinai (Exod. 20–24).[18]

God covenants with David (and "the son of David"), an everlasting covenant, on Mt. Zion (2 Sam. 7:12–13).[19] Strikingly, this is the precise location of God's covenant with Abraham—Mt. Moriah is Mt. Zion, as the *Chronicler* reveals.[20]

World Congress of Jewish Studies 9 (1986): 19. See also T. Desmond Alexander, *From Eden to the New Jerusalem* (Grand Rapids, MI: Kregel, 2008), 20–31.

17. The language of "covenant" (Hebrew: *berith*) is not explicit, yet all the dimensions of the covenant are present in these chapters. See J. Milgrom, "Covenants: The Sinaitic and Patriarchal Covenants in the Holiness Code (Leviticus 17–27)," in *Sefer Moshe: The Moshe Weinfeld Jubilee Volume*, ed. C. Cohen et al. (Winona Lake, IN: Eisenbrauns, 2004), 91–101.

18. Exod. 24:8, 24:15: "And Moses took the blood and threw it upon the people, and said, '*Behold the blood of the covenant* which the Lord has made with you in accordance with all these words' ... Then Moses went up on the mountain, and the cloud covered the mountain. *The glory of the Lord settled on Mount Sinai,* and the cloud covered it six days; and on the seventh day he called to Moses out of the midst of the cloud."

19. See 2 Sam. 7:10–16: "*the Lord will make you a house* ... I will raise up your offspring after you, who shall come forth from your body, and I will establish his kingdom. *He shall build a house for my name, and I will establish the throne of his kingdom forever* ... *your house and your kingdom shall be made sure for ever before me; your throne shall be established forever.*"

20. See 2 Chron. 3:1. S. W. Hahn, *The Kingdom of God as Liturgical Empire: A Theological*

But this mountain motif is not bound within the Old Testament canon. Viewed through the lens of temple theology, Calvary, the place of the crucifixion of Jesus, may be interpreted as the last in a long chain of holy mountains, whereupon God united himself to humanity in ever deeper and ever fuller ways. Calvary is not simply "one more mountaintop encounter" between God and humanity—it is the climactic apex of the entire covenantal story begun on Mt. Eden. The heights of Calvary is the mountain toward which the entire narrative has been leaning all along, and without which the biblical epic would remain truly incomplete.

From the perspective of Catholic biblical theology, it is atop Calvary that God unites himself in love, to all the world, through the sacrificial offering of the Lamb of God, Jesus Christ.[21] The new and everlasting covenant, brought about through the death (and Resurrection) of Jesus, rests firmly upon the foundation of the covenants of the Old Testament.

Throughout the Old Covenant, God bound himself to his people in and through various human mediators: Adam, Noah, Abraham, Moses, and David. This "binding of God" to his people took place in every instance on holy mountains. In this light, the sacrifice of Jesus Christ on Calvary reveals a new and everlasting covenant, written not on tablets of stone but, in the language of the prophet Jeremiah, on human hearts: "Behold, the days are coming, says the Lord, when I will make a new covenant with the house of Israel and the house of Judah … I will put my law within them, and I will write it upon their hearts; and I will be their God, and they shall be my people" (Jer. 31:31–33).

The Threefold Architecture of Genesis and the Jerusalem Temple

The Jerusalem Temple, whether in the form of its forerunner—that is, the Tabernacle of the wilderness—or in the form of the Temple Solomon built, or of the one that succeeded it—that is, the so-called Temple of Herod in

---

Commentary on 1–2 Chronicles (Grand Rapids, MI: Baker Academic, 2012), 112ff. "The detail that the temple was built on Mount Moriah ties the temple to the most important sacrifice in Israel's sacred history, Abraham's binding of Isaac, the Akedeh, which occurred on an unspecified mount in the land of Moriah. In later Jewish tradition, this tradition is commonplace and is connected with another tradition—the ram sacrificed in the place of Isaac remained at Moriah for many generations."

21. Luke 22:20: "And likewise the cup after supper, saying, 'This cup which is poured out for you is *the new covenant in my blood.*'"

Jesus's day—was composed of three main parts: (1) the Outer Courts, (2) the Holy Place, and (3) the Holy of Holies.

Each of these three divisions of the Temple has correspondences in the text of Genesis 1–2. As one "gazes into the Garden" of Genesis, it is not unlike "staring at the Sanctuary" of the Jerusalem Temple later in Scripture. This is no accident, but an intentional patterning and pairing of the two temples, such that the one is meant to point forward (or backward, as the case may be) to the other. Such patterning by the biblical authors reflects a genuine intent to say something about the one temple by looking at the other, and vice versa. The most crucial point is that in both temples, Eden and Jerusalem, there is a threefold pattern *of lesser to greater realms of holiness*.[22] There is a core biblical principle: that God is holy, and anything/anyone that is nearest to him must be holy.

With this in mind, consider the three parts of the "temple of Creation." First, the Outer Courts of the Jerusalem Temple correspond to the lands beyond the Garden. These lands were, like everything else in God's Creation, "good," yet inasmuch as they are the furthest point from the Holy of Holies, they are wild and unruly and in need of someone to "fill" and "subdue" them (see figure 1). This rests upon a core biblical principle: God is holy, and anything/anyone that is nearest to him must be holy.

Hence the outer courts represent the outer regions of the earth beyond the Mountain/Garden, meant to be "tamed" by Adam, as Beale explains: "The land and seas to be subdued by Adam outside the Garden were roughly equivalent to the outer court of Israel's subsequent Temple. Thus, one may be able to perceive an increasing gradation in holiness from outside the garden proceeding inward: the region outside the Garden is related to God and is 'very good' (Gen. 1:31) in that it is God's creation (i.e., the outer court)."[23]

Second, the Holy Place of the Jerusalem Temple corresponds to the Garden itself, and everything within its boundaries. This is the place where the high priest Adam, along with his wife, experiences God's presence in the Tree of Life, in the very "center" of the Garden Temple. Here, Adam was privileged to be in this place at all; God created Adam and *placed* him in the Garden (Gen. 2:8). Like the priests of the Jerusalem Temple, being in the Holy Place was a great blessing and a great responsibility:

22. See Beale, "General Symbolism of the Temple," in *The Temple and the Church's Mission*, 32–36.

23. Beale, *The Temple and the Church's Mission*, 75.

Figure 1. A Map of Eden

HOLY OF HOLIES. Eden, the place where God Himself dwells.

HOLY PLACE. The Garden, the abode of Adam and Eve—at the base of Eden, with the sustaining Tree of Life in its center. Adam's call was to 'keep and work' the Garden, and with the Woman, to enjoy the presence of God.

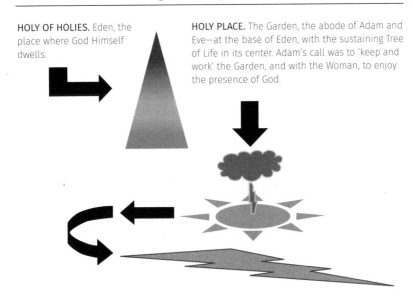

OUTER COURTS. The land and sea beyond the Garden; good, but chaotic and needing to be transformed. As they are "fruitful and multiply," God's life in them would fill the entire earth, thereby extending the Temple over the whole of creation.

Israel's Temple was the place where the priest experienced God's unique presence, and Eden was the place where Adam walked and talked with God. The same Hebrew verbal form (stem) *mithallēk* used for God's "walking back and forth" in the Garden,[24] also describes God's presence in the Tabernacle.[25]

Third and finally, the Most Holy Place of the Jerusalem Temple corresponds to Mt. Eden, the place where God dwells or, more precisely, atop which God dwells. As Beale explains, the Most Holy Place, or Holy of Holies, was unique among all the spaces within the space of the Temple. "Israel would never have dared to say simply: *God lives there*. Israel knew that God is infinitely great, that he surpasses and embraces the whole world."[26]

24. See Gen. 3:8.

25. Beale, *The Temple and the Church's Mission*, 66. See Lev. 26:12: "And I will *walk among you*, and will be your God, and you shall be my people."

26. Joseph Ratzinger, *Jesus of Nazareth, Part Two. Holy Week: From the Entrance into Jerusalem to the Resurrection* (San Francisco: Ignatius Press, 2011), 91.

It is to the centerpiece of these three spaces, to the Holy Place of the Garden itself, that the reader's attention is drawn. The concern here is not merely with *what Eden is,* for that has been made clear. Rather, at stake is *what happens to the Holy Place of Eden, to the violation of this holy place in a most cataclysmic way.* It was in the Holy Place of the Garden that God "placed the man" (Gen. 2:8), and it is here that the Man and the Woman dwelt and served God in "original holiness." Though created by God, and therefore good, "the world beyond" was wild, untamed, in need of being subdued. As such, it was the mission field of Adam along with his wife Eve.[27] In fulfilling God's command to "*be fruitful and multiply and fill the earth,*"[28] their priestly presence was meant to radiate outward, extending God's temple over the farthest regions of the earth.

Yet, as Genesis 3 opens, it should strike the reader that the Serpent appears suddenly—like a bolt from out of the blue. How did he get in? Why is he here, and what does he want to accomplish? Make no mistake: this wild creature from "beyond the Garden" does not belong. Nothing is said of Adam's naming him, welcoming him, or even *knowing* that he is now here. He is a threat from beyond, from the wilds beyond the Garden Temple. This is a discussion for chapter 4.

Concluding Remarks

As this chapter draws to a close, a core insight from the opening of the book can be reiterated: that the Creation narratives of Genesis depict Eden as the mountain sanctuary of God. Childish depictions of the Garden of Eden must be laid aside in light of the intricate beauty and complexity cast by the biblical author—of not merely a "paradise," but a Holy Place of a Holy Temple, under the watchful care of the Creator. This is confirmed by numerous pieces of biblical data. This cosmological Temple motif in Genesis 1–2 sets the stage not only for the remainder of Genesis but also for the story of God's covenantal love poured out to his people. This "mountain temple" motif is recapitulated throughout the Old Testament, particularly in the story

---

27. The reader should be aware that Eve is not being neglected here. In the biblical narrative, he—not he and Eve—is alone depicted as God's High Priest of Eden. For this reason, in subsequent discussions of temple theology, it is Adam's "temple-building" role that is decisive and of particular interest to the topic.

28. Gen. 1:28.

of God's expanding covenantal relationship with his people, from Noah to Abraham and Moses, and culminating with David. This temple theology of the Old Testament sets the stage for the climactic moment in the larger biblical story, in the crucifixion of God's own Son, Jesus, on Mt. Calvary.

Grounded in this key insight, the reader is well positioned to consider other related aspects of temple theology in the opening chapters of Genesis. Specifically, chapter 3 will examine several distinctive liturgical patterns rooted in the text, and these patterns will deepen one's understanding of the elaborate temple theology in Genesis.

THE SACRED SPACE
OF THE GARDEN SANCTUARY

The Temple of Creation (II/III)

One thing have I asked of the Lord, that will I seek after; that
I may dwell in *the house of the Lord* all the days of my life, to
behold the beauty of the Lord and to inquire in his temple.

Psalm 78:69

Deliverance from the Waters of Chaos

As was explained, the terrain of the Garden of Eden was sacred, and the
waters that flowed down from Mt. Eden watered the Garden to fructify the
land and seas beyond.[1] In numerous texts from the ancient Near East, mountains were held as sacred and functioned as proto-temples. These mountains
were typically seen as situated above the primordial waters of Creation and
chaos, that is, the outer courts. Water had a dual power: life/creation and
death/destruction.

On the one hand, the sacred mountain of God was the source of this
"living water." This water, flowing down "from above," from the mountain of
God, symbolized the living God himself, who gives and sustains life. Practi-

---

1. Gen. 2:10–14: "A river flowed out of Eden to water the garden, and there it divided and became four rivers." See also Gen. 1:2, "The earth was without form and void, and darkness was upon
the face of the deep; and the Spirit of God was moving over the face of the waters"; Psa. 24:1–3, "The
earth is the Lord's and the fullness thereof … for he has founded it upon the seas, and established
it upon the rivers"; and Psa. 18:16, "He reached from on high, he took me, he drew me out of many
waters."

cally speaking, this living water nourished not only the Garden, but also all of Creation. On the other hand was the "water below," the watery chaos from which God "created." Theologically, of course, God indeed created all that is and has ever been, *ex nihilo*. Figuratively speaking, however, the earth "rose up" above these primordial waters, as God made "an expanse in the midst of the waters above and the waters below" (Gen. 1:6). In this way, Genesis conveys the idea that God created the earth from "between the waters." It is here on the solid ground, far from natural (and supernatural) danger, that God created the Garden sanctuary and placed the man therein rising above the Garden was the mountain of God. It was the highest and farthest place from the chaotic waters below.

Consider how this imagery functions in the narrative of Genesis 1. The text indicates that at the first moments of time in Creation, the earth was "formless and void." The Spirit of God hovers, but over what? Over the "face" (*pane*) of the deep. God creates the world *ex nihilo*, out of nothing. As the days of Creation unfold, there is a movement from "forming" what is brought into being and "filling" the Creation, until it is brought to completion by God.

In this poetic description of the Creation, *something* is brought out of *nothing*; at the start of it all, the earth is something yet to be formed. Then, suddenly, light and darkness. Day and night. Then, following this, in verses 6–9, water again becomes the central motif. Dry land seems to "rise up" out of the waters beneath it. Then follows the "filling" of the earth with vegetation, plants, and trees—all fructified by the living waters. In like fashion the text describes the "seas," filled with all sorts of living things. Every sort of bird flies through the air and every manner of living creature comes into being and takes its place in the order of God's Creation. Finally and only after the climax of this orderly symphony of Creation, of life rising up from the waters, God declares, "*Let us create man in our image*" (v. 26).

All of this biblical imagery is intriguing: a mountain rises up out of the chaotic waters below. It is not just any earthly peak; it is Mt. Eden, the center and highest place on earth. It becomes the peak from which these "living waters" flow, watering the Garden and the world beyond it.[2] Here in Genesis is a key biblical pattern to which the reader should be attentive: just as the

---

2. Jon Levenson, *Sinai and Zion: An Entry into the Jewish Bible* (Minneapolis: Winston Press, 1985), 28–29.

rivers flow down and out of Eden,[3] so too do "living waters" flow out from the Temple of Solomon to the Gihon spring far below. And water flows not only from Solomon's Temple, but also from the eschatological Temple envisioned by the Book of Ezekiel[4] as well as the heavenly temple of the Book of Revelation).[5]

In Jesus's day, the Second Temple was constructed (as was the First Temple) above the Gihon Spring, which provided fresh water necessary to wash away vast amounts of blood from the Temple sacrifices. One can imagine that during feast days, such as Passover, the pilgrims and inhabitants of Jerusalem would have seen a river of blood and water flowing from the Temple.[6] This leads to the Gospel of John, in which Jesus at the Feast of the Tabernacles says, "He who believes in me, as the Scripture has said, *'Out of his heart shall flow rivers of living water.'"*[7] Jesus's statement was a partial fulfillment of Zechariah's vision of the coming Messiah. According to the prophet's vision, on the great "day of the Lord," living waters would flow from the Temple and saturate all of Jerusalem, during the Feast of Tabernacles.[8]

Commenting on the importance of ancient sanctuaries being founded on springs, one scholar writes that "the reason such springs exist in Temples is that *they are perceived as the primeval waters of creation*, Nun in Egypt, Abzu in Mesopotamia. The Temple is thus founded on and stands in contact with primeval waters."[9] In a manner consistent with this ancient motif, God created the heavens and earth *ex nihilo*, out of the watery chaos, placing Adam upon the Edenic mountain to enjoy his Divine Presence.

So, in Sacred Scripture, the mountain of Eden is God's *Sanctum sanctorum*, upon which the Divine Presence abides. Figuratively, one can say that the mountain of God represents Heaven—the Holy of Holies. Below the

---

3. Gen. 2:10–14.   4. Ezek. 47:1–12.

5. Rev. 21:1–2.

6. John 19:34: "But one of the soldiers pierced his side with a spear, and at once there came out blood and water."

7. John 7:38 (see also John 4:10).

8. "Zechariah 14:1–21 constitutes the climactic unit of the entire book with the prophet's portrayal of Yhwh's recognition as universal sovereign by the nations at Zion on the day of Yhwh, identified here as the festival of Sukkoth." Marvin A. Sweeney, *The Twelve Prophets & 2*, vol. 1, *Berit Olam Studies in Hebrew Narrative and Poetry*, ed. David W. Cotter, Jerome T. Walsh, and Chris Franke (Collegeville, MN: Liturgical Press, 2000), 697.

9. J. M. Lundquist, *What Is a Temple? A Preliminary Typology* (Winona Lake: Eisenbrauns), 208 (emphasis added).

Garden (Holy Place) and the world beyond (Outer Courts) are the depths of the sea; in Hebrew, *Sheol*. This threefold cosmology is likewise seen in a number of ancient Near Eastern creation texts, as well as in various texts from the Hebrew bible. The Psalms often celebrate God's omnipresence and "the deliverance of the righteous" in just this fashion:

> If I *ascend to heaven*, thou art there!
> If I make my bed in *Sheol*, thou art there!
> If I take the wings of the morning
> and dwell in the uttermost parts of the sea,
> even there thy hand shall lead me,
> and thy right hand shall hold me.[10]

Similarly, in the Book of Amos, the ancient prophet draws upon this imagery. Yet, for Amos, it is not the usual pattern of God's deliverance that is depicted but rather the reverse; a judgment scene of the unrighteous, who cannot hide from God anywhere in Creation: "Though they dig into Sheol, from there shall my hand take them; though they climb up to heaven, from there I will bring them down. Though they hide themselves on the top of Carmel, from there I will search out and take them; and though they hide from my sight at the bottom of the sea, there I will command the serpent, and it shall bite them" (Amos 9:2–3).

In other words, deep beneath Eden's threefold structure is *Sheol*, the chaotic, untamed waters. Still, God's control over Creation (and therefore over even these chaotic waters) includes the power to rescue souls from it, as the following texts from the Psalms indicate:[11]

In my distress I called upon the Lord; to my God I cried for help. *From his Temple he heard my voice*, and my cry to him reached his ears. He reached from on high, he took me, *he drew me out of many waters* (Psa. 18:5–6, 8:16).

When the waters saw thee, O God, when the waters saw thee, *they were afraid*, yea, the deep trembled (Psa. 77:16).

Stretch forth thy hand from on high, *rescue me and deliver me from the many waters,* from the hand of aliens (Psa. 144:7)

---

10. Psa. 139:8–10.
11. See Psa. 18, 66, 69, 88, 122, 144; 2 Sam 22, etc.

Striding high above all of these psalmic images of "rescue from the waters below" is of course the archetypal figure of Noah himself. Noah emerges from a humanity darkened by sin, as the one who was "remembered by God" (Gen. 8:1). Because of Noah's righteousness, he and his family are saved through the waters of the Flood (see 1 Pet. 3:21). This "Noahic" pattern is recapitulated numerous times over in the Psalms: the psalmist is beset by raging waters and at the same time accursed by his enemies; he protests his innocence/righteousness, beseeching God for deliverance. Finally, the psalmist is drawn out of this calamity to safety. And just as Noah built an altar to praise God for his redemption (see Gen. 8:20), so too for the psalmist; a liturgical act of worship follows, in which God is praised for his deliverance from harm.[12]

Gate Liturgies: Who May Enter the Sacred Mountain Temple

In a number of ancient Near Eastern texts beyond the Bible is a third motif closely associated with the previous two (that is, mountain temples, deliverance through the waters). The concept is known by scholars as "Gate Liturgies," which are depicted as taking place at the holies places on earth, high atop sacred mountain temples. The imagery is of a boundary—and a holy gate that separates a holy interior space from the profane outer regions. The space of interior holiness is highly revered and functions as a "Holy of Holies" of these mountain sanctuaries. The Holy Place is cordoned off by such a gate, protecting the sacredness of the god in his dwelling place from the corruption and exterior chaos beyond it. Here, the gatekeeper is all important; his role is to ensure that only the righteous freely enter, while the unrighteous are kept outside. In the event one should transgress the threshold, that person is "cast out," banished from the sanctuary altogether.

Commenting on these ancient pagan texts, one scholar writes, "There are reasons why Temple doors were considered important. They represent the entrance to the holy place, and the 'gate' was often used in pictures as a symbol of the Temple itself ... the door was the symbol for a central point ... *the meeting place between god and man*."[13] Protecting the Divine abode from

---

12. See L. Michael Morales, *The Tabernacle Pre-Figured: Cosmic Mountain Ideology in Genesis and Exodus* (Leuven: Peeters, 2012), 20–32, for more.

13. Ibid., 35.

profanation was the function of temple guardians in the ancient Near East (guards, lions, angels, cherubim, etc.)

For example, an ancient Sumerian text, known as the *Gudea Cylinder*, has an inscription over the door of the gate: "*To admit the righteous, to keep away the wrong doer.*" A similar motif is seen in Psalm 24: "Who shall ascend the hill of the Lord? And *who shall stand in his holy place*? He who has clean hands and a pure heart, who does not lift up his soul to what is false, and does not swear deceitfully" (vv. 4–6).[14]

A clarification is necessary as it pertains to the apparent literary parallels in such ancient pagan texts on the one hand and the biblical text on the other. Such parallels from pagan texts are helpful when taken for what they are, but they cease to be so when they are mistaken as the inspiration from which Genesis derived its theological content. Such is not the case—not at all. The human authors of Genesis, the Psalter, and other biblical books would have never dreamed of infusing their narratives with polytheistic pagan ideals. Biblical critics of the nineteenth and twentieth centuries, who argued for such wholesale importing of pagan myths into the biblical worldview, plainly misunderstood the core tenant within ancient Judaism—*absolute monotheism*. Make no mistake—the parallels are real. Yet the biblical authors would *never*, as faithful monotheists loyal to Yahweh, dare to defy him by, in a manner of speaking, mixing "orthodoxy with heresy." Rather, one can make sense of such echoes between the pagan and biblical worlds as follows.

In order to best communicate the truths of the Creation the author of Genesis makes subtle reference to certain symbols and images from the broader literary traditions within the ancient world. But—and this is the decisive point—in using certain images, phrases and the like, the biblical author is not paying homage to the pagan writers nor to the beliefs contained in their texts. Rather, there is a kind of "tweaking" of the pagan myths, critiquing them while simultaneously setting the record straight about the Creation of the world.

Such tweaks are in present in Genesis for all to see—provided one is conversant of how the ancient pagan stories go. For example, Genesis insists that it was not the many gods who created the world out of violence, from some

14. See R. E. Averbeck, "The Cylinders of Gudea," in *The Context of Scripture*, vol. 2, *Monumental Inscriptions from the Biblical World*, ed. W. W. Hallo and K. L. Younger (Leiden: Brill, 2000), 417–33.

preexistent matter. Rather, it was the one, true, invisible God, Yahweh, who alone created the world out of love and did so *ex nihilo*. Numerous examples could be added to the one above. The author of Genesis was shrewd and prudently distinguished the biblical understanding of God's glorious Creation from pagan conceptions. Nothing is introduced to confuse the reader; to the contrary, the hints of other mythologies are for the benefit and edification of the Jewish believer. And when the text of Genesis proclaims its own story, it does so, at least in part, *as a kind of reversal,* from darkness to light, from falsehood to truth, from myth to reality, or in Jean Daniélou's phrase concerning the relationship of the Old to the New, *"from shadows to reality."*

Twentieth-century English literary giants such as Owen Barfield, C. S. Lewis, and J. R. R. Tolkien contribute much to Daniélou's understanding of "myth" as it pertains to the proper interpretation of Genesis. For Tolkien, Genesis was just such a turn, a deliberate move by the author, a besting of the pagan myths, and a setting right of the *true telling* of Creation by the one living God. On various occasions, C. S. Lewis, Tolkien's friend and colleague at Oxford, spoke of Christ as the "true myth" of history. Tolkien, Lewis, and their fellow Inklings were, however, careful to distinguish true myth, such as in Genesis, the Gospels, and in their own writings, from pagan corollaries: "For Tolkien ... even pagan myths attempted to express God's greater truths. True myth has the power to revive us, to serve as an anamnesis, or way of bringing to conscious experience ancient experiences with transcendence. But, Tolkien admitted, myth could be dangerous, or 'perilous,' as he usually stated it, if it remained pagan. Therefore, Tolkien thought, *one must sanctify it.*"[15]

---

15. Bradley Birzer, *J. R. R. Tolkien's Sanctifying Myth: Understanding Middle-Earth* (Wilmington, DE: Intercollegiate Studies Institute, 2003), 263 (emphasis added). Birzer continues: "St. Paul attempted to convert the Athenians with reference to their statue of the 'Unknown God'; St. Augustine re-read the works of Plato and Cicero in a Christian light in his City of God; St. Aquinas uncovered the synchronies between Aristotelian and Christian thought; and on our own continent, we see that Catholic monks built a monastery on top of the highest mound-temple in Cahokia, Illinois, former site of the priest-king of a vast Native American empire. Indeed, churches throughout Europe and North America sit on formerly sacred pagan sites. In building churches in such places Christians sought, in essence, to baptize the corrupt ground, just as Sts. Augustine and Aquinas baptized pagan ideas." On "myth becoming reality," see also J. R. R Tolkien, "On Fairy-Stories," in *The Monsters and the Critics and Other Essays*, ed. Christopher Tolkien (Boston: Houghton Mifflin, 1983), 109–61; Verlyn Flieger, *Splintered Light: Logos and Language in Tolkien's World*, 2nd rev. ed. (Kent, OH: Kent State University Press), 2012.

In his masterful treatise on cosmology, Louis Bouyer describes how "myth," when properly understood, is not only an acceptable way of interpreting the Creation narratives Genesis, but also, from a wholly Catholic standpoint, an extremely fruitful one. Here he defines myth as a synthetic view of *reality*, "whose inner and native unity reemerges in the explicit discovery of [reality's] multiplicity."[16] A view of *reality*—not of fiction, fable, or magic. Bouyer explains that myth is a kind of synthetic elaboration of man's experience of the world, "reestablished in unity through the integration of successive and discrete views of reality into one intuitive and all-inclusive vision, so that the world may be formally acknowledged in its primordial unity, rather than just being mysteriously sensed."[17] Bouyer is quick to add a necessary caution— that mythopoetic knowledge must be distinguished from pagan notions of magic. In the ancient world, he explains, there was a natural human tendency for the composer of a cosmological text "to want to become, or already think that he is, the only person that counts, and to draw to himself everything in the world ... This is the temptation of *magic*, which affects all cultures in the process of becoming a civilization ... Myth, which proclaims on the contrary that *ritual*, even when practiced by man, *remains fundamentally and properly a divine activity*, contradicts this magical tendency."[18]

Here, Bouyer is contrasting the approach of the polytheistic, pagan composer of Babylonian and Egyptian cosmologies and creations myths with the Semitic composers of ancient biblical texts, for whom the notion of Creation being a byproduct of the gods or of magic was not part of their worldview whatsoever: "The most original feature in the text of Genesis ... is clearly the idea that God creates all beings *by his Word alone*. First, here is the most solemn affirmation that *the Divine Word, the source of Israel's entire history, including its existence as God's people, is the origin of all existence.* Conversely, every created being is but the expression and materialization of the omnipotent

---

16. L. Bouyer, *Cosmos: The World and the Glory of God* (Petersham: St. Bede's, 1988), 14.

17. Ibid., 14. "Mythopoetic thinking approaches cosmic reality first through a *sure instinct* that there exists a spontaneous harmony between our spirit and that reality ... which allows our spirit to grasp reality ... by means of a *deep sympathy* with its inner structure and fundamental evolution" (23, emphases added).

18. Ibid., 19. "Even in the waking state, a resurgent *mythopoetic* consciousness bursts forth *in the daydreams of poetry*, the only form of consciousness through which we continue *to hold onto the deepest realities* ... These concern our innermost being, the most secret but most authentic reality of this world, and we are perhaps ourselves only when we rediscover this reality in its proper dimension" (23, emphases added).

benevolence of the God who showed himself to Abraham and his children. This being so, the whole world exists and has a definite identity, at least in its principle, *only because God thinks and wants it.* This world is the expression of the conjoined thought and will of the Most High, the Only One."[19]

Armed with these salient insights from Bouyer, the discussion turns back to the inklings. Lewis and especially Tolkien were deeply invested in the classical mythologies of ancient Greece and Rome and in many more from ancient and medieval cultures. Tolkien was a genius with regard to philology and understood that, in myth, "language" and "symbol" are shaped by culture and its governing stories and in turn are at the service of a culture's myths. Tolkien invented his "legendarium" of Middle Earth—not only *The Hobbit* and *The Lord of the Rings* but also and especially his life's work, the lesser known *Silmarillion,* which is a Creation myth that in some subtle ways is in dialogue with Genesis 1–3. And he did so primarily to give his languages (he invented about a dozen "elven" languages) a home to inhabit.

Tolkien's innate and acquired gifts in these areas (Lewis's, too) allowed him to "see" more than many others in myth, be it *Beowulf,* Icelandic sagas, or the inspired texts of Genesis. His keen understanding of the purpose, nature, and depth of myth offer much to the interpreter of Genesis. Such a recovery of true myth, of "myth become reality," in Lewis's words, is called for today in the proper exegesis of Genesis 1–3.

Here is the key insight from these English masters: it is *only* when myth "becomes reality," *only* when it is truly sanctified and *only* when it is purged of falsehood and imbued with (Divine) truth can it lead, guide, purify, and save. It is in this sense, building upon the theological insights from Daniélou—as well as the literary contributions of Tolkien and Lewis (and other Inklings)—that a Catholic may interpret the sacred and inspired Creation accounts in Genesis in a mythic way. And do so without a false note, without conceding an inch to the secular and humanistic way of interpreting the text as a kind of "fiction," nor to the other extreme, falling into the quagmire that biblical creationists and literalists do, that is, of turning Genesis into a kind of science textbook, in which the world is a scant six thousand years old.

Undergirded with these clear distinctions (and they must be kept clear), a Catholic may indeed interpret Genesis in what Tolkien referred to as a "eucastrophe": a tragedy with an unexpected and "happy turn" at the end. One

19. Ibid., 42 (emphases added).

might say that Tolkien's grasp of myth in a positive way is enhanced, if not reliant upon, his Catholic worldview.

In sum, reading the text in a "mythopoetic" way, as advocated by Bouyer as well as Tolkien and Lewis, is thus something that may be done with no risk to the integrity of the biblical narrative, nor to Catholic biblical principles, chief among them biblical inspiration.

Put simply, not only may a Catholic interpret Genesis along such mythopoetic lines, but doing so may also provide built-in advantages over those who do not do so (particularly the biblical literalist). As Daniélou adds,

In the cosmic Temple, man is not living primarily in his own house, but in *the house of God*. This is why he knows that he should revere those creatures who do not belong to him, that he can lay hands on nothing without permission. *All is holy; the trees are heavy with sacramental mysteries.* Primitive sacrifice is simply the recognition of the sovereign realm of God. He takes the first-fruits and leaves the rest to man. But at the same time, man is part of creation and has his role to play in it. God has in some way *left creation unfinished* and man's mission is *to bring it to fulfillment*. Through his work he exploits unknown material resources and thus work is sacred, being cooperation in the task of creation. Through knowledge and art he removes it from its ephemeral condition to enable it to subsist spiritually.[20]

Returning to the text of Genesis, armed with these mythopoetic insights, the following may be seen. In Genesis 2, Adam is placed in the Garden by God (v. 8). There, he enjoys the Divine Presence. After instructing Adam to "protect and keep" the temple (Gen. 2:15), God gives him a specific command in verse 16. As Beale has shown, "the notion of divine commanding (*sawâ*) or giving of 'commandments' (*miswôt*) often follows the word guard/ keep (*shamār*) elsewhere."[21]

Yet once Adam (and Eve with him) transgresses God's commands, and he is banished from Eden and its Tree of Life. Adam is, in the imagery of the pa-

---

20. Jean Cardinal Daniélou, "The Sign of the Temple: A Mediation," *Letter & Spirit* 4 (2008): 256–57.

21. G. K. Beale, *The Temple and the Church's Mission: A Biblical Theology of the Dwelling Place of God* (Downers Grove, IL: InterVarsity Press, 2004), 68–69. "In I Kings 9:6 when both 'serving' and 'keeping' occur together, the idea of commandments is to be kept is in view … [This passage] is addressed to Solomon and his sons immediately after he had 'finished building the house of the Lord' (1 Ki. 9:1): if they do not keep My commandments … and [instead] serve other gods … I will cut off Israel from the land … and the [Temple] … I will cast them out of my sight … Accordingly, Adam's disobedience, as Israel's, results in his being cut off from the sacred land of the Garden."

gan myths, effectively "cast out" beyond the holy gate and "cut off" from the Divine Presence: "Therefore the Lord God sent him forth *from the garden of Eden*, to till the ground from which he was taken. *He drove out the man*; and at the east of the garden of Eden *he placed the cherubim, and a flaming sword which turned every way, to guard the way to the Tree of Life*" (Gen. 3:23–24).

Adam's banishment is further ironic, given that *it was Adam who was to protect Eden as its priestly gatekeeper!* This banishing of the priestly figure of Adam in Genesis has profound interpretative implications for the entire biblical narrative that follows, and particularly for Israel's yet-to-be Temple. As one theologian explains, "priestly obligations in Israel's later Temple included the duty of guarding unclean things from entering, especially in view of the unclean creature lurking on the perimeter of the Garden and who then enters."[22] Not only this, but also this depiction of Adam as Temple priest and guardian of God's sanctuary establishes a pattern adhered to in many subsequent biblical texts: "Adam's *priestly role* of 'guarding' (*shamār*) the Garden sanctuary may also be reflected in the later role of Israel's priests who were called 'guards' (1 Chron. 9:23) and repeatedly were referred to as *temple 'gatekeepers'*[23] who 'kept watch' (*shamār*) at the gates (Neh. 11:19) so that *'no one should enter who is in anyway unclean'* (2 Chron. 23:19). Consequently, *the priestly role* in both the Garden and the later Temple was to [maintain] order and keeping out uncleanness."[24]

As the Old Testament narrative unfolds, this gate-keeping pattern reemerges time and again. It is yet another way in which the fiber optics of temple theology weaves its way through the biblical drama. It is the person who pursues righteous who is "admitted" and enters the Temple and participates in its liturgies. Three examples of this pattern will suffice, one from the Law, the next from the Prophets, and the third from the Writings. The first such example is found in the Book of Exodus, near the end of the Song of Moses: "*Thou wilt bring them in,* and plant them on thy own mountain, the place, O Lord, which thou hast made for thy abode, the sanctuary, Lord, which thy hands have established" (Exod. 15:17). A second example of this

---

22. Ibid., 69 (emphases added).

23. E.g., 1 Chron. 9:17–18, "The gatekeepers were: Shallum, Akkub, Talmon, Ahiman ... These were the gatekeepers of the camp of the Levites"; 1 Chron. 9:24, "*The gatekeepers were on the four sides, east, west, north and south ...* for the four chief gatekeepers, who were Levites, were in charge of the chambers and the treasures of the house of God."

24. Beale, *The Temple and the Church's Mission*, 69 (emphases added).

sort is seen in the prophet Isaiah: "*Open the gates* that the righteous nation which keeps faith *may enter in*" (Isa. 26:2). Finally, a third example is drawn from Psalm 118: "*Open to me the gates of righteousness* that I may *enter through them* and give thanks to the Lord. This is the gate of the Lord; the righteous shall enter through it" (vv. 19–20).

This recurrent pattern effects how one reads and makes sense of the early chapters of Genesis as well as for the remainder of the book. For instance, when Genesis 11 is read in light of a temple framework, the Tower of Babel episode represents a flagrant attempt to fashion a human replica of Eden and a prefigurement of the sin of idolatry (Golden Calf, high places, etc.) In this reading, the "mountain of Babel" becomes a mirror image in reverse, a negative reflection of the original pattern established by God on the "mountain of Eden."

The same holds true far beyond the Book of Genesis. More precisely, it is asserted here that as one moves beyond the world of Genesis, this temple pattern resurfaces often. If one carefully studies the structure of the Temple in books like Leviticus and 1 Kings, it becomes clear that the various courts of the Temple represent one's nearness to God. One moves from the furthest point in the Temple, the Court of the Gentiles (the world) to the Court of Women (Israel) to the Holy Place (Israel's priests) until one finally reaches the Holy of Holies and its high priest, who was (at least in theory) the "holiest" in all of Israel. Only he and he alone dare to traverse the threshold of the Holy of Holies on the Day of Atonement, to beg God to pardon his sins and those of all of Israel.

Likewise, in the Book of Exodus, God through Moses delivers the Israelites from death as they pass through the waters of the Red Sea and are taken up to the mountain of Sinai. Later, and again, the Israelites' entry into the Promised Land can and should be viewed as a recapitulation of "passing through the waters"; as now, it is not the inhabitants that "pass through the waters, up to the mountain," but the Israelites who pass through the waters of the Jordan and come to the mountain of God:

"*But when you go over the Jordan [through the waters]* and live in the land which the Lord your God gives you to inherit [to the holy mountain], and when he gives you *rest* from all your enemies round about, so that you live in safety, then to the place which the Lord your God will choose, to make His name dwell there, thither you shall bring all that I command you: your burnt offerings and your sacrifices, your tithes and the offering that you present, and all your votive offerings which you vow to the Lord" (Deut. 12:10–11). On a spiritual level, St. Paul may be thinking along similar lines in discussing Baptism (see Rom. 6:1ff.).

To sum up: reading Genesis in a "mythopoetic" way and interpreting the biblical text as "myth become reality" are sensible in light of corresponding data from pagan texts. Not only so; such an approach, when properly deployed, is fully consistent with Catholic biblical principles. Along such lines, temple cults of the ancient Near East frequently conceived of sacred mountains as sanctuaries in which the divine presence of the gods was experienced. There is ample evidence in Genesis 1 that such a motif is in play. In Genesis, Eden is the first and foremost of many mountain temples that are depicted in such a cosmological way (e.g., Mt. Sinai, Mt. Zion). Moreover, Adam is presented as the high priest of the Garden Temple and the prototype for the subsequent priesthood of the Israel's later Tabernacle and Temple.

The ancient notion of Gate Liturgies is apparent under Genesis 3, and its pattern reveals itself in the framework of Genesis, as Adam, the one called to keep the unholy out of the Holy Place, himself becomes the one who is unholy and is subsequently "cut off" from it. This liturgical pattern, of the holy ones who can enter the Holy Place and the unholy ones as the ones who are cast out of the Holy Place, is an important biblical motif that is established in Genesis and repeated often throughout the Old and New Testaments.

Recapitulating the Temple of Eden

Convincingly, Beale shows that Israel's Tabernacle and Temple were a recapitulation of the first sanctuary of Genesis, that is, the Edenic Temple.[25] Some of the more important data in Beale's work include the following. First, Eden is the unique dwelling place of God. God's "walking back and forth" in the Garden utilizes the Hebrew verb *mithallek*, the same term used elsewhere to describe God's presence in the Temple.[26]

Second, Eden represents the Holy Place of the first high priest. After all, what is a temple without a priest? Genesis 2:15 states that God placed Adam in Eden to "till" (*'abad*) and "keep" (*shamar*) it. When *'abad* and *shamar* occur together in the Old Testament, they always refer to keeping/guarding

---

25. Ibid., 66–80.
26. Cf. Gen. 3:8 with Lev. 26:12; and Deut. 23:14–15 with 2 Sam. 7:6–7.

and serving God's word and priestly duties in the Tabernacle: "They shall *keep* (*shamar*) guard over him and over the whole congregation before the tent of meeting, as they minister at the Tabernacle. They shall guard all the furnishings of the tent of meeting, and keep guard over the people of Israel as they minister (*'abad*) at the Tabernacle" (Num. 3:7–8[27]).[28]

In fact, these two Hebrew terms *'abad* and *shamar* only occur together again in the Pentateuch in the descriptions in Numbers for the Levites' activities in the Tabernacle.[29] Adam fails the test as the gatekeeper of the Garden sanctuary, allowing unrighteousness to enter. And so he and the woman are expelled. Similarly, the Ark of the Covenant is guarded by two cherubim, stationed on either side and placed in the Holy of Holies.[30]

Eden was the place of the Tree of Knowledge of Good and Evil; likewise, the Holy of Holies was the place in which the Ark was kept, and within it the Torah, which was wisdom and light for all. Similarly, the menorah of the Temple was reminiscent of the Tree of Life—a small, flowering tree with seven protruding branches.[31]

Solomon's Temple is described with botanical and arboreal imagery, rendering it with an Eden-like appearance. Throughout the Temple, there were wood-carved gourds and flowers,[32] pomegranates,[33] and a bronze sea.[34] Likewise, as in Eden, there were precious stones, numerous items fashioned of gold,[35] as well as golden floors, walls and ceilings of the Temple. The high priest's garments were constructed of gold and onyx.[36]

Concluding Remarks

These Edenic/temple patterns not only provide the reader with an interpretative key for reading the Old Testament, but also help to make fuller sense of the life and ministry of Jesus Christ in the New Testament. As the temple thread "weaves" its way forward, Beale's assessment of things provides

27. English Standard Version (ESV).

28. Other examples: Num. 8:25–26, 18:5–6; 1 Chron. 23:32; Ezek. 44:14.

29. *Midrash Rabbah Genesis* interprets Adam's role in Gen. 2:15 as offering the kinds of "sacrifices" later required by Mosaic Law. See also *Epistle of Barnabas* 4:11, 6, for similar connotations.

30. See Exod. 25:18–22.   31. Exod. 25:31–36.

32. See 1 Ki. 6:29.   33. See 1 Ki. 7:20.

34. See 1 Ki. 7:24–26.   35. See 1 Ki. 6:20–22.

36. See Exod. 25:7, 28:6–27; 1 Chron. 29:2.

a fitting conclusion to the present discussion: "The Old Testament tabernacles and temples were symbolically designed to point [back] to the cosmic
reality that *God's tabernacling presence,* formerly limited to the holy of holies
formerly limited to the holy of holies, was to be extended through the whole
earth" (see Rev. 21).[37]

Chapter 3 will continue with more discussion of the Creation narrative.
Primary focus will be placed upon a fascinating "numerical" pattern that will
add to the reader's understanding of temple theology in the Book of Genesis.

37. Beale, *The Temple and the Church's* Mission, 74–75: "It may even be discernible that there
was a sanctuary and a holy place in Eden corresponding roughly to that in Israel's later temple. The
Garden should be viewed as not itself the source of water but adjoining Eden because Gen 2:10 says,
'a river flowed out of Eden to water the Garden.' Therefore, in the same manner that ancient palaces
were adjoined by gardens, Eden is the sources of the waters and [is the palatial] residence of God, and
the Garden adjoins God's residence. Similarly, Ezek. 47:1 says that water would flow out from under
the Holy of Holies in the future eschatological Temple and would water the earth around. Similarly,
in the end-time Temple of Revelation 22:1–2, there is portrayed a river of the water of life, coming
from the throne of God and of the Lamb, and flowing into a garden-like grove, which has been modeled on the first paradise in Genesis 2, as has been much of Ezekiel's portrayal. If Ezekiel and Revelation are developments of the first garden-temple, then Eden, the area where the source of water is
located, may be comparable to the inner sanctuary of Israel's later Temple and the adjoining Garden
to the holy place. Eden and its adjoining Garden formed two distinct regions. This is compatible
with [the] identification of the lampstand in the holy place of the Temple with the tree of life located
in the fertile plot outside the inner place of God's presence. Additionally, the Bread of the Presence,
also in the *Holy Place,* which provided food for the priests, would appear to reflect the food produced
in the Garden for Adam's sustenance ... the land and seas to be subdued by Adam outside the Garden
were roughly equivalent to the Outer Court of Israel's subsequent Temple. Thus, one may be able to
perceive an increasing gradation in holiness from outside the Garden proceeding inward: the region
outside the Garden is related to God and is very good (Gen. 1:31) in that it is God's Creation (= the
outer court); the Garden itself is a sacred space separate from the outer world (= the Holy Place),
where God's priestly servant worships God by obeying him, by cultivating and guarding; Eden is
where God dwells (= the Holy of Holies) as the source of both physical and spiritual life (symbolized
by the waters)."

"SEVEN" AND THE TEMPLE
IN THE MYSTERY OF CREATION

The Temple of Creation (III/III)

He built his sanctuary like the high heavens,
like the earth, which he has founded forever.

Psalm 78:69

What's in a Number? Numerology in Ancient Judaism

Today, for a variety of reasons, many students of the Bible are rightly suspicious of numerology (i.e., the use of numbers or numerical interpretations) in regard to the Old Testament (OT). This is, at least in part, "because of its unwise use by groups of Christians who see theological symbolism in every number in the OT."[1] Despite the fact that the (mis)use of numerology has fallen on hard times more recently,[2] the reader should understand that, for ancient writers, the use of numbers in concealing/unveiling mysteries was a common and legitimate practice. In his monumental commentary on the Book of Acts, Craig Keener discusses numerology in Acts 6, in regard to the selection of "seven" elders:

1. Walter A. Elwell and Philip Wesley Comfort, *Tyndale Bible Dictionary*, Tyndale Reference Library (Wheaton, IL: Tyndale House, 2001), 956. Elwell and Comfort provide a concise summary of the use of numeric symbolism in the Old Testament, including the prominent ones such as "three," "four," "six," "seven," "ten," and "twelve." See also M. J. J. Menken, *Numerical Literary Techniques in John: The Fourth Evangelist's Use of Numbers of Words and Syllables*, Novum Testamentum Supplement 55 (Leiden: Brill, 1985).

2. One only need mention the recent glut of books such as M. Drosnin, *The Bible Code* (New

It is not surprising that the early church, which already had a group of "the Twelve," would choose another number widely invested with significance. *Jewish people and others widely used the number seven symbolically*, but its use for groups of leaders is most significant. Given the seventy(-two)'s analogous role of receivers of delegated responsibility in Luke 10, the number might evoke the seventy elders of Num 11.[3]

In terms of the use of the number seven more broadly in the Hellenistic world, Keener explains: "The *seven planets*[4] made seven an important number for Greeks, including in the Mithras cult. Some ancients opined that seven had special power, appearing in many natural phenomena. Pythagoras had regarded the number as holy, and Pythagorean numerology had important influence in antiquity."[5]

Directing his attention to ancient Judaism, and its preoccupation with the number seven, Keener adds that the days of the week, "climaxing in the Sabbath, had already made seven an important number for Jewish people; confluence with Hellenistic and continuing Babylonian contexts would have only increased this emphasis."[6] One need to look not only to the Old Testament, but also to extrabiblical texts such as the *Dead Sea Scrolls*, pseudepigraphical texts such as *Joseph and Aseneth* and the great Jewish philosopher, Philo of Alexandria.[7]

Consider the following examples from ancient Judaism as further evidence in support of Keener's well-grounded discussion. First, a fragment from Qumran, a text from a *Dead Sea Scrolls* document known today as *4Q Songs of the Sabbath Sacrifice*:

1 The third of the chief princes. He will exalt the God of the exalted [an]gels *seven times*, with seven words of wonderful exaltations.

York: Touchstone Press, 1998). Regrettably, such unhelpful, uncritical, and sensationalistic books only increase skepticism as it pertains to the *legitimate* use of numeric symbols, *gematria*, and Pythagorean concepts from the ancient world.

    3. Craig S. Keener, *Acts: An Exegetical Commentary & 2: Introduction and 1:1–14:28*, vol. 1 (Grand Rapids, MI: Baker Academic, 2012–13), 1277–78 (emphasis added). "Some scholars argue that Jewish people associated 'seven' with the Hellenistic world, a comparison that would be apt if correct, though hard to prove given the wide range of associations for 'seven.' Greeks had their famous 'seven sages.' It is possible that Palestinian Jewish charity distributors sometimes functioned in groups of seven."

    4. See, e.g., Pliny the Elder, *Natural History*, 2.4.12, 2.6.32–41; Keener, *Acts*, 1:1278.

    5. Keener, *Acts*, 1:1278. See also Pythagoreas, *Apuleius Metamorpheses* 11.1.

    6. Keener, *Acts*, 1:1278–79.

    7. *Joseph and Aseneth*, 2.6. On the *Dead Sea Scrolls* and Philo, see the discussion below.

2 Psalm of praise, on the tongue of the fou[rth], to the Powerful One who is above all [the gods] with its *seven wonderful powers*. He will praise the God

3 of powers seven times, with seve[n] words of [wonderful] praise. [Ps]alm of [tha]nksgiving, on the tongue of the fif[th,] to the [K]in[g of] glory,

4 with its *seven wonderful thanks[giv]ings*. He will give thanks to the honoured God se*[ven times*, with se*]v[en wor]ds of wonderful thanksgivings*. [Psalm] of exultation.[8]

Second, in a number of texts in the large body of his works, Philo of Alexandria makes use of numerology in the context of intricate philosophical discussions: "And in strict consistency with himself, the lawgiver also calls the seventh day 'rest,' which the Hebrews call 'the Sabbath'; not as some persons fancy, because after six days the multitude was refrained from its habitual employments, *but because in real truth, the number seven is both in the world and in ourselves free from seditions and from wars, and is of all the numbers that which is the most averse to contention, and the greater lover of peace*."[9]

Keener explains why, for Philo, seven was the obvious number pertaining to the Sabbath: "it was the most honored number and a suitable symbol for God. He uses seven's astrological significance to confirm this claim. 'Seven' thus had widespread appeal and significance."[10]

An even more striking example is observed when Philo extols the singular perfection of the number seven in his treatise *On the Creation*: "And such great sanctity is there in the number seven, *that it has a pre-eminent rank beyond all the other numbers in the first decade*. For of the other numbers, some produce without being produced, others are produced but have no productive power themselves; others again both produce and are produced. *But the number seven alone is contemplated in no part*."[11]

---

8. See 4Q404.1–4 in Florentino García Martínez and Eibert J. C. Tigchelaar, *The Dead Sea Scrolls Study Edition (Translations)* (Leiden: Brill, 1997–98), 815.

9. Philo of Alexandria, *On Abraham* 28 (emphasis added). See Charles Duke Yonge with Philo of Alexandria, *The Works of Philo: Complete and Unabridged* (Peabody, MA: Hendrickson, 1995), 413.

10. Keener, *Acts*, 1:1278–79.

11. Philo of Alexandria, *On the Creation* 99 (emphases added). See Yonge, *Works of Philo*, 14. In §101, Philo continues to extol the singular virtues of the number seven: "Among the things then which are perceptible only by intellect, the number seven is proved to be the only thing free from motion and accident; but among things perceptible by the external senses, it displays a great and comprehensive power, contributing to the improvement of all terrestrial things, and affecting even the periodical changes of the moon. And in what manner it does this, we must consider. The number seven when compounded of numbers beginning with the unit, makes eight-and-twenty, a perfect

All of the above underscores the point that while there is for some an understandable hesitancy about the use of numerology if biblical interpretation, its use was quite widespread among ancient Jewish and Hellenistic writers. Not only that, it was skillfully employed by poets, mathematicians, and philosophers of the highest reputation. Whatever one makes of its (mis)use today, in the ancient world, numerology did not involve esoteric guesswork, but part of a larger literary craftsmanship that was rooted in the integration of philosophy, theology, cosmology, mathematics, and poetry. As seen in the above examples, numerology played a crucial role in ancient Jewish works such *Dead Sea Scrolls* and the works of Philo. As will be argued below, the author of Genesis made repetitious but careful use of the number seven in depicting God's perfecting of Creation—and the covenant he lovingly and freely entered into with humanity.

Seven: The Number of Perfection, the Number of the Covenant

Seven was a highly evocative number in ancient Judaism, and it is crucial for unlocking the deeper meaning of the Book of Genesis. In ancient Judaism, seven was widely regarded as the number of perfection.[12] For the author of Genesis, seven carried an even more particular meaning: not merely of "perfection" but that of "perfecting." Mathematically, seven is a prime num-

---

number, and one equalized in its parts. And the number so produced, is calculated to reproduce the revolutions of the moon, bringing her back to the point from which she first began to increase in a manner perceptible by the external senses, and to which she returns by waning. For she increases from her first crescent-shaped figure, to that of a half circle in seven days; and in seven more, she becomes a full orb; and then again she turns back, retracing the same path, like a runner of the diaulos, receding from an orb full of light, to a half circle again in seven days, and lastly, in an equal number she diminishes from a half circle to the form of a crescent; and thus the number before mentioned is completed. "And the number seven by those persons who are in the habit of employing names with strict propriety is called the perfecting number; because by it, everything is perfected. And any one may receive a confirmation of this from the fact, that every organic body has three dimensions, length, depth, and breadth; and four boundaries, the point, the line, the superficies, and the solid; and by theses, when combined, the number seven is made up" (§102).

12. See Umberto Cassuto, *A Commentary on the Book of Genesis Part I: From Adam to Noah. Genesis I–VI*, trans. Israel Abrahams (Jerusalem: Magnes Press, 1961 [1944]), 12–13; Carol L. Meyers, *The Tabernacle Menorah: A Synthetic Study of a Symbol from the Biblical Cult*, American Schools of Oriental Research Dissertation Series 2 (Missoula, MT: Scholars Press, 1976), 107.

ber, and in the biblical narrative it functions as an epic symbol pointing to *the perfecting of God's Temple of Creation.*

Yet this notion of perfecting is not the end of it. Two more points may be added here as it relates to the notion of "seven" in Genesis. First, in Genesis, the Hebrew term *sheba* ("seven") is closely related to the terms *shebua* ("oath"),[13] as in an oath "sworn" in sealing a covenantal treaty.[14] This connection is important, as it suggests that in Genesis the number seven signifies not only the perfecting of God's Temple of Creation but also *the ratification of a covenant between God and Creation.* In effect, God "sevens" himself to Creation, and he does so through his chosen mediator, Adam, who is called to enact the covenant in all of God's priestly duties.[15]

Second, beyond the notions of *perfecting the Temple of Creation* and *the ratification of a covenant between God and Creation covenant,* the number seven had another layer of hidden meaning for the author of Genesis. This last notion may be the most familiar of all to the reader: seven revealed *the mystery of the Sabbath.* Seven is the number of *Shabbat,* the pinnacle of Creation; the seventh day is set apart from all other days, as the day in which God "rested," having brought his creation to perfection. The Sabbath is a divine call for all of Creation to enter God's holy rest, and in fact it continues as a perpetual ordinance throughout Judaism.[16] The Sabbath is crucial to Adam's experience in Eden, and throughout the Abrahamic covenant(s), right

---

13. Also note the Hebrew verb *nisba* ("to swear").

14. While the Hebrew term *berith* ("covenant") occurs in covenantal formulas through the Old Testament (e.g., Gen. 6:18, 9:9, 15:8, etc.) the term *shebua* ("oath") is often substituted for it, such that they often function as synonyms. Numerous texts bear this out, most notably Abraham's covenant with the Canaanite known as Abimilech: "Therefore that place was called *Beer-sheba*; because there both of them swore an *oath*. When they had made a *covenant* at Beer-sheba" (*Gen.* 21:31–32). The place where the oath to the covenant was sworn was literally called "beer-sheba," the well of the oath. See Ezek. 17:13–19; also Deut. 29:12, 29:14; Josh. 9:15; Judg. 2:1; 2 Ki. 11:4; Ezek. 16:8, 16:59; Hos. 10:4; Psa. 89:3.

15. More will be said later about the particulars of the covenantal relationship between God and Adam (and Eve). Here, it may simply be added that Adam was given all of the provisions to "keep" the covenant with Go, and to ensure its effects on behalf of God's Creation, as God's mediator. Put another way, God's own faithfulness to the covenant ensured the aid of his divine power assist Adam to perform his duties. Yet, at the same time, in light of the gift of "free will," it remained a possibility that Adam would *not* fulfill his covenantal duties. And in ancient covenantal terms, when a duty remains unfulfilled, the oath sworn ensures *divine retribution.*

16. See Exod. 20:8, 31:14–15, 35:2; Lev. 23:3; Deut. 5:12.

through the Old Testament.[17] Finally, in the New Testament, the Sabbath is redefined and taken up by Jesus.[18] Later, in the Book of Hebrews,[19] the idea recurs—again, in a transformed way.[20]

One number, three hidden meanings. Such is the significance of the number seven within the text of Genesis. In the remainder of this chapter, literary and theological evidence will be brought forward in support of the above.

The Predominance of "Seven" in Genesis 1

As Gordon Wenham explains, "the number seven dominates this opening chapter [of Genesis] in a strange way."[21] Genesis 1:1 contains precisely seven words: *bərеshîth bārā 'elōhim; 'ēṯ-hashshāmayim wə'eth hā'āreṣ.*[22] There is a doubling from the first to the second verse; there are fourteen words (2 × 7) in Genesis 1:2.[23]

Following verse 1, which stands apart, the next section of Genesis 1 is divided into seven paragraphs, each of which pertains to one of the seven days.[24] There are three nouns in Genesis 1:1: God (*Elohim*), heavens (*shamay-*

---

17. See Exod. 16:23–29, 20:8, 20:10; Lev. 16:31, 23:3, 23:11, 23:15–16, 24:8; 1 Chron. 9:32; Isa. 56:2, 56:6; Jer. 17:21–22, 17:24; Amos 8:5; 2 Macc. 5:26.

18. E.g., Matt. 12:1–8; Mark 1:21–28; Luke 4:16–21, 6:1–9, 13:13–16, 14:1–5; John 5:9, 5:10, 5:16, 5:18, 7:22–23, 9:14, 9:16.

19. See Heb. 4:3–5.

20. Clearly the "rest" offered to Israel was the Sabbath rest offered to Adam. Heb. 4:9–10 states: "There remains a Sabbath rest for the people of God; for whoever enters God's rest also ceases from his labors as God did from his," that is, on the seventh day of the creation week. So, then, the "rest" lost by Adam and Israel was offered by God once again through the voice of David (Psa. 95:7–8), but he offers more perfectly now, through Jesus, who has inaugurated the "today" (Heb. 1:5, 3:13–15, 4:7) in which "rest" is available. The Old Covenant is associated with unfaithful Adam and Israel under Moses, the New with David, who spoke of it and received the promise of it.

21. Gordon J. Wenham, *Genesis 1–15*, vol. 1, *Word Biblical Commentary* (Waco, TX: Word Books, 1987), 6.

22. Gen. 1:1: וְאֵת הָאָרֶץ אֵת הַשָּׁמַיִם בָּרָא אֱלֹהִים בְּרֵאשִׁית׃

23. This is not evident in English but crystal clear in Hebrew. While it appears that there are twelve words, in Hebrew, two words may be joined by a hyphen, as two are here. Hence fourteen words comprise Gen. 1:2: *wə-hā-'ā-reṣ, hā-yə-ṭāh ṯō-hū wā-ṯō-hū, wə-ḥō-šeḵ 'al-pə-nê ṯə-hō-wm; wə-rū-aḥ 'ĕ-lō-hîm, mə-ra-ḥe-pheṭ 'al- pə-nê ham-mā-yim.* "The earth was without form and void, and darkness was upon the face of the deep; and the Spirit of God was moving over the face of the waters."

24. An obvious indicator of this division is seen in the repeating formula, "And there was evening and there was morning, such-and-such day."

im), and earth (*arets*). These nouns are key in the section that follow, and each of them recur in multiples of seven. The name of *God* occurs thirty-five times (7 x 5), the noun *earth* occurs twenty-one times (7 x 3), and the noun *heavens* occurs twenty-one times (7 x 3).

The terms "light" (*ôr*) and "day" (*yôm*) occur seven times in the first paragraph, and there are seven references to light in the fourth paragraph. "Water" (*mayim*) occurs seven times within paragraphs two and three. "Creatures" (*ayyā*) occurs seven times within the fifth and sixth paragraphs. The phrase "it was good" (*ki-tôv*) occurs seven times; the seventh occurrence is "as it was very good" (*ki-tov meōd*). In the seventh paragraph, which deals with the seventh day, are the following three sentences, each of which consists of seven words and contains in the *very middle* the expression "the seventh day":

> And on *the seventh day* God finished His work which He had done,
> And He rested on *the seventh day* from all His work which He had done.
> So God blessed *the seventh day* and hallowed it.

Finally, the sum of words in the seventh paragraph totals thirty-five (7 x 5). Even more evidence could be marshaled, yet the significance of the number seven in Genesis 1 is obvious. As Umberto Cassuto concludes, "To suppose that all this is a mere coincidence is not possible."[25]

The many occurrences of the number seven underscore three great themes in Genesis 1. First, the utter perfection of God's creation: the beauty of creation emerges in a cascade of sevens. Second, the covenantal bond between God and creation: God sevens himself to his people. Third, the Sabbath as the sign of this covenant: a perpetual command for humanity to enter God's rest on the seventh day.

A few remarks need to be made about the relationship between this pattern of sevens and the Sabbath. This intriguing repetition in Genesis 1, this "architecture of 7's," conveys something remarkable and powerful. The Creation culminates with God's "rest" on the seventh day, Shabbat (Sabbath). Shabbat is the key to unlocking the mystery of 7's. As the *Catechism* put it, the Sabbath is "the heart of Israel's law."[26] Along these lines, Ratzinger is spe-

---

25. Cassuto, *Commentary on the Book of Genesis*, 15.

26. *Catechism of the Catholic Church*, §348. See also Exod. 20:8, 20:11, "Remember the Sabbath day, to keep it holy … for in six days the Lord made heaven and earth, the sea, and all that is in them, and rested the seventh day; therefore the Lord blessed the Sabbath day and hallowed it"; Exod. 31:14, "You shall keep the Sabbath, because it is holy for you; everyone who profanes it shall be put to

cific in stating that the entire Creation "is oriented towards worship."[27] He adds, "In the Creation account the Sabbath is depicted as the day when the human being, in the freedom of worship, participates in God's freedom, in God's rest, and thus God's peace. To celebrate the Sabbath means to celebrate the covenant."[28]

In Scripture, the Sabbath is and always has been about much more than "taking a break" and "going to Church" because God ordained a day of rest. It is about God's perfecting of Creation. One other key point needs to be added: in Hebrew, the terms for "Sabbath" and "seven" are uncanny in relation to one another *shabbat* and *shibbith*. This suggests that, all along, from Day One right through Day Seven, all of the "sevening" was pointing forward to the Sabbath, to the perfecting of God's Creation. The cacophony of *shibbiths*, of sevens in Creation, prepares the reader for the perfecting of Creation: when the newly created Man enters into God's perfection, into the Shabbat.

Even more stunning is that the noun *shibbith*, the number of "perfection" in Scripture, has a verbal form: *sheba*. To "seven" something is to swear an oath, to bind something (e.g., *Beer-sheba* = "well of the oath"). In other words, as God creates, his glorious acts of creation cry out that he is "sevening" himself to Creation; God is covenanting with Creation, through Creation, binding himself, sevening himself to his Creation.

The climax of God's sevening is in Genesis 1:27–28: "So God created man in His own image, in the image of God he created him; male and female he created them. And God blessed them, and God said to them, 'Be fruitful and multiply, and fill the earth and subdue it; and have dominion over the fish of the sea and over the birds of the air and over every living thing that moves upon the earth.'"

Only then does God declare (for the seventh time), *ki-tov meōd*, "it is very good." All of Creation—every creature, the stars, the seas, the mountains and valleys, and each and every person—is part of the grand design of God and

---

death; whoever does any work on it, that soul shall be cut off from among his people"; Lev. 16:31, "It is a Sabbath of solemn rest to you, and you shall afflict yourselves; it is a statute forever"; Isa. 56:2, "Blessed is the man who does this, and *the son of man* who holds it fast, who keeps the Sabbath, not profaning it, and keeps his hand from doing any evil."

27. Joseph Ratzinger, *In the Beginning: A Catholic Understanding of Creation and the Fall* (Grand Rapids, MI: Eerdmans, 1995) 27.

28. Ibid., 30–31.

is created and designed for worship. Creation—and Man in particular—is created in such a way that is oriented to divine worship. God brings Creation and Man into existence, into relationship with himself, and that the "perfecting" of Creation, for which it was created is worship.

As further support, scholars have noted many parallels between the seven days of creation in Genesis 1 and Moses's construction of the Tabernacle in Exodus 25–39.[29] The most important parallels are evident: the concept of Sabbath rest links the Temple with Creation. Construction of Solomon's Temple begins only after God gave David rest from his enemies on every side.[30] Similarly, the story of Solomon repeats this theme of entering more deeply into God's rest through the construction of the Temple.[31] Moreover, Psalm 132 describes the Temple as God's "resting place":[32] "For the Lord has chosen Zion; he has desired it for his habitation: 'This is my resting place forever; here I will dwell, for I have desired it.'"[33]

There is notable sevenfold correspondence between the creation in Genesis 1 and the construction of Solomon's Temple.[34] The dedication of Solomon's Temple's occurs during the Feast of Tabernacles, a seven-day festival[35]

---

29. See Jon Levenson, *Sinai and Zion: An Entry into the Jewish Bible* (San Francisco: Harper & Row, 1985), 143–44; Jeffrey L. Morrow, "Creation and Liturgy: The Liturgical Background of Genesis 1–3" (presented at the Annual Meeting of the Society for Biblical Literature, San Diego, CA, November 2007).

30. See 2 Sam. 7:1–6: "The word of the Lord came to Nathan, *Go and tell my servant David, 'Thus says the Lord: Would you build me a house to dwell in?* I have not dwelt in a house since the day I brought up the people of Israel from Egypt to this day, but I have been moving about in a tent for my dwelling.'"

31. See 1 Ki. 5:4–5: "*And so I purpose to build a house for the name of the Lord my God,* as the Lord said to David my father, 'Your son, whom I will set upon your throne in your place, shall build the house for my name.'"

32. Levenson, *Sinai and Zion*, 143–44.

33. Psa. 132:13–14.

34. See Levenson, *Sinai and Zion*, 143–44. Summarizing the most important ones here: (1) The construction of the Solomonic Temple in Jerusalem takes seven years to complete (1 Ki. 6:38). In Lev. 25:3–7, the seventh year is called a Sabbath, thus forming a connection between the *seven days of the week* and *the seven years of, in the case of Leviticus, agricultural labor* and, in the case of *I Kings, temple labor*. (2) The Temple dedication occurs during the Feast of Tabernacles, which was a *seven-day festival* (Deut. 16:13) that fell on the *seventh month* of the year (1 Ki. 8:2); Solomon's speech during the Temple's dedication included seven petitions (1 Ki. 8:31–53). (3) The concept of "rest" also links the Temple with creation. Rest occurs at the completion of each project (Psa. 132:13–14 associates the experience of the Temple with rest).

35. See Deut. 16:13.

that fell on the seventh month of the year;[36] Solomon's speech during the Temple's dedication included seven petitions.[37] The construction of the Solomonic Temple was completed in the *seventh year* after construction begins.[38] In Leviticus 25:3–7, the seventh year is designated as a "Sabbath year," a year of rest. Not only does this represent another connection between the seven days of creation and the construction of the Temple, but it also likens the laborers of the Temple to the image of God, resting when their creative work is complete. Like Solomon's Temple, the consecration of the earlier Tabernacle in the wilderness lasted seven days.[39] Note the following sets of parallels, from Genesis and Exodus, respectively:

- And God saw everything that he had made, and behold, it was very good (Gen. 1:31).
- And Moses saw all the work and behold, they had done it; as the Lord had commanded, so had they done it. And Moses blessed them (Exod. 39:43).
- Thus the heavens and the earth were finished, and all the host of them (Gen. 2:1).
- Thus all the work of the Tabernacle of the tent of meeting *was finished*; and the people of Israel had done according to all that the Lord had commanded Moses; so had they done (Exod. 39:32).
- And *God blessed* ... (*Gen.* 2:3).
- And *Moses blessed* them ... (Exod. 39:43).
- And *sanctified* it ... (Gen. 2:3).
- And to *sanctify* it and its furnishings (Exod. 40:9).

It is only left to ask what difference these patterns make as it pertains to temple theology. A sound answer has become clear over the course of this chapter: all of these patterns point to *the perfecting of God's Temple* and to

---

36. See 1 Ki. 8:2. 37. See 1 Ki. 8:31–53.
38. See 1 Ki. 6:38.

39. Cf. Gen. 1:31, "And God saw everything that he had made, and behold, it was very good," with Exod. 39:43, "And Moses saw all the work, and behold, they had done it; as the Lord had commanded, so had they done it. And Moses blessed them"; Gen. 2:1, "Thus the heavens and the earth were finished, and all the host of them," with Exod. 39:32, "Thus all the work of the Tabernacle of the tent of meeting was finished; and the people of Israel had done according to all that the Lord had commanded Moses; so had they done"; Gen 2:3, "And God blessed," with Exod. 39:43, "And Moses blessed them"; Gen. 2:3, "And sanctified it," with Exod. 40:9, "and to sanctify it and its furnishings."

God's *ratification of a covenant between God and Creation. These* mysteries come to their climax on *the seventh day, the Day of the Sabbath.*

One only need recall the various pieces of evidence presented earlier, all of which support the claim that Genesis 1–2 depicts Eden as a cosmological temple. Added to that data is the present discussion of "seven" in Genesis 1. Perhaps more data could be piled on, but for now the evidence presented will have to suffice. In place of more static notions of a two-dimensional Garden, a fresh portrait of Eden has emerged: God has created his holy temple of Eden and has brought Man into this perfection, to protect it, dwell in it, and multiply it over the face of the earth.

Before turning to chapter 4, it is worth pausing here to examine an early Christian writer and his impressions of Eden. Using symbolic and allegorical language, the fourth-century deacon and liturgical poet of Syria St. Ephrem[40] expresses this mystery of Eden as a temple. In his *Hymns on Paradise*, he turns his attention to Genesis 3. Here, he speaks of the Tree of Life as the Holy of Holies of the Garden, and how Satan deceived the Man (and Woman) to enter unworthily. In so doing, they experienced deep remorse. As such, Ephrem creates a "negative" parallel, inasmuch as he compares the sin of Adam (and Eve) in terms of the high priest of the temple who is prevented from trespassing the veil:

When the accursed one learned, how the glory of that inner tabernacle, as if in a sanctuary, was hidden from them and that Tree of Knowledge, clothed with an injunction, served as the veil for the sanctuary, he realized that its fruit was the key of justice that would open the eyes of the bold—and cause them great remorse.[41]

Elsewhere, St. Ephrem speaks of Adam's shame at beholding the *"glory of the Holy of Holies"*:

But when Adam boldly ran and ate of its fruit. This double knowledge straightaway flew toward him, tore away and removed both veils from his eyes: He beheld the Glory of the Holy of Holies and trembled; He beheld, too, his own shame and blushed groaning and lamenting because the twofold knowledge he had gained had proved for him a torment.[42]

---

40. Ephrem the Syrian (306–73 AD), saint and writer of poetic commentaries and liturgical hymns, was regarded by Pope Benedict XVI as being the author of the greatest examples of Christian poetry prior to Dante.

41. St. Ephrem the Syrian, *Hymns on Paradise* (New York: St. Vladimir's Press), 92 (Hymn III, §5).

42. Ibid., 93 (Hymn II, §7).

Near the end of the hymn, St. Ephrem comments on the priest-king Adam, cut off from the glory of God's presence in the Holy of Holies:

God to not permit Adam to enter that innermost Tabernacle this was withheld, so that first he might prove pleasing in his service of that outer Tabernacle like a priest with fragrant incense. Adam's keeping of the commandment was to be his censer; that he might enter before the Hidden One into that hidden Tabernacle.[43]

Finally, in the last stanza, St. Ephrem compares the high priesthood of Adam with the High Priest of the Old Testament. He does so to draw a theological parallel between the two, in that both are excluded from the Holy of Holies (the latter enters only once a year):

The symbol of Paradise was depicted by Moses who made the two sanctuaries, the sanctuary and the Holy of Holies; into the outer one entrance was permitted, but into the inner, only once a year. So too with Paradise, God closed off the inner part, but He opened up the outer wherein Adam might graze.[44]

Concluding Remarks

The present chapter as well as chapter 2 focused on the temple of Creation, of how the biblical authors present Eden as the Holy Place, of the temple. In the midst of it is the Tree of Life, the symbol of God's perfecting of Creation and of God's own life that nourishes and sustains the divine grace upon Adam and Eve. Chapter 3 turns from a discussion of the archetypal *temple* to its *archetypal priest Adam*, the one who not only inhabits God's cosmological temple, but who is also called to "protect" and to "multiply" God's temple presence.

43. Ibid., 96 (Hymn II, §16).
44. Ibid., 96 (Hymn III, §17).

4

THE PRIEST OF
EDEN IN ALL OF HIS GLORY

Temple Priesthood in the Old and
New Testaments (I/IV)

And the Lord God made *garments of glory* for Adam and for
his wife from the skin which the serpent had cast off.

Targum Pseudo-Jonathan on Genesis 3:21

Until this point, the biblical theology undertaken in the book has dealt
with the cosmological temple of the Creation narratives in Genesis. The discussion now turns to a related matter—to the biblical theology of "mediation" within this temple, that is, to priesthood in Sacred Scripture.[1] Far from
presenting the reader with a detour into some unrelated subject, the notion
of priesthood is integral to a proper understanding of temple theology in Sacred Scripture.

And just as the broader inquiry into the temple began with Genesis, so
too does this next step require a return "to the beginning." As will be shown,
it was the first Man who was called by God to participate in the holiness
of the temple of Creation. Specifically, Adam was "ordained" as one formed

---

1. It is beyond the scope of the book to assert a theology of the priesthood in the Old and New
Testaments, or to trace every key development of this theme in Scripture. In accord with the theme
of the book, discussions of priesthood will focus especially on the sacerdotal (i.e., salvific) role of the
high priest, especially as it relates to the Temple. For a fresh and helpful look at the topic of priesthood in Scripture, see Thomas A. Lane, *The Catholic Priesthood: Biblical Foundations* (Steubenville,
OH: Emmaus Road Press, 2016).

by God and placed into the Garden sanctuary as God's high priest. Adam's obedience to this call would ensure that the temple of Creation was revered by him and his wife—and by all the Creation—as absolutely holy. In fact, Adam was called to *guard and protect* the "temple gates" to assure that nothing unholy entered in to the Garden sanctuary. Finally, Adam—and Eve in relationship with him—was called to *extend God's temple presence* over the earth in the first recorded command in the Bible: "Be fruitful and multiply … fill the earth" (Gen. 1:28).

Beginning with the priesthood of Adam, forthcoming chapters will focus upon subsequent stages of priesthood in the Old Testament. From the priest-king Melchizidek and the priesthood of the patriarchs to the pivotal turn to the Levitical high priesthood, the study moves forward toward the New Testament and its presentation of Jesus as the eternal High Priest.

The Lost Priesthood of Sacred Scripture

The biblical institution of the priesthood, in all of its stages, is absolutely vital to the study of both the Old and New Testaments. As one contemporary Catholic biblical theologian writes, "If, for an ancient Jew, it would have been absurd to speak of religious worship without sacrifice, then it would be equally absurd to speak of sacrifice without priesthood. Indeed, the two are almost synonymous: the Temple is the locus of the priesthood because it is the sole place of sacrifice, and it is the sole place of sacrifice because it is the locus of the priesthood. The place of 'the priests, the ministers of the Lord,' is 'between the vestibule and the altar,' that is, in the Temple (Joel 2:17). *Hence, any attempt to understand Jesus' relationship to the ancient Jewish Temple must eventually raise the question of his relationship to the ancient Jewish priesthood."*[2]

The past several centuries of historical-critical studies of the Old Testament have produced a largely negative assessment of the priesthood in Scripture. As explained in the introduction to this volume, it was originally the source critical studies of the Five Books of Moses that led the way in the diminishment of the priesthood, with Julius Wellhausen serving as aide-de-camp.

2. Brant Pitre, "Jesus, the New Temple, and the New Priesthood," *Letter & Spirit* 4 (2008): 70–71 (emphasis added).

It is not inaccurate to say that the cumulative effect of such historical-critical investigations was a weakening of the biblical concept of priesthood. Despite various positive presentations in the twentieth century—from respected theologians such as Yves Congar, Jean Daniélou, and Joseph Ratzinger (among others)—it seems that considerable damage had been done to the biblical image of the priest.

By the late nineteenth century, source critics began to have interests in exploring the New Testament along similar lines as the Five Books of Moses. Soon, numerous scholars developed rather intricate hypotheses regarding the formation of the Synoptic Gospels. Not too surprisingly, most of the scholarly output did not treat with the notion of "priesthood" in the Synoptic Gospels in a compelling or positive way.

This sort of biblical criticism (one might add biblical skepticism) had seismic effects on the biblical interpretation of the Gospels—and primary subject of the Gospels, Jesus the Messiah. Fletcher-Louis puts it this way: "Jesus' priestly character has been ignored, first and foremost, because the priesthood itself has been ignored in modern biblical studies."[3] As he correctly observes, the actual data concerning the priesthood—beginning with the Old Testament—are remarkable in both the quantity as well as the quality of positive depictions of God's priests: "In the Old Testament the priesthood—its ordination, clothing, sacrificial and other responsibilities—is described with considerable detail."[4] Yet, as Fletcher-Louis suggests, the priestly portions of the Old Testament have been treated by many biblical scholars as "a lamentable decline in Israelite religion from the pure faith of the prophets … into a post-exilic obsession with cultic order and institutional religiosity."[5]

---

3. Crispin Fletcher-Louis, "Jesus and the High Priest," accessed November 29, 2016, http://www.marquette.edu/maqom/jesus.pdf, 2. A more accessible essay by Fletcher-Louis is "Priests and Priesthood," in *Dictionary of Jesus and the Gospels*, 2nd ed., ed. J. B. Green, J. K. Brown, and N. Perrin (Downers Grove, IL: InterVarsity Press, 2013), 696–705. Interestingly, Fletcher-Louis is a non-Catholic (Anglican) scholar and yet is one of the world's leading specialists on the priest/priesthood today (also angelology). His work is thought provoking and well worth reading. The title of the present chapter acknowledges the important work of Fletcher-Louis in his dissertation, published as *All the Glory of Adam: Liturgical Anthropology in the Dead Sea Scrolls* (Leiden: Brill Academic, 2001).

4. Fletcher-Louis, "Jesus and the High Priest," 2.

5. Ibid. Fletcher-Louis has in mind historical-critical scholars such as Julius Wellhausen, who systematically dismantled the priesthood from its primary place at the core of all Old Testament study.

It is a more than reasonable argument that such timely, negative conclusions about the priesthood, swirling as they were within circles of Old Testament critics, played some role in shaping the direction of New Testament criticism in the twentieth century, particularly as it pertained to the idea of the "priesthood of Jesus" and of his Apostles.

Positively, after well over a century of aspersions cast upon priesthood among biblical scholars, the study of the priesthood in Old Testament scholarship is at present beginning to receive a fresh look, and some of the studies being produced are turning the theological conclusions of the early source critics on their head.[6] Whether or not such positive developments in Old Testament theology result in a reevaluation of priesthood remains to be seen.[7]

What about the state of New Testament scholarship, as it relates to biblical priesthood? Sadly, the somewhat surprising and positive treatment that the priesthood of the Old Testament has been receiving of late has not been met with much excitement by New Testament scholars. The somewhat encouraging trend in Old Testament theology appears to have been slower in coming in New Testament circles.[8] As one commentator accurately summarizes, "If there is any single subject which modern historical scholarship on Jesus has almost completely neglected, it is the subject of Jesus and the Jewish priesthood."[9]

---

6. See ibid., 2–3; Lane, *Catholic Priesthood*.

7. More recently, an article in *Catholic Biblical Quarterly* examined the question of whether "Eden" is hinted at in Gen. 18:12–13. Interestingly, the question is undertaken from a source-critical view, and the author suggests that the latter is reworking the scene from Eden. See Andrew R. Davis, "Eden Revisited: A Literary Theological Reading of Genesis 18:12–13," *Catholic Biblical Quarterly* 78 (2016): 611–31.

8. Fletcher-Louis, "Jesus and the High Priest," 3. Fletcher-Louis notes some important exceptions: Bruce Chilton, *The Temple of Jesus: His Sacrificial Program within a Cultural History of Sacrifice* (University Park: Pennsylvania State University Press, 1992); N. T. Wright, *Jesus and the Victory of God* (London: SPCK, 1996); Paula Fredrickson, *Jesus of Nazareth, King of the Jews* (London: Macmillan, 2000). See also Menahem Haran, *Temples and Temple Service in Ancient Israel* (Oxford: Clarendon, 1978); Roland De Vaux, *Ancient Israel: Its Life and Institutions* (Grand Rapids, MI: Eerdmans, 1997 [1961]), 274–329; Pitre, "Jesus, the New Temple, and the New Priesthood," esp. 70–82.

9. Pitre, "Jesus, the New Temple, and the New Priesthood," 71. He adds: "This is true, despite the fact that it is widely acknowledged that the Dead Sea Scrolls have proven beyond the shadow of a doubt that Jews in the first century were not only waiting for a new Temple, but for a priestly Messiah. Indeed, several major scholars categorically deny even the possibility that Jesus saw himself as a priestly Messiah, much less that he sought to establish an eschatological priesthood. Remarkably, this

This book wishes to move beyond this theological divide and demonstrate just how vital priest and priesthood are to the fullest meaning of both the theology of the Old and New Testaments. The discussion begins with an examination of Adam's priesthood in the Book of Genesis.

The High Priesthood of Adam

The second chapter of Genesis presents clues that Adam is not merely a horticultural figure, but a priestly figure, chosen by God as the High Priest of Eden: "The Lord God took the man and put him in the Garden of Eden to till and keep it" (Gen. 2:15). The juxtaposition of two Hebrew verbs, *'abad* and *shamar* ("to till" and "to guard," respectively) is essential to understand Adam's priestly identity in Genesis. As Daniel Bock writes, "Just as priests and Levites *served* and *guarded* sacred spaces, so the man was charged *to serve and to guard* the garden."[10] Both verbs were commonly used in a religious sense of serving God.[11] They occur, often together, in early priestly texts of the Pentateuch, especially as it pertains to Tabernacle duties of the Levitical priests.[12]

Two examples from the Book of Numbers echo this biblical phenomenon: "They shall keep guard (*shamar*) over him and over the whole congregation before the tent of meeting, as they minister (*'abad*) at the Tabernacle. They shall guard all the furnishings of the tent of meeting, and keep guard over the people of Israel as they minister at the Tabernacle" (Num. 3:7–8, ESV); "They minister to their brothers in the tent of meeting by keeping guard (*shamar*), but they shall do no service (*'abad*). Thus shall you do to the Levites in assigning their duties" (Num. 8:26, ESV).[13]

---

is even true of studies that are otherwise very interested in the ancient Jewish context of Jesus' words and deeds. Such works leave one with the distinct (but historically puzzling) impression that while Jesus had a great deal to say about the Jewish Temple, he had almost nothing to say about the Jewish priesthood" (71–72).

10. Daniel Bock, "Eden: A Temple? A Reassessment of the Biblical Evidence," in *From Creation to New Creation: Essays in Honor of G. K. Beale*, ed. Daniel M. Gurtner and Benjamin L. Gladd (Peabody: Hendrickson, 2013), 11.

11. See, e.g., Deut. 4:19.

12. Wenham, *Genesis 1–15*, vol. 1, *Word Biblical Commentary* (Waco, TX: Word Books, 1987), 67, emphases added.

13. See also Num. 18:5–6 (ESV): "And you shall keep guard (*shamar*) over the sanctuary and over the altar, that there may never again be wrath on the people of Israel. And behold, I have taken

In fact, it should be stressed that wherever the two Hebrew terms appear in Scripture within an approximately fifteen-word range, they are always in reference to priestly service:[14] Wenham observes that in both Genesis 2 and in the Levitical texts, these two terms are juxtaposed, another pointer to the interplay of Tabernacle and Eden symbolism.[15]

Targum Neofiti is an early translation of Genesis from Hebrew into Aramaic, and it is likewise instructive. The rendering of Genesis 2:15 is typical of early Jewish concepts of Adam, depicted in priestly language. There, *Targum Neofiti* describes Adam as being placed in the Garden "*to toil in the Law and to observe its commandments.*" This expression is intended to evoke priestly rigor, and calls to mind similar descriptions of Levitical priests in the Book of Numbers. The translation of *Targum Neofiti* at Genesis 2:19[16] presents yet another example. At this point, the Targum explicitly states that in naming the animals, Adam used "*the language of the Sanctuary.*"

Such examples of early Jewish interpretations of Genesis are compelling evidence, and invite further inquiry into the possible intentions of the sacred author, with respect to Adam and a possible priestly role. Beale agrees, and insists that Adam's very identity was priestly and that his God-given duties involved "more than spadework in the dirt of a garden."[17] Anticipating the appearance of the Serpent in Genesis 3, Beale adds: "It is apparent that priestly obligations in Israel's later Temple including the duty of 'guarding' unclean things from entering ... and this appears to be relevant for Adam, especially in view of the unclean creature lurking on the perimeter of the Garden and who then enters."[18]

On the notion of Adam's possible priestly role—that is, in preventing that which is unclean to trespass into the "gates" of the Garden sanctuary—another text from Genesis 2 requires some attention. The Hebrew term *tardemah* ("deep sleep") in Genesis 2:21 with respect to Adam's rest suggests the author's

your brothers the Levites from among the people of Israel. They are a gift to you, given to the Lord, to do the service (*'abad*) of the tent of meeting."

14. G. K. Beale, *The Temple and the Church's Mission: A Biblical Theology of the Dwelling Place of God* (Downers Grove, IL: InterVarsity Press, 2004), 67.

15. Wenham, *Genesis 1–15*, 67.

16. Gen. 2:19: "So out of the ground the Lord God formed every beast of the field and every bird of the air, and brought them to the man to see what he would call them; and whatever the man called every living creature, that was its name."

17. Beale, *The Temple and the Church's Mission*, 69 (emphases added).

18. Ibid. (emphases added).

intention to indicate the passing of time, such that Adam—who was created on the sixth day—awakens to discover Eve, given to him by God on the seventh day.[19] In such a reading, the gift of Eve on the Sabbath would place Eve near the center Adam's perfected, priestly world. Out of his side, and by his side, he would freely roam the garden, preserving and protecting the boundaries of the Garden: seeing to the continual state of holiness all that was within the sanctuary, and that all unclean things were kept outside the sanctuary.

While the timing of the creation of Eve remains unclear, the following is clear. Adam, the high priest of Eden, failed to fulfill his end of the covenant. When the most unclean Serpent (Hebrew, *nahash*) trespassed the boundaries of the Garden sanctuary, and failed to preserve and protect the holiness of the Temple, "Adam stepped aside and did not guard the garden sanctuary or his wife from the evil it represented."[20] One Catholic theologian opines that "Adam's failure to engage this demonic serpent in battle was the result of his unwillingness to lay down his life in defense of the garden Sanctuary ... he failed to offer his life as a priestly sacrifice to God."[21]

In the New Testament, the Book of Hebrews suggests something similar when it writes of "the fear of death" that overcomes men. An identification with Adam seems plausible, if not likely: "Since therefore the children share in flesh and blood, [Jesus] himself likewise partook of the same nature, that through death he might destroy him who has the power of death, *that is, the devil*, and deliver all those who *through fear of death* were subject to lifelong bondage" (Heb. 2:14).

In any event, in the dialogue between the Serpent and the Woman, Genesis appears to portray Adam as "absent" during the dire meeting. And if he is present, he remains utterly silent.[22] For example, the apocryphal

19. See *Davis*, "Eden Revisited," 627. Davis shows that *tardemah* occurs only seven times in the Hebrew Bible, two of which are in the Pentateuch. The Pentateuchal occurrences are as follows: here in Gen. 2:21 and again in 15:12, where God casts a "deep sleep" upon Abram before a covenantal action). See also 1 Sam. 26:12; Isa. 29:10; Job 4:13, 33:15; Prov. 19:15.

20. The dire nature of this threat posed by the Serpent is sometimes lost on the reader of English translations of Genesis. In Num. 21:6, the same term, *nahash*, is used to depict the fiery Serpents that attacked Israel in the wilderness. Elsewhere, in Isa. 27:1, it is used with reference to the monstrous "Leviathan" from the deep. In a canonical sense, the Serpent of Genesis reemerges in the Book of Revelation, as the great red dragon, an image of the Satan (Rev. 12:3–4, 12:9).

21. Michael Barber, *Singing in the Reign: The Psalms and the Liturgy of God's Kingdom* (Steubenville, OH: Emmaus Road, 2001), 44.

22. See Gen. 3:1–5.

Proto-evangelion of James explicitly portrays Adam in this way:[23] "Has not the history of Adam been repeated in me? For just as Adam was in the hour of his singing praise, and the serpent came, *and found Eve alone*, and completely deceived her, so it has happened to me also. And Joseph stood up from the sackcloth, and called Mary, and said to her: O thou who hast been cared for by God, why hast thou done this and forgotten the Lord thy God? Why hast thou brought low thy soul, thou that wast brought up in *the holy of holies*, and that didst receive food from the hand of an angel? And she wept bitterly, saying: I am innocent, and have known no man."

Commenting upon this apocryphal text, Catholic theologian Gary Anderson observes, "While Adam was absent, the serpent found his way to Eve. No such story can be found explicitly in Scripture, *but it could be implied from the context.* Eve, after all, speaks to the serpent on her own; Adam appears to have no role whatsoever in the conversation."[24] Elsewhere, in apocryphal text *Life of Adam and Eve* of the second century BC, Adam is busy in another part of the Garden from where Eve was: "God, however, gave part of paradise to me [Adam], and part to your mother [Eve]: to me he gave the tree of the eastern and northern part and to your mother he gave the southern and western part. The Lord God gave us two angels to watch over us. *The hour came for the angels to ascend to the sight of God for worship. At once, the Devil, our adversary, found the place. Then she ate and gave to me to eat.*"[25]

Curiously, only in Genesis 3:6 is Adam is described as "with her."[26] Only then does he seem to return, as the woman gives him the fruit to eat. When it came time for prayer, the angels who attended Eve left Eden to worship God in heaven. In this moment, Eve was unattended, and the Serpent saw his opportunity to tempt her. According to this text, Eve ate the fruit on her own

---

23. *Proto-evangelion of James* 13:1. (Also known as the *Gospel of James/Infancy Gospel of James*, this text originates in the second century AD. It was widely read but obviously never accepted into the New Testament Canon.)

24. Gary Anderson, *The Genesis of Perfection: Adam and Eve in Jewish and Christian Imagination* (Louisville, KY: Westminster, 2001), 91. It is beyond the scope of this book to engage this idea further. But it is worth noting that the "deception" of Eve has enormous implications for early Christianity. Anderson summarizes this well—particularly the understanding of Mary as the New Eve, as the one who reverses the disobedience of Eve in her "yes" to God (91–97).

25. *Life of Adam and Eve* 32:2, 33:1–2.

26. Gen. 3:6: "So when the woman saw that the tree was good for food, and that it was a delight to the eyes, and that the tree was to be desired to make one wise, she took of its fruit and ate, and *she also gave some to her husband who was with her*, and he ate."

and later gave it to Adam. As such, Adam is depicted as a delinquent guard—allowing the unclean Serpent to gain access to the Holy Place of the Garden. As its high priest, Adam did not minister well in God's temple of Creation.

Other ancient Jewish texts reinterpret Genesis in a similar fashion. The Book of Jubilees goes further still, speculating that Adam and Eve were created outside the Garden: "And God brought her to him and he knew her and said to her, 'This is now bone of my bones and flesh of my flesh' … and *after forty days were completed* for Adam in the land where he was created *we brought him into the garden of Eden* so that he might work it and guard it."[27]

A related theme in such apocryphal texts is that Adam needed to consecrate himself before entering the Garden Temple. As Eden's priest, Adam's entrance into the sacred space of the Garden Temple occurs only after a time of consecration and purifying prayer. It may seem strange to introduce this idea into the text of Genesis, yet this hermeneutical move is perfectly consistent with the theology of Jubilees, whose priestly author was fervently loyal to the Temple.

In fact, such an exegetical choice by the author puts the text of Genesis at the service of the high priestly cult. With Scripture behind him, the author of Jubilees can urge his priestly readers of his day that just as Adam needed to consecrate himself and be holy, so must priests in Jerusalem follow his archetypal example and do the same as he.

Another astonishing interpretative move of *Life of Adam and Eve* is seen in its suggestion that Adam inappropriately consummated his marriage to Eve in the Garden Temple. For the author of the apocryphal text, their conjugal union should have taken place "beyond the holy garden." According to the text, their willful disobedience defied God—and his holy Temple. Simply put, Adam and Eve profaned the sacred space of the Garden sanctuary and warranted expulsion. They were to be "cut off" and exiled from the Temple.

The hermeneutical moves of *Life of Adam and Eve* may seem strange, but they are worth contemplation, particularly when one understands "the why" of these moves. And the reason may be summarized in this way: this apocryphal text engages the text of Genesis not to engage in fanciful speculation, but to *teach*. The author of the text wishes to promote priestly purity in their setting in the second/first century BC, and particularly laws of sexual

---

27. Book of Jubilees 3:6, 3:9.

abstinence for Levitical priests. In ancient Israel, most priests were married and served in the Temple just two weeks per year, returning to their homes afterward. Before their time of priestly duties began, all Levitical priests were to fast from their conjugal life for a period of about three days. Some followed this oral tradition, but apparently others did not. And the leaders of the Temple cult were adamant about preserving and enforcing this ceremonial law.

With this background in mind, the odd exegetical moves of the apocryphal text become much less bizarre. The allegorical message was this: priests of the Temple, do not do as Adam did. Do not profane the Temple. Instead, practice ritual abstinence before your Temple service and do not render yourself unclean in the holy Temple.

Adam, the Bejeweled High Priest of Eden

The above extrabiblical evidence confirms the high priestly identity of Adam within Genesis. In returning to the Old Testament, other texts beyond Genesis are worthy of consideration. For example, in Exodus, Moses is commanded to fashion precious gems for the Temple and for Aaron's vestments, both of which reflected the glory (*kāvôd*) of God himself, as several texts from Exodus make clear: "And you shall make holy garments for Aaron your brother, for glory (*kāvôd*) and for beauty" (Exod. 28:2); and "For Aaron's sons you shall make coats and sashes and caps. You shall make them for *glory* (*kāvôd*) and beauty" (Exod. 28:40).

The term used here for "glory" (*kāvôd*) is standard terminology "for God's glorious theophanic revelation of himself to Israel at Sinai, at the Tabernacle, and at the end of time."[28] Genesis does not portray Adam dressed in the glorious robes of the high priest of the later Temple, yet Ezekiel does,[29] and stops short of referring to him as an angelic being: "You were *an anointed guardian cherub*. I placed you; you were on the holy mountain of God; in the midst of the stones of fire you walked" (Exod. 28:14).

---

28. Beale, *The Temple and the Church's Mission*, 41–42. The word for "beauty" (*tiparâ*) is rarer, and it should not be lost on the reader that most of its occurrences are associated with the beauty of Solomon's Temple (2 Chron. 3:6: "He adorned [made beautiful, *tipārâ*] the house with settings of precious stones").

29. Ezekiel is technically describing the King of Tyre, but it is quite clear from the text that what the prophet says of the King of Tyre is really a comment about Adam himself.

Likewise, texts from the Dead Sea Scrolls depict the glory of Adam: "Adam our father, you fashioned *in the image of your glory* ... the breath of life you blew into his nostril, and intelligence and knowledge in the Garden of Eden, which you had planted. You made [him] govern ... and so that he would walk in a glorious land ... he kept. And you imposed on him not to turn away ... he is flesh, and to dust."[30] And elsewhere, "Remember Adam, please, that all of us are your people ... You are in our midst, in the column of fire and in the cloud your holy walks in front of us, *and your glory is in our midst.*"[31]

Similarly, the Aramaic Targums replace "garments of skin" in Genesis 3:21[32] with "garments of glory," as in this text: "And the Lord God made *garments of glory* for Adam and for his wife from the skin which the serpent had cast off."

As Bock explains, both the Tabernacle[33] and Temple[34] "were lavishly decorated with gold, in keeping with the surpassing glory of its resident."[35] Likewise, precious stones adorned the Tabernacle and Temple.[36] This corresponds to the depiction of gold in the Garden: "And the gold of that land is good; bdellium and onyx stone are there" (Gen. 2:12). In Genesis 3:8, the verb *hithallék* ("to walk"), used to describe God's "walking to and fro" in the Garden, is the same verb[37] used to describe God's presence in the Tabernacle: "And I will walk among you and will be your God, and you shall be my people" (Lev. 26:12).[38] Later, in the time of the Jerusalem Temple, the golden lampstand (*menorah*) was conspicuously placed just outside the Holy of Holies. This corresponds to the Tree of Life in the center of the Garden. In the Jerusalem Temple, the *menorah* was depicted as a small, flowering tree, with seven branches.[39]

Similarly, just as water flowed from the Garden of Eden and watered the

---

30. *Dead Sea Scrolls*, 4Q504. A precise translation of this document is notoriously difficult owing to the fragmentary condition of the text. For the sake of readability, "bracketing" of omissions and questionable portions of the translation have been removed.

31. *Dead Sea Scrolls*, 4Q504.   32. Gen. 3:21.

33. Exod. 25:11, 25:17, 25:24, 25:29, 25:36.   34. See 1 Ki. 6:20–22, 6:28, 6:30, 6:32, 6:35.

35. Bock, "Eden," 13.

36. E.g., Exod. 25:7, 25:11, 25:17, 25:31; Num. 11:17; 1 Chron. 29:2.

37. Not only are the terms identical, but also, strikingly, the forms of both verbs likewise are identical (*hithpael*).

38. See also Deut. 23:14; 2 Sam. 7:6–7.

39. See Exod. 25:31–37.

earth, so too is the Temple depicted with water flowing from it. This is readily seen when one compares the passage from Genesis with subsequent biblical texts:

A river flowed *out of Eden* to water the garden, and there it divided and became four rivers (Gen. 2:10).

They feast on the abundance of Your house, and *You give them drink from the river of your delights.* For with You is the fountain of life; in Your light do we see light (Psa. 36:8–9, ESV).

On that day *living waters shall flow out from Jerusalem,* half of them to the eastern sea and half of them to the western sea; it shall continue in summer as in winter (Zech. 14:8).

The entrance to the Garden sanctuary was in the east and was carefully guarded by cherubim: "He drove out the man, and at the east of the garden of Eden he placed the cherubim and a flaming sword that turned every way to guard the way to the tree of life" (Gen. 3:24, ESV).[40] This eastward pattern is notable in later texts in Ezekiel: "And you shall make a veil of blue and purple and scarlet yarns and fine twined linen … And the veil shall separate for you the *Holy Place* from the *Most Holy*" (Exod. 16:31–33, ESV).

Later in his temple vision the prophet Ezekiel writes, "Then he went into the gateway facing east, going up its steps, and measured the threshold of the gate, one reed deep" (Ezek. 40:6). Commenting on this "facing east" motif, Jean Daniélou draws a spiritual connection, as he observes, "Prayer facing east is connected with the ideas of Paradise. For does not Genesis say that 'Paradise was planted towards the east' and so to turn to the East seemed to be an expression of *longing for Paradise.* This is the reason given by St. Basil: 'It is by reason of an *unwritten tradition that we turn to the East to pray.*' But we know that we are *seeking the ancient homeland,* the Paradise that God planted in Eden in the East."[41]

One final consideration is necessary before bringing the present topic

---

40. G. K. Beale, "The Final Vision of the Apocalypse and Its Implications for a Biblical Theology of the Temple," in *Heaven on Earth,* ed. T. Desmond Alexander and Simon Gathercole (Carlisle, UK: Paternoster Press, 2004), 198: "When Adam failed to guard the Temple by sinning and letting in an unclean serpent to defile the sanctuary, Adam lost his priestly role, and the two cherubim took over the responsibility of 'guarding' the Garden Temple."

41. Jean Daniélou, *The Bible and the Liturgy* (Notre Dame, IN: University of Notre Dame Press, 1956), 32. Daniélou cites St. Gregory the Great's *On the Holy Spirit,* 27.

to a fitting close. It concerns the expansion of the Garden Temple. Specifically, Adam's high priesthood over the Garden Temple involved expanding it, in that he was called to extend God's temple presence beyond the sacred space of the Garden sanctuary, so that God's holiness would fill the ends of the earth. The following is a summary of the most crucial evidence of this important motif.

The first occurrence of 'ādām in Scripture is in Genesis 1:26–27.[42] There it occurs twice, describing the divine creation of humanity on the sixth day. It is clear that the 'ādām created is intended as a collective. In Genesis 1:27, 'ādām in the first half of the verse is set in parallel with "male and female" in the second half. The intent is to include all members of the human race in the 'ādām that God created.[43]

The First "Great Commission"

The Man and Woman were commanded to be fruitful and to subdue the earth.[44] Hess explains the significance of this duty as follows: "A royal statue at a distant corner of the empire represented the king's authority when the ruler could not be physically present. So also, at the completion of God's creation, he left 'ādām as his image to represent his authority on earth ... the function of the image is to extend God's kingdom into every area of nature, society and culture. This is exactly what happens with the first man in Genesis 2."[45]

Adding to this, Beale asserts that Genesis 1 established the biblical pattern by which this commission was to be accomplished: "Humanity will fulfill the commission by means of being in God's image ... As Adam and Eve were to begin to rule over and subdue the earth, it is plausible to suggest that they were to extend the geographical boundaries of the Garden until Eden extended throughout and covered the whole earth."[46] In other words, according to Genesis, God did not intend for Adam to passively remain in

---

42. Gen. 1:26–27: "Then God said, "Let us make man in our image, after our likeness; and let *them* have dominion over the fish of the sea, and over the birds of the air, and over the cattle, and over all the earth, and over every creeping thing that creeps upon the earth. So God created man in his own image, in the image of God he created him; *male and female he created them*."

43. R. S. Hess, *Dictionary of the Old Testament: Pentateuch*, s.v. "Adam."

44. Ibid.   45. Ibid.

46. Beale, "Final Vision of the Apocalypse," 201.

Eden and merely assure its holiness, but, as Genesis 1:28 indicates, a chief requirement of his priestly identity involved a subduing of "the entire earth."[47]

This Adamic role of expanding God's temple presence over the face of the earth did not come to a sudden and abrupt stop with the ironic turn of events, in which he himself was "cast out" of Eden with his wife Eve. No—a careful examination of the biblical data indicates that Adam's priestly role to "fill the earth," though unfulfilled at the conclusion of Genesis 3, was nevertheless passed on to humanity by virtue of God's will in the matter.

This temple-building role given to Adam is rooted in Genesis 1:26–28 and does not end with the expulsion from the Garden. Rather, the author of Genesis establishes a biblical precedent, an ongoing pattern and biblical mandate to be taken up by other priestly figures, long after the death of Adam. In other words, the formulaic language of Genesis 1 functions as what might be called the "First Great Commission." God's command extends to Adam and his offspring, and this temple-building role is taken up with other priestly figures with whom God calls. The first of these post-Adamic priestly figures is none other than Noah, in a decisive scene in Genesis 9: "And God blessed Noah and his sons, and said to them, "Be fruitful and multiply, and fill the earth ... And you, *be fruitful and multiply*, bring forth abundantly on the earth and multiply in it."[48] This temple-building commission is passed forward from Noah to the patriarchs and, eventually, to Israel herself. Again and again, the pattern of Genesis 1 repeats throughout the various stages of the covenantal story of the Old Testament: "And I will make my covenant between me and you, an*d will multiply you exceedingly ... I will make you exceedingly fruitful*."[49]

Israel inherits the priestly mantle and priestly duties given first to Adam in Eden. Israel was called by God to be a "royal priesthood,"[50] living out this same temple-building commission from God. Central to fulfilling this corporeal priestly identity was God's command for Israel's chosen king, David, to build God's "house" and thus begin to again fill the earth with God's glorious presence (2 Sam. 7:13–14).

47. Beale, *The Temple and the Church's Mission*, 81.

48. Gen. 9:1, 9:7.

49. Gen. 12:2, 17:2, 17:6, 26:4, "I will multiply your descendants as the stars of heaven"; Gen. 28:3, "God Almighty bless you and make you fruitful and multiply you"; Gen. 47:27, "[Israel] gained possessions in it, and were fruitful and multiplied exceedingly."

50. Exod. 19:6.

Extending God's Temple Presence over the Earth

A close reading of the story of Israel suggests a basic continuity with the story of Adam in this respect. Both Adam and Israel were called by God to extend his temple presence over the face of the earth, in various ways. And in various ways both ultimately failed to achieve God's plan. Yet Israel's role in this biblical drama of spreading God's temple presence is considerably more extensive. Adam's opportunity comes and goes in three chapters, yet the story of Israel's role in this temple-building drama unfolds over numerous ages and in many books of the Hebrew Bible.

Later, the prophet Ezekiel develops Israel's future-oriented role in temple building, quite literally in prophetic vision. In chapter 36, the prophet Ezekiel evokes this motif from the Creation narratives of Genesis 1 and 2. Here, the prophet writes that the whole house of Israel is to be "tilled' and "multiplied." The language of Genesis 1 is carefully deployed, as Israel is charged to *increase and be fruitful* (36:11).

The entire prophetic vision describes not only a restoration of Israel as in former days, but also an *eschatological expansion* and an entirely new creation for God's people. Again, this eschatological vision offered by Ezekiel draws decisively upon Edenic language and motifs: "For, behold, I am for you, and I will turn to you, and you shall be tilled and sown; and *I will multiply men upon you*, the whole house of Israel … I will multiply upon you man and beast; and *they shall increase and be fruitful* … Then you will know that I am the Lord" (Ezek. 36:7–11).

Elsewhere, in the prophet Isaiah, a similar recapitulation of the temple theology of Genesis is evident. Yet for Isaiah, biblical motif, in which Adam/Israel is called to "multiply" God's temple presence, is developed slightly differently. Isaiah hones in on a key theological term closely related to the temple motif in Genesis, namely, *light* (LXX: *phos*). Isaiah envisions a future time when an ever-expanding temple will create, as it were, a sanctuary with enormous courts that extend far beyond the land occupied by Israel, such that God's people would truly become "a light to the nations." Isaiah's temple-building motif anticipates the accomplishment of God's intentions, wherein Israel's lived holiness would, over time, gradually draw in Gentiles toward God's presence: "And nations shall come to your light, and kings to the brightness of your rising"[51] (Isa. 60:3–4)

51. Isa. 42:6–7; see also Isa. 60:3–4.

However, the hopes of the prophets, of Ezekiel and Isaiah, were not realized within the history of Israel. In her long story, God's people never truly fulfilled such prophetic mandates, nor did they on their own fulfill this temple-building call, becoming a "light to the nations." Instead, Israel was met by devastating losses: the division of the northern and southern kingdoms, the Assyrian invasion, and, eventually, the destruction of Solomon's Temple by the Babylonians. Along these lines, Israel's prophets conveyed the sobering message that the destruction of the Temple by the Babylonians was a chastisement for this collective failure, God's judgment on his unfaithful "kingdom of priests."

Yet, even in that dark hour, hope remained. The postexilic prophets perceived that God's glory would indeed return to Israel. God's name would be magnified throughout the earth: "Who is left among you that saw this House *in its former glory*? ... I will shake the heavens and the earth and the sea and the dry land; and I will shake all nations, so that the treasures of all nations shall come in, *and I will fill this House with splendor*, says the Lord of hosts ... *The latter splendor of this House shall be greater than the former*" (Hag. 2:2–9).[52]

Even in the latter Maccabean era, hope remained that Israel would eventually achieve the temple-expanding role that God assigned to her: "When we gain control of our kingdom, we will bestow great honor upon you and your nation and the temple, *so that your glory will become manifest in all the earth*" (1 Macc. 15:9). Yet, historically speaking, none of these hopes materialized. Zerubbabel's Second Temple was in no way as glorious as Solomon's majestic one. Israel's enemies were still Israel's enemies. And only in a symbolic way did "all the earth" come to see the glory of the Lord in his Temple, as Egyptians, Greeks, and later Romans did business in the Court of the Gentiles. Israel's priestly calling, to extend God's temple presence and to be a light of the nations, remained an unfinished business and an unfulfilled mission. Gradually, though, the prophets of Israel awakened Israel to faith. They cried out that God's glory would restore this "kingdom of priests," binding them together and giving them victory over their enemies.

All of this would take place in future days, when God's Christ, his anointed Messiah, did for them what they could not do for themselves. N. T. Wright

---

52. See Jer. 23:3: "Then I will gather the remnant of my flock out of all the countries where I have driven them, and I will bring them back to their fold, *and they shall be fruitful and multiply*."

explains why: "The cross stands ... as the arrow which marks the central point of '*the faithfulness of God.*' It is the point from which the enthroned Messiah can look to east and west, to north and south, and like Abraham gaze upon all the lands of his inheritance. Their rulers have now been defeated through his death, and they and their people can be summoned to 'faithful obedience, for the sake of his name.'[53] It is through his 'giving himself for our sins' that he has 'delivered us from the present evil age.'"[54]

The Messianic Temple Builder

The closing chapter of Zechariah envisions a future day when the Messiah-priest comes to redeem his people on the Feast of Tabernacles. It was a "day of reckoning," when God's Messiah will judge the peoples who have punished Israel. But it is also a day of triumph, when God becomes king over all of Israel and all of the earth: "On that day *living waters shall flow out from Jerusalem*, half of them to the eastern sea and half of them to the western sea; it shall continue in summer as in winter. And the Lord will become king over all the earth; on that day the Lord will be one and his name one" (Zech. 14:8–9).

As such, Jesus, Israel's true Messiah and true priest-king, was achieving for Israel what God had commissioned Israel to do but that she did not achieve—to extend the Temple over the whole of the earth. What the New Testament proclaims is that Jesus indeed recapitulated Adam and Israel's temple-building mission in a glorious, spiritual, and sacramental way. N. T. Wright explains what this means with respect to the Gospels: "Jesus, completely in line with the hope of Israel, was to be seen as *the genuine human being, the 'true Adam', the ultimate image-bearer, doing for Adam what Adam could not do for himself*, reversing the 'fall' and rein-scribing the notion that image-bearing humans were to be set in authority over God's creation."[55]

Wright goes on, "When he receives the inheritance which is his as Messiah ... this is also both the 'inheritance' which was promised to Abraham and (since Abraham's task was to reverse the problem of Adam and so to get

---

53. See Gen. 13:14; cf. Gen. 28:14; Psa. 2:8; Rom. 1:5, 8:17.

54. N. T. Wright, *Paul and the Faithfulness of God*, vol. 4, *Christian Origins and the Question of God* (Minneapolis: Fortress Press, 2013), 911 (emphasis added).

55. Ibid., 908. See Rom. 5:14–21, 8:29; 1 Cor. 1:20–28; Phil. 3:20*ff.*

the 'true humanity' project back on track) the 'inheritance' of Adam himself. Jesus as Messiah thus inherits all that God had promised to Israel in the person of the king, that is, sovereignty over the world. With that, Jesus stands, for Paul, *where Adam stood in Genesis 1:26–28*."[56]

Concluding Remarks

Throughout this chapter, four particular insights were discussed as they pertain to temple theology. First, the collective evidence of Scripture overwhelmingly suggests that Adam was more than a tiller of soil; he was a priest-king, the high priest of Eden. In Beale's words, Adam, as "God's vice-regent," was supposed to "put the finishing touches on the world" that God began, "making it a livable place for all, in order that they would achieve the grand aim of glorifying Him."[57] Second, evidence from apocryphal texts, such as Jubilees and the *Life of Adam and Eve*, not only supports this but also serves to clarify how Adam's priestly role was understood in Judaism just prior to the first century. Third, Adam's role "was to spread God's luminescent presence by extending the boundaries of the original Edenic temple outward into the earth."[58] Beale emphasizes that "Adam's kingly and priestly activity in the Garden was to be a beginning fulfillment of the original commission in 1:28 and was not limited to the garden's original earthly boundaries but was to be *extended over the whole world*."[59] Fourth and finally, just as Adam was called to be God's temple builder, so were the covenantal figures of Noah, Abraham, and the like.

Ultimately, as a "kingdom of priests," Israel was commissioned, just as Adam was before her, to extend God's temple presence over the entire earth. Historically, Israel did not fulfill this "Great Commission" first given to the high priest Adam in Genesis. Yet, typologically and prophetically, the later prophets of the Old Testament foresaw a New Creation. And in it, God's own Messiah would accomplish Israel's priestly mission, and Adam's too, in extending God's temple presence to all of humanity, beginning in Jerusalem.

56. Wright, *Paul and the Faithfulness of God*, 908.
57. Beale, *The Temple and the Church's Mission*, 82.
58. Ibid.   59. Ibid., 83.

5

PRIESTS AND PRIESTHOOD IN THE PATRIARCHAL ERA

Temple Priesthood in the Old and New Testaments (II/IV)

When they came to the place of which God had told him, Abraham built an altar there, and laid the wood in order, and bound Isaac his son, and laid him on the altar, upon the wood. Then Abraham put forth his hand, and took the knife to slay his son. But the angel of the Lord called to him from heaven, and said, "Abraham, Abraham!" And he said, "Here am I." He said, "Do not lay your hand on the lad or do anything to him; for now I know that you fear God, seeing you have not withheld your son, your only son, from me."

Genesis 22:9–12

Contrary to popular misconception, the priesthood of the Israelites did not originate with Aaron and the Levites. According to the sacred authors, the origins of the priesthood can be traced back to the high priest Adam and from there, into its patriarchal developments, and only later to the Levites. One scholar describes the religion of the patriarchs as having an "unmediatedness" in that they had no prophets or priests to act on their behalf.[1]

1. R. W. L. Moberly, *The Old Testament of the Old Testament: Patriarchal Narratives and Mosaic Yahwism* (Philadelphia: Fortress, 1992), 94. "The patriarchs have neither prophet nor priest to mediate between themselves and God, nor do they themselves fulfill the role of either prophet or priest with regard to others. There is a quality of unmediatedness about the patriarchal religion, which contrasts with the central roles that prophet and priest hold in Mosaic Yahwism."

Priests before Priesthood

The patriarchs were "without prophet and priest" strictly speaking, and enacted these respective "offices" in primeval ways. In other words, the patriarchs *did* participate in cultic, priestly actions—even if such actions, particularly the Temple sacrifices, looked quite different in the age of Levitical priesthood that was still to come.

The priesthood of the patriarchal period was of a more primitive and natural order. It was passed from father to son in a familial manner. Priestly duties were taught at home, as "mediation" was patriarchally passed from one generation to the next, from father to son. Sacrifices were not originally offered at fixed sites, but at the discretion of the patriarchs, who practiced a form of natural religion.

By way of example, consider the term *mincah* ("offering"), which seems to belong to the age of the Temple. Yet, surprisingly, it has roots that go back *well before* the patriarchal period. In fact, the term is first used in the narrative of the sacrifice of Abel: "In the course of time Cain brought to the Lord an offering [Hebrew: *mincah*] of the fruit of the ground, and Abel brought of the firstlings of his flock and of their fat portions. And the Lord had regard for Abel and his offering, but for Cain and his offering he had no regard" (Gen. 4:3–4).

An early example of this sort of early priestly figure is Noah. While he is not explicitly identified as a *kohen* ("priest"),[2] he acts the part by constructing an altar to worship God—the first alter mentioned in Scripture: "Then Noah built an altar to the Lord, and took of every clean animal and of every clean bird, and offered burnt offerings on the altar" (Gen. 8:20).

Following this Noahic example, all of the patriarchs, Abraham, Isaac, and Jacob likewise, build altars and in turn offer sacrifices to God. The "binding of Isaac" (Gen. 22:3–8) is a notable example and, from a Catholic biblical perspective, points forward in a typological way to the sacrifice of the "new Isaac," the sacrifice of God's own Son, Jesus.

Numerous patristic and medieval theologians dealt with this decisive passage of the "sacrifice" of Isaac. For many early patristic writers, the entire passage was interpreted allegorically, such that Isaac prefigured Christ, whom God the Father does not spare but is offered up for the deliverance of all.

---

2. The first figure to be identified as *kohen* in the Old Testament is Melchizidek (Gen. 14:18).

Although later theologians did not usually adhere to the allegorical framework of patristic writers before them, the Tradition is remarkably cohesive in its pattern of exegesis: the sacrifice of Isaac pointed forward to Jesus whom God willing sacrificed in atonement for the sins of humanity.

Consider the fourth-century bishop and doctor of the Church, St. Ephrem, who worked it out in an Eastern way, and in a liturgically poetic style, "In place of Isaac the just, a ram appeared for slaughter, in order that Isaac might be liberated from his bonds. The slaughter of the animal redeemed Isaac from death. In like manner, the Lord being slain, saved us."[3]

By comparison, St. Ambrose highlights the "father-son" motif in the more direct style of catechesis of the Western Church: "[Abraham] brought his beloved son to be sacrificed and him whom he had begotten so late he offered without delay. Nor was he held back by being addressed as father, when his son called him 'father' and answered 'my son.'"[4]

Even today, modern Catholic theologians generally build upon the foundations established across two thousand years of theological interpretation of the "sacrifice" of Isaac: "[Abraham] is given something else to offer instead of the son of God—a male lamb. And so representative sacrifice is established by divine command. God gives the lamb, which Abraham then offers back to him ... Somehow there always has to be a stinging reminder of this story, an expectation of the true Lamb, who comes from God and is for that very reason not a replacement but a true representative, in whom we ourselves are taken to God."[5]

Moreover, "priestly" treatments of Genesis 22 have a long and respected pedigree in the history of biblical interpretation. From earliest Christianity, Abraham's "binding" of Isaac was interpreted as priestly and sacrificial actions, actions that ultimately testified to Abraham's righteousness. Contem-

---

3. St. Melito of Sardis, *Catena on Genesis*.

4. St. Ambrose, *On His Brother, Satyrus* 2.97. See also *Summa Theologica* I–II, q. 103, a. 1, ad 1: "The patriarchs offered up these oblations, sacrifices and holocausts previously to the Law, out of a certain devotion of their own will, according as it seemed proper to them to offer up in honor of God those things which they had received from Him, and thus to testify that they worshipped God Who is the beginning and end of all."

5. Joseph Ratzinger, *The Spirit of the Liturgy*, trans. John Saward (San Francisco: Ignatius Press, 2000), 38. "The Christian theology of worship—beginning with St. John the Baptist—sees in Christ the Lamb given by God. The *Apocalypse* presents this sacrificed Lamb, who lives as sacrificed, as the center of the heavenly liturgy, a liturgy that, through Christ's Sacrifice, is now present in the midst of the world and makes replacement liturgies superfluous (see Rev. 5)."

porary theologian Margaret Barker adds, "The story of the [binding] of Isaac was important for the Church: the earliest surviving lectionaries show that it was read on Maundy Thursday or Good Friday."[6]

For its part, the *Catechism* describes Genesis 22 in a decidedly sacrificial way: "As a final stage in the purification of his faith, Abraham, 'who had received the promises'[7] is asked to sacrifice the son God had given him. Abraham's faith does not weaken ('God himself will provide the lamb for a burnt offering'), for he 'considered that God was able to raise men even from the dead.'[8] And so the father of believers is conformed to the likeness of the Father who will not spare his own Son but will deliver him up for us all."[9]

The Royal Priesthood of Melchizidek

The above discussion underscores that the author of Genesis conceived of a pre-Levitical and more natural sort of father-son priesthood. A concise look at the "sacrifice of Isaac" in Genesis 22 bears this out, and is supported by two millennia of theological reflection. Next, the discussion turns to an archetypal figure of priesthood in the pre-Levitical, patriarchal period.

Looming over the various priestly figures of the patriarchal period is that of Melchizidek (Gen. 14). Here is a singularly mysterious figure who all but vanishes from the canon as soon as he appears. Even the biblical name of this figure is enigmatic and compelling. "Melchizidek" derives from two Hebrew terms: *melek*, meaning "king," and *siddiq*, meaning "righteous." Taken as a whole, the name may be translated as "king of righteousness" or, alternatively, "my king is righteous." Genesis describes him as king of Salem, a striking fact in that the Psalter indicates that Salem is an older form of Jerusalem: "In Judah God is known, his name is great in Israel. His abode has been established *in Salem*, his dwelling place in Zion" (Psa. 76:1–2). The identification of Salem with Jerusalem in the Hebrew Bible is similarly evident in rabbinic sources and confirmed by the Jewish historian Josephus.[10]

This connection between Salem and Jerusalem is deeply important. Typologically, Melchizidek's ministry in Salem prefigures David's priesthood and Jesus's ministry in Jerusalem (as well as the "heavenly" Jerusalem). Melchizidek

---

6. Margaret Barker, *Temple Themes in Christian Worship*, 3rd ed. (London: Bloomsbury, 2013), 31.
7. Heb. 11:17.   8. Gen. 22:8; see Heb. 11:19.
9. *Catechism of the Catholic Church*, §2573; see Rom. 8:32.
10. See Josephus, *Jewish Wars* VI.10.

is the first individual in Scripture who is explicitly identified as a *kohen* ("priest").[11] Likewise, of all of the figures in Genesis, Melchizidek is the only one in the book called a priest of *'El 'Elyon*, "God Most High."[12] He further brings forth "bread and wine" in thanksgiving to Abram's God, possibly suggesting a covenantal meal between them.[13] For all of these reasons, Melchizidek represents a mysterious archetype of the Patriarchal priesthood.[14]

In Genesis, the precise identity and background of the figure Melchizidek remains a puzzle. Ancient Judaism offered forth a number of possibilities: Melchizidek the angel, heavenly judge, and so on. The most striking of all is that Melchizidek was none other than Shem, the righteous son of Noah. The literary case for such an interpretation is as follows. Genesis 11:10 indicates that Shem lived for six hundred years, into the age of Abraham. The righteous line of Shem leads from Noah to Abraham, and he, like Noah, is set apart from all humanity as a "righteous father" and a blessing to many. Numerous rabbinic texts make explicit the Melchizidek-Shem connection.[15] Elsewhere, *Targum Neophyti* refers to Melchizidek as "the Great Shem."

In patristic Christianity, St. Jerome[16] accepted this interpretation. Much later, St. Thomas did as well:[17] "What may have been more important than the form of this passage is that Yahweh in *Gen.* 9:26 is called the '*God of Shem*,' and in Gen. 14:18 Melchizedek appears as priest of *El-Elyon*, which deity the rabbis as well as Philo and Josephus identified with the true God. Between Gen. 9:26 and 14:18 *there is no other passage in which Yahweh is said to be the God of anyone other than Shem.*"[18]

11. See Gen. 14:8.

12. The title *'El 'Elyon* occurs in the Hebrew Bible only here and in Psa. 78:35. It appears to be an ancient formulation meaning "great or exalted one." Nahum M. Sarna, *Genesis: The JPS Torah Commentary* (Philadelphia: Jewish Publication Society, 1989), 381. See also Gordon J. Wenham, *Genesis 1–15*, vol. 1, Word Biblical Commentary (Waco, TX: Word Books, 1987), 318; M. H. Pope. *El in the Ugaritic Texts*, vol. 2, *Vetus Testamentum Supplements* (Leiden: Brill, 1955); F. M. Cross, *Canaanite Myth and Hebrew Epic* (Cambridge, MA: Harvard University Press, 1973), 50–51.

13. Bruce Vawter, *On Genesis: A New Reading* (Garden City, NJ: Doubleday, 1977), 196; A. Viberg, *Symbols of Law: A Contextual Analysis of Legal Symbolic Acts in the Old Testament* (Stockholm: Almqvist & Wiksell, 1992), 76. But see Wenham, *Genesis 1–15*, 316.

14. S. W. Hahn, *Kinship by Covenant: A Canonical Approach to the Fulfillment of God's Saving Promises* (New Haven, CT: Yale University Press, 2009), 131.

15. See *Genesis Rabbah* 46:7; *Leviticus Rabbah* 25:6.

16. See Jerome, *Questiones*, 14.18.

17. See Thomas's *Commentary on Hebrews*.

18. F. L. Horton, *The Melchizedek Tradition* (New York: Cambridge University Press, 1976), 117 (emphasis added).

Beyond his appearance in Genesis, the Sacred Scriptures offer sparse clues as to Melchizidek's origins and his destiny. The Psalter contains the only other explicit reference to him. Specifically, Psalm 110 indicates that David was a priest in the "order of Melchizidek" (v. 4). This is astounding, as David was not a Levite; according to the Torah, only Levites could serve as priests.[19] In this way, the psalmist asserts that David inherits the priestly mantle of Melchizidek. David is a true priestly figure, but he is not a Levitical one. This is an important development in the biblical text and one that illustrates the way in which temple theology often involves typological connections that are rooted in the Old Testament and correspond to related texts in the New Testament.

While David's priestly status is not discussed in 2 Samuel 7, it is clearly demonstrated in the previous chapter. There, David offers sacrifice (v. 13), wears an ephod (the garment of a priest, v. 14), pitches the sacred tent and sacrifices in it (v. 17), blesses the people (v. 18), and distributes bread to the people (v. 19). In these priestly actions, David represents a priest-king after the manner of Melchizidek himself, who was a bread-bringing priest-king in Jerusalem. Melchizidek's priesthood in Salem prefigures not only David's priestly identity but also Jesus's priestly ministry in Jerusalem, a matter that will be discussed in more depth later in the book. Hebrews sees in Melchizidek a prefigurement of Jesus's eternal high priesthood: "Jesus has gone as a forerunner on our behalf, *having become a high priest for ever after the order of Melchizedek*" (Heb. 6:19–20).

The message of the Book of Hebrews is clear: Jesus's high priesthood is not derived from the Levitical line, nor is it subject to the manner in which the Levitical priesthood had become corrupted over time. Instead, Jesus's priesthood is utterly unique—"holy, blameless, unstained, and separated from sinners, exalted above the heavens." Moreover, unlike the fallible and mortal high priests of the Temple, who offered sacrifices day after day, he did so "once for all when he offered up himself" (Heb. 7:26–27).

The Temple of Sinai

Collectively, the above evidence suggests that various biblical authors took for granted that there existed a kind of primordial, mysterious priesthood that

---

19. Exod. 40:12–15.

preceded the Levitical line that began with Aaron. Not only this, but a key passage in the Book of Exodus offers yet another image of a primordial temple. It is as if the narrative of Exodus, which has clearly moved on beyond Genesis, nevertheless takes certain cues from Genesis, and in a sense looks back to the cosmological temple described in the earlier book. Exodus does not envision some sort of return to Eden. Rather, as Israel leaves captivity in Egypt, it arrives at a new mountain sanctuary. There, God will forge an entirely new phase of his relationship with his people. And in a pivotal covenantal scene in the Old Testament, God binds himself to his people through the mediation of Moses, and the mountain sanctuary where it transpires is Mt. Sinai.[20]

The prophet Ezekiel refers to Sinai as "the mountain of God," a theological phrase associated with both the Garden sanctuary of Mt. Eden as well as that of Solomon's Temple on Mt. Zion.[21] God's covenant with Moses is solemnized on a mountain, on Sinai, just as the covenants with Adam and Noah were solemnized on mountains—Eden and Ararat, respectively: "So Moses rose with his servant Joshua, and Moses went up into *the mountain of God*" (Exod. 24:13). Commenting on this text, Beale observes, "Not only does the top part of Sinai approximate the *Holy of Holies* because only Israel's 'high priest,' Moses, could enter there, but it was the place where God's theophanic cloud and presence 'dwelt.'"[22]

Beale is correct in his assertion that the depiction of Sinai as a proto-temple is rooted in the theology of the Book of Exodus, with its precise instructions for the construction of the Tabernacle. The Tent of Meeting was from the outset to be the earthly representation of the *heavenly tabernacle*, "according to all that I show you" (Exod. 25:9).

In support of Beale's argument, both Jewish and Christian exegetes over the centuries have identified the Mosaic Tabernacle as a "copy" of its heavenly prototype, such that Mt. Sinai is seen as a kind of primordial temple. For instance, Philo of Alexandria writes of the correspondence that was necessary in fashioning the sacred vessels after the divine pattern revealed to Moses:

20. "The location of Sinai is debated, but wherever it is, and wherever in Midian Moses started from, the Sinai Peninsula is aptly described as "wilderness." D. W. Baker, *Dictionary of the Old Testament: Pentateuch*, s.v. "Wilderness, Desert."

21. On Eden as the "mountain of God," see Ezek. 28:14, 28:16; on Solomon's Temple as the "mountain of God," see Exod. 3:1, 18:5. See G. K. Beale, *The Temple and the Church's Mission: A Biblical Theology of the Dwelling Place of God* (Downers Grove, IL: InterVarsity Press, 2004), 105.

22. Beale, *The Temple and the Church's Mission*, 105. See Exod. 24:15–17.

Moses determined to build a most holy Sanctuary, the furniture of which he was instructed to supply by precise commands from God … for it was suitable and consistent for the task of preparing and furnishing the Temple to be entrusted to the real high priest, that he might with all due perfection and propriety make all his [actions] in the performance of his sacred duties *correspond* to the works which he was now to make.[23]

Likewise, in his allegorical commentary on the Song of Songs, Origen, arguably the most significant patristic figure of the second century, writes of the "angelic mediation" involved in the giving of the Ark of the Covenant, the mercy seat and even the Temple itself: *all given to Israel by the angels*.[24] In other words, Origen asserted that the Temple was sacred because it replicates the holiness of the true temple in heaven above: "Moses … made the tent of meeting in obedience to God's command, according to the pattern he had seen on the mountain. This means that *the earthly Temple is only a replica, not the true Temple*. It is an image and likeness, which points beyond itself."[25]

In the identification of Sinai as a proto-temple, the high priestly personage of Aaron (and, in a sense, Moses with him) is integral in the divine gift described in Exodus, in which God declares to Israel: "You shall be my own possession among all peoples; for all the earth is mine, and you shall be to me a *kingdom of priests* and a holy nation" (Exod. 19:5–6).

There is a *typological* connection here as well. In the New Testament, it is likely that the language of 1 Peter looks back to the priestly scene at Sinai—to the priesthood of the Israelites, in the image of the Church of Christ as a "chosen race, a royal priesthood" (1 Pet. 2:9). This identification of members of the Church as "royal priesthood" undoubtedly has a Christological motive: just as Moses (i.e., Aaron) is the high priest figure of Mt. Sinai, so now Jesus is the high priest of Mt. Calvary.

Beale explains that there was in the proto-temple at Sinai a threefold division, with "increasing levels" of holiness. This corresponds to the later Tabernacle of the wilderness and the Temple of Jerusalem: "As with the … Temple, so

---

23. Philo of Alexandria, *The Life of Moses*, II.74–75. *Works of Philo: Complete and Unabridged* (Peabody, MA: Hendrickson, 1995), 497. My own translation supplied here slightly modifies the text for clarity.

24. Origen, *Commentary on the Canticles*, 2. See Jean Daniélou, *The Angels and Their Mission* (Manchester, NH: Sophia Institute Press, 2009). Originally published as *Les Anges et Leur Mission* (Chevetogne, Belgium: Editions de Chevetogne, 1953), 9.

25. Ratzinger, *Spirit of the Liturgy*, 41 (emphasis added). See Exod. 25:40; Acts 7:44.

Mount Sinai was divided into three sections of increasing sanctity. The majority of the Israelites were to remain at the foot of Sinai.[26] The priests and seventy elders were allowed to come some distance up the mountain.[27] Only Moses could ascend to the top[28] and directly experience the presence of God."[29]

Ratzinger agrees and adds that the work of Moses—in constructing the Tabernacle and ordering Israel's worship there—was a unique role. Looking ahead to the New Testament, he explains that, in a similar manner as Moses, "the new Prophet, the definitive Prophet, will lead the people out of the age of the Tabernacle and its impermanence, out of all the inadequacy of sacrificial animals."[30]

A Recapitulation of Eden

Stepping back from the text of Exodus, what can be concluded about the movement from Eden to Sinai? What is the relationship between the two mountains as it pertains to temple theology? The answer is clear: the covenantal scene at Sinai represents in its entirety a *recapitulation* of the Garden Temple of Eden. What Adam (along with his wife and his descendants) had forfeited at Mt. Eden was being renewed at Sinai, and graciously gifted to Moses and the Israelites.

Recall that Adam was called to extend God's temple presence beyond the Holy Place of Eden, to extend his holiness to the "outer courts," reaching out to the ends of the earth. From a human perspective, Adam's temple-building commission was contingent upon his cooperation with Divine grace. In other words, to the extent that Adam, who was made in the image and likeness of God, was "fruitful and multiplied," God's temple presence would continue to fill the earth with holiness.

Yet such is not how the story turned out. In defying and disobeying God, Adam was "cut off" from the Tree of Life, from the primordial Holy Place, and subsequently expelled from the Garden Temple. Now, at Sinai, God renews his relationship with humanity, through the mediation of a new high priest: Moses. As at Mt. Eden, now at Sinai, in a new and fresh way, God

---

26. Exod. 19:12, 19:23.   27. Exod. 19:22, 24:1.
28. Exod. 24:2.
29. Beale, *The Temple and the Church's Mission*, 105.
30. Ratzinger, *Spirit of the Liturgy*, 41.

calls a high priestly figure and his "offspring" (Israel) to extend God's temple presence beyond the Holy Place, to the outer courts of the world (i.e., the Canaanites).

This is no small connection. In fact, the implications are far reaching. Reflecting on the connection between the Creation narrative of Genesis and its recapitulation at Sinai, Margaret Barker observes that the predominant thinking in ancient Judaism was that Moses had the mystical experience of "seeing" God's heavenly temple during his six days on Mt. Sinai: "Moses had a vision [on Sinai] of the creation which became the six days of Genesis. Day One was the state of unity underlying and sustaining the whole creation, represented by the angels and the throne of God, and in the Tabernacle/Temple it was the *Holy of Holies*. The second day was the firmament separating what was above from what was below (Gen. 1:6), represented by the veil that separated the *Holy of Holies* from the hall of the Tabernacle/temple. On the third day, the plants were created, represented by the table offerings of cereal, wine and incense. On the fourth day, the lights of heaven were created, represented by the seven-branched [menorah]."[31]

In concluding her analysis of the early Jewish tradition, Barker suggests that Moses constructed the Tabernacle in stages corresponding to the six days of Creation. This leads to an important parallel between Adam and the figure of the high priest, as she points out: "When God created [Adam] on the sixth day, he created the high priest for the Temple, the one who had access to the presence of God at the heart of creation."[32]

The Mystery of the Firstborn

The priesthood of the patriarchal era was of a *familial* sort. A pattern of primogeniture (i.e., firstborn) characterized the priesthood of this period. This primordial priesthood is implicit in the earliest biblical texts of Genesis, yet within Exodus this "priestly primogeniture" becomes explicit with respect to all of Israel. In Exodus, all of Israel is identified by God as his "firstborn" (Exod. 4:22).

This leads to a significant insight as to the deeper purpose of the priestly primogeniture with which Israel was gifted by God at the beginning of Cre-

31. Barker, *Temple Themes in Christian Worship*, 11–12.
32. Ibid.

ation. Such primogeniture had a purpose in the life of Israel. Specifically, it had an "outward looking" dimension to it: you are (to become) a kingdom of priests" (Exod. 19:6). Priest to whom? To Israel? To the world? Yes and yes.

The priestly primogeniture in the Book of Exodus appears to be yet another recurrence of the biblical pattern established back in Genesis. Just as the high priest Adam was called to "multiply," or extend, God's temple presence beyond the Garden, so too Israel, God's firstborn, was called to be a "kingdom of priests" with respect to the nations (Exod. 19:6).[33] Looking beyond the Old Testament to the New, Ratzinger addresses how this pattern of priestly primogeniture points to the person of Christ in the Gospel of Luke and later in the Captivity Epistles of St. Paul: "The lamb appears clearly as the ransom through which Israel is delivered from the death of the firstborn ... This fact should help us appreciate the emphatic way in which St. Luke in his infancy narratives describes Jesus as the first-born."[34]

The mystery of the firstborn unfolds throughout the Book of Exodus in three stages. The first stage follows after the revelation of God's name to Moses at Sinai: "And you shall say to Pharaoh, 'Thus says the Lord, *Israel is my first-born son* and I say to you, "*Let my son go that he may serve me*"; if you refuse to let him go, behold, I will slay *your first-born son*'" (Exod. 4:22–23). This can be compared with another biblical text, from the deuterocanonical Book of Sirach: "Have mercy, O Lord, upon the people called by thy name, upon Israel, *whom thou hast likened to a firstborn son*" (Sir. 36:12).

The second stage is Passover, when Israel's firstborn sons are redeemed and the firstborn sons of their enemies are slain. The redemption and forever-after memorial of this redemption is the Passover Lamb, which is slain and eaten: "They shall eat the flesh [of the Lamb] that night, roasted; with unleavened bread and bitter herbs they shall eat it" (Exod. 12:8). Thereafter, every firstborn male was consecrated to God as a sign of this great redemption: "*Consecrate to me all the first-born*; whatever is the first to open the womb among the people of Israel, both of man and of beast, is mine ... *The first-born of your sons you shall give to me*" (Exod. 13:2, 22:9). This text from the Book of Exodus may be compared with a similar passage in the Infancy

---

33. See N. H. Sarna, *Exodus: The JPS Torah Commentary* (Philadelphia: Jewish Publication Society, 1991), who comments on the identity of "the priests" in Exod. 19:22: "And also let the priests who come near to the Lord consecrate themselves, lest the Lord break out upon them" (107).

34. Ratzinger, *Spirit of the Liturgy*, 38.

Narrative in the Gospel of Luke: "When the time came for their purification according to the law of Moses, they brought him up to Jerusalem to present him to the Lord, as it is written in the law of the Lord, '*Every male that opens the womb shall be called holy to the Lord*'" (Luke 2:22).

The third and final stage transpires as the Israelites approach Sinai, and the giving of the Law: "you shall be to me a kingdom of priests (*mamleket kōhanîm*) and a holy nation." Here, God reasserts the filial identity of all Israel, with covenantal provisions. If Israel keeps the covenant with him, she will be "my own possession (*segullâ*) among all peoples."[35]

With God's revelation of the heavenly pattern of the Tabernacle, which Moses and Aaron were instructed to build (Exod. 25:9), Mt. Sinai emerges as a kind of proto-temple, recapitulating the Temple of Eden. The parallel becomes more evident as one reads the narrative of the Mosaic covenant given on Sinai; just as Adam and his descendants were called to be God's temple builders, extending his holy presence beyond Eden, so are Moses and Aaron, and all the Israelites called to become God's temple-building people among the pagan nations around them.

God's Firstborn Sons: The Light to the World

To fully grasp the greater purpose of Israel being God's "firstborn" in Exodus 4, one must read on to Exodus 19, where the priestly primogeniture of Israel is given a mission: to bless the nations of the earth. Again, the pattern established in Genesis 1–2, between God and his priest Adam, is being recapitulated in the Book of Exodus. The remarkable promises to Israel always carried—just as they once did with Adam—an outward orientation, a mission of "multiplying" God's temple holiness. Several texts from the prophet Isaiah underscore these greater responsibilities: "I will give you as a light to the nations, that my salvation may reach to the end of the earth" (Isa. 49:6); "*And nations shall come to your light, and kings to the brightness of your rising. Lift up your eyes round about, and see; they all gather together, they come to you … Then you shall see and be radiant*, your heart shall thrill and rejoice; because the abundance of the sea shall be turned to you" (Isa. 60:3–6).

As the study turns from the Old to the New Testament, a paradigmatic

35. Hahn, *Kinship by Covenant*, 140.

pattern will be seen. This priestly mandate, belonging first to Adam alone and then to all Israel, is applied to the Church. Mirroring the pattern established in the Old Testament, the "sons and daughters" of the Almighty (2 Cor. 6:18) are called to be the "light to the nations." In the Sermon on the Mount, Jesus says, "*You are the light of the world. A city set on a hill cannot be hid.* Nor do men light a lamp and put it under a bushel, but on a stand, and it gives light to all in the house. *Let your light so shine before men, that they may see your good works and give glory to your Father who is in heaven*" (Matt. 5:14–16). Here, Acts recalls the Old Testament mandate of God calling for Israel to be a "light to the Gentiles," and to "bring salvation to the ends of the earth" (Acts 13:46–49). The motif is also seen in 1 Peter: "But you are a chosen race, a royal priesthood, a holy nation, God's own people, that you may declare the wonderful deeds of him who called you out of darkness *into his marvelous light*" (1 Pet. 2:9).

Concluding Remarks

The patriarchal period was a key stage in the temple theology of the Old Testament. During this period, priestly actions were not yet defined by the characteristics of the later Levitical order, nor rooted in the institution of the Tabernacle or Temple. Rather, this more ancient form of biblical priesthood developed beyond the Garden. It was characterized and governed by the "will" to worship God—or not. Biblical figures such as Abel, Noah, Shem, and Abram typify the "priest" who offers the self back to God as a wholehearted offering of thanksgiving. In contrast, their counterparts and others found in Scripture withheld their very self or offered sacrifices half-heartedly. They have names like Cain, Lemech, and Ham—and among their "offspring" are the Canaanites, Jebusites, and other peoples that defy the living God in unholy worship.

The quintessential archetype of the holy priest of this patriarchal period is not one who "inherits" his office from any human source. Rather, his priesthood is uncompromised and unique. It is even said elsewhere that he was without father or mother. It is the enigmatic Melchizidek who almost unnoticeably offers *unmitigated praise* to the God of Abram, to *'El 'Elyon*. Similar to Mary in the New Testament, his words are few but filled with holy resolve. Like Mary, one must pay close attention to Melchizidek's faith-saturated actions, and not merely the brevity of his words.

Though Melchizidek's role in the biblical drama is brief and easily over-shadowed by the likes of Abraham, Isaac, Jacob, or even Moses, his return in Psalm 110 creates an unmistakable impression as to his importance in the temple theology of the Old Testament. For, despite his brief time onstage, it is Melchizidek—and not the aforementioned patriarchs—who reemerges in the drama of the Book of Hebrews. There, Melchizidek is held up, higher in some sense than the Holy Place of the institutional temple, as the image of the "priest of God." And in his sweeping, rhetorical critique of the "former covenant," the author of Hebrews looks back to the priest-king of Salem in extolling the eternal high priesthood of Jesus:

But when Christ appeared as a high priest of the good things that have come, then through the greater and more perfect tent (not made with hands, that is, not of this creation) he entered once for all into the Holy Place, taking not the blood of goats and calves but his own blood, thus securing an eternal redemption. (Heb. 9:11–12)

Later in chapter 19, when the focus turns from the temple theology of the Old Testament to the New, more of Melchizidek's significance will be discussed. For now, it is the complex temple theology of the Old Testament that demands much more attention. Chapter 6 will treat a decisive stage in the temple theology of the Old Testament, that of the Levitical priesthood.

6

THE PRIESTHOOD
OF THE LEVITES

Temple Priesthood in the Old and
New Testaments (III/IV)

> You shall consecrate [the priest], for he offers the bread of
> your God; he shall be holy to you; for I the Lord, who sanc-
> tify you, am holy.
>
> Leviticus 21:8

The Origins of the Levitical Priesthood

With Moses as their mediator, Israel accepts God's gracious offer of being God's firstborn sons—at least initially. The Torah is given, and the covenant is ritually sealed with a mutual oath in Exodus 24, an important passage: "Moses rose early in the morning, and built an altar at the foot of the
mountain, and twelve pillars, according to the twelve tribes of Israel ... Then
he took the book of the covenant, and read it in the hearing of the people ...
*And Moses took the blood and threw it upon the people, and said, 'Behold the
blood of the covenant which the Lord has made with you in accordance with all
these words'"* (Exod. 24:3–8).

Yet the Israelites soon broke their oath, with the great apostasy of the
Golden Calf.[1] As Moses prayed atop Mt. Sinai, many broke faith with Yahweh and fashioned an image of the Egyptian god Apis. The resulting apostasy suggests to some a correlation with the Garden: "The [Golden Calf inci-

---

1. See Exod. 33–34.

dent] brought about a massive reconfiguration in the socio-religious life and structure of Israel. Not only did it cause Israel's firstborn sons to forfeit their royal priesthood, along with the nation itself, but it also brought in its wake a whole series of catastrophic rebellions. The consequences of the golden calf for Israel are staggering. Not without truth can it be said that *what the tree was for Adam, the golden calf was for Israel.*"[2]

It is clear that God revoked earlier priestly privileges enjoyed by many in Israel, rerouting them from the "many" (firstborn) to the "few" (the Levites). Priestly privileges are granted to the Levites, who are depicted as stepping forth at the crucial hour under Moses's leadership: "And Moses said, 'Today you have ordained yourselves for the service of the Lord, each one at the cost of his son and of his brother, that he may bestow a blessing upon you this day'" (Exod. 32:26, 32:28).

Given such an interpretation, an earlier text in Exodus seems to anticipate this shift in priestly identity: "And you shall say to Pharaoh, 'Thus says the Lord, Israel is my *first-born son.*'"[3] As one scholar writes, "Israel is God's *segulla* … Israel is to exercise the privileges and the responsibilities of the first-born of all God's sons—the other nations and peoples of the world." In other words, the firstborn sons of God are called to be "the priest-nation for the nations of the world, exercising the responsibility of priestly instruction and intercession in behalf of all peoples before Yahweh."

The Threefold Structure of Clerical Service

From this point forward, priesthood in Israel reached *a new stage.* Now, it was entrusted to the Levites as a safeguard so that all Israel would have a way to approach God in holiness: "And you shall take the Levites for me … *instead of all the first-born among the people of Israel*" (Num. 3:41). The larger aim of the Levitical priesthood was to proclaim the holiness of God in ritual action and enforce holiness toward him by all Israel. There was a threefold division in the Levitical priestly system, as follows.

---

2. S. W. Hahn, *Kinship by Covenant: A Canonical Approach to the Fulfillment of God's Saving Promises* (London: Yale University Press, 2009), 174 (emphasis added).

3. Exod. 4:22. W. Harrelson, *Interpreting the Old Testament* (New York: Holt, Rinehart and Winston, 1964), 92.

The High Priesthood

The first division is the office of the high priest. As the Book of Leviticus records, Aaron, the brother of Moses, served as Israel's first high priest, and liturgically it is Moses who officiates at Aaron's ordination: "And he put on [Aaron] the coat, and girded him with the girdle, and clothed him with the robe, and put the ephod upon him ... And he placed the breast piece on him, and in the breast piece he put the Urim and the Thummim. And he set the turban upon his head, and on the turban, in front, he set the golden plate, the holy crown, as the Lord commanded Moses" (Lev. 8:6–9). More details on the high priest will be provided below. For now, the discussion turns to the priestly office under the care of the high priest, and who carried out many duties on his behalf.

The Levitical Priesthood

Only descendants of Aaron himself could enter into the priesthood. The office of the Aaronic high priest was a hereditary birthright—not a vocation, as in the modern office of the Roman Catholic priesthood, for example. The Jewish high priestly office was based upon a principle known as *qidusshat 'olam* ("lifelong sanctity").[4] The uniqueness of his office "was transmitted to him by the investiture with the eight-parts of his high-priestly vesture."[5] His vesture "possessed atoning power," and each of its eight parts atones for specific sins.

It was the high priest alone who entered into the Holy of Holies once a year, on the Day of Atonement.[6] As Josephus writes, "But for the most sacred place, none went in but the high priests, clothed in their peculiar garments."[7] As noted in Leviticus, there were four primary vestments: white linen robe, white linen trousers, turban, and girdle. There were also four specialty items: golden breastplate, ephod (i.e., apron with straps), seamless tunic (put on over the head), and golden diadem, which was fit on the turban.[8]

---

4. Joachim Jeremias, *Jerusalem in the Time of Jesus*, trans. F. H. Cave and C. H. Cave (Philadelphia: Fortress, 1969), 148.

5. Ibid., 148.

6. More will be said on the meaning of the Day of Atonement in chapter 19.

7. Josephus, *Against Apion*, II.108.

8. The full description of the high priest's vestments is found in Exod. 28–29. See Jeremias, *Jerusalem in the Time of Jesus*, 148.

Biblical theologian Joachim Jeremias explained how even the vesting of the Jewish high priest became a political ploy for the Romans who controlled them: "Neither Herod the Great ... nor the Romans later could find a more effective safeguard against rebellion than to keep the high-priestly robes in custody in the temple fortress of Antonia, handing them over to the high priest only on feast days."[9]

Next, under the high priest were the priests in his service. The first Levitical priests were the two sons of Aaron. Thereafter, aside from being a descendant of Aaron, Israelite men were to be free from physical deformities[10] and were to meet stringent demands regarding marriage and cultic purity.[11] The high priest was subject to even more demanding regulations.[12] In general, the priests had to undergo a course of instruction and were examined before being allowed to officiate.[13] When a priest's son reached the canonical age of twenty years, the Sanhedrin, in session at the Temple, in the Chamber of Hewn Stone, at the south side of the Court of Priests, examined him on his bodily fitness, and on the legitimacy of his descent before admitting him for ordination. Only after he was found fit was the man ordained.

Following his ordination, he immersed himself in a ceremonial bath of purification and was invested with priestly robes: (1) the undergarment made of fine linen; (2) pants of made of fine linen; (3) a girdle embroidered in blue, purple, and scarlet, linen breeches; (4) a white turban; and (5) a sash.[14] These solemn ceremonies lasted seven days.[15]

The priestly class was not allotted land[16] but given residence in thirteen of the forty-eight cities set aside for Levitical use. Their support was not taken directly from the land but was received through a tenth of the tithes of the people,[17] portions of sacrifices not consumed upon the altar,[18] the firstborn of flock and herd, the first fruits of the harvest, the redemption money for Israel's firstborn sons,[19] and the mysterious Bread of the Presence.[20]

---

9. Jeremias, *Jerusalem in the Time of Jesus*, 148.

10. Lev. 21:17–23. 11. See Lev. 21–22.

12. Lev. 21:10–15.

13. Alfred Edersheim, *The Temple, Its Ministry and Services as They Were at the Time of Jesus Christ* (Peabody, MA: Hendrickson, 1995), 92.

14. See Jeremias, *Jerusalem in the Time of Jesus*, 214–15; *Eerdmans Bible Dictionary* (Grand Rapids, MI: Eerdmans, 1987), 849. See also Exod. 29; Lev. 8; Sir. 50.

15. Jeremias, *Jerusalem in the Time of Jesus*, 215. 16. Num. 18:20, 18:23–24.

17. Num. 18:26–28. 18. See Lev. 5:13, 6:26, 7:31–34, 10:14–15.

19. See Num. 18:12–19. 20. See Lev. 24:5–9.

The specific number of Levitical priests is unknown. What is certain may be summarized as follows. "There was in the Temple in Jerusalem a kind of archive in which the genealogies of the priesthood were kept."[21] The number of priests at the time of Jesus is indeterminate but appears to be considerable.[22] "If the high priest was one and the high priests few, the priests were many!"[23] Each priest was on duty for only one day during his division's week, such that each of the twenty-four divisions would number about 300 priests, or a grand total of 7,200.[24] Added to this number of Levitical priests were approximately 9,600 Levites: nonpriestly laymen who assisted priests in their duties.[25] This brought the estimated total of priests and Levites in the time of Jesus to approximately 16,800.

Priestly duties varied.[26] First, "everything connected with the priesthood was intended to be symbolical and typical—the office itself, its functions, even its dress and outward support. The fundamental design of Israel itself was to be unto [Yahweh] a kingdom of priests and a holy nation."[27] The *kohenim* ("priests") were responsible for the daily sacrifices in the Temple. As indicated, they were organized into two dozen divisions, each being composed of Levites from throughout Israel.

Priests lived all over the country and only came to officiate in the temple every twenty-fourth week, "when the turn of their division came."[28] "They were obliged to follow some profession in their own district, mostly manual work. Herod had a thousand priests trained in carpentry and masonry, and

21. Jeremias, *Jerusalem in the Time of Jesus*, 214.

22. Ibid., 199–200.

23. Oskar Skarsuane, *In the Shadow of the Temple: Jewish Influences on Early Christianity* (Downers Grove, IL: InterVarsity Press, 2002), 101. According to Josephus, there were a few Sadducees, some 4,000 Essenes, and well over 6,000 Pharisees, but 20,000 priests and Levites. Regarding these figures, and for a discussion of their significance, see E. P. Sanders, *Jesus and Judaism* (London: SCM Press, 1985), 194–98, and the response in N. T. Wright, *The New Testament and the People of God* (London: SPCK, 1996), 195–97.

24. Jeremias, *Jerusalem in the Time of Jesus*. "The number 300 cannot possibly be an invention. We must regard it as the approximate number on each weekly course ... Since there were twenty-four weekly courses, *the total number of priests amounts to 24 x 300 = 7,200 priests*" (200). See also Skarsuane, *In the Shadow of the Temple*, 99–100.

25. Jeremias, *Jerusalem in the Time of Jesus*, 199–200.

26. For more detail on priestly duties, see Edersheim, *The Temple*, "The Officiating Priesthood," chap. 4, 55–73.

27. Ibid., 84 (emphasis added). See Exod. 19:5–6.

28. Skarsuane, *In the Shadow of the Temple*, 99. See 1 Chron. 24:1–19.

during the renovations to the Temple he employed them in the Temple court and in the building of the Sanctuary."[29]

Each division's duties normally lasted seven days, and priests served twice a year. During that week, each division was entirely responsible to carry out all of the daily functions in the Temple, far beyond altar service. Priests took turns throughout the year in a manner that can be compared to military reserve duty. One would come to Jerusalem for his obligatory period of service in the Temple. In the Temple, the priests' primary duty was to receive the sacrifices and offerings brought by laypeople to the Temple; to inspect the animals for blemishes; to slaughter, flay, and cut the animal; to sprinkle the blood and throw the parts to be burnt up upon the altar; to maintain the fire on the altar; and to clean the area around the altar.[30] It seems as though most of this was done outside the sanctuary, in the court of priests, where the great altar stood. In the main hall of the Temple, they probably had fewer responsibilities, "but it was there they burnt incense to accompany the daily, fixed prayers."[31]

The Levites

Men of the tribe of Levi—that is, those not descended of Aaron—were excluded from the possibility of priestly service. These laymen provided a vital supportive role as assistants to the high priest and priests,[32] and served

---

29. See Jeremias, *Jerusalem in the Time of Jesus*, 206.

30. Skarsuane, *In the Shadow of the Temple*, 100.

31. Ibid.; Jeremias, *Jerusalem in the time of Jesus*, 201–3. A good example from the New Testament is found in Luke 1:5–10, 1:21–23: "In the days of Herod, king of Judea, there was a priest named Zechariah, of the division of Abijah; and he had a wife of the daughters of Aaron, and her name was Elizabeth. And they were both righteous before God, walking in all the commandments and ordinances of the Lord blameless. But they had no child, because Elizabeth was barren, and both were advanced in years. Now while he was serving as priest before God when his division was on duty, according to the custom of the priesthood, it fell to him by lot to enter the temple of the Lord and burn incense. And the whole multitude of the people were praying outside at the hour of incense ... And the people were waiting for Zechariah, and they wondered at his delay in the temple. And when he came out, he could not speak to them, and they perceived that he had seen a vision in the temple; and he made signs to them and remained dumb. And when his time of service was ended, he went to his home."

32. See Num. 1:47–54, 18:16. The beginning of their service is reckoned variously from ages twenty (1 Chron. 23:24, 23:27; 2 Chron. 31:17; Ezra 3:8), twenty-five (Num. 8:24), and thirty (Num. 4:3; 1 Chron. 23:3).

until the age of fifty.[33] In the wilderness, the Levites had charge of the Tabernacle and its furnishings.[34] They assisted the priests in the Tabernacle service[35] and were exempted from military duty so that they could carry on with these duties.[36] "Singers and musicians formed the upper stratum among the Levites, and only for them were proof of pure descent necessary when they wished to be admitted to office."[37] The duties of the Levites appear to have later changed with their reorganization during the monarchy.[38] During the monarchy, they would assist in the care of the Temple and in the offerings, stand with the priests at prayer and offering times, and take care of the Temple treasuries.[39] Some Levites were officers and judges, others gatekeepers,[40] and still others served as Temple police.[41]

Having reviewed the main divisions of the Levitical priesthood, the discussion now returns to the high priesthood itself: first to the symbolism and meaning of the high priestly office, and second to the Day of Atonement liturgy over which he presided.

The Symbolism and Meaning of the High Priest

The high priest was bound to a higher degree of ritual holiness than other priests. He could have no contact with dead bodies, including those of his parents. Nor could he rend his clothing or allow his hair to grow out as signs of mourning. He could not marry a widow or divorced woman, but only an Israelite virgin.[42] His appointment was for life, unless he stepped down (because of illness, etc.). From the time of David to approximately 175 BC, all high priests were selected from the family of Zadok, the so-called Zadokite

---

33. Num. 4:1–3: "The Lord said to Moses and Aaron, 'Take a census of the sons of Kohath from among the sons of Levi, by their families and their fathers' houses, *from thirty years old up to fifty years old,* all who can enter the service, to do the work in the tent of meeting."

34. Num. 3:8, 3:25–26, 3:31, 3:36–37; 4:15, 4:25–26, 4:31–32.

35. Num. 18:2–4, 18:6, 18:23.

36. Num. 1:47–54.

37. Jeremias, *Jerusalem in the Time of Jesus,* 208.

38. See 1 Chron. 23:25–26, 23:28–32.

39. See 1 Chron. 26:20–28; see 2 Chron. 8:15.

40. See 1 Chron. 6:38, 6:42, 23:4, 23:5, 26:1–19, 26:29–32.

41. See 1 Chron. 23:5; 16:41–42; chapter 25; 2 Chron. 8:14. See Jeremias, *Jerusalem in the Time of Jesus,* 209.

42. Lev. 21:10–15.

line of Levitical priests. Any sin committed by the high priest brought guilt upon the entire nation and had to be countered by special sacrifice.[43]

Technically speaking, the high priest's only prescribed duties were to preside over the Day of Atonement liturgy, Israel's great annual feast. It was the only day of fasting prescribed in Mosaic Law, and the high priest was central to its celebration. Beyond the annual feast, the high priest likely presided over Sabbath services and other special liturgies, especially Passover, Pentecost, and Tabernacles.

The office of high priest took on different dimensions after the exile. It gained the qualities of prestige and dignity that had formerly been held only by the king. In 520 BC, the high priest Joshua and the Davidic governor Zerubbabel were identified as equals, the "two anointed" of Yahweh.[44]

Yet over time his political involvement became more pronounced. By the second century BC, the high priest presided over a group of chief priests, scribes, and heads of families that formed the early Sanhedrin. During the Hellenistic period, the office of high priest became highly corrupt, the target of ambitious and unscrupulous people.[45]

The Day of Atonement Liturgy

The annual Day of Atonement was observed on the tenth day of the seventh month, five days prior to the Feast of Booths.[46] From the evening of the ninth day until the evening of the tenth was a fast on which Israelites were not to work,[47] and according to the *Mishnah* were forbidden to eat, drink, bathe, put on oil or sandals, or engage in sexual relations. It was not a pilgrimage festival, but it was to be observed throughout Israel, with attention focused on confession of sin. The central enactment of the observance was carried out in the Temple. There the focus of attention was on the high priest, who performed the liturgical rite for himself and "all Israel." It served as the annual day of purification for the Temple, altars, furnishings, and priests, and as an atoning sacrifice for the sins of Israel.[48] It was the one and

43. Lev. 4:1–12.

44. Zech. 4:14; see Hag. 1:1, 1:12.

45. More on this in a later chapter.

46. The following is adapted from D. G. Reid, *Dictionary of New Testament Background: A Compendium of Contemporary Biblical Scholarship*, s.v. "Sacrifice and Temple Service."

47. See Lev. 16:29, 23:26–32; Num. 29:7.

48. See Lev. 16:30.

only day of the year on which the high priest entered the Holy of Holies; he and he alone was permitted to enter.[49]

Seven days prior to the Day of Atonement, the high priest took up residence in his chamber within the Temple[50] in order to carefully maintain ritual purity. During that time, the high priest carried out the *tamid* (daily morning and evening offerings), and under the leadership of the chief priests reviewed and memorized the liturgical rite of the coming feast.

The high priest was not allowed to sleep the night before the Day of Atonement lest he jeopardize his cultic purity by a nocturnal emission.[51] At dawn, the high priest carried out the *tamid* (daily morning offering), and when completed, he bathed, dressed in linen, and turned to the centerpiece of the day's activity: the sacrifice of a young bull for a sin offering for himself and his household and the sacrifice of two male goats for a sin offering for Israel (one a sacrifice and one a scapegoat); each of these sacrifices was accompanied by specified grain offerings.[52]

The high priest first confessed his own sins over the bull. He then cast lots to determine which of the two goats would be sacrificed, and which would become the symbolic scapegoat to be led into the Judean wilderness.[53] Following this, he returned to the bull, confessed his sins again and slaughtered it (its blood was captured in a bowl). The high priest then entered the Holy of Holies a second time to place a censer of burning incense on the stone where the Ark of the Covenant had once rested.

Entering the Holy of Holies for a third time, the high priest sprinkled the covering of the Ark, seven times in all, with some blood from the goat. He then sprinkled the veil seven times with the bull's blood and another seven with goat's blood. He mixed together the remaining blood and smeared it on the horns of the Golden Altar of Incense.[54] He retrieved the blood of the bull, reentered the Holy of Holies, and sprinkled blood in the direction of the stone.[55] He then returned to the sacrificial goat and completely slaughtered it, being careful to capture its blood.

49. "Evidence from Mishnah tractate Yoma reflects the extreme care with which the rite would have been carried out in the first century A.D., for it was fundamental to the maintenance of the status of Israel before God and, in the eyes of many, the fulfillment of Israel's promised redemption." Reid, "Sacrifice and Temple Service," 1042.

50. Located along the southern edge of the sanctuary, adjoining the Chamber of Hewn Stone.

51. See Josephus, *Antiquities*, 17.6.4 (§165–66).   52. See Lev. 16:3.

53. *Mishah Yoma* 3:9, 4:1.   54. Exod. 30:1–10; *Mishna Yoma* 5:2.

55. *Mishna Yoma* 5:3.

Ascending to the Holy of Holies, the high priest continued the liturgy by sprinkling the blood upon the stone and veil. The blood of both the bull and the goat was mixed and used to sanctify the Bronze Altar just outside the Holy Place. The blood was applied to the altar as well as sprinkled against its sides. The remainder was poured out at its base.

Following this, the high priest would put his hands on the head of the scapegoat and confess a litany of the sins of Israel. Meanwhile, a designated priest led the scapegoat out "into the wilderness." The high priest shed his linen garments, bathed, and put on his regular high-priestly garments.[56] He then placed the fat from the bull and goat on the burning altar as a sin offering along with their respective grain offerings, and the remainder of the animals, including the hide, was taken out of the Temple and burned completely on the Bronze Altar.

The penultimate step of the Day of the Atonement liturgy brought the people of God, gathered at the Temple, into proximity with the high priest himself. Specifically, the high priest processed out to the Court of Women where the people were assembled. Once within the court, he read the liturgical instructions governing the Day of Atonement from the Torah. After doing so, he uttered eight blessings to the people of Israel.[57] "While the incense was offered in the Most Holy Place the people withdrew from proximity to it, *and worshipped in silence*. At last the people saw the high-priest emerging from the sanctuary, and they knew that the sacrifice had been accepted."[58] It remained for the high priest to take off his clothes, don white garments, purify his hands and feet, and return to the Holy of Holies, where he retrieved the incense censer. After another ritual immersion and change of clothing—now in his full high-priestly vestments—he offered incense on the golden incense altar and lit the menorah for the evening.

The final stage of the liturgy involved a bath of ritual immersion. Afterward, the high priest retired to his home for a private feast with family and

---

56. Lev. 16:23–24.

57. Sir. 50:14–21: "Finishing the service at the altars, and arranging the offering to the Most High, the Almighty, he reached out his hand to the cup and poured a libation of the blood of the grape; he poured it out at the foot of the altar, a pleasing odor to the Most High, the King of all. Then the sons of Aaron shouted, they sounded the trumpets of hammered work, they made a great noise to be heard for remembrance before the Most High. Then all the people together made haste and fell to the ground upon their faces to worship their Lord, the Almighty, God Most High."

58. Edersheim, *The Temple*, 315.

friends, celebrating the accomplishment of his duties.[59] With this, the single highest feast associated with the Temple came to an end.

It is this memorial event—the great Day of Atonement—that the author of Hebrews has in mind when he writes of the high priest entering "the inner room of the earthly tabernacle once a year, but Christ entering once into the most holy place of the heavenly tabernacle with his own blood rather than the blood of bulls and goats."[60] When St. Paul speaks of Christ being set forth as the "mercy seat,"[61] he has in mind the *hilisterion*, or covering of the Ark of the Covenant, on which the blood was originally to be sprinkled in the Holy of Holies on the Day of Atonement. For him, Jesus is the mercy seat of the new Temple, and by the blood of his death he fulfills and transforms the Day of Atonement, far surpassing it in finality and scope.

The Glory of the High Priest

Extensive details are provided in the Old Testament concerning the special garments worn by the high priest (Exod. 28:2–39). Specifically, these consisted of a robe or outer garment; an ephod, breastplate, coat, or undergarment; a turban; and a girdle. The ephod and breastplate were permanently fastened together (v. 28). The robe was a sleeveless blue garment worn under the ephod, reaching perhaps to the feet and decorated along the skirt with embroidered pomegranates (Num. 15:38–41) alternated with golden bells. The coat, worn beneath the robe, had sleeves and also reached the feet (Exod. 28:39).

That the high priest was to image the holiness of God is clear throughout the Old Testament. The penultimate chapter of the deuterocanonical Book of Sirach reflects this conviction. A particularly vivid portion of Sirach 50 may be cited here at some length:

The leader of his brethren and the pride of his people was Simon the high priest ... who in his life repaired the house, and in his time fortified the temple ... *How glorious he was when the people gathered round him as he came out of the inner sanctuary!* Like the sun shining upon the Temple of the Most High ... *When he put on his glorious robe and clothed himself with superb perfection and went up to the holy altar, he made the court of the sanctuary glorious....* he reached out his hand to the cup and ... poured it out at the foot of the altar, a pleasing odor to the Most High, the King of all ... Then the sons of Aaron shouted, they sounded the trumpets of hammered

59. *Mishna Yoma* 7:4.   60. Heb. 9:6–14.
61. See Rom. 3:25.

work, they made a great noise to be heard for remembrance before the Most High. (Sir. 50:1–22)

Concluding Remarks

One final mystery needs to be mentioned. According to Exodus, the high priest did not enter the Holy of Holies by his own name, but by the name of Yahweh. A golden plate engraved with the words "Holy to the Lord" was fastened to the front of the high priest's turban with blue lace (v. 36). Known as the holy crown (Hebrew, *nēzer hāqqōdeš*; Exod. 29:6), this plate was intended to remove the iniquity of the "holy things that the sons of Israel consecrate" (Exod. 28:38). Josephus indicates that the holy crown also had a three-tiered diadem worn over the turban and decorated with a floral design reminiscent of the flora of Eden.[62]

Profoundly, he bore the name of God *upon his own head*, and all who saw him saw not him but the One whom he served. This mysterious and somewhat obscure element of the high priesthood is all but forgotten in Scripture until it returns spectacularly in the Book of Revelation: "There shall no more be anything accursed, but the throne of God and of the Lamb shall be in it, and his servants shall worship him; they shall see his face, and his name shall be on their foreheads" (Rev. 22:1–4)

St. John the Evangelist seems to anticipate that in the age to come all will finally "see God face to face." According to the Book of Revelation, and in a grand recapitulation of the high priesthood, his name will be on the forehead of every believer, as a mark of their belonging to him. Here is an indication that the "priesthood of all believers" will have finally reached its culmination in the age to come. As sons and daughters of God in Jesus Christ, Revelation seems to hint that, in Christ, the new priesthood echoes that earlier stage of the "unmediated" priesthood in the age of Melchizidek and the great patriarchs. It is not that St. John believes that believers are without a priestly mediator. To the contrary! St. John is clear that it is the Lamb, standing as though slain, who is the one, true mediator. And all who belong to him share in his priesthood. Yet, in some sense, it is as if the priesthood of believers is somehow unmediated in that each one who belongs to him is a *living sacrifice*, perfected in the resurrected Jesus. It is to this topic that the discussion turns in chapter 7.

62. Josephus, *Antiquities*, 3.7.6.

7

JESUS, GOD'S ETERNAL
HIGH PRIEST

*Temple Priesthood in the Old and
New Testaments (IV/IV)*

> Therefore he had to be made like his brethren in every re-
> spect, so that he might become a merciful and faithful high
> priest in the service of God, to make expiation for the sins of
> the people.
>
> Hebrews 2:18

Previous chapters focused upon the priesthood of the Old Testament. Now, the emphasis shifts to the New Testament and particularly to how Jesus Christ is revealed as the eternal High Priest. In a recent and insightful essay, Brant Pitre describes four aspects of the Temple that are critical to understanding the High Priesthood of Jesus in the New Testament: "(1) The dwelling-place of God on earth; (2) a microcosm of heaven and earth; (3) the sole place of sacrificial worship; (4) the place of the sacrificial priesthood."[1] As he summarizes, "Jesus saw all four of these aspects of the Temple as being fulfilled in himself and his disciples."[2] Following Pitre's argument closely, this chapter will examine each one of these aspects of the Temple.

---

1. Brant Pitre, "Jesus, the New Temple, and the New Priesthood," *Letter & Spirit* 4 (2008): 48.
2. Ibid.

The Dwelling Place of God on Earth

"Above all, it was the presence of God that made the Temple a place 'set apart': in Greek, that is what the word 'temple' (*hieron*) means. Although ancient Jews recognized that the transcendent God of the universe could not be 'contained' by any earthly dwelling, they nevertheless maintained that he had chosen in some unique way to dwell with his people in the Temple in Jerusalem."[3]

Pitre describes this theme that "runs like a golden thread" in the Old Testament, and only a few Scriptures representing many more need be offered:

Then Moses and Aaron went from the presence of the assembly to the door of the tent of meeting, and fell on their faces. And the glory of the Lord appeared to them.[4] (Num. 20:6)

And when the priests came out of the holy place, a cloud filled the house of the Lord, so that the priests could not stand to minister because of the cloud; for the glory of the Lord filled the house of the Lord. Then Solomon said, "The Lord has set the sun in the heavens, but has said that he would dwell in thick darkness. I have built thee an exalted house, a place for thee to dwell in forever."[5] (1 Ki. 8:10–13)

As the glory of the Lord entered the temple by the gate facing east, the Spirit lifted me up, and brought me into the inner court; and behold, the glory of the Lord filled the temple. (Ezek. 43:4–5)

On the motif of the "glory cloud," Josephus writes, "This cloud so darkened the place, that one priest could not discern another; but it afforded to the minds of all a visible image and glorious appearance of *God's having descended into this Temple*, and of his having gladly pitched his Tabernacle there."[6] E. P. Sanders adds that it is about the presence of the Lord himself: "*The Temple was holy not only because the holy God was worshipped there, but because he was there....* Jews did not think that God was there and nowhere

---

3. Ibid., 50–51 (emphasis added). See also N. T. Wright, *Jesus and the Victory of God*, vol. 1, *Christian Origins and the Question of God* (London: SPCK, 1996), 406–7; Craig R. Koester, *The Dwelling of God: The Tabernacle in the Old Testament, Intertestamental Jewish Literature, and the New Testament*, Catholic Biblical Quarterly Monograph Series 22 (Washington, DC: Catholic Biblical Association of America, 1989).

4. See also Deut. 5:23–24; Num. 14:10.

5. See also 1 Chron. 7:1–3.

6. Josephus, *The Antiquities of the Jews*, Book 8, chap. 4, 106, in *The Works of Josephus*, trans. William Whiston (Peabody, MA: Hendrickson, 1994), 219. See Pitre, "Jesus, the New Temple, and the New Priesthood," 51.

else, nor that the Temple in any way confined him. Since he was creator and Lord of the universe, he could be approached in prayer at any place. Nevertheless, he was in some special sense present in the Temple."[7]

What conclusion can be drawn? For his part, Pitre puts the question aptly: "Hence, the divine presence, the presence of God in the Temple, lays the foundation for all of its other aspects ... *How does it illuminate the mystery of Jesus' relationship to the Temple?*"[8]

Consider Jesus's self-understanding of his messianic mission. Jesus himself said, "At that time Jesus went through the grain fields on the Sabbath; his disciples were hungry, and they began to pluck heads of grain and to eat. But when the Pharisees saw it, they said to him, 'Look, your disciples are doing what is not lawful to do on the Sabbath.' He said to them, 'Have you not read what David did, when he was hungry, and those who were with him: how he entered the house of God and ate *the bread of the Presence*,[9] which it was not lawful for him to eat nor for those who were with him, but only for the priests? Or have you not read in the law how on the Sabbath the priests in the temple profane the Sabbath, and are guiltless? *I tell you, something greater than the temple is here*'" (Matt. 12:1–6).

Clearly Jesus's expression is self-reverential. "Should there be any doubt about this, he uses similar language elsewhere to refer to himself as prophet and king: 'Something greater than Solomon is here' (Matt. 12:42; Luke 11:31) and 'Something greater than Jonah is here' (Matt. 12:41; Luke 11:32). In this text, Jesus is not only identifying Himself *with the Temple*—as if this were not striking enough—but as *greater than* the Jerusalem Temple."[10]

This leads to more questions with profound implications of their own: "This identification immediately raises a question of no little importance: if, to an ancient Jew, the Temple is the dwelling place of God on earth, *then what could possibly be greater than it?* Although some commentators have tried to avoid the obvious, the only adequate answer is, of course, God himself, present in person, 'tabernacling' in the flesh."[11]

---

7. E. P. Sanders, *Judaism: Practice and Belief 63 BCE–66 CE* (Philadelphia: Trinity Press International, 1992), 70–71; see Pitre, "Jesus, the New Temple, and the New Priesthood," 52 (emphasis added).

8. Pitre, "Jesus, the New Temple, and the New Priesthood," 52.

9. The mysterious "Bread of the Presence" is a key element of the Temple, and will be dealt with in chapter 15. See Exod. 25:30, 35:13, 39:36; Num. 4:7; 1 Sam. 21:6; 2 Chron. 4:19.

10. Pitre, "Jesus, the New Temple, and the New Priesthood," 53.

11. Ibid. Pitre makes an astute observation about a blind spot in contemporary biblical theology (53n19): "It is fascinating to observe that many modern commentators do not even attempt to wrestle

Although there is much more evidence that could be marshaled here, only one more passage will be mentioned: "Jesus answered him, 'Because I said to you, I saw you under the fig tree, do you believe? You shall see greater things than these.' And he said to him, 'Truly, truly, I say to you, *you will see heaven opened, and the angels of God ascending and descending upon the Son of man*'" (John 1:50–51).

Here, Jesus draws upon not one but two Old Testament passages in his response to Nathanael: Daniel 7:13–14[12] and Genesis 28:10–17.[13] The first passage from Daniel, telling of the coming "son of man" is integrated with Jacob's dream of a heavenly temple. Strikingly, Jacob renames the place *Beth'el* ("house of God").[14] Later, Jacob has another mystical experience, when he wrestles with an angel (Gen. 32). There, he renames the place *Peni'el* ("the face of God").

Regarding this first aspect, "in ancient Judaism that the Temple was the dwelling place of God … Jesus, by contrast, transfers this belief to himself, thereby identifying himself as the true Temple of God. He is not only greater than the present Temple, the dwelling-place of God on earth, but at the revelation of the … Son of Man he will be shown to be the heavenly Temple of God—the dwelling place of 'the Lord' that was revealed to the patriarch Jacob … it is no wonder that Jesus both reveres the Temple and awaits its destruction. *The old Jerusalem Temple must make way for the unveiled glory of the divine presence that will be manifest in the coming of the heavenly Son of*

---

with the implications of Jesus' identification of himself as *'greater than the Temple.'* The verse is all but ignored in the otherwise extremely thorough work of W. D. Davies and Dale C. Allison, *The Gospel According to Saint Matthew* (Edinburgh: T & T Clark, 1991), 2:314–315. Similarly, the verse receives no discussion at all in Rudolf Schnackenburg, *The Gospel of Matthew* (Grand Rapids, MI: Eerdmans, 2002), 111–112. It is also lacking in works on Jesus, such as the (otherwise massive) work of James D. G. Dunn, *Jesus Remembered* (Grand Rapids, MI: Eerdmans, 2003), 566–569 who totally ignores it in his discussion of Matt. 12:1–8; Mark 2:23–28; Luke 6:1–5, *and does not mention it anywhere else in his book.* Even Ben Witherington's book, *The Christology of Jesus* (Minneapolis: Fortress, 1990), 66–71, *never even mentions this verse in his discussion.* It should be noted that this cannot be because there is a strong case for the inauthenticity of the verse, since has already been seen that it strongly coheres with Jesus' words about being *'greater than Solomon'* (Matt. 12:42; Luke 11:31) and *'greater than Jonah'* (Matt. 12:41; Luke 11:32)."

12. See Dan. 7:13–14.

13. See Gen. 28:10–17.

14. Gen. 32:30: "So Jacob called the name of the place Peni-el, saying, '*For I have seen God face to face*, and yet my life is preserved.'"

Man."[15] The discussion now moves to the remaining three aspects taken up in Pitre's essay.[16]

A Microcosm of Heaven and Earth

The concept of the Jerusalem Temple as a microcosm of heaven and earth was discussed previously and will not be repeated here. Pitre's argument moves to the New Testament, particularly in the Gospel of Matthew. In the Passion Narrative in Matthew, Jesus cries out one last time in a loud voice and surrenders his spirit. Of interest is that St. Matthew adds, "the curtain of the temple was torn in two" (Matt. 27:51). Here, one encounters a Gospel text that is fully grasped only in light of the Old Testament. Pitre explains, "Every first-century Jew would have known: on the Temple veil was depicted 'the panorama of the heavens.'[17] With the tearing of the Temple veil and the earthquake, the whole universe, 'heaven and earth,' were symbolically being torn asunder. And because the Jerusalem Temple was the sign and symbol of this universe, it was now destined to share the same fate. The old Temple would be replaced by a new one, and the old world—as Isaiah had said so long ago—would be replaced by 'a new heavens and a new earth.'[18] And all this, according to Jesus, would begin 'on the third day.'"[19]

The Sole Place of Sacrificial Worship

In the final two topics of the essay, Pitre turns to the idea of sacrificial worship and sacrificial priesthood. One of Jesus's most memorable actions was his temple action (often known as his "cleansing" of the Temple): "And He entered the temple and began to drive out those who sold and those who

15. Pitre, "Jesus, the New Temple, and the New Priesthood," 56 (emphasis added).

16. Each of these four aspects is important for grasping the New Testament's revelation of Jesus as the living Temple. Pitre correctly identifies this first aspect, just examined as the most crucial. It is the key that unlocks the other three. Therefore (and for the sake of space) the subsequent discussion will be more succinct in discussing the next three. The reader is referred to Pitre's article for complete analysis.

17. Josephus, *Wars of the Jews*, Book 5, chap. 5, 214. See also Dale Allison, *The End of the Ages Has Come: An Early Interpretation of the Passion and Resurrection of Jesus* (Eugene, OR: Wipf & Stock, 2013), 33.

18. Isa. 65:17, 66:22.

19. Pitre, "Jesus, the New Temple, and the New Priesthood," 63.

bought in the Temple, and he overturned the tables of the money changers and the seats of those who sold pigeons; and he would not allow anyone to carry anything through the Temple. And he taught, and said to them, 'Is it not written, "My house shall be called a house of prayer for all the nations"? But you have made it a den of robbers'"[20] (Mark 11:15–16).

Clearly this was a symbolic action of Jesus. But what does it mean? Often, scholars speak of the righteous indignation of Jesus the prophet.[21] But is there more than this? Most certainly. Jacob Neusner astutely explains that Jesus's actions "would have provoked astonishment."[22] The reason this is so is that "the overturning of the moneychangers' tables represents an act of rejection of the most important rite of the Israelite cult, the whole-offering, and, therefore, a statement that there is a means of atonement other than the daily whole offering [known as the *tamid*], which is now null. Then what was to take the place of the daily whole offering? It was to be the rite of the Eucharist: table for table, whole offering for whole offering."[23]

Neusner's exegesis suggests that there is something going in Jesus's temple actions, something beyond a kind of "righteous anger." According to Neusner, Jesus's actions brought about a symbolic halt to the daily whole burnt offering, which was believed to effect atonement.[24] Pitre goes even further, suggesting that when "Jesus' actions in the Temple are combined with his actions in the upper room, they lead Neusner to the conclusion that He intended the sacrifices of the Jerusalem Temple to be replaced by 'the rite of the Eucharist.'"[25]

20. See Matt. 21:12–13; Luke 19:45–46; John 2:13–21.

21. Raymond E. Brown, *The Gospel According to John (I–XII): Introduction, Translation, and Notes*, vol. 29, *Anchor Yale Bible* (New Haven, CT: Yale University Press, 2008), 121: "If the tradition is correct, then Jesus' action had precedents in the OT. A prophet like Jeremiah, whom Jesus resembled in many ways (Matt 16:14), had warned the priests of his time that the Temple had become a den of thieves (Jer. 7:11—the very text that Mark and Matthew record to explain Jesus' action)."

22. Jacob Neusner, "Money-Changers in the Temple: The Mishnah's Explanation," *New Testament Studies* 35 (1989): 287–90; here 289–90 (emphasis added), cited in Jostein Ådna, "Jesus' Symbolic Action in the Temple (Mark 11:15–17): The Replacement of the Sacrificial Cult by His Atoning Death," in *Gemeinde ohne Tempel* [Community without Temple], ed. Beate Ego, Armin Lange, and Peter Pilhofer (Tübingen: Mohr Siebeck, 1999), 461–73 (here 472n6). See Pitre, "Jesus, the New Temple, and the New Priesthood," 67–68.

23. Neusner, "Money-Changers in the Temple," 289–90 (emphasis added). See Pitre, "Jesus, the New Temple, and the New Priesthood," 67–68.

24. Num. 28:1–8.

25. Pitre, "Jesus, the New Temple, and the New Priesthood," 68.

This insight brings the present discussion to the Institution of the Eucharist itself: "Now as they were eating, Jesus took bread, and blessed, and broke it, and gave it to the disciples and said, 'Take, eat; this is my body.' And he took a cup, and when he had given thanks he gave it to them, saying, 'Drink of it, all of you; for this is *my blood of the covenant*, which is poured out for many for the forgiveness of sins'" (Matt. 26:26–28).

The phrase "my blood of the covenant" in Matthew is similar to that in Luke, "This cup which is poured out for you is the *new covenant in my blood*" (22:20). Both Gospels harken back to the "words of institution" of the Mosaic covenant at Mt. Sinai, when Moses took the blood, threw it upon the people, and said, "Behold the blood of the covenant which the Lord has made with you in *accordance with all these words*" (Exod. 24:8).

Despite these parallels in formulation, one of the striking differences between the Old and the New Covenant is the transformation of death into that of radical self-giving and something that could only be accomplished by the Son of God. On this point, Ratzinger observes, "With the institution of the Eucharist, Jesus transforms his cruel death into 'word,' into the radical expression of his love, his self-giving to the point of death. So he himself becomes the 'Temple.'"[26]

Jeremias pointed out that by utilizing the combined imagery of "body" and "blood," any ancient Jew would have recognized that Jesus is applying to himself terms from the language of sacrifice. This is especially true of the image of blood being poured out; such language is clearly sacrificial imagery drawn directly from the liturgy of the Temple (Lev. 4:5–7;[27] Deut. 12:26–27[28]).[29]

A key implication of the revelation of the "true Temple" of Jesus's body emerges here: that it is no longer from the Jerusalem Temple from which the blood will flow: "The Temple has now been replaced by the immolated body of Jesus ... the very body and blood of the crucified Messiah is now revealed as the true Temple of God."[30]

26. Ratzinger, *Jesus of Nazareth, Part Two. Holy Week: From the Entrance into Jerusalem to the Resurrection* (San Francisco: Ignatius Press, 2011), 80.

27. Lev. 4:5–7.

28. Deut. 12:26–27.

29. Pitre, "Jesus, the New Temple, and the New Priesthood," 68, citing Jeremias, *The Eucharistic Words of Jesus*, trans. John Bowden (London: SCM, 1966), 222.

30. Pitre, "Jesus, the New Temple, and the New Priesthood," 70 (emphasis added).

The Place of the Sacrificial Priesthood

Finally, the discussion turns to a fourth aspect of the Temple relevant to understanding Jesus as the new and living Temple: that of the sacrificial priesthood. Pitre begins, "If, for an ancient Jew, it would have been absurd to speak of religious worship without sacrifice, then it would be equally absurd to speak of sacrifice without priesthood. Indeed, the two are almost synonymous: the Temple is the locus of the priesthood because it is the sole place of sacrifice, and it is the sole place of sacrifice because it is the locus of the priesthood."[31] Here, Pitre's analysis is sound, though it should be pointed out that his approach flies in the face of much modern biblical scholarship, which rejects/diminishes the notion of a sacrificial priesthood in the New Testament.[32]

Jesus is called the "Holy One of God" (Mark 1:24; Luke 4:34; John 6:69), a title used "exclusively of Aaron in the Bible (Psa. 106:16; Num. 16:7; Sir. 45:6)."[33] In support of his argument, Pitre turns to a number of biblical passages in which Jesus speaks of the eschatological temple, comparing them with Old Testament counterparts: "it is no coincidence that in the very texts wherein Jesus speaks about the eschatological temple, he also speaks of the eschatological priesthood."[34]

One of first pair of texts he looks at is Jesus's temple action, and he compares it with a text from the prophet Isaiah: "And the foreigners who join themselves to the Lord, to minister to him, to love the name of the Lord,

---

31. Ibid., 70–71 (emphasis added). He adds: "The place of 'the priests, the ministers of the Lord,' is 'between the vestibule and the altar'—that is, in the *Temple* (Joel 2:17). Hence, any attempt to understand Jesus' relationship to the ancient Jewish Temple must eventually raise the question of his relationship to the ancient Jewish priesthood."

32. For important exceptions, see Crispin Fletcher-Louis, "Jesus as the High Priestly Messiah: Part 1," *Journal for the Study of the Historical Jesus* 4, no. 2 (2006): 155–75; idem, "Jesus as the High Priestly Messiah: Part 2," *Journal for the Study of the Historical Jesus* 5, no. 1 (2007): 57–79; also Albert Vanhoye, SJ, *Old Testament Priests and the New Priest*, trans. J. Bernard Orchard (Petersham, MA: St. Bede's, 1986), 47–59; André Feuillet, *The Priesthood of Christ and His Ministers*, trans. Matthew J. O'Connell (New York: Doubleday, 1975); Oscar Cullman, *The Christology of the New Testament*, trans. Shirley C. Guthrie and Charles A. M. Hall (London: SCM, 1959), 83–89. Pitre adds: "It is notable that none of these appear in major historical monographs on Jesus."

33. Crispin Fletcher-Louis, *Dictionary of Jesus and the Gospels*, 2nd ed., s.v. "Priests and Priesthood."

34. Pitre, "Jesus, the New Temple, and the New Priesthood," 72.

and to be his servants ... these I will bring to my holy mountain, and make them joyful in my house of prayer; their burnt offerings and their sacrifices will be accepted on my altar; for my house shall be called a house of prayer for all peoples" (Isa. 56:6–8).[35] This is a remarkable text: the prophet Isaiah foresees a new house of prayer, an eschatological temple, and along with it a new priesthood and eschatological priesthood.

The "foreigners"—that is to say, the Gentiles—are clearly depicted as making righteous "burnt offerings" to the Lord in a future age. As Pitre explains, "At the time Jesus, every practicing Jew would have known that it was not only totally prohibited for a Gentile to act as priest, but even the majority of Israelites, all twelve tribes, with the exception of the tribe of Levi were prohibited from acting a priests. Since the time of the Golden Calf incident, the priesthood had been taken away from the twelve tribes as a whole and given to only one: the tribe of Levi."[36]

A second set of texts examined is Matthew 12:1–8[37] and Leviticus 24:5–9.[38] The Gospel text is one of the so-called Sabbath sayings of Jesus ("For the Son of man is lord of the Sabbath"). The text from Leviticus concerns the mysterious Bread of the Presence.

The Bread of the Presence (or "face")[39] is significant to understanding

---

35. Another passage that speaks of an "eschatological priesthood" including Gentiles is Isa. 66:21: "And some of them also I will take for priests and for Levites, says the Lord."

36. Pitre, "Jesus, the New Temple, and the New Priesthood," 73. (See Exod. 32.) For corroborating evidence, see the ancient *Testament of Levi* 18:1–14: "When vengeance will have come upon them from the Lord, *the priesthood will lapse. And then the Lord will raise up a new priest, to whom all the words of the Lord will be revealed....* And the angels of glory of the Lord's presence will be made glad by him. *The heavens will be opened and from the Temple of glory sanctification will come upon him, with a fatherly voice, as from Abraham to Isaac.* And the glory of the Most High shall burst forth upon him. And the spirit of understanding and sanctification shall rest upon him in the water. For he shall give the majesty of the Lord to those who are his sons in truth forever. *And there shall be no successor for him from generation to generation forever. And in his priesthood the Gentiles shall be multiplied in knowledge upon the earth, and they shall be illumined by the grace of the Lord. In his priesthood sin shall cease* and lawless men shall rest from their evil deeds, and righteous men shall find rest in him. *And he shall open the gates of Paradise; he shall remove the sword that has threatened since Adam, and he will grant to the saints to eat of the Tree of Life.* The spirit of holiness shall be upon them. And Beliar shall be bound by him. And he shall grant his children the authority to trample on wicked spirits." Source: Charlesworth, *Old Testament Pseudepigrapha*, 1:794–795.

37. Matt. 12:1–8.

38. Lev. 24:5–9.

39. One of the reasons that this mysterious substance is overlooked by many—aside from the

Jesus's statement and how Jesus's disciples "plucked grain" on the Sabbath. As Leviticus indicates, in the Old Testament, *lehem panim* was a sign in the Temple of God's eternal covenant with Israel (hence the "twelve cakes"). *Lehem panim* was offered to God as an offering weekly, on the day of rest and worship, that is, the Sabbath. Aaron and his sons and they alone ate the *lehem panim* in the Tabernacle. This was the exclusive offering of the Sabbath. It was consumed by the priests, who also drank offerings of wine.[40]

To be clear, it is the unbloody sacrifice that Jesus refers to in the Sabbath saying. Strikingly, the person who eats the Bread of the Presence to which Jesus refers in Matthew 12 is not Aaron, nor any Levitical priest, but David. This is striking, for David is not a priest, and not even a Levite.[41] Yet, just as David and his men were "guiltless" priests (Matt. 12:5), Jesus argues that his disciples were indeed "guiltless" (Matt. 12:7). How could this be? Fletcher-Louis sees a priestly context as the solution: "The way Jesus tells the Old Testament story, David plays the role of the priest who enters the sanctuary on the Sabbath to collect the old bread and distribute it to his fellow priests."[42]

Recall in earlier discussions of the priesthood of Melchizidek, that Psalm 110 boldly declares that David was indeed a legitimate priest of an entirely different nature, "after the order of Melchizidek" (Psa. 110:4). Fletcher-Louis explains how Jesus validates the breach of the Sabbath made by his own disciples. It is because Jesus "claims to be a sacral king and high priestly Son of Man. Where *he is*, in that place there is the transcendent liturgical space and time of the true Temple in which his disciples can legitimately act as priests for whom the Sabbath prohibition does not apply."[43]

---

fact that many references to it are tucked away in Leviticus—is that it has been mistranslated. A number of English Bible translations retain the phrase "Showbread" from the Protestant term *schaubrot* (German: "shewbread"), which mistranslates the original Hebrew phrase, *lehem panim*. Literally, *lehem panim* is best translated as "bread of the face/presence."

40. See Exod. 25:29.

41. David was of the tribe of Judah. As such, he was disqualified from the Levitical priesthood, which was reserved by God for the Levites alone. (See 1 Sam. 17:12: "Now David was the son of an Ephrathite of Bethlehem in Judah, named Jesse, who had eight sons.")

42. Fletcher-Louis, "Jesus as the High Priestly Messiah: Part 2," 76. Regarding the priesthood of David, see Carl E. Armerding, "Were David's Sons Priests?" in *Current Issues in Biblical and Patristic Interpretation: Studies in Honor of Merrill C. Tenney Presented by His Former Students*, ed. Gerald F. Hawthorne (Grand Rapids, MI: Eerdmans, 1975); Anthony Phillips, "David's Linen Ephod," *Vetus Testamentum* 19 (1969): 458–87. Pitre, "Jesus, the New Temple, and the New Priesthood," 77.

43. Fletcher-Louis, "Jesus as the High-Priestly Messiah: Part 2," 77. See Pitre, "Jesus, the New Temple, and the New Priesthood," 77.

In Exodus, the Bread of the Presence, along with the Ark and Golden Lampstand, were all "patterned on the heavenly realities."[44] Next to the mysterious bread were "flagons and bowls" for sacrificial offerings of wine, apparently drunk "in a sacred meal of bread and wine."[45] If, for the sake of discussion, the Bread of the Presence was for a strong part of his argument, the question that remains how Jesus made use of it in the course of defending his disciples. What was Jesus attempting to teach his disciples through this connection?

To begin with, there is the terminology itself. A more accurate translation of *lehem panim*, often mistranslated as "showbread," is "bread of the presence" or "face." Summing up his argument, Pitre suggests important implications, stating that in Exodus "the bread itself is a visible sign of the face of God."[46]

On this last point, recall that in Exodus 24, Moses, along with Aaron, Nadab, and Abihu, are said to have "seen God" at Sinai: "they beheld God, and ate and drank" (Exod. 24:11). Later in Leviticus, the Temple priests are commanded to continually bake twelve cakes of this bread as a perpetual sign of the everlasting covenant between God and his people.[47] Moreover, texts in Ezekiel suggest that this covenantal bread was an altar and therefore a sacrifice and not merely a meal.[48] Much later, just prior to the destruction of the Temple in 70 AD, weekly Sabbath worship revolved around priestly offerings of the bread, baked in the recesses of the Temple and eaten by its priests.

Finally, some important ancient rabbinic texts testify to the fact that at the three great Temple feasts—Passover, Tabernacles, and Pentecost—the Levitical priests would remove the Bread of the Presence from the restricted space of the Holy Place, so that all of the pilgrims could "see" the Bread of the Face of God: "They [the priests] used to life it [the Golden Table] up and exhibit the Bread of the Presence on it to those who came up for the festivals, saying to them, 'Behold, God's Love for you.'"[49]

44. Brant Pitre, *Jesus and the Jewish Roots of the Eucharist: Unlocking the Secrets of the Last Supper* (New York: Doubleday, 2011), 120. See Exod. 25:23–34, 25:29–30.

45. Pitre, *Jesus and the Jewish Roots of the Eucharist*, 120.

46. Ibid., 121.

47. See Lev. 24:5–7; Pitre, *Jesus and the Jewish Roots of the Eucharist*, 123.

48. See Ezek. 41:21–22; Pitre, *Jesus and the Jewish Roots of the Eucharist*, 123.

49. Pitre, *Jesus and the Jewish Roots of the Eucharist*, 131; see Babylonian Talmud, *Menahothi* 29A.

Concluding Remarks

The Bread of the Presence is a key element of Jesus's defense of his disciples. Taken alone in his response to the Pharisees, Jesus appears to be placing himself in the tradition of David, who, as Jesus explains, was not merely "allowed an exception" to eat the Bread of the Presence, but uniquely qualified to do so as he did, along with his men. Here, a biblical case can be made that Jesus's argument rests upon David's somewhat hidden (yet no less real) priestly identity. If one reads the conflict scene in the light of the entire Gospel in which it is found, it becomes a lively lens through which to understand the institution of the Eucharist. Pitre provocatively suggests that Jesus's liturgical actions of breaking the bread harkens back to the Bread of the Presence, such that, at the dawn of the New Covenant, it constitutes "the center of the eschatological priesthood of the restored twelve tribes of Israel."[50]

---

50. Pitre, "Jesus, the New Temple, and the New Priesthood," 77–78. He clarifies: "Although there is some speculation that John ... was of a priestly family, and good reasons to believe that Matthew (Matt. 9:9; 10:3) was of Levitical heritage (also called 'Levi' in Mark 2:15; Luke 5:27) there is no evidence to my knowledge that any of the other Twelve were of priestly descent." The theory about the priestly identity of John was recently given a visible supporter, Ratzinger, *Jesus of Nazareth, Part Two*, 224–25, following Henri Cazelles, "Johannes: Ein Sohn des Zebedäus. 'Priester' und 'Apostel'" [John: A Son of Zebedee. 'Priest' and 'Apostle'] *Internationale Katholische Zeitschrift Communio* 31 (2002): 479–84.

8

THE HOLY TABERNACLE OF
THE WILDERNESS

The Presence and Transcendence of Israel's God

Then the cloud covered the tent of meeting, and *the glory of
the Lord filled the Tabernacle*. And Moses was not able to enter the tent of meeting, because the cloud abode upon it, and
the glory of the Lord filled the Tabernacle.

Exodus 40:34–35

Israel in the Wilderness

This chapter examines the reality of the Tabernacle ("tent of meeting")
and the notion of God's glory as the glorious prefiguration of Jesus.[1] Inasmuch as the Tabernacle is a "vessel" containing within it the presence of God,
we will also explore connections between the Tabernacle of the Old Testament and the Virgin Mary.[2]

The Tabernacle was the Lord's tented sanctuary and dwelling place in the
midst of Israel as they traveled from Sinai to Canaan (Num. 10–21). Some do
not realize that the Tabernacle was part of their experience even while in the
Promised Land. Right up until the time that Solomon's Temple was built,

---

1. For a verse-by-verse approach to the Tabernacle chapters, see N. M. Sarna, *The JPS Commentary: Exodus* (Philadelphia: Jewish Publication Society, 1991); also T. D. Alexander, *From Paradise
to the Promised Land: An Introduction to the Pentateuch* (Grand Rapids, MI: Baker Book House,
2002), chap. 15.

2. For an introduction, see R. E. Averbeck, *Dictionary of the Old Testament: Pentateuch*, s.v.
"Tabernacle."

it survived as a sanctuary.[3] However, the Ark of the Covenant was removed from the Tabernacle in the time of Eli[4] and never returned there. After the Lord delivered them from Egypt, he guided and protected them on their journey from Egypt through the wilderness to Sinai[5] by means of the pillar of cloud by day and the pillar of fire by night: "And the Lord went before them by day in a pillar of cloud to lead them along the way, and by night in a pillar of fire to give them light, that they might travel by day and by night; the pillar of cloud by day and the pillar of fire by night did not depart from before the people" (Exod. 13:21–22).

God revealed Moses the pattern for the Tabernacle, as these two texts from Exodus make abundantly clear: "*According to all that I show you* concerning the pattern of the Tabernacle, and of all its furniture, so you shall make it … And see that you make them after the pattern for them, *which is being shown you on the mountain*" (Exod. 25:9, 25:40).[6]

Its actual construction was undertaken by Bezalel and Oholiab with their assistants,[7] with the Israelites providing the materials through voluntary contributions.[8] The work was completed one year after the Exodus[9] and nine months after Israel had arrived at Sinai.[10] In accordance with the Lord's specific requirements,[11] they constructed the Tabernacle, from the blueprint in heaven,[12] while they camped there at Sinai for almost one year.[13]

On the day of its completion, the Lord promptly occupied the Tabernacle in all of his glory: "Then the cloud covered the tent of meeting, and the glory of the Lord filled the Tabernacle. And Moses was not able to enter the tent of meeting, because the cloud abode upon it, and the glory of the Lord *filled the Tabernacle*" (Exod. 40:35). From that point forward he continuously manifested his guiding and protecting presence to all the people in the form of "a cloud by day and with fire in it by night over the Tabernacle."[14]

---

3. See 2 Sam. 7:6; 1 Ki. 8:4; 2 Chron. 1:3–6.
4. See 1 Sam. 4–6.
5. See Exod. 13–18.
6. See also Acts 7:44; Heb. 8:5.
7. Exod. 31:1–11, 36:1.
8. See Exod. 25:1–7, 35:4–9, 35:20–29.
9. See Exod. 40:2, 40:17.
10. See Exod. 19:1.
11. See Exod. 25–31.
12. See Exod. 35–40.
13. See Exod. 19:1; Num. 10:11.
14. See Num. 9:15–23, 10:11–12, 10:33–34.

Figure 2. **The Dimensions of the Tabernacle**

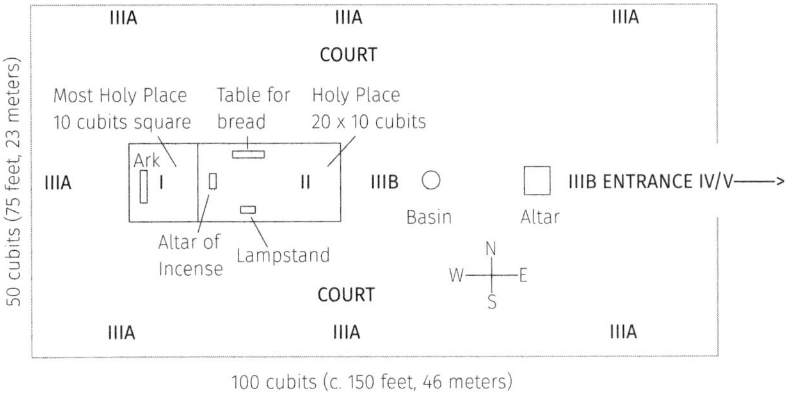

100 cubits (c. 150 feet, 46 meters)

Adapted from: R. E. Averbeck, "Tabernacle," *Dictionary of the Old Testament: Pentateuch* (Downers Grove, IL: InterVarsity Press, 2003), 808.

The Glory of the Lord in His Holy Tabernacle

Four points will be made about the Tabernacle in Scripture.[15] First, it must be understood that the larger purpose of the Tabernacle was holiness. Israel was called to exemplify absolute holiness: "For I am the Lord your God; *consecrate yourselves therefore, and be holy, for I am holy*" (Lev. 11:44). This is the basic expectation of God for his people: "In Scripture, holiness is exclusive to Yahweh; the holiness of anything else is derived, either from God's presence or from consecration to the sanctuary."[16] The Tabernacle, as has been said, was the very dwelling of God with his people: "Let them make me a sanctuary, that I may dwell in their midst" (Exod. 25:8).

Importantly, the Hebrew verb "to dwell" (*shakan*) was often used in reference to "God's presence with His people / God's glory in the midst of His people" and has the same root as the term "Tabernacle" (*mishkan*). Moreover, the word for the "glory cloud" (Hebrew: *shekinah*) is from the same root as the word for the Temple itself: *mishkan*. Both reveal the glory of God. In Scripture,

15. More will be said in future chapters about Jesus, the dwelling place of God's glory / the Word "tabernacling" among us, as well as the Virgin Mary and the glory of God. For the sake of space, these will not be discussed here.

16. J. E. Hartely, *Dictionary of the Old Testament: Pentateuch*, s.v. "Holy and Holiness, Clean and Unclean."

to speak of God's glory in the midst of his people was to speak of the Tabernacle. And to speak of the Tabernacle was to speak of God's presence with his people.

Recalling an earlier insight, of how God reveals himself on holy mountains, leads to a second a key insight concerning the Tabernacle. Specifically, it is this: the "glory" (*kavod*) of God, revealed to God's people in times past on his holy mountains (e.g., Eden, Sinai), now abides in the Most Holy Place in the Tabernacle. As Exodus describes, "Then the cloud covered the tent of meeting, and the glory of the Lord filled the Tabernacle. And Moses was not able to enter the tent of meeting, because the cloud abode upon it, *and the glory of the Lord filled the Tabernacle*" (Exod. 40:34). This pattern is repeated in the Temple of Jerusalem: "And when the priests came out of the Holy Place, *a cloud filled the House of the Lord*, so that the priests could not stand to minister because of the cloud; *for the glory of the Lord filled the house of the Lord*" (1 Ki. 8:10–11).[17]

Third, all of these Tabernacle and Temple images, describing the glory of God filling the house of the Lord, harken back to God's original covenant with Moses at Sinai. "And *Mount Sinai was wrapped in smoke*, because the Lord descended upon it *in fire*; and the smoke of it went up like the smoke of a kiln, and the whole mountain quaked greatly. And as the sound of the trumpet grew louder and louder, Moses spoke, *and God answered him in thunder. And the Lord came down upon Mount Sinai, to the top of the mountain;* and *the Lord called Moses to the top of the mountain*, and *Moses went up*" (Exod. 19:18). On this point, recall that originally Adam (and later Moses and all of Israel with him) was called to expand the temple of God over all the entire of Creation. This motif of the "multiplying" of the God's glory over the whole earth is seen in a number of texts, across the canon:

Then the Lord said, "As I live, and as *all the earth shall be filled with the glory of the Lord*, none of the men who have seen my glory and my signs which I wrought in Egypt and in the wilderness." (Num. 14:20–23)

And one called to another and said: "Holy, holy, holy is the Lord of hosts; the whole earth is full of his glory." (Isa. 6:3)

For the earth will be filled with the knowledge of the glory of the Lord, as the waters cover the sea. (Hab. 2:14)

17. See also 2 Chron. 5:14; 7:1; Ezek. 10:4, 43:5, 44:5; Rev. 15:7–8. "And one of the four living creatures gave the seven angels seven golden bowls full of the wrath of God who lives for ever and ever; *and the temple was filled with smoke from the glory of God* and from his power, and no one could enter the temple until the seven plagues of the seven angels were ended."

Fourth and finally, it follows that since the Tabernacle was the holy abode of God with his people, everything and everyone associated with it were to be carefully and faithfully revered as holy, as the following biblical texts illustrate: "Then you shall take the anointing oil, and anoint the Tabernacle and all that is in it, and consecrate it and all its furniture; *and it shall become holy*" (Exod. 40:29);[18] "And you shall make *holy garments* for Aaron your brother, for glory and for beauty" (Exod. 28:2–3); "And you shall be to me a kingdom of priests and a *holy nation*" (Exod. 19:6); "And fire came forth from the presence of the Lord and devoured [Nadab and Abihu], and they died before the Lord. Then Moses said to Aaron, 'This is what the Lord has said, "*I will show myself holy among those who are near me, and before all the people I will be glorified.*"' And Aaron held his peace" (Lev. 10:1–3).

Yves Congar on the "Glory Cloud"

Yves Congar wrote on the mystery and meaning of the Tabernacle and particularly about the presence of God in relationship to it. As Congar explains, the *Shekinah*, or "glory cloud," was "always linked to a manifestation of God."[19] In the wilderness narratives of Numbers, the *Shekinah* signified, on the one hand, the glorious presence of God; his nearness and availability to Israel upon their arduous journey. Theologically, one may speak of God's "being-with-Israel-ness" as his *immanence*.

On the other hand, the reality of the Tabernacle demanded absolute holiness, even (and especially) Israel's priests. This is evidenced by an assortment of "cautionary stories" in Scripture, such as the fate of the immoral sons of the priest Eli:[20] "Now Eli was very old, and he heard all that his sons were doing to all Israel, and how they lay with the women who served *at the*

---

18. Compare with St. Cyprian of Jerusalem: "Similarly, Saint Cyprian sees a Eucharistic pre-figurement in Psalm 103: Having learnt these things, and been fully assured that the seeming bread is not bread, though sensible to taste, but *the Body of Christ*; and that the seeming wine is not wine, though the taste will have it so, but *the Blood of Christ*: and that of this David sung of old, saying, 'And bread strengthens man's heart, to make his face to shine with oil, strengthen your heart by partaking thereof as spiritual, and make the face of your soul to shine'" (*Catecheses*, 22:9). See also St. John Chrysostom, *On the Priesthood*, 3.4: "For *when you see the Lord sacrificed, and laid upon the altar*, and the priest standing and praying over the Victim, and all the worshippers empurpled with that precious blood, *can you then think that you are still among men, and standing upon earth?*"

19. Yves Congar, *The Mystery of the Temple* (New York: Newman Press, 1962), 9.

20. See, e.g., Num. 16:1–20, 25:4–15.

entrance to the tent of meeting. And he said to them, 'Why do you do such things? For I hear of your evil dealings from all the people. No, my sons; it is no good report that I hear the people of the Lord spreading abroad. If a man sins against a man, God will mediate for him; *but if a man sins against the Lord, who can intercede for him?*' But they would not listen to the voice of their father; for it was the will of the Lord to slay them" (1 Sam. 2:22–25).

And so, in addition to revealing something of God's immanence, the Tabernacle, in all of its glory, conveyed something "wholly other" than the nearness of God. From the glory cloud of that abode upon the Tabernacle, described in its original dedication by Moses and Aaron (Exod. 40:33–35), to the judgment about to befall the sons of Eli, everything about the Tabernacle, and how one should rightly approach it (above), every detail of every narrative concerning the Tabernacle in Scripture, exudes the *transcendence* of God.

In other words, the Tabernacle is something of a paradox in Scripture, in that it simultaneously conveys both the *immanence* of God and the *transcendence* of God: "It signifies both presence and transcendence, it presupposes that God comes down to earth but that He is in heaven. This is why in Jewish and Christian eschatology the cloud is the sign of heaven descending to earth or of a return to heaven."[21]

Congar further unpacks the distinctions between the glory of God itself and the glory cloud that reveals it. While some may see this as theological hair-splitting, understanding the difference between them is necessary in order to understand the reality of the Tabernacle in the Old Testament. He writes, "The Glory [of God] is a reality closely allied with the Cloud," and in some passages Congar admits that the line between them becomes a little blurry, adding, "*in a sense,* it is the same thing."[22] Yet, as he continues, there are also important nuances between them to be kept in mind: "The cloud is rather the phenomena and by means of which the Glory is revealed. The Glory is in a sense nearer to God ... In His glory, his *kabod*, Yahweh makes His transcendent majesty and His presence visible to men by means of a phenomenon of light connected with some sacred reality: Mount Sinai; [23] the Tabernacle;[24] and later, the Temple.[25] This manifestation of God, confined

---

21. Congar, *Mystery of the Temple*, 9–10.   22. Ibid., 10.

23. See Exod. 24:15–17.

24. See Exod. 29:42; Num. 14:10, 16:19, 16:42; Heb. 17:7.

25. See 1 Ki. 8:10–11; 2 Chron. 5:13–14, 7:13.

during the period of the exile and of the Temple by the Chosen people, will later be spoken of by the prophets as destined to spread the earth."[26]

Finally, Congar explains how Yahweh really dwelt in the Tabernacle of the wilderness, despite the fact that his true home is in heaven above. As he describes this apparent paradox, notice how Congar is able to distinguish between non-Israelite concepts of "local deities" and their "presence" in various shrines, and the Israelite notion of God's *otherness*, and of his transcendent presence that *participates* in his Creation, but is not defined by nor confined in a place:

There was a certain local presence [of God in the tent or the ark or the later Temple]. God was there, since He acted and manifested His will there. God really sat upon His throne above the cherubim ... But He is not locally present absolutely speaking as were the pagan gods represented by their idols ... Above all, God is the mighty, living God who intervenes and acts here below but who is not bound to any particular place. There was a god of this spring, that tree, a god who cured men of such and such a disease in such and such a place, etc. But Yahweh is the one, omnipresent and all-sovereign God ... God is in the midst of Israel because Israel is His people, and in order to make Israel His people ... God is there to act and to make known His will; He is in the midst of His people and with them so as to fulfill His undertaking to lead them to the land of promise.[27]

Three comments need to be made about the concepts of clean and unclean in regard to the Tabernacle. First, the terms *clean* and *unclean* must be carefully distinguished from *holy* and *common*. To be clear, the notion of clean and unclean in the Old Testament has to do with ritual purity. The purpose of the various rules, which can seem arcane to modern people, was "to establish boundaries in the routine of daily life in order that the Israelites might live as a holy people serving Yahweh, who is holy. The primary boundary was to prevent any impure person or thing from entering sacred space ... all had to be ritually clean before entering the sanctuary lest holiness consume them."[28]

Second, being clean did not render something or someone to be automatically holy—only that it was pure and allowed to be used in a holy way. There are gradations of holiness, but something or someone is either clean or unclean. As such, holiness is a comparative concept—whereas the notion of clean and unclean is a concept of *polarity*; that is, one is either is clean—or

26. Congar, *Mystery of the Temple*, 10.   27. Ibid., 9–15.
28. Hartely, "Holy and Holiness, Clean and Unclean."

not. As an example, both a priest and the high priest may be ritually clean, but the high priest is holier given his office. Even if the high priest became unclean, he was still holier than the priest that serves him.

Similarly, being unclean did not necessarily render someone or something unholy; rather, the person or object was not permitted in that state to draw near God in his holiness. Most causes of uncleanness come were from within the person, not from contact with external elements or peoples.[29] Still, a pagan was always unclean and never holy. As such, they could never pass over into the space around the Tabernacle. Later, the Court of the Gentiles functioned as a space where Gentiles were welcome and could "come near" the holiness of God. As Alexander writes, "The regulations in *Leviticus* reveal that holiness and uncleanness are incompatible … is it impossible for anyone or anything to be holy and unclean at the same time."[30]

It was the duty of priests, and above all the high priest, to teach the people what is clean or unclean, and to administer over the people accordingly. This was done on a daily basis by priests who, through their sacrifices, rendered the unclean as clean once again. This was especially true of the high priest, who was to make atonement for the holy place, "because of the uncleanness of the people of Israel, and because of their transgressions, all their sins; and so he shall do for the tent of meeting, which abides with them in the midst of their uncleanness" (Lev. 16:16).

Third, to preserve the purity of Israel as a whole and so to please God, all took strident precautions with regard to things such as not eating certain unclean animals and birds;[31] the periods before, during, and after childbirth;[32]

---

29. Ibid.

30. T. Desmond Alexander, *From Eden to the New Jerusalem* (Grand Rapids, MI: Kregel, 2008), 144 (emphasis added).

31. See Lev. 11:1–38, 11:41; cf. Deut. 14:3–20. Clean animals had to be slaughtered properly; no animal could be eaten that had died of natural causes (Deut. 14:21) or had been torn by beasts (Lev. 17:15) or that still contained blood (Gen. 9:3–4; Lev. 17:11ff.; Deut. 12:23).

32. See Lev. 12:1–8; Deut. 14:3–20. The law regarding the uncleanness of childbirth (Lev. 12:2) can be understood against the backdrop of the curse put on women in the Garden (Gen. 3:16). The Old Testament relates childbirth to God's curse over mankind due to sin. When the woman delivered a male child, she would be unclean for a period of seven days. During the next thirty-three days, she was required to remain "in the blood of her purification" and was forbidden to touch holy objects or enter the holy place until the period of her purification had been completed (Lev. 12:2–4). She was excluded from participating in the sacrifices for forty days after the birth of her son (e.g., Luke 2:22). Thus Mary observed her days of purification before she and Joseph presented her son Jesus to the

Figure 3. The Spectrum of Holiness and Uncleanness

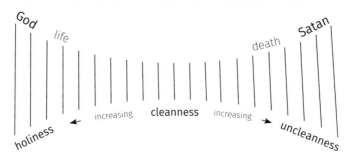

avoiding certain diseases, especially leprosy;[33] bodily discharges;[34] coming in contact with dead bodies;[35] and captured spoil.[36]

Threefold Distinction of the Interior of the Tabernacle

The Tabernacle consisted of an outer structure that defined the public court and a smaller structure, the Tabernacle proper, which was divided into the Holy Place and the Holy of Holies. The Tabernacle proper consisted of gold-plated boards, each approximately fourteen feet[37] high and twenty-six feet wide.

Twenty boards each were on the south and north sides, with eight (six plus the two corner boards) on the west side. Every board was placed in two silver pedestals, having external golden rings through which cross-boards were slid. The east side remained open, closed off by a curtain. Over the wooden frame were placed curtains made from four materials: a double layer of multicolored fine-linen curtains embroidered with cherubim, a double layer of goat's hair curtains, and an outer covering made of rams' skins dyed red and *taḥash* (goatskins).[38]

Lord in Jerusalem. Once the sacrifices of purification were made, the priest made atonement for her, and she was declared clean.

33. See Lev. 13:1–14:57. The procedure for purification procedure was quite intricate. For a detailed description, see A. Myers, *Eerdmans Bible Dictionary*, s.v. "Clean and Unclean."

34. See Lev. 15:1–33.   35. See Lev. 11:39–40.

36. See Num. 31:23–24.   37. Ten cubits.

38. See A. Myers, *Eerdmans Bible Dictionary*, s.v. "Tabernacle."

A multicolored, embroidered veil of fine linen, hanging on four pillars of acacia wood overlaid with gold, divided the Tabernacle into the most holy place, which was a cube measuring ten cubits,[39] and the Holy Place was twenty cubits wide[40] and ten cubits and high.[41] The Ark of the Covenant was sheltered in the holy of holies. In the Holy Place were the table of the Bread of the Presence on the north side, the golden lamp stand on the south side, and the golden incense altar in front of the veil of the Holy of Holies. The Holy Place was separated from the court outside by a curtain of fine linen hanging on five pillars of acacia wood.

There was a threefold dimension of the Tabernacle: the Most Holy Place, the Holy Place, and the Courts, as follows. (See figure 3.) In terms of the sacred space in the Tabernacle, the Most Holy Place (*qodesh haqqōdeshim*) was the area dedicated to God's presence; all other space was common in comparison to it.

1. The Holy Place.

2. The Courts.

3. The Exterior. People, objects, space, and time could be described as "holy." The sanctuary was holy, while the camp was common. However, when the camp was compared to the area outside the camp, the camp itself was holy, while the surrounding area was common.[42]

Yahweh appeared to Moses at "the mountain of God," where God made his special dwelling place.[43] This was "holy ground,"[44] and it was there that the Lord promised not only to be "with" Moses as he brought Israel out of Egypt but also to bring him back there to worship God "on this mountain."[45] Likewise, the Lord was traveling before them by day in a pillar of cloud to lead them on the way and by night in a pillar of fire to give them light. "Neither the pillar of cloud by day nor the pillar of fire by night departed from before the people."[46]

Like Moses, who prayed to see God's glory but was prevented from doing so, the high priest could not see the glory of God's face. As he entered the Most Holy Place on the Day of Atonement, he swung a censer, which filled

---

39. Equivalent to 14.6 feet on each side. 40. Equivalent to 29.2 feet long.
41. Equivalent to 14.6 feet wide and high.
42. Hartely, "Holy and Holiness, Clean and Unclean."
43. See *Exod.* 3:1–2, 4:27, 18:5, 19:2, 24:13. 44. Exod. 3:5.
45. Exod. 3:12. 46. Exod. 13:21–22.

the Most Holy Place with fragrant white smoke—reminiscent of Moses on Mt. Sinai. In the later Temple, the high priest not only went in to the Most Holy Place, but also actually ascended up it; like Sinai, it was at the heights of the Temple.

Recall that the Tabernacle was designed to be portable and imminently movable as the Israelites made their way through the wilderness toward the Promised Land. When the Tabernacle and its contents were moved from place to place, the boards and curtains of the tent could be carried on oxcarts, but its furnishings were to be mounted on acacia-wood poles and carried by Levites.[47] The poles used to carry the Ark of the Covenant were never to be removed from their position in the rings mounted on the sides of the ark.

The Levites who carried the Tabernacle furnishings were never to touch them, on pain of death.[48] When David retrieved the ark from its Philistine captors, it was transported by oxcart. During that journey, Uzzah put out his hand to steady the ark on the tottering cart, immediately forfeiting his life.[49]

And so Israel made its way through the wilderness with the Tabernacle of God. Perhaps the most distinctive feature of the Tabernacle, aside from the "glory cloud" that accompanied it, was its portability. The mobility of the Tabernacle served a practical purpose. The entire structure, elaborate in its own right, was nevertheless designed to be movable, from site to site. At the same time, this particular notion of portability hints at something deeper and more mysterious, namely, the *temporal* nature of the Tabernacle.

To be sure, the Tabernacle was still in play as Israel entered Canaan as the conquest and settlement periods began. In fact, the portable Tabernacle remained in operation at various sites, such as Shiloh,[50] Bethel,[51] Gilgal and Kiriath-jearim,[52] all the way up until the moment of dedication of the Temple by Solomon. Yet, once Solomon's Temple was dedicated in the year 953 BC, the purpose of the Tabernacle—that is, the "portable temple"—had now ceased.

Before moving to chapter 9, which will discuss that "permanent" Tem-

---

47. Exod. 25:12–15, 25:26–28, 27:6–7, 30:4–5; Num. 4:1–15, 7:6–9.

48. Num. 4:15: "And when Aaron and his sons have finished covering the sanctuary and all the furnishings of the sanctuary, as the camp sets out, after that the sons of Kohath shall come to carry these, but they must not touch the holy things, lest they die."

49. See 2 Sam. 6:2–7.   50. See Josh. 18:1.

51. See Judg. 20:26–27.

52. See 1 Sam. 7:1–2. In addition to the locations mentioned here, there were, for a period of

ple built by Solomon, a theological (and spiritual) insight from St. Thomas Aquinas is now offered. In the *Summa Theologica* (I–II), St. Thomas discusses the question of the cause (or purpose) of the Old Testament ceremonial law. In Question 102, the Angelic Doctor takes up the *first* of *ten objections* on the matter, which he states this way:

> It would seem that no sufficient reason can be assigned for the ceremonies of the Old Law that pertain to holy things. For Paul said (Acts 17:24): The God who made the world and everything in it, being Lord of heaven and earth, does not live in shrines made by man. It was therefore unfitting that in the Old Law a tabernacle or temple should be set up for the worship of God.[53]

In other words, St. Thomas presents an objection asserting that a sort of earthly or man-made Temple would be unsuitable for worshipping God. Immediately following this, St. Thomas proceeds to the *second objection*, closely related to the *first*: "Further, the state of the Old Law was not changed except by Christ. Yet, the Tabernacle denoted the state of the Old Law. Therefore, it should not have been changed by the building of a Temple."[54]

The *second objection* goes beyond the parameters of the *first*, as to the idea that nothing in the Old Law was changed until Christ. Given that, what accounts for the development of the Jerusalem Temple as a "change" beyond the Tabernacle.

The details of St. Thomas's responses cannot be taken up here. And yet it is worth tracing the main thought of each of the two replies, with an eye to what biblical texts St. Thomas draws upon as the foundation of each, respectively.

In terms of the *first reply*, St. Thomas underscores that there are two things involved in Divine worship, namely, (1) God, who is worshipped, and (2) men, who worship him. God is incorporeal in nature, the latter corporeal—that is, bodily—in nature.[55] Given man's bodily nature, St. Thomas

---

time prior to the dedication of the Temple in Jerusalem, some local shrines that the Israelites established to commemorate certain events, e.g., Gilgal (Josh. 4:19–24), Shiloh (Josh. 22:12), and Mizpah (1 Sam. 7:5–12). It is not also clear in the text of Scripture whether such shrines were in altogether different places, apart from the Tabernacle, or whether the Tabernacle and shrine formed a sort of single worship site.

53. St. Thomas Aquinas, *Summa Theologica*, trans. Fathers of the English Dominican Province (London: Burns Oates & Washbourne, n.d.).

54. *Summa Theologica* I-II, q. 102, a. 4, obj. 2.

55. *Summa Theologica* I-II, q. 102, a. 4, ad 1.

states, "There was need for a special Tabernacle or Temple to be set up for the worship of God." Yet God in his Divine nature "is not confined to a bodily space" (Latin: *nullo corporali loco clauditur*). In other words, in his *first reply*, St. Thomas asserts that the Tabernacle/Temple was, strictly speaking, necessary *for the sake of man* and not for the sake of God.

In terms of his Scriptural sources, St. Thomas cites 1 Kings 8:27: "But will God indeed dwell on the earth? Behold, heaven and the highest heaven cannot contain thee; *how much less this house which I have built!*" He cites several other Scripture verses, particularly v. 29, in which Solomon prays that God's eyes would be continually on the Temple, "the place of which thou hast said, *'My name shall be there,'* that thou mayest hearken to the prayer which thy servant offers toward this place."

For St. Thomas, these texts from 1 Kings underscore man's need of the Tabernacle/Temple as corporeal beings. God provides for this human need, "that God might be made known there by means of things done and said there; and that those who prayed there might, through reverence for the place, pray more devoutly, so as to be heard more readily." Strictly speaking, God has no need of such man-made sanctuaries. Additionally, St. Thomas emphasizes that it is "God's name" that is particularly praised in the Temple: "From this it is evident that the house of the sanctuary was set up, *not in order to contain God, as abiding therein locally, but that God's name might dwell there.*" In no way is St. Thomas denying God's glorious "presence" in the Holy of Holies. Rather, he is rejecting any attempt to conceive of God's "bodily" presence in the Temple. (Yves Congar made a similar point as was seen above.)

It is St. Thomas's *second reply* in which he responds to the objection that the "change" from Tabernacle to Temple seems to negate the idea of any change to the Old Law. In other words, the objection would state that there would be no necessity of "change" in the Old Law, except and until Christ comes and fulfills it. (St. Thomas's *second reply* is three paragraphs in length, the details of which cannot be discussed here.)

To sum up, St. Thomas affirms that Christ fulfilled the Old Law, and in that sense the Old Law was definitively "changed" in this way. But, he explains, it was necessary, from time to time *within* the Old Law, for God to affect the conditions of it, to suit the people living under it: "Because, at first, the people were in the desert, having no fixed abode: afterwards they were engaged in various wars with the neighboring nations; and lastly, at the time of David and Solomon, the state of that people was one of great peace. *And then for the first time the temple was built in the place which Abraham, instructed by God, had chosen for the purpose of sacrifice.*"[56]

In other words, there was no need of a permanent sanctuary while Israel was making its way through the wilderness. Such an abode would be of no use, "lest the Gentiles might seize hold of that place" or otherwise destroy it. Rather, St. Thomas says, "at the time of David and Solomon," Israel had settled into the land of Canaan, and a permanent sanctuary was now for the first time in their history as a people a true possibility. And so God gave his people a temporal sanctuary in the wilderness, until the appointed place and time at which it would be suitable for them to have a permanent sanctuary.

In support of this response, St. Thomas cites Deuteronomy 12:5–6 as Scriptural source: "But you shall seek the place *which the Lord your God will choose* out of all your tribes to put his name and make his habitation there; thither you shall go, and thither you shall bring your burnt offerings and your sacrifices." Notice too that in the text from Deuteronomy, as with the earlier text he drew upon from 1 Kings, there is the mention of God's name, that is, "*to put his name and make his habitation there.*"

Finally, near the end of the *second reply*, St. Thomas's response deals with the question slightly differently. Thomas presents what he refers to as the "figurative" (Latin: *figuralis*) meaning, by which he means what today would be called the "spiritual" sense of Scripture, specifically the allegorical.[57] He writes: "The figurative (*figuralis*) reason may be assigned to the fact that they signify a twofold state. For the Tabernacle, which was changeable (*mutabile*), signifies the state of the present changeable life (*praesentis vitae mutabilis*)."

St. Thomas then contrasts the "mutable" nature of the Tabernacle with the Temple of Solomon, and he describes the latter as "fixed and stable" and that as such it "signified the state of future life that is altogether unchangeable" (*significatur status futurae vitae, quae omnino immutabilis est*).

In the final part of the reply, St. Thomas presents a spiritual conclusion that brings these various facts together, as he applies the logic of his argu-

---

56. *Summa Theologica* I-II, q. 102, a. 4, ad 2.

57. Some readers may be surprised that St. Thomas made use of *figuralis*—i.e., spiritual exegesis—given his insistence on the "literal" sense in biblical interpretation. Yet such a false dichotomy is not found in his treatment of Scripture, either in the *Summa* or in his various works of biblical commentary. The key is to understand that, for St. Thomas, the literal sense always functioned as the *foundational* and *primary* sense of Scripture, and from which spiritual meaning could be investigated.

ment of the Tabernacle/Temple comparison to that of the Old Law/New Law: "For this reason it is said[58] that in the building of the Temple no sound was heard of hammer or saw, to signify that all movements of disturbance will be far removed from the future state (*statu futuro*)—Or else the Tabernacle signifies the state of the Old Law (*veteris legis*); while the Temple built by Solomon betokens the state of the New Law (*novae legis*)."[59]

Concluding Remarks

Approximately one thousand years before St. Thomas developed this logical and at the same time richly theological and spiritual discussion of the distinctions between the Tabernacle and Temple, St. Clement (150–215 AD), the great second-century allegorist and head of the Catechetical School of Alexandria, comments on the same text in 1 Kings and develops an equally fascinating yet very different interpretation.

In comparison to St. Thomas's replies in the *Summa*, three distinctions are seen in how St. Clement handles the biblical text. First, unlike St. Thomas, St. Clement is not obviously engaged in composing a systematic treatise, but focused solely on the Sacred Page itself. Second, his interpretation is *purely allegorical*; he does not begin with the literal sense, as does St. Thomas. Third and finally, St. Clement's interpretation of the text does not lend itself to a comparison between the "temporal" nature of the Tabernacle in contrast to the more "permanent" nature (relatively speaking) of Solomon's Temple. Instead, St. Clement sees in the Temple a *prefigurement* of the Incarnation of Jesus Christ.

St. Clement's thought is quite a fitting way to end this chapter, and the reader is reminded of the specific text in 1 Kings upon which his spiritual interpretation is based: "But will God indeed dwell on the earth? Behold, heaven and the highest heaven cannot contain thee; how much less this House which I have built" (1 Ki. 8:27). Concerning Solomon's self-styled question (and answer) about the Temple, St. Clement writes:

Solomon the son of David ... comprehending not only that the structure of the true Temple was celestial and spiritual *but had also a reference to the flesh*, which he who was both the son and the Lord of David was to build up, both for his own presence,

58. No indication is given in the text as to the specific source(s) Thomas has in mind.

59. *Summa Theologica* I-II, q. 102, a. 4, ad 2.

where, as a living image, he resolved to make his shrine, and for the church that was to rise up through the union of faith, says expressly, "Will God in very deed dwell with humans on the earth?" He dwells on the earth *clothed in flesh*, and his abode with humans is effected by the conjunction and harmony that obtain among the righteous and that build ... *a new Temple.*[60]

This concludes the present chapter on the Tabernacle. Chapter 9 is fittingly dedicated to a discussion of the Temple that the "son of David" was to build up.

60. Fragment 36, 12.3, in L. Berkowitz and K. Squiter, eds., *Thesaurus Linguae Graecae: Canon of Greek Authors and Works*, 2nd ed. (Oxford: Oxford University Press, 1986).

9

FROM THE HAND OF THE LORD

The Temple of Solomon (I/III)

Then David gave Solomon his son the plan of the vestibule of the temple, and of its houses, its treasuries, its upper rooms, and its inner chambers, and of the room for the mercy seat; and the plan of all that he had in mind for the courts of *the house of the Lord*, all the surrounding chambers, the treasuries of *the house of God*, and the treasuries for dedicated gifts; for the divisions of the priests and of the Levites, and all the work of the service in the house of the Lord … All this he made clear by the writing *from the hand of the Lord* concerning it, all the work to be done according to the plan.

1 Chronicles 28:11–13, 28:19

When Solomon had ended his prayer, fire came down from heaven and consumed the burnt offering and the sacrifices, and *the glory of the Lord filled the temple.* And the priests could not enter the house of the Lord, because the glory of the Lord filled the Lord's house. When all the children of Israel saw the fire come down and *the glory of the Lord upon the temple*, they bowed down with their faces to the earth on the pavement, and worshiped and gave thanks to the Lord, saying, *"For he is good, for his steadfast love endures forever."*

2 Chronicles 7:1–3

The Necessity of Zion

Chapter 8 examined earlier stages of temple theology in the Old Testament, in the form of the Tabernacle. Attention now shifts to the next stage and a paramount development: the Temple of Solomon.[1] The fiber optics of the Temple weaves its way forward from one mountain to another, from the sanctuary begun at Sinai to the much more glorious one called for at Zion, in Jerusalem. Along these lines, contemporary Catholic theologian Matthew Levering writes, "If Sinai were not followed by Zion, God would be related to Israel simply through the covenantal event on Sinai ... through observance of [the] Torah. God would relate to human beings fundamentally through the gift of law ... Yet Sinai is not the only covenant."[2]

Levering understands that this move is more than a geographical development—it is a deeply theological one. As one traces the story of the Temple in Scripture, it becomes apparent that the construction and dedication of the Temple as overseen by David's son Solomon signify an entirely new manifestation of God's presence with his people. The Book of 2 Samuel 7 records the establishment of the Davidic covenant, and this covenantal theology is re-presented with slight modifications in Psalm 89:[3]

When your days are fulfilled and you lie down with your fathers, I will raise up your offspring after you, who shall come forth from your body, and I will establish his kingdom. He shall build a house for my name, and I will establish the throne of his kingdom forever. (2 Sam. 7:12–13)

Thou hast said, "I have made a covenant with my chosen one, I have sworn to David my servant: I will establish your descendants forever and build your throne for all

---

1. In order to streamline/consolidate the presentation, prudential choices were necessary as to what can/cannot be discussed here.

2. Matthew Levering, *Christ's Fulfillment of Temple and Torah: Salvation According to Thomas Aquinas* (Notre Dame, IN: University of Notre Dame Press, 2002), 84. Levering's research was crucial to the present chapter.

3. Nahum Sarna, "Psalm 89: A Study in Inner Biblical Exegesis," in *Biblical and Other Essays*, ed. A. Altmann (Cambridge, MA: Harvard University Press, 1963), 29–46. Sarna suggests that the elements of the divine oath Psalm 89 "do not represent a different, independent recension of Nathan's oracle to David, ... [but] rather an exegetical adaptation of the oracle by the psalmist to fit a specific historic occasion" (39). On the relationship between 2 Sam. 7 and Psa. 89, see M. H. Floyd, "Psalm LXXXIX: A Prophetic Complaint about the Fulfillment of an Oracle," *Vetus Testamentum* 42 (1992): 442–57; T. Veijola, "The Witness in the Clouds: Ps 89:38," *Journal of Biblical Literature* 107 (1988): 413–7.

generations ... I will not violate my covenant, or alter the word that went forth from my lips. Once for all I have sworn by my holiness; I will not lie to David. His line shall endure forever, his throne as long as the sun before me." (Psa. 89:3–4, 89:34–36)[4]

In the text of 2 Samuel, there are a number of puns employed with respect to the Hebrew term *bayith* ("house"). God promises David a dynasty (a throne or royal house, v. 13) through an heir (a son; here, "house" literally means family, v. 11) who will build a Temple for Yahweh (the Lord's house, v. 13). Moreover, God swears to David's offspring the gift of divine sonship: "I will be his father, and he will be my son" (v. 14). Finally, God promises that the Davidic throne will last "forever" (vv. 13–16).

Obviously, the biblical author intends to underscore the relationship between David (and David's royal offspring) and the Temple itself. Yet what is the significance of this? In a word, *covenant*. The Book of 2 Samuel brings together David's offspring and the house he is commanded to build into a single reality, in which to see one is to see the other, as two sides of the same coin. As one scholar explains, "The Temple was *the embodiment of the covenant of David*, in which the triple relationship between Yahweh, the House of David and the people of Israel was established."[5]

If the Tabernacle of Sinai and the wilderness experience signify *God's people on the journey*, then the Temple of Zion symbolizes *God's people having arrived*. Arrived *where*? Precisely in the land God promised to David's forefathers. This fact alone is significant, but more than this, the Temple on Zion outshines the Tabernacle as the clearest image yet of the new Eden. Here, on Zion, in Jerusalem, God's holy presence would abide, and the Temple would be, generation after generation, a lasting sign of God's approval—and his invitation to all of Israel to join God in his holy Sabbath rest.[6]

For all of these reasons, Jerusalem, and more specifically Zion, is *the destina-*

---

4. In addition to Psa. 89, see Psa. 110, 132. Though Psa. 89 was written after the demise of the Davidic monarchy, its composition is dependent upon the divine promises of 2 Sam. 7, and complements it, in that the psalm yearns for the restoration of the monarchy.

5. Toomo Ishida, *The Royal Dynasties in Ancient Israel: A Study on the Formation and Development of Royal-Dynastic Ideology*, Beiheft zur Zeitschrift für die Alttestamentliche Wissenschaft 142 (New York: W. de Gruyter, 1977), 145 (emphasis added).

6. See 1 Sam. 7:1–3: "Now when the king dwelt in his house, *and the Lord had given him rest from all his enemies round about,* the king said to Nathan the prophet, 'See now, I dwell in a house of cedar, but the ark of God dwells in a tent.' And Nathan said to the king, 'Go, do all that is in your heart; for the Lord is with you.'"

tion of God's people, decreed by God himself: "From a theological perspective, the history of [Jerusalem] *has its origin in a divine choice.*[7] David conquered Jerusalem, an ancient Canaanite city.[8] He transferred the Ark of the Covenant there.[9] Solomon built the Temple there,[10] and the city ranked among the older sacred places in Judah and Israel where people went on pilgrimage. In the war of Sennacherib against Hezekiah in 701 BC,[11] Jerusalem alone among the towns of Judah was spared, although the [northern] kingdom of Israel was completely conquered by the Assyrians in 722 BC. The deliverance of Jerusalem had been prophetically announced[12] as an act of divine favor."[13]

The Temple of Jerusalem, like a glistening jewel atop Zion, is the concrete hope of Israel, in that it signifies the climax of the covenant between God and his people. To gaze upon the Temple is to gaze upon God's promises to David and all of Israel: "Jerusalem is usually designated as 'the city chosen by the Lord,'[14] 'established' by Him,[15] the 'city of God,'[16] the 'holy city,'[17] because the Lord is 'in its midst.'[18] She is promised a glorious future: assurance of divine presence 'forever' and 'from age to age,'[19] guaranteed protection[20] as well as happiness and prosperity. Certain texts even attribute an ideal perfection to this city of cities. Above and beyond its geographical location, she becomes the pole of attraction and the axis of the world."[21]

7. See 1 Ki. 8:16–20 (above).

8. See 2 Sam. 5:6–12: "And the king and his men went to Jerusalem against the Jebusites, the inhabitants of the land, who said to David, 'You will not come in here, but the blind and the lame will ward you off'—thinking, 'David cannot come in here.' Nevertheless, David took the stronghold of Zion, that is, the city of David.... And David dwelt in the stronghold, and called it the *city of David* ... And David became greater and greater, for the Lord, the God of hosts, was with him. And Hiram king of Tyre sent messengers to David, and cedar trees, also carpenters and masons who built David a house. And David perceived that the Lord had established him king over Israel, and that he had exalted his kingdom for the sake of his people Israel."

9. See 2 Sam. 6:14, 6:17–20.   10. See 1 Ki. 6:1.

11. See 2 Ki. 18:13.   12. See 2 Ki. 19:30–34.

13. Pontifical Biblical Commission, *Jewish People and Their Sacred Scriptures in the Christian Bible* (New York: Pauline Books and Media, 2003), §48.

14. See 1 Ki. 8:44.

15. Isa. 14:32: "What will one answer the messengers of the nation? '*The Lord has founded Zion*, and in her the afflicted of his people find refuge.'"

16. Psa. 87:3.   17. Isa. 48:2.

18. Zep. 3:17.   19. Joel 3:20.

20. Isa. 31:4–5.

21. Edersheim, *The Temple, Its Ministry and Services as They Were at the Time of Jesus Christ* (Peabody, MA: Hendrickson, 1995), 39.

The Design of the Temple

The discussion now turns from the divine choice of Jerusalem to the design of the sanctuary itself. The magnitude of the project is well captured in the following text of the Chronicler: "Now Solomon purposed to build a temple for the name of the Lord, and a royal palace for himself. And Solomon assigned seventy thousand men to bear burdens and eighty thousand to quarry in the hill country, and three thousand six hundred to oversee them" (2 Chron. 2:1–2).

As Edersheim aptly wrote of the Temple long ago, "The ocean surrounding the world is the white of the eye; its black is the world itself; the pupil is Jerusalem; but the image within the pupil is the Sanctuary."[22] The Book of 2 Chronicles adds a marvelous description about the construction of the Temple: "Behold, I am about to build *a house for the name of the Lord* ... The house which I am to build will be great, for our God is greater than all gods ... So now send me a man skilled to work in gold, silver, bronze, and iron, and in purple, crimson, and blue fabrics, trained also in engraving, to be with the skilled workers who are with me in Judah and Jerusalem, whom David my father provided. Send me also cedar, cypress, and timber from Lebanon *... for the House I am to build will be great and wonderful*" (2 Chron. 2:4–9).

Features and Furnishings of the Temple

Recall from earlier discussions that Genesis depicts a threefold design of the temple of Creation, and a movement from "within to beyond." Beginning from the Holy of Holies (i.e., both the mountain towering over the Garden and the Tree of Life within it), to the Garden itself, to the untamed world beyond, the concept presented there is one of increasing levels of holiness as one comes near to God (and decreasing levels of holiness as one moves away from God's presence). This pattern of holiness established

---

22. Ibid. He adds: "The purple light on the mountains of Moab was fast fading out. Across the city *the sinking sun cast a rich glow over the pillared cloisters of the Temple*, and over the silent courts as they rose terrace upon terrace. From where they stood they could see over the closed Beautiful Gate, and right to the entrance to the Holy Place, *which now glittered with gold*; while the eastern walls and the deep valley below were thrown into a solemn shadow, creeping, as the orb sunk lower, further and further towards the summit of [the Mount of Olives], *irradiated with one parting gleam of roseate light, after all below was sunk in obscurity*" (59–60).

in Genesis, repeated in the design of the Jerusalem Temple, will now be discussed.

First, the space of the Holy of Holies was depicted as an image of heaven, the dwelling place of God. The Holy Place and Most Holy Place were separated by an embroidered veil. In Genesis, one can think of God entering the Holy Place of the Garden sanctuary, as when God "walks and talks" with Adam, but not the other way around—only God dwelt in the Holy of Holies of his heaven above Eden. Symbolically, the Tree of Life in the Garden represented a reminder of God's presence above the Garden. From this Tree the Man and Woman freely ate, and, so long as they persisted in this "state of grace," received the benefits of its immortal fruit—the life of God.

Just beyond the veil inside the Holy of Holies were two massive cherubim.[23] Together, they formed a golden chariot throne of God. The Book of 1 Kings indicates that when the Ark was recovered from the Philistines, Solomon placed it in the Temple.[24] The only furnishing within the Holy of Holies was the Ark[25] (and possibly the Altar of Incense).[26] In an earthly sense, to approach the Ark was to approach the presence of God himself. This is exactly what the high priest did on behalf of the people.

As discussed, only on the great Day of Atonement (Yom Kippur) did the high priest (and only the high priest) enter this most sacred space of the sanctuary to offer sacrifices for himself and for all Israel. Only after sacrifices were offered outside the Holy of Holies would the high priest enter in, offering prayers to God in a brisk cloud of incense—lest the high priest gaze upon the presence of God directly.[27]

Next, consider the Ark itself. Prior to its placement in the Temple, the Ark contained a golden jar containing some of the manna from the Israelites' trek in the wilderness, and the rod of Aaron that budded.[28] Later, they were removed prior to the building of Temple, and there "was nothing in the Ark except the two stone tablets."[29]

The Book of 1 Kings describes Solomon worshipping before the Ark after his dream in which the Lord promised him wisdom.[30] This recalls Adam's

---

23. The cherubim were fifteen feet high with a wingspan of fifteen feet.
24. See 1 Ki. 8:6–9.   25. Exod. 26:31–34.
26. Heb. 9:3–4.
27. See the account of Zechariah in Luke chapter 1.
28. See Exod. 16:32–34; Heb. 9:4.   29. See 1 Ki. 8:9.
30. See 1 Ki. 3:15. The "Holy of Holies" was prepared to receive the Ark (1 Ki. 6:19), and when

worship of God, in his celebratory song upon awaking to the gift of the Woman. Like Solomon, Adam's experience of worship takes place just after his own solemn sleep.[31] Setting aside later Christian typology of Mary (the New Eve) as the New Ark of the Covenant, there is a fascinating parallel to be seen here, between Solomon and Adam. Just as Adam makes the Woman his own, so Solomon makes the Ark his own. When the priest emerged from the Holy of Holies, after placing the Ark there, the Temple was filled with a cloud, "for the glory of the Lord had filled the house of the Lord."[32]

Like the Garden sanctuary, the Holy Place was an enclosed sacred space.[33] It was entered through a narthex, facing east. Within the Holy Place was the golden Menorah (i.e., lamp stand), the table with the twelve cakes of the Bread of the Presence upon it (one for each of the twelve tribes of Israel), and the Altar of Incense. Both the Holy of Holies and the Holy Place were the innermost spaces deep within the interior of the Temple.

The court just beyond the Holy Place was known as the Court of the Israelites, in which only Israelite men were allowed. Obviously, only the Levites and Levitical priests were allowed into the Holy Place itself. A special gate, the so-called Nicanor Gate,[34] separated the Court of Women (where all Israelites could gather) from the inner Court of the Israelites.[35] Within the Court of the Israelites, the most prominent features were the Altar of Unhewn Stones[36] and the bronze Laver.

Some description of this remarkable altar is necessary. The Bronze Altar was a square of forty-eight feet. When its four protruding horned edges were taken into account, it stood fifteen feet high. Around it was a circuit, for use by ministering priests who "always passed round by the right, and retired by the left."[37] Whatever the meaning of the priests' movement, it underscores

---

the Temple was dedicated, the Ark—containing nothing but the two Mosaic tables of the *Torah*—was placed therein.

31. See Gen. 2:21–23.   32. See 1 Ki. 8:10–11.

33. Sometimes referred to as "The Sanctuary."

34. This was the only gate in the Temple that was not gilded, but formed of Corinthian copper.

35. "According to an inscription on a sarcophagus discovered in a cave on Mt. Scopus, it was named for the first-century A.D. Alexandrian craftsman who made the gates." A. Myers, *Eerdmans Bible Dictionary*, s.v. "New Year."

36. "They were 'whitened' twice a year. Once in seven years the high priest was to inspect the Most Holy Place, through an opening made from the room above. If repairs were required, the workmen were let down through the ceiling in a sort of cage, so as not to see anything but what they were to work at." Edersheim, *The Temple*, 54.

37. Ibid.

the sacredness of the altar. The circuit was nine feet off the ground, and one and a half feet high. Close by the altar was the great heap of salt, from which every sacrifice was salted.

Upon the Bronze Altar, three fires burned continually: the first for sacrifices, the second for incense, and the third to supply the means for kindling the other two. The four horns of the altar were straight, hollow protrusions with two openings, into whose silver funnels drink offerings were poured. On the Feast of Tabernacles, water taken from the Pool of Siloam (see John 9) for the libation ceremony was poured into them.

A red line around the middle of the Bronze Altar marked "that above it the blood of sacrifices intended to be eaten, below it that of sacrifices wholly consumed, was to be sprinkled." A drainage system lay below the altar, and its chambers could be flushed at will. This system has been described as "the most wonderful of [the Temple's] arrangements."[38] Both blood and cleansing water[39] were swept away from the altar, out of the Temple, and into Gihon Spring in the Kidron Valley far below.[40]

Near the altar was the immense laver of brass, supported by twelve colossal lions, "which drained every evening, and filled every morning by machinery, and where twelve priests could wash at the same time."[41] "If this had not been sufficient, the ground [was] perfectly honeycombed with a series of remarkable rock-hewn cisterns, in which the water, brought by an aqueduct from Solomon's Pools, near Bethlehem, was stored."[42] The cisterns were connected by a system of channels hewn from the rock. When one cistern was full the surplus ran into the next, and so on.

One of the cisterns, known as the Great Sea, is said to have held as many as two million gallons of water. Today, biblical theologians correctly ascribe Creation symbolism to the Great Sea cistern. Yet most theologians do not seem to know what to make of the image, other than an obvious reference to the Genesis account. Armed with insights from earlier in the book, one can now go further in suggesting the deeper meaning of this fantastic cistern. This unique feature of the Temple undoubtedly served more than a strictly functional purpose. True, it recalled the waters of Creation, *but in what sense?* Recalling the discussion of "deliverance through the waters" in primor-

---

38. Ibid., 54–55. 39. See John 19:34.
40. See Edersheim, *The Temple*, 54. See also *Lev.* 2:13; Num. 18:19.
41. Edersheim, *The Temple*, 55.
42. Ibid., 56.

dial temple liturgies, the Great Sea cistern echoes the deliverance through the Red Sea from the Exodus narrative.

It was fitting for ancient Israelites to remember the exodus as they participated in the Temple sacrifices, was it not? Once Moses had led Israel through the Sea to the temple of Sinai. There, in establishing God's covenant with Israel, Moses offered blood sacrifices on behalf of all of Israel: "And Moses took the blood *and threw it upon the people,* and said, 'Behold the blood of the covenant which the Lord has made with you in accordance with all these words.'"[43] Immediately afterward, Moses and what would be Israel's first Levitical priests (i.e., Aaron, with sons Nadab and Abihu), along with the seventy elders, ascended the mountain sanctuary, "and they saw the God of Israel."[44] Now, in Solomon's Temple, just outside the Holy Place, Israel would offer thanksgiving to God for deliverance—from sin, from enemies near and far, and pray for mercy.

Turning now to the Court of the Israelites, there were a number of chambers; for example, the *Golah,* "for the water apparatus which emptied and filled the laver; and the wood-chamber."[45] Above it were the residences of the high priest and the chamber of the priestly council for affairs of the Temple. The Chamber of the Hearth contained four smaller chambers. In one of the subchambers, priestly bread makers baked the Bread of the Presence. In another, six lambs were set aside for the *'olat tamid*[46] (i.e., Morning and Evening offerings). Yet another subchamber contained a *miqvaoth* (i.e., immersion baths) for priests to immerse themselves before entering the sanctuary or offering sacrifices at the altar. A final subchamber was reserved for the high priest (who had his own residence in the Court of the Gentiles). Rising above the Court of the Israelites were the *bet moked,* temporary residences for priests whose division was on duty in the Temple.

Moving beyond the Court of the Israelites (for men only) is the outer the Court of Women, which was farther from the Holy Place but still within the parameters reserved for Israelites (men and women), provided they were ritually clean and in no violation of Levitical requirements. Yet beyond the Court of Women stood the outermost court of the Temple Mount; it was the place for the unclean, the Court of the Gentiles.

43. Exod. 24:8.   44. Exod. 24:9–10.

45. Edersheim, *The Temple,* 53. For more details, see this section of Edersheim's classic work.

46. On the *tamid* offering, see Exod. 29:38–42; Num. 28:1–8; 2 Ki. 16:15; Ezek. 46:13–15; Neh. 10:34; 2 Chron. 13:11.

"The world beyond" was a place of strange creatures, an unholy terrain. It was good, in that it was created so by God, yet it was untamed and not under Adam's stewardship, as was the terrain of the Garden. The land beyond was cut off from the Garden sanctuary because it was not holy and was to be kept out. The world beyond Eden represented a kind of mission territory, in which Adam and Eve were called to *go*. In fulfilling the first command of God ("*be fruitful and multiply*"), they would extend the temple presence of God beyond Eden, and spread God's holy presence to the world beyond (recall figure 1).

Viewed in this Scriptural light, the Court of the Gentiles had a deeper meaning for the Israelite. On one hand, it was something that one passed through upon entering *into the Temple*. As one entered, the pilgrim was reminded that they belonged here, that they were God's own, and had the privilege of worshipping him in holiness—a privilege not shared by their neighbors. Likewise, as one left the Temple in the same fashion, one contemplated the ambassador-like role of bringing God's presence in the world beyond.

True—outside the Temple was Jerusalem, Judea, and the land of Israel. Yet, in a real sense, Gentiles were quite literally in their immediate vicinity. Symbolically, then, the space between the Court of the Israelites and the Court of the Gentiles was a kind of theological threshold, through which one passed into or away from the presence of God.

The immense Court of the Gentiles that formed the lowest or outer enclosure of the Temple was "paved with the finest variegated marble."[47] According to Jewish tradition, it formed a square of 750 feet. Its name derives from the fact that it was open to all—Jews or Gentiles—"provided they observed the prescribed rules of decorum and reverence."[48] The Court of the Gentiles contained apartments for the (nonpriestly) Levites, as well as a synagogue.[49] As Edersheim recounts, "The view from this 'Royal Bridge' must have been splendid. It was over it that they led the Savior, in sight of all Jerusalem, to and from the palace of the high priest, that of Herod, the meeting-place of the Sanhedrim, and the judgment-seat of Pilate. Here the city would have lain spread before us like a map. Beyond it the eye would wander over straggling suburbs, orchards, and many gardens—fairest among them the royal gardens to the south, the 'garden of roses' ... till the horizon was bounded by the hazy outline of mountains in the distance."[50]

---

47. See Edersheim, *The Temple*, 45–46.   48. Ibid.
49. Ibid., 46.   50. Ibid., 43 (emphasis added).

The Sacrifices of the Temple

"Every unprejudiced reader of the Bible must feel that sacrifices constitute the center of the Old Testament."[51] Above all, it was the Great Atonement, and its *kipporeth*, that was the solemn liturgical ritual of the entire year. As will be examined in some detail below, the Day of Atonement "constituted *the sole and decisive point of fulfillment of the priestly system of the Old Testament*: the sacred place, the sacred time, the sacred person, the sacred action."[52]

Without question, though, the core ideas related to the priesthood of Levitical priesthood were two in particular: *forgiveness* and *mediation*, "the one was expressed by typically atoning sacrifices, the other by a typically intervening priesthood." Moreover, the very term *kohen* referred to "one who stands up for another, and mediates in his cause."[53]

Holiness—this was the heart of it all. For holy priests to help all Israel be holy in the presence of God: "Israel was to be 'a holy nation'—reconciled through the 'sprinkling of blood;' brought near to, and kept in fellowship with God by that means. The priesthood, as the mediators of the people, was also to show forth the 'holiness' of Israel."[54] From this vantage point, Christians read the Old Testament looking beyond it—and viewing the priestly mediators of Solomon's Temple in the light of the New Testament: "One element only was still wanting—that this Son of David, this Sufferer and Conqueror, should be shown to be our Substitute, to whom also the sacrificial types had pointed."[55]

By the time of Jesus, the sacrificial program outlined in the Book of Leviticus had evolved considerably. In the first century, there were in fact no fewer than eleven required public sacrifices in the Jerusalem Temple.[56]

---

51. Ibid., 106. "The fundamental idea of sacrifice in the Old Testament is that of *substitution*, which again seems to imply everything else—atonement and redemption, vicarious punishment and forgiveness" (107, emphasis added).

52. Albert Vanhoye, *Old Testament Priests and the New Priest According to the New Testament* (Petersham, MA: St. Bede's, 1980), 35.

53. Edersheim, *The Temple*, 84–85 (emphasis added).

54. Ibid., 85.

55. Ibid., 124.

56. Most of the sacrifices are described in Leviticus chapters 1–7.

1. *Tamid* (daily morning and evening sacrifices)
2. An additional *tamid* for the Sabbath
3. Sacrifices for the New Moon
4. The Passover lamb itself
5. Additional Passover sacrifices
6. Pentecostal sacrifices
7. Those brought with the two first loaves
8. New Year's sacrifices
9. Day of Atonement sacrifices
10. Tabernacles sacrifices—one on the first day thereof
11. Tabernacles sacrifices—one on each successive day of the octave thereof[57]

It is worth reiterating that the entire system of the Temple provided a means of reconciliation with God through the forgiveness of sins. With the sacrifices themselves, various offerings, when properly administered, also rendered one "clean"—regardless of whether one had sinned or not.[58] Yet a clarification must be added: in ancient Israel, there did not exist the idea of forgiveness of *all* sins, of every possible sin. This is an innovation of the New Testament, in Jesus Christ. From the standpoint of the Book of Hebrews, the Old Testament priesthood was incapable of rendering *any* sin forgiven, or of bringing about a total reconciliation between God and man. Rather, sacrifices needed to be made "year after year" (Heb. 10:1).

The author of Hebrews recognized the necessity of the Temple sacrifices and Temple cult, yet emphasized its temporal status: "For if that first covenant had been faultless, there would have been no occasion for a second" (Heb. 8:7). In speaking of the Temple of the Old Covenant in this way, the author of Hebrews goes on to admit its obsolescence in light of the New Covenant: "In speaking of a new covenant he treats the first as obsolete. And what is becoming obsolete and growing old is ready to vanish away" (Heb. 8:13).

Afterward, in Hebrews chapter 9, the author describes the threefold division of the Temple, taking care to note the separation between the Holy Place and the Holy of Holies: "But only the high priest goes [in] and he but once a year, and not without taking the blood that he offers for himself and

---

57. See Edersheim, *The Temple*, 111.
58. See discussion of clean/unclean in a previous topic.

for the sins committed unintentionally by the people. By this the Holy Spirit indicates that the way into the sanctuary *has not yet been disclosed (pephaner-osthai)* as long as the first tent is still standing" (Heb. 9:10, NRSV).

Notice verse 8, and here a precise translation matters. The New Revised Standard Version (as well as the NAB, NIV)[59] renders the verb *pephaner-osthai* (from *phaneroo*) more accurately as "*has not yet been disclosed*," rather than the Revised Standard Version, which has "*not yet opened*."

This distinction is not unimportant. As Vanhoye explained, "The author did not simply write, as he is sometimes misunderstood to have said, that 'the way to the sanctuary was not opened up,' which could lead one to believe that the way was known, but forbidden."[60] Rather, as Vanhoye correctly points out, the author wrote this way because "God had not yet revealed it."[61]

Yet God did reveal it gloriously in Jesus Christ: "But when Christ appeared as a high priest of the good things that have come, then through the greater and more perfect tent (not made with hands, that is, not of this creation) he entered once for all into the Holy Place, taking not the blood of goats and calves but his own blood, thus securing an eternal redemption" (Heb. 9:11–12).

Here, the phrase "perfect tent" is key, as it translates the Greek terms *teleiosis* ("perfect") and *skene* ("tent, tabernacle"). Vanhoye's analysis is salient: "The author's expression ... implies that the result of sacrifice ought above all to be the transformation of the one who makes the sacrifice ... The author makes the point that every sacrifice ought to be a sacrifice of priestly consecration, of *teleiosis*, for its purpose is always to make a many worthy to present himself before God. *But for this the ancient rites proved unsatisfactory.* In fact, they could only confer *an external ritual transformation* which ... was limited to the hands: they sought 'to make the hands perfect.'"[62]

But, Vanhoye asks, is it enough to approach God in holiness, with only consecrated hands? "Obviously not. A transformation of the conscience is necessary. On this level, *the Old Testament worship did not provide any effec-*

---

59. The ESV version also has "opened," as does the RSV (above). In contrast, the more literal NASB has "disclosed," as does the NRSV. Although the NIV is rarely to be preferred for accuracy, it too has "disclosed." Both the older NAB as well as the NAB-RE (revised) have "revealed," which is also preferred to the RSV/ESV translations. The KJV renders the verb as "made manifest," which is also satisfactory.

60. Vanhoye, *Old Testament Priests and the New Priest*, 186.

61. Ibid.   62. Ibid., 187 (emphasis added).

tive mediation. The victim offered certainly underwent a transformation, but only in the sense of a destruction. As for the one who made the offering, he inevitably *remained outside the sacrifice ... Consequently, one is bound to admit the powerlessness of the Old Testament worship and its radical ineffectiveness.*"[63]

The possibility existed in the Old Testament economy of capital punishment due to serious sin (unrepentant blasphemy, treason, etc.). Such persons could be "cut off" from access to the Temple, placed in a state of perpetual state of "uncleanness." A frequent formula that pertains to punishment for sin is the literal expression: "That soul shall be cut off from the congregation of Israel/my presence." This referred to expulsion from the community. Reasons for expulsion from the community often included disregard of cultic regulations, such as a desecration of something sacred (e.g., sacred time, a sacred substance, a sacred place, profaning God's holy name).[64] Moreover, for outrageous sins, the Mosaic Law prescribed the physical penalty of death.[65] Still, God forgives: "The Lord, the Lord, a God merciful and gracious, slow to anger, and abounding in steadfast love [Hebrew: *hesed*] and faithfulness, keeping steadfast love for thousands, forgiving iniquity and transgression and sin" (Exod. 34:6–7).

In any case, within ancient Judaism, access to God's forgiveness clearly was through the ministry of the Temple in the form of specific types of sacrificial offerings, to which the discussion now turns.[66]

Main Types of Temple Sacrifices in Ancient Judaism

There were five distinct kinds of sacrifices offered in the Temple.[67] The first type was the burnt offering (Hebrew: *olah*), also known as a holocaust offering.[68] It was a complete offering in which an entire animal was offered upon the altar, and ascended to God "in the form of smoke and a savory scent." Its blood was sprinkled on the altar, and its hide was given to the priest. Burnt offerings symbolized total self-surrender to God. As such, it has

---

63. Ibid., 187–88 (emphasis added).

64. E. A. Martens, *Dictionary of the Old Testament: Pentateuch*, s.v. "Sin, Guilt." See Exod. 12:15, 30:33, 30:38; Lev. 7:20, 7:25, 7:27.

65. See Exod. 21:15–17; Lev. 20:10–16, 24:10–17; Deut. 21:18–21, 24:16; Num. 18:22, 27:3.

66. See Lev. 4:1–6:7.

67. See Edersheim, *The Temple*, 93–103.

68. See Lev. 1:3–7, 6:8–13; also Exod. 29:38–42.

rightly been called the *sacrificium latreuticum*, or sacrifice of devotion and service.

Day by day it formed the regular morning and evening sacrifice in the Temple, while on Sabbaths, new moons, and festivals, additional burnt offerings followed ordinary worship.[69] A bloody sacrifice involved an unblemished male lamb, goat, ram, and the like. It could be brought forth by Gentiles as well as Jews. Perhaps the classic example was the *tamid*, the daily morning and evening sacrifice.[70]

A second type of Temple sacrifice was the cereal offering (Hebrew: *mincah*, "gift").[71] This type was also known as a tributary offering, in that it was offered as a gift of gratitude to God. By definition it was an unbloody sacrifice, offered as an auxiliary sacrifice with, for example, burnt offerings. There appears to be variety in the constitution of such offerings: either unleavened wheat or barley grain was used, and it could be baked, unbaked, griddled, or uncooked altogether. If baked as bread, it was made with fine corn flour, sometimes as in the form of wafers. Grains were mixed or anointed with oil. Wine was frequently poured out with grain offerings as a libation to the Lord. In practice, the priest would throw a handful onto the fire of the altar, and the remainder was eaten as consecrated bread by priests. Examples include the *lehem panim* (Bread of the Presence)[72] as well as the grain offering during priestly ordinations.[73] It was known as "the perfect sacrifice of the Gentiles."[74]

A third type of Temple sacrifice was the peace offering (Hebrew: *zebah shelamim*).[75] It was also known as a fellowship offering or thank offering (Hebrew: *todah*). This type was similar to the burnt offering, in that it involved the sacrifice of an animal. However, it was not offered for the one's whole being, but rather for a specific action of God's deliverance, such as a serious illness. Many of the so-called Psalms of Thanksgiving likely originated from such liturgies.[76] An example of a cereal offering is as follows. According to 1 Kings, 142 lambs were offered in thanksgiving at the Temple's dedication.[77] On a more individual basis, Leviticus mentions a *todah* liturgy, offered as a

---

69. See Edersheim, *The Temple*, 126–27.

70. See Exod. 29:38–46.

71. See Lev. 2:1–16, 6:14–23.

72. See Exod. 25:30; Num. 4:7.

73. See Lev. 6:19–22, 8:25–29.

74. Mal. 1:11; see Lev. 6:20.

75. See Lev. 3:1–17, 7:11–36.

76. Psa. 50, 51:17, 54:6, 56:12, 116:17–18.

77. See 1 Ki. 8:63.

sacrifice of thanksgiving once the person recovered from the ailment or hardship and was able to come to the Temple.[78]

A flock or herd animal was divided into several parts, its blood sprinkled upon the altar. One-third of the offering was consumed by the fire of the altar itself. Another third was reserved for the priest as consecrated food. Most importantly, the final third was to be eaten by the worshipper, along with his family members with him. In terms of early Christianity, several points can be added regarding this Temple sacrifice. First, rabbinic tradition considered this the sole sacrifice of the coming messianic age.[79] Second, from the vantage point of the Eucharist of the early Christians, the fact that the worshipper ate the bread offering is especially significant. Third and finally, in the Greek Old Testament (LXX), the Hebrew word *todah* ("thanksgiving") is represented by the Greek term *eucharistia*.

A fourth type of Temple sacrifice was known as the sin offering (Hebrew: *hattat*).[80] It was also known as a purification offering, as in repentance and purification from some specific sin. It involved a bloody sacrifice. The animal offered up depended upon who it was in substation of: if a priest, a bull was offered; if a ruler, a male goat; if a layperson, a female goat or, in the case of the poor, a turtledove or pigeon. If for the entire congregation, a bull was offered. Blood was sprinkled on the altar. The fat portions and kidneys of the animal were burned. A meat portion given to the priest and the remainder was burned or destroyed.

The entire rite conveyed forgiveness upon individuals. Accordingly, blood was smeared on the worshipper by the priest. The sin offering was also the primary offering for those in a state of uncleanness that was not necessarily the result of sinning. To clarify: in such cases, the sin-offering function was for cultic purification and not for the forgiveness of sins. Examples include a woman's return to Temple life after childbirth,[81] a person recovering from leprosy,[82] or a person with some sort of bodily emission.[83] Above all of these was Yom Kippur, the Day of Atonement.[84] Here, one also thinks of the

---

78. See Lev. 7:11.

79. More will be said about this in chapter 13.

80. See Lev. 4:1–5:13, 6:24–30.

81. Lev. 12:6; see Mary in the Temple ("purification") in Luke 2:22: "And when the time came for their purification according to the law of Moses."

82. See Lev. 14:19.   83. See Lev. 15:1–33.

84. Lev. 16:3. In the case of the Day of Atonement liturgy, one male goat was sacrificed on the

Suffering Servant who is a messianic sin offering in Isaiah's Servant Songs.[85]

A fifth and final type of Temple sacrifice was the guilt offering (Hebrew: *asham*),[86] which was offered as a kind of reparation or penance. These were occasional bloody sacrifices, in which the animal's blood was dashed against the side of the altar. It offered atonement for one specific circumstance of guilt, for instance, the profanation of a holy thing some sort of unjust appropriation of personal property. The worshipper paid a 20 percent tithe to the Temple in reparation. Examples include penance for impurity or unwitting sin,[87] cleansing of a healed leper,[88] and penance made after restitution of stolen goods.[89]

Before leaving this chapter on the Jerusalem Temple, one final question needs to be raised. What was—in a single word—the object of all of these sacrifices, whether bloody or unbloody? The word *forgiveness* springs quickly to mind, though in truth not all sacrifices were presented for those in need of forgiveness. *Prayer* is another possibility, for the very design of the offerings, especially those involving animal sacrifice, produced smoke and incense that rose above the heights of the Temple, lifting up prayers from the worshippers below. A still better word is *liberty*, the liberty of the prayerful, forgiven, thankful worshipper who is freed from mortal concerns in the space of the Temple, and whose love for God is rekindled near the hearth of the altar.

Concluding Remarks

As this chapter draws to a close, it is worth pausing to consider a spiritual and ecclesial application as it pertains to temple building. Long after the Temple's final destruction, in the High Middle Ages, St. Bernard of Clairvaux wrote to a friend about a similar kind of liberty. That friend was the pope of his day, Eugene III. In a spiritual classic called *Five Books on Consideration: Advice to a Pope*, St. Bernard challenges his disciple and friend, and now the reigning Pontiff, to consider the practical and theological demands of his new office. Early on, St. Bernard writes, "Love knows no master. It rec-

---

altar; a second goat ("Azazel") was sent into the desert in order to "remove" Israel's sins (see Lev. 16:8, 16:10, 16:26).

85. Isa. 53:12.
86. See Lev. 5:14–6:7, 7:1–7.
87. See Lev. 5:14.
88. See Lev. 14.
89. See Lev. 6:1–17.

ognizes a son, even though he wear the tiara."[90] In *Book V*, in one of the most intimate passages, St. Bernard writes of the liberty on Christ that he wishes for his friend, the pope.

Although St. Bernard's spiritual advice may seem at first glance a long way from the Jerusalem Temple, there are in fact several direct and indirect references to the Temple and Temple worship in the passage. Moreover, the larger message of the passage can be read against the backdrop of the Temple, in terms of the liberty that lay behind the blood, smoke, and incense of the sacrifices offered in the Temple:

O Eugene, how good it is for us to be here ... Our affections lie weighted down by this bodily mass, and cling to desires while only consideration, dry and delicate, flies before. And still with so little granted it as yet, it freely cries out, '*Lord, I have loved the beauty of your House and the place where Your glory dwells.*'[91] What if the soul were ... recalled from all the places they were held captive by fearing what should not be feared, loving what was unworthy, grieving vainly and more vainly rejoicing ... And when the soul has begun to move about the illumined mansions and to examine carefully even the bosom of Abraham, and to look again at the souls of the martyrs,[92] dressed in their first robes,[93] and patiently awaiting their second,[94] will it not say much more insistently with the Prophet, '*One thing I have asked of the Lord, this will I seek, that I may dwell in the House of the Lord all the days of my life, that I may see the will of the Lord, and visit His Temple?*'[95] ... His heart of mercy lies open, His thoughts of peace lie revealed, the riches of His salvation, the mysteries of His good will, the secrets of His kindness, which are hidden from mortals and beyond the comprehension of even the elect. This, indeed, is for the good of their salvation, so they do not cease fearing before they are found suited for loving worthily.[96]

90. St. Bernard of Clairvaux, *Five Books on Consideration: Advice to a Pope*, trans. John D. Anderson and Elizabeth Kennan (Kalamazoo, MI: Cistercian, 1976), 23. (From the preface.)

91. Psa. 26:8.   92. Rev. 6:9–10.

93. Luke 15:22–24.   94. Rev. 6:11.

95. Psa. 27:4: "One thing have I asked of the Lord, that will I seek after; that I may dwell in the house of the Lord all the days of my life, to behold the beauty of the Lord, and to inquire in his Temple."

96. St. Bernard of Clairvaux, *Five Books on Consideration*, 148–49, Book V, 8.

INTERNALIZING AND UNIVERSALIZING GOD'S LAW

Temple Theology in the Psalms and Wisdom Literature,
The Temple of Solomon (II/III)

Surely goodness and mercy shall follow me all the days of my
life; and I shall dwell in the house of the Lord forever.

Psalm 23:6

Chapter 9 examined the theological movement from Sinai to Zion, the movement from Tabernacle to Temple. The present chapter delves into several types of biblical literature, closely associated with God's covenant with David, and with the key earthly symbol of that covenant, the Jerusalem Temple, constructed under the reign of David's son.

Specifically, this part of the book will examine the influence of the Temple upon the theology of both the Psalter and the Wisdom books of the Old Testament. As is common knowledge, the figures of David and Solomon stand at the head of a long tradition of temple songs—the Psalms—and temple knowledge—Jewish Wisdom literature.

The collection of psalms that eventually became the Psalter—along with the Old Testament Wisdom books—together represents a kind of *internalizing* and *universalizing* of the earlier Mosaic covenant, which was characterized by a less interior dimension of religious adherence and a far less universal—in fact, an *exclusive to Israel*—Law. These new dimensions of the covenant are foreseen by the prophet Jeremiah (Jer. 31:30–33) and are key characteristics of the life of the Temple, once the Temple is actually established in Jerusalem. This chapter examines some of the biblical evidence regarding two characteristics.

According to the testimony of 1–2 Samuel, as well as 1–2 Chronicles, the early Davidic Kingdom was an era of manifold blessings: a new land, new temple, and, above all, God's promise of an everlasting dynasty. For God's people, it is a new faith and optimism, new forms of instruction, and new liturgical music and feasts.

Beyond the Law of Moses: The Songbook of the Temple

The Psalter of the Old Testament is permeated with a Davidic ethos and echoes many of the promises of the Davidic covenant. As one scholar writes, "The Psalms are a vast temple in which God is worshiped. Each individual psalm is like a room in the temple, full of God's presence but not exhausting it. Praising God in one psalm one hear echoes of songs from other rooms. The psalms in their totality are the 'script' for the people of God, themselves a temple wherein God is worshiped, so that in the singing of the psalms the two temples come together."[1]

For the ancient Jewish composers of the Psalter, life was meaningless apart from the spiritual refreshment and communion with God, which one encountered in visiting the Temple. A good example of this is seen in Psalm 73, one of St. Augustine's favorites in the entire Psalter. In the opening words of the psalm, the author speaks in a sober and anxious tone, not unlike the

---

1. Laurence Krieghauser, OSB, *Praying the Psalms in Christ* (Notre Dame, IN: University of Notre Dame Press, 2009), 13. From a Catholic perspective, Krieghauser adds, "Because the ongoing psalmody of the Church on earth is *a participation in the action by which all men and women are reconciled to God*, no other action of the Church, apart from the Eucharist from which [the Psalter] flows, surpasses it in efficacy" (12). Vatican II's Constitution on Sacred Liturgy, *Sancrosanctum Concilium* (*SC*), speaks to the centrality of the Psalter to the whole people of God today: "To promote active participation, the people should be encouraged to take part by means of acclamations, responses, psalmody, antiphons, and songs, as well as by actions, gestures, and bodily attitudes. And at the proper times all should observe a reverent silence" (*SC* §30). Likewise, the Psalter plays a central role in the Church's in the Liturgy of the Hours: "The divine office, because it is the public prayer of the Church, is a source of piety, and nourishment for personal prayer. And therefore priests and all others who take part in the divine office are earnestly exhorted in the Lord to attune their minds to their voices when praying it. The better to achieve this, let them take steps to improve their understanding of the liturgy and of the bible, *especially of the Psalms*" (*SC* 90). See also Jean Corbon, *The Wellspring of Worship*, trans. M. J. O'Connell (New York: Paulist Press, 1988).

author of Ecclesiastes, who comes to perceive the search for meaning in life as "vanity of vanities" (Eccles. 1:1–2).

The situation is as follows. The psalmist is perplexed and angry at an outrageous injustice: the ungodly who prosper while ignoring and even mocking God. Meanwhile, he goes about his life, honoring God while growing increasingly confounded at the last of punishment of such unrighteous people by God. This leads to inner turmoil, expressed beautifully in the psalm. At one point, the psalmist gives up his pursuit of righteousness and even contemplates "bad mouthing" God to his friends (e.g., "What's the point of trying to be holy?") Then, in a moment, things take a dramatic turn for the better. A spiritual epiphany occurs to the psalmist, which centers him, giving him new reason for optimism that God is indeed just. He reverses the course he was on and praises God's goodness, exclaiming, "Whom have I in heaven but You?" (v. 25). But what is most significant about this change of heart is *where* it takes place.

The pivotal verse in the psalm reads, "But when I thought how to understand this, it seemed to me a wearisome task, *until I went into the sanctuary of God"* (v. 17).[2] In other words, worship—Temple worship—brought the psalmist back to God and back to his senses. In coming near to the Almighty, the psalmist's anxieties, frustrations, and fears melt away in the presence of God's glory. Not only so, his inner turmoil was also transformed into faithful devotion and witness.

Yet what was the larger purpose of the Psalter in ancient Israel? Texts from Psalm 9 ("The Lord dwells in Zion"[3]) and Psalm 43 ("on His holy hill"[4]) make it clear that the Psalter was "the songbook of the Temple, and in them we glimpse something of the ancient [Jewish] liturgy."[5] The theology of the Psalter corresponds to the idea that the Temple is the dwelling place of God's glory.[6]

This leads to an insight about the meaning and value of song and singing from the perspective of temple theology. "Singing," it turns out, is one of the most repeated verbs in the Bible, occurring 399 times in the Old Testa-

2. Psa. 73:16–17.

3. Psa. 9:11: "Sing praises to the Lord, *who dwells in Zion!"*

4. Psa. 43:3: "Oh send out thy light and thy truth; let them lead me, *let them bring me to thy holy hill and to thy dwelling!"*

5. Margaret Barker, *Temple Themes in Christian Worship*, 3rd ed. (London: Bloomsbury, 2013), 137.

6. Psa. 26:8: "O Lord, I love the habitation of thy house, and *the place where thy glory dwells."*

ment and 36 times in the New Testament. What does this reveal? That when man comes into contact with God, "mere speech is not enough," as Ratzinger writes. "Indeed, man's own being is insufficient for what he has to express, and so he invites the whole of creation to become a song with him: 'Awake, my soul! Awake, O harp and lyre! I will awake the dawn! I will give thanks to you, O Lord, among the peoples; I will sing praises to you among the nations. For your steadfast love is great to the heavens, your faithfulness to the clouds'" (Psa. 57:8).[7]

About the theological contributions of the Psalter, St. Hippolytus writes, "The Book of Psalms contains new doctrine after the Law of Moses. After the writing of Moses, it is the second book of doctrine ... [David] introduces the new hymn and a new style of jubilant praise in the worship of God ... [David] teaches many other things beyond the Law of Moses."[8] In the Psalter, one sees that God has put a "new song" in the mouth of Israel: "O sing to the Lord a new song; sing to the Lord, all the earth!"[9] "O sing to the Lord a new song, for he has done marvelous things!"[10]

What St. Hippolytus is tapping into is important to this study of temple theology; what the great saint recognized is that, collectively, the Psalms represent a *deeper and more interior encounter* of God than previously in the story of Israel. The developments of the Davidic covenant are a "going beyond" the Sinai covenant. But make no mistake: this covenantal development, as evidenced in the Psalms, is not a repudiation of the earlier Mosaic Law given at Sinai. Rather, the Psalms express God's desire as part of the Davidic covenant, and the Law now would be "written on the hearts" of all Israel.[11]

This going beyond Sinai to Zion is an arresting development, as it pertains to *both* covenantal theology *and* temple theology. In a sense, these two dimensions of biblical theology (i.e., covenant, temple) powerfully converge in the Psalter. The Davidic covenant is not merely a continuation of God's covenant with Israel at Sinai, another chapter. Rather, it is a "bringing closer" of God to his people—and God's people to himself in new and more personal encounters—in "new songs" of the heart and in "new laws" for the mind.

---

7. Joseph Ratzinger, *The Spirit of the Liturgy*, trans. John Saward (San Francisco: Ignatius Press, 2000), 136 (emphasis added).

8. Cited in M. Barber, *Singing in the Reign: The Psalms and the Liturgy of God's Kingdom* (Steubenville, OH: Emmaus Road, 2001), 15.

9. Psa. 96:1. 10. Psa. 98:1.

11. Jer. 31:33.

Yet it is not only the Psalter that plays a special role in this regard. In fact, both the Psalms and the Wisdom literature of the Old Testament were instrumental in God's invitation to all of Israel to *actualize* the covenant, to enact it and live it out, as never before. What these two biblical traditions of Psalms and Wisdom represent is *the further reach* of God's covenantal love for all humanity. These are fresh biblical approaches of encountering God. In short, the Psalter is a call to *internalize* the Law, to make it one's own, to "taste and see that the Lord is good."

From Sinai to Zion: The Law Universalized

Like the Psalter, the Wisdom literature of the Old Testament represents a theological development of the Davidic covenant not possible earlier, that is, at Sinai. And, also like the Psalter, the Wisdom literature represents, in its own distinct fashion, a "going beyond" from Sinai to Zion. As explained, in the Psalter, one can say that the Law moves inward; there is a call to *internalize* the Law, and that this call is cast out to all of Israel.

The paradigm shift in the Wisdom literature is similar to—and different from—that of the Psalter. The two biblical traditions are similar in several ways. First, both traditions are closely connected to the expression of the Davidic covenant and its promises, and to the institution of the Temple. Both are part of this "Sinai to Zion" development, the going beyond, the expanding, and deepening of the Law. Second is the output of the Davidic and Solomonic eras; both begin to develop in the time of the monarchy and gradually continue to develop long after the time of David and Solomon, in fact, long after Solomon's Temple is standing. These traditions can generally be dated from approximately 1000 to 400 BC. (Some of the later Wisdom books, like Sirach and Wisdom of Solomon, are later still, in the second and first centuries.)

So much for the similarities. There are numerous differences between these two biblical genres, which lie beyond the scope of this book. One key distinction relevant to this discussion is this. Whereas the Psalter represents an interiorizing and internalizing of the Law, in the heart of the Jewish believer, the Wisdom tradition represents an *expanding* of the Law of Moses *beyond Jerusalem*, and in fact *beyond Israel*.

Many aspects of the Wisdom tradition reflect the later influence of Hellenization. Books like Sirach and Wisdom of Solomon are clearly aimed at Greek-speaking Jews, living in Diaspora locales like Alexandria. One can think of the Wisdom tradition as a *universalizing* of the Mosaic Law. To be clear, it is still for Israel, yet packaged and presented in a way that Hellenistic Jews and the curious non-Jew could *access it*, in a way that was not as possible with the Mosaic Law.

First, such books were, like the Pentateuch itself, put into the Greek. In fact, Sirach was translated a generation after its original composition, from Hebrew into Greek, for dissemination among Hellenized Jews. And Wisdom of Solomon was composed from the outset in Greek.

Second, it is more than the accessibility of language, crucial as that was. The Wisdom books are conveyed in such a way that they compress and carefully conceal traditional Jewish motifs, in favor of a more atomized and nuanced presentation. For example, in a classic text, Proverbs 8, it is through "Sophia" (i.e., Lady Wisdom) that God creates the world. There, Lady Wisdom "speaks," and instructs the reader that "the Lord created me *at the beginning of his work*" (v. 22). God is there "at the first, before the beginning of the earth" (v. 23). One can hardly imagine such a text at the beginning of Genesis, or anywhere in the Pentateuch.

Likewise, Wisdom of Solomon recasts the story of the Exodus, although the hero of the story is different. It is not Moses who delivers Israel from the hands of Pharaoh in Egypt; rather, "*she* [i.e., Lady Wisdom] brought them over the Red Sea," leading Israel "through the waters" while "drowning their enemies" (Wisd. 10:18–19). Elsewhere, Adam is only referred to indirectly (and in a rather Platonic fashion) as the "first-formed father of the world" (Wisd. 10:1).

These are striking moves and make sense only in the context of a Jewish Diaspora audience; one that had lost the Temple, lost the land, and were in danger of losing their way, Jewishly speaking. But, again, the Wisdom tradition emerges as not only an appeal to Hellenized Jews, but also in some sense "all who have ears to hear." At one point early in the book, the author of Wisdom of Solomon addresses his audience this way: "Listen therefore, *O kings*, and understand; learn, *O judges of the ends of the earth*. Give ear, you that rule over multitudes, and boast of many nations. For *your dominion was given you from the Lord*, and your sovereignty from the Most High, who will search out your works and inquire into your plans" (Wisd. 6:1–3).[12]

There is much complexity in the Wisdom tradition that cannot be dis-

---

12. It is possible that the author is addressing non-Jewish leaders and influential members of a Greek *polis* (city). Another more subtle possibility is that the author is addressing the Greek-speaking

cussed here. Many more texts could be added to the ones above, all of which underscore this "universalizing" of the Mosaic covenant. One scholar writes, "There is a clear movement from Sinai to Zion represented by the Davidic covenant. Sinai represents the Mosaic tradition, a national covenant, especially linked with ceremonial laws. Zion, however, represents an *international* arrangement." He adds that God's covenant with David "brings His law to the nations, not through an exclusive Israelite law code [as at Sinai], but through the universality of the Wisdom literature."[13]

All of this pertains to temple theology in the following sense: *the Wisdom books correspond to the expansive nature of the Davidic Kingdom.* Put another way, in the Davidic Kingdom, the call of God to Adam to "be fruitful and multiply" takes on a deeper meaning. In the context of temple theology, it is possible to suggest that the "first great commission" that God gave to Adam—that is, to extend his temple presence beyond the land in which Adam dwelt—finds renewed expression in the Davidic covenant. Like the "first-formed father of the world," David is the priest-king called to lead the way, and to "spread Eden beyond Eden" that God's temple presence would fill the whole earth.

The Wisdom literature exhibits this sort of universalizing or internationalizing quality in a way that was more or less unseen in older, more traditional Old Testament texts that precede it. In Proverbs, a personified Lady Wisdom is depicted as "readily available," not merely to Israel but also seemingly to all who respond to the sound of her voice: "Wisdom cries aloud in the street; in the markets she raises her voice; on the top of the walls she cries out; at the entrance of the city gates she speaks" (Prov. 1:20–21)

Where does all of this lead, from a New Testament perspective? The universalization of the Mosaic Law in the Wisdom tradition bears striking similarity to sayings of Jesus in the Gospels, as in John 18:20: "Jesus answered him, 'I have spoken openly to the world ... I have said nothing secretly.'" Elsewhere, one can see a connection between the presentation of Lady Wisdom in Sirach and Jesus in the Gospel of Matthew:

Jews in a rhetorical way, for example, a colony of Jews in Alexandria who are in search of self-governance, empowerment, and advancement within a foreign society. If this is the case, the vocative expression "O Kings" could be taken as a subtle nod, not to Jewish power in the Diaspora but to the desire for it, and to a "kingdom" where none is immediately in sight (see Wisd. 6:17–22). In either case, this text is a striking example of the "internationalizing" notion being discussed here.

13. Barber, *Reign*, 67, 74 (emphasis added).

Come to me, you who desire me, and eat your fill of my produce. For the remembrance of me is sweeter than honey, and my inheritance sweeter than the honeycomb. Those who eat me will hunger for more, and those who drink me will thirst for more. (Sir. 24:19–21)

Come to me, all who labor and are heavy laden, and I will give you rest. Take my yoke upon you, and learn from me; for I am gentle and lowly in heart, and you will find rest for your souls. For my yoke is easy, and my burden is light. (Matt. 11:28–30)

A comment is warranted about the above parallels between the Wisdom and Gospel texts. Specifically, such universal availability was not the case with the Mosaic Law, which was concealed in the Ark of the Covenant and kept out of sight, in the Holy of Holies inside the inner recesses of Israel's holy Tabernacle. This shift says something about the expansive, invitational dimension of worship that was gradually but steadily coming to be associated with the Temple in each successive generation. In stark contrast, such was not the case with the Mosaic Law, kept in the Ark and preserved out of sight, in Israel's Tabernacle. Again, the Davidic period represents a renewed stage of "filling the earth" with God's temple presence. In this way, Zion goes further than Sinai at recovering Eden.

The Righteousness Triumph through Wisdom

The above discussion focused on Wisdom's availability as a universalizing characteristic of Judaism in the age of Mt. Zion. Another way that this universalizing tendency is seen is in the very manner in which many wisdom sayings are presented. More specifically, in the Wisdom literature, the righteous who prevail are often *unnamed*. They could come from any cultural background, and not necessarily Judaism. No mention is made of ethnicity, gender, or other descriptions. They are simply the righteous. In this way, the Wisdom literature reflects a new, international dimension of the Davidic covenant. Unlike the earlier covenant initiated at Mt. Sinai, the Davidic covenant, ratified on Mt. Zion, is not presented in the form of the ritual laws of Torah or for Israel alone; it is presented in a more expansive form, available to all who seeks righteousness: "Zion represents both the reunification of Israel and [the reunification] of all the nations. Zion represents the great accomplishment of the Davidic rule—a Pan-Israelite kingdom that includes all the nations."[14]

14. Ibid., 70.

Examples abound: "Love righteousness, you rulers of the earth, think of the Lord with uprightness" (Wisd. 1:1); "But the souls of the righteous are in the hand of God, and no torment will ever touch them" (Wisd. 3:1); "But the path of the righteous is like the light of dawn, which shines brighter and brighter until full day. The way of the wicked is like deep darkness; they do not know over what they stumble" (Prov. 4:18–19).

Wisdom Dwells in God's Temple

Despite the universalizing tendency of Temple wisdom of the Davidic covenant, another pattern needs to be mentioned alongside in the Wisdom literature. More specifically, it is Israel's "chosenness," that is, God's relationship with his elect people that counterbalances the universalizing theme. Within this chosenness, the primacy of Zion is clearly evident. For instance, in Sirach, Lady Wisdom (Greek: *Sophia*) has royal access to the entire world. In a clear instance of personification, Wisdom describes her heavenly origins: "I came forth from the mouth of the Most High, *and covered the earth like a mist.* I dwelt in high places, and my throne was in a pillar of cloud" (Sir. 24:3–4). Yet it is not access to the world that Lady Wisdom searches for. She seeks a "home" on earth: "In the waves of the sea, in the whole earth, and in every people and nation I have gotten a possession. Among all these I sought a resting place; I sought in whose territory I might lodge" (Sir. 24:6–7).

While Lady Wisdom depicts herself as being present in "every people and nation," it is in Jerusalem and specifically in the holy tabernacle on Mt. Zion that she finds her true "resting place" (v. 11). And it is precisely *in the Temple*, and nowhere else that she dwells, where she tabernacles:

Then the Creator of all things gave me a commandment, and the one who created me assigned a place for my tent [Greek Old Testament (LXX): *skene*]. And he said, 'Make your *tabernacle*[15] in Jacob, and in Israel receive your inheritance.' From eter-

---

15. Sirach was originally composed in Hebrew but translated into Greek a generation later by the grandson of the author (see the Prologue to Sirach). The term in the Greek Old Testament (LXX) for "tabernacle" is *skene*. Strikingly, it shares the same root as the verb "to dwell/to tabernacle" in John 1:14: "And the Word became flesh and *dwelt* [Greek: *skeneoō*] among us." In Hebrew, the corresponding term for "tabernacle" is *mishkan*. It will be recalled that the *mishkan* is directly related to the verb *shakan* ("to dwell"), especially as in God's glory cloud that "dwelt" or "abode" upon the Tabernacle. The point: there was a "family" of Hebrew terms, and corresponding Greek terms, that were often used in the Old Testament with respect to God's glory, the Tabernacle, dwelling place. This

nity, in the beginning, he created me, and for eternity I shall not cease to exist. In the holy *tabernacle* [Greek Old Testament (LXX): *skene*] I ministered before him, and so I was *established in Zion*. In the beloved city likewise he gave me a resting place, and in Jerusalem was my dominion. (Sir. 8–11)

This is a remarkable passage about which three comments need to be made. First, here in Sirach, Lady Wisdom is a commanding, cosmic presence. One might wonder whether there is a conflict between her self-adulating statements on one hand, and a strict monotheism on the other. Such is not the case. Certainly, the language is perplexing from the vantage point of Jewish monotheistic faith. Yet, in a highly Hellenized context, Lady Wisdom's language is less enigmatic, and in fact quite at home among depictions of the Greek "logos" of Platonic philosophers, or even that of the Jewish philosopher, Philo of Alexandria.[16]

Second, Lady Wisdom is summoned not merely to Jerusalem, but also to the Temple. There, she would dwell among God's people so near his own presence and who personify God's own glory, and is so closely linked with God's glory that one cannot easily discriminate between *her glory* and that of the Almighty. Third, the language of the Gospel of John is remarkably similar: "And the Word became flesh and *tabernacled* among us" (John 1:14a). This last point is significant to the temple theology of the Gospel, and will be taken up in a later chapter.[17]

Elsewhere in the Wisdom tradition, other startling revelations are made about Lady Wisdom. For example, the author of Wisdom of Solomon learns "what is pleasing" to God from Lady Wisdom, "For she knows and understands all things, and she will guide me wisely in my actions and guard me with her glory" (Wisd. 9:10–12). The author of Sirach makes it abundantly clear that she glorifies God; even so, he writes that "Wisdom will *praise her-*

---

terminology was seized upon by the Evangelist to make the point that, whereas in the Old Covenant, the Law/Wisdom was the "place" where God's glory "tabernacled," now in the New Covenant that "place" is the Logos/Jesus.

16. In his *On the Creation of the World* (§25), Philo speaks of the mediating role of the Reason in Creation: "Accordingly [God], when recording the creation of man, in words which follow, asserts expressly, that he was made in the image of God ... It is manifest also, that the *archetypal seal*, which we call that world which is perceptible only to the intellect, must itself be the archetypal model, the idea of ideas, the Reason (*logos*) of God." Charles Duke Yonge with Philo of Alexandria, *The Works of Philo: Complete and Unabridged* (Peabody, MA: Hendrickson, 1995), 5.

17. In chapter 16, more will be said about the fascinating literary and theological parallel between Sir. 24:8–11 and John 1:14.

self" (Sir. 24:1–2). By placing Lady Wisdom so high above all of Israel—and all of humanity—the whole notion of acquiring wisdom is elevated to heaven itself. She functions as an "intermediary," for the one who embraces Lady Wisdom is drawing near to the Almighty: "I inclined my ear a little and received her, and I found for myself much instruction. I made progress therein; to him who gives wisdom I will give glory" (Sir. 51:16–17).

One of the most eloquent and enigmatic descriptions is found in Wisdom of Solomon 7. There, the superlatives about her qualities reach new heights, bathed in honorific language that resembles developments in Middle Platonism: "For she is a breath of the power of God, and a pure emanation of the glory of the Almighty; therefore nothing defiled gains entrance into her. For she is a reflection of eternal light, a spotless mirror of the working of God, and an image of his goodness" (Wisd. 7:25–26). In the metaphor that immediately follows, Lady Wisdom surpasses the beauty of the sun and moon: "For she is more beautiful than the sun, and excels every constellation of the stars. Compared with the light she is found to be superior, for it is succeeded by the night, but against wisdom evil does not prevail" (Wisd. 7:29–30).[18] The final clause of verse 30 ("against wisdom evil does not prevail") is particularly notable, as she is greater than the light of the sun, "superior" to it, yet the darkness of night does not "prevail" against her.

Such language is approximate enough to what St. John writes about the Logos in his Prologue Gospel, to raise the possibility that the passage in John is alluding to the passage in Wisdom of Solomon: "The light shines in the darkness, and the darkness has not overcome it" (John 1:4). It is not at all clear whether the Evangelist intends for his audience to hear such an allusion to the earlier text, or whether the expression from Wisdom was simply "in the air" in his day. If either possibility were in play, and somehow "beneath" the text of the Prologue, then it would seem likely that the Evangelist was making a comparison or, better, a contrast between Lady Wisdom and the logos. Such a contrast would work something like this: Lady Wisdom is true wisdom, surpassing all forms of human knowledge; "she" existed before all things, and emanates from God himself. Moreover, Wisdom of Solomon will make clear before the book ends that Lady Wisdom *is* the holy Torah.[19]

---

18. Compare with John 1:5: "The light shines in the darkness, and *the darkness has not overcome it.*"

19. In re-presenting Israel's flight from Egypt, the author of Wisdom writes: "But for thy holy ones [i.e., Israel] there was *very great light* [as previously stated in the text, this light is Lady Wisdom]. Their

Concluding Remarks

The traditions of the Psalter and the Jewish Wisdom literature are far more complex than could be commented on here. This chapter could have examined other aspects of temple theology in the Psalter and Wisdom books, but it intentionally focused more narrowly upon Israel's covenant with God. Moreover, many texts within these traditions do not necessarily flow in the direction suggested here. Nevertheless, they contribute to the larger discussion by highlighting the influence that the Jerusalem Temple had upon the liturgical and intellectual life of ancient Israel.

With regard to the covenant, the above texts indicate a paradigmatic shift that comes about with the emergence of then Temple and thereafter. This shift is characterized by two trends, an *internalizing* of the Law (in the Psalter) and at the same time a *universalizing* of the Law, beyond Israel to the nations (in the Wisdom books). Biblical theologians refer to this phenomenon as the move "from Sinai to Zion," in that the latter represents a fuller flowering of the earlier covenantal promises. This blossoming could not have taken place outside of the Promised Land, nor would it have been possible apart from the presence of the Jerusalem Temple.

If the above analysis is essentially correct, then the following two conclusions may be drawn. First, the very presence of the Temple (or its absence, that is, in its destruction) represented a kind of recapitulation of Eden—not a return to Eden, as all ancient readers perceived that was beyond the grasp of Israel. Nevertheless, it was a *fresh participation* in the original promises of the Garden, accessed by partaking in the sacrifices of the Jerusalem Temple. Exactly *how* some ancient Jews reconciled a new participation of Eden with their Second Temple reality is a bit allusive; *that* many did so is not questioned. One important clue to the puzzle is found within the biblical prom-

---

enemies [i.e., the Egyptians] heard their voices but did not see their forms, and counted them happy for not having suffered, and were thankful that thy holy ones, though previously wronged, were doing them no injury; and they begged their pardon for having been at variance with them. Therefore thou didst provide a *flaming pillar of fire* as a guide for thy people's unknown journey, and a harmless sun for their glorious wandering [see Wisd. 10:17–20]. For their enemies deserved to be *deprived of light* and imprisoned in *darkness*, those who had kept thy sons imprisoned, *through whom the imperishable light of the law was to be given to the world.*" Here, at the end of the book, the author has revealed that Lady Wisdom is the "imperishable light of the law." Not only that, but also she (Wisdom/Torah) was "given to the world," not only to Israel but also *to the world*. This last phrase is a good example of the "universalizing" of the Mosaic Law within the Jewish Wisdom tradition.

ises of the Davidic covenant (2 Sam. 7; Psa. 89). In the language of the covenant, God is a "father" to the Davidic king; in turn, the Davidic king is a "son" to the Lord (2 Sam. 7:13–14). This language recalls God calling all of Israel his "firstborn son" (Exod. 4:22).[20] Further back than Exodus is the filial relationship of Adam to God as son to Father (see Luke 3:38).

Pulling these strands together, it can be concluded that Wisdom literature is a decisive step beyond the Pentateuch, in that David, in some sense, achieved something Adam did not. One scholar puts it this way: "The truth that Adam failed to realize is finally understood by the Davidic king. If the Mosaic Torah, which was meant to make Israel a light to the nations, is identified with Sinai, the Wisdom literature [is] identified as the Torah of the Davidic covenant that comes forth from Zion."[21]

Second, these patterns yield profound possibilities as it pertains to the New Testament, and open up a set of new questions: To what extent did these new characteristics of temple theology, inaugurated in the age of David and Solomon (*internalizing, universalizing*), affect later biblical authors, for example, postexilic prophets? To what extent was a future judgment upon the corrupted Temple cult predicated upon these hopes? To what extent was Ezekiel's vision of a new, "world-filling" Temple connected to or influenced by these characteristics from Sinai to Zion? To what extent do the *internalizing* and *universalizing* concepts "clash" with other more traditional convictions in Second Temple Judaism, for example, the beliefs of the Sadducees? Moreover, does their acceptance or rejection by Jews in Jesus's day enable the reader to make more sense of tensions within Judaism to define the soul of Judaism? How important are these concepts to Jesus, John the Baptist, the Evangelists, and, more generally, followers of Jesus? Do these concepts from the Psalter and Wisdom tradition in some sense prepare the soil for the teachings of Jesus, which seem to build upon these Edenic hopes?

20. "In a brilliant pairing of the themes of Israel's election and the ultimate defeat of the Egyptian oppressors, Israel is declared to be Yahweh's own firstborn son (v. 22), and Pharaoh's firstborn son is threatened with death, should Pharaoh be disobedient to Yahweh's request (v. 23). Inserted between these two great themes, there is a glimmer of the exodus itself in the request that Yahweh's son be sent out, so that he might worship his *divine father* (v. 23). Israel is lovingly called '*my son, my firstborn,*' and the Pharaoh's son, in an exact parallel, is poignantly called '*your son, your firstborn.*'" John I. Durham, *Exodus*, vol. 3, *Word Biblical Commentary* (Dallas: Word Books, 1998), 56.

21. Barber, *Reign*, 75.

11

THEY BURNED THE HOUSE OF THE LORD

The Destruction of the Temple of Solomon (III/III)

The word that came to Jeremiah from the Lord: "Stand in the gate of the Lord's house, and proclaim there this word, and say, Hear the word of the Lord, all you men of Judah who enter these gates to worship the Lord." Thus says the Lord of hosts, the God of Israel, "Amend your ways and your doings, and I will let you dwell in this place. Do not trust in these deceptive words: '*This is the temple of the Lord, the temple of the Lord, the Temple of the Lord.*'"

Jeremiah 7:1–4

The focus of the book shifts to that epochal event in the history of ancient Israel, the destruction of the Solomon's Temple. Emphasis here will be less upon historical or technical aspects of the Temple's destruction and more upon the theological implications of this epochal event. The crucial question that this chapter leads to is this: *What did the absence of the Temple mean for the authors of Sacred Scripture?* The discussion begins with a central character leading up to these events, namely, the rise and fall of King Solomon.

The Wisdom—and Folly—of Solomon

According to 1 Kings, Solomon was bequeathed vast sapiential knowledge from God. Even as he and his great wisdom became synonymous, it was his expanding power, influence, and wealth that became world renown—and a seismic problem for Israel.[1] "And God gave Solomon wisdom and understanding beyond measure, and largeness of mind like the sand on the seashore, so that Solomon's wisdom surpassed the wisdom of all the people of the east, and all the wisdom of Egypt ... And men came from all peoples to hear the wisdom of Solomon, and from all the kings of the earth, who had heard of his wisdom" (1 Ki. 4:29, 4:34)

When God first appeared to the new king in a dream and granted him one request, Solomon elected to pray for wisdom.[2] Solomon's wisdom was so celebrated that he became the figure most associated with the wisdom tradition of ancient Judaism, even beyond Israel. Attributed to him are two large sections of Proverbs,[3] Song of Songs, Ecclesiastes, Psalm 127, Wisdom of Solomon, as well as apocryphal texts, such as *Psalms of Solomon* and *Odes of Solomon*. In the New Testament, Jesus himself mentions Solomon by way of contrast: "The queen of the South will arise at the judgment with this generation and condemn it; for she came from the ends of the earth to hear the wisdom of Solomon, and behold *something greater than Solomon is here*" (Matt. 12:42).

It will be helpful to retrace the critical steps of Solomon's kingship and later decline, which led to the split of the United Kingdom of David. As his father David grew old, two factions fought for succession to his throne. On one side was David's eldest living son Adonijah, helped along by David's general Joab as well as his high priest, named Abiathar.[4] This was the first powerful faction. On the other side was Solomon himself, supported by included Bathsheba, his own mother, along with the prophet Nathan. Also in his entourage of key supporters was Benaiah, who served as captain of David's personal security. The last crucial figure in the Solomonic camp was the high priest Zadok. As will be seen in chapter 12, it was the priest Zadok and his descendants who held the high priestly throne from the time of David and Solomon until the age of the Maccabees, nearly a full millennium later.

According to 1 Chronicles, Zadok (Hebrew: *ṣāḏôq*, "righteous") served as priest of the Tabernacle at Gibeon in the early days of David's kingship.[5] There was a military figure of the same name who joined himself to David at Hebron: "These are the numbers of the divisions of the armed troops, who

---

1. *Catechism of the Catholic Church*, §2580.
2. See 1 Ki. 3:5–15.
3. Prov. 10:1–22:16, 25:1–29:27.
4. See 1 Ki. 1:5–10.
5. See 1 Chron. 16:39–40.

came to David in Hebron, to turn the kingdom of Saul over to him, according to the word of the Lord ... [and with them] Zadok, a young man mighty in valor, and twenty-two commanders from his own father's house."[6]

It is unclear whether Zadok the young warrior of David and Zadok the priest were one and the same.[7] Regardless, both Zadok and Abiathar were leading priests under David's rule.[8] Together, Zadok and Abiathar carried the Ark of the Covenant back into Jerusalem[9] and served as David's *intelligentsia*, keeping him apprised of intrigue in Jerusalem.[10]

The decisive split seems to have occurred when Abiathar joined Adonijah, David's eldest living son, in Adonijah's attempt to claim the David's throne. For his part, Zadok smartly kept clear of the conspiracy: "Adonijah conferred with Joab the son of Zeruiah (David's nephew and a military commander)[11] and with Abiathar the priest; and they followed Adonijah and helped him. But Zadok the priest, and Benaiah the son of Jehoiada (another military commander)[12] and Nathan the prophet ... and David's mighty men were not with Adonijah."[13]

The controversy ended when David approved of and chose Solomon. It was the priest Zadok and the prophet Nathan who anointed Solomon king.[14] Once he ascended to the throne of his father David, Solomon immediately banished Abiathar to a nearby city, stripping him of his power: "And to Abiathar the priest [Solomon] said, '... you deserve death. But I will not at this time put you to death, *because you bore the Ark of the Lord God before David my father*, and because you shared in all the affliction of my father.' So Solomon expelled Abiathar from being priest to the Lord, thus fulfilling the word of the Lord" (1 Ki. 2:26–27).[15]

Solomon then transferred Abiathar's priesthood to Zadok: "[Solomon] put Benaiah the son of Jehoiada over the army in place of Joab, and the king put Zadok the priest in the place of Abiathar." That the high priestly office

6. See 1 Chron. 12:23, 12:28.
7. See Josephus, *Antiquities*, VII.2, 2.
8. See 2 Sam. 20:25.
9. See 2 Sam. 15:24–29.
10. See 2 Sam. 17:15–16.
11. See 1 Chron. 2:16; 2 Sam. 8:16.
12. See 2 Sam. 8:18.
13. See 1 Ki. 1:7–8.
14. See 1 Ki. 1:32–40.

15. The Book of 1 Samuel depicts the priestly line of Eli as corrupted and doomed. It was Eli who did not perceive Hannah, the soon-to-be holy mother of the prophet Samuel, to be praying. Eli also mistakes Samuel's encounter with the voice of God, and tells Samuel to return to sleep. Later, Eli's two sons humiliate themselves and their father, and commit acts of sacrilege. Eli, who is first depicted as "sitting," later meets his own demise by falling off of a chair (see 1 Sam. chapters 1–3).

was now firmly in the hands of Zadok and his offspring is clear from the text of 1 Kings, where Zadok's son is listed among Solomon's other high officials: "King Solomon was king over all Israel, and these were his high officials: Azariah the son of Zadok was the priest" (1 Ki. 2:35).

The key point is that, when the dust settled, Solomon emerged as king and Zadok as his loyal high priest. And just as David and Solomon became emblematic of the high point of the monarchy and United Kingdom, so too it was the Zadokite line of Levitical priests that held the power of the high priestly office, long after David and Solomon. And whereas the Davidic kingship definitively ended at the time of the Babylonian captivity, the high priestly line of Zadok *did not*. It continued for several more centuries, and as such the Zadokite line represented a kind of continuity with the Davidic covenant and Davidic Kingdom. (This will be a subject that is dealt with more, later in the book.)

In fact, the high priesthood of the Zadokites endured—uninterrupted—all the way until the second century BC. By the time of the prophet Ezekiel, the line of Zadok is synonymous with the high priesthood going back to David himself, and as such, they are the only line permitted to serve as high priest of the Temple: "The chamber [of the Temple] which faces north is for the priests who have charge of the altar; these are the sons of Zadok, who alone among the sons of Levi may come near to the Lord to minister to him" (Ezek. 40:46).

Before returning to the story of Solomon, several other questions factor in here. Once the Temple collapses, and with it the Davidic line of kings, how important is the preservation of the high priestly Zadokite line? What effect would the eventual usurping of the Zadokite line have, given that it endured over so many centuries and came to represent the holiness of God's Temple from the time of David and Solomon? These topics will be addressed in chapter 12. Meantime, it was this Solomonic faction that gained favor with David and bested the faction of Adonijah. Such political intrigue never ends amicably, so that even as Adonijah and his group were claiming victory, Solomon was proclaimed David's co-regent and successor.[16]

As new ruler, Solomon divided all of the territory except for Judah into twelve districts, ignoring the old tribal allotments, and centralized power in Jerusalem. Each district was responsible for supporting his government and the Temple for one month of the year.[17] Solomon used foreigners, many of

16. See 1 Ki. 1:11–49.
17. See 1 Ki. 4:7–28, 5:1–8.

them captives, as forced labor in his extensive building projects. Eventually this levy included Israelites.[18] In the eleventh year of his reign, after seven years of building (950 BC), he completed and dedicated the Temple.[19] By all accounts, the first Temple was glorious, composed of the finest gold, mahogany from the sea-faring Phoenicians, cedars from Lebanon, and other exquisite materials. He added to it his own his own magnificent palace.[20]

Solomon's ships sailed to the ends of the known world, a three-year journey.[21] From these expeditions he acquired gold and other treasures. He brokered a number of treaties with neighboring states, such as that with Hiram of Tyre.[22] Many of these negotiations were cemented by marriage alliances. He even married the daughter of the Egyptian pharaoh, an indication of the greed of his kingdom (1 Ki. 3:1). The author of 1 Kings makes it perfectly clear that Solomon did this "despite the command of God not to do so" (1 Ki. 11:1–2). Such foreign entanglements led Solomon away from the pure worship of the God of Israel,[23] and 1 Kings lays the blame for the division of the Davidic Kingdom at Solomon's feet. God informs Solomon that he will indeed "tear" the kingdom from him (1 Ki. 11:11).

Yet, in a remarkable display of *hesed* (i.e., covenantal faithfulness), God shows mercy to Solomon and vows that "for the sake of David *your father,*" he would not do so in Solomon's lifetime but afterward, when the Davidic Kingdom passed into the hands of his son. In effect, all of the tribes of the Davidic Kingdom would be "torn away," except for that of Judah: "I will *give one tribe to your son,* for the sake of David my servant and for the sake of Jerusalem which I have chosen" (1 Ki. 11:13). This sets in motion the events that solidify the permanence of the "divided kingdom."

Despite the assertion of blame ascribed to Solomon noted here, an overall assessment of the books of Kings and Chronicles suggests a favorable portrait of Solomon. In fact, one has to wait until much later in the biblical canon to hear any sharper criticism of Solomon. But when the criticism of him does come, as in the deuterocanonical Book of Sirach, it is deliciously served, following some passing praise:

Your name reached to far-off islands, and you were loved for your peace. For your songs and proverbs and parables, and for your interpretations, the countries mar-

---

18. See 1 Ki. 5:13–18, 5:27–32.
21. See 1 Ki. 9:26–28, 10:22.
23. See 1 Ki. 11:1–8.

19. See 1 Ki. 6:38.20. See 1 Ki. 7:1–8.
22. See 1 Ki. 5:1–12, 5:15–26.

veled at you. In the name of the Lord God, who is called the God of Israel, you gathered gold like tin and amassed silver like lead. But you laid your loins beside women, and through your body you were brought into subjection. You put stain upon your honor, and defiled your posterity, so that you brought wrath upon your children *and they were grieved at your folly*, so that the sovereignty was divided and a disobedient kingdom arose out of Ephraim. (Sir. 47:16–22)

One could hardly imagine anything close to such a devastating critique in Kings or Chronicles. Nothing of the sort is found in those books, even as Solomon's sins are held up as the root cause of the division of the Davidic Kingdom. Context is crucial in understanding the shift in tone, from that of positive, restrained language about Solomon (Kings, Chronicles) to that of sharp critique and abject shame (Sirach). An explanation is as follows. Centuries passed between the composition of Kings and Chronicles, which were composed nearer to the events, and to the writing of Sirach, which was much more removed chronologically and geographically. On the latter, it should be kept in mind that when Ben Sira's grandson translated the Book of Sirach into Greek, it was with the express intent of dispersing his grandfather's wisdom to Hellenistic Jews living far from Jerusalem (likely in Alexandria).

Such recipients, living in far-off places during the Diaspora were, generally speaking, well assimilated into Hellenistic culture. As such, they would have accepted and likely embraced such a scathing assessment of Solomon as given in Sirach. The attitude of Hellenized Jews would have likely have been one of agreement with the author of the books (e.g., "Shall we talk further about the *wisdom* of Solomon; or shall we recall the *folly* of Solomon which led to the collapse of the kingdom!").[24] Additionally, Sirach describes the Northern Kingdom, whose capital was Ephraim, as a "disobedient kingdom," showing his allegiance to David and his Judean loyalties.[25]

Though it is a shaper criticism of Solomon, is not a sustained one. Sirach quickly shifts to a more optimistic tone, one of trust in God's providence. With clear messianic overtones, he intimates that God would vindicate the children of David, despite Solomon's failures:

But the Lord will never give up his mercy, nor cause any of his works to perish; he will never blot out the descendants of his chosen one, nor destroy the posterity of him who loved him; so he gave a remnant to Jacob, and to David a root of his stock. (Sir. 47:22)

24. The author of Sirach shows its allegiance to the Southern Kingdom of Judah, to which belonged the promises of the Davidic covenant.

25. Sir. 47:21.

In the final judgment, though, Sirach definitely indicts Solomon for being the reason, prima facie, of the division of David's kingdom. While the blame is squarely laid at the feet of Solomon (as well as that of his son, Reheboam), Sirach emphasizes that the everlasting kingdom promised to David[26] remained in full effect, and that there will be a remnant of faithful ones. From this lineage, according to Sirach, would eventually come the "remnant of David."

The Fall of the Temple, the Great Invasion

Rehoboam[27] was the son of Solomon and his successor as king. He reigned as first king of Judah (922–915 BC) after the division of the Northern Kingdom (Israel) and the Southern Kingdom (Judah). He is listed among the ancestors of Jesus (Matt. 1:7). He was just forty-one years old when he began to reign over Judah after the death of Solomon (1 Ki. 14:21). He was initially to become king of all Israel.[28] Yet, because he refused to reduce the burden of forced labor that Solomon had imposed, the northern tribes revolted (see below).

In his place, the representatives of the northern tribes proclaimed a man named Jeroboam as king of Israel. Only Judah and (and the tribe of Benjamin) supported Solomon's son Rehoboam, the rightful king. As a result of the uprising, Rehoboam fled to Jerusalem. The Book of 1 Kings records this, and remarks that the northern tribes (i.e., Israel) were in rebellion against "the house of David" (i.e., the Davidic and Judean kings).[29] The text adds: "There was none that followed the house of David, but the tribe of Judah only."[30]

Theologically, the division of the kingdom was viewed as God's response to Solomon's idolatry, fulfilling what had been spoken earlier through the prophets.[31] The faithful priests and the Levites in the north came south to live in Judah, yet Rehoboam himself was faithful to God for only the first three years of his reign.[32] Afterward, he and many in Judah engaged in idolatry, constructing "high places" (i.e., pagan shrines and alters). In response, God punished Rehoboam by sending the Egyptian pharaoh Shishak, who took the Temple treasures of Jerusalem, and by causing continuous conflicts between Rehoboam and Jeroboam.[33]

---

26. See 2 Sam. 7:12–13.

27. Hebrew: "The people are numerous."

28. See 1 Ki. 12:1.

29. See 1 Ki 12:18–20.

30. See 1 Ki. 12:21.

31. See 1 Ki 12:15.

32. See 2 Chron. 11:13–17.

33. See 2 Chron. 12:1–4.

The first king of the Northern Kingdom was Jeroboam[34] (922–901 BC). As a young man, he led a revolt against Solomon:[35] "And there was war between Rehoboam and Jeroboam continually" (1 Ki. 14:30). Originally an officer on the Solomon's building projects, he was made head of forced labor because of his abilities.[36] Such forced labor had long irritated many in Israel.[37] The prophet Ahijah fanned such discontent into open revolt,[38] and promised kingship to Jeroboam.[39] Following this, Jeroboam escaped Solomon's wrath by fleeing to Egypt: *Solomon sought therefore to kill Jeroboam; but Jeroboam arose, and fled into Egypt, to Shishak king of Egypt, and was in Egypt until the death of Solomon*" (1 Ki. 11:40).

After learning that Rehoboam went to Shechem to be confirmed as successor to Solomon's throne, Jeroboam returned from Egypt.[40] Meanwhile, Rehoboam foolishly rejected the northern tribes' request to lighten their burdens,[41] and vowed to add to their burdens: "Whereas my father laid upon you a heavy yoke, *I will add to your yoke. My father chastised you with whips, but I will chastise you with scorpions*" (1 Ki. 12:11). Naturally, northern Israel rejected his rule, ending the dual monarchy.[42] Instead, they acclaimed Jeroboam as king over the ten tribes: "And when all Israel heard that Jeroboam had returned, they sent and called him to the assembly and made him king over all Israel. *There was none that followed the house of David, but the tribe of Judah only*" (1 Ki. 12:20).

Jeroboam made Shechem his first capital, fortifying it. His reign was marked by continual warfare with Judah.[43] Afraid that the Temple worship in Jerusalem would erode his support, Jeroboam erected golden calves at Bethel and Dan for Israel's worship;[44] the calves were soon enmeshed in a syncretistic blend with Baalism, the symbol of which was the bull. Jeroboam appointed new priests representing all strata of society except the Levites.[45]

---

34. Hebrew: "may the people multiply."

35. See 1 Ki. 12:21: "When Rehoboam came to Jerusalem, he assembled all the house of Judah, and the tribe of Benjamin, a hundred and eighty thousand chosen warriors, *to fight against* the house of Israel, to restore the kingdom to Rehoboam the son of Solomon."

36. See 1 Ki. 11:27–28.   37. See Deut. 26:6–7.

38. See 1 Ki. 11:29–39.   39. See 1 Ki. 11:30–32, 11:34–35.

40. See 1 Ki. 12:1–2.   41. See 1 Ki. 12:3.

42. See 1 Ki. 12:4–19.

43. See 1 Ki. 14:19, 14:30, 15:6–7; 2 Chron. 12:15.

44. See 1 Ki. 12:26–30.

45. See 2 Ki. 12:31.

On occasion he himself officiated at the sacrifices.[46] He reorganized the cultic calendar, moving the date of the Feast of Booths and the like.

Such innovations drew the ire of the orthodox and came to typify "the sins of Jeroboam,"[47] and they eventually led to Israel's fall to the Assyrians in 722 BC: "When he had torn Israel from the house of David they made Jeroboam king ... *So Israel was exiled from their own land to Assyria until this day*" (2 Ki. 17:21–23). Jeroboam persisted in this apostasy despite repeated warnings; neither "oracles of doom,"[48] nor the word of the old prophet Ahijah, nor even the death of his own son[49] made Jeroboam repent.[50] His obstinacy became the sin of his house and ended with its destruction: "[The] King of Assyria came and captured ... Kedesh, Hazor, Gilead, and Galilee, all the land of Naphtali; and he carried the people captive to Assyria" (2 Ki. 15:29).

In the early 700s BC, Assyria, under Tiglath-Pileser, began to conquer the Israelites. Ultimately, the battle was lost by the Northern Kingdom.[51] Continued idolatry would bring severe judgments upon both idolatrous nations. And in 722 BC—a key date—the Assyrians invaded northern Israel, plundering Ephraim and deporting many Israelites. This is known as the Assyrian invasion.[52] Although the Assyrians attempted to seize Jerusalem, Judah's King Hezekiah staved it off by smartly fortifying the walls of Jerusalem. Even more shrewdly, Hezekiah had his team of engineers construct a secret tunnel deep underground. The tunnel, which brought fresh water from the Gihon spring into the walls of the city, spared Jerusalem from destruction.[53] Many scholars consider Hezekiah's tunnel as instrumental to the retreat of the Assyrians and the sparing of Jerusalem.

Meanwhile, the Jewish inhabitants of the north were deported and forced to intermarry. The people that eventually resettled in this region became known as *Samaritans*—half Israelite, half pagan in ancestry. In reality, they were the lost tribes of Israel. They were alienated from Judah, and, theologically, this meant that they were "cut off" from the Davidic promises, of land, temple, and covenant. The Samaritans rewrote the Pentateuch, editing it in keeping with the northern mind-set. They established their own temple on Mt. Gerazim. They remained cut off from the house of David throughout the rest of Israel's history.

---

46. See 2 Ki. 12:32–33.

47. See 1 Ki. 15:30, 15:34, 16:26, 16:31.

48. Spoken by an unknown Judean prophet; see 1 Ki. 13:1–10.

49. See 1 Ki. 14:1–18.

50. See 1 Ki. 13:33.

51. See 2 Ki. 15:29.

52. See 2 Ki. 15.

53. See 2 Ki. 20:20.

From all of this, anger and resentment continued between Jews and Samaritans, generation after generation. In the eyes of the Judeans, the Samaritans had cut themselves off from the Davidic promises. Jesus's encounter of the Samaritan women at the well (John 4) should be read as his desire to bring salvation to all Israel—and to restore the lost tribes of Israel—and all wayward Israelites from exile.

The Destruction of the Jerusalem Temple—and the Exile

Later, in 587 BC—another crucial date—came the final blow to the Kingdom of Judah. Nebuchadnezzar invaded Judah, captured Jerusalem, and completely destroyed Solomon's Temple. This was a most cataclysmic event in the long history of Israel, and its importance cannot be emphasized enough: "Nebuchadnezzar king of Babylon came with all his army against Jerusalem, and laid siege to it … Then they captured the king [Zedekiah, the last Judean king], and brought him up to the king of Babylon … who passed sentence upon him. They slew the sons of Zedekiah before his eyes, and put out the eyes of Zedekiah, and bound him in fetters, and took him to Babylon … Nebuchadnezzar, king of Babylon came to Jerusalem … *And he burned the house of the Lord, and the king's house and all the houses of Jerusalem*; every great house he burned down. And all the army of the Chaldeans, who were with the captain of the guard, broke down the walls around Jerusalem … So Judah was taken into exile out of its land" (2 Ki. 25:1, 2:6–10, 2:21b).

The theological import of this most cataclysmic episode in the life of ancient Israel is captured in a number of texts, such as Psalm 137: "*By the waters of Babylon, there we sat down and wept, when we remembered Zion …* There our captors required of us songs, and our tormentors, mirth, saying, 'Sing us one of the songs of Zion!' How shall we sing the Lord's song in a foreign land? … Let my tongue cleave to the roof of my mouth, if I do not remember you, if I do not set Jerusalem above my highest joy!" (Psa. 137:1–6).

Even as the anguish and loss of the Temple is well captured in Psalm 137, the theme of anger at Israel's enemies, along with a cry for God's justice to be dealt and a deep yearning for God to somehow undo the Temple's destruction, accompanies such laments over the Temple's loss. Notice the desperate longing of Psalm 74: "O God, why dost thou cast us off forever? … Thy foes have roared in the midst of thy Holy place … At the upper entrance they hacked the wooden trellis with axes. And then all its carved wood they broke down with hatchets and hammers. They set thy Sanctuary on fire; to the ground they desecrated the dwelling place of thy name ... We do not see our signs; there is no longer any prophet, and there is none among us who knows how long. How long, O God, is the foe to scoff? Is the enemy to revile thy name forever? Why dost thou hold back thy hand, why dost thou keep thy right hand in thy bosom? Yet God my King is from of old, working salvation in the midst of the earth."

In the above psalm, the cry for vindication is accompanied by images associated with the Creation: "Thou hast established the luminaries and the sun. Thou hast fixed all the bounds of the earth; thou hast made summer and winter." In addition, it includes victorious images of the exodus: story (*"Thou didst divide the sea by thy might"*). There is a sense in which the restoration of the Temple, at least according to Psalm 74, would involve nothing short of a New Creation and a New Exodus.

All of this was a most remarkable tragedy for all of Israel thereafter, and it led to many lingering questions for centuries:

- How could God allow this to happen? What did it all mean?
- Where was our God in our hour of need—and why did his glorious presence leave the Temple? Would he return? When? How?
- Would he have us rebuild the Temple? Would he restore the Temple? Restore our fortunes? Restore us to the land?

Such concerns are taken up by the classical biblical prophets, and not infrequently the response of the prophets integrated hopes for a restoration of the Temple with *messianic* hopes. "The prophets who followed Moses were the great witnesses to the impermanence of all these customs. Raising their voices, they pushed history forward toward the New Moses."[54] In truth, understanding the reasons for—and implications of—the destruction of Solomon's Temple became the primary preoccupation of nearly all of the prophets of the Old Testament (and their audiences).

The preexilic prophets warned of what was about to happen, of the immanence of the Temple's destruction, due especially to the corruption of Israel's king, which in turn led many away from the ways of God, as in Isaiah's "Song of the Vineyard":

---

54. Joseph Ratzinger, *The Spirit of the Liturgy*, trans. John Saward (San Francisco: Ignatius Press, 2000), 42.

Let me sing for my beloved a love song concerning his vineyard: My beloved had a vineyard on a very fertile hill. He digged it and cleared it of stones, and planted it with choice vines; he built a watchtower in the midst of it, and hewed out a wine vat in it; and he looked for it to yield grapes, but it yielded wild grapes. And now, O inhabitants of Jerusalem and men of Judah, judge, I pray you, between me and my vineyard. What more was there to do for my vineyard that I have not done in it? When I looked for it to yield grapes, why did it yield wild grapes? *And now I will tell you what I will do to my vineyard. I will remove its hedge, and it shall be devoured; I will break down its wall, and it shall be trampled down.*[55]

The exilic prophets sought to make sense of what was happening as the just judgment of God and foresaw a new Temple, functioning in a future age, with the purified people of God. Ezekiel writes of how the Northern Kingdom of Israel defiled the land *"by their ways and their doings"* (Ezek. 36:16). Like the archetypal Adam who was banished from Eden, they were "cast out" of the land of the Temple: "I scattered them *among the nations*, and they were dispersed through the countries; in accordance with their conduct and their deeds I judged them" (v. 19). Even the Gentiles, Ezekiel writes, comprehended that these were "the people of the Lord," but because of their deeds, *"they had to go out of his land"* (v. 20). The prophet Baruch embodies the woes of Israel in exile and, speaking in the first person, depicts *even Israel's dead* as participating in the banishment from the land of the Temple:

But we did not obey thy voice, to serve the king of Babylon; and thou hast confirmed thy words, which thou didst speak by thy servants the prophets, that the bones of our kings and the bones of our fathers would be brought out of their graves; and behold, *they have been cast out* to the heat of day and the frost of night. (Bar. 2:24–25)

Baruch's dire assessment turns to the subject of Solomon's Temple itself, as he laments its destruction: "And the house which is called by thy name thou hast made as it is today, because of the wickedness of the house of Israel and the house of Judah" (Bar. 2:26).

So the postexilic prophets continued to chastised Israel for what had happened and this "judgment" upon them would serve as a witness to all of the nations:

The house of Israel shall know that I am the Lord their God, from that day forward. And the nations shall know that the house of Israel went into captivity for their iniq-

---

55. Isa. 5:1–5. Cf. Luke 20:9–18.

uity, *because they dealt so treacherously with me that I hid my face from them* and gave them into the hand of their adversaries. (Ezek. 39:22–23)

And yet they foresaw that "the great Day of the Lord is at hand" (Zeph. 1:14) and told of a coming Messiah who would vindicate Israel among her enemies (Zechariah). "On that day there shall be a fountain opened for the house of David and the inhabitants of Jerusalem to cleanse them from sin and uncleanness" (Zech. 13:1–2).

Ezekiel sees a future reversal of Israel's fortunes and envisions a day when "they will forget their shame" (Ezek. 39:25) and they will again *dwell in their land* with none to make them afraid" (v. 26). In calling Israel back to the land they were "cast out" from, God's name and holiness would be vindicated "in the sight of many nations" (v. 27):

Then they shall know that I am the Lord their God because I sent them into exile among the nations, and then *gathered them into their own land* ... I will not hide my face any more from them, when I pour out my Spirit upon the house of Israel, says the Lord. (vv. 28–29)

Concluding Remarks

The capture of Jerusalem led to a generation of over forty years of captivity and slavery in Babylon (587–539 BC), known as the Babylonian captivity or, simply, the exile. Many of the most influential, wealthy Jews were deported along with artisans and the like.

In 539 BC, as the subsequent Persian Empire overtook the Babylonians, they gained control of the region, and King Cyrus of Persia decreed that the Jewish people could return to their land, resettle it, and rebuild their Temple (i.e., the Edict of Cyrus). Many Jews did not return—and never resettled Judea. This is often considered the beginning of the great dispersion (Diaspora) of the Jewish people, though, in truth, it first began during the Assyrian captivity in 722 BC.[56]

It is to the Second Temple period of Judaism that the discussion now turns.

---

56. By the first century AD, due to these "forced" dispersions—as well as voluntary migrations—many Jews were now, for the first time, living across the region of the Mediterranean and beyond, in Alexandria, Egypt, Asia Minor, Rome, etc. Fascinatingly, from a Christian perspective, this Diaspora assured that the missionary journeys of St. Paul and other Christian preachers had an "immediate" audience of Jewish hearers, in the synagogues and communities of these cities and regions.

12

REBUILDING THE
HOUSE OF THE LORD

*Judaism in the Period of the
Second Temple*

And also let the gold and silver vessels of the house of God,
which Nebuchadnezzar took out of the temple that is in Jerusalem and brought to Babylon, be restored and brought
back to the temple which is in Jerusalem, each to its place;
you shall put them in the house of God.

Ezra 6:5–6

Return and Restoration:
Second Temple Judaism

The discussion now turns to the aftermath of the crisis that was the destruction of Solomon's Temple and the resulting exile in Babylon. In light of
the Edict of Cyrus, a remnant of fervent and faithful Jews did return to Judea
and the city of Jerusalem that lay in ash and ruins. Under the leadership of
the prophet Nehemiah, the walls of Jerusalem were repaired. The cry of broken hearts came, in some sense, to take the place of the sound of the Temple
sacrifices in Jerusalem. Here, Ratzinger aptly summarizes the arduous situation of the Jewish people, following the destruction of the Temple: "The Exile came as a challenging opportunity to formulate clearly a positive doctrine
about worship and the new thing that was to come. There was no Temple any
more, no public and communal form of divine worship as decreed in the law.

Deprived as she was of worship, Israel was bound to feel immeasurably poor and pathetic. She stood before God with empty hands. There was no expiation any more, no 'holocausts' ascending to God."[1] He adds:

The cry of [Israel's] broken heart, her persistent pleading before the silent God, had to count in his sight as "fatted sacrifices" and whole burnt offerings. It was the very emptiness of Israel's hands, the heaviness of her heart that was now to be worship, to serve as a spiritual equivalent of the missing Temple oblations.[2]

Aside from Nehemiah, the great scribe and priest Ezra loomed large in the era of the return from exile. He proclaimed the word of God publicly, and in many ways a reform and revival of Judaism had begun. It was hoped that a prince of Judea, Zerubbabel,[3] would emerge as a new Davidic king, but these hopes were quickly dashed. Meanwhile, construction of the Second Temple—sometimes called the Temple of Zerubbabel, the so-called prince of Judea—was begun. It was not as glorious as Solomon's, and it was completed and dedicated in 518 BC (with far less spectacle).

This was a time of great oppression, as the Jewish people lived under the rule of one Gentile power after another: the Babylonians, followed by the Persians, and then the Greeks, and finally the Romans:

- 587–539 BC: Babylonian rule
- 539–323 BC: Persian rule
- 323–167 BC: Hellenistic rule (Alexander, followed by his successors)
- 66 BC (and beyond): Roman rule

All of this brought to the Jewish people fear, violence, strife, heavy taxation, and much uncertainty. Even though their Temple was rebuilt, and daily sacrifices continued, some Jews speculated that God was not present in his sanctuary. Even the Ark itself was absent, never to be reclaimed physically.

---

1. Joseph Ratzinger, *The Spirit of the Liturgy*, trans. John Saward (San Francisco: Ignatius Press, 2000), 45.

2. Ibid., 45.

3. Ezra 2:2: "They came with Zerubbabel, Jeshua, Nehemiah, Seraiah, Re-el-aiah, Mordecai, Bilshan, Mispar, Bigvai, Rehum, and Baanah." See also Sir. 49:11: "How shall we magnify Zerubbabel? He was like a signet on the right hand ... in their days they built the house and raised a temple holy to the Lord, prepared for everlasting glory."

The Corruption of the High Priesthood

For only a brief period of about a century, out of their long sojourn through history, did the ancient Jewish people enjoy a form of self-governance. This occurred just after the period of the Maccabean revolt of 167–166 BC.[4] Prior to 167 BC, the Jewish people were ruled by the Babylonians, Persians, and Greeks, respectively. After 66 BC, they were ruled by the Romans.[5] Yet even this interregnum of about a century was filled with violence and corruption in the Jewish political dynasty known as the Hasmoneneans.[6]

From the time of Solomon (970–931 BC) until just prior to the Maccabean revolt (167 BC), the high priestly line was strictly chosen from within one Levitical family. That elite family was that of the *Zadokites*. Century after century, every subsequent high priest was selected from the Zadok clan.[7] In fact, 1 Chronicles 6:3–15 traces the Zadokite line from Aaron all the way to the Exile, though it extended well beyond the fourth century into the second.[8]

Astonishingly, in 175 BC, and in order to flex his political and military muscles, Antiochus Epiphanies IV, ruler of Egypt and de facto leader of Israel, intervened in the Temple procedures: he made the fateful decision to elect Jerusalem's high priest—by himself.[9] He broke the continual tradition of *fourteen generations* such that the last Jewish high priest chosen by proper appointment was Onias III, who reigned from 185 to 75 BC. Antiochus replaced him, appointing Jason in his stead in 175 BC. To be clear, Jason was also a Zadokite, but the shocking fact was that he was chosen not within ruling class of the Jerusalem Temple, but by the Hellenistic king. Jason vied for this position, promising Antiochus "a considerable sum of money" and in

---

4. Specifically, the period of Judean self-rule was from 152 to 37 BC.

5. Roman rule technically began in 66 BC. In 37 BC, however, Herod usurped the long-standing process of the appointment of the Jewish high priest, the main topic of this section.

6. "The Hasmoneans were a Jewish family that became instrumental in freeing Judea from Seleucid rule, beginning in 167 b.c. Several generations served as high priests, governors and kings, until Roman intervention in 63 b.c. curtailed their role and Herod the Great ousted the last Hasmonean king in 37 b.c." J. Sievers, *Dictionary of New Testament Background: A Compendium of Contemporary Biblical Scholarship*, s.v. "Hasmoneans."

7. See 2 Sam. 8:17, 15:24; 1 Ki. 1:8, etc. See also Joachim Jeremias, *Jerusalem in the Time of Jesus*, trans. F. H. Cave and C. H. Cave (Philadelphia: Fortress, 1969), 183. "There was in the Temple in Jerusalem a kind of archive in which the genealogies of the (high) priesthood were kept" (214).

8. But see Jeremias, *Jerusalem in the Time of Jesus*, 182n105, who suggests that the idea of the Zadokite priesthood going back to Aaron is "erroneous."

9. Ibid., 183.

return for his appointment, "implemented many Greek customs into Jerusalem."[10]

More boldly still, in 171 BC, Antiochus appointed Menelaus *the first non-Zadokite high priest* since the time of Solomon, "an unheard of outrage to the religious feelings of the people."[11] Menelaus reigned from 171 to 162 BC.[12] Jason, his predecessor, obtained the high priesthood from the Greek Seleucid ruler Antiochus IV Epiphanes. And so a radical program of the Hellenization of Jerusalem was underway.[13]

Ultimately, it was Jewish corruption *from within*—even more so than Hellenistic forces from the outside—that led to the Maccabean revolt. It was Menelaus and subsequent non-Zadokite high priests, selected by the Greeks, that ultimately led to the crisis, more than the desecration of the Temple by Antiochus IV. Regardless, Jerusalem's Temple and her high priesthood had become corrupted, and the priesthood would be forever tainted in the eyes of many Jews.

What happened following this, historically speaking, is as follows. A figure named Jacim was appointed as high priest by the Hellenistic overlords. Jacim was high priest from 162 to 159 BC. He was not the rightful heir, but at least he was a Zadokite. Onias III, the lawful successor, fled to Egypt, where he was warmly received by a group of diaspora Jews who had constructed an alternative Temple to the one in Jerusalem at Leontopolis.[14] Following Jacim,

---

10. Ibid., 184.

11. Ibid., 185.

12. "The forced Hellenization program of the high priests Jason and Menelaus (175–164 b.c.), the rise of the Hasmonean family as the saviors of Israel and the combining of the high priesthood and kingship under that one dynasty had long-lasting ramifications for the period." D. A. DeSilva, *Dictionary of New Testament Background: A Compendium of Contemporary Biblical Scholarship*, s.v. "Apocrypha and Pseudepigrapha."

13. For more on the Hellenization of the Jewish people in the Second Temple/Maccabean periods, see especially E. Schürer, *The History of the Jewish People in the Age of Jesus Christ (175 b.c.–a.d. 135)*, 2nd ed., ed. G. Vermes, F. Millar, and M. Goodman (Edinburgh: T & T Clark, 1973–87); J. M. G. Barclay, *Jews in the Mediterranean Diaspora* (Edinburgh: T & T Clark, 1996); V. Tcherikover, *Hellenistic Civilization and the Jews* (Philadelphia: Jewish Publication Society, 1961); E. P. Sanders, *Judaism: Practice and Belief, 63 b.c.–a.d. 66* (Philadelphia: Trinity Press International, 1992); E. J. Bickerman, *The Jews in the Greek Age* (Cambridge, MA: Harvard University Press, 1988); M. Hengel, *The "Hellenization" of Judaea in the First Century after Christ* (London: SCM, 1989).

14. Jeremias, *Jerusalem in the Time of Jesus*, 185; Josephus, *Jewish War*, 1.33. See also Richard Gottheil and Samuel Krauss, *Jewish Encyclopedia*, s.v. "Leontopolis," accessed December 17, 2016, www.jewishencyclopedia.com/articles/9772-leontopolis. Jeremias observes: "The fact that Onias III re-

there was a period of seven years when there was in fact no high priest in Jerusalem (159–152 BC). Little is known about whether the Temple sacrifices were even active at this time, including during the annual Day of Atonement sacrifices.

From that point time and until early Roman rule,[15] the high priest was chosen from the Levites but, strikingly and importantly, *from non-Zadokite families* among the Jewish "Hasmoneans," a powerful Pharisaical political party. Astonishingly, and breaking from the centuries-old precedent leading all the way back to David himself, there was not in this 115-year period (152 to 37 BC) *a single Zadokite who served as high priest.*

Later, in 37 BC, Herod the Great put to death the remaining Hasmonean line and seized control of the high priesthood. As Jeremias explains, "Herod wallowed in blood. He put to death even the distant relatives of the Hasmonean line, so that no single male Hasmonean was left alive to be considered as ruler and consequently, high priest."[16]

Herod's bold and violent actions effectively ended the life-long nature of the Jewish high priesthood altogether. He appointed and deposed high priests at will. With two exceptions, Herod chose high priests from "insignificant persons who were merely of priestly descent" for the high priesthood.[17] From the vantage point of most faithful Jews in the lifetime of Jesus, the theological impact of all of this was traumatic. The holy line of the high priesthood, and his divine appointment by Temple leaders, specifically from the holy family of Zadok, had stretched back to the time of King David. Now, a millennium later, the office of the high priesthood had become a political football, tossed this way and that, with all of the inherent corruption that accompanies dirty politics.

On a spiritual level, the fallout of these conditions was enormous. It led in large part to a factionalism within Judaism and the emergence of a handful

---

solved to *build a temple in a heathen land*, and moreover found priests, Levites, a community and the very considerable resources necessary to pursue his plan, and finally that this rival temple in a heathen land *existed for 243 years,* until its destruction by the romans in AD 73, *all would be completely incomprehensible if we did not know how ingrained in the Jewish race was the awareness that Onias III, as the son of the last rightful Zadokite high priest, Onias II, was the legitimate heir to the high priesthood …* In the meantime, the storm of religious persecution broke over Israel (167–164 B.C.), with the Maccabean revolt, and in December 164 the *desecrated Temple was re-consecrated*" (186).

15. Roman rule of Judea began in 66 BC.   16. Jeremias, *Jerusalem in the Time of Jesus,* 190.

17. Josephus, *Antiquities,* 20.247.

of distinct religious groups, among which were disparate and even opposing ideas of what it means to "live righteously before God," and of what were the "essentials" of religious belief and practice. For many Jews of the Second Temple period, these tensions led to the formulation of pressing questions:

- How could God allow this to happen to his Temple, to us his people?
- How long will God forget us?
- How would God remedy the injustices and hardships we now face?
- What does God expect of us—and how are we now to live and please him, so that he might one day bless us?
- Finally, who would God use to enact justice—and restore his Temple to a "house of prayer?" (Matt. 21:13; Mark 11:17; Luke 19:46)

The Many Judaisms of the Second Temple Period

The Second Temple period, which can be dated from the dedication of Zerubbabel's Temple in 518 BC to its destruction by the Romans in 70 AD, was broadly speaking a tumultuous period for the Jewish people. During these centuries, what would emerge can only be described as a multifaceted Judaism, or, better, many "Judaisms."[18] It is these distinct movements that will now be discussed in light of temple theology. As the various "ways of living Jewishly" in the first century are discussed, the group values were, among other factors, shaped by the destruction of the Temple and subsequent exile, by the loss of the Davidic Kingdom, and last but in no way least by the growing corruption of the Temple priesthood. The religious beliefs and practices of each particular movement may be seen as the expression of that groups determined effort to "live righteously" before God, and ultimately bring about a restored and renewed relationship of Israel to God and God to his people.

The popular movement of *the Pharisees*[19] was a "holiness" movement, im-

18. On the "plurality" within first-century Judaism, see Lee Levine, *Jewish Sects, Parties and Ideologies in the Second Temple Period* (Jerusalem: Hebrew University, 1978); Schürer, *History of the Jewish People in the Age of Jesus Christ*; E. P. Sanders, *Judaism: Practice and Belief 63 BCE-66 CE*, rev. ed. (London: SCM Press, 1992).

19. On the Pharisees, see Oskar Skarsuane, *In the Shadow of the Temple: Jewish Influences on Early Christianity* (Downers Grove, IL: InterVarsity Press, 2002), 177–22; John Bowker, *Jesus and the Pharisees* (Cambridge: Cambridge University Press, 1973); Louis Finkelstein, *The Pharisees: The Sociological Background of Their Faith*, 2 vols., 3rd. ed. (Philadelphia: Fortress, 1962); Jacob Neusner, *The Rabbinic Traditions about the Pharisees before 70*, 3 vols. (Leiden: Brill, 1971; reissued in the South

posing a radical ceremonial purity upon all the people, not just the priestly class, so that all Israel would be pleasing to God.[20] They saw themselves as a leaven from within. It was a movement of the people, a populist movement, and despite its rather harsh and imposing expectations, it attracted many. Like Jesus, they embraced the Law and the Prophets, and professed hope in the resurrection. Yet, unlike Jesus, they prescribed many oral laws that became a burden upon many.

The party of the Scribes[21] has been commonly been limited to that of copyists of the Law, though in reality they were primarily the legal scholars and interpreters who shaped the Torah. Most of the scribes were adherents of the Pharisees' interpretation of the Torah, which is why they were lumped together. But while most scribes were Pharisees, certainly not all Pharisees were scribes, or even that scholarly. Many ordinary rabbis were of the Pharisaical party and were not scholars as such. The scribes were the academic elite of the Pharisaical movement.

The Sadducees were a smaller group of priestly elites who sought to consolidate the power of the (corrupt) priestly line. They were the old guard of aristocratic, priestly temple authority. They were the conservative party who, unlike the Pharisees, held to just the Five Books of Moses (i.e., Torah) and rejected the prophetic books, and with them the belief in angels and in resurrection. The group had elements of fundamentalism within it.

The Sanhedrin was the governmental body of the Temple and was composed of both Pharisees and Sadducees, as well as those of neither party. The high priest was its president and the chief priests and leading Levites made up much of the body, and so there was priestly and lay representation. At the end of the day, it was the current high priest along with former high priest who had most of the influence over the Sanhedrin. It was the seat of Temple power.

The Essenes[22] were a community of dissatisfied priests, angry about many

---

Florida Studies in the History of Judaism Series, 202–4 (Atlanta: Scholars Press, 1999). E. P. Sanders, "Did the Pharisees Have Oral Law?," in *Jewish Law from Jesus to the Mishnah: Five Studies* (London: SCM Press, 1990).

20. On this point, see especially E. P. Sanders, "Did the Pharisees East Ordinary Food in Purity?," in *Jewish Law*, 97–130.

21. See Anthony J. Saldarini, *Pharisees, Scribes, and Sadducees in Palestinian Society* (Wilmington, DE: Michael Glazier, 1988).

22. The Qumran community of the Essenes and their manuscripts (*Dead Sea Scrolls*) are, in reality, massive topics. For a brief introduction to some of the leading issues and themes, as well as a

things, especially the corruption of the Temple's high priesthood. They withdrew to a sort of proto-monastic life in the Judean desert at Qumran. Their leader was the Teacher of Righteousness, likely a deposed priest of the Zadokite line. They were an apocalyptic community and expected a final battle between themselves (Sons of Light) and corrupt Jews and pagan nations, who would align together against them (Sons of Darkness). They eagerly awaited a priestly Messiah who would vindicate them and with them cleanse the Temple of unrighteousness and empower their Teacher as the rightful high priest. The Essenes followed a strict Community Rule and composed the Dead Sea Scrolls, which contained many manuscript copies of every Old Testament book (except the Book of Esther), along with an array of non-biblical texts (legal texts, community texts, Temple prayers, etc.). Although there is speculation that John the Baptist was at one time a member of this separatist movement, there is no definitive evidence to necessitate it.

Those known as *the Zealots*[23] were in all actuality a complex web of smaller movements that had one larger and common aim: the violent overthrow of the Roman occupation and the political restoration of the Davidic Kingdom. "They hid daggers in their clothes and used the cover at festival crowds to get at their victims—hence their nickname Sicarii, dagger men."[24]

In some sense, all of these ways of being Jewish can be understood through the matrix of the Temple. That is, their Jewish identity, their vision of Judaism, and future hope for their religion and society had particular hopes for the Temple: from keeping the status quo to restoring the Temple through radical, ritual purity to awaiting a deliverer figure in the Judean desert. Still, one should refrain from thinking of these categories as all-inclusive.

Many Jews, the common folk of the land, unless they ascribed to the populist movement of the Pharisees, were not likely aligned, at least not formally, with any of these parties. They were simply *Ioudaioi*—Jews living in

---

short history of the Qumran community, see Geza Vermes, *The Dead Sea Scrolls in English*, 7th ed. (London: Penguin, 2014), 1–64; James VanderKam, *The Dead Sea Scrolls Today* (Grand Rapids, MI: Eerdmans, 1994).

23. See Skarsuane, *In the Shadow of the Temple*, 126–28; Martin Hengel, *The Zealots: Investigations into the Jewish Freedom Movement in the Period from Herod I until 70 A.D.* (Edinburgh: T & T Clark, 1989).

24. Skarsuane, *In the Shadow of the Temple*, 126–27. He notes that the *Sicarii* were distinguished from other nationalistic zealot groups prior to 70 AD. It remains unclear whether Judas's nickname, "Iscariot," is an indication that he belonged to such a group. For discussion of both possibilities, see ibid., 127.

or near Judea, perhaps in Galilee or further abroad. They worked as laborers, craftsman, and artisans or in the marketplace. They raised their children, went to synagogue, paid their taxes, and occasionally made the trip up to the Temple in Jerusalem for the great feasts, like Tabernacles and Passover. Like these more defined groups, they too had hopes of a renewed temple, a restored temple, a temple in which their children would find forgiveness from God, and a hope and a future.

There are any number of texts from the Second Temple period that deserve to be "put under the magnifying glass" for closer analysis: the prophet Zechariah, and his vision of a man called Branch (Hebrew: *netzer*) who would restore the Temple and fight Israel's enemies "as when he fights on a day of battle" (Zech. 14:3). A good starting point is with the prophet Ezekiel and his vision of a coming eschatological temple.

Ezekiel's Eschatological Temple Vision

Following the destruction of the Temple of Solomon, the prophet Ezekiel—a priest as well as a prophet[25]—had an eschatological, heavenly vision of a perfected and renewed Temple.[26] As one scholar explains, "The purpose of [Ezekiel's] temple is to provide access to Yahweh, who is the source of life and blessing in a new Eden.[27] The renewal of the environment is a further result of the return of Yahweh and the restoration of the Temple. The Temple is also at the center of the city,[28] which is called 'Yahweh is there,'[29] a fitting conclusion to the theme of God's presence that is so central to the theology of Ezekiel."[30]

The vision of Ezekiel must be read against the recent destruction of the Second Temple and fall of Jerusalem—along with a fervent hope that God's glorious presence would return to the Temple. This portion of the complex Book of Ezekiel can be approached as a pronouncement of hope for postexilic Jews that God would concretely restore holiness to their land—and their Temple. Helpfully, Beale points out that a kind of literalism about this prophetic text should be avoided at all costs.[31] No small number of theologians

---

25. See Ezek. 1:3.

26. See Ezek. chapters 40–44.

27. See Gen. 2:10.

28. See Ezek. 48:21.

29. See Ezek. 48:35.

30. P. P. Jenson, *Dictionary of the Old Testament: Prophets*, s.v. "Temple."

31. Some today mistakenly await a rebuilding of the Temple according to the pattern established

have pointed out that a literalistic reading of Ezekiel's vision "would violate the principle of Hebrews: the Old Testament sacrifices pointed to Christ's 'one for all' sacrifice ... so that to go back to those sacrifices would indicate the insufficiency of Christ's sacrifice."[32]

So, while on one hand the prophet's vision is not to be interpreted in a literalistic fashion, on the other hand, Ezekiel's hope is grounded in the firm conviction that God would bring about a real and legitimate end of the exile. Wright explains: "Israel's God, having abandoned Jerusalem and the Temple at the time of the Babylonian exile, would one day return. He would return in person. He would return in glory. He would return to judge and save. He would return to bring about a new Exodus, overthrowing the enemies that had enslaved his people. He would return to establish his glorious, tabernacling presence in their midst. He would return to rule over the whole world. He would come back to be king."[33] In this way, Wright clarifies, "Jesus' movement was itself a new-exodus movement, a liberation-movement, *a return-from-exile movement* ... To affirm the resurrection was to affirm the fact that Israel's God was at work in a new way, turning the world upside down."[34]

The Details of Ezekiel's Vision

The basic inspiration for the layout of Ezekiel's temple was Solomon's Temple, though there are a number of differences. In Ezekiel 37, God promises a future, restored sanctuary in the midst of a resurrected people: "I will make a covenant of peace with them; it shall be an everlasting covenant with them; and I will bless them and multiply them, *and will set my Sanctuary in the midst of them for evermore. My dwelling place shall be with them; and*

---

in Ezekiel. Certain fundamentalist groups (both Jewish and Christian) interpret the prophet's vision in a literalistic fashion, such that the rebuilding of the Temple according to Ezekiel's pattern will herald in the coming of the Messiah/return of Christ. These interpretations distort the message of Ezekiel and entirely miss the way in which New Testament writers view the Incarnation of Christ as the true and living Temple. See John 2:19–22.

32. G. K. Beale, *The Temple and the Church's Mission: A Biblical Theology of the Dwelling Place of God* (Downers Grove, IL: InterVarsity Press, 2004), 343.

33. N. T. Wright, *Paul and the Faithfulness of God*, vol. 4, *Christian Origins and the Question of God* (Minneapolis: Fortress Press, 2013), 653.

34. N. T. Wright, *The Resurrection of the Son of God*, vol. 3, *Christian Origins and the Question of God* (London: Society for Promoting Christian Knowledge, 2003), 427.

I will be their God, and they shall be my people. Then the nations will know that I the Lord sanctify Israel, *when my Sanctuary is in the midst of them for evermore"* (Ezek. 37:26–28).

This bold declaration serves as the foundation for the prophet's vision of an entirely new temple in Ezekiel 40–48. The bulk of the prophet's vision concerns the measurements of the Temple and its ceremonial practices, both of which underscore the realized perfection and holiness of the Temple. Geographically, Ezekiel is brought to a very high mountain,[35] the antithesis of the "valley of dry bones" (Ezek. 37:1–14).

Like the Tabernacle before it, Ezekiel's vision of the restored temple has a layer of sacred spaces that symbolize greater holiness. Ezekiel's Temple adhered to the characteristic "threefold division" of the Temple.[36] But it did not correspond to either the original Tabernacle or Solomon's Temple. Instead, "square" outer and inner courts[37] dominated, and symbolized the perfection of holiness. In addition, layers of vertical holiness complemented these three layers of horizontal holiness. They recalled the cosmic mountain temples of Eden, Ararat, Sinai, and Zion.[38] The outer wall of the Temple had three massive gates; none lie to the west, as the temple and a mysterious building occupy that side.[39] The eastern gate is where the glory of Yahweh enters the temple. This is striking, especially given the discussion of the expulsion of Adam and Eve to the east of Eden:[40] "Afterward he brought me to the gate, *the gate facing east.* And behold, *the glory of the God of Israel came from the east*; and the sound of his coming was like the sound of many waters; and the earth shone with his glory. And the vision I saw was like the vision which I had seen when he came to destroy the city ... and I fell upon my face" (Ezek. 43:1–3).

Commenting on this key passage in Ezekiel, St. Jerome develops a spiritual connection to the New Testament when he writes: "The earth shone with his glory, which really takes place at the coming of Christ, when the sound of the Apostles goes forth on the whole earth and their words to the ends of the earth."[41]

---

35. Ezek. 40:2.

36. Ezek. 40:48, 41:1, 41:4.

37. Ezek. 40:17–19, 40:44.

38. Ezek. 40:6, 40:34, 40:49.

39. Ezek. 41:12.

40. Gen. 3:24: "He drove out the man; and *at the east of the garden of Eden* he placed the cherubim, and a flaming sword which turned every way, to guard the way to the tree of life."

41. St. Jerome, *Commentary on Ezekiel* 13.43.1–9.

The east gate remained closed, indicating the continual presence of Yahweh in his temple.[42] This was a dramatic reversal of Yahweh's departure from the Temple before its destruction.[43] Moreover, it is likely that the prophet Zechariah, writing later, draws upon this "eastern" motif in his depiction of God's coming Messiah: "On that day his feet shall stand on the Mount of Olives which lies before Jerusalem on the east; and the Mount of Olives shall be split in two from east to west ... Then the Lord your God will come, and all the holy ones with him. On that day living waters shall flow out from Jerusalem ... And the Lord will become king over all the earth; on that day the Lord will be one and his name one" (Zech. 14:4–10).[44]

Within Ezekiel's vision, Gentiles could not enter the Temple,[45] and Levites carefully guarded the other gates where sacrifices are brought in by all the faithful of Israel.[46] Ezekiel makes no mention of the high priest in the temple vision, but only Zadokite priests offer sacrifices, since they remained faithful to Yahweh.[47]

In a sense, the vision Ezekiel puts forth is of a temple city: "[The Lord] set me down *upon a very high mountain*, on which was *a structure like a city* opposite me" (Ezek. 40:2). Commenting on the inaugural vision of the temple in Ezekiel 40 (above), Beale makes an important contribution in observing that what was once the case for the Holy of Holies would one day be true for all of Jerusalem: "the Temple is equivalent to the city because the whole city will be filled with God's presence that was formerly limited to the innermost sanctuary of Israel's temple."[48]

---

42. At least some of the early Church fathers took this as a prefiguration of the Virgin Mary. St. Theodoret of Cyr (393–466 AD): "It is very likely that these words *refer to the womb of the Virgin*, through which no one enters and from which no one departs other than the only one who is the Lord" (*Commentary on Ezekiel* 16.44); St. Ambrose (333–97 AD): "What is that gate of the sanctuary, that outer gate facing the east and remaining closed? *Is not Mary the gate through whom the Redeemer entered this world?*" (*Letter* 44).

43. See Ezek. chapters 8–11.

44. Regarding the eastern gate, St. Gregory the Great allegorically extends the image: "Each preacher can be understood under the name 'gate' because whoever opens for us the door of the heavenly kingdom through his speech is a gate." *Homilies on Ezekiel*, 2.3.2.

45. Ezek. 44:4–8. 46. Ezek. 44:10–14.

47. Ezek. 44:10–16.

48. Beale, *The Temple and the Church's Mission*, 340.

Awaiting the True and Definitive David

After the death of Solomon, the United Kingdom soon dissolved into two distinct and rival kingdoms. The possibility of a reunited Davidic Kingdom already unlikely because of civil war now became unthinkable and unworkable. The Northern Kingdom despised the Kingdom of Judah, which it saw as prideful, greedy, and economically and religiously oppressive. The Southern Kingdom saw the Northern Kingdom as apostates—those that left the house and promises of David and Judah.

Meanwhile, the world empires of Assyria and Babylon laid siege to the Northern and Southern Kingdoms, respectively. The northern tribes were taken captive to Assyria, dispersed, and forced to intermarry. They eventually repopulated the region and became known as the Samaritan peoples. The conquest of Jerusalem and the destruction of the Temple were together *the* defining moment of the people of Judah, and indeed of all Israel.

After the exile ended in Babylon in 539 BC, a small percentage of zealous Judeans began to return to Judea in three waves. Within a generation, Jerusalem was functioning, fortified, and the Temple of Solomon was rebuilt. It was smaller, less grand and opulent, but at last Temple sacrifices returned to Jerusalem.

This was the time of fervent revival, the time of Second Temple Judaism. Still, many remained in faraway places of the Diaspora. For Jews of this period, there were many unanswered questions, especially concerning God's presence with them in the Temple, and holiness of the holy priesthood. Over these centuries, there was a massive corruption of the high priesthood, from the holy Zadokite family, so that in the Maccabean era it was the Greek overlord Antiochus IV and his successors who appointed the high priest.

Later, and worse still, Herod the Great abolished the lifelong nature of the high priesthood. Slaying his enemies of the Hasmonean line, he appointed and deposed high priests at will—none of which were from the Zadokite line going back to David and Solomon. Each diverse form of Judaism that emerged—the Pharisees, the Sadducees, the Essenes, and so on—saw themselves as the solution to the big question: *What is God doing now, and how is he intending to save us?*

It was into this period of great complexity—mixed with despair and hope, with confusion and confidence—that various biblical prophets began to boldly proclaim that God had not abandoned his people, that he will be victorious among Israel: *God will vindicate us and deliver us by his own hand through the One to Come, the Messiah.*

Concluding Remarks

The multifaceted world of first-century Jewish was the rather complex world that Jesus of Nazareth stepped into. His ministry was, first and foremost, as a Jew and to the Jewish people. Jesus proclaimed that "salvation is from the Jews" (John 4:22). Yet he presented himself as the savior of many, "to all who believed in His name" (John 1:12). His ministry of healing and proclamation of Good News begins with the healing of the wounds experienced by his own people, including the lost tribes of Israel. It should strike the reader that Jesus's inaugural ministry lie in the old Northern Kingdom, in Galilee, precisely where Isaiah prophesized the Messiah would emerge.[49]

In fact, much of Jesus's ministry may be more fully understood if one thinks of him as the "faithful and true Israelite"—God's own Son[50]—who comes to restore God's people to God, and God to his people. He came to unify his people in the House of the Lord, in his holy Temple. He came "that they may be one, even as you and I are one."[51] Jesus enters Jerusalem and its Temple as the Son of David,[52] as the one who surpasses David, who is the "true" and definitive David[53] who would restore the glory of God with his people.

---

49. See Isa. 9:1.   50. See Exod. 4:22.

51. See John 17:11.

52. Matt. 1:1, 1:20, 9:27, 12:23, 15:52, 20:30–31, 21:9, 21:15; Mark 10:47–48, 12:35; Luke 3:31, 18:38–39.

53. Joseph Ratzinger, *Jesus of Nazareth, Part Two. Holy Week: From the Entrance into Jerusalem to the Resurrection* (San Francisco: Ignatius Press, 2011), 255–56. "The tomb containing his corpse is the proof of his not having risen. Yet the psalm text is still true: it applies to *the definitive David*. Indeed, Jesus is revealed here as the *true David*, precisely because in him this promise is fulfilled: 'You will not let your Holy One see corruption.'"

II

TEMPLE THEOLOGY IN THE
NEW TESTAMENT

13

TEMPLE, MESSIAH,
AND KINGDOM

*Temple Theology in the
Four Gospels (I/V)*

Oh that you would rend the heavens and come down,
that the mountains might quake at your presence—
as when fire kindles brushwood and the fire causes water to boil—
to make your name known to your adversaries,
and that the nations might tremble at your presence!

From of old no one has heard or perceived by the ear,
no eye has seen a God besides you, who acts for those who wait for him.
You meet him who joyfully works righteousness, those who remember you in your
ways. *Behold, you were angry, and we sinned; in our sins we have been a long time,*
and shall we be saved?

There is no one who calls upon your name, who rouses himself to take hold of you;
for you have hidden your face from us, and have made us melt in the hand of our
iniquities.
But now, O Lord, you are our Father; we are the clay, and you are our potter;
we are all the work of your hand.
Be not so terribly angry, O Lord, and remember not iniquity forever.

Behold, please look, we are all your people.
Our holy and beautiful house, where our fathers praised you,
has been burned by fire, and all our pleasant places have become ruins.
Will you restrain yourself at these things, O Lord?
Will you keep silent, and afflict us so terribly?

Isaiah 64:1–12

From the Old to the New Temple

This chapter represents a paradigm shift in the book. The temple fibers have indeed woven their way from Creation to New Creation. Up to this point, the discussion of temple theology was primarily anchored within Old Testament, from the Holy Place of Eden clear through to the Temple of Solomon and its eventual destruction. This study had not hesitated to indicate various ways in which the long road that runs from the Old Testament leads to the New runs "through the Sanctuary." Significant points of connection between the canons have been presented to the reader, where necessary and appropriate to do so. Certain typological parallels between Old and New were indicated, with support from theologians such as Matthew Levering and, before him, Jean Daniélou and Yves Congar. Additionally, allegorical insights from patristic masters such as Origen or St. Ephrem the Syrian were brought into the discussion. Other times in the study, likely connections between the two testaments were stressed by the inclusion of meritorious arguments of contemporary biblical theologians, such as Gregory Beale, Gary Anderson, and Crispin Fletcher-Louis, to name a few. Even though primary emphasis has been placed upon the Old Testament, the attentive reader will have some appreciation of how, biblically speaking, the fiber optics of temple theology weave their way from the Old to the New Testaments.

Yet now the discussion of temple theology turns a decisive corner. From this chapter forward, the above pattern of study will be inverted; it will be the New Testament that is in the foreground, while the Old Testament is placed behind it, and in the background. Now, primary attention will be given to explicating temple theology within the New Testament.

Extensive consideration will be placed upon the "new beginning" of the Four Gospels, each of which, in particular ways, builds upon temple theology from Eden onward. Specifically, the next four chapters will investigate numerous ways that temple theology unfolds within the Four Gospels. Following them, the book will take up the theme as found in Acts of the Apostles, followed by the Pauline epistles, and the remainder of the New Testament.

Any attempt to articulate the temple theology of the New Testament without reference to the Old Testament would in the end leave the reader baffled and dissatisfied. To the reader, it must be stressed that a sense of continuity is called for as the study moves forward. The salient conclusions from earlier in the book cannot and will not be left behind. Rather, the conclusions drawn in this chapter and all subsequent ones build upon those of the previous chapters. The temple theology of the New Testament will be seen with far greater clarity when approached in the context of the temple theology in the Old Testament, rather than apart from one another.

The diligent and close inquiries made into the temple theology of the Old Testament now will pay large dividends, paving the way for a rich discussion of the New Testament and its distinct temple theology. Many nuances might not be as readily seen or as sufficiently grasped had the reader begun at this chapter without the benefit of the previous ones.

This is not to suggest the temple theology of the Old Testament be viewed as merely a preliminary step before examining that the temple theology of the New Testament. To the contrary, it is hoped that the reader now possesses a sound understanding of temple theology within the Hebrew Scriptures *in its own right*, even as it provides the necessary foundation as the focus of the study shifts to the Four Gospels and the remainder of the New Testament.

A word about the substance of this chapter and the next three, all of which provide, in one way or another, a treatment of temple theology on the Four Gospels. First, the present chapter examines the relationship between three interconnected concepts: the coming Messiah, the Kingdom of God, and the Jerusalem Temple. Chapters 14 and 15 assess temple theology as found in the Synoptic Gospels and the Gospel of John, respectively. Then in chapter 16, attention will be given to the temple theology with the Passion narratives of the Four Gospels. As such, the first three chapters of the series will refrain from any discussion of the Passion (and Resurrection) of Jesus, reserving that critical topic as the focus of its own chapter.

The Mystery of Revelation in the Four Gospels

As the book now shifts to the New Testament, and the Four Gospels in particular, the reader is reminded of the multiplicity of meaning that is possible in examining a biblical text. In my previous book, *The Word of the Lord*, due consideration was given to an important element of Catholic biblical interpretation, namely, the Four Senses of Scripture:

According to an ancient tradition, one can distinguish between two *senses* of Scripture: the literal and the spiritual, the latter being subdivided into the allegorical, moral, and anagogical senses. The profound concordance of the four senses guarantees all its richness to the living reading of Scripture in the Church.[1]

The present study has searched and will continue to search for meaning in biblical texts according to this vital rubric from the Church's tradition, and all the more as the Four Gospels come into focus. A few remarks will be made about the senses of Scripture as it relates to the book.

First, all sound and balanced exegesis must first seek to discover the literal and rational meaning of the text before going deeper into various spiritual possibilities. This cannot be emphasized enough. Citing St. Thomas Aquinas, the *Catechism* goes on to define the literal sense as: "The meaning conveyed by the words of Scripture and discovered by exegesis, following the rules of sound interpretation: 'All other senses of Sacred Scripture are based on the literal.'"[2]

Second, and related to the idea that St. Thomas himself underscored, is that the literal sense is primary because it is essentially the meaning intended by the human author of Scripture. Inasmuch as the human author and the Holy Spirit are united in inspired Scripture, to search for the literal is to seek the voice of God. For all of these reasons, the literal is and always will be the foundational sense, without which the reader would be disoriented and apt to not discover *any additional meaning* of another sort, as the spiritual senses flow, in a manner of speaking, out of the river of the literal headwaters.

A third and final point about the Four Senses should be added. Modern students of Scripture are sometimes wary of searching for a spiritual dimension of a text. It is true that eisegesis (i.e., reading into the text something that is not legitimately relevant, but imposed by the interpreter) is all too common in an age of much biblical illiteracy, and to be avoided. It is also true that even in the "Golden Age" of patristic exegesis, this or that allegorist occasionally put forth speculative assertions about a text. And yet the vast amount of spiritual interpretations of the Gospels over the centuries is a treasure trove that the Church has not nor ever should ignore.

True spiritual readings of Scripture are a vital organ in the body of the Church's body of reflection upon the Sacred Page. In further defining the spiritual sense, the *Catechism* speaks of how the realities and events of Scrip-

---

1. *Catechism of the Catholic Church*, §115.
2. *Catechism of the Catholic Church*, §117; Thomas Aquinas, *Summa Theologica* I, q. 1, a. 10, ad 1.

ture can themselves be signs that point to deeper realities still.[3] Within the spiritual sense are three types of spiritual senses: the *allegorical*,[4] the *moral*,[5] and the *heavenly* (or anagogical).[6] According to a medieval expression, "The Letter [literal] speaks of deeds; Allegory to faith; The Moral how to act; Anagogy our destiny."[7]

St. Basil—and Unwritten Mysteries

St. Basil the Great (330–79 AD) spoke of two ways in which dogma was handed down: "Of the dogma and kerygma which are preserved in the Church, we have some from teaching in writing, and the others we have received from the tradition of the apostles, *handed down in a mystery*."[8] In other words, St. Basil taught that there were at times meanings in biblical texts— intended by their authors yet remained obscure or at least not obvious to the reader. As an example, he mentions the practice of facing east when praying. The written arguments for this custom were less known in St. Basil's time, *but the oral tradition was prolific.* Christians understood that it was not only facing Calvary in Jerusalem but also the paradise of Eden. Here, St. Basil adds, "*A whole day would not be long enough for me to go through all the unwritten mysteries of the Church.*"[9]

Well earlier than St. Basil the Great in the east, in the west, St. Irenaeus (early second century AD) spoke of how Christ *recapitulated* what had been formerly done by Adam.[10] On the notion of recapitulation, Daniélou clari-

---

3. *Catechism of the Catholic Church*, §117.

4. Ibid. "The *allegorical sense*. We can acquire a more profound understanding of events by recognizing their significance in Christ; thus the crossing of the Red Sea is a sign or type of Christ's victory and also of Christian Baptism."

5. Ibid. "The *moral sense*. The events reported in Scripture ought to lead us to act justly. As St. Paul says, they were written 'for our instruction.'"

6. Ibid. "The *anagogical sense* [Greek: *anagoge*, "leading"]. We can view realities and events in terms of their eternal significance, leading us toward our true homeland: thus the Church on earth is a sign of the heavenly Jerusalem."

7. Ibid. Latin: "Littera gesta docet, quid credas allegoria, moralis quid agas, quo tendas anagogia." Attributed to Augustine of Dacia, *Rotulus pugillaris* I, Angelicum 6, ed. A. Walz (Rome, 1929).

8. St. Basil the Great, *On the Holy Spirit*, 66.

9. Ibid., 67. See Margaret Barker, *Temple Themes in Christian Worship* (London: Bloomsbury: 2007), 2.

10. For examples of "recapitulation" in St. Irenaeus, see especially *Against Heresies*, IV, 14; III, 22, 23. The Greek term used by Irenaeus is *anakephalaiosis.*

fies: "Christ both *accomplishes* and *restores* what had been done by Adam. This is the exact meaning of recapitulation."[11] As Daniélou explains, the mystery of recapitulation involved, in some sense, biblical typology, in which a person, place, thing, or event from the Old Testament prefigures a person, place, thing, or event in the New Testament. One might think of the Bronze Serpent as a type of Christ or the Ark of Noah as a type of Christian Baptism.[12]

Yet, in a sense, the mystery of recapitulation is a fuller and deeper way in which the Old and New Testament are connected. Deeper than biblical typology, recapitulation thrusts the reader into the mysteries of Christ's life in search of more than typology's one-to-one correspondence. Recapitulation may involve but is not dependent upon the presence of type/antitype pairs. Rather, it is "a new beginning that is a *resumption* of the first, while at the same time it *restores* the broken harmony ... and *surpasses* the original work."[13]

The value of approaching Scripture with the mystery of recapitulation in hand helps the assiduous reader to apprehend more. In addition, the reader will come to appreciate the deep connections between the Old and New Testaments: "It is precisely when we read the New Testament in terms of cultic theology that we see how much it is bound up, in its deepest implications, with the Old. The New Testament corresponds to the inner drama of the Old. It is the inner mediation of two elements that at first are in conflict with one another and find their unity in the form of Jesus Christ, in his Cross and Resurrection."[14]

In approaching temple theology within the Four Gospels, this study is committed to the above principles and proceeds with them firmly in hand.

---

11. Jean Daniélou, *From Shadow to Reality: Studies in the Typology of the Fathers* (London: Burns and Oates), 30.

12. Ibid., 30.

13. *Catechism of the Catholic Church*, §518. "Christ's whole life is a *mystery of recapitulation*. All Jesus did, said, and suffered had for its aim restoring fallen man to his original vocation: When Christ became incarnate and was made man, he *recapitulated in himself the long history of mankind and procured for us a 'short cut' to salvation, so that what we had lost in Adam, that is, being in the image and likeness of God, we might recover in Christ Jesus*. For this reason Christ experienced all the stages of life, thereby giving communion with God to all men." According to the *Catechism*, the Four Gospels are best approached in light of a *threefold* mystery, of which "recapitulation" is one. The other two are mysteries are: "*revelation*" and "redemption." (See §§516–18 for details.)

14. Joseph Ratzinger, *The Spirit of the Liturgy*, trans. John Saward (San Francisco: Ignatius Press, 2000), 49.

With St. Thomas, the approach adopted here will begin with the foundation, the literal sense. At the same time, in keeping with the wisdom of Saints Irenaeus and Basil, as well as modern theologians such as Daniélou, *this study will seek to go beyond the literal alone.* As the Four Gospels are engaged, due attention must be paid to the unique voice of each Evangelist, and how each develops his own temple theology as Jesus is proclaimed. As such, the reader is advised to contemplate various spiritual possibilities, to search for the presence of typology and/or recapitulation in Gospel texts, and other "unwritten mysteries" of the Church (i.e., Basil), in order to plunge adequately into the depths of the topic.

The Temple, the Messiah, and the Coming Kingdom of God

The remainder of this chapter will examine selected texts from the Four Gospels that concern the Davidic Messiah—and the hopes of what the Messiah would accomplish. This requires a bit of explanation, as it may seem like this is irrelevant to temple theology. In reality, nothing could be more relevant to the study of the Temple than the related themes of Messiah and kingdom.

First, the Messiah was the figure who would, in God's timing, unite all of Israel. Second, the Messiah would restore the Temple, and—given the corruption of the priesthood and the various groups vying for the allegiance of Jews at the Temple—this is equally important. Third, and beyond these first hopes, some prophetic texts of the Old Testament postulated that God—or his Messiah—would cleanse Israel of all of their sins in a single day. While this sounds like the familiar Day of Atonement ritual, the prophet Zechariah had something—someone—more mysterious and still very real in mind. Fourth, first-century Jews longed for justice. This Messiah would somehow right all the wrongs that had been done to Israel over the ages. Specifically, he would fight Israel's enemies—and triumph over them.

Fifth and finally, the Messiah would gather all of the nations to worship the One True Living God. He, the Lord, would do this, in his Messiah, or he was not the Anointed One, the Messiah, at all. In accomplishing these divine mysteries, the Messiah would truly deliver Israel, as God had done in the period of the Old Testament, as in the days of Abraham, Moses, or David.[15]

---

15. *Catechism of the Catholic Church,* §702. "From the beginning until 'the fullness of time' (Gal. 4:4), the joint mission of the Father's Word and Spirit remains hidden, but it is at work. *God's Spirit*

And, speaking of David, this was one of the most crucial hopes of all: the full restoration of the Davidic Kingdom.

The picture, then, is of a priestly figure—one that forgives sins and restores the Temple and the welfare of Israel. Yet he is also a kingly figure, a descendant of David, one qualified in every way to assume the throne of David as the legitimate heir and son. As such, this Messiah would liberate Israel from its great foes, set it on the path of peace that leads to life, and importantly restore the glory of the Lord in the Temple. Here, Barker adds the following detail: "The original Temple vessels that had been looted by the Babylonians were returned with the first group of [returning exiles]. Basins, bowls, and censers are listed, but there is no mention of the major items: the menorah, the ark, the golden altar ... Later Jewish tradition hoped that [these items of significance] would be restored in the temple in the time of the Messiah: the fire, the ark, the menorah, the Spirit [of God] and the cherubim ... the faith of the first Temple would be restored by the Messiah."[16]

These five hopes were not the *only* desires of God's people in the first century concerning the Messiah, nor did all agree in the particular details. And yet they are representative of the kinds of messianic expectations that were "in the air." Each in their own way represents a strain of thought about how God might act to deliver his people and bring justice and salvation. Each adds to the complex picture of messianic expectation. Each is crucial to understanding not only Jewish expectations of the coming Messiah but also the temple theology within the Four Gospels. Finally, and importantly, each of the above hopes can be seen in various texts from the Old Testament as well as in extrabiblical literature.

In order for the reader to see more concretely the connections between these expectations and their fulfillment in Jesus, each "hope" will be discussed below, along with textual examples from the Old Testament that reference or allude to that expectation. Old Testament texts will be immediately followed by relevant textual examples from the Gospels, which in one way or another suggest some type of "fulfillment" by Jesus. Rather than adding

---

prepares for the time of the Messiah. Neither is fully revealed but both are already promised, to be watched for and welcomed at their manifestation. So, for this reason, when the Church reads the Old Testament, she searches there for what the Spirit, 'who has spoken through the prophets,' wants to tell us about Christ."

16. Barker, *Temple Themes in Christian Worship*, 57 (emphasis added). See *Numbers Rabbah* XV.10.

commentary, the reader may contemplate the texts together, for himself or herself. Before that presentation of textual examples, two points of clarification need to be made about the manner in which the Four Gospels seem to articulate the fulfillment of these various hopes by Jesus. First, the Gospel writers recognized something that others did not, that in some surprising way, Jesus was *symbolically* and yet at the same time *really fulfilling* these various expectations of what the Messiah would do. As such, for the Evangelists, each of these five hopes that go back to the period of the Old Testament, was, as they expressed, "coming to be" before their very eyes. These hopes were understood by the Evangelists as antecedents and prefigurements waiting to be consummated in Jesus. Jesus brought them from "shadow into reality" during their lifetime. In saying that, the reader should *not* think of the Evangelists (worse still, Jesus himself) as somehow "play acting." The Gospel writers did not perceive Jesus as somehow "performing" actions and words predetermined for him by the prophets—no. Nor should one imagine such about Jesus's public ministry. Yet, as one reads the Four Gospels, it is clear that in a new and at the same time mysteriously familiar way, Jesus *embodied* the story of Israel, giving "flesh" to the sincere but abstract hopes. In so doing, he took the hopes and fears of Israel upon himself, and in Divine charity completed the will of his Father to transform them from future hope to present reality.

A second clarification is as follows. Jesus did not fulfill these hopes in a literalistic fashion. Often, his actions and words were but a hint that *something messianic had begun*. Even so, his actions and words were anything but mere symbols; Jesus was indeed affecting his reality—and Israel's—in truly real and historical ways. The age of the Messiah had come. With these two remarks in mind, what follows is a further unpacking of each of the five hopes, along with textual examples of Jewish (Old Testament) expectation, immediately followed by their fulfillment in Jesus, as seen textual corollaries from the Four Gospels.

God's Messiah Will Unite "All Israel"

In some ways, this hope encompasses the others that follow. By the time of Jesus, the Davidic Kingdom had long since split into two kingdoms. This was the sign of disunity. Moreover, there had emerged a number of alternative and competing ways of being Jewish. The following texts show in various ways how, especially in the period of Second Temple Judaism, the voices of the prophets and other biblical writers grew louder and clearer that, in the coming Day of Judgment and Visitation, God would unite all Israel.

More precisely, the reunification of Israel, of brothers amending their ways, forgiving one another's debts, and so forth would be a sign of that the messianic age had arrived. Above all, God would reunite both the Northern Kingdom of Israel and the Southern Kingdom of Judah under the rulership of his Messiah. Three examples support this claim.

In the first example from the prophet Isaiah, what was once shattered and fragmented would be made whole again when God's Messiah comes: "In that day[17] from the river Euphrates to the Brook of Egypt the LORD will thresh out the grain, and *you will be gathered one by one, O people of Israel.* And in that day a great trumpet will be blown, and *those who were lost in the land of Assyria and those who were driven out to the land of Egypt will come and worship the LORD on the holy mountain at Jerusalem*" (Isa. 27:12–13).[18]

A second example is seen in the prophet Jeremiah. Like Isaiah, the Jerusalem prophet envisions a future day when "the house of Judah shall join the house of Israel," such that the "lost tribes" of the Northern Kingdom would reunite with Judah as one (see Jer. 3:18).

A third and final example of this uniting hope is seen in the prophet Ezekiel, who envisions a day of future restoration of the two rival kingdoms. Speaking on the Lord's behalf, he writes of a future day time when the "shepherd" will seek out his flock that were scattered abroad: "I will seek out my sheep; and I will rescue them from all places where they have been scattered on a day of clouds and thick darkness" (see Ezek. 34:11–12).

Turning to the New Testament, this Jewish hope of the Messiah unifying a renewed Israel is found in numerous places within the Gospels. Two examples from the Gospel of Matthew will suffice. First, in calling "the Twelve," Jesus recapitulates the twelve tribes of Israel, unified as one nation under Moses: "And he called to him his twelve disciples and gave them authority over unclean spirits, to cast them out, *and to heal every disease and every infirmity.*

---

17. Phrases such as "in/on that day," "in those days," etc. are common Old Testament (OT) expressions that anticipate to the time of the Messiah. They are important in that they represent the sure and certain fulfillment of the blessings and judgments associated with the coming Messiah. Be alert for OT phrases such as "day of the Lord" (Isa. 13:6, 58:13; Jer. 46:10; Amos 5:18; Zech. 14:1, etc.) and New Testament expressions such as "the one who is to come" (Matt. 11:3) that are rooted in messianic expectations.

18. See also Isa. 11:1–3.

The names of the *twelve apostles* are these: first, Simon, who is called Peter, and Andrew his brother; James the son of Zebedee, etc.... *These twelve Jesus sent out,* charging them, 'Go nowhere among the Gentiles, and enter no town of the Samaritans, *but go rather to the lost sheep of the house of Israel'"* (Matt. 10:1–6).

Jesus began to unite his disciples around himself as "one body." At the center of this communion were the Twelve. Just as the twelve tribes of Israel were united as one under Moses, so now, the Twelve (apostles) were united as one under the New Moses. To choose *twelve,* Jesus deliberately and symbolically took this hope of restoration upon himself, fulfilling it in a partial sense in his earthly ministry, and in a "perfecting" way that continues until he comes again in glory.

A second example, taken from the same Gospel, is highly eschatological in nature. In Matthew 19, Jesus says, "Truly, I say to you, in the new world, when the Son of man shall sit on his glorious throne, you who have followed me will also sit on *twelve thrones, judging the twelve tribes of Israel"* (Matt. 19:28). Here is another instance of Jesus uniting all of Israel in himself. But this text goes beyond the above calling of the Twelve. In this text, the apostles are told by Jesus of their future, heavenly role as prince-judges who will dispense God's divine justice upon Israel.

God's Messiah Will Restore the Jerusalem Temple

The second of the five Jewish hopes, given expression in the biblical prophets, is that the coming Messiah would somehow initiate a restoration of the Temple itself.[19] Here, "restoration" is best understood not in physical terms, but in regard to the "glory of God." In the centuries following the destruction of Solomon's Temple—long after the Babylonian ended, long after a "remnant" of Jews returned to Jerusalem, and after the Second Temple was dedicated in 518 BC—deep questions remained as to the "status" of the Temple.

A number of texts in the prophetic tradition of the Old Testament explicitly or implicitly look forward to the messianic age as a glorious future age in which all of Israel is renewed and gathered around a purified sanctu-

---

19. Given the importance that this particular Jewish hope has in relation to the chapter as a whole, the discussion of it will be more extensive than the other four Jewish hopes as it pertains to the messiah and temple theology. Regardless, all five of the Jewish hopes will be discussed amply in their own right.

ary, teeming with holiness. *In those days*, the prophets announced, the righteous ones will be justified, and Israel's enemies vanquished. *In those days*, the prophets proclaimed, the *Shekinah*, the glory of God, will pervade the Temple, and all will know that Israel's God is the one true living God. *In those days*, Israel will offer sacrifices to God, and the merciful God will accept them and show mercy to Israel.

In sum, *in those days*, God's Messiah will govern and guide Israel, ushering in a new age, a new world order, in which Jerusalem is the "center of the world," and the gleaming Temple abounds with the glory of God, and many will flock to Jerusalem to praise the earth's true King in all of his glory.

All of these eschatological hopes were simultaneously grounded in such a "restoration" of the Temple and, importantly, *in the one who would usher in this age, namely, God's priest-king, God's anointed, God's Messiah*. For these reasons, the Evangelists, who came eventually came to believe what Peter first expressed, that Jesus is "the Christ, the Son of the Living God" (Mark 8:29), described Jesus in the Gospels as not only on par with Moses—that is, the "prophet like Moses" (Deut. 18:18)—but also as the one who surpassed Moses. St. John writes, "For the Law was given through Moses, but grace and truth came through Jesus Christ" (John 1:17). Along these lines, Catholic theologian Matthew Levering writes, "Christ was not merely another prophet, as if he had been sent to simply confirm the teachings of Moses. Rather, the Messiah's obedience to the Old Law *enabled him to fulfill and to transform the Old Law*."[20]

Turning now to the biblical evidence itself, the theme of a coming restoration of the Temple is apparent in the prophet Isaiah. Early in the book, the prophet writes:

It shall come to pass in the latter days that the mountain of the house of the Lord shall be established as the highest of the mountains, and shall be raised above the hills; and all the nations shall flow to it, and many peoples shall come, and say: "Come, let us go up to *the mountain of the Lord*, to *the house of the God of Jacob*; that he may teach us his ways and that we may walk in his paths." For out of Zion shall go forth the Law, and the word of the Lord from Jerusalem. (Isa. 2:1–3)

Three comments may be mentioned about the "restoration" theme in this text. First, recall the phraseology "*It shall come to pass in the latter days*" cues

---

20. Matthew Levering, *Christ's Fulfillment of Temple and Torah: Salvation According to Thomas Aquinas* (Notre Dame, IN: University of Notre Dame Press, 2002), 46.

the reader to the "day of visitation" of God's justice, rooted in the expectation of the coming Messiah. Second, Isaiah speaks of how the *mountain* of the Temple will be established as "the highest of the mountains." In the logic of the text, this eschatological elevation that is being described serves a practical purpose in the prophet's vision: it allows the nations to see and "flow to it" (v. 2). It is the Gentiles who, in this time, will say, "Come, let us go up to *the mountain of the Lord*, to the house of the God of Jacob; that he may teach us his ways and that we may walk in his paths." But there is another way of interpreting Isaiah's incredible image, one that recalls the temple theology in the Creation narratives. In Genesis 1–2, the land rises up, up above the watery chaos, and soon the mountain of Eden emerges as a place of safety, tranquility, and perfect order. Isaiah's image is, in some sense, rooted in the biblical symbolism of the "high mountain," as a place of divine majesty and divine God's presence. As Mt. Zion rises up in the future time of the Messiah, it is as if Eden itself will be recapitulated, and all will see this holy mountain and be drawn to it.

A third point, and one that directly related to the previous one, is that the passage in Isaiah anticipates a renewal in devotion to the Law, for as the mountain of Zion rises up, and Gentiles flock to it, they respond by exclaiming that they will go up to the house of the Lord, "that he may teach us his ways." God's truth, in other words, will have its way with the wayward Gentiles, who will, in this coming day, be drawn to "the word of the Lord" that flows out of Zion, just as the living waters flowed out of Eden, "watering" the earth with nourishment. This "drawing in" of the Gentiles to the heights of Mt. Zion is expressed in positive terms in verse 2, but then in verse 4 Isaiah recognizes this as a coming judgment upon the nations, long overdue in the prophet's eyes. And so, in what follows, in verses 5–11, Isaiah admonishes God's people to embrace the Law, that such devotion to God's word would precipitate, in some sense, the coming judgment upon the Gentiles: "O house of Jacob, come, let us walk in the light of the Lord ... The haughty looks of man shall be brought low, and the pride of men shall be humbled; and the Lord alone will be exalted in that day."

Much later, in Isaiah 66, the prophet again foresees, in the coming messianic age, a turning of the nations to Zion: "For I know their works and their thoughts, and I am coming to gather all nations and tongues; and they shall come and shall see my glory" (66:18). This theme, of God drawing "all nations," overlaps with another hope that will be discussed below. Yet it is mentioned here because of an astonishing statement made about the future priesthood:

And they shall bring all your brothers from all the nations as an offering to the Lord, on horses and in chariots and in litters and on mules and on dromedaries, to my holy mountain Jerusalem, says the Lord, just as the Israelites bring their grain offering in a clean vessel to the house of the Lord. *And some of them also I will take for priests and for Levites, says the Lord.* (Isa. 66:20–21)

This is an extraordinary promise in Isaiah. One is not surprised, at this point, to hear the prophet announce that in the messianic age to come, Gentiles will be drawn to the "highest of mountains," to the Temple on Zion. Yet it is quite astonishing to hear Isaiah's announcement that the Lord will accept some of these *Gentiles as priests.* There is almost a whiplash effect as this text is read; how can this be? How can one reconcile this with the Mosaic Law, and the strict commands of all priests being from the tribe of Levi? And yet, in the prophet's vision, the remark is made without warning or explanation. How does one interpret this text? One's interpretation of this perplexing riddle is helped considerably by temple theology, beginning in Genesis. There, Adam was originally called to "be fruitful and multiply" and so spread God's holiness beyond the temple of Eden.

And so the enigmatic text in Isaiah becomes more sensible in light of the archetypal temple pattern established in Genesis. Those Gentiles and "sons of Adam," who were once separated from God because of unrighteousness, are called home and respond. Those formerly "cut off" from the holiness of the Temple hear the Word of the Lord, and in penitence and humility seek the Lord in Zion. In Isaiah's eschatological vision, they come to the Temple and worship the living God there. Not only that, but also "some" among them (the prophet gives no indication of few or how many) will be "taken as priests and Levites." What a reversal of Eden! Those who were "cast out" not only "enter in" to the Temple, in a just and holy way, but are also accepted by God, in the fashion of the Father embracing the prodigal in Luke 15. Herein lies a remarkable hope, that the Messiah overcomes the banishment of Adam (and Eve) from Eden. That which was formerly off-limits to a fallen humanity will again become accessible. And not merely "accessible"; those formerly cut off will come to play an integral role in the future worship of God, who draws all men to his Temple in the messianic age.

Another book of the Old Testament with strong, consistent themes pertaining to temple theology is Zechariah. In a remarkable text, the postexilic prophet envisions a messianic figure, named "the Branch," who will restore the corrupted Temple: "Behold, the man whose name is the Branch: for he shall grow up in his place, *and he shall build the temple of the Lord.* It is he who shall build the temple of the Lord, and shall bear royal honor, and shall sit and rule upon his throne ... And those who are far off shall come and help to build the Temple of the Lord; and you shall know that the Lord of hosts has sent me to you" (Zech. 6:12–15).

Several comments about this text are necessary. First, the reader is told that there is no ambiguity as to *how* the Temple will be restored; it would happen by God's temple builder, the Messiah. He would bring Israel together in a unifying way, through the "rebuilding" of the Temple. The Messiah is not only a priestly figure but also a royal one, "who shall sit and rule upon his throne." This is a clear allusion to the Davidic covenant, and the "everlasting kingdom" that God promised to David and his sons (see 2 Sam. 7:13–14).

A second point, related to the above, is that Zechariah employs an interesting term in describing the coming Messiah. He writes, "Behold the man whose name is *netzer* [Hebrew: Branch]." *Netzer* is a highly symbolic term pertaining to the Davidic Messiah, with the emphasis on *Davidic.* It is rooted in God's promises to David and his offspring. The term *netzer* (and others like it) rests upon the Davidic covenant. It occurs elsewhere in the biblical prophets,[21] and while Jeremiah does use not the term, he captures the same idea when he twice refers to the coming Messiah as the *sedeqah shemah*, the "righteous *branch*" (Jer. 23:5, 33:15).

Along with *netzer*, the prophets use similar terms to communicate the same type of messianic expectation. For example, elsewhere, Isaiah describes the servant of the Lord as the *shoresh* ("root") of Jesse, the father of David (Isa. 11:1). Earlier in the same chapter, the prophet writes of how a *hoter migeza* ("shoot from the stump"), and a *netzer* shall grow out of Jesse's roots.

Zechariah does not use terms other than *netzer*, and it is employed twice in the book, here in Zechariah 6 as well as earlier, in chapter 3: "behold, I will bring my servant the *Branch*" (Zech. 3:8). The *netzer* term is particularly evocative for another possibility it raises, one that scholars have not seized upon. Jesus is raised in *Nazareth*, and the name of the village shares a certain congruency with *netzer.*

---

21. See also Isa. 4:2, 11:1; Jer. 23:5; Dan. 11:7; Zech. 3:8.

This raises a possible question as to whether this is sheer coincidence, or if the name of Jesus's village, Nazareth, is in any way connected to the term *netzer*, a term that recurs in the biblical prophets and that is used to depict the coming Messiah as the "Branch" of David, and whether the "branch of David" is then the rightful heir to the Davidic throne.

This is an interesting thesis, but only a thesis. It is beyond the scope of this book to marshal evidence in support of this possible connection, and it is not claimed here that anything decisive can be adduced from such apparent correspondence between *netzer* and *Nazareth*. Yet it offers some compelling possibilities for understanding the "motives" of not only Mary and Joseph, who made Nazareth their home for many years, but also other Nazoreans. It appears that, in addition to the Holy Family, there were some first-century Jews, Jews who might be more precisely described as "loyal David-ists"—that is, Judean families of Davidic ancestry—who had roots in or near Judea but deliberately *chose* to make their home in faraway Galilee. Though living in small towns like Nazareth, these Davidic Jews remained sympathetic to Judean values and beliefs, were supportive of the Jerusalem Temple, and above all eagerly awaited the fulfillment of the prophetic hopes that are being discussed here.

For his part, St. Luke goes out of his way to inform his audience that Joseph and Mary journeyed to Jerusalem *kata etos* ("year after year") for the Feast of Passover (Luke 2:41). In their devotion to the Jerusalem Temple, Joseph and Mary were not alone; certainly, thousands of Jewish pilgrims from the Diaspora made annual religious pilgrimages of this sort to Jerusalem, from a variety of locations far from Jerusalem. Others who could not make the journey nevertheless paid the Temple tax. Yet what distinguished Jews in Galilee from other far-flung Jewish colonies is that attached to Galilee were a number of specific promises from the biblical prophets as to *where* the Messiah would come from. In the context of the Emmanuel Prophecy in Isaiah 9, the prophet writes:

But there will be no gloom for her that was in anguish. In the former time he brought into contempt the land of Zebulun and the land of Naphtali, but in the latter time he will make glorious the way of the sea, *the land beyond the Jordan, Galilee of the nations*. (Isa. 9:1)

In this text, the prophet Isaiah offers a ray of light for people who "walk in darkness" (v. 2). Specifically, in the "latter time"—that is, the messianic age—God will bring forth "a son" (v. 6), upon whom the governance of God's people will rest. He will be called Wonderful Counselor, Mighty God, Everlasting Father, Prince of Peace. And this "child" who would be born (v. 6) would come from "the land of Zebulun and Naphtali," two of the northern most tribal allotments of ancient Israel. Verse 1 points not only to a Galilean, but also to the *derek hayam* ("Way of the Sea"). The Way of the Sea was a Roman highway that ran from Assyria in the north down to Egypt, and the so-called Via Maris passed close by the western shore of the Sea of Galilee. From this information some interesting questions may be formulated:

- Did such displaced Judeans as Joseph (and Mary, a likely Judean by ancestry) and other Judeans who lived with zealous messianic expectations "anticipate" that the Messiah would come from the north, from the Galilee, as Isaiah indicates, and orient their life in such a way as to welcome him?
- Were there small villages across Galilee, insignificant in size and influence but composed largely, perhaps almost chiefly, of Judean families that longed to usher in the messianic age at God's appointed time?
- Is it plausible that such Jews "clustered" together—for example, around a common synagogue—and that as they shared these messianic hopes with one another, and devoted themselves to the writings of the prophets, that their mind-set and even manner of speaking was shot through with biblical words and phrases from the Jewish Scriptures, phrases that reminded them of these sure hopes?

Given the above, it does not seem entirely unfathomable to imagine that at some point the small hamlet of Nazareth was so named (or renamed) in part because of the "branch" connotations of the Old Testament prophets, and in part because a small group of Davidic Jews settled there, awaiting the coming Messiah. If such a scenario could be bolstered by sufficient facts, and not theological conjecture (as is the case here), then the following could be cautiously suggested. Specifically, by some point in the early part of the first century, the small hamlet known as Nazareth became home to a sort of "community of the Branch"—that is, a Galilean cluster of Judeans—Davidic loyalists who settled there. In time, it may have germinated into a small but dedicated "messianic seedbed" of like-minded northern Judeans awaiting what the prophets foretold.

The above proposal concerning Nazareth is presented for the reader's consideration. While it proposes a number of interesting possibilities, they need not be embraced either in part or as a whole. What is *not supposition* are the strong expectations, as evidenced in numerous texts from the prophetic tradition of the Old Testament, that the coming Messiah would restore the Jerusalem Temple to its former glory.[22]

Before turning to texts in the Four Gospels that correspond to the Jewish hopes that the coming Messiah would restore the Jerusalem Temple, one more text may be added to the above discussion, also from the prophet Zechariah. In chapter 14, the book draws to a close with one final and colorful prophetic image of the messianic age: "On that day living waters shall flow out from Jerusalem ... it shall continue in summer as in winter. And the Lord will become king over all the earth; on that day the Lord will be one and his name one" (Zech. 14:8–10). Four remarks may be offered about this text.

First, note that the inauguration of the messianic age is depicted *in Jerusalem.* While the surrounding context in Zechariah 14 mentions the Mount of Olives, in an equally stirring way this text seems to have the city of Jerusalem—and particularly the Temple on Mt. Zion—in mind. The evidence for this is in the text itself; Zechariah speaks of "living waters" flowing out of Jerusalem, waters not subject to climate, rains, or floods (v. 9).

Second, the image of living waters is associated with the Feast of Tabernacles, and the high priestly ritual of processing from the Temple to the Pool of Siloam, and returning to the Temple with a golden cistern filled with water. In a Temple liturgy at Tabernacles, the high priest would pour the running water upon the Bronze Altar. This action symbolized God's saving actions in the wilderness period, when Moses and the Israelites wandered through the desert. In those wilderness years, *God provided for them*; he fed them the supernatural "bread from heaven," the Manna (see Exod. 16), and he quenched

---

22. As discussed, the "Nazareth/Branch" possibility is presented for the reader's consideration only. The arguments in this chapter related more directly to the messianic restoration of the Temple do not necessarily lead to the supposition, nor do they depend in any way upon the scenario. That said, the supposition is not without its merits. In the second century, a messianic movement began in Galilee, swirling around the historical figure known as Simon Bar Kochba, also known as the "Son of the Star." Bar Kochba led an uprising that ultimately contributed to the so-called Second War with Rome in 103–32 AD. The revolt of Bar Kochba and his sympathizers was put down, but not without much violence and loss of life. For a related study that deals in part with the Nazareth/Branch possibility, see Bargil Pixner, *Paths of the Messiah and Sites of the Early Church from Galilee to Jerusalem: Jesus and Jewish Christianity in Light of Archaeological Discoveries* (San Francisco: Ignatius Press, 2010).

their thirst by miraculously bring "living water" forth from the rock.[23] The Feast of Booths, or Tabernacles, was a kind of "holy remembering" of God's saving deeds of the past, and the eight-day festival culminated with a liturgical reenactment of this "water ritual." This water rite was performed along with a "ritual of light," in which the large torches were lit over the Court of Women. The entire Temple mount was illuminated at night by bright light. This symbolized God's provision of the "pillar of fire" that guided the Israelites on their wilderness pilgrimage.[24]

Third, according to Zechariah's description of this "eschatological Feast of Tabernacles," the Messiah emerges as a priestly figure who is "at home" in the Temple and purifies it. And yet, at the same time, the "man called Branch" is simultaneously a *royal* figure. Zechariah writes, "And the Lord will become king over all the earth; on that day the Lord will be one and his name one" (14:10).

Further consideration of texts from Nazareth must now be concluded in order to continue with the main discussion at hand, of the five hopes concerning the Messiah in the Old Testament, and how they find resonance in the fulfillment in the ministry of Jesus, as described by the Four Gospels. Insights from Zechariah as it pertains to temple theology may be summed up as follows. God will send his Messiah, a man called "Branch," and this messianic figure will restore the Temple to its former glory. As a priestly figure, he is "at home" in the Temple and appears to preside over a special Feast of Tabernacles liturgy. If this were not enough, the coming of the Messiah and the purification of the Temple lead to a renewed sense of the Lord's "kingship" over all the earth, as all of God's people are united under God's sovereignty, and as his name is "one" and his people are "one."

Having examined various promises of this second messianic hope in the Old Testament (i.e., that the coming Messiah would restore the Jerusalem Temple), the discussion now turns to the "fulfillment" of the hope, as seen in the Four Gospels.

There are a number of texts in the Gospels in which the "restoration of the Temple" is taken up, as it relates to the identity and mission of Jesus as Israel's true messiah. For the sake of this discussion, two pertinent texts will be examined from Matthew and John. Both texts have some commonalities and oc-

23. See Exod. 17:6; Num. 20:8–11.
24. See Exod. 13:21–22, 14:19, 14:24; Num. 14:14, etc.

cur in the immediate context of the Temple (or the precincts immediately surrounding the Temple). Both texts deal with scenes in the Temple; the former has to do with Jesus's temple action, commonly known as his "cleaning of the Temple."[25] The latter is a saying of Jesus, of how he would "raise it up" in three days:

And Jesus entered the Temple of God and drove out all who sold and bought in the Temple, and he overturned the tables of the money-changers and the seats of those who sold pigeons. He said to them, "It is written, 'My house shall be called a house of prayer'; but you make it a den of robbers." And the blind and the lame came to him in the Temple, and he healed them. (Matt. 21:12–15)

Jesus answered them, "Destroy this temple, and in three days I will raise it up." The Jews then said, "It has taken forty-six years to build this temple, and will you raise it up in three days?" But he spoke of the temple of his body. When therefore he was raised from the dead, his disciples remembered that he had said this; and they believed the scripture and the word which Jesus had spoken. (John 2:19–22)

These texts and their implications have perplexed many; this is not the occasion to engage in an exegesis of these texts in an extended way. Yet some analysis is warranted in order to arrive at a reasonable understanding of how these texts represent a kind of fulfillment of the prophets' hopes, that God's Messiah would indeed "restore the Temple."

Regarding the first text, located in the Gospel of Matthew, three observations may be made. First, notice that Jesus "entered the Temple." The act of his entering so readily and freely speaks volumes as to Jesus's being "at home" in the Temple. Jesus was in his element in the Temple, about which he once remarked to Mary and Joseph that he must be "in His Father's house" (Luke 2:19).

Second, however one interprets the meaning of Jesus's actions, one thing is clear: his actions disrupt the order of the day, and presumably "Temple business." Third, and most strikingly, Matthew concludes the passage with a comment that may appear to be—but is not—incidental. Specifically, the Evangelist writes, "And the blind and the lame came to him in the Temple, and he healed them." As to the meaning of this brief comment, there should be little doubt as to how it relates to Jesus's actions in the Temple, narrated just prior to Matthew's remark.

---

25. Given the extensive nature of the second messianic hope (i.e., God's Messiah Will Restore the Temple), remarks concerning the details of the two Gospels passages that evince this particular hope will be kept succinct. Additionally, Jesus's temple actions will be discussed in chapters 14 and 15.

The healing ministry of Jesus, carried out in the immediate context of his temple actions, demonstrates several things. First, it shows that despite Jesus's indignation at some figures in the Temple, he is and remains open, loving, and compassionate to those in need; he is merciful upon them and healed them. Second, the Temple miracles of Jesus represent, at least on a deeper symbolic level, *the renewal of the ministry of the Temple.* Jesus appears disturbed that the Temple has become a "den of robbers" (Matt. 21:14). His actions telescope a "negation" and critique of such temporal business within the Temple.[26]

Turning to the other passage, in the Gospel of John, three things deserve to be mentioned as it pertains to this chapter. First, as in the passage just examined from the Gospel of Matthew, the Johannine text has its setting within the precincts of the Jerusalem Temple. This fact only amplifies the message that John is conveying in the text, given the setting is at the Temple itself.

Second, and this point must be strongly underscored, Jesus never asserts that he would in any way harm or destroy the Temple. This charge is falsely brought against him later at his trial, yet nothing of the sort is uttered by Jesus himself.[27]

Third, St. John underscores the "temple Christology" in play here in the final editorial remark that he makes (John 2:23). Specifically, St. John explains that sometime following Jesus's Resurrection (precisely when he does not indicate), his disciples "remembered" that Jesus had said, "[If you] de-

---

26. As will be argued in a later chapter, Jesus's temple action, as described in Matthew (and parallels), need not be construed, *at least not primarily,* as a kind of spontaneous outburst of righteous anger, e.g., signifying his horror over his discovery of the "unholy" business and commerce taking place within the Temple. Rather, the actions are better seen as symbolic and carefully handled gestures, in line with the prophetic tradition of the Old Testament. The prophets of the Old Testament sharply critiqued Temple corruption—and warned that such practices would bring about God's judgment upon the Temple. In a similar fashion, here is "Jesus, God's anointed Prophet," decrying such common marketplace activities being comingled with the holiness of the Temple. *As a result of Jesus's controlled actions, the Temple sacrifices would have, at least temporarily, "ceased" during the ensuing chaos.* The "cleansing" of the Temple is really something altogether different than how it is often portrayed. In other words, Jesus's symbolic actions were not as much a "cleansing" of the Temple as much as they were a "disruption" of the sacrificial economy of the Temple. In this sort of reading, Jesus's actions prophetically anticipates, in a spectacular, symbolic gesture, the "cessation" of Temple sacrifices. What was soon to become the "old temple," just one generation after Jesus's crucifixion, was about to be supplanted by the New Temple—the Temple of Jesus's body. Again, more will be said about the scene in chapter 17.

27. See Matt. 27:40; Mark 14:58, 15:29.

stroy this Temple, in three days I will raise it up again" (John 2:19). A significant closing comment follows, one that crystalizes everything that the Evangelist wishes his audience to know: "*But [Jesus] spoke of the temple of his body.*" In this expression of the Evangelist, the fullness of hopes as longed for by the Old Testament prophets is realized in the Resurrection of Jesus Christ. In "raising up the Temple" in three days—a clear nod to the Passion of Jesus—Jesus has fulfilled, but in an unanticipated way, what it meant that the Messiah would indeed "restore the Temple."

This concludes the discussion of the prophetic hope that the Messiah would "restore the Temple" and the various questions that surround it. We now turn to a third Jewish expectation.

God's Messiah Will Forgive Their Sins (in a Single Day)

The idea that anyone could forgive sin apart from God was blasphemy in ancient Judaism, and it is this very concern that often lands Jesus in trouble with his adversaries. For ancient Jews, the concept of the forgiveness of sin was bound up with the Temple sacrifices, through the mediatorial service of the Temple priests. The culminating liturgy was the annual Day of Atonement. It took place in the autumn of the year, when the high priest would offer sacrifice for himself and all of Israel on that day.

The postexilic prophet Zechariah anticipates a future time of an outpouring of forgiveness of sins and closely associates this with the hope of the Messiah. The text does not indicate explicitly that the messianic figure would forgive sins, for only God could do so. And yet the proximity of the Messiah to God's outpouring of forgiveness is brought remarkably close in the following text:

Hear now, O Joshua the high priest ... behold, I will bring my servant the Branch. For behold, upon the stone which I have set before Joshua, upon a single stone with seven facets, I will engrave its inscription, says the Lord of hosts, and I will remove the guilt of this land in a single day. In that day, says the Lord of hosts, every one of you will invite his neighbor under his vine and under his fig tree. (Zech. 3:8–9)

Note that in the prophet's vision God brings forth his servant, the "Branch," as God addresses the *high priest*, whose name is Joshua (interestingly enough), who stands before him (v. 8). The following seven details from the surrounding context of Zechariah 3 help fill out the picture. First, Satan is also present in this heavenly scene, and ready to accuse the high priest

(vv. 1–2). Second, in verse 5, Zechariah describes Joshua as being clothed in *soim begadim* ("filthy garments)." Third, God takes away the high priest's sins, and the "angel of the Lord" commands that Joshua now be clothed in *mahasalot* ("clean vestments," v. 4).[28] Fourth, Zechariah comes to the high priest's defense as well, calling for a *tahor sanip* ("clean turban") to be placed upon his head (v. 5). Fifth, the "angel of the Lord" then conveys God's message to the high priest, calling the high priest to holiness and obedience: "*If* you walk in My ways and keep My charge, then you shall *rule My house*," a clear reference to the Temple. Sixth, all of the various garments are priestly language, rooted in the Temple. In fact, although the scene is depicted in a heavenly context, the entire scene is simultaneously highly evocative of the Jerusalem Temple and the high priesthood. Seventh and finally, notice the classical biblical if, enjoined upon the high priest, a conjunction that warns of the conditional nature of God's protection of the high priest, and a portent of things to come.

These contextual details lead the reader to a greater understanding of the issues involved in Zechariah 3:8–10. Now, Zechariah's vision looks not so much heavenward but forward in time, to the future messianic age. The prophet introduces a new image at this point, that of a "stone with seven facets" (v. 9). The stone is engraved with an untold inscription. Here, it seems likely that both the term *netzer* ("Branch") and *eben* ("stone") point to one and the same individual, the priestly and kingly Messiah:

> By using the two metaphors of "branch" and "stone" to refer to the coming Messiah, Zechariah or the editor saw him as both *king* and *priest*. The idea of a priest-king may go back to the ancient concept of the priesthood of Melchizedek, king of Salem.[29]

Zechariah does not look to the "rehabilitation" of the high priest Joshua, nor is any hope expressed about the Temple that will happen through *that* high priest. However, Zechariah does see *another* priestly figure that is a great source of hope. Specifically, Zechariah's hope is channeled toward the future, to the coming of the man called "Branch"—the Davidic Messiah.

The reference to the "stone" ("rock"?) with seven facets (v. 9) is likewise

---

28. See Ralph L. Smith, *Micah–Malachi*, vol. 32, *Word Biblical Commentary* (Dallas: Word Books, 1998), 200. "The reason given for the cleansing of the high priest and Israel is that God has chosen Israel (3:2; cf. 1:17; 2:16, Eng. 2:12). Yahweh had snatched the high priest and Israel from destruction as a piece of wood is snatched from the fire."

29. Ibid., 201. On Melchizedek, see Gen. 14:17–20; Psa. 110:4.

a fascinating image, with connections in the two canons, both Old and New. In terms of the Old Testament, the image recalls the wilderness narratives in Exodus and Numbers, which describe several occasions in which Moses (the latter to his own detriment) strikes the "rock," producing a gush of running water.[30] Elsewhere in the canon, the prophet Ezekiel, in describing his vision of the eschatological Temple, uses the imagery of water "rushing out of the Temple" (Ezek. 47:1–2).

For his part, Zechariah concludes his book with a vision of the priest-king Messiah presiding over an eschatological the Feast of Tabernacles, as follows. In chapter 13 of the book, Zechariah announces that in the messianic age there will be a *maqor* ("fountain") opened up for the house of David (13:1). Zechariah identifies the purpose of this "fountain" (which may alternatively be translated "spring"[31]); it is to cleanse God's people from "sin and uncleanness." "Sin and uncleanness" are terms readily associated with the Temple, whereas "fountain" is not. Yet in the next and final chapter of the book, as Zechariah's messianic vision comes to a close, the prophet explicitly mentions Tabernacles: "On that day," the prophet writes, "living waters (*hayyim mayim*) shall flow out from Jerusalem … and the Lord will become king over all the earth; on that day the Lord will be one and his name one" (14:8–9).

Zechariah's image of the Messiah as "stone" not only has resonances elsewhere in the canon of the Old Testament, but there are also resonances within the canon of the New Testament. What leaps immediately to mind is St. Paul's image of Christ as the "cornerstone" of the Temple,[32] a theme crucial to the temple theology of the New Testament, and one that will be discussed at length later in the book. St. Paul will refer to Christ in other places as *rock*: "And all [Israel] ate the same supernatural food and all drank the same supernatural drink. *For they drank from the supernatural Rock which followed them, and the Rock was Christ*" (1 Cor. 10:4).

One culminating remark needs to be made, as it relates to the Jewish hope of a "special outpouring of forgiveness" in the coming messianic age. Specifically, Zechariah declares that when the man called Branch comes, God will *remove the guilt of this land in a single day*" (Zech. 3:9).

At face value, this is an astonishing (if not perplexing) statement, on many levels. One may ask the prophet: Does not God *already* forgive sins? Is

---

30. See Exod. 17:1–8; Num. 20:11.

31. *Enhanced Brown-Driver-Briggs Hebrew and English Lexicon*, s.v. "מָקוֹר (*maqor*)."

32. See esp. Eph. 2:20; also Rom. 9:32–33.

there not an outpouring of forgiveness in the Temple that happens, in some sense, *on a daily basis*, through the ministry of sacrificial offerings? Above all, is not the Day of Atonement the annual solemn occasion in which, through the ministry of the high priest, God "forgives Israel's sins *on a particular day?*" The answers to these questions is yes, indeed; God does, and he is forgiving Israel's sins. Whatever Zechariah intends in this saying must be something further, something beyond that which *God is already doing*.

Getting beyond those perplexing questions, one may call to mind possible New Testament parallels, specifically the crucifixion of Jesus. The astute reader may recall that it is Zechariah himself who prophetically writes, "They will look upon him who they have pierced" (12:10). It is well understandable to ascertain a possible connection between Zechariah 3 and "Good Friday" when, in the context of the New Covenant, God forgives the sins of the world "in a single day." But to immediately clarify: one need not axiomatically connect Zechariah's expression of forgiveness of sins "in a single day" to the Passion Narratives of the Gospels, at least not in a static way. Rather, it may be prudent to think about this in a slightly different and stepwise fashion.

Recall what was said earlier in the book about the duties of the high priest. His was indeed a ministry of the "forgiveness of sins," and one that took place on a particular day, the Day of Atonement (Lev. 16). Obviously, forgiveness is tied to an oblation, to a sacrificial offering. And such take place in *one and only one place:* the Jerusalem Temple. So the outpouring of divine forgiveness that would come about in a special way in the messianic age would by definition involve *sacrifice*. The Messiah would be a priest-king. He would be the rightful heir to the Davidic throne, in other words, a *royal Messiah*. At the same time, he would be intimately involved (one way or another) with a special dispensation of God's mercy and forgiveness, and therefore a *sacerdotal Messiah,* a *priestly Messiah*.

In addition to everything else Zechariah puts forth in regard to the Messiah's mission of "restoring the Temple" (i.e., Hope 2), it seems that his announcement of this future outpouring of forgiveness was meant to draw a sharp contrast between the *repeated and continual actions* of the high priest, and a kind of spectacular and special "moment" of forgiveness that would take place in and through the coming One, the Messiah.

It is unclear from the text itself whether Zechariah has something particular in mind as to *how God will forgive* Israel's sins in a way that is different from the high priest's actions in the Temple on the Day of Atonement. What is clear from the text is that, for Zechariah, it is enough to believe that *God will do so*, that he will see to this when the Messiah comes. The question of precisely *how* this future "Day of Atonement" will be different from the present state of things in the Temple does not seem to be in the prophet's purview to know or at the least to reveal. From the text itself, it is safe to say that for Zechariah, while the "how" of this special outpouring of divine grace is not unveiled,[33] it is enough to know that *God will do so*.

The reader is told in Zechariah 3 is that, like the Day of Atonement liturgy of the Temple, what will happen will happen "on a single day." Needless to say, whatever was going to happen in the messianic age would somehow *eclipse* the present Day of Atonement; otherwise, this "forgiveness event" would offer nothing new, nothing more than Israel already had. Somehow, *it would be different*. Somehow, *it would bring God closer to Israel, and Israel closer to God* than in Zechariah's age. Yet Zechariah does not further elaborate.

What springs to mind is the contrast drawn in the Book of Hebrews, between the high priest of the Temple, who offered sacrifices for his own sins and those of all of Israel "year after year" (Heb. 10:1), as opposed to the "once for all" sacrifice of Jesus (Heb. 7:27). Just what sort of "lesser than, greater than" distinctions Zechariah may have in mind with respect to the present Day of Atonement of the high priesthood of his day and the "eschatological Day of Atonement" with the priestly Messiah is unknowable.

A final clarification: Zechariah does not state that it would be the messiah who actually "forgives sins." Strictly speaking, that would be tantamount to blasphemy, "for who can forgive sins *but God alone*?" (Luke 5:21).[34] And yet the close connection between an unprecedented outpouring of forgiveness of sins on one hand and the messiah on the other cannot be ignored.

Summing up, Zechariah 3 is a fascinating example of temple theology, and the discussion of the text wove together half a dozen fibers of temple theology from the Old and New Testaments: (1) a scene of heavenly judgment and restoration of a priestly figure; (2) terminology rooted in the priesthood of the Temple (garments, turban, etc.); (3) a "conditional" promise of the

33. But see Zech. 12:10.

34. See Luke 5:24: "But that you may know that the Son of Man has authority on earth to forgive sins."

protection of the high priest and by extension the Temple that he governs, *provided* that high priest "walks in My ways;" (4) names or descriptions of the coming messiah (*branch, stone*) that connote a priestly as well as a kingly figure; (5) the motif of "living water" flowing out from a restored Temple, at the Feast of Tabernacles; and, lastly, (6) a special outpouring of the forgiveness of sins in the messianic that would take place "in a single day."

While the prophet Zechariah may offer the most intriguing description of a future outpouring of forgiveness in the messianic age, he was not the only biblical prophet to put forth such a hope. Both Ezekiel and Jeremiah include similar hopes in their respective books. In the following text from Ezekiel, what is especially noteworthy is that the "forgiveness" associated with the coming messiah will somehow heal the *land*, and this restoration of the land is described in Edenic language: "Thus says the Lord: *On the day that I cleanse you from all your iniquities* ... And the land that was desolate shall be tilled ... And they will say, 'This land that was desolate *has become like the Garden of Eden*'" (Ezek. 36:33–36).

Yet one more prophetic text may be mentioned, which associates the future messiah with the forgiveness of sins. In a well-recognized passage from Jeremiah the prophet writes, "This is the *covenant* which I will make with the house of Israel after those days, says the Lord: *I will put my law within them, and I will write it upon their hearts;* and I will be their God, and they shall be my people. And no longer shall each man teach his neighbor and each his brother, saying, 'Know the Lord,' for they shall all know me, from the least of them to the greatest, says the Lord; *for I will forgive their iniquity, and I will remember their sin no more*" (Jer. 31:33–34). The only comment to be added about this text from Jeremiah is his insistence that in the messianic age, the Law itself will penetrate deeper than ever before, reaching to the interiority of the believer; the Law will be "written on their hearts."

One last point needs to be made concerning this third Jewish hope, concerning this unprecedented outpouring of forgiveness of sins in the messianic age. Specifically, the point concerns the Gospels. While primary emphasis was placed upon various Old Testament texts that evoked this particular Jewish expectation, numerous texts from the Gospels (and elsewhere in the New Testament) were brought into the discussion. But just before turning to a discussion of the next Jewish expectation regarding the messiah (i.e., Hope 4), it need only be stated that there are *explicit* texts in the Gospels in which

Jesus is described as "forgiving sins." In fact, collectively, the Four Gospels are *replete* with texts that display Jesus's power to forgive sins. The following are just three examples from the Gospels:

She will bear a son, and you shall call his name Jesus, for he will save his people from their sins. (Matt. 1:22)

When Jesus saw their faith he said to the paralytic, "Take heart, my son; your sins are forgiven." (Matt. 9:2)

Therefore I tell you, "*her sins, which are many, are forgiven*, for she loved much; but he who is forgiven little, loves little." And he said to her, "Your sins are forgiven." Then those who were at table with him began to say among themselves, "Who is this, who even forgives sins?" And he said to the woman, "Your faith has saved you; go in peace." (Luke 7:47–50)

God's Messiah Will Defeat İsrael's Enemies

Jewish expectations of the coming messiah not only included a "unifying" of all of Israel, a "restoring" the Jerusalem Temple, and a special outpouring of the forgiving sins just described. The messianic age was also depicted as a time of "visitation" and future judgment. Every Israelite was admonished to repent and return to the Lord, lest he face the terrible condemnation awaiting Israel's enemies, who persecuted Israel and rejected Israel's God, as Jeremiah, Zechariah, and Isaiah make clear:

In that day, says the Lord of hosts, *I will break the yoke from off their neck, and I will burst their bonds, and strangers shall no more make servants of them.* They shall serve the Lord their God *and David their king, whom I will raise up for them.* (Jer. 30:8–9)

Then the Lord will go forth *and fight against those nations as when he fights on a day of battle.* On that day his feet shall stand on the Mount of Olives which lies before Jerusalem on the east; and the Mount of Olives shall be split in two ... *Then the Lord your God will come, and all the holy ones with him.* (Zech. 14:3–4, 14:6)

In that day the remnant of Israel and the survivors of the house of Jacob *will no more lean upon him that smote them, but will lean upon the Lord, the Holy One of Israel, in truth.* (Isa. 10:20–24)

And the Lord will smite Egypt, smiting and healing, and they will return to the Lord, and *he will heed their supplications and heal* (!) *them.* (Isa. 19:22–25)

In the New Testament, it is clear that the words and deeds of Jesus do not perfectly correspond to the messianic judgments as in the above prophetic texts. True, Jesus warns of a coming judgment,[35] that he has come to "cast fire" upon the earth,[36] and warns of the destruction of the Temple itself.[37] Yet to understand the way in which the New Testament understood Jesus fulfilling this Jewish hope requires more explanation than the previous one discussed above.

Here, there is a radical transformation in the definition of Israel's enemies from the vantage point of Jesus and his Apostles. Whereas the Old Testament prophets point in the direction of the pagan nations that often waged war against Israel, the enemy of Israel is not the other nations but *sin and death*, which create a chasm between God and Israel. In the Gospels, there are few texts that explicitly talk about Jesus vanquishing death as an enemy.[38] However, this idea is common enough in St. Paul:

For if *while we were enemies* we were reconciled to God by the death of his Son, much more, now that we are reconciled, shall we be saved by his life. (Rom. 5:10)

For he must reign until he has put all his enemies under his feet. *The last enemy to be destroyed is death*. (1 Cor. 15:25)

"O death, where is thy victory? O death, where is thy sting?" The sting of death is sin, and the power of sin is the law. But thanks be to God, *who gives us the victory* through our Lord Jesus Christ. (1 Cor. 15:55–57)

---

35. E.g., Matt. 25:41: "Then he will say to those at his left hand, 'Depart from me, you cursed, into the eternal fire prepared for the devil and his angels.'" See also Mark 13:19; Matt. 11:24; Luke 10:14; etc.

36. See Luke 12:49.

37. See Mark 13:1ff.

38. An exception is found in Matt. 16:18: "And I tell you, you are Peter, and on this rock I will build my church, and the powers of death shall not prevail against it." As far as the rarity in the Gospels, the *Catechism* underscores Jesus's victory over death, on full display in various ways in the Gospels (not least of which is his glorious Resurrection). The *Catechism* concurs that the motif is found more extensively in the letters of St. Paul: "Indeed, Jesus raises the dead, gives life to the dead, and preaches about *zoe*, eternal life. He promises the Twelve that they will rule over the twelve tribes 'in the new world.' Indeed, Jesus' death on the Cross atones for the sins 'of many,' and the Resurrection narratives can and must be understood as the Messiah's decisive victory over the grave. Yet, the more developed teaching of Jesus the Messiah's victory over sin and death are located in Paul's epistles." See *Catechism of the Catholic Church*, §438.

God's Messiah Gathers All Nations
to the One, True Living God

Finally, the last Jewish hope to be examined is that of the Messiah drawing all of the nations to Israel and specifically to the Temple in Jerusalem. Here again, there are numerous texts in the Old Testament prophets that contain such characteristics:

It shall come to pass in the latter days that *the mountain of the house of the Lord* shall be established as the highest of the mountains, and shall be raised above the hills; *and all the nations shall flow to it, and many peoples shall come, and say: "Come, let us go up to the mountain of the Lord, to the house of the God of Jacob; that he may teach us his ways and that we may walk in his paths."* For out of Zion shall go forth *the Law*, and *the word of the Lord from Jerusalem. He shall judge between the nations* ... and they shall beat their swords into plowshares, and their spears into pruning hooks; nation shall not lift up sword against nation, neither shall they learn war any more. *O house of Jacob, come, let us walk in the light of the Lord.* (Isa. 2:4)

The LORD will have compassion on Jacob and will again choose Israel, and will set them in their own land, *and aliens will join them and will cleave to the house of Jacob.* (Isa. 14:1)

In those days ten men from the nations of every tongue shall take hold of the robe of a Jew, saying, *"Let us go with you, for we have heard that God is with you."* (Zech. 8:23)

In the Four Gospels there are corresponding actions of Jesus that symbolically—but at the same time, in a very real way—inaugurate this "ingathering of the Gentiles" in his public ministry. Consider the following examples:

Now the woman was a Greek, a Syro-phoenician by birth. And she begged him to cast the demon out of her daughter. And he said to her, "Let the children first be fed, for it is not right to take the children's bread and throw it to the dogs." But she answered him, "Yes, Lord; yet even the dogs under the table eat the children's crumbs." And he said to her, *"For this saying you may go your way; the demon has left your* daughter." And she went home, and found the child lying in bed, and the demon gone. (Mark 7:26)

There came *a woman of Samaria* to draw water. Jesus said to her, "Give me a drink." For his disciples had gone away into the city to buy food. The Samaritan woman said to him, *"How is it that you, a Jew, ask a drink of me, a woman of Samaria?" For Jews have no dealings with Samaritans.* Jesus answered her, "If you knew the gift of God, and who it is that is saying to you, 'Give me a drink,' you would have asked him, and he would have given you living water." (John 4:7–11)

Now among those who went up to worship at the feast were *some Greeks*. So these came to Philip, who was from Beth-saida in Galilee, and said to him, *"Sir, we wish to see Jesus." Philip went and told Andrew; Andrew went with Philip and they told Jesus.* And Jesus answered them, "The hour has come for the Son of man to be glorified." (John 12:20–24)

And Jesus came and said to them, "All authority in heaven and on earth has been given to me. *Go therefore and make disciples of all nations,* baptizing them in the name of the Father and of the Son and of the Holy Spirit, teaching them to observe all that I have commanded you; and lo, I am with you always, to the close of the age." (Matt. 28:18–20)

Concluding Remarks

The above discussion is a fitting transition from the examination of temple theology of the Old Testament to that of the New Testament. Each of the five hopes and the textual examples related to them reflect a yearning for God to act in a decisive way. At the very roots of such yearning was the destruction of the Jerusalem Temple and the ensuing exile in Babylon. It should come as no surprise to the reader that all five of the hopes associated with the coming Messiah can be traced back, in one way or another, to the Davidic covenant and to the establishment of the House of the Lord, the Temple.

The life of Israel under the rule of the coming messiah would have meant, among other things, that with a new David on the throne, Israel would be reunited as before. Not only so, but also that the corruption of the Temple would be definitively dealt with and that in some inexplicable way, God himself would return to the Temple and cleanse it, so that all of Israel would be pure in the eyes of God. It would further mean that forgiveness of sin would be efficacious and powerful in a renewed way, *in a singularly atoning way*, that seemed hollow following the catastrophe of the exile.

Moreover, under the messiah, Israel's enemies became God's enemies, and just as in the days of Pharaoh and Egypt, God would fight on behalf of Israel (Exod. 14:14). Through his messiah, God would enact a triumphant eschatological victory over Israel's foes, and as a final and decisive victory, Israel would enjoy the Sabbath rest of God in true and lasting peace. Finally, the coming messiah would extend God's mercy far beyond Israel, so that through the messiah, the nations of the earth would come to acknowledge Israel's God *as their own*, and as such, God's divine kingship would "fill the earth."

As one steps back from these collective promises, their Edenic meaning becomes clear. Their eventual fulfillment would somehow bring about a renewal of the whole creation, with Israel in the very center of things. A sanctified Jerusalem and its restored Temple would draw all to it, and to God. A wave of holiness would radiate over the earth. The coming of God's messiah would be nothing less than a renewal of Paradise and a recapitulation of the life with which Adam had originally been gifted—in order to fill the earth with God's temple presence.

14

IN MY FATHER'S HOUSE

Temple Theology in the Four Gospels (II/V)

Did you not know that I must be in my Father's house?

Luke 2:49

The Infancy Narratives

To begin, the Infancy Narratives of Matthew and Luke are replete with temple theology. Only the most important aspects will be included here. The appearance of the Magi in Matthew 2:1–13 reflects the Evangelist's concerns to show that the Son of God is the Savior of the world.[1] The infant Jesus is the son of Adam, the New Adam, whose kingdom—unlike the first Adam—fills the earth, even as he "draws all nations to Himself."[2] St. Thomas explains, "As Augustine says, the shepherds were Israelites, the Magi were Gentiles. The former were near to Him, the latter far … Both hastened to Him together as to the cornerstone. There was also a point of contrast: for the Magi were wise and powerful; the shepherds simple and lowly. He was also made

---

1. *Catechism of the Catholic Church*, §528. "The magi's coming to Jerusalem in order to pay homage to the king of the Jews shows that they seek in Israel, in the messianic light of the star of David, the one who will be king of the nations. Their coming means that pagans can discover Jesus and worship him as Son of God and Savior of the world only by turning toward the Jews and receiving from them the messianic promise as contained in the Old Testament. The Epiphany shows that 'the full number of the nations' now takes its 'place in the family of the patriarchs,' and acquires *Israelitica dignitas* (are made 'worthy of the heritage of Israel').

In the magi, representatives of the neighboring pagan religions, the Gospel sees the first-fruits of the nations, who welcome the good news of salvation through the Incarnation."

2. John 12:32.

known to the righteous as Simeon and Anna; and to sinners ... so as to show no condition of men to be excluded from Christ's redemption."[3]

On the role of the Magi in Scripture, Pope Benedict XVI draws relevance for today: "My particular greeting goes to those who, like the Magi, have come from the East. You are the representatives of so many of our brothers and sisters who are waiting, without realizing it, for the star to rise in their skies and lead them to Christ, Light of the Nations, in whom they will find the fullest response to their hearts' deepest desires."[4]

Turning to the Gospel of Luke, it is evident that he structures the entirety of his Gospel according to the Temple. In this Gospel, one encounters Jesus by "entering in" and "exiting out" of the Jerusalem Temple. Specifically, Luke begins the narrative of his Gospel in the Temple with the vision of Zechariah,[5] and concluded his Gospel in the Temple[6] with the Twelve returning to Jerusalem after Jesus's Ascension, where they were "continually in the Temple blessing God."[7]

---

3. Thomas Aquinas, *Summa Theologica* III, q. 36, a. 3.

4. Pope Benedict XVI, *God's Revolution: World Youth Day and Other Cologne Talks* (San Francisco: Ignatius Press, 2006), 35. In an earlier work, he reflects on the coming of the Magi: "By way of summary, we can say: Old and New Testaments, Jesus and the Sacred Scripture of Israel, appear here as indivisible. The new thrust of his mission to unify Israel and the nations corresponds to the prophetic thrust of the Old Testament itself. Reconciliation in the common recognition of the kingdom of God, recognition of his will as the way, is the nucleus of Jesus' mission, in which person and message are indivisible. *This mission is efficacious already at the moment when he lies silent in the crib.*" Joseph Ratzinger, *Many Religions—One Covenant: Israel, the Church, and the World*, trans. Graham Harrison (San Francisco: Ignatius Press, 1999), 28 (emphasis added).

5. See Luke 1:1-23.

6. Joseph A. Fitzmyer, *The Gospel According to Luke I–IX: Introduction, Translation, and Notes*, vol. 28, *Anchor Yale Bible* (New Haven, CT: Yale University Press, 2008), 165. "Unlike the compositions of the other evangelists, the Lucan Gospel begins and ends in Jerusalem: after the prologue, the first scene is that of Zechariah offering incense in the Jerusalem Temple (Luke 1:9), where he learns of the birth of a son, and at the end Luke tells how the Eleven and the others returned to Jerusalem from Bethany to spend their time in the Temple (24:53). In its own way the infancy narrative strikes the chord of the journey-to-Jerusalem motif in depicting the child Jesus taken there twice by his parents (2:22, 42). The scene of the twelve-year-old Jesus sitting among the Temple teachers, who were astounded at his understanding and his answers, foreshadows in a sense not only his Temple teaching-ministry (19:47), but identifies him as one who has to be in his Father's house (2:49; cf. 19:45–46). Moreover, the angel's words to Mary reveal that the child to be born to her will sit on the throne of David and be king over the house of Jacob (1:32–33)—implying a special relationship to Jerusalem."

7. Luke 24:53.

As one reads the text of the Presentation of Jesus,[8] several facts are clear as it pertains to temple theology. First, St. Luke depicts Jesus as the faithful Israelite in the holy Temple, whose mother[9] dedicates him as the firstborn to the Lord, reminiscent of Hannah's mother Samuel. Recall the earlier discussion concerning the firstborn of Israel.[10] Ratzinger adds: "The lamb appears clearly as the ransom through which Israel is delivered from the death of the firstborn. Now this ransom serves also as a reminder. It is ultimately the firstborn itself to which God lays claim: 'Consecrate to me all the first-born; whatever is the first to open the womb among the people of Israel, both of man and of beast, is mine' (Exod. 13:2) ... This fact should help us appreciate the emphatic way in which St. Luke in his infancy narratives describes Jesus as the first-born."[11]

Second, the figures of Simeon and Anna recapitulate the faith of Israel at its best, as they expectantly await the Messiah.[12] In gazing at the newborn Savior, Simeon, who awaited the "consolation of Israel," bursts into joyful and prophetic song.[13] For her part, Anna, a prophetess of the northern tribe of Asher—represents the lost tribes of Israel, whom the Messiah will deliver out of their long spiritual exile. This consecrated virgin and widow did not depart from the Temple, worshiping with fasting and prayer night and day.[14]

As with the scene of the Presentation, the Finding in the Temple[15] is a

---

8. Luke 2:22–40; *Catechism of the Catholic Church*, §527: "Jesus' *circumcision*, on the eighth day after his birth, is the sign of his incorporation into Abraham's descendants, *into the people of the covenant*. It is the sign of his submission to the Law and his deputation to Israel's worship, in which he will participate throughout his life. This sign *prefigures that 'circumcision of Christ' which is Baptism*."

9. St. Jerome: "All heretics have gone astray by not understanding the mystery of his nativity. The statement 'he who opens the womb shall be called holy to the Lord' is more applicable to the special nativity of the Savior than to that of all men, for Christ alone opened the closed doors of the womb of virginity, which nevertheless remained permanently closed. This is the closed east door, through which only the high priest enters and leaves, and nevertheless it is always closed." *Against the Pelagians* 2.4. St. Jerome writes of the mystery of Christ as the first—and only—born of Mary, ever Virgin.

10. As discussed in chapter 5; see Exod. 13:2, 13:12–13.

11. Joseph Ratzinger, *The Spirit of the Liturgy*, trans. John Saward (San Francisco: Ignatius Press, 2000), 38.

12. "With Simeon and Anna, all Israel awaits its *encounter* with the Savior—the name given to this event in the Byzantine tradition." *Catechism of the Catholic Church*, §529.

13. See Luke 2:25–32.

14. Luke 2:37.

15. Luke 2:41–52.

mystery of Christ's life recorded only in Luke. With respect to temple theology, three points need to be made.

First, in this brief scene, Luke once again depicts the Holy Family as in the Temple, having gone up *kat etos* ("every year") at the feast of Passover (Luke 2:41). Luke does not specify whether the Holy Family would have traveled to Jerusalem for the other two great feasts (i.e., Tabernacles, Pentecost).[16] Regardless, this Lucan detail is reminiscent of the family of the prophet Samuel, going to the Temple faithfully each year for the great Temple feasts.[17] Importantly, this fact underscores the faithfulness of the Holy Family to the Temple; that is, these Galilean residents are loyal Judeans, true to David and David's God.

Second, at the heart of the text's meaning, the climax of the passage occurs in the Temple. After diligently searching for their missing son for three days,[18] he is not merely discovered safe and sound, but in a striking reversal and display of divine lucidity, he is found among *ton didascalon* ("teachers, doctors"), conversing with them and asking them questions. Here, it is he who ultimately questions them:

After three days they found him in the Temple, sitting among the teachers, listening to them and asking them questions; and all who heard him were amazed at his understanding and his answers. And when they saw him they were astonished; and his mother said to him, "Son, why have you treated us so? Behold, your father and I have been looking for you anxiously." And he said to them, *"How is it that you sought me? Did you not know that I must be in my Father's house?"* (Luke 2:46–49)

---

16. "It is difficult to know how widely the law of the three feasts was observed in Jesus' time: many Jews living outside Palestine may have made the pilgrimage only once in a lifetime, and many Palestinian Jews may have come only once a year." Raymond E. Brown, *The Birth of the Messiah: A Commentary on the Infancy Narratives in the Gospels of Matthew and Luke*, New updated ed. (New York: Yale University Press, 1993), 472.

17. See 1 Sam 1:3, 1:7, 1:21, 2:19. John Nolland, *Luke 1:1–9:20*, vol. 35A, *Word Biblical Commentary* (Dallas: Word Books, 1998), 129.

18. This detail of "three" days is disputed among scholars. While some see a symbolic prefigurement of Jesus's Resurrection, others suggest that the phrase is only meant to heighten the tension as to the whereabouts of the child Jesus: "The three days of anxiety prepare for the intensity behind Mary's rebuke in v 48." Nolland, *Luke 1:1–9:20*, 35A:130. In favor of Resurrection symbolism, see R. René Laurentin, *Jésus au temple: Mystère de PaÆques et foi de Marie en Luc 2,48–50*, *Etudes bibliques* (Paris: Gabalda, 1966), 95–109; Cornelius à Lapide, *The Great Commentary of Cornelius À Lapide: S. Luke's Gospel*, vol. 4, 4th ed., trans. Thomas W. Mossman (Edinburgh: John Grant, 1908), 131; *Saint Luke's Gospel, The Navarre Bible* (Dublin: Scepter, 2005), 51.

What preoccupied the twelve-year-old Jesus is not told and has been explored among theologians over the centuries. On a spiritual level, Lapide provided a rich possibility: "The whole of these three days, then, Jesus spent in praying ... His food He received from the doctors, who, being present, and admiring His wisdom, invited Him."[19]

Third and finally, paradoxically, Luke Timothy Johnson points out both the comprehensibility and incomprehensibility of this Temple scene: "Why should this cause incomprehension? His parents had been told that he would be Lord and Messiah and Savior and *assume the throne of his father David* ... No matter how much they had been told of the child's special character, having [the young Jesus refer to] *God as his Father* would come as a shock. But the incomprehension of the parents also serves a broader literary function ... Luke shows the reader how *even the most faithful of the people 'did not understand' in the time of the prophet's first visitation* ... so must those who follow his story ... like Mary, '*keep these words in their heart.*'"[20]

The Virgin Mary and the Temple

The mystery of Christ is inexplicable apart from the Virgin who bore him in her womb. Like her Son, the mystery of Mary's life is unveiled in the shadow of the Temple. In the above Presentation scene, Simeon tells Mary in the Temple Courts that "a sword will pierce her heart."[21]

Commenting on this mystery, Ratzinger writes, "The sword shall pierce her heart—this statement foreshadows the Son's Passion, which will become her own passion. This passion already begins with her next visit to the Temple: she must accept the precedence of Jesus' true Father and of his house, the Temple; she must learn to release the Son she has borne. She must complete the Yes to God's will that made her a mother by withdrawing into the background and letting Jesus enter upon his mission. Jesus' rebuffs during his public life and her withdrawal are an important step that will reach its goal on the Cross with the words 'behold, your son.'"[22]

---

19. Lapide, *Great Commentary*, 131.

20. Luke Timothy Johnson, *The Gospel of Luke*, vol. 3, *Sacra Pagina Series*, ed. Daniel J. Harrington (Collegeville, MN: Liturgical Press, 1991), 61 (emphasis added). Johnson observes that this expression "is the first note in the theme of 'ignorance' that plays such an important role in *Luke-Acts*."

21. Luke 2:35.

22. Joseph Ratzinger, *Mary: Church at the Source* (San Francisco: Ignatius Press, 2011), 76. He

The Annunciation[23] is replete with temple theology, but it requires careful attention to see it more fully. In the Annunciation, the Angel Gabriel declares to Mary, "*Hail, full of grace.*" "Hail" is from the Greek *chaïré* and is not merely a simple salutation (i.e., "hello") but "an invitation to joy."[24] As such, Gabriel's greeting represents an invitation to messianic joy. The age of the New Temple has arrived at last. There are only four occurrences of *chaïré* in the Greek Old Testament (LXX), specifically in Zechariah 9:9[25] as well as in Joel 2:21,[26] Zephaniah 3:14,[27] and Lamentations 4:21.[28] In each context, *chaïré* is associated with messianic joy.

Here is a clear prophecy about the coming Messiah—a clear fulfillment of the prophecy as to the coming of the anointed Davidic Messiah in Zechariah 9.[29] Mary is the faithful Israelite, the Daughter of Zion, whose yes to God is the reversal of Eve's refusal to align her will to God's will. Justin Martyr explains this typological mystery: "[Jesus] became man by the Virgin so that the course which was taken by disobedience in the beginning through the agency of the serpent might be also the very course by which it would be put down. Eve, a virgin and undefiled, conceived the word of the serpent and bore disobedience and death. But the Virgin Mary received faith and joy when the angel Gabriel announced to her the glad tidings that the Spirit

---

adds, "It is no longer Jesus but the disciple who is her son. To accept and to be available is the first step required of her; to let go and to release is the second. Only in this way does her motherhood become complete: the 'blessed is the womb that bore you' comes true only when it enters into the other beatitude: 'Blessed rather are those who hear the word of God and keep it' (Luke 11:27–28). But this means Mary is prepared for the mystery of the Cross, which does not simply end on Golgotha. Her Son remains a sign of contradiction, and she is thus kept to the very end in the pain of this contradiction, in the pain of her messianic motherhood."

23. See Luke 1:46–55.

24. Ignace De La Potterie, *Mary in the Mystery of the Covenant*, trans. Bertrand Buby (Staten Island, NY: Alba House, 1992), 55. The form of the term is *chaïré* is imperative, and stronger than the "present active" form. As such, it implores action; a simple greeting is not tenable.

25. Zech. 9:9: "Rejoice greatly (*chaïré*), O daughter of Zion! Shout aloud, O daughter of Jerusalem! Lo, your king comes to you; triumphant and victorious is he, humble and riding on an ass, on a colt the foal of an ass."

26. Joel 2:21: "Fear not, O land; be glad and rejoice (*chaïré*), for the Lord has done great things!"

27. Zeph. 3:14: "Sing aloud, O daughter of Zion; shout, O Israel! Rejoice (*chaïré*) and exult with all your heart, O daughter of Jerusalem!"

28. Lam. 4:21: "Rejoice (*chaïré*) and be glad, O daughter of Edom, dweller in the land of Uz."

29. A further Davidic connection is evident: Solomon, the *son of David*, when he is anointed as king, rides on a donkey of his father David (see 1 Ki. 1:38–40).

Hannah's Hymn (1 Sam 2:2-10)	Mary's Magnificat (Luke 1:46-55)
"*MY HEART EXULTS IN THE LORD*; my strength is *EXALTED IN LORD*, my mouth derides my enemies because I rejoice in thy salvation." (2:1a)	"*MY SOUL MAGNIFIES THE LORD*, and my spirit *REJOICES IN GOD MY SAVIOR*, for he has regarded the low estate of his handmaiden." (1:46-48)
"There is no one *HOLY LIKE THE LORD.*" (2:2a)	"*HOLY IS HIS NAME.*" (1:49b)
"Talk no more so very *PROUDLY* . . . for the Lord is a God of knowledge and by him *ACTIONS ARE WEIGHED.*" (2:3)	"He had showed strength in his arm. He has *SCATTERED THE PROUD* in the imagination of their hearts." (1:52)
"The *BOWS OF THE MIGHTY ARE BROKEN*, but the *FEEBLE GIRD ON STRENGTH.*" (2:4)	"He has *PUT DOWN THE MIGHTY FROM THEIR THRONES*, and *EXALTED THOSE OF LOW DEGREE.*" (1:52)
"Those who were full have hired themselves out for bread, but *THOSE WHO WERE HUNGRY HAVE CEASED TO HUNGER.*" (2:5a)	"He has *FILLED THE HUNGRY WITH* good things." (1:53a)
"He will *GUARD THE FEET OF HIS FAITHFUL ONES.*" (2:9)	"And *HIS MERCY IS ON THOSE WHO FEAR HIM* from generation to generation" (1:50)

of the Lord would come upon her and the power of the Most High would overshadow her, for which reason the Holy One being born of her is the Son of God. And she replied 'Be it done unto me according to your word' [Luke 1:38]."[30] Additionally, Mary's Magnificat contains a number of literary and theological parallels with the "Song of Hannah" in 1 Samuel 2 (see figure 4). At Shiloh, Hannah, the barren yet faithful Israelite, vows to dedicate her "firstborn" to the Lord.[31] Her son Samuel becomes the holy prophet, priest, and judge who "anoints" (Greek: *christos*) Saul, Israel's first king, and later David himself. Thus Mary and Hannah share a number of fascinating Davidic and Messianic connections.

"The power of the Most High will *overshadow* you" (Luke 1:35). This expression of Gabriel to Mary likewise reverberates with temple theology, par-

---

30. St. Justin Martyr, *Dialogue with Trypho the Jew*, 100.

31. See 1 Sam. 1:11: "And she vowed a vow and said, 'O Lord of hosts, if thou wilt indeed look on the affliction of thy maidservant, and remember me, and not forget thy maidservant, but wilt give to thy maidservant a son, *then I will give him to the Lord all the days of his life*, and no razor shall touch his head.'"

ticularly the term "overshadow." St. Luke intends an allusion to the *shekinah* (i.e., glory cloud), the abode that overshadowed the Ark of the Covenant at the end of Exodus: "And Moses was not able to enter the tent of meeting, because the [glory] cloud abode [Greek: *epeskiasen*] upon it, and the glory of the Lord filled the Tabernacle" (Exod. 40:35). The Greek verb *episkiazo* ("to dwell, abide, overshadow") occurs just twice in Luke: the first occurrence is in 1:35, at the Annunciation scene, in which the Holy Spirit overshadows Mary—a clear allusion to the Tabernacle of Exodus. Interestingly, the second occurrence of the *epeskiazo* occurs in the Transfiguration scene, where a cloud "overshadows" Peter, James, and John—another clear reference to the Tabernacle of Exodus.

St. Luke's point in the present instance[32] registers loud and clear: Mary is the new Tabernacle, the new Ark of the New Covenant, as patristic, medieval, and modern theologians all describe. St. Athanasius writes, "O noble Virgin, truly you are greater than any other greatness. For who is your equal in greatness, O dwelling place of God the Word? To whom among all creatures shall I compare you, O Virgin? *You are greater than them all O Covenant, clothed with purity instead of gold! You are the Ark in which is found the golden vessel containing the true manna, that is, the flesh in which divinity resides.*"[33] For his part, St. Thomas explained in the *Summa* that God "prepares and endows" those that he chooses for special purposes, so that they are equipped to accomplish his will. Accordingly, he states, "The Blessed Virgin was chosen by God to be His Mother. Therefore, there can be no doubt that God, by His grace, made her worthy of that office."[34]

Even contemporary Catholic theologians, while they might give different expression to such discussions, will describe Mary in a comparative way with respect to the Tabernacle. Gary Anderson is a good example of this: "Mary does not become God, of course, but she does 'house' God in the most intimate way imaginable. The extrinsic manner of relating God to temple is put to good use: Mary both receives the divine Son and gives birth to him. But in the logic of the Incarnation this moment transforms her forever. Her

---

32. Similarly, in the Transfiguration scene, *episkiazo* recalls the glory cloud of Yahweh in the wilderness; now, on the mountain, it prepares the disciples for *the revelation of the Son's own glory*, which he shares with the Father.

33. St. Athanasius, *Homily of the Papyrus of Turin*, 71:216.

34. Thomas Aquinas, *Summa Theologica* III, q. 27, a. 4.

body remains holy forever thereafter as a result of housing the Holy One of Israel. *And as the Temple could be revered and praised on its own terms without any worry of committing some form of idolatrous apostasy, so Mary could be revered and adored.* Not as a goddess, *but as the one who housed God.* If one could turn to the Temple and say, 'how lovely is thy dwelling place,' and attend to its every architectural detail, *why would one not do the same with the Theotokos?*"[35]

"All generations will call me blessed" (Luke 1:48). As Ratzinger explains, this saying of Mary is no invention by the first Christians: "This phrase from the *Magnificat*, the spirit-filled prayer of praise that Mary addresses to the living God, is thus one of the principal foundations of Christian devotion to her. *The Church invented nothing new of her own when she began to extol Mary*; she did not plummet from the worship of the one God to the praise of man. The Church does what she must; she carries out the task assigned her from the beginning. At the time that St. Luke was writing this text, the second generation of Christianity had already arrived, and the '*family*' of the Jews had been joined by that of the Gentiles, who had been incorporated into the Church of Jesus Christ. The expression '*all generations, all families*' was beginning to be filled with historical reality.

The Evangelist would certainly not have transmitted Mary's prophecy if it had seemed to him an indifferent or obsolete item. He wished in his Gospel to record 'with care' what '*the eyewitnesses and ministers of the word*'[36] had *handed on from the beginning*, in order to give the faith of Christianity, which was then striding onto the stage of world history, a reliable guide for its future course."[37]

The discussion now turns from the Virgin Mary to another key figure in the Gospels and one closely related to the Temple: John the Baptist.

John the Baptist: The Beginnings of a Counter-Temple Movement

The life and ministry of John the Baptist may be viewed as a counter-temple movement. As the forerunner of Jesus, he prepares Israel for the com-

---

35. Gary Anderson, "Mary in the Old Testament," in *Pro Ecclesia*, vol. XVI, no. 1 (Lanham, MD: Rowan & Littlefield, 2007), 33–55; here 50 (emphases added).

36. Luke 1:2–3.

37. Ratzinger, *Mary*, 61–62 (emphases added).

ing of the New Temple in Jesus. If John represents its beginnings, Jesus's life and ministry are the completion of the counter-temple movement, as he fulfills and transfigures Israel's Temple in himself. The following evidence reflects this counter-temple motif in the Synoptic Gospels.[38] Nicholas Perrin lists seven indisputable features of the ministry of John the Baptist,[39] among them that he "lived an ascetical lifestyle which took him to the desert."[40] This

38. The phrase "counter-temple movement" must be clearly distinguished from "anti-temple movement"—the two are not at all the same. To say that John (and Jesus) implemented a counter-temple movement is uncontroversial, given the preponderance of evidence in the Four Gospels. However, it would be incorrect and unhelpful to suggest that John (and/or Jesus) was implementing an anti-temple movement in Israel. This is *not* the case. John and Jesus envisioned a restoration and renewal of the Temple, beginning with John's ministry and culminating in the coming of the Messiah. Jesus did prophesy of the Temple's destruction, yet he never said "*I* will destroy this temple" (John 2:19); his opponents bring forth a false charge (see Matt. 26:61; Mark 14:58). Jesus was a faithful Jew who loved the Temple and longed for its full restoration—and understood that his mission from the Father would inaugurate a new age of the Temple, culminating in his death and Resurrection.

"Like the prophets before him *Jesus expressed the deepest respect for the Temple in Jerusalem.* It was in the Temple that Joseph and Mary presented him forty days after his birth. At the age of twelve he decided to remain in the Temple to remind his parents that he must be about his Father's business. He went there each year during his hidden life at least for Passover. His public ministry itself was patterned by his pilgrimages to Jerusalem for the great Jewish feasts." *Catechism of the Catholic Church*, §83.

39. Nicholas Perrin, *Jesus the Temple* (Grand Rapids, MI: Baker Academic, 2010), 38. On disputes about the historical ministry of John the Baptist, see pp. 37–38. See also Jean Daniélou, *Jean-Baptiste. Témoin de l'agneau* (Paris: Seuil, 1964); J. A. T. Robinson, "The Baptism of John and the Qumran Community," and "Elijah, John, and Jesus," in *Twelve New Testament Studies* (London: SCM, 1962), 11–27 and 28–52; Raymond E. Brown, "John the Baptist in the Gospel of John," in *New Testament Studies* (Garden City, NY: Image, Doubleday, 1968 [1965]), 174–84; John P. Meier, "John the Baptist in Matthew's Gospel," *Journal of Biblical Literature* 99 (1980): 383–405; idem, *A Marginal Jew, Rethinking the Historical Jesus: Volume Two, Mentor, Message, and Miracles* (New Haven, CT: Yale University Press, 1994), 19–62. Meier writes, "Our study of the chronology of Jesus' life at the end of Volume One had a somber result. It placed two historical figures, both connected with two striking symbols of judgment and death, at two dates that bracket the ministry of Jesus: John the Baptist with his baptism at the beginning of a.d. 28 and Pontius Pilate with the cross on April 7, a.d. 30" (2:19).

40. Nicholas Perrin, *Jesus the Temple* (Grand Rapids, MI: Baker Academic, 2010), 38. The remaining six features are: (2) he preached the necessity of a baptism of repentance in light of Israel's sin; (3) he expected the near-arrival of "eschatological judgment"; (4) he attracted large crowds; (5) he included Jesus among his adherents through baptism—until Jesus broke off to start a new movement; (6) he was not embraced by the ruling temple authorities of his day; and (7) he died at the hands of Herod Antipas.

particular feature alone suggests a challenge on the part of John to the political powers in Jerusalem: "But going into the desert and starting a movement is to do anything but hide or retreat, especially in first-century Israel ... in effect he was saying, 'Yahweh is beginning again with a new Exodus and starting a new nation. It is starting under my auspices—here and now' ... John knew that his activities could only be interpreted as being politically charged."[41]

At the very beginning of the Gospel of Mark, one encounters John the Baptist in the wilderness. What is he doing? Preaching—but what? "A baptism of repentance for the forgiveness of sins."[42] Perrin explains the significance of this as it pertains to the Temple, and the insight is important: "Since in the normal course of things, the Temple was the place where one confessed one's sins and offered the prescribed sacrifice, *John's invitation to receive forgiveness outside of the temple apparatus essentially rendered the Jerusalem institution redundant.* Apparently, like his religious competitors down the road at Qumran, John had come to believe that *a new Temple was already taking shape* ... Under the Baptizer, Israel is starting afresh, and with this new start comes, as a matter of course, a new Temple."[43]

In *The Bible and the Liturgy*, Daniélou explains the typological significance of Christian Baptism in numerous ways, moving beyond the data of the New Testament and into the sacramental reality of the early Church. He writes: "The baptismal rites constitute a drama, in which the candidate, who up to this time has belonged to the demon, strives to escape his power."[44] Engaging patristic thinkers as diverse as St. Cyril of Jerusalem, St. Augustine, and Theodore of Mopsuestia, Daniélou explains how the early Church drew upon typology to *catechize* to reveal how the candidate was indeed part of

41. Ibid., 38. Perrin includes numerous citations from Josephus of first-century "desert-based insurgency movements" by way of example. Incidentally, Perrin is *not* painting John's ministry as an insurgency as such. Nor does Perrin presume that John's break with Jerusalem and the Temple were "absolute." He agrees with Meier that "all claims to salvation on the basis of racial solidarity with Abraham were unavailing." Ibid., 40n86.

42. Mark 1:4. See also Matt. 3:1–3: "In those days came John the Baptist, preaching in the wilderness of Judea, '*Repent, for the kingdom of heaven is at hand.*' For this is he who was spoken of by the prophet Isaiah when he said, 'The voice of one crying in the wilderness: Prepare the way of the Lord, make his paths straight.'"

43. Perrin, *Jesus the Temple*, 41.

44. Jean Daniélou, *The Bible and the Liturgy* (Notre Dame, IN: University of Notre Dame Press, 1956), 21.

the larger biblical drama: "This drama begins with the enrollment and is not concluded ... until the actual Baptism ... The trial that the candidate undergoes [relates] on the one hand to the *temptation of Adam*, on the other hand to that of Christ."[45] As Daniélou stresses, "We are now in the center of biblical typology."[46]

The discussion now turns from John the Baptist to Jesus himself and various motifs within the Gospels pertinent to temple theology.

Jesus, the New Adam

A number of strands of evidence in the Gospels[47] indicate that the Evangelists present Jesus as the New Adam, ruling over a new Creation,[48] as in Luke's genealogy, which concludes: "The son of Enos, the son of Seth, *the son of Adam, the son of God*" (Luke 3:38). Commenting on the latter, Beale writes: "The reason ... that Luke's genealogy ends with 'Adam, the son of God' is to identify Jesus as an end-time Adam, the true Son of God, resisting the temptations to which Adam and Eve succumbed."[49]

The Temptation of Jesus

Jesus's forty days in the wilderness recapitulates Adam's temptations and Israel's forty years in the wilderness.[50] Along with St. Prudentius, the Catechism correctly reads the Temptation narrative as a "new Eden," in which the victory by the New Adam reverses the defeat of the first Adam. Here, St. Prudentius writes, "Still the pinnacle stands, outlasting the Temple's destruction. For the corner raised up from that stone which the builders rejected will remain throughout all ages forever and ever. *Now it is head of the Temple*

---

45. Ibid.

46. Ibid.

47. The letters of St. Paul—and the Book of Revelation—must be added to this "New Adam/New Creation" topic but will be discussed separately in chapters 18 and 19.

48. See G. K. Beale, *The Temple and the Church's Mission: A Biblical Theology of the Dwelling Place of God* (Downers Grove, IL: InterVarsity Press, 2004), 171.

49. Ibid., 172. See subsequent discussion for more examples.

50. "Jesus succeeds in facing the same temptations to which Israel succumbed." Ibid. Cf. Deut. 8:3 and Matt. 4:4; Deut. 6:16 and Matt. 4:7; Deut. 6:13 and Matt. 4:10.

and holds the new stones together."[51] That "the angels ministered to him"[52] is likely a comment by the Evangelists to underscore Satan's (Lucifer's) disobedience in contrast to the holy angels.[53] As the Catechism states, "Christ is the center of the angelic world. They are his angels.[54]

The Coming of the Kingdom: The World beyond the Garden

Adam's vocation was to be God's temple builder, extending the temple of Creation out to the whole world—the world beyond the Garden. As Adam (and Eve) fulfilled his mission to "be fruitful and multiply," and to "fill the whole earth and subdue it,"[55] the glory of God's presence would be extended over the face of the earth. Adam's disobedience disrupted this pattern, as he and Eve were expelled from Eden. They and their offspring indeed began to "fill the earth." But not always in ways that brought God's temple presence to the world, or the world to God's temple presence.

Later, Abraham, Moses, and eventually David were each in their respective eras in salvation history called to recapitulate Adam's temple-building mission. In various ways, this mission was fulfilled in half measures, over and

---

51. St. Prudentius (348–410 AD), *Scenes from Sacred History*, 31. The *Catechism of the Catholic Church* adds: "Driven by the Spirit into the desert, Jesus remains there for forty days without eating; he lives among wild beasts, and angels minister to him. At the end of this time *Satan tempts him three times, seeking to compromise his filial attitude toward God.* Jesus rebuffs these attacks, *which recapitulate the temptations of Adam in Paradise* and of *Israel in the desert,* and the devil leaves him 'until an opportune time'" (§538). See also §539: "*Jesus is the new Adam who remained faithful just where the first Adam had given in to temptation. Jesus fulfills Israel's vocation perfectly:* in contrast to those who had once provoked God during forty years in the desert, Christ reveals himself as God's Servant, totally obedient to the divine will. In this, *Jesus is the devil's conqueror:* he 'binds the strong man' to take back his plunder. *Jesus' victory over the tempter in the desert anticipates victory at the Passion, the supreme act of obedience of his filial love for the Father.*"

52. Cf. Matt. 4:11 and Mark 1:13.

53. "The angels were always on earth to minister to him … At the Lord's behest they withdrew from him so that the devil might have room to work against Christ. If the devil were to see angels around him, he might not approach him. In this same way the devil comes invisibly to tempt the faithful." Anonymous (fifth century AD), *Opus Imperfectum* [*Incomplete Commentary on Matthew*], Homily 5.

54. *Catechism of the Catholic Church*, §331. See also §414: "Satan or the devil and the other demons are fallen angels who have freely refused to serve God and his plan. Their choice against God is definitive. They try to associate man in their revolt against God."

55. Gen. 1:28.

over again. With this temple-building motif in mind, the discussion returns to an idea raised in chapter 13, closely connected to temple theology, specifically the Messiah and the coming Kingdom of God.

Now the study can add this: whereas Adam ultimately failed in his temple-building vocation, Jesus, the New Adam, recapitulates Adam's mission and brings it to humanity as a divine and growing reality for all people, at all times, in all places. Jesus announces the Kingdom of God, and in countless words and deeds reveals that with his Incarnation the kingdom is now here. Jesus is God's divine temple builder, and through his Cross and Resurrection, it has reached the furthest ends of the earth.

Moreover, through the power of the Holy Spirit, the Church, built on the Apostles appointed by Jesus himself, continues his temple-building mission, proclaiming that the Kingdom of God is indeed at hand.

"Not Made with Human Hands": Daniel's Heavenly Temple Image

Beneath the Kingdom of God/temple-building paradigm of the Gospels are several texts in the prophet Daniel specifically: Daniel 2:31–45 and 7:13–14. In Daniel 2:31–45, the prophet correctly interprets Nebuchadnezzar's dream. In fact, Daniel explains that it is not the prophet himself, but that "there is a God in heaven who reveals mysteries, and he has made known to King Nebuchadnezzar what will be in the latter days."[56]

Daniel's vision of the statue, made of gold, silver, bronze, and iron (mixed with clay), represent "the kingdoms of this world."[57] The vision culminates with the mysterious stone that fills the whole earth: "But the stone that struck the image became a great mountain and filled the whole earth" (Dan. 2:33). Here is a vivid image and prefiguration of the Kingdom of God.

---

56. Dan. 2:28.

57. While there is healthy debate among scholars, the kingdoms depicted *appear* to be Babylonian, Persian, Hellenistic, and Roman empires, respectively, though there is some debate: "The periodization of history into a sequence of empires reflects the shaping of the political history of the ancient Near East by a succession of empires, *Assyria, Media/Babylon* (respectively to the north/east and to the south/west of the old Assyrian empire), *Persia, Greece, and Rome* ... By c. 300 [BC], this historical outline has become a formal scheme of four empires, *Assyria, Media or Babylon, Persia,* and *Greece,* to which *Rome* is later added." John E. Goldingay, *Daniel,* vol. 30, *Word Biblical Commentary* (Dallas: Word Books, 1998), 40–41.

The prophet goes on how explain that this heavenly kingdom, despite its small stature at the outset, will nevertheless shatter the mighty man-made kingdoms, as it "fills the earth" with its holy presence. Recall from an earlier discussion in the book that in the ancient world, the phrase "not made with human hands" was prominent in the depiction of "cosmic temples." Here, in Daniel is an example of this sort:

And in the days of those kings (*malkayya*), the God of heaven will set up a kingdom (*malkú*) which shall never be destroyed, nor shall its sovereignty be left to another people. It shall break in pieces all these kingdoms and bring them to an end, and it shall stand forever; just as you saw that a stone was cut from a mountain by no human hand (*di la bi-yadin*) and that it broke in pieces the iron, the bronze, the clay, the silver, and the gold. A great God has made known to the king what shall be hereafter. The dream is certain, and its interpretation sure. (Dan. 2:44–45)

In the above text it is striking that *malkayya* ("those kings") is juxtaposed with *elah shamayya* ("the God of heaven"). Here, the divine King of heaven above triumphs over the mortal kings of earth. In other words, in Daniel 2, a connection is established between kingship and kingdom; the two go hand in hand. Later, in chapter 7 of the book, the prophet envisions "one like a Son of Man" coming on the "clouds of heaven." Here, the earlier kingdom imagery is recalled, now with the royal Son of Man in the midst of it, as its unending king: "And to him was given *dominion and glory and kingdom*, that all peoples, nations, and languages should serve him; his dominion is *an everlasting dominion,* which shall not pass away, and *his kingdom one that shall not be destroyed*" (Dan. 7:14).

Together, these texts indicate a deep connection between the vision of Daniel and the many references to the Kingdom of God in the Gospels. To this something else can be added: when the Gospels are examined in light of temple-building insights discussed earlier, it becomes clear that in Jesus's proclamation the Kingdom of God is "at hand," that Adam's and Israel's temple-building vocation is finally being realized, recapitulated in Jesus, the New Adam, and true Israelite.

Kingdom/Temple Building in the Gospels

There are many numerous kingdom passages in the Gospels that, in one way or another, portray Jesus as God's divine temple builder. Space does not permit any sort of exhaustive study. Still, the following examples demonstrate the diversity of literary forms of Kingdom of God passages[58] (sayings, parables, etc.) that contain temple-building motifs. With each example, a few brief remarks will be made.

"Now after John was arrested, Jesus came into Galilee, preaching the Gospel of God, and saying, 'The time is fulfilled, and the kingdom of God is at hand; repent, and believe in the Gospel'" (Mark 1:14–15).

Here, immediately after his Temptation in the wilderness (recalling Israel's wilderness experience), St. Mark presents Jesus's inaugural message: "the Kingdom of God is at hand." Jesus's disciples are given the opportunity—and power to do so in his name—to do what Adam and later Israel had failed to do, namely, to repent and believe: "And he said, '*With what can we compare the Kingdom of God*, or what parable shall we use for it? It is like a grain of mustard seed, which, when sown upon the ground, *is the smallest of all the seeds on earth*; yet when it is sown it grows up and becomes the greatest of all shrubs, and puts forth large branches, so that the birds of the air can make nests in its shade'" (Mark 4:30–32).

The Parable of the Mustard Seed is an excellent example in parabolic form, of the motif of "filling of the earth" with God's temple presence—in and through the Kingdom of God. Like Daniel's small stone, the mustard seed begins in a miniscule way, yet becomes the greatest of shrubs. "Truly, I say to you, not even in Israel have I found such faith. I tell you, many will come from east and west and sit at table with Abraham, Isaac, and Jacob in the kingdom of heaven, while the sons of the kingdom will be thrown into the outer darkness; there men will weep and gnash their teeth.' And to the centurion Jesus said, 'Go; be it done for you as you have believed.' And the servant was healed at that very moment" (Matt. 8:10–13).

The Healing of the Centurion's Servant confirms that the "filling of the earth with God's temple-presence" knows no barriers—his faith is rewarded, while the faithless in Israel are warned of God's judgment. Note that the context is in the form of a miracle story, and that "healing" is primarily associated with the Temple: "And Jesus came and said to them, 'All authority in heaven and on earth has been given to me. *Go therefore and make disciples of all nations*, baptizing them in the name of the Father and of the Son and of the Holy Spirit, teaching them to observe all that I have commanded you; and lo, I am with you always, to the close of the age'" (Matt. 28:18–20).

---

58. Or "Kingdom of Heaven," as in Matt. 3:2, 4:17, 5:3, 5:10, 5:19, 5:20, 7:21, etc.

In many ways, the Great Commission is a classic temple-building motif in a proto-Trinitarian formula: the Apostles are called to continue the "fill the earth" with the Father's presence in them—by the authority of the Son—as they baptize and teach through the power of the Holy Spirit.[59]

"Thy kingdom come. Thy will be done, On earth as it is in heaven. Give us this day our daily bread; And forgive us our debts, As we also have forgiven our debtors" (Matt. 6:10–11). In the context of the Sermon on the Mount, these petitions from the Lord's Prayer reflect the necessity of forgiveness, in order for God's temple presence to grow. Jesus teaches his disciples to pray "Our Father" and to ask for his forgiveness, to the extent that they forgive others.[60]

As they were going along the road, a man said to him, "I will follow you wherever you go." And Jesus said to him, "Foxes have holes, and birds of the air have nests; but *the Son of Man* has nowhere to lay his head." To another he said, "Follow me." But he said, "Lord, let me first go and bury my father." But he said to him, "Leave the dead to bury their own dead; *but as for you, go and proclaim the kingdom of God.*" Another said, "I will follow you, Lord; but let me first say farewell to those at my home." Jesus said to him, "No one who puts his hand to the plow *and looks back is fit for the kingdom of God.*" (Luke 9:57–62)

59. Beyond this, Beale amply shows that the Great Commission is a recapitulation of 2 Chron. 36:23: "Thus says Cyrus king of Persia, 'The Lord, the God of heaven, has given me all the kingdoms of the earth, and he has charged me to build him a house at Jerusalem, which is in Judah. Whoever is among you of all his people, may the Lord his God be with him. Let him go up.'" His reasons are as follows: (1) in the Hebrew Bible, 2 Chron. was the last book in the (developing) canon, and so 36:23 becomes the last verse of the Scripture, just as the Great Commission concludes Matthew's Gospel; (2) Matthew's genealogy is based, in part, on the genealogy in 1 Chron. 1–3; and (3) elsewhere, Scripture refers to Cyrus as a "Messiah" (Isa. 44:28–45:1). As Beale summarizes, "Thus, the concluding [Great Commission] is not spoken by a *pagan king to theocratic Israel but spoken by the true, divine king to the beginning remnant of true Israel, 'the Twelve.'*" *The Temple and the Church's Mission*, 177.

60. Perrin suggests that the Jewish theology of "The Jubilee Year" stands behind this saying (see Lev. 25; Deut. 15:1–11). A root cause of the exile was "economic injustice." He writes: "This falls in line with the burden of the prophetic witness which closely links *exile* with *Israel's failure* to observe the 'seventh seven', that is, the radical program of debt remission laid out in the jubilee requirements." *Jesus the Temple*, 135. He adds: "The dramatic announcement of return from exile and restitution through a much-delayed release was no pie-in-the-sky matter, for in receiving alms and re-dispensing them to the poor, Jesus was *doing* jubilee … Jubilee was not an end in itself … The main point of land distribution and debt forgiveness was that *God's temple might soon pick up where it left off.* The time, however … *Israel would find that their temple had a whole new look. Through Messiah, Israel's God was building a temple whose treasure would neither decay or go missing.* The breathtaking news for Jesus' peers lay in His claim that *temple-building was going on in the present*" (emphases added). See also Gary Anderson, *Sin: A History* (New Haven, CT: Yale University Press, 2010).

Here, recall Adam's and Israel's reluctance to be God's temple builder, placing his own fleshly concerns over the expansion of the God's temple of Creation. Spiritually, "looking back" is like Israel's desire to return to Egypt or Lot's wife to Sodom. Such double-mindedness leads to death, not life. In order for God's temple presence to radiate through the earth, it must possess the believer in full measure: "And he called the twelve together and gave them power and authority over all demons and to cure diseases, and he sent them out to preach the kingdom of God and to heal" (Luke 9:1–2).

Finally, Jesus's proclamation of the kingdom does not end with the Twelve—it is only the beginning. In their apostolic ministry, the Father's temple-building mission, enjoined by the Son, continues in the power of the Holy Spirit,—to the ends of the earth.

Concluding Remarks

This chapter provided an ample number of examples of temple theology in the Synoptic Gospels. Included in the discussion were texts from the Infancy Narratives, the coming of the Magi, and the Presentation and the Finding of Jesus in the Temple. The special role of Mary and her relationship to the Temple was also highlighted as it relates to temple theology. The reader came to see John the Baptist as setting in motion a *counter-temple movement* in advance of Jesus. A composite of texts indicated that the Gospel authors portrayed Jesus as the New Adam.

Finally, the discussion returned to the temple-building motif from earlier in the book. Significant pieces of data from the Synoptic Gospels were explained, specifically how Jesus's proclamation of the Kingdom of God represents a temple-building mission; Jesus is God's *divine* temple builder, recapitulating and perfecting the vocation of Adam and Israel in himself.

Chapter 15 will examine still more examples of temple theology within the Synoptic Gospels, and how they are employed by the Evangelists in various ways to portray Jesus as the new Temple.

SOMETHING GREATER THAN THE TEMPLE IS HERE

Temple Theology in the Four Gospels (III/V)

At that time Jesus went through the grain fields on the Sabbath; his disciples were hungry, and they began to pluck heads of grain and to eat. But when the Pharisees saw it, they said to him, "Look, your disciples are doing what is not lawful to do on the Sabbath." He said to them, "Have you not read what David did, when he was hungry, and those who were with him: how he entered the house of God and ate the bread of the Presence, which it was not lawful for him to eat nor for those who were with him, but only for the priests? Or have you not read in the law how on the Sabbath the priests in the temple profane the Sabbath, and are guiltless? I tell you, something greater than the Temple is here."

Matthew 12:1–6

Calling the Twelve: Recapitulating the True Israel

In calling the Twelve, Jesus "begins to re-gather the tribes of Israel by beginning to call his twelve Apostles ... [they] represent the microcosmic true Israel under their true leader, Jesus (i.e. Yahweh), though Jesus is also portrayed as a latter-day Moses."[1] This action reveals Jesus as the New Mo-

---

1. G. K. Beale, *The Temple and the Church's Mission: A Biblical Theology of the Dwelling Place of God* (Downers Grove, IL: InterVarsity Press, 2004), 174.

ses who leads the true Israel toward a New Exodus. Yet, as one greater than Moses, Jesus is not only prophet but also priest and king: "Soon afterward he went on through cities and villages, preaching and bringing *the good news of the Kingdom of God. And the Twelve were with him*" (Luke 8:1).[2]

"The Lord Jesus chose men to form the college of the twelve apostles, and the apostles did the same when they chose collaborators to succeed them in their ministry."[3] This catechetical summary of the ministry of the Apostles finds early support from St. Clement of Alexandria: "So preaching everywhere in country and town, [the Apostles] appointed their first-fruits, when they had proved them by the Spirit, to be bishops and deacons unto them that should believe. And this they did in no new fashion; for indeed it had been written concerning bishops and deacons from very ancient times; for Scripture says in a certain place, 'I will appoint their bishops in righteousness and their deacons in faith.'"[4]

In the Four Gospels, the concentric circles of disciples around Jesus— from the many, to the seventy, to the Twelve, and his inner circle of three— recapitulates the concentric circles of Moses and his disciples of Israel:

The many disciples	The nation of Israel
The seventy disciples	The seventy elders (Exod. 24:1; Luke 10:1, 10:17)
The Twelve apostles	The twelve tribes / pillars (Exod. 24:4; Matt. 10:1)
Peter, James, John	Aaron, Nadab, Abihu (Exod. 24:9; Matt. 17:1)[5]

This parallel is important for a number of reasons, not least that Moses's actions on Mt. Sinai are themselves, as discussed earlier, a recapitulation of Eden. Just as Moses ascends the mountain of God, so too will the New Moses ascend mountains: the Mount of Beatitudes, to proclaim the Kingdom of God; the Mount of Transfiguration, where he prefigures his resurrected glory in the flesh; and ultimately Mount Calvary, where he "ascends" to his Cross and reverses the disobedience of Adam, making peace with God possible for all of humanity.

2. On the Twelve, see Matt. 10:1–4, 19:28, 20:17, 26:14, 26:20, 26:47; Mark 4:10, 6:7, 9:35, 10:32, 11:11, 14:10, 14:17, 14:20, 14:34; Luke 8:1, 9:1, 9:12, 18:31, 22:3, 22:30, 22:47; John 6:67, 6:70, 6:71. 20:24.

3. *Catechism of the Catholic Church,* §1577. "The Church is apostolic. She is built on a lasting foundation: the twelve apostles of the Lamb (Rev. 21:14)." See §§230, 869.

4. St. Clement, *The First Epistle to the Corinthians,* 42.4–5.

5. On Peter, James, and John, see also Mark 5:37, 9:2, 13:3, 14:33.

It may be added that Jesus assigned an eschatological role to the Twelve as priestly judges over the true Israel. This is seen in Matthew, "Truly, I say to you, in the new world, when the Son of Man shall sit on his glorious throne, you who have followed me will also sit on *twelve thrones, judging the twelve tribes of Israel*" (Matt. 19:28),[6] and in Luke, "You are those who have continued with me in my trials; and I assign to you, as my Father assigned to me, a kingdom, *that you may eat and drink at my table in my kingdom, and sit on thrones judging the twelve tribes of Israel*" (Luke 22:28–30). How could such a new order of the priesthood develop?

Such eschatological expressions of Jesus concerning the future role of the Apostles in the "new world" as priestly judges would be difficult to sort out, were there not also a radical transformation of the Temple itself. Jesus (and later St. Paul) had much to say about this as well (see John 2:19–22; Eph. 2:20). So the new Temple would have its new priesthood; the two are intimately connected. It would take some time, into the patristic era, for biblical thinkers to work out the details of this, but the essential idea, which would later find expression from figures such as St. Irenaeus, St. Jerome, and others, was that the priestly function of the Apostles transcends the Temple in Jerusalem, since it is his body that is the true and living Temple of God. As such, in the heavenly kingdom, as the end of the Book of Revelation describes, the priestly apostles are the foundations of the new temple city: "And the wall of the city had twelve foundations, and on them the twelve names of the twelve apostles of the Lamb" (Rev. 21:14).

St. Peter and the Keys of the New Temple

The discussion turns from that of the Apostles in general to St. Peter in particular. St. Peter's role as the head of the Twelve recapitulates the Davidic Kingdom.[7] Speaking of the divine authority by the Apostles, and specifically Peter, to "bind and loose," the *Catechism* concisely synthesizes the Tradition in stating, "The power to 'bind and loose' connotes the authority to absolve

---

6. The phrase "you who have followed me" is not to be taken as a generic reference to *all disciples*, but rather an implicit remark about the betrayal (and subsequent replacement) of Judas among the Twelve.

7. *Catechism of the Catholic Church*, §552. "Simon Peter holds the first place in the college of the Twelve;" "When Christ instituted the Twelve, 'he constituted [them] in the form of a college or permanent assembly, at the head of which he placed Peter, chosen from among them'" (§880).

sins, to pronounce doctrinal judgments, and to make disciplinary decisions in the Church.

In short, Jesus entrusted this authority to the Church through the ministry of the apostles and in particular through the ministry of Peter, the only one to whom he specifically entrusted the keys of the kingdom."[8]

This leads to a discussion of a well-known biblical text in the Gospel of Matthew. In turning to the following passage, one is reminded of its geography context, up in the far northern reaches of Upper Galilee, at Caesarea Philippi: "Simon Peter replied, 'You are the Christ, the Son of the living God.' And Jesus answered him, 'Blessed are you, Simon Bar-Jona! For flesh and blood has not revealed this to you, but my Father who is in heaven. *And I tell you, you are Peter, and on this rock I will build my church, and the powers of death shall not prevail against it.* I will give you *the keys of the kingdom of heaven,* and *whatever you bind on earth shall be bound in heaven, and whatever you loose on earth shall be loosed in heaven*'" (Matt. 16:18–20).

Why does Jesus take Peter and the Twelve to such a far-flung, out-of-the-way location as this? After all, it was in the rocky hill country of Upper Galilee, and well north of the region surrounding Capernaum in Lower Galilee, where most of Jesus's Galilean ministry was located. It would have been no easy journey on foot. The answer that presents itself as most likely is that Caesarea Philippi had one main attraction: the Roman Temple of Pan.[9] It was here at this *ekklesia* (Greek: "assembly") that Jesus declares that Peter is the "rock" upon which *his ekklesia* will be built.[10] The contrast could not be

---

8. *Catechism of the Catholic Church*, §553.

9. "The Greeks dedicated the cave from which the water flows to the deity Pan, naming the city Paneas, a name which survives as Banias, the modern city built on the same location as ancient Caesarea Philippi. The Romans assigned the district to King Herod the Great (20 B.C.), who erected a white marble temple there in honor of Augustus and placed the image of the emperor near the altar of Pan. After Herod's death in 4 B.C. Philip the tetrarch beautified the city and named it *Caesarea*; it became known as *Caesarea Philippi* to distinguish it from the city with the same name on the Palestinian coast to the southwest [Caesarea Maritima]. In New Testament times Caesarea Philippi was a place to worship Pan as well as to honor Caesar." *Eerdmans Bible Dictionary*, s.v. "Caesarea Philippi."

10. "'*This rock*' has been identified variously with Peter's faith or confession, with Peter's preaching office, with the truth revealed to Peter, with the twelve apostles, with Jesus, with Jesus' teaching, and even with God himself. *All this is special pleading. The most natural interpretation is that of Roman Catholic tradition: the rock is Peter.*" W. D. Davies and Dale C. Allison Jr., *A Critical and Exegetical Commentary on the Gospel According to Saint Matthew*, International Critical Commentary (London: T&T Clark International, 2004), 627 (emphases added). Neither Davies nor Allison is Roman Catholic.

more striking: at "the gates of hell" of this Roman *ekklesia*, Jesus declares that Peter is the foundation stone upon which the Church will be built. *Jesus—not Caesar is Lord*[11]—and the Kingdom of God are breaking into the violent, idolatrous empire of the world.[12]

The keys of this kingdom belong not to Caesar's power structure, but to the fisherman from Galilee, and just as Rome had the power to govern, to "bind and loose," so will the prince of the Apostles (and those in fellowship with him) have power from heaven—divine power—to not only govern but also truly forgive sins, in the power of God working through Christ in the Holy Spirit.

Finally, on the notion of *ekklesia*, Jesus's expression is not only a contrast with the Roman temple, but also a likely recapitulation of Israel under Moses's authority at Sinai, according to the analysis of Allison and Davies: "The early Christians—like the Qumran [community], thought of themselves as a counterpart to the Sinai-Congregation,[13] which in Deuteronomy is called the *ekklesia* [in the Greek Old Testament (LXX)].[14] That Matthew himself perceived the connection we need not doubt."[15] They add that the biblical typology in Matthew 1–5, as well as numerous parallels between Jesus and Moses, is indicative of a Matthean leitmotif, of the Church being led out a New Exodus by Jesus, the New Moses.

Setting this possibility aside, it is likewise evident that, from the outset of his Gospel, St. Matthew develops a *Davidic Christology*. It is this Christology that is of concern, particularly in making sense of the text in Matthew 16, concerning Peter's confession along with Jesus's response. The question to be

---

11. "When Paul said, '*Jesus is lord*,' a good many of his hearers must have known at once that this meant, 'So Caesar isn't.' And *that* was the 'good news', the *euangelion* which Paul announced around the world." N. T. Wright, *Paul and the Faithfulness of God*, vol. 4, *Christian Origins and the Question of God* (Minneapolis: Fortress Press, 2013), 384 (emphases added). Wright suggests that the proclamation "Jesus is Lord" along with the belief that God raised him from the dead was, at least for St. Paul, was a fulfillment of Deuteronomy: "What Paul has done is to say: *now at last we see what it means to 'fulfil Torah' in the sense Deuteronomy 30 had in mind.* Professing that Jesus is lord, and believing that God raised him from the dead, together constitute the reality towards which Deuteronomy 30 was pointing. This is the real 'return from exile', the lifting of the covenantal curse, the giving of the life which Torah itself had promised but by itself could not give" (514–15).

12. *Ekklesia* ("assembly, church") occurs only twice in the Four Gospels—here and at Matt. 18:18.

13. See 1 Cor. 10:1–5; Heb. 12:18–24.

14. See Exod. 4:10, 9:10, 18:16, 31:30; Philo, *Decalogue*, 32.

15. Davies and Allison, *Critical and Exegetical Commentary*, 629.

pursued is, how does this Davidic Christology work in Matthew, and what conclusions can be reasonably drawn from the confession scene in light of it?

To begin a response, numerous times in the Gospel, Jesus is called son of David,[16] and the first such occurrence is in Matthew 1:1: "The genealogy that follows further underscores Jesus' Davidic lineage. As scholars note, its division into three sets of fourteen generations also seems to highlight its Davidic nature, since fourteen is the numeric value of David's name in Hebrew. This reading is supported by the recognition that David's name is the fourteenth name in the list."[17]

Adding to this initial evidence of the Davidic pattern in Matthew are the following: (1) Jesus was born in Bethlehem, the "city of David."[18] (2) The baptism of the Son of God; just as the Spirit of the Lord came upon Solomon at his anointing, so the Spirit comes down upon Jesus at his baptism.[19] (3) Jesus embodied "Davidic exorcistic and healing powers."[20] (4) The Son of David enters Jerusalem.[21] (5) The "Passion of the Davidic king."[22]

There is more compelling evidence that space does not permit here, though one final remark may be added, from a recent essay called "Peter, the

16. Matt. 1:1, 1:20, 9:27, 12:23, 15:22, 20:30, 20:31, 21:9, 21:15, 22:42.

17. M. Barber, "Jesus as the Davidic Temple Builder and Peter's Priestly Role in Matthew 16:16–19," *Journal of Biblical Literature* 132, no. 4 (2013): 933–51, here 935. See also Davies and Allison, *Critical and Exegetical Commentary*, 161–88. "The section offers proof of the title: Jesus is the son of Abraham and the Son of David. More particularly, because 'the heritage of the king is from son to son only' (Sir. 45:25), and because Jesus is, through his father, a descendant of King David, in this respect *he qualifies as the Davidic Messiah*" (187).

18. Matt. 2:4; 1 Sam. 16:11; see John 7:42.

19. Matt. 3:16; 1 Sam. 16:13. "That Davidic allusions are in play is strongly supported by the fact that the voice from heaven identifies Jesus as God's son." Barber, "Jesus as the Davidic Temple Builder," 936.

20. "Those seeking healing specifically address him as [*son of David*] (Matt. 9:27; 20:31). This title is also linked to his role as an exorcist (Matt. 15:22). Notably, David was associated with exorcistic and healing abilities (see 1 Sam. 16:14–23; Josephus, *A.J.* 166–68; 11QPsa XI, 2–11; *L.A.B.* 60:1). Solomon also had a reputation as an exorcist and healer (see Josephus, *A.J.* 8:42–49; *Apoc. Adam* 7:13; cf. also Wisd. 7:17–22). That Matthew links such activity to Jesus' messianic role is clear." Ibid.

21. Jesus's "triumphal entry into Jerusalem (Matt. 21:9) recalls Solomon's royal coronation (1 Ki. 1:33, 38). Matthew explicitly ties Jesus' entry into the city to Zechariah's eschatological prophecy of a coming king (Zech. 9:9), a passage modeled on Solomonic traditions. The crowd's acclamation flows naturally from such allusions: [*hosanna to the son of David*] (Matt. 21:9)." Ibid.

22. "Jesus' royal identity is especially underscored in Matthew's passion narrative. Jesus suffers as [*king of the Jews*] (Matt. 27:29, 37). Caiaphas also directly links Jesus' supposed identity as the '*Christ*' with divine sonship status (Matt. 27:63: [*the Christ, the son of* God])." Ibid., 937.

Keys and the Priestly Eliakim,"[23] in which numerous parallels between Matthew 16:19[24] and Isaiah 22:22[25] are closely analyzed. Three insights from the essay are pertinent to us.

First, both texts in Isaiah and Matthew express the giving of royal authority using motifs of "opening and shutting" (Isaiah) and, similarly, "binding and loosing" (Matthew). Second, both passages refer to Davidic motifs, that is, house of David (Isaiah) and Son of God/Messiah (Matthew). Third and finally, the role of Peter by St. Matthew is juxtaposed with Isaiah's Eliakim. In the essay, Barber convincingly argues that Eliakim is not merely a royal figure in David's kingdom (as most all scholars agree), but also a priestly figure.[26] If the evidence presented is correct, it represents one of the strongest examples of temple theology in Matthew, with Jesus as a messianic temple builder and Peter as a priestly figure over the temple community: "In sum, the imagery comes together to form one coherent picture. *Jesus is the Davidic Messiah, who, like the son of David, will build a temple, understood as the community.* Given that the community is described as a temple, it is no wonder that Jesus describes Peter's leadership role over it in terms of priestly authority; as God appointed the priestly Eliakim in Isaiah, *Jesus establishes Peter as a priestly figure over the Temple community.*"[27]

23. Ibid., 942–45. See especially "The Son of David and Temple Building" (937–40) and "Temple-Community Imagery Elsewhere in Matthew" (940–41).

24. Matt. 16:19: "I will give you the keys of the kingdom of heaven, and whatever you bind on earth shall be bound in heaven, and whatever you loose on earth shall be loosed in heaven."

25. Isa. 22:22: "And I will place on his shoulder the key of the house of David; he shall open, and none shall shut; and he shall shut, and none shall open."

26. Barber, "Jesus as the Davidic Temple Builder," 942–43. As evidence, he cites a number of texts from Second Temple Judaism that describe Eliakim in priestly garb, invested with priestly dignity and engaged in priestly actions. (Examples include *Targum on Isaiah* 22; *Leviticus Rabbah* 5:5.) He argues, "How did ancient interpreters come to the conclusion that Eliakim was a priestly figure? This view appears to be rooted in the language of the Hebrew text of Isaiah 22 itself. Eliakim is portrayed as wearing the garments [a tunic] and a [sash]—two garments specifically associated with the high priest (see for example, Exod. 28:4) Indeed, his role in the sanctuary may be suggested by Isa. 22:24, where he is given authority over 'every small vessel, from the cups to all the flagons'" (943). Priestly responsibility for "the keys of the temple" is attributed to in rabbinic literature (*2 Bar.* 10:18; *4 Bar.* 4:4–5; *Leviticus Rabbah* 19:6).

27. Ibid., 943 (emphases added).

Jesus's Miracles and Exorcisms as "Temple Actions"

The discussion now turns to the ministry of Jesus described in the Synoptic Gospels pertaining to miracles and exorcisms. In keeping with the temple theology already presented in the Synoptic Gospels, such texts represent important data that need to be considered in a fresh light.

But how, exactly? First, Beale puts in healing and exorcistic ministry of Jesus in context as it pertains to the new creation: "The restoration [of Israel] involves various kinds of healings, which were prophesied to occur when Israel would undergo her true end-times restoration to God ... Jesus is re-establishing the *new creation and kingdom, which Adam should have established.* Seen within the framework of the new creation, Christ's miracles of healing *not only established the end-time kingdom but signaled the beginning of the new creation,* since the healings were a reversal of the curse of the old fallen world. *The miracles were a sign of the inbreaking new creation,* where people would be completely healed."[28]

Beale's insight is sound, but inadequate. Not only do Jesus's miracles and exorcisms indicate the in-breaking of a New Creation, but they also suggest that his messiahship would bring about the restoration of the Temple. The messianic age would represent an unprecedented outpouring of forgiveness and mercy, formerly associated with God's presence in the Temple and sacrifices offered to God in the Temple, for especially for the forgiveness of sins.

The following is but one example in which a Gospel text, in this instance from Matthew, builds upon Old Testament expectations of the coming Messiah. The prophet Isaiah writes, "Then the eyes of those who see will not be closed, and the ears of those who hear will hearken. The mind of the rash will have good judgment, and the tongue of the stammerers will speak readily and distinctly" (Isa. 32:3–4). Earlier in the text, Isaiah uses language that is familiar to any reader of the Gospels: "I have given you as a covenant to the people, a light to the nations, to open the eyes that are blind, to bring out the prisoners from the dungeon, from the prison those who sit in darkness" (Isa. 42:7). Consider the Gospel of Matthew in light of these Old Testament texts: "And he went about all Galilee, teaching in their synagogues and preaching the gospel of the Kingdom and healing every disease and ev-

28. Beale, *The Temple and the Church's Mission,* 174 (emphases added).

ery infirmity among the people. So his fame spread throughout all Syria, and they brought him all the sick, those afflicted with various diseases and pains, demoniacs, epileptics, and paralytics, and he healed them" (Matt. 4:23–24).

It is worth pointing out that in Jesus Judean ministry, many of his miracles and/or exorcisms took place in or near the Temple. Here is an example elsewhere in Matthew: "And the blind and the lame came to him in the Temple, and he healed them. But when the chief priests and the scribes saw the wonderful things that he did, and the children crying out in the temple, 'Hosanna to the Son of David!' they were indignant" (Matt. 21:14–15); another is seen in the Gospel of John, as Jesus heals the paralytic man on the Sabbath. In that familiar text from John, note the author's comments at the end of the miracle story, along with Jesus's comments: "Now the man who had been healed did not know who it was, for Jesus had withdrawn, as there was a crowd in the place. *Afterward, Jesus found him in the Temple,* and said to him, 'See, you are well! Sin no more, that nothing worse befall you'" (John 5:13–14).[29]

One may object to the suggestion that Jesus's teachings were done primarily in the Temple. In fact, this is not what was claimed, only that when he was in Judea. It is quite true that many of Jesus's miracles and exorcisms are done *far from the Temple*, particularly in the Galilean ministry. In affirming this, it must be quickly added that a considerable number of the non-Temple contexts of Jesus's miracles and exorcisms take place in *local synagogues*.[30]

This is a significant detail, as the local synagogue was understood as *an extension of the Temple*. As such, given that Jesus's many healings and exorcisms take place in synagogues—and, it may be added, wherein he was frequently challenged by *Temple authorities*—such texts may be added into the Temple category, broadly speaking.[31] As Perrin states, "When it came to divine healing, there was no better place to find it than in the Temple. Jesus' acts of healing easily lend themselves to being interpreted within just this [Temple] context."[32] He adds: "That the itinerant Jesus attained his fame primarily through his therapeutic abilities, *together with the fact that the Temple*

---

29. See also Matt. 21:12.

30. See Matt. 12:9–14; Mark 1:23–28, 3:1–5, 5:22*ff*.; Luke 6:6–11, etc.

31. Matt. 12:9–15. Similarly, see Jesus's synagogue-related healings in Mark 1:21–28, 3:1–6, 5:21–24; Luke 4:16–30 (esp. v. 18), 8:40–42, 8:49–56, 13:8–17.

32. Nicholas Perrin, *Jesus the Temple* (Grand Rapids, MI: Baker Academic, 2012), 153.

was the primary venue for healing within Judaism, makes it altogether plausible that Jesus' healing ministry, which he shared with his disciples, was meant to make off the movement as the mobile embodiment of the Temple."[33]

As Perrin suggests, Jesus's itinerant ministry provided a ministry of healing and reconciliation to God previously associated with the building of the Temple. Now, through his divine actions and therapeutic power, his ministry, like John the Baptist before him, took on a counter-temple quality. However, unlike John, who announced and awaited the renewal of the Temple, Jesus's healing actions displayed God's cleansing actions, associated in the past with the Temple in Jerusalem, *everywhere he went*.

In a manner of speaking, the Gospels portray Jesus as having a kind of "contagious holiness"[34] that both echoed God's merciful power within the Temple and yet transcended it, making it available to more people than ever before, even (and especially) to those who were "cut off" from the Temple, the tax collectors and sinners, as well as the unclean of various sorts, who in his day remained at a distance from the Temple itself. Now, with Jesus, this was no longer the case, as his ministry unfolded as a kind of "contagious holiness" to all who desired it. In addition, Fletcher-Louis suggests that examples of individuals experiencing healing power by merely touching his garments recall the power of the high priest in his own anointed garments: "You shall consecrate [the high priest's garments], that they may be most holy; *whatever touches them will become holy*" (Exod. 30:29).[35]

An echo of the contagious holiness of priestly garments is seen in reverse, in a text from Ezekiel: "And when they go out into the outer court to the people, they shall put off the garments in which they have been ministering, and lay them in the holy chambers; and they shall put on other garments, *lest they communicate holiness to the people with their garments*" (Ezek. 44:19).[36]

33. Ibid., 154 (emphasis added).

34. Crispin Fletcher-Louis, *Dictionary of Jesus and the Gospels*, 2nd ed., s.v. "Priests and Priesthood." I am indebted to Fletcher-Louis for the apt phrase. See also Perrin, "Jesus the Exorcistic High Priest," in *Jesus the Temple*, 168–70: "The eschatological high priest will restore Israel by *delivering the remnant from the demonic power and sitting in judgment on the Gentiles*" (168). Perrin cites a related text from the Dead Sea Scrolls (11Q13) that depicts the Messiah as the priest-king Melchizidek of Psa. 110, who delivers the righteous "from the power of Belial."

35. See also Wisd. 18:20–25.

36. Notice it is "they" and not "he" in the above text. Given Ezekiel's theology and his ongoing critique, it is not surprising that the garments described belong to Levitical (Zadokite) priests, not the high priest.

Compare these Old Testament texts to a miracle story, recorded in all three Synoptic Gospels:[37] "As he went, the people pressed round him. And a woman who had had a flow of blood[38] for twelve years and had spent all her living upon physicians and could not be healed by any one, came up behind him, and touched the fringe of his garment; and immediately her flow of blood ceased. And Jesus said, '*Who was it that touched me?*' When all denied it, Peter said, 'Master, the multitudes surround you and press upon you!' But Jesus said, '*Someone touched me; for I perceive that power has gone forth from me.*' And when the woman saw that she was not hidden, she came trembling, and falling down before him declared in the presence of all the people *why she had touched him, and how she had been immediately healed. And he said to her, 'Daughter, your faith has made you well; go in peace'*" (Luke 8: 42–48).

The account of the miracle as recorded by St. Mark adds something of the woman's awareness and belief of the healing power of Jesus, available to her even from coming in contact with his clothing: "She had heard the reports about Jesus, and came up behind him in the crowd and touched his garment. For she said, '*If I touch even his garments, I shall be made well*'" (Mark 5:27–28).

The confirmation of the miracle is given in the next verse, and St. Mark adds: "and *she felt in her body that she was healed of her disease.*"[39] St. Matthew's version is particularly striking in that it adds the detail of "the fringe" (Greek: *kraspedou*) of Jesus's garment as being touched. This likely refers not merely to the edge of Jesus's garment "but to the tassels (Hebrew: *tsisit*) required by Num. 15:38–41[40] and Deut. 22:12[41] for the four corners of one's outer garment (cf. 23:5)."[42] In this way, St. Matthew underscores Jesus's obedience to the whole of the Law.[43]

Matthew contains one other instance in which people attempt to "touch"

37. See also Matt. 9:20–22; Mark 5:24–34.

38. "A uterine hemorrhage is undoubtedly meant." Davies and Allison, *Critical and Exegetical Commentary*, 2:128. They add: "For other miracle stories in which the duration of the sickness is given—something that indicates both the difficulty of the cure and the despair of the sufferer—see Mark 9:21; Luke 13:11; John 5:5; 9:1; Acts 3:2; 4:22; 9:33; 14:8, etc."

39. Mark 5:29.   40. Num. 15:38–41.

41. Deut. 22:12.

42. Donald A. Hagner, *Matthew 1–13*, vol. 33A, *Word Biblical Commentary* (Dallas: Word Books, 1998), 248–49.

43. "Jesus is thus faithful to the Torah in his dress." Ibid., 249.

Jesus, probably toward a similar end. It is located near the end of the exorcism account at Gennesaret (Matt. 14:35–36), a passage that will be discussed in more detail below.

Elsewhere, St. Mark describes the similar desire of people with diseases seeking to touch Jesus: "And he told his disciples to have a boat ready for him because of the crowd, lest they should crush him; for he had healed many, so that all who had diseases pressed upon him to touch him" (Mark 3:9–10). Another example occurs just a few chapters later: "And wherever he came, in villages, cities, or country, they laid the sick in the market places, and besought him that they might touch even the fringe (*kraspedou*) of his garment; and as many as touched it were made well" (Mark 6:56).

Jesus's Exorcisms: Purifying the Unclean from the Land of the Temple

The discussions now turn to a second type of healing stories within the Synoptic Gospels. Though different in substance and form, these healings have the same interest as that of Jesus exorcisms. In ancient temples, a key priestly duty was guarding the gates of the temple, determining who could enter and who was banned from entering.[44] In Judaism, the priest was the guardian of the Jerusalem Temple, admitting the clean and expelling the unclean. Recall that Adam's failure in the Garden, in admitting in the serpent, may be interpreted as a dereliction of just this priestly duty.

In this way, Jesus's exorcisms may be seen as a recapitulation of Adam's role in Genesis, as well as the high priest's role throughout the Old Testament. Added to this starting point is a key text in Zechariah: "On that day there shall be a fountain opened for the house of David and the inhabitants of Jerusalem to cleanse them from sin and uncleanness. And on that day, says the Lord of hosts, I will cut off the names of the idols from the land, so that they shall be remembered no more; and also I will remove from the land the prophets and the unclean spirit" (Zech. 13:1–2).[45]

As Perrin observes, "Jesus' conflict with the Temple dignitaries at his ar-

---

44. See the earlier discussion of "gate liturgies" in chapter 2.

45. "Here is a passage [Zech. 13] which tells of the clash between the *true, Davidic 'shepherd'* of Yahweh (v. 7), on the one side, and the 'false prophets' (vv. 2–6) who abuse their charge as they are carried along by the 'unclean spirit' (v. 2), on the other." Perrin, *Jesus the Temple*, 162.

rest, a moment ... he seems to have anticipated and interpreted in light of Zechariah 13:7."[46] He goes on to explain: "In situating Jesus' *exorcistic activity* within the context of Zechariah 13, that is, as a symbolic expression of Yahweh's imminent intention to purify the land of idolatry and dark spiritual forces, we recognize its inextricable political [power] within the first-century context ... As pious first-century Jews saw it, linking hands with the Romans was the steep slippery-slope to the incursion of idolatry, demonic spirits, and ultimately, the desecration of the land, which had been one of the central precipitating causes of the exile."[47]

A textual example from the Gospel of Mark will now be examined in light of Perrin's insights. Mark 5:1–20 records one of Jesus's most prolific miracles, the healing of the demoniac of the region of Gerasene and the expulsion of the unclean spirit(s) into the herd of swine.

The passage apparently has a complex literary history[48] as well as a number of features that are not analyzed here, except one: its locale.[49] Specifically, the sight of the exorcism is depicted as being the eastern shore of the Sea of Galilee.[50] This fact is significant in that it placed Jesus *in Hellenistic territory*, near the site of the ancient city of Hippos, one of the twelve cities of the Decapolis and the locale of one of Herod's fortresses. Perrin argues for a sociopolitical bearing upon this exorcism report, and possibly for Jesus exorcistic ministry more broadly: "Jesus' exorcism ... would have not only effected a

---

46. Zech. 13:7: "Strike the shepherd, that the sheep may be scattered." Perrin, *Jesus the Temple*, 162: "I conclude that it was the master himself who pulled the phrase 'unclean spirit' from Zechariah 13:2 and pushed it to the forefront of the community's consciousness ... he applied the phrase ... not only to fill out the scriptural interpretative grid which he commanded, *but to give distinctive significance to his own exorcistic powers.*"

47. Perrin, *Jesus the Temple*, 164 (emphasis added).

48. "As it stands in Mark, our colourful tale is difficult to unravel. It contains both doublets and inconsistencies ... and one scholar has even managed to unearth four hypothetical pre-*Markan* stages through which it has allegedly passed. Even if a complex tradition-history seems called for, one hesitates to think we can now accurately reconstruct it. Is Mark 5:1–20: really a literary onion whose skin can be peeled off layer by layer?" Davies and Allison, *Critical and Exegetical Commentary*, 2:77.

49. For more on this passage, see Robert A. Guelich, *Mark 1–8:26*, vol. 34A, *Word Biblical Commentary* (Dallas: Word Books, 1998), 271–89; John R. Donahue and Daniel J. Harrington, *The Gospel of Mark*, vol. 2, *Sacra Pagina Series*, ed. Daniel J. Harrington (Collegeville, MN: Liturgical Press, 2002), 162–71; Adela Yarbro Collins and Harold W. Attridge, *Mark: A Commentary on the Gospel of Mark*, Hermeneia: A Critical and Historical Commentary on the Bible (Minneapolis, MN: Fortress Press, 2007), 263–74.

50. Davies and Allison, *Critical and Exegetical Commentary*, 2:78–79.

substantial loss of animal property, but also, given that the Roman soldiers garrisoned at nearby Hippos would have likely depended upon the swine as a food source, served to deprive the legionnaires of a staple delicacy. In this respect, Jesus' measures amounted, albeit in an indirect way, to an act of political sabotage. The symbolic irony could hardly have been lost on those present."[51]

This is a fascinating possibility. Perrin's work, which is stimulating in its own right, supports one of the primary points made earlier in the book. Specifically, if the narrative of the Garden of Eden is read within the framework of temple theology, then Genesis 2–3 presents the unholy one being cast out of the Edenic temple. Adam is banished from this temple, and "cut off" from the Tree of Life, the symbol of God's own presence. This "being cast out" motif is repeated many more times in the Old Testament, particularly in the exile of unholy Israel, which is "cast out" of the Promised Land as it is brought under God's judgment.

Strikingly, this "cast out" motif is not limited to Genesis, or even to the canon of the Old Testament. It recurs in the New Testament, where it recasts the exile motif in the Jesus story. The Gospels portray Jesus as the New Moses, leading God's people out of captivity in a New Exodus. Seen in this light, the episode of Jesus encountering the Garasene demoniac has insights that, as Perrin shows, fit into this exilic pattern. More specifically, Perrin's interpretation suggests a deeper level of meaning of the exorcism (and satire) to the exorcism account, beyond Jesus's deliverance of the man from evil. Specifically, it suggests the possibility that the entire scene is an "expulsion" motif, that is, of removing that which is unclean from the holy sanctuary (of Israel).

Regardless of Perrin's suggestion, which is an intriguing possibility, one thing is clear: Jesus's exorcistic activity clearly joins his larger healing ministry of miracles as deeply symbolic actions that signal the advent of the Kingdom of God, of his messianic and salvific role in it, and with this a new reality of healing previously associated with the ministry of the Temple, and now associated with the new Temple of Jesus's person.

51. Perrin, *Jesus the Temple*, 164.

The Transfiguration of Jesus, the Glorious High Priest

Discussion now turns to another key scene in the Synoptic Gospels: the Transfiguration of Jesus. All who have spent any time with it realize that it is, along with the Baptism of Jesus, a crucial, revelatory scene in the Gospels. The Transfiguration of Jesus reveals the divine glory of Jesus, as confirmed in the confession by Peter atop Mt. Tabor. It prepares Jesus's disciples for the darkness that awaits Jesus in Jerusalem, as they "beheld His glory" (John 1:14). As Moses and Elijah appear before Jesus, the disciples contemplate Jesus as they have never before seen him—as the fulfillment of the Old Covenant, of the Law and the Prophets, as the glorious Son of God. As the *Catechism* sums up, the Transfiguration is, for Jesus's disciples then as now, a sign of Christ's Resurrection—and that of the Christian believer. "On the threshold of the public life: the baptism; on the threshold of the Passover: the Transfiguration. Jesus' baptism proclaimed 'the mystery of the first regeneration,' namely, our Baptism; the Transfiguration 'is the sacrament of the second regeneration:' our own Resurrection."[52]

Going further into the depth of the Transfiguration and its meaning, Origen developed an allegorical reading about the Christian life, building upon the image of light (and darkness): "But when He is transfigured, His face also shines as the sun that he may be manifested to the children of light who have put off the works of darkness and put on the armor of light,[53] and are no longer the children of darkness or night but have become the sons of day, and walk honestly as in the day.[54] Being manifested, He will shine unto them not simply as the sun, but as demonstrated to be the sun of righteousness."[55]

And yet one may ask whether the Transfiguration of Jesus belongs in a discussion of temple theology. The answer is an unqualified yes. This is true for several key reasons. First, the Transfiguration plunges the reader deep into the reality of the Old Testament, in which the entire history of Israel is being mysteriously recapitulated. As Davies and Allison write, "When Jesus, in circumstances strongly reminiscent of Exod. 24 and 34, goes up on

---

52. *Catechism of the Catholic Church*, §555. See Thomas Aquinas, *Summa Theologica* III, q. 45, a. 4, ad 2.

53. See John 12:36.   54. See Rom. 13:13.

55. Origen, *Commentary on Matthew*, 12.37.

a mountain and is transfigured into light, the reader is to infer that history has come full circle, that the eschatological expectations of Judaism have begun to find their fulfillment. The eschatological prophet, the one like Moses and Elijah, has appeared, and the light of the Resurrection and *parousia* has already shone forth. Israel's primal history is being recapitulated by her Messiah, God's Son, the eschatological embodiment of true Israel."[56]

Second, and more pointedly, Jesus's ascending the "high mountain"[57] recalls Moses's going up Mt. Sinai to meet God,[58] which in turn recapitulates Adam's experiencing the presence of God in Eden.[59] It may be added that Jesus's ascent also recalls the high priest's ascent to the Holy of Holies, which, it will be recalled, was not only the inner most place in the Temple, but also the upper most place in the Temple.

Third, Jesus's dazzling appearance recalls the high priest, who radiated the glory of God. Luke 9:29: "And as he was praying, the appearance of his countenance was altered, and his [garments] became dazzling white."[60] In his treatise *On Dreams*, Philo of Alexandria writes about the vestments of the high priest of the Temple as images of incorruptibility and immortality: "When this same high priest enters into the innermost parts of the holy Temple, he is clothed in the variegated garment, and he also assumes linen robe, made of the very finest flax. And this is an emblem of vigor, and *incorruptibility*, and the most brilliant light. For such a veil is a thing very difficult to be broken, and it is made of *nothing mortal*, and when it is properly and carefully purified it has a most clear and brilliant appearance."[61]

Here, some insights from Crispin Fletcher-Louis are helpful, on how the high priest radiated the image of Yahweh in his luminescent garments: "[This recalls the] light-giving properties of the high priest's garments in general and, in particular, his dazzling white linen garments of the Day of Atonement."[62] "We also regularly find the view that the high priest's garments, par-

56. Davies and Allison, *Critical and Exegetical Commentary*, 2:684.

57. See Matt. 17:1; Mark 9:2; Luke 9:28.   58. See Exod. 19:20, 24:12–15.

59. See Gen. 3:8.   60. Cf. Matt. 17:2 and Mark 9:23.

61. Philo, *De Somnis* [*On Dreams*] I:126–27: "When this same high priest enters into the innermost parts of the holy temple, he is clothed in the variegated garment, and he also assumes another linen robe, made of the very finest flax. And this is an emblem of vigor, and incorruptibility, and the most brilliant light. For such a veil is a thing very difficult to be broken, and it is made of nothing mortal, and when it is properly and carefully purified it has a most clear and brilliant appearance."

62. Fletcher-Louis, s.v. "Priests and Priesthood." Moreover, "language in Matthew's version [of

ticularly the stones, are iridescent, light-giving garments, which means that … the Urim (and Thummim) are identified with the garments and that an association with God's own glorious light-filled garments is implied … And, so, also Yahweh is 'clothed with honor and majesty, wrapped in light as with a garment'" (Psa. 104:1–2).[63]

Fourth, Jesus's Transfiguration is a scene that is not only crucial to the glorious identity of Jesus in the Synoptic Gospels, but it is also a crucial passage that connects the temple theology of the Old Testament to the temple theology of the New Testament. On Mt. Tabor, Jesus radiates with the glory of the Only Son, recapitulating the glorious robes of the high priest of the Temple in his very being. It is not the "robes" of any priest that shine with blinding, glorious light on Tabor, but also the very flesh of Jesus, in his total being. For the early Jewish disciples of Jesus, who lived in the shadow of a "lesser" Temple with a growingly corrupted high priesthood, this scene, foreshadowing the resurrected, radiant eternal high priest, must have been truly decisive in their recognition of Jesus as *their* true Mediator.

A further point may be added: for the astute Jewish hearer of the Gospel, the Transfiguration must have called to mind a high priest more glorious than Aaron himself—the high priesthood of Adam, in the temple of Eden. Unlike Adam, these Gospel recipients would have grasped that, unlike Adam, Jesus did not exchange his "garments of glory" for "garments of skin," but by fulfilling the will of the Father in his oneness with him (John 10:30), Jesus is seen as the New Adam.

Jesus's temple action (commonly known as "the cleansing" of the Temple") will be treated in chapter 16. Similarly, since the temple theology of Christ's Passion will be dealt with in a separate chapter, only one category remains to be examined at present: various temple sayings of Jesus.

The majority of temple sayings in the Gospels concern the coming judg-

---

the Transfiguration] associates the mountaintop revelation of Jesus' identity with the installation of a new (royal) high priest at the New Year's festivals." See 1 Macc. 10:21; Josephus, *Antiquities* XIII.303–8; XV.50–52; *Jewish Wars* 3.73; *Jubilees* 32:2–9.

63. Crispin Fletcher-Louis, "God's Image, His Cosmic Temple and the High Priest," in *Heaven on Earth*, ed. T. Desmond Alexander and Simon Gathercole (Carlisle, UK: Paternoster Press, 2004), 91. He adds: "In one Qumran text the Urim and Thummim [of the Temple] is somehow identified with the primal light, the perfect light ('ortm) which God himself creates for his dwelling on the first day of creation (4Q392 frag. 1 lines 4–5 … The gods of Israel's neighbors are clothed in light or luminescent garments."

ment upon the Temple. As such, they are prophetic utterances of the end of era of the natural, physical Temple and the inauguration of the supernatural Temple—Jesus himself. Yet there are two other sayings that will be mentioned here, each of which is pertinent to a discussion of temple theology.

Something Greater Than the Temple Is Here

As mentioned, the miracles and exorcisms of Jesus, when read in light of the Temple, provide the Gospel authors with radiant and powerful examples of the "transference of divine power, from the old Temple of Jerusalem to the new one, of Jesus' body." The above saying operates in a different manner, but the principle in Jesus's saying is similar, if not identical, to that of Jesus's miracles and exorcisms. In fact, this is not really one saying but two independent sayings brought together in Matthew 12:[64] "I tell you, *something greater than the Temple is here* ... The queen of the South will arise at the judgment with this generation and condemn it; for she came from the ends of the earth to hear the wisdom of Solomon, and behold, *something greater than Solomon is here*" (Matt. 12:6, 12:42).

In this saying, Jesus announces the arrival of the new Temple. What could possibly be "greater than the Temple" other than the Deity himself? This seems to be Jesus's point precisely. As such, St. Matthew uses it to underscore Jesus's divinity and articulate that, as the Son of God, Jesus is indeed greater than the Temple itself. Such attestations were common in the patristic era, as in this example from St. Hilary: "Christ also reminded them of another prophecy so that they might learn that all things that were spoken of previously were accomplished in him through the Law, that the priests in the Temple broke the Sabbath without offense, *clearly revealing that Jesus himself was the Temple*."[65]

The second saying in Matthew 12 is equally important. Jesus's suggestion that "something greater than Solomon" is here is not mere repetition. This addition does two things. In its context, it first suggests a future judgment of Israel for its persistent disobedience. This is evident in the phrase "the Queen of the South," a Gentile, rising up and judging "this generation." Second, the reference to Solomon in particular indicates an added contrast between Je-

---

64. See Davies and Allison, *Critical and Exegetical Commentary*, 2:314.
65. St. Hillary of Poitiers (315–367 AD), *On Matthew* 12.4.

sus, the Son of David, and Solomon, David's son. In this way, St. Matthew presents Jesus as the new Solomon: "Jesus is 'greater than Solomon' because He is a greater king and had more wisdom ... Similarly, Jesus is greater than the Temple because God's presence is more manifest in the Him than in the Temple. On Him, not the Temple rests the shekinah *glory*."[66]

The second saying in Matthew 12 is related to the first, but not given in the immediate context of the Sabbath.[67] "Queen of the South" is likely a reference to the queen of Sheba. Davies and Allison add several helpful insights here: "Note that, according to 1 Kings 10:1, the queen of Sheba came to Solomon 'to test him with hard questions.' So like the Pharisees she tested a king. But unlike them, she could see the truth ... Israel has had the opportunity to see and hear one greater than Jonah and *one greater than Solomon*. All to no avail. Therefore her judgment will be the harsher."[68]

To the above insights a keen point from Davies and Allison may be added in concluding the analysis of this biblical text. Both independent sayings, brought together by Matthew, are given in the context of Jesus and his disciples, walking through the grain fields on the Sabbath. They emphasize that the entire controversy unfolds as a result of the disciples' plucking some of the heads of grain to eat. This is significant for understanding St. Matthew's theology: "This and the next two verses are Matthew's own work, without parallel in Mark or Luke. The point [of the addition is] this: if the priests who serve in the Temple on the Sabbath are innocent of wrong-doing ... how much more innocent are the disciples, who are serving Jesus, one greater than the Temple?"[69]

The True Cornerstone

The focus now shifts to another temple saying of Jesus, also located in the Gospel of Matthew: "Jesus said to them, 'Have you never read in the scrip-

---

66. Beale, *The Temple and the Church's Mission*, 178, citing A. Cole, *The New Temple* (London: Tyndale, 1950), 12 (emphasis added).

67. The basic context is as follows: "After Jesus is asked by the scribes and Pharisees for a sign, he responds with a speech which takes up three points, the first being the sign to 'this generation' (the sign of Jonah; 39–40), the second being the sayings about past generations (41–42), the third being the fate of 'this generation' (vv. 43–45)." Davies and Allison, *Critical and Exegetical Commentary*, 351.

68. Ibid., 360 (emphasis added).

69. Ibid., 313, citing D. J. Moo, "Jesus and the Authority of the Mosaic Law," *Journal for the Study of the New Testament* 20 (1984): 16–17.

tures: The very stone which the builders rejected has become the head of the corner; this was the Lord's doing, and it is marvelous in our eyes'" (Matt. 21:42). The context in which the saying is given is crucial, as the immediate setting is again *in the Temple*: "And when he entered the Temple, the chief priests and the elders of the people came up to him as he was teaching, and said, 'By what authority are you doing these things, and who gave you this authority?'" (Matt. 21:23–24).

Jesus responds to the chief priests and elders of the Temple with two parables, the Parable of the Two Sons (Matt. 21:28–32) and the Parable of the Vineyard (Matt. 21:33–41). Recall that Jesus had asked them about the origins of John's baptismal ministry.[70] They are trapped; they cannot assert with Jesus that John's ministry is from God in heaven, knowing that he would respond by saying, "Why then did you not believe him?" (Matt. 21:25). Neither can they outright assert that John's ministry is not divine in origin, for fear of the crowd. Therefore they balk (vv. 26–27). The point of the first parable is that the Temple leaders did not accept John the Baptist or his prophetic ministry. They failed to recognize John's baptismal ministry as a counter-temple movement as "from God." Rather, in hypocrisy, they feared and detested John and subsequently Jesus, for the same reasons.

The details of the following parable, the Parable of the Vineyard, need not be mentioned here. Like the parable preceding it, the point is clear. It is a scathing critique of the Temple authorities. In this parable, however, there is a judgment of all of Israel, for rejecting God's Son, similar to the way Isaiah depicts the coming judgment of Israel and Judah in the Song of the Vineyard (Isa. 5:1–7): "And now, O inhabitants of Jerusalem and men of Judah, judge, I pray you, between me and my vineyard. What more was there to do for my vineyard?"

It is immediately *after* these two parables, given in the Temple, to the Temple authorities, that Jesus's saying is found, "Jesus said to them, 'Have you never read in the scriptures: The very stone which the builders rejected has become *the head of the corner*; this was the Lord's doing, and it is marvelous in our eyes?'" (Matt. 21:42).

Davies and Allison argue that Jesus "proverbial-sounding line ... emphasized Jesus' rejection by unbelievers and his vindication by God. In the OT it

---

70. Matt. 21:25: "The baptism of John, whence was it? From heaven or from men? And they argued with one another, "If we say, 'From heaven,' he will say to us, 'Why then did you not believe him?'"

appears to be about Israel, rejected by the nations ... *Here the subject is Jesus himself,* rejected by the Jewish leaders [yet] vindicated by God."[71]

Later in the Gospel, the motif comes up yet again. As Jesus and his disciples made their way to Jerusalem for his final Passover, they would have sung the Psalms of Ascent.[72] "These are hymns of thanksgiving to God for liberating Israel from Egypt [which] speak of *the stone rejected by the builders that wondrously turned out to be the cornerstone.*"[73] For his part, St. Peter draws upon this cornerstone imagery in his first epistle:[74] "Come to him, to *that living stone,* rejected by men but in God's sight chosen and precious; and *like living stones be yourselves built into a spiritual house,* to be a holy priesthood, to offer spiritual sacrifices acceptable to God through Jesus Christ. For it stands in scripture: 'Behold, I am laying in Zion a stone, a cornerstone chosen and precious, and he who believes in him will not be put to shame.' To you therefore who believe, he is precious, but for those who do not believe, 'The very stone which the builders rejected has become the head of the corner,' and '*A stone that will make men stumble, a rock that will make them fall*'; for they stumble because they disobey the word, as they were destined to do" (1 Pet. 2:4–8).

Throughout later ages of the Church, many theologians drew upon this "cornerstone" motif as a means of explaining the relationship of the disciple to Christ. In discussing the necessity of Christian baptism, St. Augustine appropriates the passage "Without the cornerstone which is Christ, I do not see how men can be built into a house of God, to contain God dwelling in them, without being born again, which cannot happen before they are born the first time."[75]

In the twentieth century, at Vatican II, *Lumen Gentium* articulated its ecclesiological vision in no small part upon this cornerstone imagery: "Often the Church has also been called the building of God.[76] The Lord Himself compared Himself to the stone which the builders rejected, but which was

---

71. Davies and Allison, *Critical and Exegetical Commentary,* 185, emphasis added.

72. Psa. 120–34.

73. Ratzinger, *Jesus of Nazareth, Part Two. Holy Week: From the Entrance into Jerusalem to the Resurrection* (San Francisco: Ignatius Press, 2011), 145–46. See Psa. 118:22: "The stone which the builders rejected has become the head of the corner."

74. This New Testament text makes allusions to Isa. 8:14 and 28:16: "Behold, I am laying in Zion for a foundation a stone, a tested stone, *a precious cornerstone,* of a sure foundation."

75. St. Augustine, *Letters* 187.31.

76. See 1 Cor. 3:9.

made into the cornerstone.[77] On this foundation the Church is built by the apostles,[78] and from it the Church receives durability and consolidation. This edifice has many names to describe it: the house of God[79] in which dwells His family; the household of God[80] in the Spirit; the dwelling place of God among men; and, especially, the holy temple. This Temple, symbolized in places of worship built out of stone, is praised by the Holy Fathers and, not without reason, is compared in the liturgy to the Holy City, the New Jerusalem. As living stones we here on earth are built into it."[81]

The Coming Destruction of the Temple

The discussion now turns to passages in the Synoptic Gospels that deal, in one way or another, with the coming destruction of the Temple and Jesus's prophetic announcements pertaining to it. Understood within a broader Catholic theological framework, the importance of these sayings is twofold. First, such sayings place Jesus squarely in the prophetic tradition of the Old Testament who preceded him. Reminiscent of prophets such as Micah[82] and Jeremiah,[83] Jesus warned that the sinful neglect of the Temple amounted to the sinful neglect of the God who dwelt within it. As the prophets before him, Jesus warned that such stubborn and unrighteous behavior would lead to the imminent demise of the Temple.

This prophetic role of Jesus in regard to the destruction of the Temple holds a second level of importance of these Synoptic sayings. They prepare the Gospel audiences for the Passover of Jesus: "On the threshold of his Passion Jesus announced the coming destruction of this splendid building, of which there would not remain 'one stone upon another.'[84] By doing so, he announced a sign of the last days, which were to begin with his own Passover."[85]

---

77. Matt. 21:42. See Acts 4:11; 1 Pet. 2:7; Psa. 117:2.

78. See 1 Cor. 3:11.   79. See 1 Tim. 3:15.

80. See Eph. 2:19–22.

81. *Lumen Gentium*, 6. "Dogmatic Constitution on the Church: *Lumen Gentium*," in *Vatican II Documents* (Vatican City: Libreria Editrice Vaticana, 2011).

82. E.g., Mic. 3:12: "Therefore because of you Zion shall be plowed as a field; Jerusalem shall become a heap of ruins, and the mountain of the house a wooded height." See also Mic. 1:1–3.

83. E.g., Jer. 7:4: "Do not trust in these deceptive words: 'This is the temple of the Lord, the temple of the Lord, the temple of the Lord.'" See also Jer. 6:2, 11:9–13, 26:18, 51:11–12.

84. See Matt. 24:1–2.

85. *Catechism of the Catholic Church*, §585.

None of the Temple sayings in the Synoptic Gospels are as explicit as that of the Gospel of John. There, it will be recalled, in presenting Jesus's Temple action (John 2:13–22), the Evangelist adds the remarkable comment that Jesus "spoke of the temple of His body" (v. 22). Jesus's prophetic statements concerning the Temple in the Synoptics anticipate a definitive end of the Jerusalem Temple surrounded by the judgment of God. It is only when one reads such temple warnings in light of the Institution of the Eucharist in the Upper Room Discourse that they can be seen, in Catholic theology, as the great foreshadowing of a new liberation from sin, which will take place apart from the stone edifice of the Jerusalem Temple. "The new Passover ... is Jesus himself, and the true liberation is taking place now, through his love that embraces all mankind."[86]

Before examining some of these Synoptic texts, a word of caution is in order. One must not mistake the prophetic utterances of Jesus as a displeasure *with the Temple itself*. It is rather the pride and corruption of those entrusted with the care of the Temple at which Jesus takes aim—at those who have neglected their duties before God and before Israel, not the daily sacrifices, the feasts, or the priestly office. The Temple authorities are the recipients of some of Jesus's sharpest barbs.[87] Such conflict scenes with Temple authorities set the stage for Jesus's prophetic words about the coming judgment of God upon such theological delinquency.

Such sayings may be categorized as follows. First, there are those that are said in or near the Temple itself. These tend to be among the most direct and explicit. A second type of pronouncement about the Temple's destruction takes place further from the Temple and is often presented in less direct, more cryptic ways.

Among the first type, the most explicit text is undoubtedly found in Mark 13, often known as the Little Apocalypse, so called because of the revelatory language and that St. Mark presents Jesus's warnings as tantamount to a transformation of the world order.[88] "And as he came out of the Temple, one of his disciples said to him, 'Look, Teacher, what wonderful stones and what wonderful buildings!' And Jesus said to him, 'Do you see these great buildings? There will not be left here one stone upon another that will not be thrown down'" (Mark 13:1–2).

86. Ratzinger, *Jesus of Nazareth, Part Two*, 147.
87. E.g., Matt. 3:7, 12:34, 22:18, 23:13; Luke 3:7, 12:56, 13:15.
88. See, e.g., Donahue and Harrington, *Gospel of Mark*, 378. "The conviction that the world

This prophecy of the coming destruction of the Temple by Jesus must have certainly dismayed his disciples. First, on a purely physical level, the beauty and grandeur of Herod's Temple exceeded most of the seven wonders of the ancient world. It was more than twice the size of the Acropolis in Athens. How could it be "thrown down," and by whom? The Romans? Would not God spare them such a catastrophe? Jesus's prophecy came to fruition just a generation after his death, precisely in 70 AD, when the Romans conquered Jerusalem under Titus, who burned the Temple to the ground. Second, and more deeply, the notion that this could happen in the future was so cataclysmic to the disciples' worldview that it could only happen as part of the end of the age altogether.

As Adela Yarbro Collins observes in her commentary on this text, Jesus's saying as preserved by Mark offers no hope of a new Temple or later rebuilding of any sort.[89] Yet, unlike Pesch, Yarbro Collins views the text as a *vaticinium ex eventu*, a "prophecy after the fact," corresponding to events that subsequently took place a generation after the crucifixion of Jesus.[90] Her argument rests upon the notion that "the western wall is, in effect, part of the foundation of the temple and still stands today."[91] Yet this seems too strict of a judgment against the prophetic dimension of the saying; by any reasonable standard, the Temple was gone. Whereas Yarbro Collins expresses skepticism about the prophetic nature of Mark 13, choosing to refer to the saying instead as "hyperbolic," Pesch and others interpret the text as true prophecy—or at least leave open the possibility of such.[92]

---

would be transformed and that [Jesus's disciples] would reign with the risen Jesus in glory gave them a horizon of hope against which they could interpret their present sufferings, and the insistence on constant vigilance helped them to find significance and ethical direction in their actions in the present" (382).

89. Collins and Attridge, *Mark*, 601.

90. Rudolf Pesch, *Das Markusevangelium* I. Teil: *Einleitung und Kommentar zu Kap. 1,1–8,26* (HTK 2.1; Freiburg: Herder, 1976 [5th ed., 1989]), and *Das Markusevangelium* II. Teil: *Kommentar zu Kap. 8,27–16,20* (HTK 2.2; Freiburg: Herder, 1977 [4th ed., 1991]): 2:271.

91. Collins and Attridge, *Mark*, 601. In contrast, see Pesch and Gerd Theissen, *The Gospels in Context: Social and Political History in the Synoptic Tradition* (Minneapolis: Fortress, 1991). Evangelical Theology of Gerd Theissen, *Lokalkolorit und Zeitgeschichte in den Evangelien: Ein Beitrag zur Geschichte der synoptischen Tradition*, NTOA 8 (Freiburg: Universitätsverlag Freiburg; Göttingen: Vandenhoeck & Ruprecht, 1989), 259.

92. "Jesus, standing in the prophetic tradition, may very well have prophesied the destruction of the Second Temple." Craig A. Evans, *Mark 8:27–16:20*, vol. 34B, *Word Biblical Commentary* (Dallas: Word Books, 2001), 300. See also Donahue and Harrington, *Gospel of Mark*, 368.

Those who view the saying as an authentic prophetic saying, rooted in Jesus's self-identification with the earlier prophets, have made the better argument. For now, this question will be set aside in order to consider St. Mark's placement of this saying in the Gospel. Jesus's saying is "the hinge on which the Passion Narrative turns. By predicting the doom of the Temple, Jesus makes clear to his disciples that he is fully prescient of what lies ahead, and by reporting this the evangelist makes Jesus' prior knowledge clear to his readers, as they live on the eve of the prophecy's fulfillment."[93]

One final point needs to be made about this text. Even prior to Mark 13, Jesus engaged the Temple authorities who, upon delivering his Parable of the Vineyard, seek to kill him (Mark 12:10). Earlier, in Mark 11, when arriving in Jerusalem from Bethany, and being hungry, Jesus seeks sustenance but finds none on the fig tree (Mark 11:12–14). His "curse" upon the tree ("May no one ever eat fruit from you again") is heard by the disciples, a detail by St. Mark that indicates its theological significance.

Importantly, the temple action of Jesus (Mark 11:15–19) is deliberately wedged between Jesus's first encounter of the barren fig tree and his return past the same tree the next day, when it is found to have "withered away" (Mark 11:20). This intentional "sandwiching" of Jesus's action in the Temple provides a decisive lens for reading his actions in the Court of the Gentile— like the about-to-be-withered fig tree, the days of the Temple and its barren fruit are numbered. In a sense, these three scenes in Mark represent both the first (i.e., direct) and second (i.e., indirect) types of sayings about the destruction of the Temple.

The next example is of the second type: sayings in the Synoptic Gospels that do not take place in the precinct of the Temple but clearly warn of its coming destruction. Here, the conversation moves from Mark to the Gospel of Matthew. The text reads as follows: "Thus, when you give alms, sound no trumpet before you, as the hypocrites do in the synagogues and in the streets, that they may be praised by men. Truly, I say to you, they have received their reward. But when you give alms, do not let your left hand know what your right hand is doing, so that your alms may be in secret; and your Father who sees in secret will reward you" (Matt. 6:2–5).

First, it should be made clear that at issue here is not the giving of alms as an extension of the Temple's ministry to the poor. Such would be un-

---

93. Evans, *Mark 8:27–16:20*, 300.

characteristic of Jesus's love of the poor, and expectation for their care and well-being.[94] Moreover, it would fly directly in the face of such commandments in the Torah (e.g., Deut. 15:11). What is at stake is the heart of the one who gives alms: "What is being criticized is its misuse for self-glorification."[95]

Second, the above saying, which is presented in the context of the Sermon on the Mount in Galilee, mentions "synagogues and streets," while Jesus's saying may have origins closer to the Jerusalem Temple. More specifically are the "trumpet-shaped" collection boxes for the poor, located in in the Court of Women: "The larger Court of Women covered a space upwards of approximately 200 feet square. All around ran a simple colonnade, and within it, against the wall, the thirteen chests, or 'trumpets,' for charitable contributions were placed ... It was probably into one of these that the poor widow dropped her 'two mites' (Luke 21:2). These thirteen chests were narrow at the mouth and wide at the bottom, shaped liked trumpets, whence their name. Their specific objects were carefully marked on them. Nine were for the receipt of what was legally due by worshippers; the other four for strictly voluntary gifts ... It is probably in ironical allusion to the form and name of these treasure-chests that the Lord, making use of the word 'trumpet,' describes the conduct of those who, in their almsgiving, sought glory from men as 'sounding a trumpet' before them—that is, carrying before them, as it were, in full display one of these trumpet-shaped alms-boxes (literally called in the Talmud, 'trumpets'), and, as it were, sounding it."[96]

With this background in mind, a connection begins to emerge, between the more explicit saying about the destruction of the Temple in Mark 13 and Jesus's temple action in the preceding chapter, which is deliberately wedged between the discussion of the fig tree that was barren and about to be destroyed. About this, Davies and Allison conclude that St. Matthew is attempting to explain "what exactly is characteristic of the community of

---

94. See Matt. 5:3, 11:5, 19:21; Mark 10:21; Luke 4:18, 7:22, etc.

95. Davies and Allison, *Critical and Exegetical Commentary*, 578.

96. "Into Trumpet Three, those women who had to bring turtledoves for a burnt—and a sin—offering dropped their equivalent in money, which was daily taken out and a corresponding number of turtledoves offered. This not only saved the labor of so many separate sacrifices, but spared the modesty of those who might not wish to have the occasion or the circumstances of their offering to be publicly known. *Into this trumpet Mary the mother of Jesus must have dropped the value of her offering when the aged Simeon took the infant Savior 'in his arms, and blessed God.'*" Alfred Edersheim, *The Temple: Its Ministry and Services as They Were at the Time of Jesus Christ* (Peabody, MA: Hendrickson, 1995), 48, 49.

believers in Jesus the Messiah; that is, he is attempting to show us what is new."[97]

The contrasts between what is inward and what is outward, between the heart and that which is external, and between receiving praise not from men but from God are precisely those that appear again in the section in the Gospel of Matthew.[98]

Again, such sayings within the Synoptic tradition are eclipsed by such a full-throated Christological expression found in John, namely, that Jesus was speaking of the "temple of His body" (John 2:19). Nevertheless, the above statement from the Sermon on the Mount reflects the strong critique Jesus had for the corruption of holy Temple practices, such as almsgiving, which apparently devolved both in the Temple, and far from the Temple, in "synagogues and the streets."

The point is crystal clear: the Temple was to be a place of intense holiness because of the presence of God there. When almsgiving or other related activities of charity become "about the external rewards," they lose their inherent value, and become detestable in the eyes of God, evoking Jesus's saying.

A final point may be added about Jesus's words about the coming destruction of the Temple. On the surface of things, it appears that the explanation given to the disciples conflates the destruction of the Temple with the end of the age as two connected events that would occur together. This is not simply the case; the Temple's demise and the "end of the age" were not one in the same event, nor were their fates tied.

To be sure, there is an immanence to *both* future events as described in the Gospel. Yet each had its own "event horizon" as well as distinct characteristics. The truly immanent event was the destruction of the Temple, which would be immediately preceded by its own discrete signals and would happen in the next generation. The "end of the age," while included in the same discourse, was not tied directly to the Temple.

Here, Evans helpfully clarifies the important distinction between Jesus's warnings about the destruction of the Jerusalem Temple and the end of the age: "Jesus' disciples are not to be unduly alarmed; these must happen, but the end time is yet to come. This is because there are many more events that

---

97. Davies and Allison, *Critical and Exegetical Commentary*, 1:620.

98. For yet another example from the Synoptic Gospels, this time in the Gospel of Luke, see the critique of the Pharisee "standing alone" in the Temple praying (Luke 18:9–14).

must take place: nations and kingdoms at war, earthquakes, and famines are among the 'beginning of birth pains.'"[99] He adds that the birth pangs are not an indication of the end, but rather of the need for vigilance by the disciples, as they signify "the crumbling of the old order as it gives way to the kingdom of God, which will finally manifest itself in its fullness."[100] As the disciples await the unfolding of these events, they must look to themselves and be ready.

In sum, what this discussion confirms is that in ways both direct and indirect, Jesus readily critiqued the lack of holiness in the Temple and its official practices. It is best understood as hyperbolic redaction of a later time, of a "looking back" by the Church to what Jesus *would* have said. They are best seen as prophetic words, rooted in Jesus's deep convictions about the Temple and his self-identification with the prophets of the Old Testament and their statements about the Temple.

Conclusion

The Synoptic Gospels made effective use of temple motifs in portraying Jesus as the Divine prophet of God, who anticipated the end of the Jerusalem Temple. The Evangelists express this by presenting Jesus's warnings and critiques of God's coming judgment of the Temple and its artifice. Importantly, these prophecies precede the Passion of Jesus and become a hinge between what proceeds them and the Passion of Jesus. As such, the meaning of these prophetic sayings deepens when read in anticipation of the New Passover, which Jesus inaugurates at the Institution of the Eucharist.

Chapter 16 turns from the temple theology within the Synoptic Gospels to that within the Gospel of John.

99. Evans, *Mark 8:27–16:20*, 313.
100. Ibid.

THE TEMPLE OF HIS BODY

The Gospel of John, Temple Theology in the Fourth Gospel (IV/V)

> The Johannine Prologue makes us realize that the Logos is
> truly eternal, and from eternity is himself God. *God was nev-
> er without his Logos.* The Word exists before creation. Con-
> sequently, at the heart of the divine life there is communion,
> there is absolute gift.
>
> Pope Benedict XVI, *Verbum Domini* §6

Chapter 15 examined temple theology within the Synoptic Gospels. Now
the discussion turns to a new fold, to its presence in the Gospel of John.[1]
Two particular aspects of Johannine theology will be considered: (1) the motif of *doxa* ("glory") and (2) the manner in which Jesus fulfilled the various
Temple feasts.

Jesus Reveals the "Glory of God": A Crucial Theme in St. John's Christology

The recurrent motif of *doxa* (Greek: "glory") is a significant theme
throughout the Gospel of John.[2] It is used far more often than in the Syn-

---

1. As with the previous chapters dealing with the Synoptic Gospels, only those texts prior to the
Passion will be discussed. Temple theology in the Passion Narratives is the topic of chapter 17.

2. "The concept of the glory of God in OT thought offers important background for Johannine
use. In the OT there are two important elements in the understanding of the glory of God: it is a *visible* manifestation of His majesty in *acts of power* ... Since Jesus is the incarnate Word of God, he is an

optic Gospels, "indicating that the concept is of particular importance for Johannine Christology."[3] John 1:14 associates the glory of the Logos with the unique glory of Yahweh of the Old Testament:[4] "And the Word became flesh and dwelt among us, full of grace and truth; we have beheld his glory, glory as of the only Son from the Father."

Numerous other times, St. John makes clear that Jesus manifests the glory of God. The Evangelist's closing remark in the Cana sign underscores that at the heart of the meaning of the miracle is Jesus who now begins to reveal the glory of God: "This, the first of his signs, Jesus did at Cana in Galilee, *and manifested his glory*; and his disciples believed in him" (John 2:11). Later, in chapter five, St. John records what amounts to a Christological discourse, of Jesus "sent-ness" by the Father (John 5:19–30). There, Jesus explains that it is not he who glorifies himself, but the Father who glorifies Jesus: "Jesus answered, '*If I glorify myself, my glory is nothing; it is my Father who glorifies me*, of whom you say that he is your God … Your father Abraham rejoiced that he was to see my day; *he saw it and was glad*'" (John 8:54, 8:57). It is striking that both the first sign of Jesus at Cana heralds the revelation of his glory—as does the final sign recorded by John, that of the raising of Lazarus.

Note the double reference of glory: "But when Jesus heard it he said, 'This illness is not unto death; it is for the glory of God, so that the Son of God may be glorified by means of it'" (John 11:4–5).

In the second half of the Gospel, which is commonly described by biblical theologians as the "Book of Glory," the motif becomes even more central than in the first half. Things take a decisive turn in chapter 12, when Jesus declares, "For this purpose I have come to this hour [see below]. *Father, glorify thy name*. Then a voice came from heaven, '*I have glorified it, and I will glorify it again*'" (John 12:27–29).

Outside of the Passion narrative in John, one of the richest examples of the glory motif is found just prior to it, as Jesus prays to the Father in chapter 17: "When Jesus had spoken these words, he lifted up his eyes to heaven and said, Father, the hour has come; *glorify thy Son that the Son may glorify thee*,

---

embodiment of divine glory (1:14). The two elements of *kabod* are present in him. He represents the visible divine presence exercising itself in mighty acts." Raymond E. Brown, *The Gospel According to John (I–XII): Introduction, Translation, and Notes*, vol. 29, *Anchor Yale Bible* (New Haven, CT: Yale University Press, 2008), 503.

3. J. A. Dennis, *Dictionary of Jesus and the Gospels*, 2nd ed., s.v. "Glory."
4. Ibid.

since thou hast given him power over all flesh, to give eternal life to all whom thou hast given him. And this is eternal life, that they know thee the only true God, and Jesus Christ whom thou hast sent. *I glorified thee on earth*, having accomplished the work which thou gavest me to do; and now, Father, *glorify thou me in thy own presence with the glory which I had with thee before the world was made*" (John 17:1–5).

Above all, St. John depicts the Passion of Jesus "as the event that reveals both Jesus' glory[5] and the Father's glory,[6] so that in Jesus' death the Father's glorification of the Son and the Son's glorification of the Father are inextricably connected."[7] Given this emphasis on glory, to what end is it employed in the Gospel of John?

The Evangelist's use of glory depicts Jesus as the divine agent of God, who alone reveals the glory of God. For St. John, this revelation of God's glory is, in some sense, dispensed to all who come into contact with Jesus; for example, John the Baptist, Nicodemus, the Samaritan woman, those he healed and taught, and even his adversaries.

Above all, the revelation of God's glory in Jesus is manifest in a special way to his apostles (referred to as "disciples" throughout this Gospel). This mystery is unfolded in John's Prologue (1:1–18). In the opening stanza of the Prologue, the Evangelist begins not with the genealogy of Jesus nor Infancy narratives—as in Matthew and Luke—nor does he start with Jesus's Baptism, as does Mark. Instead, he takes the reader up into the heavenly realms. From the outset, "in the beginning" (1:1), he evokes the language of Genesis.[8]

---

5. See John 7:39, 11:4, 12:16, 12:23.

6. See John 12:28, 13:31–32.

7. Dennis, *Dictionary of Jesus and the Gospels*, 2nd ed., s.v. "Glory." "The second division [of the Gospel], which narrates what happened from the Thursday evening of the Last Supper until Jesus' appearance to his disciples after the resurrection, has all through it the theme of Jesus' return to his Father (13:1, 14:2, 28, 15:26, 16:7, 28, 17:5, 11, 20:17). This return means *the glorification of Jesus* (13:31, 16:14, 17:1, 5, 24), so that the resurrected Jesus appears to his disciples as Lord and God (20:25, 28)— whence our title '*The Book of Glory.*'" in Brown, *Gospel According to John*, cxxxix (emphasis added).

8. Raymond Brown, Ben Witherington, Craig Keener, and a number of other modern biblical scholars have suggested that the language of John's Prologue is reminiscent of the Jewish Wisdom tradition and should not be overlooked. Such "Wisdom Christology" is not new—Origen was one of the first to recognize connections between books like Sirach and Wisdom of Solomon and the Fourth Gospel. Brown writes: "Wisdom is said to be a pure emanation of the glory of the Almighty (Wisd. 7:25)—so also Jesus has the Father's glory which he makes manifest to men (1:14, 8:50, 11:4, 17:5, 22, 24). Wisdom is said to be a reflection of the everlasting light of God (Wisd. 7:26); and in

For St. John, the Gospel is a new Genesis, an entirely New Creation. As such, earlier insights concerning the temple of Creation should already begin to reverberate loudly: "The Gospel begins, as did both the theology and rituals of the Davidic kingship, in the Holy of Holies."[9]

The opening verse of the Prologue (1:1) goes on to declare: "and the Word was with God." In the Greek, the precise language of this important clause is *kai ho logos en pros ton theon.* The Greek phrase that is pertinent here is *pros ton theon* ("with God"). What exactly does St. John mean by this?

Raymond Brown argued that the phrase connotes "accompaniment, accord," that the Logos/Jesus was "with God" in the sense that he was in his company, in happy accord and union, in heaven.[10] Yet Ignace de la Potterie strongly argued for a more nuanced reading, in which *pros ton theon* indicates something more like "towards God," that is, "in the Father's presence" or "at the Father's side."[11] De la Potterie's translation is preferred, not only because of his sound, textually based argument, but also because of the very placement of the phrase at the beginning of the Prologue. To explain: at the end of the Prologue, in verse 18, the Evangelist makes an astounding statement: "No one has ever seen God; the only Son, *who is in the bosom of the Father*, he has made him known."

In the closing verse of the Prologue, it is clear that the Evangelist is not merely depicting the Logos/Jesus as "with God," merely in the sense of his being in God's company, but as in the manner which de la Potterie suggests back in 1:1, that is, "*towards God,* in the Father's presence, at the Father's side."

This is precisely how John 1:1 should be understood, too—so that the opening and closing lines provide an experiential framework for understanding the identity of the Logos, and the relationship of the Logos with the Father: "The Johannine Prologue makes us realize that the Logos is truly eternal, and from eternity is himself God. *God was never without his Logos.*

---

lighting up the path of men (Sir. 50:29), she is to be preferred to any natural light (Wisd. 7:10, 29)—in Johannine thought, God is light (1 John 1:5); and Jesus who comes forth from God is the light of the world and of men (John 1:4–5, 8:12, 9:5), ultimately destined to replace all natural light (Rev. 21:23)." *Gospel According to John*, cxxiii.

9. Margaret Barker, *Temple Theology in John's Gospel* (London: SPCK, 2014), 159.

10. Brown, *Gospel According to John*, 4.

11. Ignace de la Potterie, "L'emploi dynamique de *eis* dans Saint Jean et ses incidences théologiques" [The dynamic use of *eis* in Saint John and its theological implications], *Biblica* 43 (1962): 366–87.

The Word exists before creation. Consequently, at the heart of the divine life there is communion, there is absolute gift."[12]

Coupling John 1:1 and 1:18 together with these insights, St. John's dynamic, relational Christology of the Divine Logos begins to emerge. And the Christology of the Prologue is decisive for understanding the way the Evangelist makes use of "glory" in all that follows in the Gospel. More than that, it bears heavily on understanding the Evangelist's temple theology—all of which justifies close attention to it.

The One Who "Gazes at God" Now "Gazes at His Apostles"

Pope Benedict XVI stressed the point that "God was never with without his Logos," and this Logos, the Evangelist explains, has indeed *seen* God. This is an extraordinary statement, for Scripture is clear elsewhere—as is the Evangelist here—"no one has ever seen God."[13] Yet this raises another theological riddle; according to Scripture, has anyone ever "seen God" or not?

The pertinent theological evidence appears to point in both directions at once, and a sound understanding of what is really contained in the Scriptures requires a nuanced response. On the one hand, Scripture is clear that God is being itself, yet a nonvisible Spirit.[14] He appeared in various theophanic ways in the Old Testament, for example, to Moses in the "burning bush"[15] and in the form of the "angel of the Lord."[16] Moses "spoke with the Lord";[17] Elijah heard him in the "still small voice";[18] and Jacob "wrestled" with God[19] and after the encounter, named the place *Peni-el,* which means "the face of God."

The final words about Moses in the Pentateuch are that "there has not

---

12. Pope Emeritus Benedict XVI, *Verbum Domini* [The Word of the Lord], Apostolic Exhortation (Vatican City: Libreria Editrice Vaticana, 2010), 6.

13. Exod. 33:18, 33:30: "Moses said, 'I pray thee, *show me thy glory'* ... [but God] said, 'you cannot see my face; *for man shall not see me and live.'*"

14. Col. 1:14, "[Jesus] is *the image of the invisible God,* the first-born of all creation"; Rom. 1:20, "Ever since the creation of the world *his invisible nature,* namely, his eternal power and deity, has been clearly perceived in the things that have been made"; 1 Tim. 1:17, "To the King of ages, *immortal, invisible,* the only God, be honor and glory for ever and ever. Amen."

15. See Exod. 3:1–6.

16. The phrase "angel of the Lord" occurs seventy-one times in the canon of the Old Testament: in the Old Testament: Gen. 16:7, 16:9, 16:10, 16:11, 22:11; Num. 22:22; Judg. 2:1, 2:4; 2 Sam. 24:16; Tob. 12:22, etc.

17. Exod. 6:13, 6:28; Lev. 16:1; Num. 1:1, 3:1, etc.

18. See 1 Ki. 19:12.   19. See Gen. 32:22–32.

arisen a prophet since in Israel like Moses, whom the Lord knew *face to face*."[20] All of this seems to suggest a tradition in the Old Testament that certain elect figures; that is, Moses and the prophets did on occasion "see God."

Yet, on the other hand, Scripture is equally clear that one not dare look upon God's countenance—lest he die. God is *"holy, holy, holy."* The high priest, when going into the holy of Holies on the Day of Atonement would shield his own face, lest he see God's countenance over the mercy seat by accident. (He was no doubt helped by massive amounts of incense smoke, flung in every direction!) Even the Seraphim "covered their face" in the Almighty's glorious presence.[21] And again, when Moses prays "Show me thy glory," recall that God does not grant his prayer but says in response, "You cannot see my face; for man shall not see me and live."[22]

Only one tenable solution to this riddle appears possible: while God's special mediators—such as Moses, Jacob, and Elijah—came closer than anyone in Israel to "seeing God," they did not actually see him. Not really, not ever. Deuteronomy's claim that Moses saw God "face to face" is intended to convey the privileged position of God's anointed prophet, Moses, who ascended the mountain of God, delivered the Law to his people, and ransomed them from the evil king. Yet he did not see God face to face.

Returning to the Prologue: the Evangelist appears well aware of this theological dilemma for his Gospel audience—and constructs his Prologue to communicate that the issue is settled. Decisively settled. Only the One who was "with God" in the beginning—from all eternity, Jesus, the Logos of God—he and he alone has indeed seen God.[23] Not only so, but also Jesus sees God in a filial way: as the divine Son. Not Moses, not Jacob, "no one" enjoys that divine status except for Jesus alone. Finally, all of this helps the reader approach the pinnacle of the Prologue, the Incarnation of the divine Son in verse 14: "And the Word became flesh and dwelt among us, full of grace and truth; *we have beheld his glory, glory as of the only Son from the Father.*"

---

20. Deut. 34:10.　　　　　　　　　　21. See Isa. 6:2.

22. Exod. 33:18, 33:30.

23. "St. John implicitly establishes a strong link between the ideas of *Sonship* and *knowledge*. It is precisely because Christ is the Son, that He knows the Father, and can *relate what He sees with the Father*; and it is because He alone is the Son (the only-begotten, the only Son) *that He alone can see and know the Father: Himself excepted, no one has ever seen God ...* This primitive text may possibly have run: '*He has led into the Father's bosom, that is to the Kingdom of Heaven, by giving us to be reborn to the divine life.*'" Marie-Emile Boismard, OP, *Saint John's Prologue* (Bath, UK: Pitman, 1957), 67, 70 (emphases added).

Four points need to be made here. First, and most importantly, it should not be missed that the passage literally reads, "The Word became flesh and tabernacled [Greek: *skeneō*] among us." This expression recalls a passage reminiscent of the Wisdom books. Specifically, Sirach 24:8–10 depicts the Torah, the Law, as Lady Wisdom. She "dances" around the throne of God, and makes the circuit of Heaven. Then, God issues a command to her: make your dwelling among men. Lady Wisdom "finds a habitation" among all people, a nod to the "universality" of true wisdom. But, in particular, she makes her home in Zion, that is, within the Temple. In other words, God's holy Wisdom, Lady Wisdom, tabernacles in the holy Temple. St. John carries this image to its Christological destination, applying the theological movement of Wisdom to the Word, to Jesus. Whether or not John directly alludes to Sirach or whether this journey of Lady Wisdom was merely "in the air" in the first century need not concern the reader.

What is crucial is that the connection is made: Jesus is the new Torah, the Law of God in the flesh. That which "tabernacled" among God's people in the Jerusalem Temple is now *enfleshed* in the person of God's Logos. Jesus is Wisdom incarnate, who tabernacles among humanity.

A second point concerns the "we" of the passage. To whom is St. John referring? This "we" is not likely a reference to the world or even to all of Israel. Rather, as Brown concluded, it likely refers to Jesus's Apostles.[24] Here, the St. John underscores to his hearers the very essence of his apostolic credentials. It is as if he is saying, "The One who from all of eternity has been *gazing at God*—God the Son—has in His boundless grace now *gazed upon me, John, and my fellow apostles*." What stronger claim could St. John assert as to the credibility and power of his eyewitness testimony?[25]

Third, and related, is the phrase "we have seen" in the text. In contrast to the confidence about the "we" (above), this textual phrase is somewhat unclear. Some scholars believe it refers to Christ's miracles, others to the

---

24. Brown, *Gospel According to John*, 13. "This is a more confined use of the first person, for the 'we' is not mankind but the apostolic witnesses, as in the Prologue of 1 John." See 1 John 1:1–3: "That which was from the beginning, *which we have heard, which we have seen with our eyes, which we have looked upon and touched with our hands*, concerning the word of life— the life was made manifest, *and we saw it, and testify to it, and proclaim to you* the eternal life which was with the Father *and was made manifest to us*—that which *we have seen and heard we proclaim also to you*, so that you may have fellowship with us; and our fellowship is with the Father and with his Son Jesus Christ."

25. See John 21:24.

Transfiguration. Given that both are possible, or even that the "whole span" of Christ's public ministry is in view, these various solutions remain as possible interpretations.[26]

Fourth—and this point brings the reflection on the Prologue to a conclusion—why does Moses unexpectedly enter the discussion in verse 17? The verse reads, "For the law was given through Moses; grace and truth came through Jesus Christ." Is this statement out of place? No; to the contrary, the Evangelist introduces Moses to make a startling contrast: Moses is said to have "seen God," but only the Logos/Jesus, the divine Son, has "truly seen God," and only he is capable of "revealing God" to us. In other words, Jesus is greater than Moses. Jesus is the New Moses, the true Revealer, the true Law Giver, the true Redeemer.

And so it follows in his Gospel: just as Moses's first sign was turning the water of the Nile into blood,[27] Jesus's first sign was turning water into wine—prefiguring the chalice of the Last Supper—and the holy Eucharist.[28] Moses built the Tabernacle according to the heavenly pattern.[29] Jesus is the heavenly pattern, the Temple in the flesh.[30] Moses parted the Sea[31]—Jesus walks upon the waves.[32] Moses called down the manna from heaven[33]—Jesus is the true Bread from Heaven.[34] And so on.

Obviously, the above findings are crucial for interpreting John 1:1–18, but given that the Prologue is a kind of overture of the Gospel, the Evangelist's intentions appear to be preparatory: all that is said in the Prologue, of Jesus's "seeing God" and as the One greater than Moses, prepares the reader for the revelation of his glory throughout the Gospel—in his signs and, above all, as he is "lifted up" on the Cross in his Passion.

26. On the view that "we have seen" refers to the Transfiguration, see: Barker, *Temple Theology in John's Gospel*, 173. Boismard holds that it may be either the Transfiguration or Christ's miracles. *Saint John's Prologue*, 70. The approach taken here—informed by 1 John 1:1–3—is that "we have seen" refers to the company of the Twelve.

27. See Exod. 7:20.

28. See John 2:1–11.

29. See Exod. 25:9, 25:40.

30. See John 2:19–22.

31. See Exod. 14:21–22; see chapter 15.

32. See John 6:19–21.

33. See Exod. 16:4.

34. See John 6:31–58.

The Christological Temple

St. John wastes no time in developing his temple theology. In the first chapter alone there are at least three occurrences.

1. "Behold, the Lamb of God" (John 1:29, 1:36). The lamb was the primary sacrificial animal of the Temple and was especially associated with Passover.[35] In John, the expression is delivered by John the Baptist about Jesus, and it is worth noting that this is Jesus's first appearance in the Gospel.

2. "Ascending and Descending" (John 1:51).[36] Jesus makes a direct reference to Jacob's dream, of the ladder reaching from earth to heaven, with angels "ascending and descending" upon it.[37] Jacob renames the place Beth-el, literally "House of God."[38] As such, the sanctuary at Bethel was a prefigurement of the Tabernacle/Temple. Yet, in John, Jesus replaces the figures of angels with the figure of the Son of Man. St. John could not be clearer here: Jesus is the ladder of God, the Holy of Holies, the new Temple. As St. Ambrose writes, "Jacob set out and slept—evidence of tranquility of spirit—and saw angels of God ascending and descending. This means he foresaw Christ on earth; the band of angels was descending to Christ and ascending to him, so as to render service to their rightful master in loving service."[39]

3. "The Holy One of God" (John 6:69). Later, in the Bread of Life Discourse, Peter will declare that Jesus is "the holy one of God."[40] This phrase was used "exclusively of Aaron in the Bible (Psa. 106:16; Num. 16:7; Sir. 45:6)."[41]

---

35. See Exod. 12:3, 12:4, 12:5, 12:21, 13:13; Lev. 3:7, 4:32, 4:35; 5:6, 5:7, 12:6, 12:8; Num. 6:12, 6:14, 7:15, 7:21, 7:27, 7:33, 7:39, 7:45, 7:51, 7:63, 7:75, 7:81; 2 Chron. 30:15, 30:17; Ezra 6:20; Ezek. 46:13; Mark 14:12; Luke 22:7.

36. John 1:51: "Truly, truly, I say to you, you will see heaven opened, and *the angels of God ascending and descending upon the Son of man.*"

37. See Gen. 28:10–17.

38. Gen. 28:17: "How awesome is this place! This is none other than the house of God, and this is the gate of heaven."

39. St. Ambrose, *Jacob and the Happy Life* 2.4.16 87.

40. John 6:69.

41. Crispin Fletcher-Louis, *Dictionary of Jesus and the Gospels*, 2nd ed., s.v. "Priests and Priesthood."

Jesus's Temple Action (John 2:13–22)

How is one to interpret Jesus's actions in the Temple?[42] A more conventional approach is to view Jesus's activity as a "righteous indignation," along the lines of the Old Testament prophets. This is true, but it stops well short of the deeper meaning.

Perrin suggests that Jesus's action is less about just anger, and is rather more parabolic, a "carefully orchestrated gesture."[43] First, Jesus's action has a twofold meaning: it is indeed "a prophetic indictment against the regnant temple administration" but also indicates "his own role of (re)builder of the eschatological temple."[44] Driving out the merchants and money changers, he rebukes them for making "His Father's house a house of trade." Jesus's actions and words here should be understood in light of Zechariah 14:21, which says of the eschatological temple: "there shall no longer be a trader in the house of the Lord of hosts on that day."

Second, and on an all-too-often overlooked note, Jesus's action would have brought chaos to the normal transactions in the Temple, thereby disrupting the daily sacrifices. If Perrin is correct, the parabolic nature of Jesus's actions would have spoken louder than words: the sacrifices of this Temple *will one day cease*. Soon thereafter, they did, in 70 AD, when the Romans destroyed the Temple.

Third, St. John provides the Christological meaning of the scene to a head: "The Jews then said, 'It has taken forty-six years to build this temple, and will you raise it up in three days?' *But he spoke of the temple of his body.* When therefore he was raised from the dead, his disciples remembered that he had said this; and they believed the scripture and the word which Jesus had spoken" (John 2:20–22). Here, the Evangelist could not be clearer— Jesus spoke of the Temple of his own body? St. John has established that Je-

---

42. It is beyond the scope of this chapter to enter the debate over the "placement" of the Temple scene at the beginning of the Gospel of John, whereas all three Synoptic accounts have it at the end of their respective Gospels. On this debate, see Lucius Nereparampil, *Destroy This Temple: An Exegetico-Theological Study on the Meaning of Jesus' Temple-Logion in Jn 2:19* (Bangalore: Dharmaram, 1978); Brown, *Gospel According to John*, 113–25.

43. Nicholas Perrin, *Jesus the Temple* (Grand Rapids, MI: Baker Academic, 2012), 91.

44. Ibid., 92. Perrin adds: "There was no room for half-measures. Those who witnessed the temple action would be forced to respond, either to oppose Jesus and all he stood for, or to stand courageously with Him and His movement until the end. But woe, Jesus intimates, to the one who chooses poorly" (113).

sus is the Son of God, the Messiah, the One who reveals God ... but how was his body a Temple? His meaning is inexplicable apart from his sacrificial death as the Passover lamb of the New Covenant.

Jesus Transforms the Temple Feasts

The Temple was the place of Jewish pilgrimage. Three times a year, all the men of Israel were required to journey to the Temple to celebrate the feasts of Passover, Pentecost, and Tabernacles.[45] For Israelites, participating in these feasts meant undergoing water washings (ablutions) to enter a state of ritually purity.[46] Only then were Israelites able to offer sacrifice[47] and participate in the feast, which principally involved eating:[48] usually the meat of the sacrifice,[49] with bread[50] and wine,[51] the fruits of the Promised Land.[52]

Passover. As noted, Jesus's temple action ("cleansing") occurs at Passover—the first of three mentions of consecutive Passover feasts in this Gospel.[53] The second Passover in John is the backdrop for the Bread of Life Discourse.[54] The theology of the Bread of Life Discourse is highly Eucharistic. Four points may be stressed.

1. Unlike the Synoptic Gospels, St. John does not include the narrative of the institution of the Eucharist in his Upper Room Discourse (chaps. 13–17). Yet his language closely parallels the narratives of the institution of the Eucharist in the Synoptic Gospels and in St. Paul.[55] The Evangelist engages the tradition in a distinctly Johannine way, yet he engages it nonetheless. One

---

45. See Deut. 16:1–17.

46. See Exod. 19:10–11; 2 Chron. 30:17–20; Lev. 11–15, esp. 15:31.

47. See Deut. 16:2, 16:6; Lev. 23:8.

48. See Deut. 16:3, 16:7–8; see also Lev. 7:11–17; 2 Chron. 30:22; Isa. 25:6.

49. See Deut. 16:4, 16:7.

50. See Deut. 16:3; Lev. 23:6.

51. See Isa. 25:6; Luke 22:18, 22:20.

52. See Deut. 16:13. It is not possible to engage in a lengthy discussion of each of Jesus's feast; only those elements that pertain to temple theology will be dealt with here.

53. See John 2:13, 6:4, 11:55, 12:1. This signals a three-year ministry according to John's narrative. In contrast, the Synoptic Gospels indicate one Passover: Matt. 26:2ff.; Mark 14:1ff.; Luke 22:1ff.

54. See John 6:35–71.

55. Cf. John 6:11; Mark 14:22; Luke 22:19; 1 Cor. 11:23–24, observing the correlation of terms, usually in sequence: "take" (*lambano*), "bread" (*artos*), "give thanks" (*eucharisteia*), and "gave/distributed" (*didimi*). See Brown, *Gospel According to John*, 247–48.

might add the St. John's treatment of the scene is deeply Christological and sacramental.

2. There is an array of motifs in the Discourse that are highly evocative of the Institution, including: the proximity of Passover, the body of Christ *given for* others, and the equation of Jesus's body with bread and the eating of his body and drinking of his blood.

3. Jewish expectations for the coming Messiah included the hope that the manna—the supernatural food that God provided for his people on the way to the Promised land, and which ceased once they crossed into the Promised Land—would return when the Messiah came: "And it shall come to pass when all is accomplished that was to come to pass in those parts, that the Messiah shall then begin to be revealed ... And those who have hungered shall rejoice ... And it shall come to pass at that ... that the treasury of manna shall again descend from on high, and they will eat of it in those years, because these are they who have come to the consummation of time" (2 Bar. 29:3, 2:6–8).[56]

4. Finally, there is a close connection between the Upper Room Discourse and the Bread of Life Discourse. The Bread of Life Discourse is immediately preceded by the "sign" of the Multiplication of the Loaves.[57] In other words, there is an anticipation of Jesus's New Passover already in John 6. Hahn explains, "The sign takes place in the context of the Passover and anticipates, in its very language (John 6:11, 23), the last Passover that Jesus will celebrate with his disciples. In the aftermath of this great sign, Jesus engages the crowd in a *mystagogical dialogue* attempting to lead them from the 'fleshly' understanding of the physical miracle[58] to the 'spiritual' realities of Jesus' identity,[59] and to how his presence is continued in the sacrament of the Church[60] through the power of the Spirit."[61]

---

56. See Pitre's helpful discussion of "The Manna of the Messiah," in *Jesus and the Jewish Roots of the Eucharist: Unlocking the Secrets of the Last Supper* (New York: Doubleday, 2011), 77–115. Later, his discussion returns to insights on "The New Passover" (48–76).

57. See John 6:1–14.

58. John 6:26: "you ate your fill of the loaves."

59. John 6:35: "I am the bread of life."

60. John 6:56: "He who eats my flesh and drinks my blood abides in me."

61. S. W. Hahn, "Temple, Sign, and Sacrament: Towards a New Perspective on the *Gospel of John*," *Letter & Spirit* 4 (2008): 124–25. The final Passover will not be discussed here; the Passion narratives are the subject of chapter 17.

The Feast of Tabernacles[62] (John 7:1–10:21) is interspersed between the second and third (and final) Passovers in the Gospel. Clearly, while it is the Temple feast of Passover that dominates in this Gospel, the Feast of Tabernacles is also crucial because it shows the intrinsic connection between the Temple and the sacramental motifs in the Gospel of John. Tabernacles (or Booths, Feast of Ingathering) was originally an annual a seven-day autumn feast, celebrated just five days after the Day of Atonement.[63] It commemorated the wilderness period, when their ancestors lived in booths. There were two liturgical ceremonies that took place in the Temple at the Feast of Tabernacles. The first was a water libation ceremony, in which each day Temple priests would fill a golden pitcher with water from the *Pool of Siloam* and, in a liturgical procession, return to the Temple and pour it over the altar. Theologically, it recapitulated God's provision of water in the desert. Prophetically, it was influenced by the Prophet Zechariah's messianic vision of an eschatological Feast when "living waters"[64] would flow forth from the time of the triumphant Messiah.[65]

The second liturgical custom was a torch-lighting ceremony. Nightly, temple priests would light four massive menorahs in the Court of Women, chanting the *Psalms of Ascent* as they did. The menorahs lit up much of the city with their blazing light. In the time of Jesus, pilgrims lived in booths made of palm branches.[66] Each day there were solemn sacrifices, and in the time of Jesus, an eighth day was added, the Great Day of the Feast.[67] It is pre-

62. "The most joyous of all festive seasons in Israel was that of the 'Feast of Tabernacles.' It fell on a time of year when the hearts of the people would naturally be full of thankfulness, gladness, and expectancy." Alfred Edersheim, *The Temple, Its Ministry and Services as They Were at the Time of Jesus Christ* (Peabody, MA: Hendrickson, 1995), 268. See Edersheim's lengthy and informative discussion of the Feast (268–87).

63. See Exod. 34:22–23; Lev. 23:43; Deut. 16:13–15.

64. Zech. 14:8: "On that day *living waters shall flow out from Jerusalem*, half of them to the eastern sea and half of them to the western sea; it shall continue in summer as in winter."

65. See the description in Craig R. Koester, *Symbolism in the Fourth Gospel: Meaning, Mystery, Community*, 2nd ed. (Minneapolis: Augsburg Fortress, 2003), 157–58. See also Rafael Patai, *Man and Temple* (Bloomington: Indiana University, 1947), 105–17, esp. 117: "The Temple corresponds to the whole world and to the creation of man who is a small world."

66. See Lev. 23:42.

67. Edersheim's description: "It was the last day, that great day of the feast. It obtained this name, although it was not one of 'holy convocation,' partly because it closed the feast, and partly from the circumstances which procured it in Rabbinical writings the designations of '*Day of the Great Hosannah*,' on account of the sevenfold circuit of the altar with '*Hosannah*;' and '*Day of Willows*,' and

cisely then, on the Great Day—and there, in the Temple courts—that Jesus declares two remarkable statements: "On the last day of the feast, the great day, Jesus stood up and proclaimed, '*If any one thirst, let him come to me and drink.*' He who believes in me, as the Scripture has said, '*Out of his heart shall flow rivers of living water*'" (John 7:37).[68] Likewise, in chapter 8, "Again Jesus spoke to them, saying, '*I am the light of the world*; he who follows me will not walk in darkness, but will have *the light of life*'" (John 8:12).

Many Johannine scholars agree that Jesus draws upon the imagery of Tabernacles' liturgical rituals and associates their fulfillment in himself. To make these claims during the feast was tantamount to *declaring himself to be the eschatological Temple.*

In John 9, the theological symbols of water and light are brought togeth-

---

'*Day of Beating the Branches*,' because all the leaves were shaken off the willow boughs, and the palm branches beaten in pieces by the side of the altar. It was on that day, after the priest had returned from Siloam with his golden pitcher, and for the last time poured its contents to the base of the altar; after the '*Hallel*' had been sung to the sound of the flute, the people responding and worshipping as the priests three times drew *the threefold blasts from their silver trumpets*—just when the interest of the people had been raised to its highest pitch, that, from amidst the mass of worshippers, who were waving towards the altar quite a forest of leafy branches as the last words of Psa. 108 were chanted—a voice was raised which resounded through the Temple, startled the multitude, and carried fear and hatred to the hearts of their leaders. *It was Jesus, who 'stood and cried, saying, If any man thirst, let him come unto Me, and drink.' Then by faith in Him should each one truly become like the Pool of Siloam, and from his inmost being 'rivers of living waters flow.'" The Temple*, 280–81.

68. To which the Evangelist adds: "Now this he said about the Spirit, which those who believed in him were to receive; for as yet the Spirit had not been given, because Jesus was not yet glorified" (v. 39). We should add that a similar scene filled with temple theology is located in John 4:4–42, i.e., Jesus and the Samaritan woman. John 4:10, 4:13–14: "Jesus answered her, 'If you knew the gift of God, and who it is that is saying to you, "Give me a drink," you would have asked him, and he would have given you living water'" and "Everyone who drinks of this water will thirst again, but whoever drinks of the water that I shall give him will never thirst; the water that I shall give him will become in him a spring of water welling up to eternal life." Here, Jesus reaches out to the Samaritan woman, who recognizes that "Messiah is coming" (v. 25), and through her he reaches to the Samaritans—part of the "lost tribes" of northern Israel. In the course of the dialogue, they discuss the "proper place of worship." Her ancestors established an alternative temple on "this mountain" (v. 20, i.e., Mt. Gerazim) and not on Mt. Zion in Jerusalem. Jesus's cryptic answer in vv. 23–24 ("The hour is coming, and now is, when the true worshipers will worship the Father in spirit and truth, for such the Father seeks to worship him. God is spirit, and those who worship him must worship in spirit and truth") does not diminish the true sanctuary in Jerusalem. In fact, he declares that "Salvation is from the Jews" (v. 22), a clear reference to the Davidic covenant (and Temple). Yet his response lifts her mind beyond the geography of physical temples to the nature of God, and the reality that his body is the "location" of the new Temple for all of humanity.

er in the sign that Jesus performs here. Just previously, Jesus proclaimed that he is the "light of the world" (8:12). Now, in the healing miracle of the man born blind, Jesus "spits" upon the ground (9:6) and performs other actions. In highlighting these symbolic gestures, St. John is indicating that in this sign following the Feast of Tabernacles, Jesus is recapitulating key elements of the first Creation in Genesis, and in the aftermath of the Feast, announcing the New Creation has already begun. Following the great patristic tradition, St. Thomas has much to add to the theological understanding of this pivotal scene: "Here five things were done by Christ. First, he moistens the earth, *he spat on the ground.* Secondly, he made the clay, as we read, he *made clay of the spittle.* Thirdly, Christ smeared the man's eyes *and anointed the man's eyes.* Fourthly, he commands the man to wash, with *go, wash in the pool of Siloam.* And fifthly, the man's sight is restored, *and he came back seeing.* Each of these has both *a literal and a mystical explanation.*"[69] Finally, Jesus compels the man to "wash in the pool of Siloam" (9:1), the same water source for Tabernacles.

Feast of Dedication. Finally, the Evangelist shows how Jesus recapitulates and elevates the Feast of Dedication ("Hanukah"),[70] which commemorated the rededication of the Temple in the time of the Maccabees.[71] The context is again in the Temple; specifically, the Evangelist writes that "Jesus was walking in the

69. Thomas Aquinas, *Commentary on the Gospel of John: Chapters 1–21*, vol. 2, trans. Fabian Larcher and James A. Weisheipl (Washington, DC: Catholic University of America Press, 2010), 162. Drawing upon St. Chrysostom, St. Gregory, and especially St. Augustine, St. Thomas first draws out the literal meaning and, in the following excerpt, the mystical: "Augustine gives the mystical and allegorical explanation. He says that the spittle, which is saliva that descends from the head, signifies the Word of God, who proceeds from the Father, the head of all things: '*I came forth from the mouth of the Most High*' (Sir. 24:3). Therefore the Lord made clay from spittle and the earth when the Word was made flesh. He anointed the eyes of the blind man, that is, *of the human race.* And the eyes are the eyes of the heart, anointed by faith in the Incarnation of Christ. But the blind man did not yet see, because the anointing produced a catechumen who has faith but has not yet been baptized. So he sends him to the pool of Siloam to wash and receive his sight—i.e., to be baptized—and in baptism to receive full enlightenment. Thus, according to Dionysius, baptism is an enlightenment: 'I will sprinkle clean water upon you, and you shall be clean from all your uncleanness' (Ezek. 36:25). And so this Gospel is appropriately read in Lent, on Holy Saturday, when those about to be baptized are examined. Nor is it without reason that the Evangelist adds the meaning of the pool, saying, *which means Sent,* because whoever is baptized must be baptized in Christ, who was sent by the Father: 'As many of you as were baptized in Christ have put on Christ' (Gal. 3:27). For if Christ had not been sent, none of us would have been freed from sin."

70. See John 10:22–42.

71. See 1 Macc. 4:36–59; 2 Macc. 6:1–2, 6:19, 10:1–8. "From then onwards, on the twenty-fifth day of the month of Kislev (November–December) and throughout the following week, all Judea

Temple, in the portico of Solomon."[72] Keener explains: "Jesus declares here, 'I am the Good Shepherd,'[73] assuming a role commonly assigned to the Lord himself in earlier Scripture. By contrast, those who have abused him are not Israel's rightful leaders but rather are predators (thieves, robbers, wolves) who do not have the sheep's best interest in view; they resemble the false shepherds of Israel as denounced by the prophets ... Ultimately, Jesus' sheep would include those scattered beyond the Holy Land; they would become one flock with one shepherd ... This mission 'beyond Israel' [was already] prefigured in Jesus' ministry to the Samaritans, who recognize Him as 'Savior of the world.'"[74]

Concluding Remarks

This chapter covered considerable ground, yet it is likely that this discussion merely scratched the surface, as the temple theology within the Gospel of John is quite rich. The motif of *doxa* ("glory") was examined, and how in his Prologue John expresses that the Logos was "with God" in a divine and intimately personal—filial—way. As such, he and only he—and not Moses, Jacob, Elijah, or any Old Testament figure that had a close encounter with God—is the One who "sees" God and reveals God to his holy apostles.

The discussion moved on to assess a number of Christological expressions in the Gospel of John. As the "Lamb of God," Jesus is the new and eternal sacrifice of the New Passover—already in John 1, the Evangelist prepares his readers for the revelation of God's glory, as the Lamb of God and Son of God sheds his blood for the sake of Israel, for the sake of all the world. Jesus's response to Nathanael recalls Jacob's ladder at Beth-el, and, again, the Evangelist depicts Jesus as the Son of Man, the "house of God" in person, the One in whom angels ascend and descend. Peter's response to Jesus in the Bread of Life Discourse, "You are the Holy One of God," takes language reserved for Aaron and applies it to Jesus, the eternal High Priest.

Finally, this chapter analyzed major feasts in first-century Judaism and

---

celebrated the anniversary of the dedication of the new altar. It was also known as the 'festival of lights' because it was customary to light lamps, a symbol of the Law, and put them in the windows of the houses (cf. 2 Macc. 1:18)." *Saint John's Gospel, The Navarre Bible* (Dublin: Scepter, 2005), 122.

72. John 10:23.

73. John 10:11, 10:14.

74. Craig Keener, "Johannine Theology," *Dictionary of Jesus and the Gospels*, 2nd ed., s.v. "John, Gospel of."

how, through them, St. John presents Jesus as the fulfillment of each one in his Gospel. First, Jesus "cleanses" the Temple at Passover, a prophetic indication of the demise of the physical Temple and its replacement by "the Temple of His body" (John 2:21).

Even more, the cessation of Temple sacrifices, caused by his unexpected actions, prefigures his sacrifice on the Cross, which surpasses and fulfills the meaning of all earlier sacrifices, which, in his death, are rendered obsolete. The Second Passover was the occasion for the Bread of Life Discourse, in which Jesus presents himself as *the new manna*, the true Bread from Heaven, given for the life of the world. He does this immediately after the *multiplication of the loaves*, along with a number of highly Eucharistic features.

Second, Jesus transforms the meaning of the Feast of Tabernacles, declaring that the "living water" of the Spirit will flow out of believers' hearts, and that he is the "light of the world." As such, he transforms and elevates the meaning of Tabernacles, filling them with fresh meaning and the hope of eternal life.

Third and finally, at the Feast of Dedication, Jesus reveals himself to be the True Shepherd, recapitulating a traditional image from the Old Testament ascribed to God himself. He is contrasted with the temple leaders as the "Good Shepherd" who lays down his life for his sheep—another allusion to his coming Passover. Moreover, the Good Shepherd unites his flock in the eternal love of the Father, surpassing Moses, David, and all of the shepherds of Israel's past and present.

On a personal and spiritual note, the reader may find it of interest that the final editing of this chapter, concerning temple theology in the Gospel of John, was actually done on a stone slab *inside the fourth-century Capernaum synagogue*, which stands directly over the first-century synagogue, where Jesus himself uttered those very words.[75]

Chapter 17 turns from the temple theology of the Gospel of John to that within the Passion and Resurrection narratives of all Four Gospels.

---

75. This tremendous privilege presented itself during my ninth pilgrimage to the Holy Land in January 2017. Though the chapter had been written, it seemed almost wrong, when the opportunity presented itself and having the electronic version of the manuscript with me at the time, *to not work out the finishing touches* in the Capernaum synagogue itself.

17

BLOOD AND WATER

*The Passion of the Christ, Temple Theology
in the Four Gospels (V/V)*

Jesus of Nazareth, the Messiah of Israel, takes *up and transforms Israel's Temple and Torah* by His saving work, culminating in His Paschal mystery of suffering, death and Resurrection.

Matthew Levering

Having closely examined the Four Gospels in the previous chapters, the
reader is now armed with numerous examples of temple theology within
them—except for the Passion of Jesus. Restraint has been made from crossing the threshold of the Passion narratives until now, so that it might be presented in a more singular and concentrated manner. This is the purpose of
the present chapter, and here the Passion narratives of all Four Gospels will
be considered together. Attention will be paid to the Resurrection and Ascension of Jesus as well. Finally, in order to properly understand the meaning
of the Passion as it pertains to the Temple, the narrative of the Last Supper
will be taken into account in the context of the Cross.

Note that the sole criterion that determines which texts from the Passion,
Resurrection, and Ascension narratives are included here is that they bear
upon temple theology *in some direct fashion*. As a result, a number of texts of
interest to the reader are absent from the discussion based upon this measure.

Epigraph. Matthew Levering, *Christ's Fulfillment of Temple and Torah* (Notre Dame, IN: University of Notre Dame Press, 2002), 128.

The Significance of the Cross in Temple Theology

In a sense, all of the strands of temple theology that have been examined so far in the book—clear back to the discussion of the cosmic temple of Eden, right through to the many developments concerning the Tabernacle and Jerusalem Temple—all converge here. They all lead to the Cross; not just to the ministry of Jesus, *but all the way to the Cross* and beyond it. Here is why: "The rejection and crucifixion of Jesus means at the same time the end of this Temple. The era of the Temple is over. A new worship is being introduced, in a Temple not built by human hands. This Temple is His body, the Risen One, who gathers the peoples and unites them in the sacrament of his body and blood. He himself is the new Temple of humanity. The crucifixion of Jesus is at the same time the destruction of the old Temple. With his Resurrection, a new way of worshipping God begins, no longer on this or that mountain, but 'in spirit and truth' (John 4:23)."[1]

Yves Congar agrees and adds: "Jesus truly transferred to His own Person the privilege, long held by the Temple, of being the place where man would find God's presence and salvation, and the starting point of every form of holiness ... Christ's body will be true sanctuary only by passing through death and resurrection ... By stating that His body would become this sanctuary by way of condemnation and a glorious resurrection, he also made it clear that the one true sanctuary is the immolated body ... [Here] we are at the heart of the whole work of Jesus, the work which His Father had given Him to do. It is to this that all God's plans leads, it is here that all its strands are gathered together."[2]

What Happened on Good Friday?

What happened on Good Friday? Consider this exercise: try to imagine oneself as a Jewish bystander near Calvary. What explanation could be offered to a passerby as to who Jesus was, what happened to him, and why? A natural tendency would be to answer as a twenty-first-century Christian, yet a first-century Jewish response would be well different. In fact, it is highly un-

---

1. Joseph Ratzinger, *Jesus of Nazareth, Part Two. Holy Week: From the Entrance into Jerusalem to the Resurrection* (San Francisco: Ignatius Press, 2011), 21–22.

2. Yves Congar, *The Mystery of the Temple* (New York: Newman Press, 1962), 138–41.

likely that any modern conception would be as accurate as the first-century Jew.

A modern believer might use phrases like sacrificial death, his atonement, or the grace that flows from the Cross. Yet a first-century Jew—perhaps even a follower of Jesus—would not likely offer such a response. Such a person would likely respond as a shocked witness to more Roman cruelty. He or she might tearfully protest his innocence, or of how his mock trial was hurriedly assembled. A courageous believer might even ascribe him honor, referring to him as Lord, perhaps as Prophet or even Son of God.

Yet the language of sacrifice would not likely have dawned upon the Jewish bystander. Nor the Greek: "Sacrifice was permitted in only one city, the holy city of Jerusalem; yet Jesus was crucified outside the city walls. Sacrifice could be offered *in only one place in that holy city:* in the Temple, on the altar, by a priest of the tribe of Levi; yet Calvary was a hill far from the Temple, and it had no altar and no offering priest."[3]

As such, the entire event would have appeared to the observer as a horrific event, another gruesome Roman execution. In the deepest reality, the meaning of Good Friday as a sacrifice—which it surely was—is only explicable in light of the Last Supper: Christ, our paschal Lamb has been sacrificed. St. Paul interpreted Christ's death as a true sacrifice earlier than Gospels.[4] In writing to the church at Corinth, he explains: "Your boasting is not good. Do you not know that a little leaven leavens the whole lump? Cleanse out the old leaven that you may be a new lump, as you really are unleavened. *For Christ, our paschal lamb, has been sacrificed.* Let us, therefore, celebrate the festival, not with the old leaven, the leaven of malice and evil, but with the unleavened bread of sincerity and truth" (1 Cor. 5:6–8).

From a Christian perspective, one can rightly say that St. Paul, illuminated by the Spirit of God, grasped that the Cross was not an "instrument of

---

3. S. W. Hahn, *Consuming the Word: The New Testament and the Eucharist in the Early Church* (New York: Image, 2013), 24.

4. Ibid. "The [New Testament] documents weren't complete till the end of the first century; even then they were not called the 'New Testament' till the end of the second century. The documents only gradually took that name … because of their liturgical proximity to the covenant sacrifice, the Eucharist. They were the *only* books approved to be read in the Eucharistic liturgy, *and they were 'canonized' for that very reason.* Thus, precisely as *liturgical books*, they were called the New Testament." Ibid., 40–41 (emphasis added). He adds: "In all of Jesus' sayings, we find *just one instance* when He used the phrase we translate as 'New Testament,' and He used it to describe neither a will nor a book, *but rather a sacramental bond*" (21).

torture" but an altar of sacrifice. His words are explicable only in light of the Last Supper. Christ, he says, is our *pascha* ("paschal lamb") and has been sacrificed. St. Paul perceived that Jesus's actions in the Last Supper meal transformed his ensuing crucifixion from a state execution to a Temple sacrifice.

But the present study can go further—much further. From an ancient Jewish perspective, St. Paul's insight was not based solely on the inspiration of the Spirit, as essential as that was. Nor was it based on his being present at the Last Supper, as he was not. Rather, it was St. Paul's deep understanding of the Passover of the Old Testament Scriptures. Exodus 12 presents the narrative of the first Passover from Egypt, and with it the precise instructions for its "perpetual memorial"[5] from that point forward. There were five particular steps of instruction in the institution of the original Passover[6] and how Jesus fulfilled this at the Last Supper.[7]

1. Choose an unblemished lamb.[8]
2. Sacrifice the lamb.[9]
3. Spread the blood of the lamb.[10]
4. Eat the lamb.[11]
5. Keep the Passover as a "Day of Remembrance."[12]

A one-year-old unblemished male lamb, free from all defect, was selected. On the fourteenth day of Nisan (March/April), on the eve of Passover, the father of each household sacrificed the lamb for his household.[13] Blood

---

5. Exod. 12:14: "This day shall be for you a memorial day, and you shall keep it as a feast to the Lord; *throughout your generations you shall observe it as an ordinance forever.*"

6. Obviously, these customs evolved over time; e.g., the spreading of the blood was done in the original action but not thereafter. Nevertheless, the basic "pattern" of the Passover was established, and the sacrifice of the Lamb—which was eaten—continued at the time of Jesus.

7. Brant Pitre, *Jesus and the Jewish Roots of the Eucharist: Unlocking the Secrets of the Last Supper* (New York: Doubleday, 2011), 51–76.

8. Exod. 12:1–6. See Pitre, *Jesus and the Jewish Roots of the Eucharist*, 51.

9. Exod. 12:6. See Pitre, *Jesus and the Jewish Roots of the Eucharist*, 52–53.

10. Exod. 12:21–23. See Pitre, *Jesus and the Jewish Roots of the Eucharist*, 53–55.

11. Exod. 12:8–12. See Pitre, *Jesus and the Jewish Roots of the Eucharist*, 53–55.

12. Exod. 12:14. See Pitre, *Jesus and the Jewish Roots of the Eucharist*, 57–59.

13. Beginning in the age of the Jerusalem Temple, worship became centralized. So, in the time period of Jesus, fathers of households did not perform the sacrificial action. Rather, Levitical priests did. Each family would purchase a lamb in Jerusalem and bring it to the priest. See Joachim Jeremias, *Jerusalem in the Time of Jesus*, trans. F. H. Cave and C. H. Cave (Philadelphia: Fortress, 1969), 77–84; Pitre, *Jesus and the Jewish Roots of the Eucharist*, 61; Josephus, *Jewish War*, 6:432–27.

was spread upon the doorposts of every Israelite home with a branch of hyssop.[14] This lamb was roasted with unleavened bread and eaten.

Importantly, "the Passover sacrifice was not complete by the death of the lamb, *but by eating its flesh.*"[15] Finally, this sacrifice was a "perpetual ordinance," a "day of remembrance" to be kept forever more. The Passover traditions evolved over time, such that all sacrifice was done in the Temple at the time of Jesus. Importantly though, on the 14th of Nisan, the lambs were sacrificed in the Temple, and that evening each family consumed the lambs. On the eve of his crucifixion, Jesus celebrated the Passover meal with his disciples in the Upper Room:[16] "And when the hour came, he sat at table, and the apostles with him. And he said to them, '*I have earnestly desired to eat this Passover with you before I suffer;* for I tell you I shall not eat it until it is fulfilled in the kingdom of God.' *And he took a cup,* and when he had given thanks he said, 'Take this, and divide it among yourselves; for I tell you that from now on I shall not drink of the fruit of the vine until the kingdom of God comes.' *And he took bread, and when he had given thanks he broke it and gave it to them, saying, 'This is my body which is given for you. Do this in remembrance of me.' And likewise the cup after supper, saying, 'This cup which is poured out for you is the new covenant in my blood'*" (Luke 22:14–20).

This is the definitive moment that links the Last Supper/New Passover with Jesus's death on the Cross. Jesus is transforming the Old Passover into a "new and everlasting covenant." As such, he is both the eternal High Priest who offers the sacrifice, and the sacrifice itself. Moreover, the Institution of the Eucharist is given specifically to his apostles as a memorial. It was their task to "perpetuate it" just as the priests did in the Temple. As such, Jesus institutes a New Priesthood for the New Temple: "The Eucharist that Christ institutes at that moment will be the memorial of his sacrifice.[17]

---

14. See John 19:29.

15. Pitre, *Jesus and the Jewish Roots of the Eucharist*, 56. This command is stated five times in Scripture.

16. See Matt. 26:26–29; Mark 14:22–25; Luke 22:14–20; John 13:1–2.

17. The Book of 1 Cor. 11:23–26 is considered to be the most primitive tradition of the Institution narrative: "**23** For I received from the Lord what I also delivered to you, that the Lord Jesus on the night when he was betrayed took bread, **24** and when he had given thanks, he broke it, and said, 'This is my body which is for you. Do this in remembrance of me.' **25** In the same way also the cup, after supper, saying, 'This cup is the new covenant in my blood. Do this, as often as you drink it, in remembrance of me.' **26** For as often as you eat this bread and drink the cup, you proclaim the Lord's death until he comes."

Jesus includes the Apostles in his own offering and bids them perpetuate it. By doing so, the Lord institutes his apostles as priests of the New Covenant: 'For their sakes I sanctify myself, so that they also may be sanctified in truth.'"[18] Ratzinger describes how, in Christianity, "Jesus is the Torah in person."[19] In making this point, he asserts that the Gospel of John brings us into direct contact with the truth that Jesus's Apostles are united to Jesus's priestly mission: "we may recognize in these words of John's Gospel the institution of the priesthood of the Apostles, *the institution of the New Testament priesthood*, which at the deepest level is service to the truth."[20]

At the same time, this "New Passover" sacrifice recapitulates the Day of Atonement, in that it accomplishes the "forgiveness of sins" for the sake of the world: "Christ's death is both the Paschal sacrifice that accomplishes the definitive redemption of men, through 'the Lamb of God, who takes away the sin of the world,'[21] and the sacrifice of the New Covenant, which restores man to communion with God by reconciling him to God through the 'blood of the covenant, which was poured out for many for the forgiveness of sins.'"[22]

In *The Spirit of the Liturgy*, Ratzinger explains how the sacrifices of the Old Testament were not like the pagan religions, with the horror of human sacrifice.[23] And yet Israel's "sacrifices, like other ancient near eastern religions, rested on the principle of 'representation,' such that sacrificial animals (or the fruits of harvest) represented man." But how, he asks, does this accomplish atonement? Actually, it cannot: "This is *not representation* but *replacement*, and worship with replacements turns out to be *a replacement for worship*. Somehow the real thing is missing."[24]

To this discussion may be added the Cross of Jesus, as the crucifixion of Jesus is understood as "sacrificial" in Catholic theology. Accordingly, is Jesus's death best understood as "representation" or "replacement"? In a manner of

---

18. *Catechism of the Catholic Church*, §611. See John 17:19.

19. Ratzinger, *Jesus of Nazareth, Part Two*, 90.

20. Ibid., 90 (emphasis added).

21. John 1:29; cf. 8:34–36; 1 Cor. 5:7; 1 Pet. 1:19.

22. *Catechism of the Catholic Church*, §613. See Matt. 26:28; also Exod. 24:8; Lev. 16:15–16; 1 Cor. 11:25.

23. Joseph Ratzinger, *The Spirit of the Liturgy*, trans. John Saward (San Francisco: Ignatius Press, 2000), 37.

24. Ibid. (emphasis added).

speaking, *neither term* is sufficient. The Cross is the ultimate vicarious atonement for humanity. It is not mere representation, nor is the concept of replacement tenable. Rather, the sacrificial death of Jesus involves something—Someone—who transforms sacrifice through love: "The idea of the sacrifice of the Logos becomes a full reality only in the *Logos incarnatus,* the Word who is made flesh and draws 'all flesh' into the glorification of God. When that happens, the Logos is more than just the 'meaning' behind and above things. *Now he himself has entered into flesh, has become bodily.* He takes up into himself our sufferings and hopes, all the yearning of creation, and bears it to God."[25]

Two great themes of Psalm 51, sacrifice and prayerful obedience, are not fully reconciled in that text. Throughout the Old Testament, they keep running toward one another, yet never fully resolved. Now in Jesus, they are brought into perfect harmony. "The Word is no longer just the representation of something else, of what is bodily. In Jesus' self-surrender on the Cross, the *Word is united with the entire reality of human life and suffering.* There is no longer a replacement cult. Now the vicarious sacrifice of Jesus takes us up and leads us into that likeness with God, that transformation into love, which is the only true adoration ... the Eucharist is the meeting point of all the lines that lead from the Old Covenant, indeed from the whole of man's religious history. Here at last is *right worship,* ever longed for yet still surpassing mortal capacity: adoration in spirit and truth. *The torn curtain of the Temple is the curtain torn between the world and the countenance of God.* In the pierced heart of the Crucified, God's own heart is opened up—here we see who God is and what he is like. Heaven is no longer locked up. God has stepped out of his hidden-ness."[26]

The Mystery of the New Passover in the Early Church

The discussion of the Last Supper/New Passover began with a question: how would one explain what happened to Jesus on Good Friday? Biblically speaking, only with assistance from St. Paul, reflecting on the Passion of Jesus, is it possible to perceive the deepest meaning of the Cross, that it was more—much more—than a Roman execution. It was the will of God, to

25. Ibid., 47.
26. Ibid., 48–49 (emphases added).

bring about the salvation of his people and all the world. It was the recapitulation of Passover.

The New Covenant was instituted at the Last Supper, and with it the New Passover and New Priesthood. Also examined, with help from Ratzinger, was how the Cross was not merely another sacrifice, nor was it a mere representation or replacement like the pagan religions, or even in a similar yet different sense the sacrifices of the Old Testament. No—Jesus's death on the Cross was a vicarious, atoning sacrifice, offered in love for the salvation of the whole human race. His death truly accomplished the forgiveness of sins, a ministry that was given to the Apostles, the New Priesthood, to continue to carry out for Jesus's sake and in Jesus's name.

So, while an interesting exercise, the modern believer would not likely have reached the deepest meaning at the foot of the Cross *based solely upon one's own powers of perception*. Thanks especially to St. Paul and Evangelists, and the early Church, which ruminated upon these mysteries, the modern believer has a trustworthy apparatus: Sacred Scripture and Sacred Tradition with which to come to a fuller understanding of the mystery of Jesus's death on the Cross.

And in regard to the early Church's reflection on the deeper meaning of Jesus, it was not long before numerous patristic figures began to articulate its meaning in Scriptural and at times poetic ways. One such example follows, in a hymn of St. Melito of Sardis, an early second-century figure about which little is known. And yet his meditation on the New Passover is a masterful text, infused with typology, recapitulation, and spiritual depth. In reading it, keep in mind that while the truths that St. Melito professes are well established for the modern believer, in this period of the very early Church, such descriptions of Christ were yet rare. Put differently, for the modern, St. Melito's poem is "settled doctrine." Be that as it may, for the first generation of readers of the text, it was *mystagogy*—doctrine wrapped in mystery and spiritual beauty. For this reason, the text is cited at length:

The law is old, but the gospel is new; the type was for a time, but grace is forever. The sheep was corruptible, but the Lord is incorruptible, who was crushed as a lamb, but who was resurrected as God ... The one was the model; the other was found to be the finished product. For God replaced the lamb, and a man the sheep; but in the man was Christ, who contains all things ... This one is the Passover of our salvation. This is the one who patiently endured many things in many people: This is the one who was murdered in Abel, and bound as a sacrifice in Isaac, and exiled in Jacob, and sold in Joseph, and exposed in Moses, and sacrificed in the lamb, and hunted down in David, and dishonored in the prophets. This is the one who became human in a virgin, who was hanged on the tree, who was buried in the earth, who was resurrected from among the dead, and who raised mankind up out of the grave below to the heights of heaven.[27]

This does not exhaust all of the temple theology within the Passion narratives; the following are other notable examples warranting further consideration.

"In Paradise": Reversing Adam's Expulsion from Eden (Luke 22:43)

The discussion begins with a rather mysterious saying of Jesus, to the thief on the Cross: "He said, 'Jesus, remember me when you come into your kingdom.' And he said to him, '*Truly, I say to you, today you will be with me in Paradise*'" (Luke 23:42–43).[28]

How is one to interpret this? First, the text should not be treated as though Jesus were holding out some utopic vision for the thief, of an "earthly paradise." John Nolland maintains that there is no literary basis or theological precedent for such a reading.[29] Second, and along these lines, the Vulgate's translation of Genesis 3:23 translates "garden" (of Eden) as *paradisio*.[30] St. Jerome relied upon the Greek Old Testament (LXX) in developing the new text of the Latin Vulgate. The Greek rendering of Genesis 3:23 does not use the term *kepos* ("garden") as other biblical texts do[31] but alternatively as *paredeisos*—paradise. As a result, it seems clear that the "Bible of Jesus' day,"

---

27. St. Melito of Sardis (early second century), *Peri Tou Pascha* [Concerning the Passover], 4–5, 67–70.

28. "In the NT, 'Paradise' is found only here and in 2 Cor 12:4; Rev 2:7." John Nolland, *Luke 18:35–24:53*, vol. 35C, *Word Biblical Commentary* (Dallas: Word Books, 1998), 1152.

29. "There is no sufficient reason for finding a martyr theology here: though in Jewish thought others may go to a heavenly destiny as a reward for martyrdom (Wisd. 3:1–9), *the word 'paradise' is not used in this connection, and it is not on the basis of martyrdom that Jesus gains entry to paradise.* Furthermore, the criminal is no martyr." Ibid., 1152.

30. Gen. 3:23 [Vulgate]: "Emisit eum Dominus Deus de paradiso Eden, ut operaretur humum, de qua sumptus est." RSV: "Therefore the Lord God sent him forth from the garden of Eden, to till the ground from which he was taken." See *Nova Vulgata Bibliorum Sacrorum Editio*, Editio Typica Altera (Vatican City: Libreria Editrice Vaticana, 1986), 9.

31. See, e.g., John 18:1 or Luke 13:19, both of which use the more prevalent term *kepos*.

the Septuagint, was in the background of Jesus's expression in St. Luke. As Nolland summarizes, "In time this becomes, through reflection on the Genesis account, a hope for an eschatological reversal of the expulsion from the garden."[32]

Here, a text from the apocryphal Jewish *Testament of Levi*, commenting on the Book of Leviticus, is instructive: "And he shall open the gates of paradise, and shall remove the threatening sword against Adam. And he shall give to the saints to eat from the tree of life, and the spirit of holiness shall be on them" (*Testament of Levi* 18:10–11).[33]

Some question whether portions such as this from *Testament of Levi* are merely Christian interpolations[34] or strictly Jewish apocalyptic texts. Regardless, *Testament of Levi* connects the "opening of the gates of Paradise" (Eden) with *a priestly Messiah*: "And after their punishment shall have come from the Lord, the priesthood shall fail. *Then shall the Lord raise up a new priest.* And to him all the words of the Lord shall be revealed; and *he shall execute a righteous judgment upon the earth* for a multitude of days. And *his star shall arise*[35] in heaven as of a king. Lighting up the light of knowledge *as the sun the day,* and he shall be magnified in the world. He shall shine forth as the sun on the earth, and shall remove all darkness from under heaven, and *there shall be peace in all the earth* ... And the angels of *the glory of the Presence of the Lord* shall be glad in him. The heavens shall be opened, and from *the Temple of glory* shall come upon him sanctification" (*Testament of Levi* 18:1–4, 5b–6).[36]

Consistent with such interpretations—and this is a third point about the Lucan text—a number of Fathers and Doctors of the Church interpret Christ's words in a spiritual and nonliteral fashion, drawing heavily on the Eden parallel. For example, Origen explained the saying in an allegorical fashion, reminding of the "Temple gatekeeper" that God called Adam to be—and, in his expulsion from the garden—how Adam too was barred access to the Tree of Life in the Garden temple: "'*Today you will be with me in*

---

32. Nolland, *Luke 18:35–24:53*, 1152.

33. *Testament of Levi* 18:10–11, in Robert Henry Charles, ed., *Pseudepigrapha of the Old Testament*, vol. 2 (Bellingham, WA: Logos Bible Software, 2004), 315.

34. "Christian interpolation": an earlier (Jewish) text reedited by Christian believers in a manner consistent with Christian beliefs about the Risen Jesus.

35. See Num. 24:17: "*A star shall come forth out of Jacob,* and a scepter shall rise out of Israel."

36. Charles, *Pseudepigrapha of the Old Testament*, 314.

paradise.' Through saying this, [Christ] also gave to all those who believe and confess *access to the entrance that Adam previously had closed by sinning.* Who else could remove 'the flaming turning sword which was placed to guard the tree of life' and the gates of paradise? What other sentinel was able to turn the cherubim from their incessant vigil, except only he to whom 'was given all power in heaven and in earth?' No one else besides him could do these things."[37]

Similarly, St. John Chrysostom looks to the Garden for further clarity of Jesus's words to the thief: "In the beginning, God shaped man, and man was an image of the Father and the Son. God said, 'Let us make man to our image and likeness.' Again, when he wished to bring the thief into Paradise, he immediately spoke the word and brought him in. Christ did not need to pray to do this, although he had kept all people after Adam from entering there. God put there the flaming sword to guard Paradise. By his authority, Christ opened paradise and brought in the thief."[38]

St. Thomas also looks to the spiritual understanding of *paradisio:* "Our Lord's expression is not to be understood of the earthly corporeal paradise, but of a spiritual one, in which all are said to be who enjoy the Divine glory. Accordingly, the thief descended locally into hell with Christ, because it was said to him: *This day thou shalt be with Me in paradise*; still as to reward he was in paradise, because he enjoyed Christ's Godhead just as the other saints did."[39]

Finally, in his volume of *Jesus of Nazareth* dealing with the Lucan scene, Ratzinger explains that Jesus's self-knowledge was a definitive "leading back" of humanity to Paradise:

This too is a mysterious saying, but it shows us one thing for certain: Jesus knew he would enter directly into fellowship with the Father—that the promise of "Paradise" was something he could offer "today." He knew he was leading mankind back to the Paradise from which it had fallen: into fellowship with God as man's true salvation. So in the history of Christian devotion, the good thief has become an image of hope—an image of the consoling certainty that God's mercy can reach us even in our final moments, that even after a misspent life, the plea for his gracious favor is not made in vain.[40]

37. Origen, *Homilies on Leviticus,* 9.5.

38. St. John Chrysostom, *Against the Anomoeans,* 9.15.

39. Thomas Aquinas, *Summa Theologica* III, q. 52, a. 4, ad 3–a. 5.

40. Ratzinger, *Jesus of Nazareth, Part Two,* 212–13.

The Torn Veil (Matt. 27:51). "And behold, the veil of the temple was torn in two, from top to bottom; and the earth shook, and the rocks were split; the tombs also were opened, and many bodies of the saints who had fallen asleep were raised, and coming out of the tombs after his resurrection they went into the holy city and appeared to many." Here, Origen adds: "Anyone who searches the Scriptures with some diligence will see that there were two curtains, an inner curtain which covered the Holy of Holies and another curtain exterior to either the Tabernacle or the Temple. These two curtains are figures of the holy Tabernacle which the Father prepared from the beginning.[41] Of the two curtains, one 'was torn into two parts from the top all the way to the bottom.' This happened at the time when Jesus 'cried out with a loud voice and gave up his spirit.'[42] Thereby the divine mystery was revealed that in the Passion of the Lord our Savior the outer curtain was torn from the top, which represents the beginning of the world, to the bottom, representing the end of the world. Thus by the tearing of the curtain the mysteries were disclosed, which with good reason had been hidden until the coming of Christ ... But 'when the perfect comes' [the imperfect will pass away][43] and the other things which now remain hidden are revealed, then the second curtain may also be removed. We will then see even the things which were hidden within the second curtain: the true Ark of the Covenant, the cherubim, the true mercy seat and the storehouse of manna in a golden bowl, and all these clearly and even things greater than these.[44] All of this has been revealed through the law of Moses when God said to him, 'Make everything according to their forms which were shown to you on the mountain.'"[45] To Origen may be added the voices of several modern theologians. In his book-length study of the Temple, Yves Congar writes, "The rending of the veil signifies in the first place the end of the former system of worship. *It is, in a sense, the first breech in the Temple whose destruction Jesus foretold.*[46] It is a sign that the Temple is to lose its sacred character, is, we might almost say,

---

41. See Exod. 25:9. 42. Matt. 27:50.

43. See 1 Cor. 13:10.

44. Heb. 9:3–5: "Behind the second curtain stood a tent called the Holy of Holies, having the golden altar of incense and the ark of the covenant covered on all sides with gold, which contained a golden urn holding the manna, and Aaron's rod that budded, and the tables of the covenant; above it were the cherubim of glory overshadowing the mercy seat. *Of these things we cannot now speak in detail.*"

45. Origen, *Commentary on Matthew*, 138. See Exod. 25:9.

46. See Mark 13:1–37; Matt. 24:1–2.

to be profaned. It signifies, in a more positive way ... that access to the true Holy of Holies is henceforth free."[47]

Along similar lines, Ratzinger explains the distinction between the old and new Temple: "It becomes apparent that the era of the old Temple and its sacrifices *is over*. In place of symbols and rituals that point ahead to the future, the reality has now come, the crucified Jesus who reconciles us all with the Father. At the same time, though, the tearing of the Temple veil means that the pathway to God is now open. Previously God's face had been concealed. Only in a symbolic way could the high priest once a year enter his presence. Now God himself has removed the veil and revealed himself in the crucified Jesus as the one who loves to the point of death. The pathway to God is open."[48]

The Seamless Robe (John 19:23–24). "When the soldiers had crucified Jesus they took his garments and made four parts, one for each soldier; also his tunic. But the tunic was without seam, woven from top to bottom; so they said to one another, 'Let us not tear it, but cast lots for it to see whose it shall be.' This was to fulfill the scripture, 'They parted my garments among them, and for my clothing they cast lots.'"

A brief comparison with the Synoptic Gospels indicates that only St. John emphasizes this scene. They all mention it, but in passing and with no special emphasis as in John.[49] Nor do the Synoptic Gospels (and this is also significant) quote Psalms 22:18 as St. John does.[50] So why does St. John expand the Synoptic accounts? Ratzinger offers a sound explanation: "The reference to the *seamless tunic (chiton)* is formulated in this precise way because St. John evidently wanted to highlight something more than a casual detail. Some exegetes make a connection here with a piece of information provided by Josephus, who points out the high priest's *chiton* was woven from a single thread."[51] Thus we may detect in the Evangelist's passing reference an allusion

47. Congar, *Mystery of the Temple*, 142–43 (emphasis added).

48. Ratzinger, *Jesus of Nazareth, Part Two*, 209.

49. Cf. Matt. 27:35–36 and Mark 15:20; Luke 23:34.

50. Psa. 22:18 mentions *nothing about this*, so it is not part of the explicit "fulfillment" of Scripture. Why, then, does John introduce this small element? Clearly it is of great symbolic and theological significance for John.

51. Josephus, *Antiquities* 3.7.4: "The high priest is indeed adorned with the same garments that we have described, without abating one; only over these he puts on a vestment of a blue color. This also is a long robe, reaching to his feet and is tied round with a girdle, embroidered with the same colors and flowers as the former, with a mixture of gold interwoven. To the bottom of which garment

to Jesus's high-priestly dignity, which John had expounded theologically in the high-priestly prayer of chapter 17. Not only is this dying man Israel's true king, but he is also the high priest who accomplishes his high-priestly ministry precisely in this hour of his most extreme dishonor.[52]

St. Augustine had a similarly spiritual impression of the text's deeper meaning: "That they cast lots for his tunic alone, 'woven from the top without seam,' rather than dividing it, demonstrated clearly enough that the visible sacraments, even though they too are the garments of Christ, can still be had by anybody, good or bad. But that sincere and genuine faith, which 'works through love'[53] to achieve the integrity of unity—because 'the love of God has been poured out in our hearts through the Holy Spirit who has been given to us'[54]—that this faith does not belong to anybody at all but is given by God's hidden grace as by lot. Thus to Simon, who had baptism but did not have this, Peter could say, 'You have no lot or part in this faith.'"[55]

Blood and Water (John 19:34). "But one of the soldiers pierced his side with a spear, and at once there came out blood and water." Above all, this imagery from St. John would have conjured up the Gihon spring, which ran along the Temple mount, down in the Kidron valley below. For Jewish readers, this would have called to mind the Temple sacrifices. Here's why: functionally, the sacrifices required an efficient manner in which to wash away vast amounts of

---

are hung fringes, in color like pomegranates, with golden bells, by a curious and beautiful contrivance; so that between two bells hangs a pomegranate, and between two pomegranates a bell. *Now this vesture was not composed of two pieces, nor was it sewed together upon the shoulders and the sides, but it was one long vestment so woven as to have an aperture for the neck; not an oblique one, but parted all along the breast and the back.* A border also was sewed to it, lest the aperture should look too indecently: it was also parted where the hands were to come out."

52. Ratzinger, *Jesus of Nazareth, Part Two*, 216–17.

53. Gal. 5:6.

54. Rom. 5:6.

55. St. Augustine, *Sermon* 218.9. Ratzinger's interpretation of the seamless tunic includes a second possibility, more of the sort as St. Augustine's, having to do with the "unity" of the Church. "The Church Fathers drew out a different aspect in their consideration of this passage: in the seamless garment, which even the soldiers were reluctant to tear, they saw *an image of the indestructible unity of the Church.* The seamless garment is an expression of the unity that Jesus the high priest implored for his followers on the evening before he suffered. *Indeed, Jesus' priesthood and the unity of his followers are inseparably linked together in the high-priestly prayer.* At the foot of the Cross we hear once more the poignant message that Jesus had held up before us and inscribed on our souls in the prayer that he uttered before setting out on that final journey." Ratzinger, *Jesus of Nazareth, Part Two*, 217 (emphasis added). This latter solution is likewise preferred by Ignace de la Potterie, *The Hour of Jesus* (Staten Island: Alba House, 1990), 139–43.

blood from the Temple. The Gihon spring "was connected to the Temple altar by a guttering system that channeled down the enormous amounts of blood from the thousands of Passover lambs being slaughtered, producing a torrent of bloody water. At the cross, Jesus has become, in fulfillment of John 2:19–21, the new Temple from which flows this river of sacrifice."[56]

The legs of the thieves were broken with a mallet (v. 32). On a *historical* level, that Jesus's legs are not broken indicates he had already expired. On a *theological* level, this is a direct fulfillment of Psalms 34:20: "He keeps all his bones; not one of them is broken." St. Augustine observed, "The prophecy was fulfilled in our Lord, because as he hung on the cross he expired before the soldiers arrived; they found his body already lifeless, so they had no wish to break his legs; thus the Scripture was fulfilled. But the promise was made to all Christians."[57]

Additionally, it is an allusion to Exodus: "In one house shall it be eaten; you shall not carry forth any of the flesh outside the house; *and you shall not break a bone of it*" (Exod. 12:46).

The Torah was strict that Passover lambs must be unblemished—with no broken bones. Chrysostom sees a prefigurement of Christ, the unblemished Lamb of God: "That well-known prophecy likewise was fulfilled: '*Not a bone of him shall you break.*' For even if this was spoken with reference to the lamb among the Jews, the type preceded for the sake of truth and was, rather, fulfilled in this event. Moreover, that is why the Evangelist cited the prophet … *He summoned Moses to testify that this not only did not take place by accident but that it had been foretold in writing from of old.*"[58]

St. Augustine looked back to the story of the Flood, and the Creation of Eve: "That blood was shed for the remission of sins, that water tempers the cup of salvation. [It] was prefigured when Noah was commanded to make *a door in the side of the ark, by which the animals that were not to perish by the deluge entered; which animals prefigured the Church.* To [prefigure] *this, the woman was made out of the side of the sleeping man; for this second Adam bowed His head, and slept on the cross,* that out of that which came forth, there might be formed a wife for Him. O death, by which the dead are quickened, what can be purer than that blood, what more salutary than that wound!"[59]

56. S. W. Hahn, "Temple, Sign, and Sacrament," *Letter & Spirit* 4 (2008): 133.

57. St. Augustine, *Exposition of the Psalms* 34.24.

58. St. John Chrysostom, *Homilies on the Gospel of John* 85.

59. St. Augustine, *Tractates on John*, CXX. St. Thomas Aquinas and John Henry Newman, *Cat-*

On the creation of Eve, the *Catechism* adds: "The Church is born primarily of Christ's total self-giving for our salvation, anticipated in the institution of the Eucharist and fulfilled on the cross. 'The origin and growth of the Church are symbolized by the blood and water which flowed from the open side of the crucified Jesus.'[60] For it was from the side of Christ as he slept the sleep of death upon the cross that there came forth the 'wondrous sacrament of the whole Church.'[61] As Eve was formed from the sleeping Adam's side, so the Church was born from the pierced heart of Christ hanging dead on the cross."[62]

Likewise, two different texts (one personal, one magisterial) draw the connection between the sleeping Adam, the creation of Eve, and the Holy Eucharist: "In this double outpouring of blood and water, the Fathers saw an image of the two fundamental sacraments—Eucharist and Baptism—which spring forth from the Lord's pierced side, from his heart. This is the new outpouring that creates the Church and renews mankind. Moreover, the opened side of the Lord asleep on the Cross prompted the Fathers to point to *the creation of Eve from the side of the sleeping Adam*, and so in this outpouring of the sacraments they also recognized the birth of the Church: *the creation of the new woman from the side of the new Adam.*"[63]

In his Apostolic Exhortation, Pope Benedict XVI wrote, "Through the sacrament of the Eucharist Jesus draws the faithful into his '*hour*;' he shows us the bond that he willed to establish between himself and us, between his own person and the Church. Indeed, in the sacrifice of the Cross, Christ gave birth to the Church as his Bride and his body. The Fathers of the Church often meditated on the relationship between *Eve's coming forth from the side of Adam as he slept*[64] and the coming forth of the new Eve, the Church, from the open side of Christ sleeping in death: *from Christ's pierced side, John recounts, there came forth blood and water*, the symbol of the sacraments."[65]

Without question, then, the image is infused with both Christological

---

ena Aurea. Commentary on the Four Gospels, Collected Out of the Works of the Fathers: St. John, vol. 4 (Oxford: John Henry Parker, 1845), 589.

60. *Lumen Gentium*, 3.

61. *Sancrosanctum Conciliam*, 5.

62. *Catechism of the Catholic Church*, §766; St. Ambrose, *Commentary on Luke*, 2, 85–89.

63. Ratzinger, *Jesus of Nazareth, Part Two*, 226 (emphases added).

64. See Gen. 2:21–23.

65. Pope Benedict XVI, *Sacramentum Caritatis*, Apostolic Exhortation (Vatican City: Libreria Editrice Vaticana, 2007).

significance and sacramental significance for the early Church: "The blood and water is the link between the events narrated and the community of believers of later generations ... When Jesus is no longer a physical presence with them, the community can still be drawn into his filial relationship with God and participate *in the sacrificial gift of his life in their sacraments of baptism and Eucharist.*"[66]

Finally, this ancient hymn poetically reflects on the mystery of the blood from Christ's side:

> *At the Lamb's high feast we sing*
> *Praise to our victorious King,*
> *Who has washed us in the tide*
> *Flowing from his pierced side.*
> *Praise we him whose love divine*
> *Gives the guests his blood for wine,*
> *Gives his body for the feast,*
> *Love the victim, love the priest.*
> *Where the Paschal blood is poured,*
> *Death's dark angel sheathes his sword;*
> *Israel's hosts triumphant go*
> *Through the wave that drowns the foe.*
> *Christ, the Lamb whose blood was shed,*
> *Paschal victim, Paschal bread;*
> *With sincerity and love*
> *Eat we manna from above.*
> *Mighty victim from the sky,*
> *Powers of hell beneath you lie;*
> *Death is conquered in the fight;*
> *You have brought us life and light.*
> *Alleluia!*[67]

---

66. Mary L. Coloe, *God Dwells with Us: Temple Symbolism in the Fourth Gospel* (Collegeville, MN: Liturgical Press, 2001), 200.

67. Ambrosian Hymn Writer, *Easter Hymn, At the Lamb's High Feast.*

Temple Theology in the Resurrection
and Ascension Narratives

At first glance, one might think that the Resurrection[68] and Ascension[69] narratives are not as pertinent to a discussion of temple theology, yet this is not the case. There are some significant connections in the Resurrection narratives, and in Luke's Ascension narrative, and both are worth consideration.

First, in the Gospel of John, Jesus's temple action is placed at the beginning, not the end, of the Gospel. Here, the scene concludes with a reference to the Resurrection: "Jesus answered them, '*Destroy this temple, and in three days I will raise it up.*' The Jews then said, 'It has taken forty-six years to build this temple, and will you raise it up in three days?' But he spoke of the temple of his body. When therefore he was raised from the dead, his disciples remembered that he had said this; and they believed the scripture and the word which Jesus had spoken" (John 2:19–22).

About this passage, it's interesting that in the final verse the Evangelist draws open the curtains and allows the reader to learn something of how the Apostles came to "remember" Jesus and, in so doing, compose the inspired texts of the Gospels. According to St. John, it appears that Jesus's temple saying was roundly perplexing in its original context, even among his own disciples, yet alone for other onlookers. St. John reveals here that the mystery became understandable *only after Jesus was "raised from the dead."*

This is a helpful insight as far as it goes; John does not disclose what form such rumination took, only that, through some fashion of (divinely inspired) recollection, what is remembered about Jesus takes on deeper, more comprehensible meaning after the experience of Easter. Without getting too far afield from the main topic, this is an insight worth holding on to, for all who study the Gospels. Catholic biblical interpretation rests upon certain inviolable foundations, and this is one of them: that the Resurrection of Jesus Christ, amidst all of its many glorious effects, contributed to what might be called an "Easter hermeneutic" in terms of how Jesus's Apostles began to remember all that Jesus had said and done in light of the Easter event. The Resurrection was the matrix through which *holy recollection* led to *faithful proclamation* and the eventual composition of the Four Gospels.

68. Matt. 28:1–20; Mark 16:9–18; Luke 24:49; John 20:1–32, 21:1–25.
69. Luke 24:50–53.

Moreover, "by calling the destruction and raising of his Temple-body a 'sign,' St. John establishes a strong link between this narrative and the account of Jesus' death and Resurrection. Jesus' death and subsequent Resurrection may be seen as a 're-building' of the Temple. The 'destruction' of His body (crucifixion) and 'raising up' of His body in glory (Resurrection) is the definitive signpost of His true identity: 'In the context of the definitive sign that Jesus speaks about, all the other 'signs' take on their significance' … By this great sign, Jesus will replace the stone Temple (with his body, the new Temple), and will fulfill the Passover, himself becoming the 'Lamb of God.'"[70]

The Resurrection as the Eighth Day of Creation

Earlier chapters discussed both the significance of the temple of creation as well the number seven in the Creation narratives of Genesis, especially as it pertains to God's covenant with all creation, and the sign of that covenant, the Sabbath. Turning to the Resurrection narratives, particularly that of St. John, it is clear that the New Creation has already begun.[71] In his glorified Resurrection body, he speaks, cooks breakfast, and eats with his disciples.[72] Moreover, he "breathes" on them, an image reminiscent of Genesis 1.[73]

"Jesus said to them again, 'Peace be with you. As the Father has sent me, even so I send you.' And when he had said this, he breathed on them, and

---

70. Celestino Lingad, *The Problems of Jewish Christians in the Johannine Community* (Rome: Gregorian & Biblical Press, 2001), 270.

71. "Resurrection is a full-blown new creation notion, since the way the righteous were to enter in and become part of the *new heavens and new earth is through recreating their bodies* … Christ is the New Adam, or the 'Son of Man,' *who has begun to do what the first Adam should have done and to inherit what the first Adam should have, including the glory reflected in God's image* … Part of Jesus' doing what Adam should have done included *establishing the new temple and extending it obediently.* In reality, he was the beginning of the new temple of the new creation, especially in the new creation." G. K. Beale, *The Temple and the Church's Mission: A Biblical Theology of the Dwelling Place of God* (Downers Grove, IL: InterVarsity Press, 2004), 175–76. Beale's quote reveals keen insight, and yet the present study, by necessity, goes further than Beale by taking his last sentence of the quote toward a sacramental conclusion. Through the sacraments, especially the Holy Eucharist, but indeed through all of them, Jesus is *extending the New Temple* of His Body over the creation, through the Church, and into the soul his disciples.

72. See John 21:1–14.

73. Recall that John begins with the opening words of Genesis ("in the beginning"). In the Greek Old Testament (LXX), the first three words of Genesis and John are identical.

said to them, 'Receive the Holy Spirit. If you forgive the sins of any, they are forgiven; if you retain the sins of any, they are retained'" (John 20:21–23). On the theme of filial adoption, Hahn writes, "Christ, by virtue of his divine-human constitution and by means of his saving actions, is the center and locus of that redemption. He is the Second Adam who renews our nature in himself, thus inaugurating a new humanity, and breathes his Spirit into us, causing us to be adopted as sons of the Father."[74]

N. T. Wright and Ratzinger help to fill out the picture on the New Creation motif in the light of Christ's Resurrection. As usual, Wright does so by asking provocative questions: "Where did resurrection show up in what the early Christians habitually did? Briefly and broadly, they behaved as if they were in some important senses *already living in God's new creation.* They lived as if the covenant had been renewed, as if the kingdom were in a sense already present, though, to be sure, future as well ... If challenged about their lifestyle, or their existence as a community, the early Christians responded by telling stories of Jesus, particularly of his triumph over death."[75]

Similarly, Ratzinger explains the "new worship" that came about with the end of Temple sacrifices: "Here the new worship is established that brings the Temple sacrifices to an end: God is glorified in word, but in a Word that took flesh in Jesus, a Word that, by means of this body which has now passed through death, is able to draw in the whole man, the whole of mankind—thus heralding the beginning of the new Creation."[76]

St. John depicts Christ's post-Resurrection appearance to the disciples as the second Sunday after the Resurrection, or the "eighth day."[77] A number of early Church fathers seized upon St. John's language of the "eighth

---

74. "This declaration to the disciples must be understood in relation to *John* 1:29, Jesus' first appearance in the gospel, where he is hailed by John the Baptist: '*Behold, the Lamb of God, who takes away the sin of the world!*' Although in this way the evangelist introduces Jesus to the reader as the one who 'takes away sin,' there is not a single instance of Jesus *explicitly* forgiving sin in the entire Gospel ... The evangelist regards those in sin as spiritually sick, blind, and dead; thus Jesus' miracles of healing may rightly be seen as *types* of liberation from sin. Nonetheless, the fact remains that, although Jesus' mission is announced from the start as the '*taking away of sin,*' *this is never enacted personally by Jesus in the Gospel ... Rather, the power to forgive is explicitly devolved upon the disciples through the power of the Spirit at the end of the Gospel.*" Hahn, "Temple, Sign, and Sacrament," 137 (emphasis added).

75. N. T. Wright, *The Resurrection of the Son of God: Christian Origins and the Question of God* (London: Society for Promoting Christian Knowledge, 2003), 578–79.

76. Ratzinger, *Jesus of Nazareth, Part Two*, 141.

77. See John 20:26: "Eight days later, his disciples were again in the house, and Thomas was with them. The doors were shut, but Jesus came and stood among them, and said, 'Peace be with you.'"

day"—presumably language common in the early Church, too—and used it liturgically and sacramentally to talk about the importance of Christian worship on Sunday, the new Sabbath, and of the Eucharist, which was the sign of the New Covenant.[78] This is evident in the *Epistle of Barnabas*: "After I have given rest to all things, *I will make the beginning of the eighth day, which is the beginning of another world.* It is for this reason that we celebrate on the eighth day, the day on which Jesus also rose from the dead, appeared and ascended into heaven."[79]

In homiletic fashion, St. Augustine taught that "it was perfectly reasonable that it should have been on the first, *which is also the eighth day—Sunday*—that our Lord chose to give us an example in his own flesh of bodily resurrection. 'Christ being raised from the dead will never die again; death no longer has dominion over him.' To this exalted state of his we must go with humility."[80]

For the Venerable Bede, Jesus's circumcision announced Jesus's Resurrection in an anticipatory way: "[Jesus's] circumcision clearly set forth an image of the Lord's resurrection because it too occurred on the eighth day, that is, on the day after the Sabbath. And just as the former was wont to release people from the punishable state of everlasting death, so the latter displayed the perfect newness of immortal life in our Creator, and revealed that it is to be hoped for in us."[81]

St. Cyril of Alexandria discusses the eighth day in the context of the liturgy: "With good reason, then, are we accustomed to have sacred meetings in churches *on the eighth day*. And, to adopt the language of allegory ... *we indeed close the doors, but Christ still visits us and appears to us all, both invisibly as God and visibly in the body. He allows us to touch his holy flesh and gives it to us. For through the grace of God we are admitted to partake of the blessed Eucharist*, receiving Christ into our hands, to the intent that we may firmly believe that he did in truth raise up the temple of his body."[82]

Coming from a modern vantage point, Daniélou sets forth a kind of theology of Sunday: "The Day of the Lord is the future age, the eighth day

---

78. See Oskar Skarsuane, *In the Shadow of the Temple: Jewish Influences on Early Christianity* (Downers Grove, IL: InterVarsity Press, 2002), 375–84.

79. *Epistle of Barnabas*, 15.8–9.

80. St. Augustine, *Sermon* 260c.5.

81. Venerable Bede, *Homilies on the Gospels* 2.20.

82. St. Cyril of Alexandria, *Commentary on the Gospel of John* 12:1.

which is beyond the cosmic week … The whole theology of Sunday is now seen clearly; it is the cosmic day of creation, the biblical day of circumcision,[83] the evangelical day of Resurrection, the Church's day of the Eucharistic celebration, and finally, the eschatological day of the age to come."[84]

Conclusion: Jesus Ascends to His Kingdom

Finally, just a few words on the Ascension. The Ascension is treated briefly in only one of the Gospels—Luke—and also in the companion volume, Acts. None of the other Gospels include the scene, yet the Ascension of Jesus was, from the beginning days of Christianity, a crucial confession of faith (i.e., Apostle's Creed).

In his first volume, St. Luke describes it this way: "Then he led them out as far as Bethany, and lifting up his hands he blessed them. While he blessed them, he parted from them, and was carried up into heaven. And they worshipped him, and returned to Jerusalem with great joy, and were continually in the Temple blessing God" (Luke 24:50–53). Similarly, he returns to the theme of Jesus's Ascension in the first chapter of Acts: "But you shall receive power when the Holy Spirit has come upon you; and you shall be my witnesses in Jerusalem and in all Judea and Samaria and to the end of the earth. And when he had said this, as they were looking on, he was lifted up, and a cloud took him out of their sight. And while they were gazing into heaven as he went, behold, two men stood by them in white robes, and said, 'Men of Galilee, why do you stand looking into heaven? This Jesus, who was taken up from you into heaven, will come in the same way as you saw him go into heaven'" (Acts 1:8–11).

How is the Ascension of Jesus informed by temple theology? First, it may be read in accord with what was said above concerning the Resurrection—it follows the Resurrection and is "contingent" upon it, chronologically speaking. Second, notice in Luke, following the Ascension, that the apostles are "filled with great joy" and return not merely to Jerusalem, but to the Temple, were they "continually blessed God."

---

83. Circumcision was normally performed on the "eighth day." See Lev. 12:3. John the Baptist was circumcised on the eighth day (Luke 1:59), as was Jesus: "And at the end of eight days, when he was circumcised, he was called Jesus, the name given by the angel before he was conceived in the womb" (Luke 2:21).

84. Jean Daniélou, *The Bible and the Liturgy* (Notre Dame, IN: University of Notre Dame Press, 1956), 267.

Given the proximity of the Ascension to the saying about the Temple, it seems likely that it is strategic, and may suggest St. Luke's interest in showing how the story of the Messiah came full circle, from the perplexed Zechariah in the Temple in chapter 1, to the "overjoyed apostles" following the Ascension.

Another connection between the Ascension and temple theology has to do with the image of the high priest "ascending" to the Holy of Holies. Recall that in the earlier discussion of the Transfiguration, Jesus's ascent "up the high mountain" parallels the high priest, who "ascends" to the Holy of Holies in a cloud of incense. Similarly, Jesus ascends to "His Father's house" on the clouds. (More will be said about the eternal high priesthood of Jesus in chapter 19.)

Finally, returning to the concept of Messiah, the Ascension is the fulfillment of the true Davidic king coming into his kingdom: "The *lifting up of Jesus on the cross* signifies and announces his lifting *up by his Ascension into heaven*, and indeed begins it. Jesus Christ, the one priest of the new and eternal Covenant, 'entered, not into a sanctuary made by human hands ... but into heaven itself, now to appear in the presence of God on our behalf.'[85] There Christ permanently exercises his priesthood, for He 'always lives to make intercession' for 'those who draw near to God through him.' As 'high priest of the good things to come' He is the center and the principal actor of the liturgy that honors the Father in heaven."[86] Henceforth Christ is *seated at the right hand of the Father*: "By 'the Father's right hand' we understand the glory and honor of divinity, where he who exists as Son of God before all ages, indeed as God, of one being with the Father, is seated bodily after he became incarnate and his flesh was glorified."[87] "Being seated at the Father's right hand signifies the inauguration of the Messiah's kingdom, the fulfillment of the prophet Daniel's vision concerning the Son of man: '*To him was given dominion and glory and kingdom, that all peoples, nations, and languages should serve him; his dominion is an everlasting dominion, which shall not pass away, and his kingdom one that shall not be destroyed.*'[88] After this event the apostles became witnesses of the 'kingdom [that] will have no end.'"[89]

Having completed a detailed study of the fiber optics of temple theology throughout the Four Gospels, subsequent chapters trace the pattern as it makes its way through the remainder of the New Testament.

---

85. See Heb. 9:24.

86. *Catechism of the Catholic Church*, §662.

87. *Catechism of the Catholic Church*, §663 (emphasis added).

88. Dan. 7:14.

89. *Catechism of the Catholic Church*, §664 (emphasis added).

18

THE SPIRIT AND THE BODY

Temple Theology in Acts and Pauline Epistles, the New Creation

> And day by day, attending the Temple together and breaking bread in their homes, they partook of food with glad and generous hearts, praising God and having favor with all the people. And the Lord added to their number day by day those who were being saved.
>
> Acts 2:46–47

Temple Theology in the New Testament beyond the Four Gospels

In moving beyond the Gospels, there is much more to examine in the remainder of the New Testament—there are significant strands of temple theology in virtually every book. This chapter will examine the temple theology within the Acts of the Apostles, followed by the letters of St. Paul.

Much like the Gospels themselves, the temple theology found in the remaining books of the New Testament is generally of a Christological sort, pertaining to the person and work of Jesus Christ. Yet, at the same time, temple theology will develop in other ways too. For example, St. Paul will characterize the Church itself as the "Temple of God." Along with this, Paul will write that the heart of the believer mirrors, in an even more personal way, the "sanctuary" of the new Temple. As Desmond Alexander explains, "In moving from the Old Testament to the New Testament, we discover that the Jerusalem Temple is replaced by the church and, with its outward expansion from Jerusalem to the ends of the earth, God's dwelling place also spreads outward."[1]

Additionally, other forms of temple theology—or, better, temple Christology—will be seen in other places within the New Testament. This is particularly the case in the Book of Hebrews, with its bold thesis that Jesus is both eternal High Priest and the "perfect" sacrifice. Finally, the first steps of temple theology, taken far back at the "mountain of God" in Genesis, will reach their decisive and triumphant conclusion as the reader encounters the mysteries of the Lamb of God, "standing as though slain" (Rev. 5:6), in a discussion of St. John's Apocalypse.

Temple Theology in the Early Church: The Book of Acts

Pentecost and the Unity of the Church are reflected in the Holy Spirit (Acts 2:1–13). The coming of the Holy Spirit is already hinted at the end of the Gospel of John. In chapter 14, St. John writes, "But *the Counselor, the Holy Spirit*, whom the Father will send in my name, he will teach you all things, and bring to your remembrance all that I have said to you" (John 14:25).[2] Following Jesus's Resurrection, St. John anticipates the coming of the Holy Spirit at Pentecost: "And when he had said this, he breathed on them, and said to them, 'Receive the Holy Spirit'" (John 20:22).

The true birth of the Church happens in Jerusalem, of course, at Pentecost, about which St. Luke writes, "When the day of Pentecost had come, they were all together in one place. And suddenly a *sound came from heaven like the rush of a mighty wind*, and it filled all the house where they were sitting. And there appeared to them tongues as of fire, distributed and resting on each one of them. And they were all filled with the Holy Spirit and began to speak in other tongues, as the Spirit gave them utterance" (Acts 2:1–3).

This new experience of God, of being "filled" and guided by the Holy Spirit, is foretold by the Old Testament prophets in various ways. Ezekiel writes, "And I will give them *one heart, and put a new spirit within them*; I will take the stony heart out of their flesh and give them a heart of flesh, that

---

1. Desmond Alexander, *From Eden to the New Jerusalem* (Grand Rapids, MI: Kregel, 2008), 60.

2. See also John 16:13–14: "When the Spirit of truth comes, he will guide you into all the truth; for he will not speak on his own authority, but whatever he hears he will speak, and he will declare to you the things that are to come. He will glorify me, for he will take what is mine and declare it to you."

they may walk in my statutes and keep my ordinances and obey them; and they shall be my people, and I will be their God" (Ezek. 11:19–20).

In Ezekiel, the "new spirit within them" brings about a unifying dimension for God's people, giving them "one heart." On one hand, this anticipates the future Pentecost. Yet on the other hand, it hearkens back to the original Creation, even before the Babel episode (see below), when, in the Garden sanctuary, the first man could exclaim of the first woman, "this is flesh of my flesh and bone of my bones."[3] In the Garden temple, the Man and Woman shared a common identity as the son and daughter of God, and in their union became "one flesh."[4]

On a moral level, St. Paul sees the reality of this Edenic unity, but only because of Christ, and to the extent that the baptized believer cooperates with the Holy Spirit and lives in a way that promotes the "bond of peace" and unity in the Holy Spirit and in Christ. "I therefore, a prisoner for the Lord, beg you to lead a life worthy of the calling to which you have been called, with all lowliness and meekness, with patience, forbearing one another in love, eager to maintain the unity of the Spirit in the bond of peace. There is one body and one Spirit, just as you were called to the one hope that belongs to your call, one Lord, one faith, one baptism, one God and Father of us all, who is above all and through all and in all" (Eph. 4:1–6).

Another Old Testament text that anticipates the coming Holy Spirit is in Jeremiah: "But this is the covenant which I will make with the house of Israel after those days, says the Lord: *I will put my law within them*, and I will write it upon their hearts; and I will be their God, and they shall be my people. And no longer shall each man teach his neighbor and each his brother, saying, 'Know the Lord,' for they shall all know me, from the least of them to the greatest, says the Lord; *for I will forgive their iniquity, and I will remember their sin no more*" (Jer. 31:33–34).[5]

This text is striking for at least two reasons. First, as discussed elsewhere, the idea of God putting his law within them is a characteristic of the Davidic covenant and memorialized in the temple music of the Psalms. There, the Law is internalized as never before. At the same time, this promise recalls the Edenic Temple, when the law of Creation was indeed sealed upon the

---

3. Gen. 2:23.
4. Gen. 2:24.
5. See also Joel 3:1–5; Ezek. 36:25–38, 37:1–14.

hearts of the Man and the Woman. Second, Jeremiah's reference to the "forgiveness of sins" anticipates a future time when God's forgiveness somehow *transcends the forgiveness offered in the Temple*. In this way, Jeremiah's words point to the messianic age and, at the same time, the outpouring of the Spirit. As the *Catechism* summarizes, these promises—and more—came to fruition in the Church of the Apostles, beginning that day in Jerusalem, not far from the Temple: "The prophetic texts that directly concern the sending of the Holy Spirit are oracles by which God speaks to the heart of his people in the language of the promise, with the accents of 'love and fidelity.' St. Peter will proclaim their fulfillment on the morning of Pentecost.[6] According to these promises, at the 'end time' the Lord's Spirit will renew the hearts of men, engraving a new law in them. He will gather and reconcile the scattered and divided peoples; he will transform the first creation, and God will dwell there with men in peace."[7]

Finally, St. Cyril associates the coming of the Spirit at Pentecost with Christian baptism. This is not at all surprising, but what is noteworthy is his description of "divine garments." If one recalls the discussion of Adam, and the glory that was upon him in the Garden sanctuary, then Cyril's text underscores the connection between the first Creation and that of Pentecost: "And lest people should be ignorant of the greatness of the mighty gift coming down to them, there sounded as it were *a heavenly trumpet*. For suddenly there came from heaven a sound as of the rushing of a mighty wind, signifying the presence of him who was to grant power to people to seize with violence the kingdom of God, that both their eyes might see the fiery tongues and their ears hear the sound. And it filled all the house where they were sitting; for the house became the vessel of the spiritual water; as the disciples sat within, the whole house was filled. Thus they were entirely baptized according to the promise and invested soul and body with a *divine garment of salvation*."[8]

A Recapitulation of Babel

As the Spirit comes upon the diversity of believers, each one hears, according to his own language, "Now there were dwelling in Jerusalem Jews,

---

6. See Acts 2:17ff.   7. *Catechism of the Catholic Church*, §715.
8. St. Cyril of Jerusalem, *Catechetical Lecture* 17.15.

devout men from every nation under heaven. And at this sound the multitude came together, and they were bewildered, because each one heard them speaking in his own language. And they were amazed and wondered, saying, 'Are not all these who are speaking Galileans? And how is it that we hear, each of us in his own native language? Parthians and Medes and Elamites and residents of Mesopotamia, Judea and Cappadocia (etc.) … we hear them telling in our own tongues the mighty works of God.' And all were amazed and perplexed, saying to one another, 'What does this mean?'" (Acts 2:5–12).

A key phrase is found in verse 5: "Devout men from every nation under heaven." Here, at Pentecost, there is a great diversity—and great faith. This is important, as it is a full *reversal* of Babel in Genesis, where there was an original unity but a lack of faith. Thus Pentecost recapitulates the *disintegration* of humanity, and the coming of the Spirit brings a new beginning, a new reintegration from the Father:[9] "And he made *from one every nation of men* to live on all the face of the earth, having determined allotted periods and the boundaries of their habitation."[10]

For Gordon Wenham, the day of Pentecost represents not merely a "new unity" in the Holy Spirit of a sort that humanity never before enjoyed. Rather, Pentecost brought about a kind of "restoration" of an original unity that was forsaken long ago at Babel: "And Luke evidently looked on the day of Pentecost when all could understand each other's speech as a sign of the last days when all who call on the name of the Lord shall be saved (Acts 2:8–21). The hopelessness of man's plight at Babel is not God's last word: at least the prophets and NT look forward to a day when sin will be destroyed and perfect unity will be restored among the nations of the world."[11]

One may ask: as fascinating as this is, wherein is the temple theology? The answer: precisely in recalling one of the first temple motifs from the early chapters of Genesis. Specifically, of Adam's (and Eve's) divine mandate to "extend the temple" across the face of the earth, we see that at Pentecost,

---

9. See *Gen.* 11:1–9; *Catechism of the Catholic Church*, §57: "This state of division into many nations [at Babel] is at once *cosmic, social, and religious*. It is intended to limit the pride of fallen humanity, united only in its perverse ambition *to forge its own unity* as at Babel.' But, because of sin, both polytheism and the idolatry of the nation and of its rulers constantly threaten this provisional economy with the perversion of paganism."

10. Acts 17:26.

11. Gordon J. Wenham, *Genesis 1–15*, vol. 1, *Word Biblical Commentary* (Waco, TX: Word Books, 1987), 246.

through faith, God succeeds in creating human unity, whilst man on his own had sadly failed.[12]

Adam failed as the descendants of Ham failed at Babel in their broken attempt at a manmade temple, a manmade unity: "There is no mistaking the fact that the Pentecost account presents a counterpart to the story of the tower of Babel (Gen. 11:1–9). The prehistory of mankind ends there with the fact that its unity shatters; more precisely, God himself *smashes a false unity in mankind*."[13]

Ratzinger's observation is helpful, as he contrasts the two forms of "false unity" of ancient Babel: "If we are to grasp correctly the deeper message of the Pentecost story, we must measure precisely the difference between the two sorts of universality. The unity of Babel is *uniformity*. The men there are only one people and have only one language. The multiplicity intended by the Creator is stifled by *a false form of unity*. It is a unity that is aligned with power, self-assertion, and 'fame.' Men build themselves a way to heaven. In fame they create for themselves their own immortality. They do not need God; rather, they content themselves with their power and their abilities."[14]

The false unity is contrasted with the "unity of diversity," in the Holy Spirit in the Church in Jerusalem at Pentecost: "The unity of Pentecost is of an entirely different nature: they all hear their own language. It brings about unity in variety. Their unity does not lie in the unity of making or of external know-how; rather, *it lies in being touched from within, in a way that does not extinguish the variety but enriches all instead in a mutual give-and-take*. For now everything belongs to everyone, and for that very reason the gifts of all, the unique endowments that the Creator has given to each one, necessarily prove their worth."[15]

---

12. *Catechism of the Catholic Church*, §696: "In the form of tongues '*as of fire*,' the Holy Spirit rests on the disciples on the morning of Pentecost and fills them with himself. The spiritual tradition has retained this symbolism of fire as one of the most expressive images of the Holy Spirit's actions." See St. John of the Cross, *The Living Flame of Love*, in *The Collected Works of St. John of the Cross*, trans. K. Kavanaugh, OCD, and O. Rodriguez, OCD (Washington, DC: Institute of Carmelite Studies, 1979), 577*ff.*

13. Joseph Ratzinger, *On the Way to Jesus Christ*, trans. Michael J. Miller (San Francisco: Ignatius Press, 2005), 137–38 (emphases added). In addition to a recapitulation of Babel, G. K. Beale interprets Pentecost "as a recapitulation of the Sinai sanctuary ... and that the 'tongues of fire' in turn represent in the Old Testament a theophany of the heavenly sanctuary." *The Temple and the Church's Mission: A Biblical Theology of the Dwelling Place of God* (Downers Grove, IL: InterVarsity Press, 2004), 204–9

14. Ratzinger, *On the Way to Jesus Christ*, 139 (emphasis added).

15. Ibid. (emphasis added).

Other Examples of Temple Theology in Acts

Another text worthy of mention is found in Acts 4, where the risen Christ is proclaimed as the Christ as "cornerstone" of the new Temple: "This is the stone which was rejected by you builders, but which has become the head of the corner" (Acts 4:11).

A similar text from the Gospels was previously discussed.[16] Here it need only be added that in Peter's speech in Acts 4, it is *Christ's death* that is focal point, that which makes him the true cornerstone of the new Temple—the Temple of the united believers at Pentecost. The Venerable Bede sees in this image a divine strength, a divine foundation, which is capable of uniting even the pronounced divisions between Jew and Gentile: "The builders were the Jews, *while all the Gentiles remained in the wasteland of idols.* The Jews alone were daily reading the law and the prophets for the building up of the people. As they were building, *they came to the cornerstone,* which embraces two walls—that is, they found in the prophetic Scriptures that Christ, who would bring together in himself two peoples, was to come in the flesh. And, because they preferred to remain in one wall, that is, to be saved alone, they rejected the stone, which was not one-sided but two-sided. *Nevertheless, although they were unwilling, God by himself placed this [stone] at the chief position in the corner, so that from two Testaments and two peoples* there might *rise up a building of one and the same faith.*"[17]

One final temple aspect of temple theology in Acts may be added to the present discussion. It is found in the context of Stephen's Speech.[18] "Our fathers had *the tent of witness in the wilderness,* even as he who spoke to Moses directed him to make it, *according to the pattern that he had seen.* Our fathers in turn brought it in with Joshua when they dispossessed the nations which God thrust out before our fathers. So it was until the days of David, who found favor in the sight of God and asked leave to find a habitation for the

---

16. See the discussion in chapter 15 (cf. Matt. 21:42 and Mark 12:10).

17. Venerable Bede, *Commentary on the Acts of the Apostles,* 4.11. On the use of "the Jews," see *Catechism of the Catholic Church,* §597: "The historical complexity of Jesus' trial is apparent in the Gospel accounts. The personal sin of the participants (Judas, the Sanhedrin, Pilate) is known to God alone. Hence we cannot lay responsibility for the trial on the Jews in Jerusalem as a whole, *despite the outcry of a manipulated crowd and the global reproaches contained in the apostles' calls to conversion after Pentecost.* Jesus himself, in forgiving them on the cross, and Peter in following suit, both accept 'the ignorance' of the Jews of Jerusalem and even of their leaders."

18. See Acts 6:13–14.

God of Jacob. But it was Solomon who built a house for him. Yet the Most High does not dwell in houses made with hands; as the prophet says, 'Heaven is my throne, and earth my footstool. What House will you build for me, says the Lord, or what is the place of my rest?'" (Acts 7:44–49).

Here, Stephen is on trial in the Temple before the Sanhedrin, and he vigorously contrasts the old Temple, the physical Temple in which they stand, and the true temple of Christ's (now resurrected and ascended) body. Beale explains the point: "The purpose ... is to conclude that 'as Moses was rejected and the people's worship became blasphemous thereby, so with *Christ* rejected, the *Temple worship* becomes blasphemous.' But there is more. Discernible in these verses also is *the hope of a new temple that has arisen in place of the old* ... Stephen's terminology is in line with the rest of the New Testament, where ['made with hands,' v. 48] refers to *the old creation* [whereas 'made without hands'] refers to the *new creation, most specifically to the resurrection state as the beginning of the new creation.*"[19]

St. Paul, the Temple Builder

The discussion now turns from the Book of Acts to one its primary characters within the book: St. Paul. There are a number of places to examine in St. Paul that pertain to temple theology. First, some background on the Apostle himself is offered.

Paul was born and raised in Tarsus[20] in 8 AD,[21] an important city in the Roman province of Cilicia in southeastern Asia Minor. Prior to Roman rule, Tarsus was a self-governing Greek state.[22] The influence of Hellenistic education and civilization made the city a center of Greek intellectual culture. Paul himself received a thoroughly classical/Greek education. As such, he was immersed in Hellenistic and Roman culture, politics, religion, and philosophy, which were all around him from birth.[23] Yet to be immersed in it is not the

---

19. Beale, *The Temple and the Church's Mission*, 223 (emphasis added). "The Word 'handmade' ['made with hands'] (Acts 7:48) *always* refers to idols in the Greek Old Testament and is without exception a *negative reference in the New Testament*" (224, esp. n43).

20. Acts 9:11, 9:30, 11:25, 21:39, 22:3.

21. Ephesians was written in 60–62 AD, making Paul about 52–54 years old when he wrote the epistle.

22. The renowned Roman statesman Cicero was governor of Tarsus in 50 BC.

23. One cannot read Ephesians or any of Paul's epistles without sensing Greek influence. Yet

same as saying he embraced it: "For Christ did not send me to baptize *but to preach the gospel, and not with eloquent wisdom, lest the cross of Christ be emptied of its power.* For the word the cross is folly to those who are perishing, but to us who are being saved it is the power of God. For it is written, 'I will destroy the wisdom of the wise, and the cleverness of the clever I will thwart.' Where is the wise man? Where is the scribe? Where is the debater of this age? Has not God made foolish the wisdom of the world? For since, in the wisdom of God, the world did not know God through wisdom, it pleased God through the folly of what we preach to save those who believe."[24]

St. Paul was likewise immersed in the Roman world. He enjoyed Roman citizenship,[25] and a number of his epistles involve Roman-style rhetoric.[26] Numerous Pauline expressions were politically charged, and sensible only in the first-century Roman landscape in which he lived and moved and had his being: "But if you confess with your lips that Jesus is Lord and believe in your heart that God raised him from the dead, you will be saved" (Rom. 10:9–10).

The phrase *Iesus Kyrios* ("Jesus is Lord") may sound purely religious to a modern person. Yet for the Apostle Paul, it was countercultural—fighting words. Throughout the Roman Empire, all those who said *Kaiseros Kyrios* swore allegiance to Caesar and his power. Wright explains: "When Paul said, 'Jesus is lord' … his hearers must have known at once that this meant, 'So Caesar isn't.' And that was the 'good news', the *euangelion* that Paul announced around the world. Was that a subversion of the symbolic world of the empire? How could it not be?"[27]

St. Paul was a Pharisee, zealous for God: "As to the law a Pharisee."[28] His love of Torah and faithful adherence to it guided him to become a leading Pharisee: "I am a Jew, born at Tarsus in Cilicia, but brought up in this city [Jerusalem] at the feet of Gamali-el, educated according to the strict manner of the law of our fathers, being zealous for God as you all are this day."[29]

---

it was his faith in Christ, undergirded by Jewish beliefs, that drove Paul's preaching and persuaded many Jews as well Greeks. See Acts 17: 1–4.

24. See 1 Cor. 1:17–21.

25. Acts 22:27–29.

26. See below for the styles of rhetoric in Ephesians.

27. N. T. Wright, *Paul and the Faithfulness of God*, vol. 1, *Christian Origins and the Question of God* (London: SPCK, 1996), 384 (emphasis added).

28. Phil. 3:5.

29. Acts 22:3.

Interestingly, St. Paul's mentor, Gamali-el, was a philosopher opposed to violence toward/oppression of Jewish heretics.[30] Like his mentor, Paul was a brilliant scholar of Torah. But unlike Gamali-el, he held a fervent, take-no-prisoners approach to Judaism and persecuted heretical Jews, including many Christians:[31] "You have heard of my former life in Judaism, *how I persecuted the church of God* violently *and tried to destroy it*; and I advanced in Judaism beyond many of my own age among my people, so extremely zealous was I for the traditions of my fathers" (Gal. 1:13–14).

Wright clarifies and adds: "Saul may have learned a lot from Gamali-el, but he did not share his particular position."[32] This leads to a discussion to St. Paul's "conversion" experience. Meeting the risen Christ was of course the paradigm shift for Paul and his entire way of seeing the world.[33] As heavenly light "flashed about him," the voice of Jesus instructed Paul to rise and go into the city of Damascus. There, upon meeting Ananias, the scales "fall from Paul's eyes" and he regains his sight (see Acts 9:1–9). In this crucial text of Paul's "conversion," there are at least three points that need to be made relevant to this study:

1. *Paul was called by Christ as his Apostle.* First, Paul's dramatic encounter with Jesus set him apart. The crucified and risen Lord *saved* Paul—and set him on a mission to proclaim the Good News as God's chosen apostle. Though not one of the Twelve, Paul's mission was identical: to proclaim the Kingdom of God.

2. *Paul was totally transformed by Christ.* Second, Paul became fully devoted to Jesus, and he was radically changed—in mind and heart. Everything he longed for had met him in the person of Jesus. At the center of his apostolic message was that *a truly transformed life* was now possible through faith in Christ. "St. Paul saw the crucified Christ as the true and living 'place of expiation,' of whom the 'mercy seat', the *kapporeth* lost during the Exile, was

---

30. See Acts 5:34–39.

31. Saul was responsible for the death of the first Christian martyr, Stephen, as recorded in Acts: "But they cried out with a loud voice and stopped their ears and rushed together upon [Stephen]. Then they cast him out of the city and stoned him; *and the witnesses laid down their garments at the feet of a young man named Saul*" (Acts 7:57–58).

32. N. T. Wright, *What Saint Paul Really Said: Was Paul of Tarsus the Real Founder of Christianity?* (Grand Rapids, MI: Eerdmans, 1997), 30.

33. Though described matter-of-factly in Acts, this was the seminal event of his life.

but a foreshadowing. In him God has now, so to speak, lifted the veil from His face."[34]

3. *Paul was caught up in the Great Mystery.* Third and lastly, Paul came to see that Christ was the great mystery of God *in the flesh.* Christ himself was "the great reversal"—undoing Adam's sin through his death on the Cross. He recognized that, in Jesus, *God definitively revealed his faithful love for all men.* Salvation was now possible for both Jews *and* Gentiles.

St. Paul's "New Perspective"

What changed after Paul's conversion? Following his dramatic encounter with the risen Christ, Paul became a missionary and evangelist of volcanic intensity, but not immediately: "But when he who had set me apart before I was born, and had called me through his grace, was pleased to reveal his Son to me, in order that I might preach Him among the Gentiles. I did not confer with [men], nor did I go up to Jerusalem to those who were apostles before me, *but I went away into Arabia*; and again I returned to Damascus. Then *after three years* I went up to Jerusalem to visit Cephas [Peter] and remained with him fifteen days."[35]

What exactly was Paul doing in Arabia for these three years? Meditating on what had happened to him, now that he was "in Christ."[36] Notwithstanding his dramatic conversion to Christ, the roots of Paul's Jewish theology remained intact. His Jewish worldview of Yahweh "becoming king over all Israel and all creation" were in no way diminished, but had rather found their true home in Christ.

To his astonishment, Paul came to realize that Israel's hopes and destiny had been summed up and achieved in Jesus the Messiah. Yet the terms "call/calling" fit better than "conversion," which suggests a pulling away from his

---

34. Ratzinger, *Spirit of the Liturgy,* 116.

35. Gal. 1:15–18.

36. The phrase "in Christ" (Greek: *en Christō*) is at the very core of St. Paul's understanding of the "new identity" in the risen Lord, with whom every believer is now eternally bonded. It occurs eighty times in his letters: Rom. 3:24, 6:11, 6:23, 8:1, 8:2, 8:39, 9:1, 12:5, 15:17, 16:3, 16:7, 16:9, 16:10; 1 Cor. 1:2, 1:4, 1:40, 3:1, 3:10, 3:15, 3:17, 15:18, 15:19, 15:22, 15:31, 16:24; 2 Cor. 1:21, 2:14, 2:17; 5:17, 5:19, 12:2, 12:19; Gal. 2:4, 2:16, 2:17, 3:14, 3:26, 3:28, 5:6; Eph. 1:1, 1:3, 1:9, 1:12, 1:20, 2:6, 2:7, 2:10, 2:13, 3:6, 3:11, 3:21, 4:32; Phil. 1:1, 1:26, 2:1, 2:5, 3:3, 3:9, 3:14, 4:7, 4:19, 4:21; Col. 1:2, 1:4, 1:28, 2:5; 1 Thess. 2:14, 4:16, 5:18; 1 Tim. 1:14, 3:13; 2 Tim. 1:1, 1:9, 1:13, 2:1, 2:10, 3:12, 3:15.

Jewish roots. Such is not the case. Krister Stendahl agrees that "conversion" is inadequate—it implies Paul that "changed his religion: the Jew became a Christian."[37] As he explains, the "I" in Paul's letters is *not the Christian but the Jewish Apostle to the Gentiles.*"[38]

Concluding Remarks: "Woe to Me If I Do Not Preach the Gospel"

Previously, "Saul the Pharisee," like the Old Testament prophets, expected that at the end of time God would vindicate Israel, restore the Temple, right the world's wrongs, and—only then—usher in the new age of the Kingdom of God. Now, "Paul the Christian" came to see that, somehow, God already did this in Jesus Christ—not at the end of time, but in the middle of history, in Paul's present reality, and for all future time to come, until God comes again. All of this filled Paul with evangelical zeal: "Woe to me if I do not preach the gospel!"[39]

In some mysterious way, Paul now "saw" what previously evaded his sight. He now perceived that something had happened that changed everything; the new age of God had definitively begun in Jesus Christ—the New Adam, the "last Adam."[40] He longed to persuade his Jewish contemporaries that the new temple had been "destroyed and raised" in three days— in the death and Resurrection of Jesus, the Messiah.[41]

At the same time, Paul understood that the New Adam was indeed the Divine temple builder who was calling Paul to help him "fill the earth" with the presence of God. And so St. Paul's Gospel was not to the Jew only, but also to the Greek: "To the Jews I became as a Jew, in order to win Jews; to those under the Law *I* became *as one under the Law*—though not being myself under the Law—that I might win those under the Law. To those outside the Law I became as one outside the Law—not being without Law toward God but under the Law of Christ—that I might win those outside the Law. To the weak I became weak, that I might win the weak. I have become all things to all men that I might by all means save some. I do it all for the sake of the Gospel, that I may share in its blessings" (1 Cor. 9:20–23).

St. Paul grasped that, through the ministry of the Holy Spirit, the New

---

37. Krister Stendahl, *Paul among Jews and Gentiles* (Minneapolis: Fortress Press, 1976), 11.
38. Ibid., 12.
39. See 1 Cor. 9:16.
40. See 1 Cor. 15:45.
41. See John 2:19–21.

Adam was building his new Temple—one that would fill the earth—and that this Temple had a name: *ekklesia*, "church," and the New Adam, raised by God in the flesh, was now divinely guiding this temple-building mission from his heavenly glory.

From this point forward, St. Paul's firm hope, that God would vindicate Israel, was more resolute than ever; only now, this hope was greatly expanding, in ways that he could have never seen or comprehended before the Damascus road experience. Now it was the risen Lord, seated in glory at the right hand of the Father, who would vindicate Israel. Not only this, but the risen Christ was also renewing the whole of Creation, in fact. He had inaugurated a New Creation—a drama in which the whole of humanity was caught up, in which every person would hear the Good News of God's salvation and, by believing in his name, receive the gift of salvation.

Yet none of this negated every truth that St. Paul deeply believed about God; in some hidden way, Christ was part of God's plan from all of eternity, and Paul recognized that he was blessed—called to be at the inception of this new ordering of Creation. Nothing would ever be the same, not for St. Paul, not for the entire world. As he began to teach and preach the Gospel, every belief and hope he had ever grasped, and was now grasping, converged in Jesus Christ. For St. Paul, every reason for ever "going to Temple" was now fulfilled—and surpassed in Jesus Christ, who *was* the New Temple in Person. This grand theme runs through the Pauline epistles. It was as if the fiber optics of the entire Old Testament—of the entire sweep of salvation history from Creation onward—ran through St. Paul's heart and mind, and out of his mouth and pen.

St. Paul instructs Timothy; for example, that if he is delayed, not to fear. He writes to Timothy in order that he may know how he ought to live and behave *"in the household of God, which is the church of the living God, the pillar and bulwark of the truth"* (1 Tim. 3:14–16). The above remarks serve as introduction to the temple theology of St. Paul, to which the study now turns.

Temple Theology in St. Paul's Letters

How does one begin to describe St. Paul's "temple optics?"[42] To begin with, he believed and taught that the New Creation had begun in Jesus

---

42. It is not possible to discuss every temple-related text in Paul. The following represent some of the more important examples.

Christ, who was the New Adam. He makes this connection clear in Romans 5: "Yet death reigned from Adam to Moses, even over those whose sins were not like the transgression of Adam, who was a type of the one who was to come." Yet it is not a comparison that St. Paul speaks of with regard to Adam and Christ; rather, it is a contrast of seismic proportions. He continues, "The free gift is not like the trespass. *For if many died through [Adam's] trespass, how much more has the grace of God and the free gift in the grace of that one man Jesus Christ abounded for many.*" Christ's work exceeds that of Adam's in every way: "The free gift is not like the effect of that one man's sin. For the judgment following one trespass brought condemnation, but the free gift following many trespasses brings justification. *If, because of one man's trespass, death reigned through that one man, much more will those who receive the abundance of grace and the free gift of righteousness reign in life through the one man Jesus Christ*" (Rom. 5:14–17).

For St. Paul, these two men—the first Adam and Jesus, the new and definitive Adam— brought together and summarized all of salvation history: "The first man Adam became a living being; the last Adam became a life-giving spirit" (1 Cor. 15:45).

St. Paul's entire theology of humanity's future resurrection is based upon this fact: that in Adam, all men inherit death, but in Jesus, the new, all men may inherit life, eternal life: "For as in Adam all die, so also in Christ shall all be made alive" (1 Cor. 15:22).

As the *Catechism* explains, "St. Paul tells us that the human race takes its origin from two men: Adam and Christ. The first man, Adam, he says, became a living soul, the last Adam a life-giving spirit,"[43] adding further that the first Adam *"was made by the last Adam, from whom he also received his soul, to give him life.*... The second Adam stamped his image on the first Adam when he created him. That is why he took on himself the role and the name of the first Adam, in order that he might not lose what he had made in his own image. The first Adam, the last Adam: the first had a beginning, the last knows no end. The last Adam is indeed the first; as he himself says: 'I am the first and the last.'"[44]

The new Temple was built on the foundation of the risen Jesus. And if Jesus is the New Adam, the he recapitulates Adam's temple-building role. Yet

---

43. *Catechism of the Catholic Church*, §360.
44. *Catechism of the Catholic Church*, §360.

where Adam (and later Israel) ultimately failed in his God-given, earth-filling vocation, Jesus, the New Adam, succeeded. Jesus was conceived by the Holy Spirit in the Virgin Mary's womb because he is the New Adam who inaugurates the new Creation.

Yet this work of temple building, of filling the earth with God's glorious presence, is ongoing. The task has been given to St. Peter and the Twelve[45] — and, sustained by the Holy Spirit, it has in a sense only begun at Pentecost. In this way, the Church is the new Temple on the foundation of the Risen Christ, and its mission was to transform the Creation, for the sake of the Son, fulfilling the mission of the Father, in the power of the Spirit. St. Paul's promise to the Church at Corinth is that anyone who is "in Christ is a new creation" (2 Cor. 5:17) rests in part upon his theology of Baptism ("the old has passed away, behold, the new has come"), and in part upon his firm conviction that in Christ, the age of the new Creation has in present in the very body of the believer.

This is seen in 1 Corinthians, in St. Paul's treatment on the resurrection of the body: "For as in Adam all die, so also in Christ shall all be made alive" (1 Cor. 15:22). It is seen again in 2 Corinthians, given in a context of St. Paul summoning the Church to moral courage—the courage even to face death: "We are afflicted in every way, but not crushed; perplexed, but not driven to despair; persecuted, but not forsaken; struck down, but not destroyed; always carrying in the body the death of Jesus, so that the life of Jesus may also be (*phanerothe en hemon to somati*) manifested in our bodies" (2 Cor. 4:8–10).

This New Creation motif, as the reader has come to better understand over the course of this book, is itself rooted in Second Temple Jewish eschatological hopes for a new Exodus and a new Temple, which St. Paul came to see as being fulfilled in and through the risen Christ. With respect to the mention of baptism as it relates to the preceding text, it should be quickly added that the New Creation that he wrote about emanated from the sacramental and priestly ministry of the Church.

St. Paul came to understood that the New Creation is bursting into the old through the power of the Holy Spirit, being unleased in the life-giving sacraments: "In Christ God was reconciling the world to himself, not counting their trespasses against them, and entrusting to us the message of recon-

---

45. See Matt. 28:18–20.

ciliation. So we are ambassadors for Christ, God making his appeal through us. We beseech you on behalf of Christ, be reconciled to God. For our sake he made him to be sin who knew no sin, so that in him we might become the righteousness of God" (1 Cor. 5:19–21).[46]

For St. Paul, *this really was Good News*—for him, for his churches, indeed for all of humanity—and Paul became preoccupied with its urgent proclamation to Jew and Gentile alike: "According to the grace of God given to me, like a *skilled master builder* [Greek: *sophos architekton*] I laid a foundation, and another man is building upon it. Let each man take care how he builds upon it. For no other foundation can anyone lay than that which is laid, which is Jesus Christ" (1 Cor. 5:10–12).[47]

St. Paul had been admonishing the Corinthians with an image of a "vineyard,"[48] but several verses later, his metaphor shifts—not just to a building, but to the Temple. This seems like an unnatural shift—why? As Beale suggests, "The shift from the agricultural metaphor … to a temple may be viewed to be more natural in the light of our prior study that *the Garden of Eden, Israel's garden-like promises land, and Israel's future restoration in a garden-like land were either equated or associated with a Temple*."[49]

"Paul identifies the 'foundation' of the new Temple to be Jesus Christ. Paul 'laid' this 'foundation' among the Corinthians when they first believed, and now Apollos and others are 'building upon it.'"[50] Moreover, following

46. *Catechism of the Catholic Church*: "The apostles and their successors carry out this '*ministry of reconciliation*', not only by announcing to men God's forgiveness merited for us by Christ, and calling them to conversion and faith; *but also by communicating to them the forgiveness of sins in Baptism, and reconciling them with God and with the Church through the power of the keys, received from Christ*" (§981); "In imparting to his apostles his own power to forgive sins the Lord also gives them the authority to reconcile sinners with the Church. This ecclesial dimension of their task is expressed most notably in Christ's solemn words to Simon Peter: "I will give you the keys of the kingdom of heaven, and whatever you bind on earth shall be bound in heaven, and whatever you loose on earth shall be loosed in heaven" (§1444). See Matt. 16:19; Matt. 18:18, 28:16–20; John 20:19–23.

47. See 1 Cor. 3:10–12.

48. See 1 Cor. 5:9.

49. Beale, *The Temple and the Church's Mission*, 246. Joseph A. Fitzmyer agrees: "The phrase, 'God's temple,' is an OT term found in Dan 5:3 … and Judith 4:2 for the actual Temple in Jerusalem, but *Paul uses it now in a metaphorical sense*, which does not imply any antagonism for the Jerusalem Temple. The Christian congregation is *no longer just a building belonging to God* (3:9), but is *God's very dwelling place, 'the temple of God,' the place where God's presence with Christians is to be found. First Corinthians: A New Translation with Introduction and Commentary*, vol. 32, *Anchor Yale Bible* (New Haven, CT: Yale University Press, 2008), 202 (emphases added).

50. Beale, *The Temple and the Church's Mission*, 249.

the Temple metaphor, Paul draws on imagery used in the Old Testament formerly associated with the building of Solomon's Temple: "So I have provided for *the house of my God*, so far as I was able, the *gold* for the things of *gold*, the *silver* for the things of *silver*, and the *bronze* for the things of *bronze*, the *iron* for the things of *iron*, and *wood* for the things of *wood*, besides great quantities of *onyx* and *stones* for setting, *antimony*, *colored stones*, all sorts of *precious stones*, and *marble*" (1 Chron. 29:2).[51]

Similarly, a parallel of this sort is seen in 1 Corinthians: "Now if any one builds on the foundation with *gold, silver, precious stones, wood, hay, straw*" (1 Cor. 3:12). There is no doubt that, for Paul, the Church at Corinth is the new Temple of God, with Christ as its foundation: "Do you not know that *you are God's temple* and that God's Spirit *dwells* in you? If anyone destroys *God's temple*, God will destroy him. For *God's temple is holy, and that temple you are*" (1 Cor. 3:16–17).[52] St. Cyprian, the martyred bishop of Carthage was himself rooted in this sort of Pauline thought: "Let those who have been redeemed by the blood of Christ submit to the rule of our Redeemer with the absolute obedience of servants. Let us take care not to bring anything unclean or defiled *into the Temple of God*, lest He be offended and *leave the abode where He dwells*."[53]

The End-Time Temple in the Present Age

In the above text, Paul urges the Church at Corinth to see themselves as they are: the new Temple built upon the foundation of Christ. St. Paul's second letter to the church is yet another example of temple theology, and in this reference he describes the Church as an "end-time Temple": "What agreement has the temple of God with idols?" Here, Paul seems to allude to the utter incompatibility of right worship mixed with pagan idolatry, as seen often in the story of Israel in the Old Testament. Christ's grace demands something more, a true break from the former life and in its place "a sacred

---

51. "The only other place in Scripture were a 'foundation' of a building is laid and 'gold,' 'silver,' and 'precious stones' are 'built' upon the foundation is Solomon's temple." Beale, *The Temple and the Church's Mission*, 247. See 1 Ki. 5:17, 6:20–21, 26:8, 6:30, 6:35; 1 Chron. 22:16, 29:2–7.

52. "Three times [Paul] calls the Corinthians 'the temple of God.'" Beale, *The Temple and the Church's Mission*, 250. Additionally, Beale suggests Malachi chaps. 3–4, which speak of silver, gold, etc. being purified in a "furnace" appears to be behind the text.

53. St. Cyprian of Carthage, *The Dress of Virgins*, 2.

space," a sanctuary of holiness in the heart of every believer: "For we are the temple of the living God; as God said, 'I will live in them and move among them, and I will be their God, and they shall be my people. Therefore, come out from them, and be separate from them, says the Lord, and touch nothing unclean; then I will welcome you, and I will be a father to you, and you shall be my sons and daughters,' says the Lord Almighty" (2 Cor. 6:16–18).

Several Old Testament texts lie under St. Paul's metaphor,[54] including Leviticus 26. Like Paul's message to the Corinthians, verse 12 contains the covenantal phrase "I will be your God, and you shall be my people." Moreover, the verse includes the verb *halak*, and the text may be translated as something like, "I will live/move among you."[55] For St. Paul, as in Leviticus, the charge to God's people is to "holy worship," and turning away from idolatry. This temptation to turn away to other gods, a perennial problem for Israel, was similarly a problem for St. Paul's Corinth.

Such covenantal language in Leviticus would be helpful to St. Paul's argument to the Corinthians, in that he was exhorting the Church *to internalize the covenant*; to become, as the new people of God, *the holy temple of God* that he might truly and rightly dwell therein. In other words, Paul is urging the Corinthians not simply to *offer* the sacrifices in the Temple, as in the Old Covenant, but to *become the Temple sacrifices* through holy living in the New Covenant.

A second text that likely influenced St. Paul's thought in 2 Corinthians 6 is found in the Book of Ezekiel. In chapter 37, God explicitly affirms, "I will make a covenant (*berith*) of peace with them; it shall be an *everlasting covenant* with them" (Ezek. 37:26). Like the other text in Leviticus, Ezekiel contains the covenantal phrase "I will be their God, and they shall be my people" (v. 28).

Strikingly, though, this text from Ezekiel contains several additional fibers of temple theology that are more explicit still. First, this is seen in the use of the prophet's term *miqdashi*, as in, "I will set *my sanctuary* in the midst of them" (v. 26). This motif is repeated in verse 27, but instead uses the term *miskani*, literally "my dwelling place." Here, as in Leviticus, is clear evidence of temple language. Yet in Leviticus 26 the "temple" that is in view is the Tabernacle of the wilderness. In contrast, the prophet Ezekiel is thinking in terms of a temple

---

54. Beale, *The Temple and the Church's Mission*, 254–56.

55. Technically, *halak* is translated, often enough, as "walk," although the range of meaning is much closer to "live/move" than to the mechanical notion of "walking."

that is yet to come, that is, the future sanctuary of the eschatological age. This point should be kept in mind, and its significance will become clear shortly.

There is a second fiber in which the temple theology of Ezekiel surpasses that in Leviticus. Specifically, in verse 26, there is a clear echo of Eden in the use of the prophet's use of the phrase, "I will *bless them* and *multiply them*" (see Gen. 1:28). Although English translations of Ezekiel 37:26 allow for "bless them" as in Genesis 1:28, the two texts use distinct verbs, *natah* versus *barak*, respectively. Still—and this must be emphasized—both Ezekiel 36 and Genesis 1 do use the identical verb for "multiply," *raha*. Moreover, Ezekiel 37:28, in keeping with the prophet's eschatological theology, envisions a kind of multiplying and expanding of the future Temple, such that the holiness of God's people will "radiate" outward to all of the earth, in a manner consistent with the original temple-building call of Adam in Genesis 1: "*Then the nations will know* that I the Lord sanctify Israel, when my sanctuary is in the midst of them for evermore."

If Ezekiel 37 (along with Leviticus 26) lies underneath St. Paul's message to the Corinthian church, as is argued here, then this theme of "multiplication" becomes not merely interesting but also decisive. Here is why: in 2 Corinthians 6, St. Paul urges the church to live in a way that surpasses the people of the Old Covenant—not only to *go* to the Temple, but also to *become* the Temple. And not only to become the Temple (i.e., for one another), but also *to recapitulate and complete the failed call of Adam, to multiply the holiness of the New Temple "beyond Eden," spreading it "beyond Israel" and out to all the earth.*

The church, as St. Paul understands it, has not only the *ability* to do what Adam did not, but also the *responsibility* to do so as the new people of God. Thankfully, they also have the *power* to do so, inasmuch as the Holy Spirit "lives and moves" among them. In Christ, the church *is* the "temple of the living God." Paul brings together three fibers of temple theology: from Leviticus, Ezekiel, and Genesis. St. Paul's message now becomes clear: in the age of the New Covenant, the Church is the fulfillment of the Old Testament hopes for a coming new Temple. For St. Paul, the Father has accomplished— in Christ—the beginning of his eschatological sanctuary in the midst of them, forever more: "Paul is not merely making an analogy between a *temple ideal* and that of Christians [rather, Paul is saying] that Christians *are* the beginning fulfillment of the actual prophecy of the end-time temple."[56]

56. Beale, *The Temple and the Church's Mission*, 254.

345

From Tradition, St. Ambrosiaster adds spiritual depth to the above discussion of 2 Corinthians 6, as he writes, "No one can serve two masters. Christ has proclaimed that we should go away from the devil ... *He has forbidden the worship of idols because they are incompatible with the Temple of God. We are temples of the living God.* There is nothing more damaging to us than idols, because they tempt us to depart from our faith in the one true God."[57]

Growing into the Temple of the Lord

The next example of temple theology in St. Paul is also "one of the most explicit descriptions of the Church as the temple in all of the New Testament."[58] The Apostle writes, "So then you are no longer strangers and sojourners, but you are fellow citizens with the saints and members of *the household of God, built upon the foundation of the apostles and prophets*, Christ Jesus himself being the *cornerstone*, in whom the whole structure is joined together and grows into a holy temple in the Lord; in whom you also are built into it for a dwelling place of God in the Spirit" (Eph. 2:19–23).

Here, once again, St. Paul introduces this new development beyond the Gospels, which primarily[59] present Jesus as the Temple; the Apostle presents the Church as the temple—the temple built upon the foundation stone of Christ. Notice the importance of the apostles (and prophets) in the text; for St. Paul, there is no space, no distance whatsoever between the "foundation" of the new Temple, which is the Apostles, and the foundation stone, which is Christ. The foundation fills out the structure of the Temple, of which the foundation stone is the sure basis of everything.

With the Apostles as the foundation of the Temple, St. Peter the apostle to the Jews, and St. Paul the apostle to the Gentiles, all of the Church is "built together" upon the true cornerstone, Christ, and it is thereby united as one, as St. Jerome insisted: "This cornerstone joins together both walls and restores two peoples to unity, concerning which God said through Isaiah:

57. Ambrosiaster (ca. 366–84 AD), *Commentary on Paul's Epistles*. "Ambrosiaster" is the name given to an anonymous Pauline commentator, once thought to have been composed by St. Ambrose.

58. Beale, *The Temple and the Church's Mission*, 259.

59. But recall Matt. 21:42: "Jesus said to them, 'Have you never read in the scriptures: "*The very stone which the builders rejected has become the head of the corner*"; this was the Lord's doing, and it is marvelous in our eyes?'"

'Behold, I will lay a cornerstone in Zion as its foundation, elect and precious; the one who believes in it will not be ashamed.' It was His will to build further upon this cornerstone and other cornerstones, so that the Apostle Paul would be able to say boldly, 'built upon the foundation of the apostles and the prophets, with Jesus Christ himself being the chief cornerstone.'"[60]

The Temple of the Holy Spirit

What the above Pauline texts all share in common is that the New Temple is not described as Christ alone, but *Christ and the church*. This begs the question: Does this development contradict or diminish the temple theology of the Four Gospels, wherein it is consistently the case that Jesus is identified as the new Temple? No; to the contrary, Paul actually underscores the theology of the Gospels. By describing Christ as the cornerstone of the Temple, upon which (along with his holy Apostles) the new Temple of the Church is built, Paul has applied the theology of the Gospels, and in so doing "built" upon it, so to speak, extending the imagery to its ecclesiological conclusion. Just as the head is united to the members, the body,[61] so is Christ, the cornerstone united to his temple, the Church.

Now, with this trajectory of temple theology in St. Paul made clear, one final example remains. Here again the reader encounters what amounts to a fresh way of applying the temple theology of the Old Testament within early Christianity. And it is precisely this: not only is the Church *the new Temple*, but also with this and from this, he will add that each member of the Church, by virtue of their baptism, and being "in Christ," is now *individually* a temple of the Holy Spirit: "Do you not know that your body is a temple of the Holy Spirit within you, which you have from God? You are not your own; you were bought with a price. So glorify God in your body" (1 Cor. 6:19).

Fitzmyer explains St. Paul's interpretative move in 1 Corinthians: "In [1 Cor.] 3:16, Paul called the Christian community of Corinth '*the temple of God*' and said that '*the Spirit of God*' *dwelt in it*, but now he teaches something very similar about *the individual Christian and his or her body*. Thus St. Paul affirms not only the corporate, but also the individual sense of the indwelling Spirit of God."[62]

---

60. St. Jerome, *Commentary on Zechariah* 3.14.10–11.
61. See Eph. 5:23; Col. 1:23, 2:18–19.   62. Fitzmyer, *First Corinthians*, 269–70.

On a practical and spiritual level, the *Catechism* adds the sacramental dimension of all of this to the life of the believer: "The Holy Spirit is '*the principle of every vital and truly saving action in each part of the Body.*' He works in many ways to build up the whole Body in charity:[63] by God's Word '*which is able to build you up;*'[64] by Baptism, through which he forms Christ's Body;[65] *by the sacraments*, which give growth and healing to Christ's members; by '*the grace of the apostles, which holds first place among his gifts;*'[66] by the *virtues*, which make us act according to what is good; finally, by the *many special graces* (called '*charisms*'), by which he makes the *faithful 'fit and ready to undertake various tasks and offices for the renewal and building up of the Church.*'"[67]

Along similar lines is an insightful papal reflection in the following text. Pope Pius XII drew upon St. Paul's image to encourage a new purity among young people: "For modesty foresees threatening danger, forbids us to expose ourselves to risks, demands the avoidance of those occasions which the imprudent do not shun. It does not like impure or loose talk, it shrinks from the slightest immodesty, it carefully avoids suspect familiarity with persons of the other sex, since it brings the soul to show due reverence to the body, as being a member of Christ and *the temple of the Holy Spirit*. He who possesses the treasure of Christian modesty abominates every sin of impurity and instantly flees whenever he is tempted by its seductions."[68]

More recently, St. Pope John Paul II applied St. Paul's teaching to those called to the vocation of marriage as well as to those called to the priesthood or religious life: "Through what we discover in a clear-sighted reading of 1 Corinthians ... we discover the whole realism of the Pauline theology of the body. While the Apostle proclaims in the letter that 'your body is a temple of the Holy Spirit within you' (1 Cor. 6:19), he is at the same time fully aware of the weakness and sinfulness to which man is subject precisely by reason of the concupiscence of the flesh ... In fact, in one as well as the other way of living—today we would say, in one as well as the other vocation—the 'gift' is at work that each one receives from God, that is, *grace, which brings it about that the body is 'a temple of the Holy Spirit'* and remains such *in virginity* (con-

---

63. See Eph. 4:16.
64. See Acts 20:32.
65. See 1 Cor. 12:13.
66. Citing *Lumen Gentium* 7, §2.
67. *Catechism of the Catholic Church*, §798.
68. Pope Pius XVII, *Sacra Virginitas*, Encyclical on Consecrated Virginity, March 25, 1954.

tinence) *as well as in marriage*, if man remains faithful to his own gift and, in conformity with his state or vocation, *does not 'dishonor' the 'temple of the Holy Spirit,' which is his body."*[69]

Concluding Remarks

In the Book of Acts and in St. Paul, one sees remarkable development of temple theology beyond the Four Gospels. Like the Gospels, these New Testament texts take up the importance of the Temple from the Old Testament, from the life of Israel, and show its fulfillment in light of the life, death, Resurrection, and Ascension of Christ.

At the same time, St. Paul's letters, along with Acts, bring out new dimensions of temple theology not realized in the Gospels, especially that the Church is the continuing presence of Christ on the earth and, inasmuch as it has the Apostles as its foundation, rests upon the true cornerstone, which is Christ himself. This image of the Church as the new Temple is profoundly important, not only for understanding the message of the New Testament but also in terms of ecclesiology, the nature of the sacramental life of the Church, Christian morality, Christian hope, and much more. Finally, added to the image of the Church as the new temple is the body of the individual, baptized believer: each Christian is called to be a "little sanctuary" within the larger temple of the Church.

With this, the study of temple theology in Acts and St. Paul comes to a close. Chapter 19 is the final reflection on the temple theology within the New Testament.

---

69. St. Pope John Paul II, *Man and Woman He Created Them: A Theology of the Body*, trans. Michael Waldstein (Boston, MA: Pauline Books and Media, 2006), 455 [*TOB* 85.2], emphases added.

19

THE SPIRIT AND THE BRIDE

Temple Theology in Hebrews and the Book of Revelation,
Eternal Priest, Heavenly Temple

> The new Temple, not made by human hands, *does exist, but*
> *it is also still under construction.* The great gesture of embrace
> emanating from the Crucified *has not yet reached its goal; it*
> *has only just begun.* Christian liturgy is liturgy on the way, a
> liturgy of pilgrimage toward the transfiguration of the world,
> which will only take place when God is "all in all."[1]
>
> Cardinal Joseph Ratzinger

The Book of Hebrews: Jesus, the Eternal High Priest

This study of temple theology began with the first book of the Old Testament and in this chapter concludes with a look at the last book of the New Testament. This chapter will discuss Christ, the "eternal" High Priest of the Book of Hebrews, followed by the heavenly Temple of the New Jerusalem in the Book of Revelation.

First, a few introductory and contextual remarks are necessary:[2] Hebrews

---

1. Joseph Ratzinger, *The Spirit of the Liturgy*, trans. John Saward (San Francisco: Ignatius Press, 2000), 50.

2. Among the best modern introductions to Hebrews, see: (1) Ceslas Spicq, C. *L'Épître aux Hébreux* [The Epistle to the Hebrews], 2 vols. Biblical Studies (Paris: Gabalda, 1952–53); (2) Albert Vanhoye, *Old Testament Priests and the New Priest*, trans. J. Bernard Orchard (Petersham, MA: St. Bede's, 1986), esp. 91–238; and (3) Craig R. Koester, *Hebrews: A New Translation with Introduction and Commentary*, vol. 36, *Anchor Yale Bible* (New Haven, CT: Yale University Press, 2001). Additionally, see Harold Attridge, *The Epistle to the Hebrews* (*Hermeneia*) (Philadelphia: Fortress, 1989); William L. Lane, *Hebrews*, 2 vols. Word Biblical Commentary (Dallas: Word Books, 1991); Andre Feuillet,

begins by contrasting the past with the author's present: "In many and various ways God spoke of old to our fathers by the prophets; but in these last days he has spoken to us by a Son, whom he appointed the heir of all things, through whom also he created the world" (Heb. 1:1–2).

Here, at the opening of the letter, all of the periods of the past—from Creation through Moses and David, up the birth of Christ—are consolidated and summed up various ways in the expression "God spoke." The author of Hebrews declares that God has definitively "spoken to us *by a Son*."[3]

In Hebrews 1–2, Christ is shown as "superior to the angels." Christ is above them in sovereignty by virtue of being "lower than the angels"[4] in his Incarnation, by which he perfects the Old Covenant that God made with Israel, so that all the sons of Adam may be saved.

Later, in Hebrews 5, the author asserts that Christ is High Priest, "just as Aaron was,"[5] yet to Christ alone, and to no other high priest, has God ever said, "Thou art a priest forever, after the order of Melchizedek."[6] This phrase "after the order of Melchizedek," which occurs five times in Hebrews,[7] is crucial to understanding the entire letter. As discussed in chapter 5, Genesis links the mysterious Melchizedek with the pre-Levitical patriarchal priesthood, in the epoch of the natural, father-son priesthood (see Num. 3:13–17).

Melchizedek is identified as the righteous priest-king of *Salem* (an earlier term for Jerusalem)[8] who brings "bread and wine" to Abram's (i.e., Abraham's), to sacrifice to Abram's God. For the author of Hebrews, Jesus is, like Melchizidek, both king and high priest. As such, Melchizidek's ministry in Salem prefigures Jesus's ministry in the "heavenly Jerusalem" later in the Epistle: "But you have come to Mount Zion and to the city of the living God, *the heavenly Jerusalem*, and to innumerable angels in festal gathering" (Heb. 12:22).

"Le 'commencement' de l'économie chrétienne d'après He ii.3–4; Mc i.1 et Ac i.1–2 ["The 'beginning' of the Christian dispensation from ii.3 He-4; I.1 Mc and Ac i.1–2"] *New Testament Studies* 24 (1977–78): 163–74.

    3. Vanhoye suggests that the *Epistle* is subdivided into three larger sections: Heb. 1:1–4:16, where one "looks in vain for the slightest allusion to the priesthood," and Heb. 5:1–10:18, the central section of the epistle, which unfolds "the priesthood of Christ." Although Vanhoye does not treat the remainder of the epistle in such an extended way, the third section is Heb. 10:19–13:25, in which the New Covenant of the New Priesthood is developed, along with an encouragement to faith and perseverance. *Old Testament Priests and the New Priest*, 90–94.

    4. Heb. 2:7, 2:9.   5. Heb. 5:4.

    6. Heb. 5:6.   7. Heb. 5:6, 5:10, 6:20, 7:11, 7:17.

    8. Psa. 76:1–2: "In Judah God is known, his name is great in Israel. His abode has been established in Salem, his dwelling place in Zion."

Before going further, recall that it was Israel's *apostasy*—the catastrophe of the Golden Calf incident[9]—that brought about "a change in the priest-hood"[10] from the earlier father-son model to the Levitical priesthood. This fact is significant for the author of Hebrews, who reaches back, long before the institution of the Levitical priesthood, to the earlier "primordial" priest-hood, of whom the mysterious Melchizidek is the definitive archetype. Here, Hebrews makes this extraordinary claim vital: "Now if perfection had been attainable through the Levitical priesthood … what further need would there have been for another priest to arise after the order of Melchizedek, rather than one named after the order of Aaron? For when there is a change in the priesthood, there is necessarily a change in the law as well" (Heb. 7:11–14).

The "change in the priesthood" to which the author of Hebrews refers is foretold in Psalm 110, which ascribes the Melchizedekian priesthood to Da-vid: "The Lord has sworn and will not change his mind, 'You are a priest forever after the order of Melchizedek'" (Heb. 7:11–14).

To be clear, it is David who the psalm identifies as the priest in the or-der of Melchizedek. This is the only explanation of how David—of the tribe of Judah—could have legitimately offered "sacrifices" to the Lord—actions that the Levitical priests—and only the Levitical priests may do.[11] Jesus—like David—is of the "tribe of Judah" and, according to the Levitical order, "disqualified" to offer priestly sacrifices.[12]

Hebrews explains that the Levitical priesthood was not established by "di-vine oath."[13] Yet the priesthood of Melchizidek *was established with an oath*, referring to Psalm 110. As such, Hebrews explains, "This makes Jesus the sure-ty [ESV: "guarantor"][14] of *a better covenant*." What does the author of He-brews mean that Jesus is the "guarantor of a better covenant?" In his commen-tary on the epistle, Koester explains, "People [in the ancient world] regularly agreed that life is better than death.[15] Therefore, instead of identifying the line of Jewish priests with tradition, Hebrews associates them with *mortality*."[16]

---

9. See Exod. 32.

10. Heb. 7:12.

11. See 1 Chron. 21:28; also Matt. 12:1–8; 1 Sam. 21:1–6.

12. See Matt. 1:2, 2:3, 2:6; Luke 3:30–33; 1 Sam. 17:12.

13. Heb. 7:20.

14. Koester: "A surety was often a relative or friend" (Heb. 363). See Sir. 29:14; Plutarch, *Alcibi-ades* 5.4.

15. See Deut. 30:15; Prov. 14:27; Jer. 8:3.   16. Koester, *Hebrews*, 371 (emphasis added).

Here the rich Christology of Hebrews again emerges, contrasting the eternal high priesthood of Jesus with that of the Levitical high priests. The author of the book emphasizes that the high priests of the Old Covenant were "many in number," because death itself prevented any one of them from continuing in office in perpetuity." In contrast, Christ "holds his priesthood permanently because *He continues forever*" (Heb. 7:22–23). This is the case, as Koester clarifies, because "Like Israel's priests, Jesus did die, yet death did not terminate His priesthood, but rather inaugurated it. Jesus 'offered himself' through death,[17] yet death did not mean that He ceased to exist, for through His exaltation he continues forever."[18]

Margaret Barker correctly situates the distinction between the priesthood of the Old and New Covenants in terms of Resurrection: "When Hebrews compared the two priesthoods—Melchizidek's and Aarons—*the difference between them was the resurrection* ... [the author of Hebrews] explained that the sons of Aaron were priests due to 'descent,' but Melchizidek was a priest of 'ascent.' He 'arises'—the word means 'resurrection' by the 'power of an indestructible life.'[19] The Aaronic priests die and have successors, but Melchizidek is a priest forever, because he is already resurrected."[20]

In summarizing key theological distinctions between the eternal priesthood of Jesus and the former, mortal priesthood of Aaron, Hebrews comes to a high point in the following text from chapter 7: "For it was fitting that we should have such a high priest, holy, blameless, unstained, and separated from sinners, exalted above the heavens. He has no need, like those high priests, to offer sacrifices daily, first for his own sins and then for those of the people; He did this once for all when He offered up himself. Indeed, the law appoints men in their weakness as high priests, but the word of the oath, which came later than the law, appoints a Son *who has been made perfect forever*" (Heb. 7:26–28).[21]

---

17. See Heb. 7:27.

18. There is an implied contrast between the many priests of the Levitical order and the singular priesthood of Jesus. This is reinforced by the instances of *hoi men ... ho de* in Lev. 7:20–21, 7:23–24.

19. Heb. 7:16.

20. Margaret Barker, *Temple Themes in Christian* Worship, 3rd ed. (London: Bloomsbury, 2013), 112. See Heb. 7:23–24.

21. "What is really new in this whole paragraph is its *polemical tone*. The author is *no longer content* with peacefully setting forth his subject; *he launches an offensive*. From the first phase (7:11) *he attacks the Levitical priesthood*. He questions its values and hints at its suppression: 'If a perfect conse-

Following this, in chapter 9, the author of Hebrews builds upon his depiction of Christ as Israel's true and perfect high priest. He does so by comparing the sacrifice of Christ on the Cross to the sacrifice of the high priest of the Old Covenant on the Day of Atonement. To begin with, the high priesthood of Jesus comes to the Church through "the greater and more perfect [tabernacle]²² not made with hands, that is, not of this creation" (Heb. 9:11). Unlike the Levitical high priests of old, Jesus had no need of using the blood of animals; rather, the atonement brought about is accomplished *dia de tou idou* ("by his own") blood (v. 12). Jesus accomplished the redemption of all humanity *ephaphax eis* ("once for all").

In other words, the sacrifice of Christ is not merely a difference in *degree*—that is, one sacrifice over the many—but a spectacular difference in *kind*. Unlike the Levitical high priests, who could only procure a limited and temporal atonement, Christ's sacrifice made possible for humanity an *aionian lytrosin* ("eternal redemption").

The author of Hebrews brings this home by way of contrast; if the temporal sacrifices of the Old Covenant brought about a sanctification of the flesh, "how much more shall the blood of Christ, who through the eternal Spirit offered himself without blemish to God" (v. 14). Moreover, it is not only "the flesh" that is purified by Christ, but also *the whole man*, body and soul, expressed by Paul in the phrase *ten syneidesin hemon* ("our conscience"). As a result of this holistic and total purification of the person, rendered possible by the sacrifice of Christ, Paul can admonish the church to leave behind "dead works to serve the living God" (v. 14).

From all of this it becomes clear that the author of Hebrews decries the inefficacious nature of the corrupt and temporal priesthood of the Old Covenant. In fact, he blames it, in good measure, for the downfall of the Temple, which was destined to be replaced by the new Temple in the person of the risen Jesus. According to its author, now and forevermore the former manifestations of priesthood were but a shadow of a greater reality—the eternal high priesthood of the Risen Christ: "The Christian claim is unmistakable:

---

cration had truly been conferred by the Levitical priesthood ... what need would there still have been *to raise up a priesthood of another kind?*'" Vanhoye, *Old Testament Priests and the New Priest*, 163.

22. "Some take the tent to be *Christ's body* [gives examples] since God's Word became 'flesh' and 'tented' in Jesus (John 1:14), whose body was a '*temple*' (John 2:21). Some identify the tent with *Christ's humanity* [gives examples]; *His resurrected body*, His *eucharistic* body ... or the church as his body." Vanhoye, *Old Testament Priests and the New Priest*, 193–96. See also Koester, *Hebrews*, 409.

the corruption of the priesthood has brought the downfall of the temple, and Jesus was the new high priest."[23]

The true sanctuary of Jesus, the eternal High Priest, is at the right hand of the Father, where he continually "lives to make intercession."[24] As such, Christ has accomplished what the Aaronic high priests could not: the inner sanctification on the believer, making them into a dwelling place for the Holy Spirit. "And every priest stands daily at his service, offering repeatedly the same sacrifices, which can never take away sins. But when Christ had offered for all time a single sacrifice for sins, He sat down at the right hand of God, then to wait until his enemies should be made a stool for his feet. For by a single offering *He has perfected*[25] for all time those who are sanctified" (Heb. 10:11–14).

In light of this perfection of the eternal High Priest, the author of Hebrews admonishes his readers to "enter the sanctuary of God's rest." In the following, note that phrases such as "the confession of our hope" (10:23) and "meeting together" (10:25) are liturgical language, rooted in the weekly Sunday worship ritual of the earliest Christians.[26]

The mystery deepens, as explained by the author, as believers need not live in perpetual uncertainty, but with *parresian* ("confidence") to enter the sanctuary of the New Temple (10:19). Here, the temple theology of Hebrews becomes highly sacramental, as its author explains that one "enters" this new sanctuary *en to haimati Iesou* ("by the blood of Jesus"), a clear reference to the Eucharist of the early Christian believers.

The author further crystalizes this Eucharistic motif through the use of the term *katapetasmatos*, translated as "curtain" or "veil" (v. 20). This term is

---

23. Barker, *Temple Themes in Christian Worship*, 56.

24. See Heb. 7:25; *Catechism of the Catholic Church*, §662: "The lifting up of Jesus on the cross signifies and announces his lifting up by his Ascension into heaven, and indeed begins it. Jesus Christ, the one priest of the new and eternal Covenant, '*entered, not into a sanctuary made by human hands ... but into heaven itself, now to appear in the presence of God on our behalf*' (Heb. 9:24) There Christ *permanently exercises his priesthood*, for he '*always lives to make intercession*' for 'those who draw near to God through him' (Heb. 9:24). As '*high priest of the good things to come*' he is the center and the principal actor of the liturgy that honors the Father in heaven." See also Heb. 9:11; *Rev.* 4:6–11.

25. Vanhoye remarks that Christ was previously "made complete," but now he "makes others complete" in relation to God. See *Old Testament Priests and the New Priest*, 218.

26. *Catechism of the Catholic Church*, §2178: "This practice of the Christian assembly dates from the beginnings of the apostolic age. The *Letter to the Hebrews* reminds the faithful 'not to neglect to meet together, as is the habit of some, but to encourage one another.'"

common in the Septuagint (i.e., Greek Old Testament).[27] This term is rare in the New Testament, occurring just six times; three of these occurrences are in the Synoptic Gospels, and the remainder are in Hebrews.[28] In all three instances in the Gospels, *katapetasmatos* refers to the veil that separates the Holy Place from the Holy of Holies—in the Temple. Similarly, in Hebrews, the first two instances refer to the Temple veil. Yet it is the final occurrence of *katapetasmatos* in Hebrews that is of greatest importance.

Earlier in Hebrews, in 6:19 and in 9:3, the use of the term is consistent with that of the Gospels—the physical, material veil in the Temple. However, in 10:20 there is a crucial shift in the meaning of the term compared with *all* other occurrences in the New Testament. Specifically, the meaning of *katapetasmatos* at first appears to be consistent with the other "Temple veil" occurrences discussed above. However, it is followed by the dependent clause *tout estin tes sarkos autou*, literally translated as "that is, through his flesh (*sarkos*)." A closer look of the technical usage of the term within the context of Hebrews 10:20 indicates that it indeed refers to "the physical body as a functioning entity."[29] This clause changes everything! It is as if the author has been patiently biding time, making use of the traditional "Temple veil" meaning of *katapetasmatos* until now.

Here, in Hebrews 10, the author surprises the reader by using the term as a *metaphor* to describe the true flesh (*sarkos*) of Jesus. In the Old Covenant, the Levitical high priest would "open up" the curtain of the Holy Place and enter with the blood of goats to perform the liturgical rite of the Day of Atonement. His priestly actions, and the sacrifice associated with it, did, according to the Mosaic Law, bring about "the forgiveness of sins" for himself and all of Israel. Still, these atoning actions involved a *limited* and *temporal* experience of forgiveness, one needing to be repeated over and over again for the cleansing of sins.

What Jesus accomplished on the Cross was a difference in kind from

---

27. The Greek term *katapetasmatos* occurs thirty-eight times in the Septuagint. Over 90 percent of these are located in Exodus–Numbers (e.g., Exod. 37:16, 38:18, 39:4, 40:3; Lev. 4:6, 4:17; Num. 3:10). The few remaining occurrences are found in 1 Samuel, 2 Chronicles, Sirach and 1 Maccabees. In the vast majority, the context is the veil in the Temple.

28. Matt. 27:51; Mark 15:38; Luke 23:45; Heb. 6:19, 9:3, 10:20.

29. BDAG, entry for σάρξ (*sarks*), 914. William Arndt, Frederick W. Danker, and Walter Bauer, *A Greek-English Lexicon of the New Testament and Other Early Christian Literature* (Chicago: University of Chicago Press, 2000).

all acts of sacrificial atonement that also have a place in the liturgy of the Temple. In his sacrificial death on the Cross, Jesus opened up the veil, so that God's mercy might flow out, and that veil is *his own flesh*. Put another way, the sacrifice of Jesus accomplished a *once for all* atoning for sins, one that was opened up for all of humanity, not Israel alone, to enter into. Moreover, Jesus's sacrifice accomplished for humanity an eternal (*zoe*) redemption—and not merely temporal/passing forgiveness of sins.

Six specific remarks need to be brought out here concerning this important development in Hebrews 10. First, no other high priest could accomplish what Jesus did. Only Jesus, the sinless Son of God, could offer himself *amomos* ("without blemish").

Second, this revelation, made by the author of Hebrews in 10:20, is added to the Eucharist language of Jesus's of *himati* ("blood") in 10:19. The *only* way one could "enter into the sanctuary" by the blood of Jesus after his death and Resurrection would be in the sacramental sense. The following verse (10:20) underscores the Eucharistic motif already present in the passage; the bringing together of *sarkos* ("flesh") with *himati* ("blood") only makes this clearer.

Third, the author of Hebrews, though he has intentionally veered in a Eucharist direction, has not lost sight of the priestly and Temple contexts of the passage as a whole. Rather, he brings things immediately back around to the Temple, referring to Jesus as the *megan heiran* ("great high priest") over the "house of God" (v. 21).

Fourth (a point that should be obvious by now): Jesus is *not only* the eternal High Priest but also the Temple sacrifice offered up to God. He is not only the Temple sacrifice, offered for the forgiveness of sins; he is also the eternal and spotless High Priest who offers up the "once for all" sacrifice of his own flesh.

Fifth, yet another sacramental motif is added to the one in 10:19-20. The author of Hebrews evokes baptismal language in stating that, in Jesus, believers have had their hearts "sprinkled clean" and their bodies washed with *katharos hydor* ("clean water").

Sixth and finally, this discussion in Hebrews 10 has taken into account the crucifixion and the Resurrection of Jesus. Yet the Ascension of Jesus is also crucial to the unfolding of this mystery. Specifically, Jesus's Ascension to the right hand of the Father allows these mysteries to work endlessly; through time and unbound by space, the "once for all" offering of the eternal High Priest continues. Thus Christ *permanently* exercises his priesthood, for he *"always lives to make intercession"* for "those who draw near to God through Him."[30] As *"high priest of the good things to come"* he *is the center and the principal actor of the liturgy* that honors the Father in heaven.[31]

All of these Christological insights hold enormous implications for the worship of the audience of Hebrews, implications too many to be enumerated here. The following point should be made: that because Christ is both the "center and principal actor" of the heavenly liturgy, the New Covenant in his blood eternally surpasses the Old Covenant. For this reason, the demise of the physical Temple, while a loss worthy of true lamentation, is nevertheless the sign of a coming Temple far more glorious, more perfect more praiseworthy than the first, and indeed more glorious than even the eschatological temple envisioned by the prophet Ezekiel.

The Temple of the New Covenant is not a "copy and shadow" of the heavenly sanctuary, as in Exodus. Christ "abolishes the first [covenant] in order to establish the second [i.e., New Covenant]."[32] Indeed, it is far greater than that holy (but ultimately temporal) sanctuary, for the sanctuary of the New Covenant is *the very embodiment of God in the flesh.* As St. John wrote in his Gospel: "The Word became flesh and dwelt among us, full of grace and truth; we have beheld his glory, glory as of the only Son from the Father."[33]

The author of Hebrews would likely share St. John's theology, yet he might have put it this way: "The Word became the eternal High Priest and perfect offering—in every way He is the Temple of God." In other words, the New Covenant is not better because it is "new," it is better because it *is better than the prior one*, infinitely so. The eternal High Priest of this New Covenant is (1) eternal, the Divine Son, who (2) now "sits at the right hand of the Father." What high priest of ancient Israel could claim either of these qualities? Christ's life is unstained by sin, and held together "by the power of an indestructible life."[34] Moreover, the sanctuary in which He "ministers" is not one "made with human hands" but was arranged "by the Lord."

When could such words have been previously uttered of the Temple in any of its earthly forms? Never, "for here we have no lasting city, but we seek the city which is to come."[35] As the author of Hebrews explains, "Now the point in what we are saying is this: we have such a high priest, one who is

30. Heb. 7:25.
32. Heb. 10:9.
34. Heb. 7:16.

31. *Catechism of the Catholic Church, §662.*
33. John 1:14.
35. Heb. 13:14.

seated at the right hand of the throne of the Majesty in heaven, a minister in the sanctuary and the *true tent* which is set up not by man but by the Lord ... But as it is, Christ has obtained a ministry which is as much more excellent than the old as *the covenant he mediates is better*, since it is enacted on better promises. For if that first covenant had been faultless, there would have been no occasion for a second" (Heb. 8:1–7).

But it *was* necessary. And efficacious, leading to life—eternal life, something not experienced under the Old Covenant, not even through the holy ministry of the high priest in God's holy Temple: "Therefore he is the mediator of a new covenant, so that those who are called may receive the *promised eternal inheritance*, since a death has occurred which redeems them from the transgressions under the first covenant" (Heb. 9:15).

The deep mystery is that, for the author of Hebrews, Christ is simultaneously *the offering* and *the one offering it*. Rupert of Deutz, a monk and biblical exegete from the medieval period, echoes the author of Hebrews when he writes, "Haec pontifex summus propiator ipse et propitiatorium, sacerdos et sacrificium, pro nobis oravit."[36] Translation: Jesus Christ is "the high priest who was himself *the one making atonement as well as the expiatory offering*, both priest and sacrifice, implored for us."

While more could be said concerning the many fiber optics of temple theology that beautifully and mysteriously interconnect within the Letter to the Hebrews, the focus now turns to the final book of the New Testament, the Book of Revelation.

The Book of Revelation: The Heavenly Temple

What kind of book is Revelation? The first thing that needs to be said about Revelation is that, in its beauty and complexity, it is composed of multiple literary genres.[37] As is well recognized,[38] Revelation obviously con-

---

36. André Feuillet, *The Priesthood of Christ and His Ministers* (New York: Doubleday, 1975), 245. Citing a text by the medieval Benedictine and biblical exegete, Rupert of Deutz (1075–1129).

37. "Genre criticism is that aspect of comparative literature that attempts to understand a literary work in relation to other similar works ... A literary genre consists of a group of texts that exhibit a coherent and recurring pattern of features constituted by the interrelated elements of form, content, and function." David E. Aune, *Revelation 1–5*, vol. 52A, *Word Biblical Commentary* (Dallas: Word Books, 1998), lxxi.

38. For an introduction to issues in the Book of Revelation, see ibid.; *Revelation 6–16*, vol. 52B;

tains apocalyptic themes, with highly symbolic imagery, all of which must be approached with great care.[39] Revelation also contains prophecy,[40] which requires a similar (yet distinct) treatment as Old Testament books such as Daniel, Ezekiel, and Isaiah, each of which Revelation makes extensive reference to throughout its twenty-two chapters.

Lastly, and above all, Revelation must be approached for what it is: a circular letter to seven churches, offering words of comfort, hope, and admonition in times of persecution and apostasy.[41] It is saturated with liturgical imagery and symbolism,[42] and its context is as proclamation in the Eucharistic liturgies of the churches to which it is addressed.[43]

Some of the more important examples of the liturgical symbolism in Revelation include the following: (1) the Apostle's vision begins "on the Lord's day,"[44] and (2) the book is filled with imagery straight out of the Temple, with its mention of "altars,"[45] "golden lamp stand,"[46] "incense,"[47] and priestly figures in white vestments.[48] In addition, there is a reference to (3) "[hidden] manna"[49] and numerous references to (4) "wine."[50] In chapter

---

Revelation 17–22, vol. 52C (Nashville, TN: Thomas Nelson, 1997); Richard Bauckham, *The Climax of Prophecy: Studies on the Book of Revelation* (Edinburgh: T & T Clark, 1993); *The Theology of the Book of Revelation* (Cambridge: Cambridge University Press, 1993); Oscar Cullmann, *Early Christian Worship*, trans. A. S. Todd and J. B. Torrance (London: SCM, 1953); André Feuillet, *The Apocalypse* (New York: Alba House, 1965); Craig Koester, *Revelation and the End of All Things* (Grand Rapids, MI: Eerdmans, 2001); G. K. Beale, *The Book of Revelation: A Commentary on the Greek Text* (Grand Rapids, MI: Eerdmans, 1999); G. R. Beasley-Murray, *Revelation*, rev. ed. (London: Marshall, Morgan & Scott, 1978); David Chilton, *Days of Vengeance* (Tyler, TX: Dominion Press, 1987).

39. See "Revelation as an Apocalypse," in Aune, *Revelation 1–5*, lxxviiff.

40. See "Revelation as a Prophetic Apocalypse," in Aune, *Revelation 1–5*, lxxxixff.

41. See "Revelation as a Letter" in Aune, *Revelation 1–5*, lxxxixff.

42. *Catechism of the Catholic Church*, §1139: "It is in this *eternal liturgy* that the Spirit and the Church enable us to participate whenever we celebrate the mystery of salvation in the sacraments."

43. "It is well to keep in mind that Revelation was meant to be *heard*, to be listened to: 'blessed they who hear' (Rev. 1:3). It has a dramatic dimension. Heard in the setting of an early Eucharistic liturgy, the scenes would have unfolded with theatrical effect." Wilfrid J. Harrington, *Revelation*, vol. 16, *Sacra Pagina Series*, ed. Daniel J. Harrington (Collegeville, MN: Liturgical Press, 2008), 6.

44. See Rev. 1:10.

45. See Rev. 6:9, 8:3, 8:5, 9:13, 11:1, 14:18, 16:7.

46. See Rev. 2:5.

47. See Rev. 5:8, 8:3, 8:4, 18:13.

48. See Rev. 1:6, 5:10, 7:9, 7:13, 7:14, 20:6, 22:14.

49. See Rev. 2:17.

50. See Rev. 6:6, 14:8, 14:10, 14:19, 14:20, 17:2, 18:3, 18:13, 19:15.

4, in the heavenly throne scene is (5) the "holy, holy, holy" of Isaiah's temple vision.[51] Scattered throughout the book are (6) "doxologies," seven in number, to be precise.[52] Near the end of the Book of Revelation is (7) the "wedding supper of the lamb."[53]

Theologia Gloriae

The entire Book of Revelation is, in some sense, a *theologia gloriae*, a "theology of glory," inasmuch as the vision of St. John is a vision of heavenly mysteries and heavenly liturgy:[54] "After this I looked, and lo, in heaven an open door! And the first voice, which I had heard speaking to me like a trumpet, said, 'Come up hither, and I will show you what must take place after this'" (Rev. 4:1). Barker stresses here that Revelation is not in its essence a book about when future calamities will threaten humanity, but about early Christian worship: "The earliest picture of Christian worship is found in the Book of Revelation, set in the temple. This is how the first Christians imagined their worship; they joined, as we do today, with the angels and archangels."[55]

Additional help in approaching the mysteries in Revelation is found in the writings of the Angelic Doctor, Thomas Aquinas. In the *Summa Theologica*, Thomas cites four stages in man's *reditus* (Latin: "return") to God:

1. the state before the Mosaic Law
2. the state of the Old (Mosaic) Law

---

51. See Rev. 4:8; Isa. 6:3.

52. See Rev. 1:5–6, 4:9, 4:11, 5:12–14, 7:12, 11:13, 19:1.

53. See Rev. 19:9. For more on the liturgical imagery in Revelation, see Margaret Barker, *The Revelation of Jesus Christ: Which God Gave to Him to Show to Servants What Must Soon Take Place (Revelation 1.1)* (Edinburgh: T & T Clark, 2000); R. Bauckham, "The Worship of Jesus in Apocalyptic Christianity," *New Testament Studies* 27 (1980–81): 322–41; "The Role of the Spirit in the Apocalypse," *Evangelical Quarterly Review* 52 (1980): 66–83; Craig Koester, "The Distant Triumph Song: Music and the Book of Revelation," *Word and World* 12 (March 1992): 243–49; O. A. Piper, "The Apocalypse of John and the Liturgy of the Ancient Church [Rev 5]," *Church History* 20 (March 1951): 10–22; G. K. Beale, *The Use of Daniel in Jewish Apocalyptic Literature and in the Revelation of St. John* (New York: Lanham, 1984); E. Cothenet, "Earthly and Heavenly Liturgy According to the Book of Revelation," in E. Cothenet, *Roles in the Liturgical Assembly*, trans. M. J. O'Connell (New York: Pueblo, 1981), 115–35.

54. This should not to be confused with the second half of the Gospel of John, which is frequently described as the "Book of Glory."

55. Barker, *Temple Themes in Early Christian Worship*, 20.

3. the state of the New Law (of Christ)

4. the state of heavenly Glory[56]

Biblically, one can restate St. Thomas's "stages" in temple language as follows. Stage 1 is the period from Mt. Eden to Mt. Sinai—that is, from Adam to Moses—just prior to the giving of the Law at Sinai. Stage 2 corresponds to the time from the early Tabernacle to the Temple of Herod—that is, from Moses's receiving the Law at Sinai to the time of Christ.[57] Stage 3 is the age of the new Temple, and the sacrifice of Christ[58] in the New Covenant,[59] sealed

56. See Matthew Levering, *Christ's Fulfillment of Temple and Torah: Salvation According to Thomas Aquinas* (Notre Dame, IN: University of Notre Dame Press, 2002), 110.

57. St. Thomas does not consider the time of the temple and Mosaic Law as a time *before grace.* Rather, "he argues that in all times and places there are 'two kinds of men,' good and evil, and that in all places and times the good accept God's call and the wicked reject it. Furthermore, [Thomas] does not conceive of a time before Christ *that lacked grace.* On the contrary … the New Law (which is the grace of the Holy Spirit) *infuses the period of the Old Law, even though grace does not belong to the Old Law per se.*" Ibid., 23 (emphases added). Thomas: "*I answer that,* It was most fitting for the Law to be given at the time of Moses. The reason for this may be taken from two things in respect of which every law is imposed on two kinds of men. Because it is imposed on some men who are hard-hearted and proud, whom the Law restrains and tames: and it is imposed on good men, who, through being instructed by the law, are helped to fulfil what they desire to do. Hence it was fitting that the Law should be given at such a time as would be appropriate for the overcoming of man's pride … Wherefore, after those times, it was necessary for a written law to be given as a remedy for human ignorance: because *by the Law is the knowledge of sin* (Rom. 3:20).—But, after man had been instructed by the Law, his pride was convinced of his weakness, through his being unable to fulfill what he knew. Hence, as the Apostle concludes (Rom. 8:3, 4), *what the Law could not do in that it was weak through the flesh, God sent* (Vulg.,—*sending*) *His own Son, … that the justification of the Law might be fulfilled in us* … With regard to good men, the Law was given to them as a help; which was most needed by the people, at the time when the natural law began to be obscured on account of the exuberance of sin: for it was fitting that this help should be bestowed on men in an orderly manner, so that they might be led from imperfection to perfection; wherefore it was becoming that the Old Law should be given between the law of nature and the law of grace." *Summa Theologica* I-II, q. 98, a. 6 *sed contra.*

58. St. Thomas clarifies: "It would seem that the ceremonies of the Old Law did not cease at the coming of Christ. For it is written (Baruch 4:1): This is the book of the commandments of God, and the law that is forever. But the legal ceremonies were part of the Law. Therefore, the legal ceremonies were to last forever." *Summa Theologica* III, q. 83, a. 1; see Rev. 13:8.

59. Levering explains that "the '*state of the New Law*' begins after the Incarnation, while the New Law itself, as the grace of the Holy Spirit, is found in all places and all times. Given this distinction, it follows that the '*state of the Old Law*' does not preclude the New Law's already being active. The 'sacraments' of the Mosaic Law [circumcision, sacrifice, etc.], while they do not *cause grace,* nonetheless belong to the movement whereby men and women under the state of the Old Law *participated in the New Law.* As Thomas remarks, 'The ancient Fathers, *by observing the sacraments of the law,* were brought towards Christ through the same faith and love by which we are still brought to Him.' The

at the Last Supper and consummated on the Cross of Christ. (As such, this stage continues until the Second Coming.)[60] Thus Stage 4 is the future age of the heavenly Temple, inaugurated with Christ's Second Coming—the Day of Judgment and the consummation of history, when God will be "all in all."[61] Levering explains, "The first three 'states' are ordered to the fourth and are therefore intended to prepared human beings for the perfect worship of God. The Temple and the community of Israel organized around the Temple prefigures such worship."[62]

Revelation: "The Apocalyptic Exodus"

How does all of this contribute to a study of the Book of Revelation— especially as it relates to temple theology? Revelation lifts the reader up to Stage 4, as revealed by God to St. John, when He "made it known by sending his angel to his servant John, who bore witness to the word of God and to the testimony of Jesus Christ, even to all that he saw."[63]

This means that Revelation invites the reader to reflect upon all earlier stages of salvation history, contemplating how the various manifestations of the temple prepared for the coming of Christ—and ultimately for the "supper of the Lamb," which is yet to come. Putting this another way, the various periods of salvation history, the stages before the Incarnation of Christ, reveal in various shadowy ways the glory of the risen Christ.

This is what the Tabernacle and Jerusalem Temple were in their purest form—a shadow of the reality of glory that was to come: "The Johannine

---

Mosaic Law and the New Law are thus *intrinsically linked*." *Christ's Fulfillment of Temple and Torah*, 23. Levering's quotation of Thomas is from *Summa Theologica* I-II, q. 8, a. 3, ad 3, using the translation of Colman O'Neill found in "St. Thomas on the Membership of the Church," *Thomist* 49 (1985): 88–442 (here 94).

60. Thomas Aquinas, *Summa Theologica* I-II, q. 103, a. 3. Levering: "Aquinas holds that the ceremonial precepts are indeed observed forever, but only in their *fulfilled* reality, the end that God had in the beginning." Moreover, "Jewish Christians, sharing in Christ's fulfillment of the Mosaic Law, do not lose their identity. Rather, they enter into the (supernatural) fullness of their identity." *Christ's Fulfillment of Temple and Torah*, 28 (emphases added). On this last point, see *Summa Theologica* III, q. 40, a. 4.

61. See 1 Cor. 15:28. An important clarification: Stage 4 is eternal and timeless—it is in no way bound by time and space, as it pertains to God himself. As such, it is *only* from a human perspective of salvation history that it "begins" with Christ's Second Coming.

62. Levering, *Christ's Fulfillment of Temple and Torah*, 111.

63. Rev. 1:1–2.

Gospel appears as a kind of Paschal catechetical instruction, to show those baptized on the night of Holy Saturday that the Sacraments they then received were divine interventions which continued the magnolia [Latin: "great things"] of Yahweh at the time of the Exodus and also at the time of the Passion and Resurrection of Christ. From the beginning of the Prologue, the Word appears as the *Shekinah*, the abode of Yahweh's glory, which dwelt in the midst of the people in the desert."[64]

In the same fashion as seen in the Gospel of John, in Revelation, St. John draws back to the time of the Exodus,[65] to present a kind of "apocalyptic version of the *Exodus*."[66] Here, it is worth quoting Daniélou at some length: "The *Apocalypse* describes the history of the Christian people in terms borrowed from that of the Chosen Race [Israel]. The whole story [of Revelation] is dominated by the sacrifice of the lamb.[67] The twelve tribes represent the whole Church,[68] while their deliverance is explicitly compared to the crossing of the Red Sea[69] ... The Revelation of God is heralded by the signs of Sinai: the noise of trumpets[70] and thunder and lightning.[71] [Moreover] the

---

64. Jean Daniélou, *From Shadow to Reality: Studies in the Typology of the Fathers* (London: Burns and Oates, 1960), 161.

65. St. John's vision of God is rooted in the Old Testament. For example, God's glory is depicted with vivid imagery of precious gems (jasper, carnelian) and a rainbow of color is lifted right out of Ezek. (1: 26–28). The rainbow is reminiscent of the covenant with Noah in Gen. (9:12–17); the gems of the heavenly Jerusalem are closely connected with the Garden of Eden (Gen. 2). St. John's imagery of "flashes of lightning, and voices and peals of thunder" in his inaugural vision (Rev. 4:5–6) is lifted from Exod. 19:5–6: "On the morning of the third day there were *thunder and lightning*, and a thick cloud upon the mountain, and a very loud trumpet blast, so that all the people who were in the camp trembled." Along with this imagery in Exod. 19, note the "cloud of glory" and the "very loud trumpet blast" that also occupy the Book of Revelation. The "sea of glass" (Rev. 4:6) may recall the firmament of Gen. 1:7, but more likely is the *pavement of sapphire stone*, which Moses and the seventy elders "saw" in their vision of God in heaven. Finally, staying with stay with the Exodus motif, it is worth noting that the Mosaic covenant is sealed with a meal: "They beheld and ate and drank" (Exod. 24:11). Likewise, the Book of Revelation culminates with a final heavenly meal: "And the angel said to me, 'Write this: Blessed are those who are invited to the marriage supper of the Lamb'" (Rev. 19:9).

66. Daniélou, *From Shadow to Reality*, 164–65.

67. Rev. 5:12.

68. Rev. 7:4–8.

69. Rev. 15:2: "And I saw what appeared to be a sea of glass mingled with fire, and those who had conquered the beast and its image and the number of its name, standing beside the sea of glass with harps of God in their hands."

70. See Rev. 8:7.

71. See Rev. 8:5.

punishments which are meted out to the enemies of God are repetitions of the plagues of Egypt: hail,[72] the changing of the sea into blood,[73] darkness,[74] locusts.[75] This is an Apocalyptic version of the Exodus ... It is John who affirms that this Apocalyptic Exodus is fulfilled in Jesus Christ."[76]

It should be quite clear by this point that Revelation is a kind of "apocalypticizing" of the exodus story. Along these lines, this part of the discussion can be brought to a close by examining one such text from near the end of the Apocalypse: "There shall no more be anything accursed, but the throne of God and of the Lamb shall be in it, and his servants shall worship him; *they shall see his face, and his name shall be on their foreheads*" (Rev. 22:3–4). In terms of verse 3, much has already said much about the "renewal" of the whole creation.

Several things are notable in verse 4. First, in this age of the eschatological temple, God's faith will finally see him "face to face." Recall in the discussion of the Gospel of John that this notion of "seeing God" was of great importance to understanding the Evangelist's larger Christological portrayal of the Logos/Jesus. In short, only Jesus, God's only begotten Son, had the eternal joy and experience of gazing at the Father face to face.

This was a decisive move for St. John, as he not so subtly underscored that *none* of Israel's heroes—not Jacob, not Abraham, not even Moses—had actually "seen" God face to face: "*No one* has ever seen God; the only Son, who is in the bosom of the Father, he has made him known."[77] John's urgent message for the readers of the Gospel: only Jesus has "seen" God, and in his mercy this same Jesus has "revealed" himself to us, so that you too may "believe."[78] But now—in the age of the eschatological temple—the believer will see God just as he is, "*face to face.*" From verse 4, it seems clear that St. John's theology in Revelation is in touch with the Prologue of his Gospel. In some sense, it is actually a step beyond it, as Jesus's Disciples finally have the experience he desired they would: "that ... which we have seen with our eyes, which we have looked upon ... and was made manifest to us ... we proclaim also to you ... that your joy may be complete."[79]

---

72. See Rev. 8:7.
73. See Rev. 8:8, 16:3.
74. See Rev. 8:12, 16:10.
75. See Rev. 9:3.
76. Daniélou, *From Shadow to Reality*, 164–65 (emphases added).
77. John 1:18.
78. See John 1:14b.
79. See John 1:1–4.

This is a fascinating dimension of Revelation's Christology, to which something further must be added. Recall that in the cultic life of the Jerusalem Temple, the high priest went into the Holy of Holies but once a year, on the Day of Atonement. And what of him; did he see God? Naturally, the answer is a resounding "no!" In fact, he would shield his eyes, like the seraphim of Isaiah 6. In a "cloud" of thick incense, swung all around, the high priest was, much like Moses before him, "protected" from accidentally catching a glimpse of the glory of God on his throne, much less his holy face.

This brings the examination of Revelation 22:3–4 to a fitting end. After declaring that God's saints will indeed "see his face," he ends with the mysterious expression "and his name shall be on their foreheads." What could this possibly mean?

There are many ciphers and unresolved riddles in Revelation. Is this one more example? No. In fact, when examined in light of Exodus, it appears to fit well with what has just been discussed above. In the Book of Exodus, in the context of Yahweh's giving Moses the commands for constructing the Tabernacle according to the "heavenly pattern"[80] shown to him, Moses is told to prepare a turban for the high priest, bearing the expression "Holy to the Lord" upon it: "And you shall make a plate of pure gold, and engrave on it, like the engraving of a signet, 'Holy to the Lord.' And you shall fasten it on the turban by a lace of blue; it shall be on the front of the turban. *It shall be upon Aaron's forehead*, and Aaron shall take upon himself any guilt incurred in the holy offering which the people of Israel hallow as their holy gifts; it shall always be upon his forehead, that they may be accepted before the Lord" (Exod. 28:36–38).

This is a profound image. With this engraving of gold, the high priest bears the very name of God upon his own head. Holy to the Lord! He was for the people, the "image" of God for the people. The "name" reminded him too, that it was not his power, but God's, that forgave Israel's iniquities.

Just as Adam was called to image God as the priest of the cosmic temple, "filling the earth" with the glorious presence of God, so too was Israel's high priest to image God, and in "atoning" for the guilt of Israel, they would be cleansed, forgiven, and restored in their likeness to God. As the high priest returned to the people of the Temple, having completed the liturgy of atone-

---

80. See Exod. 25:9, 25:40; Num. 8:4; see Acts 7:44.

ment, Israel would "see" God, inasmuch as their high priest bore his name, and imaged his glory in a human way. They were now free—forgiven and free to extend God's glory further and further into the world.

Returning to Revelation 22, it seems quite clear that St. John has once again apocalypticized Exodus and its high priest. Here is the point: by the death and Resurrection of Jesus, the veil has been brought down, and every believer is before God a high priest who bears his name and his image. They shall all see his face, and his name shall be on all of their foreheads—forever more. Daniélou summarizes superbly: "A deep impression forms itself in our mind after reading these many texts. It was the clear intention of the New Testament writers to show the mystery of Christ as at once continuing and surpassing the outstanding events in the story of Israel at the time of Moses. We are thus led to see in history *the fulfillment of the divine plan*, baffling from our human point of view, yet offering a coherence and inner harmony which allows man's faith to rest therein as upon an immovable rock."[81]

The Lamb Standing as Though Slain

Throughout the Book of Revelation, amidst all of the liturgical imagery, reminiscent of the Jerusalem Temple, no image is more pervasive than the Lamb.[82] The first and most important of its many occurrences is in Revelation 5: "And between the throne and the four living creatures and among the elders, I saw a Lamb standing, as though it had been slain, with seven horns and with seven eyes, which are the seven spirits of God sent out into all the earth" (Rev. 5:6).[83]

First, consider the symbolism of "standing as though slain." This image of the lamb is strange, yet it points to something beyond the lamb of the

---

81. Daniélou, *From Shadow to Reality*, 165 (emphases added). St. Thomas: "It is true to say that Christ was sacrificed, even in the figures of the Old Testament: hence it is stated in the Apocalypse, 'Whose names are not written in the Book of Life of the Lamb, which was slain from the beginning of the world.'" *Summa Theologica* III, q. 83, a. 1; see also Rev. 13:8.

82. The term "lamb" (Greek: *arnion*) occurs twenty-nine times in Revelation: 5:6, 5:8, 5:12, 5:13, 6:1, 6:16, 7:9, 7:10, 7:14, 7:17; 8:1, 12:11, 13:8, 13:11, 14:1, 14:4, 14:10, 15:3, 17:14, 19:7, 19:9, 21:9, 21:14, 21:22, 21:23, 22:1, 22:3.

83. Although it cannot be pursued further, note that the Holy Spirit was depicted in a *sevenfold* manner, recalling the earlier discussion of the number seven as the number of the Sabbath, of the perfection, and of God's covenant with his people.

Temple. This phraseology "does not mean that the Lamb only appeared to have been slaughtered but rather that the Lamb had been slaughtered and was now alive, thus combining the two theological motifs of death and resurrection."[84]

St. John's Christological title is linked with temple theology and explicitly calls to mind temple sacrifice: "behold the Lamb of God."[85] For St. John, it is Christ who now embodies true temple sacrifice. It is he who paradoxically "offers and is offered, who gives and is given."[86] In this short expression, "Lamb of God," the entire temple cult has been radically reevaluated; not rebuked or rejected, but nevertheless *changed and surpassed* by the figure of Christ. The Christological title assigned to Christ by St. John took the temple sacrifices to purpose higher than the holiest of high priests could have imagined. Now, in the Lamb of God, the Father is *truly satisfied* with man's offering. The very reason for the Temple's existence has been transfigured in the slain Christ, and made "new," recapitulated in the risen Christ.

In one sense, one can surmise that John's firsthand encounter with Jesus allows him an extraordinary and rather unique vantage point from which to teach about the mysteries of the Temple, the mysteries of God-with-us. In another sense, it is as if John's experience, and indeed his image of the Lamb of God, is not completely unexpected or out of the blue. In fact, the image of the lamb is a familiar and almost common one, biblically speaking. As Ratzinger describes, "It is remarkable how important a part is played in the Bible by the image of the lamb. We come across it in the very first pages, in the account of the sacrifice of Abel, the shepherd; and in the last book of Holy Scripture the Lamb is at the very center of heaven and earth. According to the book of Revelation, the Lamb alone can open the seals of history. *It is the Lamb, who appears as slain and yet lives, who receives the homage of all creatures in heaven and earth.*"[87]

Elsewhere in St. John's writings, near the end of the Book of Revelation, the reader is taken up into one last bit of fantastic and vivid imagery: "Then he showed me the river of *the water of life,* bright as crystal, flowing from the

---

84. David E. Aune, *Revelation 1–5*, vol. 52A, 353.

85. See John 1:29, 1:35.

86. *Catechism of the Catholic Church*, §1137.

87. Joseph Ratzinger, *Behold The Pierced One: An Approach to a Spiritual Christology*, trans. Graham Harrison (San Francisco: Ignatius Press, 1986), 114.

throne of God and of the Lamb through the middle of the street of the city; also, on either side of the river, *the tree of life* with its *twelve kinds of fruit*, yielding its fruit each month; and the leaves of the tree were for the healing of the nations" (Rev. 22:1–2).

Here, at the end of the biblical narrative, *the reader is carried back to the beginning*, back to Paradise and the Tree of Life in the Holy of Holies of Eden: There it is stated that in the early church there were *two trees*, just as there had been in Paradise; the tree of life, and the tree of the knowledge of good and evil. "The tree of life is Christ Himself. This tree becomes accessible in the spiritual understanding of Scripture" (Rev. 22:1–2).[88]

It is as if all temple theology from Genesis onward is flashed before the reader's eyes one last time. In a manner of speaking, it is as if the Scriptures have been leaning forward toward this glorious vision all along—toward the recapitulation of Mt. Eden. Here is the "river," reminiscent of the rivers of Genesis 2—the Pishon, the Gihon, the Tigris, and the Euphrates—flowing down and out from the mountain of God, Mt. Eden.[89] They fructify the garden of the Man and Woman, and give life to the whole earth. In Revelation, they pour forth the "water of life," recalling the Spirit moving over the "waters of creation,"[90] the water God provided in the wilderness,[91] the water poured over the altar of the Temple at Tabernacles, which Christ drew upon in his temple saying.[92]

Above all, this recalls the "blood and water" flowing from the side of the crucified Christ, the new temple, as it did in the old Temple, when the lambs were sacrificed Passover after Passover.[93] Now, it reflects the waters of baptism, "which plunge the Christian down into the depths of death with Christ," rising to new life, Resurrection life in the risen Christ.[94]

Finally, here is the Lamb himself—not slain but risen, triumphant, standing next to the "tree of life," the Holy of Holies of Genesis. Upon the Tree are "twelve kinds of fruit"—a recapitulation of the true Israel, now living

---

88. Joseph Ratzinger, *The Theology of History in St. Bonaventure*, trans. Zachary Hayes (Chicago, IL: Franciscan Herald Press, 1989), 152 (emphasis added).

89. See Gen. 2:11, 2:13, 2:14.   90. See Gen. 1:2.

91. See Num. 19:11.

92. John 7:38: "He who believes in me, as the Scripture has said, 'Out of his heart shall flow rivers of living water.'" See Zech. 14:8.

93. See John 19:34.

94. See esp. Rom. 6:1–11; also 1 Pet. 3:21.

in faith, nourished by the Lamb himself, just as Adam "ate" from the Tree provided by God for his sustenance. Now, the Church is *illuminated* by the Lamb itself: "And night shall be no more; they need no light of lamp or sun, for the Lord God will be their light, and they shall reign for ever and ever."[95] But who is it that ultimately "conquers?"

In *The Spirit of the Liturgy*, Ratzinger offers this suggestion: "The *Apocalypse* of St. John draws the bow back even farther. The final enemies of the People of God have stepped onto the stage of history: the satanic trinity, consisting of the beast, its image, and the number of its name. *Everything* seems lost for the holy Israel of God in the face of such overwhelming odds. But then the Seer is given the vision of the conquerors, 'standing beside the sea of glass with harps of God in their hands. And they sing the song of Moses, the servant of God, and the song of the Lamb' (Rev. 15:3). The paradox now becomes even more powerful. It is not the gigantic beasts of prey, with their power over the media and their technical strength, who win the victory. *No, it is the sacrificed Lamb that conquers.* And so once again, definitively, there resounds the song of God's servant Moses, *which has now become the song of the Lamb.*"[96]

The World-Filling Temple of the Lamb

The present study began in Eden, with an extensive discussion of the temple of Creation in the opening chapters of Genesis. There the biblical author described Adam as not just the "first formed father of the earth,"[97] but as the gloriously robed high priest of Mt. Eden. He, along with Eve, was called to "be fruitful and multiply,"[98] a command frequently echoed throughout the biblical narrative.[99] And yet, whereas Adam's willful disobedience caused him

---

95. Rev. 22:5.

96. Ratzinger, *Spirit of the Liturgy*, 137 (emphases added).

97. Wisd. 10:1.

98. Gen. 1:28.

99. Most literally, this command to "be fruitful and multiply" is evident in texts like Gen. 8:17, 9:1, 9:7, 26:22, 35:11; Jer. 23:3; Ezek. 36:11. Implicitly, it is evident in God's call for Abraham to "go" (Gen. 12:1): "so that he by you all the families of the earth shall bless themselves" (Gen. 12:3). From this foundation, every stage of the covenantal story is seen as an echo of Adam's failed call, and Abraham as the "New Adam" figure through whom God's temple presence will reach the ends of the earth. As noted, there are numerous New Testament parallels to this "filling" motif, such as the

to fail in his vocation to "*fill the earth*" with the holy presence of God, Abraham (cast as a kind of New Adam) succeeded in extending God's temple vision—but partially, always partially. The same is true for Isaac and Jacob.

In the same fashion as her great forefathers and patriarchs, Israel was called and chosen to manifest God's glory to the nations. Here too there were great victories and sacrifices that brought Israel closer to truly fulfilling her God-given mission of his name and his glory. Yet even as the Kingdom of David reached its zenith, so too would Israel's willful disobedience ultimately lead, just like Adam's, to a failure to "fill the earth" with God's holy presence. By the close of the Maccabean era, and by the end of the Old Testament period, the mission remained incomplete and in doubt. Still, the prophets imagined and proclaimed that it would happen through a new David, through God's anointed Christ.

Looking back over the biblical epic, it ought to be clear that, in various ways, each of the Four Gospels and the rest of the New Testament seize upon this never forgotten mandate, declaring that the mission is about to be fulfilled by a New Adam, by the true and definitive Adam, who through his crucifixion and Resurrection, and now in his ascended glory at the right hand of the Father is filling the earth with God's holy temple presence, through the Church.[100]

The glorious presence of God is "tabernacling" throughout the earth, in the Word of God, and in the sacramental power of Christ alive in the Church, especially in the Eucharist. All of this temple building is not the work of the humanity alone. That would only be part of the story. The ongoing "filling of the earth" is ultimately powered along, driven by the divine Spirit of God, and not by the might or creativity of the human spirit alone.

Consider Revelation 21, with its remarkable vision of the New Jerusalem: "Then I saw *a new heaven and a new earth*; for the first heaven and the first earth had passed away, and the sea was no more. And I saw *the holy city, new Jerusalem, coming down out of heaven from God,* prepared as a bride adorned for her husband" (Rev. 21:1–2). Here is another example of the "culminat-

---

spread of the Kingdom of God: "*Go* therefore and make disciples of all nations, baptizing them in the name of the Father and of the Son and of the Holy Spirit" (Matt. 28:19).

100. *Catechism of the Catholic Church*, §1045: "For man, this consummation will be the final realization of the unity of the human race, which God willed from creation and of which the pilgrim Church has been 'in the nature of sacrament'"; see also *Lumen Gentium*, §1.

ing vision" discussed above. Yet there appears to be a riddle in this particular text: Why is it that here St. John sees a new heaven and a new earth, yet later (chapter 22) there is no such description of this new heaven and new earth?

To put a fine point in it, why does St. John not provide details of "the many forests, mountains, streams, valleys, and the many other features of a fertile worldwide new creation?"[101] Clearly such descriptions are absent from this otherwise vivid book. St. John sees a gardenlike temple, but not a "full panorama" of the new heavens and new earth.[102] Why? Beale's suggestion is sound: "the new creation and Jerusalem are *none other than God's taber-nacle*. This tabernacle is the true Temple of God's special presence portrayed throughout [Rev.] chapter 21."[103] As the *Catechism* puts it, "In this new universe, the heavenly Jerusalem, God will have his dwelling among men."[104]

Relevant to this discussion is an earlier text from the Book of Revelation: "Behold, I stand at the door and knock; if any one hears my voice and opens the door, I will come in to him and eat with him, and he with me" (Rev. 3:20). This image in Revelation ought to remind the reader of the temple theology of Genesis, and the concept of "Temple gatekeepers." Whereas the first Adam failed to keep out the "unrighteous" (i.e., wicked Serpent), thereby guarding God's holy temple, the Last Adam recapitulates this failure in his inviting in all the righteous into the glorious presence of God.

Moreover, as the true "Door,"[105] he has the "keys" of David: "And to the angel of the church in Philadelphia write: 'The words of the holy one, the true one, who has the key of David, who opens and no one shall shut, who shuts and no one opens'" (Rev. 3:7).

The present argument finds further support from another text in Revelation 21: "But as for *the cowardly, the faithless, the polluted, as for murderers, fornicators, sorcerers, idolaters, and all liars,* their lot shall be in the lake that burns with fire and sulphur, which is the second death" (Rev. 21:8). The Lamb, the "True One," who has the "keys of David," lets in the righteous but keeps out ("cuts off") the unrighteous from entry into God's holy Temple.

---

101. G. K. Beale, *The Temple and the Church's Mission: A Biblical Theology of the Dwelling Place of God* (Downers Grove, IL: InterVarsity Press, 2004), 23 (emphasis added).

102. Ibid. (emphasis added).   103. Ibid. (emphasis added).

104. *Catechism of the Catholic Church*, §1044.   105. See John 10:1, 10:2, 10:7, 10:9.

Concluding Remarks

In the Book of Revelation, the fiber optics of temple theology has reached its glorious destination: the wedding supper of the Lamb, in the heavenly Jerusalem. The entire Creation has been made radiant by the presence of Christ—the eternal High Priest, the New Adam, the New Moses, and New Aaron—who fills the new heavens and new earth with the glory of God. This is the definitive realization of God's plan to bring under a single head "all things in [Christ], things in heaven and things on earth."[106]

This brings the larger study of temple theology to an end, at least as it concerns Sacred Scripture. In the conclusion to this volume, some final remarks will be offered regarding implications of temple theology and some key ways in which it is taken up in the early Church.

---

106. *Catechism of the Catholic Church*, §1043. See Eph. 1:10.

CONCLUSION

Heirs of the Temple, the Influence of Temple Theology
upon Architecture, and Worship
in the Early Church

> But the Father having proved Him now as well as then, has
> established Him as the head of the corner of this our com-
> mon church. This, therefore, *the living temple of the living*
> *God,* formed of yourselves, I say, is *the greatest and the truly*
> *divine sanctuary*, whose inmost shrines, though invisible to
> the multitude, are really holy, a *Holy of Holies.*
>
> Eusebius, Bishop of Caesarea

Jewish Influences upon Early Christianity:
The Church as the Temple of God

A considerable amount of theological ground has been covered in this
book. In keeping with the stated purpose, the focus was kept close to the
contours of Sacred Scripture and biblical theology. Before bringing the entire book to its end, one final consideration remains: the impact and reception of the temple theme within the early Church. To be clear, there are likely
a number of implications of temple theology as it pertains to the patristic
period, most of which cannot be treated here. The aims of this conclusion
are modest: to simply show a few elements of Christian liturgy and worship
practices that may be traced back to—or at the least may have been influenced by—the fiber optics of temple theology within Sacred Scripture.

In his majestic work on the Eucharist, Louis Bouyer mentions some of

---

Epigraph. Eusebius, *An Ecclesiastical History 10:4.* Edited by S. E. Parker (London: Samuel Bag-
ster and Sons, 1847), 416.

the Jewish influences on the early Church that will be touched on here: "Finally we must add (and this is a capital point) that it is not only in the prayer texts that the Church's dependence on the [Temple] and Synagogue seems to be noticeable. It is also in *all aspects of worship: architecture, sacred music,* and even in an area which up until recent discoveries was never even considered, *iconography.*"[1]

The early Church drew upon the nuptial imagery in the Song of Songs and throughout the Scriptures to explain the marriage bond that existed between Christ and the Church. In *The Bible and the Liturgy,* Daniélou calls attention to the *Procatechesis* of Cyril of Jerusalem, in which Cyril explains the nuptiality present in the Baptismal rite: "Already the *perfume of blessedness* awaits you, O catechumens. Already you gather spiritual flowers to weave heavenly crowns. Already the sweet perfume of the Holy Spirit is poured out. *You are in the vestibule of the royal dwelling.*"[2] Commenting on this ancient text, Daniélou writes, "The allusions to the *Canticle of Canticles* are clear: 'The flowers have appeared' (2:120); 'The perfume is poured out' (1:2); 'The king leads into his dwelling' (1:4). The [baptismal] catechumens are on the threshold of the *Garden of Paradise, where the wedding is ready to take place.*"[3]

Consider the interpretation of Psalm 45[4] in the early Church. As one commentator explains, the substance of the psalm is clear: "it is a wedding song, celebrating the marriage of a king to a princess. In its original sense and context, it is not in any sense a messianic psalm. And yet within the context of early Christianity (and in Judaism before that), it becomes a messianic psalm par excellence."[5]

Even prior to the patristic age, the author of the Book of Hebrews drew

---

1. Louis Bouyer, *Eucharist: Theology and Spirituality of the Eucharistic Prayer,* trans. Charles Underhill Quinn (Notre Dame, IN: University of Notre Dame, 1968), 24 (emphasis added).

2. Jean Daniélou, *The Bible and the Liturgy* (Notre Dame, IN: University of Notre Dame Press, 1956), 193 (emphasis added).

3. Ibid. (emphasis added).

4. On Psa. 45, see P. C. Craigie, *Psalms 1–50,* vol. 1, *Word Biblical Commentary* (Waco: Word Books, 1983), 335–41; M. L. Barre, "Hearts, Beds, and Repentance in Psalm 45 and Hosea 7:14," *Biblica* 76, no. 1 (1995): 53–62; R. D. Rowe, *God's Kingdom and God's Son: The Background in Mark's Christology from Concepts of Kingship in the Psalms* (Leiden: Brill, 2002); A. M. Harman, "The Syntax and Interpretation of Psalm 45:7," *Journal of Semitic Studies* 13 (1968): 58–63; J. R. Porter, "Psalm XLV.7," *Journal of Theological Studies* 12 (1961): 51–53; C. S. Lewis, *Reflections on the Psalms* (New York: Harcourt Brace, 1958), 101–15.

5. Craigie, *Psalms 1–50,* 340.

upon the same psalm, highlighting its image of God anointing the righteous with the "oil of gladness" (v. 7). Hebrews applies the royal imagery and applies it to God's Son: "But of the Son he says, 'Thy throne, O God, is for ever and ever, the righteous scepter is the scepter of thy kingdom. Thou hast loved righteousness and hated lawlessness; therefore God, thy God, *has anointed thee with the oil of* gladness *beyond thy comrades'*" (Heb. 1:8–9).

St. Cyril of Jerusalem would likewise interpret Psalm 45 Christologically, taking cues from the author of Hebrews and asserting that this anointing of Christ with the "oil of gladness" was none other than the Holy Spirit: "Christ was not anointed by people with oil or material ointment, but the Father, having before appointed him to be the Savior of the whole world, anointed him with the Holy Spirit ... As he was anointed with *an ideal oil of gladness, that is, with the Holy Spirit,* called oil of gladness, because he is the author of spiritual gladness, so you were anointed with ointment, having been made partakers and 'fellows of Christ.'"[6]

Elsewhere, Theodore of Mopsuestia would draw upon Psalm 45's imagery of the king's robes "all fragrant with myrrh and aloes and cassia" (v. 8), apply it to the Passion of Christ, and, building upon it, add an ecclesiological dimension to the Church itself: "In his wish to imply both the passion and the glory of the passion [the psalmist] says 'myrrh, resin, and cassia from your garments,' suggesting by myrrh the Passion, and by mention of 'resin and cassia' implying the fragrance and splendor of the Passion ... *We are the fragrance of Christ* among those who are being saved and among those who are perishing."[7]

Yet the great fourth-century Antiochene theologian Diodore of Tarsus would carry the ecclesiological implications one step further still. Whereas the psalmist exclaims, "From ivory palaces stringed instruments make you glad" (Psa. 45.8), Diodore applies it to *the churches themselves*, such that the radiance of Christian churches was likened to this explicit temple imagery: "By 'palaces' [the psalmist] means houses, and by 'ivory' the splendor of the houses, by this implying the churches." So his intention is to say that after the

---

6. St. Cyril of Alexandria, *Catechetical Lectures* 21.2. For similar patristic interpretations, see St. Justin Martyr, *Dialogue with Trypho* 63; St. Irenaeus, *Against Heresies* III.6.1; St. Augustine, *Exposition on the Psalms* XLV.6.

7. Theodore of Mopsuestia, "Commentary on Psalm 45," in *Writings from the Greco-Roman World* (Atlanta: Society of Biblical Literature Press), 2001, 5:581–83.

death of Christ splendid and beautiful temples will be erected to him, like the churches to be seen in the present day.[8]

Diodore's interpretation clearly applies the opulence of the Temple forward, to the design and beautification of Christian churches. In such patristic thought it was not a matter of merely "imitating" the pristine example of Solomon's Temple. No, Christologically speaking, for such patristic thinkers, the design of churches *ought to surpass the splendor of the Temple*, in the same manner that Christ surpasses the Old Covenant.

One caution is in order. The reader should be vigilant not to indiscriminately arrive at hasty conclusions by overlaying the early Christian cathedrals with the blueprint of the earlier Jewish Temple. The earliest Christians clearly saw their worship of the crucified and Resurrected Christ as decisively new, and not a continuation of Judaism with its Torah and Temple: *"Behold, I make all things new."*[9]

Yet if the roots of Christian theology plunge deep into the soil of the Old Testament, as they surely do, then the question may be asked: *Which "sacred space" from ancient Judaism was closest to the form and function of Christian sanctuaries—the temple or the synagogue?*

Synagogue or Temple?

Little has been discussed about ancient Jewish synagogues in the study, and this is not the place to engage the topic extensively. A few clarifying remarks will suffice. First, the Jewish synagogue movement likely began in earnest after the Babylonian exile, in the 500s BC. As a matter of necessity, Jews living in the Diaspora needed places for prayer, fellowship, and community. In their most basic sense, this was the function of the ancient synagogue.[10] It should be made clear that the synagogue was not a replacement for the Temple in Jerusalem.[11]

---

8. Diodore of Tarsus, "Commentary on Psa. 45," in *Writings from the Greco-Roman World*, 9:145.

9. Rev. 21:5.

10. For more on Jewish synagogues, see Dan Urman and Paul V. M. Flesher, eds., *Ancient Synagogues: Historical Analysis and Archeological Discovery*, vol. 1, Studia Post-Biblica 47, 1 (Leiden: Brill, 1995); Lee I. Levine, *The Ancient Synagogue: The First Thousand Years* (New Haven, CT: Yale University Press, 2000); Oskar Skarsuane, *In the Shadow of the Temple: Jewish Influences on Early Christianity* (Downers Grove, IL: InterVarsity Press, 2002), 68–85.

11. "Only a small fraction of the total Jewish population lived so near the [Jerusalem] Temple

Second, it was in the Temple—and *only* in the Temple—that sacrifices were offered. Only there did the high priest and those men in his service—priests and Levites—offer slain animals to God. It was in only in the Temple—and not in the many smaller synagogues that dotted the landscape—that the presence of God, the glory of God, dwelt in the Holy of Holies.

And so the synagogue may rightly be seen as a kind of "extension" of the Temple, but only inasmuch as those nonsacrificial dimensions of the temple were concerned: prayer, reading of Torah, Sabbath services, community fellowship.

As imperfect as most analogies are, here is one that may be useful: consider the difference between the Temple and the synagogue as the difference between the sanctuary of the local Catholic parish, and its parish hall/center. Today, many Catholic parishes have some sort of parish hall for adult faith formation as well as for council meetings, receptions, and other "all-purpose" functions.

In many instances, as in the case of my own town's local parish, the "parish center" is even a separate building from the church proper, with its sanctuary as the center of the campus. In other cases, the parish center may be in a basement or another separate space, apart from the sanctuary. Both sanctuary and hall play important roles in the life of the parish, but the one is not the other. Many Catholics disdain when the Mass is celebrated in the parish hall, for example, as an "overflow" room at a Christmas or Easter liturgy. Conversely, no one in their right mind could imagine a children's birthday party, with magician and all, playing out in front of the tabernacle in the sanctuary.

From Analogy to Reality

The above is meant to illustrate, however imperfectly, key distinctions between the Jewish Temple and the Jewish synagogue. By way of analogy, one may liken the Catholic sanctuary to the Temple, with the Catholic altar and tabernacle echoing the altar of the Temple's Holy Place and the Tabernacle for the Blessed Sacrament echoing the presence of God himself in the Tem-

---

that they could visit it and take part in the Temple [liturgy] on a regular basis … [for many, it was] something that required a week or two, and was … something one did only once or twice a year, or less. For distant Diaspora Jews, pilgrimage to the Temple may have been a once-in-a-lifetime experience." Ibid., 83.

ple's Holy of Holies. Along similar lines, one may liken the Catholic parish hall/parish center to the Jewish synagogue. Both are places of religious life and yet are better characterized by things like prayer, discussion, fellowship, even laughter and refreshment.

The reason the above analogy is offered is that in the rest of this chapter the reader is asked to keep a clear distinction between temple and synagogue so that a sensible discussion can be undertaken as to the extent to which temple theology (not "synagogue theology") may have influenced early Christian worship. In fairness, there is a legitimate and necessary purpose of the synagogue (both ancient and modern) and the parish hall/center. But make no mistake, it is the Temple, not the synagogue, that is of concern in what follows.

Here, Ratzinger offers an insightful reflection on the distinctions between Temple and synagogue: "Christian worship, or rather the liturgy of the Christian faith, *cannot be viewed simply as a Christianized form of the synagogue service*, however much its actual development owes to the synagogue service. *The synagogue was always ordered toward the Temple and remained so, even after the Temple's destruction.* The synagogue's liturgy of the Word, which is celebrated with magnificent profundity, regards itself as incomplete, and for that reason it is very different from the liturgy of the Word in Islam, which, together with pilgrimage and fasting, constitutes the whole of divine worship as decreed by the Koran. By contrast, the synagogue ... service is the divine worship that takes place *in the absence of the Temple and in expectation of its restoration.* Christian worship, for its part, regards the destruction of the Temple in Jerusalem as final and as theologically necessary. Its place has been taken by the universal Temple of the risen Christ, whose outstretched arms on the Cross span the world, in order to draw all men into the embrace of eternal love. The new Temple already exists, and so too does the new, the definitive sacrifice: the humanity of Christ opened up in his Cross and Resurrection. *The prayer of the man Jesus is now united with the dialogue of eternal love within the Trinity. Jesus draws men into this prayer through the Eucharist, which is thus the ever-open door of adoration and the true Sacrifice, the Sacrifice of the New Covenant.*"[12]

12. Joseph Ratzinger, *The Spirit of the Liturgy*, trans. John Saward (San Francisco: Ignatius Press, 2000), 49 (emphases added).

Aftershocks: The Impact of Temple Theology within the Early Church

Before going further, a clarification is in order: by the beginnings of the patristic era, there is both continuity and discontinuity between ancient Judaism and its "offspring," Christianity. The reader has already been given many examples of the ways that Christianity drew upon the story and "sacraments" of the Old Covenant.

A New Testament example is seen in Jesus's transforming the Feast of Tabernacles with his temple saying, "I am the light of the world."[13] Beyond Scripture, St. Melito's hymn on the Eucharist as the "new Passover" comes to mind,[14] which was examined earlier. In such examples as these, and in numerous patristic writings, early Christianity reflected a decided continuity with the Old Testament. It became the "playbook" for early apologists like St. Justin Martyr and St. Irenaeus of Lyons.[15] They proclaimed Christ as the Jewish Messiah, and as the fulfillment of Israel's Torah and Temple.

On the other hand, even before the end of the first century there were serious hostilities between Jews and Christians that would persist long into the patristic era. Without question, the Gospel of John contains a decided polemic against the Jewish authorities who bore much responsibility for his death.[16] Within the truth of the Gospel, the Temple authorities indeed had Christ crucified (by the Romans). This is found the Evangelist's phrase, "the Jews," which clearly cannot be directed at all Jewish people of the time (much less thereafter).

Nevertheless, it is indicative of the tensions between Jews and Christians in the era of the early Church. Likewise, the wicked and hypocritical depic-

---

13. John 8:12.

14. St. Melito of Sardis (early second century), *Peri Tou Pascha* [Concerning the Passover] (above).

15. In fairness, both of these figures were highly proficient in Hellenistic philosophy, and in no way should one construe their defense of Christ as simply a proof texting from the Hebrew Scriptures. Even when their arguments run along primarily Scriptural lines, with various "proofs" from the prophets, etc., it is accomplished on an impressive rhetorical footing.

16. See John 7:1; also 1:19, 2:13, 2:18, 2:20, 3:1, 5:15, etc. See the discussion in the *Catechism of the Catholic Church*: "The personal sin of the participants (Judas, the Sanhedrin, and Pilate) is known to God alone. Hence we cannot lay responsibility for the trial on the Jews in Jerusalem as a whole, despite the outcry of a manipulated crowd and the global reproaches contained in the apostles' calls to conversion after Pentecost" (§597).

tion of the Pharisees in the Synoptic Gospels surely is not the whole picture of this popular Jewish group. Still, none of the Evangelists should in any way be faulted for their rhetorical portrayal of the dramatic encounters between Christ and the Pharisees.[17] A final example may be the clearest one of all. Recall the earlier discussion of the "eighth day of creation." On one hand, this expression is undeniably dependent upon the Jewish Sabbath (the *seventh* day) if it is to be sensible at all. And yet the very image of the *eighth day*—and not the *seventh*, as the day of Christian worship—represents a kind of "over and against" move, a surpassing of the one by the other. The Lord's Day is *the new Sabbath*, yet it is *more than the Sabbath* of the Old Covenant.

Thus there was in the early Church a continuity with Judaism, and at the same time a "parting of the ways" with it as well.[18] Given these realities, any discussion of Jewish Christianity, or of the influences of temple theology upon early Christianity, must be approached with sensitivity and in light of this both/and situation.

Moreover, any apprehension of temple theology by the early Church—be it in the life of the sacraments or the architecture of its churches—would never simply "pass over" the thought of the New Testament. The early Church would be interested in *both*—and would likely begin with the mysteries of Christ in the New Testament—before "mining" the Old Testament for its important contributions. Following this wisdom, this book has considered the influence of temple theology of both Old and New Testaments in light of their canonical unity.

In the remainder of this chapter, the reader is asked to consider one final possible dimension of temple theology: that the "aftershocks" of centuries of biblical temple theology were felt in the early centuries of Christianity. The nearer one is to the epicenter of a great earthquake, the more powerful its waves continue to be felt. The same phenomenon is true with regard to the temple theology of Scripture: it continued to "radiate" throughout the early

---

17. *Catechism of the Catholic Church*, §575: "To be sure, Christ's relations with the Pharisees were not exclusively polemical. Some Pharisees warned him of the danger he was courting; Jesus praises some of them, like the scribe of Mark 12:34, and dines several times at their homes. Jesus endorses some of the teachings imparted by this religious elite of God's people: the resurrection of the dead, certain forms of piety (almsgiving, fasting, and prayer), the custom of addressing God as Father, and the centrality of the commandment to love God and neighbor."

18. See James D. G. Dunn, *The Partings of the Ways: Between Christianity and Judaism and Their Significance for the Character of Christianity* (London: SCM; Philadelphia: Trinity, 1991).

Church in a number of important ways for some time to come, and in many respects its tremors are still being felt.

Nearest the Epicenter: The Churches of the Holy Land

In keeping with the above metaphor, a few comments will be made about the early basilicas churches of the Holy Land, as they were nearest "the epicenter" of the Jerusalem Temple—and temple theology. No attempt will be made here to offer a comprehensive history of the period, or to deal with every Christian sanctuary in the Holy Land. To the contrary, just a few examples will be cited here. A few examples will illustrate that the aftershocks of temple theology were felt well after the end of the first century, and the close of the apostolic age.

To begin with, from the earliest days of Christianity, those who bore the name of Christ made pilgrimages to the land of Israel, namely, to Jerusalem to worship and pray at the places where Christ instituted the Eucharist, was on trial, was crucified, and laid in the Tomb from which he arose on the third day and from where he later ascended to heaven.[19]

Eusebius writes of Alexander, Bishop of Cappadocia, who visited Jerusalem in 212 AD "to see the historic sites."[20] He writes of Bethlehem as "The

19. See esp. Eusebius, *Ecclesiastical History*, Books 8–10. One of the finest studies is that of Bargil Pixner, who served as prior of the Benedictine Abbey on Mt. Zion for many years: *Paths of the Messiah and Sites of the Early Church from Galilee to Jerusalem: Jesus and Jewish Christianity in Light of Archaeological Discoveries* (San Francisco: Ignatius Press, 2010). Also by Pixner: "Church of the Apostles Found on Mount Zion," *Biblical Archaeology Review* 16, no. 3 (1990): 16–35. Additionally, see Bernardino Amico, *Plans of the Sacred Edifices of the Holy Land*, SBF Collectio Maior 10, trans. T. Bellorini and Eugene Hoade (Jerusalem: Franciscan Printing Press, 1953); David Kroyanker, *Jerusalem Architecture* (New York: St. Martin's Press, 1994); Richard M. Mackowski, *Jerusalem: City of Jesus* (Grand Rapids, MI: Eerdmans, 1980); W. Telfer, "Constantine's Holy Land Plan," in *Studia Patristica*, vol. 1, Texte und Untersuchungen 63 (Berlin: Akademieverlag, 1955), 696–700; Robert Wilken, *The Land Called Holy: Palestine in Christian History and Thought* (New Haven, CT: Yale University Press, 1992); Peter W. Walker, *Holy Land, Holy Places? Christian Attitudes to Jerusalem and the Holy Land in the Fourth Century*, Oxford Early Christian Studies (Oxford: Clarendon, 1990); Blake Leyerle, "Pilgrims to the Land: Early Christian Perceptions of Galilee," in *Galilee through the Centuries: Confluence of Cultures*, Duke Judaic Studies 1, ed. Eric M. Meyers (Winona Lake, IN: Eisenbrauns, 1999), 345–58; Oded Irshai, "The Christian Appropriation of Jerusalem in the Fourth Century: The Case of the Bordeaux Pilgrim," *Jewish Quarterly Review* 99 (2009): 465–86; J. W. Wilkinson, *Jerusalem Pilgrims before the Crusades* (Warmister: Aris and Phillips, 2002).

20. Eusebius, *An Ecclesiastical History* 6.10: "He performed a journey from Cappadocia, where he was first made bishop, to Jerusalem, in consequence of a vow and the celebrity of the place. Whilst

place of His birth, which is to-day so famous *that men still hasten from the ends of the earth to see it*, but shouted it out with the greatest clearness."[21] Elsewhere, Eusebius remarks that the ruins of Jerusalem were of significance for those visiting Jerusalem, specifically "objects of Jewish reverence," by which he means the Temple: "And I have pointed out that only from the date of our Savior Jesus Christ's Coming among men have the objects of Jewish reverence, *the hill called Zion and Jerusalem, the buildings there, that is to say, the Temple, the Holy of Holies, the Altar, and whatever else was there dedicated to the glory of God*, been utterly removed or shaken."[22]

One of the earliest records of visitors to the Christian sanctuaries and holy sites in ancient Jerusalem was that of the Bordeaux Pilgrim, who in 333 AD saw a great stone that was revered by the Jews, "the *foundation stone* that had been under the *Holy of Holies*. At the temple site stand two statues of Hadrian, and not far from them, a pierced stone, which the Jews come and anoint every year. They mourn and rend their garments and then depart."[23]

Yet many Christian shrines were destroyed during the persecutions of the Roman emperor Diocletian (302–5 AD): "The destruction had begun after the Imperial Council at Nicomedia in 302 [AD] which resolved to suppress Christianity throughout the empire ... After Diocletian abdicated in 305 [AD], the persecution continued under Galerius and Maximian until the Edict of Milan, issued by Constantine in 313 [AD] established religious freedom throughout the empire."[24]

This is sad and fascinating in its own right, but it is not the primary point; rather, as Barker puts it, "*in their new-found freedom, Christians built many churches and described them with temple imagery.*"[25] Just how exactly did early Christians depict churches with temple imagery? "Texts from the *Psalms*

he was there, most cordially entertained by the brethren, who would not suffer him to return home, another revelation also appeared to them at night, and uttered a most distinct communication to those that were eminent for a devoted life."

21. Eusebius of Cæsarea, *The Proof of the Gospel: Being the Demonstratio Evangelica of Eusebius of Cæsarea*, vol. 1, *Translations of Christian Literature. Series I: Greek Texts*, ed. W. J. Sparrow-Simpson and W. K. Lowther Clarke, trans. W. J. Ferrar (London: Society for Promoting Christian Knowledge; Macmillan, 1920), 3.

22. Eusebius of Cæsarea, *Proof of the Gospel* 8:1.

23. Pilgrim of Bordeaux, cited in Wilkinson, *Jerusalem Pilgrims before the Crusades*. See Margaret Barker, *Temple Themes in Christian Worship*, 3rd ed. (London: Bloomsbury, 2013), 61.

24. Ibid., 64.

25. Ibid.

about 'entering the house of the Lord' were applied in the new churches, but Eusebius also included the older belief *that the Christian community was the living temple* ... The Cathedral at Tyre was *described as a temple,* and *the place of the altar described as a temple:* there were fountains in the courtyard before the 'temple' and the place of the altar was called the *Holy of Holies.* Its doors were in the east end, and its sanctuary in the west, *exactly as it was in the Second Temple.*"[26]

Rebuilding the Christian "Temples"

It was St. Helena, Constantine's devout mother, who traveled to Jerusalem at her emperor-son's behest "along with Constantine's architects and master builders and they immediately began three great building projects."[27] First, in Bethlehem, the cave of the Nativity of Christ was cleaned and renovated, "and above it an enormous basilica was raised."[28] Second, in Jerusalem, the so-called Temple of Jupiter, which was constructed near Golgotha in 132 AD, at the order of Hadrian, the Roman emperor at the time, was demolished. "They started digging away the temple platform beneath it."[29]

Third, on the Mount of Olives a sanctuary was raised, dedicated to the Ascension of Christ:[30] "In the years following Constantine's reign, other large basilicas were erected, one after the other, on all the important scenes of the Gospel stories, and even on many Old Testament sites. Just as the [liturgy] was formed to celebrate the entire history of salvation, so the land of Israel became the living illustrated Bible, containing the scenes ... of sacred history—first and foremost scenes of the Word-become flesh."[31]

The Church of the Holy Sepulchre in Jerusalem was intended as a new temple, with its Holy of Holies in the west and its doors facing east:[32] "[Constantine] first of all decked out the sacred cave ... On the side opposite the cave, which looked towards the rising sun, *was connected to the royal temple,* an extraordinary structure of immense height and very extensive in depth and breadth."[33]

---

26. Ibid.
27. Skarsuane, *In the Shadow of the Temple,* 434.
28. Ibid.   29. Ibid., 184.
30. Ibid., 434.   31. Ibid., 435.
32. Barker, *Temple Themes in Christian Worship,* 64.
33. *Life of Constantine* 3.33, as cited in Barker, *Temple Themes in Christian Worship,* 65.

It was dedicated in 335 AD, on September 13, "just as Solomon had dedicated his Temple at the great autumn festival."[34] As the early traveler to Jerusalem, named Egeria, writes: "Those are called the days of dedication when the holy church which is in Golgotha, and which they call the *martyrium*, was consecrated to God; the holy church also which is at the *Anastasis*, that is, in the place where the Lord rose after His Passion, was consecrated to God on that day. The dedication of these holy churches is therefore celebrated with the highest honor, because the Cross of the Lord was found on this same day. And it was so ordained that, when the holy churches above mentioned were first consecrated, that should be the day when the Cross of the Lord had been found, in order that the whole celebration should be made together, with all rejoicing, on the self-same day. *Moreover, it appears from the Holy Scriptures that this is also the day of dedication, when holy Solomon, having finished the House of God which he had built, stood before the altar of God and prayed, as it is written in the books of the Chronicles.*"[35]

In addition, there is an apocryphal story in the *Testament of Solomon*, a Jewish text attributed to Solomon but composed in the first to third centuries AD. The strange story relates how Solomon was bothered in the building of his Temple by demons, and had allegedly obtained power over them by a "magic ring."[36] The reason that this apocryphal tale is worth any mention at all is this: the so-called Pilgrim of Egeria testified that she was shown the ring in her visit to the Holy Sepulcher: "And as all the people pass by one by one, all bowing themselves, they touch the Cross and the title, first with their foreheads and then with their eyes; then they kiss the Cross and pass through, but none lays his hand upon it to touch it. When they have kissed the Cross and have passed through, a deacon stands *holding the ring of Solomon* and the horn from which the kings were anointed; *they kiss the horn also and gaze at the ring.*"[37]

---

34. Barker, *Temple Themes in Christian Worship*, 65. See 1 Ki. 6:37–38.

35. Pilgrim of Egeria, *Diary*, 48.2. (Source: http://www.ccel.org/m/mcclure/etheria/etheria.htm.) See 2 Chron. 7:8–9: "At that time Solomon held the feast for seven days, and all Israel with him, a very great congregation, from the entrance of Hamath to the Brook of Egypt. And on the eighth day they held a solemn assembly; for they had kept the dedication of the altar seven days and the feast seven days." For the precise date of the dedication of Solomon's Temple, see 1 Ki. 6:37–38.

36. See *Testament of Solomon*, in James Charlesworth, ed., *The Old Testament Pseudepigrapha*, vol. 1 (London: Darton Longman and Todd, 1983).

37. Pilgrim of Egeria, *Diary*, 48.2. (Source: http://www.ccel.org/m/mcclure/etheria/etheria.htm.)

Moreover, according to a Jewish Targum[38] known as *Pseudo-Jonathan*, the death of Adam took place on the Temple Mount. Thus Egeria was likely shown the place in the Holy Sepulchre that commemorated the death of Adam, strategically placed directly under the altar of Golgotha. Whatever historical validity this legend has is dubious, but the theology of it is splendidly developed in an early Christian homily from Holy Saturday, which is offered is its entirety:

What is happening? Today there is a great silence over the earth, a great silence, and stillness, a great silence because the King sleeps; the earth was in terror and was still, because God slept in the flesh and raised up those who were sleeping from the ages. God has died in the flesh, and the underworld has trembled. Truly he goes to seek out our first parent like a lost sheep; he wishes to visit those who sit in darkness and in the shadow of death. He goes to free the prisoner Adam and his fellow-prisoner Eve from their pains, he who is God, and Adam's son.

The Lord goes in to them holding his victorious weapon, his cross. When Adam, the first created man, sees him, he strikes his breast in terror and calls out to all: "My Lord be with you all." And Christ in reply says to Adam: "And with your spirit." And grasping his hand he raises him up, saying: "Awake, O sleeper, and arise from the dead, and Christ shall give you light.

I am your God, who for your sake became your son, who for you and your descendants now speak and command with authority those in prison: Come forth, and those in darkness: Have light, and those who sleep: Rise. I command you: Awake, sleeper, I have not made you to be held a prisoner in the underworld. Arise from the dead; I am the life of the dead. Arise, O man, work of my hands, arise, you who were fashioned in my image. Rise, let us go hence; for you in me and I in you, together we are one undivided person.

For you, I your God became your son; for you, I the Master took on your form; that of slave; for you, I who am above the heavens came on earth and under the earth; for you, man, I became as a man without help, free among the dead; for you, who left a garden, I was handed over to Jews from a garden and crucified in a garden.

Look at the spittle on my face, which I received because of you, in order to restore you to that first divine inbreathing at creation. See the blows on my cheeks, which I accepted in order to refashion your distorted form to my own image. See the scourging of my back, which I accepted in order to disperse the load of your sins which was laid upon your back. See my hands nailed to the tree for a good purpose, for you, who stretched out your hand to the tree for an evil one.

38. A Targum was an Aramaic translation (and interpretation) of the Hebrew Scriptures. The one under consideration here is known as the *Targum of Pseudo-Jonathan*.

I slept on the cross and a sword pierced my side, for you, who slept in paradise and brought forth Eve from your side. My side healed the pain of your side; my sleep will release you from your sleep in Hades; my sword has checked the sword which was turned against you ... But arise, let us go hence. The enemy brought you out of the land of paradise; I will reinstate you, no longer in paradise, but on the throne of heaven. I denied you the tree of life, which was a figure, but now I myself am united to you, I who am life. I posted the cherubim to guard you as they would slaves; now I make the cherubim worship you as they would God."

The cherubim throne has been prepared, the bearers are ready and waiting, the bridal chamber is in order, the food is provided, the everlasting houses and rooms are in readiness; the treasures of good things have been opened; the kingdom of heaven has been prepared before the ages.[39]

Along with this splendid homily is the Holy Saturday Responsorial:

Our shepherd, the source of the water of life, has died. The sun was darkened when he passed away. But now man's captor is made captive. This is the day when our Savior broke through the gates of death. He has destroyed the barricades of hell, overthrown the sovereignty of the devil. This is the day when our Savior broke through the gates of death.

Temple Theology and Early Christian Worship

Having examined some of the ways in which the early Christians understood their "sacred spaces"—especially those of the Holy Land—in the light of the Temple, a few remarks will be offered about the Sacraments within the early Church. According to Eusebius, when Constantine had a statue of himself erected in Rome, his figure was depicted holding a cross in his hand "In the most public place at Rome, he commanded the following inscription to be written in the Roman tongue, as follows: '*By this salutary sign, the true ornament of bravery, I have saved your city,* liberated from the yoke of the tyrant. Moreover, I have restored both the Senate and the Roman people to their ancient dignity and splendour.'"[40]

Eusebius's account goes some distance to show the "triumph" of the Cross, especially as it concerns its eventual vindication from Roman perse-

---

39. *Ancient Homily for Holy Saturday*. (For an abbreviated version, see *Catechism of the Catholic Church*, §636.)

40. Eusebius, *Ecclesiastical History* 9.9.

cution, paradoxically from the decree of one of its own emperors. Ratzinger summarizes: "The most basic Christian gesture in prayer *is and always will be the sign of the Cross.* It is a way of confessing Christ crucified with one's very body, in accordance with the programmatic words of St. Paul: '[W]e preach Christ crucified, a stumbling block to Jews and folly to Gentiles, but to those who are called, both Jews and Greeks, Christ the power of God and the wisdom of God'[41] ... Whenever we make the sign of the Cross, we accept our Baptism anew; Christ from the Cross draws us, so to speak, to himself and thus into communion with the living God."[42]

In other words, Christians who "sign" themselves place their lives under its protection, "like a shield that will guard us in all the distress of daily life and give us the courage to go on."[43] With the early Christians, one begins to grasp how the Cross was, especially for Jewish believers, "Something more than the wood on which Jesus was crucified. It is *a spiritual, mysterious, living reality* which accompanies the risen Christ."[44] In like fashion, St. Justin Martyr writes of the Cross as "the greatest symbol of [Christ's] power and rule."[45] He sees the sign of the Cross in countless examples of the visible world: "For consider all the things in the world, whether without this form they could be administered or have any community. For the sea is not traversed except that trophy which is called a sail abide safe in the ship; and the earth is not ploughed without it: diggers and mechanics do not their work, except with tools which have this shape."[46]

Jewish Christians especially, in meditating upon the Cross of Christ, saw in the Old Testament a typology of the Cross. One is reminded here of Je-

---

41. See 1 Cor. 1:23*ff.*

42. Ratzinger, *Spirit of the Liturgy*, 178 (emphasis added). "The sign of the Cross is a confession of faith: *I believe in him* who suffered for me and rose again; in him who has transformed the sign of shame into a sign of hope and of the love of God that is present with us. The confession of faith is a confession of hope: *I believe in him* who in his weakness is the Almighty; in him who can and will save me even in apparent absence and impotence" (177).

43. Mark 8:34: "And he called to him the multitude with his disciples, and said to them, "If any man would come after me, let him deny himself and take up his cross and follow me."

44. Jean Daniélou, *The Theology of Jewish Christianity*, trans. and ed. John A. Baker (London: Darton, Longman and Todd, 1964), 270.

45. Justin Martyr, *First Apology*, 55, in *The Apostolic Fathers with Justin Martyr and Irenaeus*, vol. 1, *The Ante-Nicene Fathers*, ed. Alexander Roberts, James Donaldson, and A. Cleveland Coxe (Buffalo, NY: Christian Literature, 1885), 186.

46. Justin Martyr, *First Apology*, 55.

sus's words in the Gospel of John: "And as Moses lifted up the serpent in the wilderness, so must the Son of man be lifted up" (John 3:14).[47]

Another typology of the Cross from the Hebrew Scriptures is the following: "And the Lord said to him, 'Go through the city, through Jerusalem, and *put a mark* [Hebrew: *tau*] *upon the foreheads* of the men who sigh and groan over all the abominations that are committed in it'" (Ezek. 9:4). Strikingly, in the above example from Ezekiel, the term translated in the English as "mark" is the last letter of the Hebrew alphabet—tau [ת]. In Revelation, this "mark" on the forehead of the elect reappears: "They shall see his face, and his name shall be on their foreheads."[48]

Not only so, but rightly sensing this interpretative move from the Old to the New Testament, Daniélou adds, "That this mark was thought of as representing the name of God is clear from [the text of Revelation]. But once the move had been made to Greek territory, the X[49] the sign of the divine Name, was no longer thought of as standing for Yahweh, but for Christ, and regarded as the first letter of *Xristos*."[50]

The Didache and the Holy Eucharist

Recall the earlier discussion of Sunday, the Lord's Day; there, it was indicated that the early Christians distinguished their worship of Jesus, placing it on "the eighth day" of Creation, rather than upon the Sabbath of their Jewish counterparts.[51] To this it may be added that Sunday was also the integration on one day of three disparate elements of Jewish worship, which took place on different occasions. Specifically, in Judaism, "we have to distinguish (1) the daily prayer; (2) the weekly [liturgy]; and (3) the annual festivals."[52]

First, in Judaism, the first element—*prayer*—was typically private and daily. This aspect of worship took place in the Jerusalem Temple. Second, *weekly liturgy* consisted of a Liturgy of the Word, similar to the weekly Sabbath service in the synagogue. Finally, the third element—*annual festivals*,

---

47. See Num. 21:8–9. Daniélou: "The type is found in all the collections [of the Church fathers]." *Theology of Jewish Christianity*, 271.

48. Rev. 22:4.

49. Here, the letter X stands for the Greek letter Chi.

50. Daniélou, *Theology of Jewish Christianity*, 154.

51. See the discussion in chapter 17.

52. Skarsuane, *In the Shadow of the Temple*, 378–79.

especially Passover, Tabernacles and Weeks (Pentecost)—were the high holy days in which case holy sacrifices were offered. This aspect of worship took place in the Temple.[53] In a unique elevation of these three Jewish traditions, the weekly Eucharistic liturgy of the early Christians preserved and integrated all three elements into one liturgy—the Sunday Mass. It is worthwhile to reconsider these three elements in light of the Mass of the early Christians.

First, in the Mass, the early Christians gathered weekly for prayer, which was also private, *but now decisively public*, as an act of "confession," and expressly offered in the body of the gathered Church. On the public nature of the Mass, Daniélou looks back to St. Gregory the Nazianzen, who "develops this symbolism of the procession as a figure of the entrance *into the heavenly sanctuary*."[54] As Daniélou shows, in drawing upon Christ's Parable of the Wise and Foolish Virgins (Matt. 25:1–13), St. Gregory makes an eschatological connection between the Eucharistic liturgy and the heavenly sanctuary: "The station which you will make immediately after Baptism, *before the great throne*, is the prefiguration of *the glory on high*. The chant of the psalms, with which you will be received, is the prelude to *the hymns of heaven*. The candles which you hold in your hands are the sacrament (*mysterion*) of the escorts of the lights on high, with which we shall go *to meet the Bridegroom*, our souls luminous and virgin, carrying the lighted candles of faith."[55] Daniélou explains how, in St. Gregory's catechesis, the Easter vigil "opens out into eternity ... All the details of the rite, the psalms, the procession, the candles, *are all interpreted in connection with the heavenly liturgy*."[56]

Elsewhere, St. Cyril of Alexandria takes up the image of the Tabernacle of the Israelites, and draws the connection to the Eucharistic liturgy. Commenting on the narrative of the Tabernacle in the Book of Numbers, he writes, "A type of Christ was seen in the holy Tabernacle which led the people in the wilderness [as well as] that the ark that was in it, the Menorah and the altar, as well as incense as that of sacrifice, *signified Christ Himself*."[57] Drawing these strands together, Cyril asserts, "Therefore ... the tabernacle

---

53. All three elements are discussed in ibid., 379.

54. Daniélou, *The Bible and the Liturgy*, 129.

55. Ibid.

56. Ibid. (emphasis added).

57. Cyril of Alexandria, *Commentary on the Gospel According to St. John*, vol. 1 (Oxford: James Parker; Rivingtons, 1874), 447.

that was brought up signifies *the Holy Body of Christ* and the pitching of His Precious Tabernacle, wherein *it was well pleasing that all the fullness of the Godhead should dwell bodily*."[58]

Second, in the Mass, the early Christians participated in weekly liturgy, which included the Liturgy of the Word, with readings from the Old Testament and most notably, as St. Justin Martyr referred to the Four Gospels, the "memoirs of the Apostles." This was an act of proclamation of the Good News of Jesus Christ, and it was followed by exhortation, that is, the homily: "And on the day called Sunday, all who live in cities or in the country gather together to one place, and the memoirs of the apostles or the writings of the prophets are read, as long as time permits; then, when the reader has ceased, the president verbally instructs, and exhorts to the imitation of these good things."[59] Summing up the many typological connections addressed in his careful assessment of the Eucharist in the early Church, Daniélou writes, "If we go through the principal [patristic] catecheses, we find that two chief themes constantly recur in explaining the significance of the sacrament: the Mass is a sacramental representation of the Cross, and *the Mass is a sacramental participation of the heavenly liturgy* ... As we have noticed, the baptismal liturgy takes us in succession through the themes of *Creation, of Paradise, of the Circumcision, of the Covenant, of the Exodus, of Kingship* ... so the Eucharist is seen to coincide with one further aspect [of the Old Testament], that of *priestly [and Temple] worship*."[60]

Third and finally, in the Mass, the early Christians participated in the Eucharistic sacrifice, the liturgy of the Eucharist. Whereas Jewish worshippers engaged in occasional sacrifices, for most, it was an annual pilgrimage to the Temple. In contrast, the early Christians gathered *each week*, on "the eighth day of creation," to eat the Body and Blood of the Lamb of the New Passover, as St. Justin Martyr describes:

Then we all rise together and pray, and, as we before said, when our prayer is ended, bread and wine and water are brought, and the president in like manner offers prayers and thanksgivings, according to his ability and the people assent, saying Amen; and there is a distribution to each, and a *participation* of that over which thanks have been given and to those who are absent a portion is sent by the deacons.[61]

---

58. Cyril of Alexandria, *Commentary on St. John*, 447.

59. St. Justin Martyr, *First Apology*, 67, in *Apostolic Fathers with Justin Martyr*, 186.

60. Daniélou, *The Bible and the Liturgy*, 128 (emphasis added).

61. St. Justin Martyr, "The First Apology of Justin," in *Apostolic Fathers with Justin Martyr*, 186.

St. Justin Martyr's use of the term of "participation" is significant, as it expresses not only the distribution of the Sacrament but also the "communion" that the Church shared, in the risen Christ. As Louis Bouyer has shown, the *Didache* preserves "the most ancient [of] formulations of the Eucharist" and one that is rooted in earlier Jewish formulations of prayers of blessing, or *berakah*.[62] The Eucharistic prayer in the *Didache* reads:

> We thank thee, our Father, for the holy vine of David Thy servant, *which Thou madest known to us through Jesus Thy Servant*; to Thee be the glory forever. And concerning the broken *bread:* We thank Thee, our Father, for the life and knowledge which Thou madest known to us *through Thy Servant Jesus*. To Thee be the glory forever. Even as this broken *bread* was scattered over the hills, and was gathered together and became one, *so let Thy Church be gathered together from the ends of the earth into Thy kingdom*; for Thine is the glory and the power *through Jesus Christ forever.*[63]

Bouyer has ably shown that "the whole [of the prayer] is in continuity, and follows the traditional succession of the meal *berakoth* ["blessing"] over the initial cu, blessing over the broken bread, threefold blessing over the last cup) ... In their final state, they obviously apply to a sacred meal of a Christian community *that is still very close to Judaism, and it could only be its eucharist* ... The Christians kept the *Jewish prayers practically intact* since this form of those prayers represented a special form of them proper to the communities *dominated by the expectation of the Messiah.*"[64]

---

62. Bouyer, *Eucharist*, 115. It is beyond the limits of this study to elaborate on the history and theology of the Eucharistic prayers and its Jewish underpinnings. See Bouyer's classical discussion of the Jewish *berakah* (50–90, 91–135). See also Brant Pitre, *Jesus and the Jewish Roots of the Eucharist: Unlocking the Secrets of the Last Supper* (New York: Doubleday, 2011), 374–443; 444–511.

63. *Didache* 9.2–4. See Alexander Roberts, James Donaldson, and A. Cleveland Coxe, eds., "The Lord's Teaching through the Twelve Apostles to the Nations," in *Fathers of the Third and Fourth Centuries: Lactantius, Venantius, Asterius, Victorinus, Dionysius, Apostolic Teaching and Constitutions, Homily, and Liturgies*, vol. 7, *The Ante-Nicene Fathers* (Buffalo, NY: Christian Literature, 1886), 380; Bouyer, *Eucharist*, 116. Joseph Ratzinger: "The connection between the *berakha* (Greek: *eucharistia*, thanksgiving prayer) of the Last Supper and the Eucharistic Prayers of the Mass has been demonstrated in detail by Louis Bouyer, *Eucharistie: Théologie et spiritualité de la prière eucharistique*." *On the Way to Jesus Christ*, trans. Michael J. Miller (San Francisco: Ignatius Press, 2005), 110. Later, as Pope Benedict XVI, he adds: "This is the context in which Jesus introduces the newness of his gift. In the prayer of praise, the *Berakah*, he does not simply thank the Father for the great events of past history, but also for his own 'exaltation.' In instituting the sacrament of the Eucharist, Jesus anticipates and makes present the sacrifice of the Cross and the victory of the Resurrection. At the same time, he reveals that he himself is the *true* sacrificial lamb, destined in the Father's plan from the foundation of the world." *Sacramentum Caritatis* (Vatican City: Libreria Editrice Vaticana, 2007), §10.

64. Bouyer, *Eucharist*, 117 (emphases added). Italicized portions of the Eucharistic prayer in the

One final point about the Eucharistic prayer from the *Didache* may be added here, concerning its closing words: "Even as this broken *bread* was scattered over the hills, and was gathered together and became one, *so let Thy Church be gathered together from the ends of the earth into Thy kingdom*; for Thine is the glory and the power *through Jesus Christ forever.*"[65] In *The Theology of Jewish Christianity*, Daniélou suggests that this "celebrated passage" may be one of the earliest and rarest extant texts from early Christianity.[66] Daniélou recognizes the influence of in fragment from a text in Isaiah 18, which refers to a "gathering in" of those who were scattered, when a signal upon a mountain is blown.[67]

Daniélou suggests another influence upon the Eucharistic prayer in the *Didache*. It comes from the ancient Jewish Temple and synagogal prayer known as the *Shemoneh Esreh* (*Eighteen Benedictions*), of which the tenth benediction reads: "*Blow the great trumpet* for our liberation, and lift a banner to gather our exiles, *and gather us into one body from the four corners of the* earth; blessed be Thou, O Lord, who gatherest the dispersed of Thy people Israel."[68] Additionally, Daniélou points out that the Greek term *klasma* ("bread") is archaic, and that the *Didache's* imagery of "corn on the hills seems especially suited to the land of Judah, with its hills covered in wheat fields."[69] Based upon all of the evidence, Daniélou suggests that the Eucharistic prayer of the *Didache* is an early formulation and likely represents "the Eucharistic devotions *of the Christians of the Mother Church in Jerusalem.*"[70]

The Celebration of Easter

Easter celebrates the Resurrection of the Lord. Therefore "the question whether the feast was retained from Judaism does not arise, for it is purely a celebration of the anniversary of Christ's Passion and Resurrection."[71] On

---

Didache follow Bouyer's own, as he wished to stress certain "Christian additions" from the underlying Jewish *berakah* upon which the Eucharistic prayer is grounded.

65. *Didache* 9.2–4.

66. Daniélou, *Theology of Jewish Christianity*, 334.

67. Isa. 18:3: "All you inhabitants of the world, you who dwell on the earth, when a signal is raised *on the mountains,* look! When a trumpet is blown, hear!"

68. Daniélou, *Theology of Jewish Christianity*, 335 (emphasis added).

69. Ibid.   70. Ibid., 334.

71. Ibid., 344. Daniélou explains: "[Judaism] at the time of Christ had two calendars, the official

the other hand, it must be readily acknowledged that events of Holy Week are inextricably linked with the Jewish Passover, as all Four Gospels fully attest.[72] As Daniélou expresses, "The real problem concerns *the date of Easter.* From the second century onward there were two opposing opinions. Now this difference of opinion sees to go back to Judaism … Whatever discussion there may be about the date, there is no doubt that *Passover time was observed by Jewish Christians as the feast of Christ's Resurrection.*"[73]

In the Jewish piety of Jesus's day, prayers were recited three times a day.[74] Beyond daily prayer, Jewish faithful prayed on Mondays and Thursdays in synagogues, homes, and small gatherings.[75] Early Christians "fasted on Wednesdays and Fridays"[76] to distinguish themselves from Jews, who fasted on Mon-

---

one, based on the lunar calendar, and the archaic priestly calendar. The Asiatic Christian use seems to correspond to the official Jewish calendar, in which the celebration of Passover *always fell on the evening of the 14th Nisan.* Here is a tradition, *certainly one of the oldest,* which *definitely goes back to Jewish Christianity;* but the other tradition, which was finally to oust the first, *and which placed Easter always on a Sunday,* also has a venerable authority. Eusebius sees it as an *Apostolic tradition* (see below). It represents the immemorial practice of Palestine, Alexandria and Rome, *and appears to be related to the priestly calendar,* which always began the celebration of the Feast of Weeks on the Sunday after the Passover." The reference to Eusebius is as follows: "There was a considerable discussion raised about this time, in consequence of a difference of opinion respecting the observance of the paschal season. *The churches of all Asia, guided by a remoter tradition, supposed that they ought to keep the fourteenth day of the moon for the festival of the Savior's Passover,* in which day the Jews were commanded to kill the paschal lamb; and it was incumbent on them, at all times, to make an end of the fast on this day, on whatever day of the week it should happen to fall. *But as it was not the custom to celebrate it in this manner in the churches throughout the rest of the world, who observe the practice that has prevailed from apostolic tradition until the present time,* so that it would not be proper to terminate our fast on any other but the day of the resurrection of our Savior. *Hence there were synods and convocations of the bishops on this question; and all unanimously drew up an ecclesiastical decree, which they communicated to all the churches in all places, that the mystery of our Lord's resurrection should be celebrated on no other day than the Lord's day;* and that on this day alone we should observe the close of the paschal fasts." *Ecclesiastical History,* 5.23.1.

72. See also Matt. 26:2, 26:17, 26:18, 26:19; Mark 14:1, 14:12, 14:14, 14:16; Luke 22:1, 22:7, 22:8, 22:11, 22:13, 22:15; John 12:1, 13:1, 18:28, 18:39, 19:14.

73. Daniélou, *Theology of Jewish Christianity,* 343–44 (emphasis added).

74. Dan. 6:10: "When Daniel knew that the document had been signed, he went to his house where he had windows in his upper chamber open toward Jerusalem; and he got down upon his knees three times a day and prayed and gave thanks before his God, as he had done previously"; see also Psa. 55:17. Skarsuane, *In the Shadow of the Temple,* 387.

75. Skarsuane, *In the Shadow of the Temple,* 387.

76. Skarsuane is correct in suggesting the suitability of Friday for Christian fasting, as a memorial of the Lord's Passion. As to the reason he gives for Wednesday fasts: "It seems Wednesday as

days and Thursdays. They prayed "at the times of temple prayer, at the third, sixth and ninth hour."[77] The *Didache* presents instructions for prayer, including its version of the Lord's Prayer.[78] The text instructs that the Lord's Prayer should be recited "three times each day."[79] Just prior to the prayer itself, it specifies the days of fasting as Monday and Thursday: "You must not let your days of fasting be at the same time as those of the hypocrites. They fast on the second day of the Sabbath [*Monday*] and on the fifth day of the Sabbath [*Thursday*], so you should hold your fasts on the fourth day of the Sabbath [*Wednesday*] and on the Day of Preparation [*Friday*]."[80]

Going Up to "The House of the Lord"

Regarding the Holy Sepulchre, the original first-century shrine at Golgotha and the Tomb of Christ were excavated from under Hadrian's Temple of Jupiter, imposed upon the Christians by the Roman emperor as a desecration and sign of his powerful persecution against them. "[Early] Christians in Jerusalem already knew that Calvary and Jesus' tomb had been buried under Hadrian's shrine. This is why Constantine's architects launched their excavations in the first place. They knew what they were digging for."[81]

well as Friday were days of special importance in the Essene calendar of the Qumran scrolls. Maybe *Didache's* two days of fasting are closer to Judaism than the author would make us think." Ibid., 388. This is possible, but inconclusive. "What *is* sure is the early Christians developed their own weekly 'rhythm' of set days of prayer and fasting from the earlier practices of Judaism. It is also sure that the 'shift' in these days from Monday/Thursday to Wednesday/Friday were symbolic 'breaks' with the practices of Judaism." *In the Shadow of the Temple*, 387. Likewise, Daniélou: "It has been noticed that these two days had a special importance in the priestly calendar used at Qumran ... it is therefore very probable that the choice of these two days of fast and assembly for worship is of Essene origin." *Theology of Jewish Christianity*, 343. See also Annie Jaubert, *The Date of the Last Supper* (New York: Alba House, 1965).

77. Barker, *Temple Themes in Christian Worship*, 20. See *Didache* 20; Acts 2:15, 3:1, 10:9.

78. See *Didache* 8:2.

79. *Didache* 8:3. Thomas O'Loughlin, *The Didache: A Window on the Earliest Christians* (London: Society for Promoting Christian Knowledge; Grand Rapids, MI: Baker Academic, 2010), 166.

80. *Didache* 8:1. O'Loughlin, *Didache*, 166.

81. As to the precise location of Golgotha, Skarsuane is helpful: "There are several indications that local [early] Christians knew the location of Calvary and [Christ's] tomb ... and some of this evidence *may point to Jewish believers.* First, in Constantine's day, as in ours, the place [of Calvary] is in the middle of the [Old City of Jerusalem], *in clear contradiction to the New Testament record that Christ was crucified and buried outside the city.* But this speaks to the location's *authenticity: if anyone*

In 1974, excavations revealed a portion of a pagan altar from Hadrian's Roman temple under the bedrock of Calvary, near the Chapel of the True Cross, in the Armenian section of the Holy Sepulchre.[82] Interestingly, these excavations also unearthed a small piece of Christian graffiti near the pagan altar. It is from the second century and bears the image of a small boat, presumably a symbol of the Christian pilgrims' mode of transportation. This graffiti includes a brief inscription, in Latin *Domine Ivimus*, "Lord, Let us go." The words of this inscription parallel the opening words of one of the Psalms of Ascent:

> Laetatus sum in eo, quod dixerunt mihi:
> «In domum Domini ibimus»

In English, Psalm 122 reads: "I was glad when they said to me, 'Let us go to the House of the Lord!'" In the time of Jesus, the words of this psalm of David were chanted by Jewish pilgrims on their way up to Jerusalem, to "the house of the Lord," the holy Temple! Now, the early Christian pilgrims who made the inscription chanted them at the risk of martyrdom. They were not going to Solomon's Temple for Passover or Tabernacles, but to the temple of the New Solomon, the crucified Jesus, whose Passover meal prepared his disciples for the full meaning of his crucifixion.

Early Christians, like these pilgrims journeying to Jerusalem, came to see the events of Good Friday as the new Day of Atonement—of the eternal High Priest, the true "lamb without blemish" (Exod. 12:5), whose blood was shed to take away the sins of the world. It was at this rock, the rock of Calvary, that the full meaning of the early Christians' inscription now becomes crystal clear. This rock was the new Holy of Holies—the place of sacrifice had moved, from the Temple mount, to the site of a Roman execution. Re-

---

at a later time freely should invent the place of Jesus' death, he would choose a place outside the city of his own time, that is, outside of Agrippa's third wall and outside Hadrian's [*Aelia Capotolina*, the name given to Jerusalem in the time of Hadrian, in the 130s AD]. In the 150s or 160s A.D. Melito of Sardis visited the Holy Land. Afterwards, he wrote in his *Paschal homily* [see above] that Christ was crucified '*in the middle*' of Jerusalem. It contradicts the New Testament, *but it agrees perfectly with Hadrian's temple within Aelia Capotolina!* Most likely, local Christians had pointed out precisely this place to Melito." *In the Shadow of the Temple*, 184 (emphases added).

82. While in Jerusalem on pilgrimage, I was given the opportunity to stand on top of this pagan altar on several different times. Both occasions provided unforgettable and special memories. I am grateful to the kindness of the Armenian priests at the Church of the Holy Sepulchre.

gardless of how powerful Roman emperors could ignore or profane the altar of Calvary, this was the temple of the true king, the true high priest. Despite the risk even of death, countless more just like them would come, again and again, singing, "I was glad when they said to me, 'Let us go to the House of the Lord!'"

The reader may be interested to know that final revisions of this concluding chapter of *The House of the Lord* were composed inside the Basilica of the Holy Sepulchre itself, during a pilgrimage to Jerusalem in early 2017. More specifically, they were composed in the lower recesses of the church while observing an all-night vigil—just a few steps from the remains of the pagan altar that once stood just outside the Roman Temple of Jupiter and just below the altar of the Rock of Calvary. The pagan altar of Hadrian is evidently in ruin. Moreover, it is, paradoxically, a powerful witness of the historicity of the site. Yet it is not because of the pagan altar that many thousands come from around the globe to the Holy Sepulchre. In fact, it is possible that most pilgrims are unaware of its presence down in the Armenian section of the church. Rather, it is to the altar of Calvary that pilgrims journey, to the place where the Lamb of God was slain for the life of the world.

AFTERWORD

Temple Theology Today

The overall content of *The House of the Lord* may be useful to readers in differing ways, and there are likely a wide array of interests among its audience. This book is tightly focused on biblical theology, yet there may be applications in other related fields of theology (and perhaps other fields beyond theology).

It is hoped that some readers, as a result of working through this topic, will go beyond it and consider its bearing upon related topics at some future point, including the following:

- First and foremost, *the recovery and advancement of Catholic biblical theology*, and the introduction of seminarians and all students of Scripture to ancient and modern master practitioners of Catholic biblical theology.
- *The proper and rigorous deployment of principles of Catholic biblical exegesis* by teachers and students of the Word (including many of the methodological precepts brought out over the course of this book).
- *Jesus's relationship with the Jerusalem Temple* and the many ways not touched upon in this book by which temple theology informs our understanding of Jesus of Nazareth.
- *The Church and the entire Body of Christ* as "members" of the New Temple, with Christ as the chief cornerstone.
- *A deeper appreciation of the biblical roots of "priesthood,"* and the manner in which some forms of scholarship diminish its centrality to both the Old and New Testaments.
- *A deeper understanding and celebration of the Tabernacle and Temple of ancient Judaism* and the many ways in which these realities affect people of faith today.
- *Biblical intertextuality*, especially *typological* readings of the Old and New Testaments; sacramental theology and its relationship to biblical

typology; and the Jewish roots of the sacramental realities, especially as they relate to temple theology.

- *The import of temple theology upon other theological* disciplines—for example, the nature of Sacred Liturgy today—as it relates to God's temple presence in Sacred Scripture, as well as systematic and moral theology and the degree to which temple theology/biblical theology informs such discussions.
- *The biblical concept of "holiness"* and the loss of the holy in some precincts of Church life (and, more broadly, in contemporary society).
- *The biblical concept of beauty* and confusion about/abstraction of that which is intrinsically beautiful in the Church (as well as in modern and secular society).
- *Music, art, and iconography,* and the commitment of educators to help train young people in various forms of sacred music and sacred arts and iconography.
- *Church architecture* and the preservation and renewal of sacred spaces.

On an intellectual and academic level, it is hoped that this book challenged the reader to engage the entire biblical narrative on a historical as well as theological level in search of God's temple presence. It is also hoped that this particular study reinvigorated the need for not merely biblical exegesis but also biblical theology and their proper, integrated relationship. Hopefully the tide has finally turned with respect to critical and negative assessments of the Temple (and priesthood) by some scholars of previous generations. Perhaps the present volume will be of some value in that regard, that this unfortunate choice of earlier scholars is not repeated in the future. May others build upon this study (and others like it), to ensure that the place of the Temple remains properly near the center of the biblical drama.

On more of a spiritual level, it is hoped that this book has assisted the reader to experience, in a fresh light, the great lengths to which the living God has gone and continues to go in inviting us closer and closer toward his holy, temple presence. In the words of Pope Benedict XVI, that "God has never been without His Logos," and through Divine revelation and natural reason, he has been drawing all people to his own glorious presence through Jesus Christ, in the power of the Holy Spirit. It is hoped that *The House of the Lord* gives the reader fresh zeal for reading the Sacred Page, *being attentive to the literal and spiritual senses.* Finally, may all readers better appreciate the many ways in which the living God invites all of humanity (and each soul) into his glorious presence, ultimately in Jesus, who is the heavenly sanctuary in the flesh.

Whatever the greatest contributions of this book may be, it is not asserted here that temple theology is the only means of approaching or developing a coherent biblical theology—only that its influence can no longer be ignored in attentive reading and study of the Old and the New Testaments.

INDEX

Aaron. *See* priesthood

Abel, 96, 107, 311, 368

Abraham, 13, 44, 45, 49, 58, 69–70, 93–94, 95–99, 108, 129n36, 146, 166, 215, 243, 251, 253, 256, 264, 288, 351, 365, 370n99, 371

Acts of the Apostles, 18–19, 65, 66n4, 67n10, 102n25, 107, 134n6, 144, 210, 269n39, 280n77, 325, 327, 328, 330n6, 331, 333–34, 335n25, 336, 348n64, 349, 366n80, 396n77

Alexander, T. Desmond, 5n3, 10n8, 38n3, 43n16, 88n40, 133n1, 140, 275n63, 327, 328n1

allegory/allegorical interpretation of Scripture, 75, 86, 96–97, 102, 146–47, 204n44, 210–12, 273, 301n69, 313, 324. *See also* four senses of Scripture

Allison, Dale, 125n17; and W. D. Davies, 124n11, 263, 271n48, 273, 276n64, 277, 278n70, 279, 284, 285n97

almsgiving, 284–85, 382n17

altar(s), 10, 43, 78, 15, 112, 114, 116, 119, 128–29, 131, 137n18, 156, 183, 299, 318, 360, 369, 386, 391; bronze, 118, 155, 156, 163–65, 216, 226; of Calvary, 306–07, 384, 387, 398; golden of incense, 117, 142, 154, 155, 315; horned, 156; pagan (i.e., high places), 14, 42, 61, 175, 186, 262, 397–98; patriarchal, 40, 54, 95, 96, 109; Roman Catholic, 379, 385; of unhewn stones, 155

Ambrose, St., 97, 204n42, 295, 319n62, 346n57

Ambrosian hymn writer, 320

Ambrosiaster, St., 346

Anderson, Gary, 84, 166n90, 210, 248, 249n35, 257n60

angel(s), 55, 60, 63, 79n3, 84, 86, 88, 95, 99, 102, 104, 124, 129n36, 139, 141, 154, 199, 203n40, 216, 231, 237n35, 242n6, 246–47,

253, 219–92, 295, 302, 313–15, 320, 325n83, 351, 361, 363, 364n65, 366, 372, 388

Apocalypse. *See* Revelation, Book of

apocalyptic literature (Jewish and Christian), 200, 313, 360, 361n53, 363–65, 367

Apostles, 7, 16–17, 25, 28n53, 29n56, 66, 80, 203, 213, 218–19, 237, 242, 254, 257, 259, 260–63, 280, 289, 293, 302, 308–9, 311, 321, 325–26, 330, 337, 342n46, 346–49, 381n16, 392. *See also* Twelve, the

Aquinas, St. Thomas, xii, 10n8, 30, 99, 144–47, 150, 212, 215, 220, 241–42, 248, 257n59, 258, 259–62, 294n26, 273n52, 301, 314, 336, 341, 381n59, 361–63, 367n81

Ark of the Covenant, 63, 102, 117, 119, 134, 142, 143, 152, 155, 174, 182, 248, 315

Athanasius, St., 248

Attridge, Harold, 350n2

Augustine, St., xii, 30, 56n15, 168, 169–70, 216n16, 241, 251, 279, 301n69, 317, 318, 324n80, 377n6

Aune, David, 359n37, 364n38–41, 368n84

Babel, Tower of, 13, 19, 61, 329–32

Baptism, sacrament of, 26n47, 27, 29n57, 62, 213n4, 214, 243n8, 250n39, 251, 252, 264, 273, 279, 289, 301n69, 317, 319, 320, 329, 330, 341, 342n46, 347, 348, 357, 369, 376, 389, 391, 392

Barber, Michael, 10n8, 31, 83n21, 173n13, 174n14, 179n21, 264n17, 265

Barclay, John, 196n13

Barker, Margaret, 31, 38n3, 98, 104, 169n5, 213n9, 216, 290n9, 294n26, 355n23, 351, 384–85, 386n34

Barron, Robert, 28n51

Basil, St., 88, 213–15

Bauckham, Richard, 359–60

403

The House of the Lord: A Catholic Biblical Theology of God's Temple Presence in the Old and New Testaments was designed in Garamond Premier Pro and composed by Kachergis Book Design of Pittsboro, North Carolina. It was printed on 60-pound Natures Book Natural and bound by Thomson-Shore of Dexter, Michigan.